ROUTLEDGE HANDBOOK OF VIOLENT EXTREMISM AND RESILIENCE

At a time of great global uncertainty and instability, communities face fracturing from the increasing influence of extremist movements hostile to democratic and multicultural norms. Europe and the West have grown increasingly polarised in recent years, beset with financial crises, political instability, the rise of malicious actors and irregular violence, and new forms of media and social media. These factors have enabled the spread of new forms of extremism and suggest a growing need for a response sensitive to inequalities and divisions in wider society – a task made even more urgent by the COVID-19 pandemic.

The *Routledge Handbook of Violent Extremism and Resilience* brings together research conducted throughout Europe and the world, to analyse various articulations of violent extremism and consider the impact that such groups and networks have had on the wellbeing of communities and societies. It examines different theories, factors, and national case studies of extremism, polarisation, and societal fragmentation, drilling deep into national examples to map trends across Europe, North America, and Australasia, to provide regional and state-level comparative analysis. It also offers a thorough exploration of resilience – a recent addition to counter-extremism policy and practice – to consider how it has come to play this increasingly central role in Preventing and Countering Violent Extremism (P/CVE), the limitations and opportunities of such approaches, and how it could be shared, developed, problematised, and deployed in response to violence and polarisation.

The Handbook details new trends in both violent extremism and counter-extremism response, within this increasingly fractured global context. It critically explores the latest theories of community violence, extremism, polarisation, and resilience, mapping them across case study countries. In doing so, it presents new findings for students, researchers, practitioners, and policymakers seeking to understand these new patterns of polarisation and extremism and develop community-driven responses.

Richard McNeil-Willson is a research fellow in the field of terrorism and political violence at the Institute of Security and Global Affairs (ISGA) at Leiden University, Netherlands and Visiting Scholar at King's College, the University of Cambridge, United Kingdom. His work critically examines the interconnections between groups labelled 'extremist' and counter-extremism legislation, as well as the impact of counterterrorism on democratic and human rights. He is also a former Max Weber research fellow at the Robert Schuman Centre for

Advanced Studies at the European University Institute, Florence, Italy, and holds a UK Research Council-funded PhD from the Institute of Arab and Islamic Studies, Exeter University. He has worked on several European Commission projects and has advised the European Commission directly in developing policy responses to far-right violence.

Anna Triandafyllidou holds the Canada Excellence Research Chair in Migration and Integration at Toronto Metropolitan University (formerly Ryerson University), Canada. Her interdisciplinary research focuses on the governance of migration and asylum; nationalism and identity issues; and overall, the contemporary challenges of migration and integration across different world regions. Her authored books include *What is Europe?* (with Ruby Gropas, Second Edition, Routledge, 2022), *Migration and Return in Southeastern Europe* (with E. Gemi, Routledge, 2021), *Migrant Smuggling* (with T. Maroukis, McMillan, 2012), and *Immigrants and National Identity in Europe* (Routledge 2001). She recently edited a volume on *Migration and Pandemics* (Springer, 2022). Her recent journal publications have appeared in the *Comparative Migration Studies* (2021, 2022), *Environment and Planning A: Economy and Society* (2022), *Ethnicities* (2022), *International Migration* (2021), *Journal of Ethnic and Migration Studies* (2022), and *Nations and Nationalism* (2020).

ROUTLEDGE HANDBOOK OF VIOLENT EXTREMISM AND RESILIENCE

Edited by Richard McNeil-Willson and Anna Triandafyllidou

LONDON AND NEW YORK

Designed cover image: © Loretta Lizzio/Richard McNeil-Willson/Bruno Figueiredo

First published 2023
by Routledge
4 Park Square, Milton Park, Abingdon, Oxon OX14 4RN

and by Routledge
605 Third Avenue, New York, NY 10158

Routledge is an imprint of the Taylor & Francis Group, an informa business

© 2023 selection and editorial matter, Richard McNeil-Willson and Anna Triandafyllidou; individual chapters, the contributors

The right of Richard McNeil-Willson and Anna Triandafyllidou to be identified as the authors of the editorial material, and of the authors for their individual chapters, has been asserted in accordance with sections 77 and 78 of the Copyright, Designs and Patents Act 1988.

With the exception of Chapter 10, no part of this book may be reprinted or reproduced or utilised in any form or by any electronic, mechanical, or other means, now known or hereafter invented, including photocopying and recording, or in any information storage or retrieval system, without permission in writing from the publishers.

Chapter 10 of this book is available for free in PDF format as Open Access from the individual product page at www.routledge.com. It has been made available under a Creative Commons Attribution-Non Commercial-No Derivatives 4.0 license.

Trademark notice: Product or corporate names may be trademarks or registered trademarks, and are used only for identification and explanation without intent to infringe.

British Library Cataloguing-in-Publication Data
A catalogue record for this book is available from the British Library

Library of Congress Cataloging-in-Publication Data
Names: McNeil-Willson, Richard, editor. | Triandafyllidou, Anna, editor.
Title: Routledge handbook of violent extremism and resilience / edited by Richard McNeil-Willson and Anna Triandafyllidou.
Description: Abingdon, Oxon ; New York, NY : Routledge, 2023. | Includes bibliographical references and index. | Identifiers: LCCN 2022060909 (print) | LCCN 2022060910 (ebook) | ISBN 9781032211695 (hardback) | ISBN 9781032211701 (paperback) | ISBN 9781003267102 (ebook)
Subjects: LCSH: Radicalism. | Political violence. | Polarization.
Classification: LCC HN49.R33 R68 2023 (print) | LCC HN49.R33 (ebook) | DDC 320.53–dc23/eng/20230210
LC record available at https://lccn.loc.gov/2022060909
LC ebook record available at https://lccn.loc.gov/2022060910

ISBN: 978-1-032-21169-5 (hbk)
ISBN: 978-1-032-21170-1 (pbk)
ISBN: 978-1-003-26710-2 (ebk)

DOI: 10.4324/9781003267102

Typeset in Bembo
by Newgen Publishing UK

The Open Access version of chapter 10 was funded by the University of Oslo.

CONTENTS

List of figures	*viii*
List of tables	*x*
Contributors	*xi*
Acknowledgements	*xvii*

PART I
Core issues on violent extremism and resilience 1

1 Violent extremism and resilience in the 21st century 3
  Richard McNeil-Willson, Anna Triandafyllidou, and Vivian Gerrand

2 Assessing our understanding of (violent) extremism 17
  Richard McNeil-Willson

3 Resilience to violent extremism at the crossroads 33
  Michele Grossman

4 European trends in polarisation and resilience 51
  Sheryl Prentice and Paul Taylor

5 Young people, radicalisation, and resilience 71
  Vivian Gerrand

6 Online extremism and resilience 92
  Amy-Louise Watkin

PART II
Country cases   111

Western Europe

7 France   113
   Francesca Scrinzi

8 United Kingdom   125
   Tahir Abbas, Richard McNeil-Willson, and Lianne Vostermans

Northern Europe

9 The Netherlands   139
   Maria Vliek and Martijn de Koning

10 Norway   153
    Rune Ellefsen and Martin M. Sjøen

Central and Eastern Europe

11 Germany   168
    Fabian Virchow

12 Hungary   181
    Zsuzsanna Vidra and Michael C. Zeller

13 Poland   196
    Michael C. Zeller and Jana Hrckova

Southern Europe

14 Italy   210
    Francesca Scrinzi

15 Greece   221
    Eda Gemi

Australasia and North America

16 Australia   236
    Michele Grossman and Vivian Gerrand

17	New Zealand *Jacinta Carroll*	254
18	Canada *Sara K. Thompson*	270
19	United States of America *Brian Hughes*	286

Index *300*

FIGURES

2.1	The ratio of the use of 'extremism' to 'terrorism' (and associated terms) as mentioned in British media	24
3.1	Transactional risk economy: prosocial and antisocial resilience	43
4.1	Showing a comparison of socio-economic abstracts and objectives with the BNC Informative Writing Sampler	53
4.2	Showing a comparison of historic abstracts and objectives with the BNC Informative Writing Sampler	55
4.3	Showing a comparison of cultural abstracts and objectives with the BNC Informative Writing Sampler	58
4.4	Showing a comparison of communication-based abstracts and objectives with the BNC Informative Writing Sampler	59
4.5	Tracing relative frequencies of concepts over time in 100 randomly selected academic article abstracts	63
4.6	Tracing relative frequencies of concepts over time in 100 randomly selected practitioner project objective summaries	64
4.7	Tracing relative frequencies of concepts over time in 100 randomly selected government policy objective summaries	66
5.1	Meme reflecting intergenerational inequality and diminished prospects for the future	75
5.2	Mapping violent radicalisation	77
5.3	Either/or antagonistic narratives of incompatibility. French officers police the Burkini ban in France	81
5.4	Either/or antagonistic narratives of incompatibility. IS propaganda promotes a similar polarising narrative	81
5.5	Both/and agonistic narratives of belonging. Somali American supermodel Halima Aden: A role model for young Muslim women in the West	82

5.6	Representative Ilhan Omar with her then 17-year-old daughter and activist, Isra Hirsi, on the cover of *Teen Vogue*, November 2020	83
5.7	'Everything I've learned about Incels.' Vulgadrawings Instagram post, 2021	85
5.8	'Everything I've learned about Incels.' Vulgadrawings Instagram post, 2021	86
16.1	COMPACT Resilience-based model	247

TABLES

5.1	Exclusivist and prosocial radical movements	78
12.1	Legal infrastructure relevant to right-wing extremist activity	189
13.1	Variants of right-wing radicalism/extremism and contemporary Polish examples	199
13.2	Social resilience processes	206

CONTRIBUTORS

Tahir Abbas holds the Chair in Radicalisation Studies at the Institute of Security and Global Affairs at Leiden University in The Hague, Netherlands. His recent books are *Countering Violent Extremism* (Bloomsbury-IB Tauris 2021), *Islamophobia and Radicalisation* (Hurst/Oxford University Press 2019), and *Contemporary Turkey in Conflict* (Edinburgh University Press 2017). His recent edited books are *Political Muslims* (co-ed., with S. Hamid, Syracuse University Press 2019) and *Muslim Diasporas in the West: Critical Readings in Sociology* (4 vols., Routledge Major Works Series 2016). He has been a visiting scholar at the London School of Economics (2017–2019) and New York University (2015–2016). He is a Fellow of the Academy of Social Sciences.

Jacinta Carroll joined the National Security College, Australia, as the Director, National Security Policy, in August 2017. She is a member of NSC's Futures Council and works across the NSC's professional development, policy and academic programmes. Previously, Jacinta was the inaugural Head of ASPI's Counter Terrorism Policy Centre, a position she held since August 2015. Jacinta joined ASPI from the Australian Government where she had held a variety of Senior Executive appointments and worked in the Department of Defence and the Attorney-General's Department. Her career experience includes working on national security, counter-terrorism, strategic policy, border security, military operations, campaign planning and scenario development, information management, and international policy with a particular focus on the Middle East and Afghanistan; she has served in Iraq. Jacinta is a graduate of the Australian National University, has post-graduate qualifications in management from Flinders University, and holds Masters' degrees from the University of Sydney and Deakin University. Her Masters' theses examined United Nations Peacekeeping, and Asia-Pacific Regional Security. She is a graduate of the Australian Defence College's Centre for Defence and Strategic Studies and the Australian Institute of Company Directors and the Australian Graduate School of Management, and serves on a number of boards including the United Service Institute-ACT and John XXIII College ANU. She has completed the Defence and Industry Study Course, the Australian Public Sector Management course, and the Middle East Diplomats course at the Truman Institute, Hebrew University of Jerusalem. She is a member of the AVERT (Addressing Violent Extremism and Radicalisation to Terrorism) Research Network and the National Security and Terrorism Program Advisory Council, Deakin University.

Martijn de Koning is engaged in research on activism among Muslims in Europe, on Dutch Muslims in the UK, and on the racialisation of Muslims. He has published about militant activism among Muslims, Dutch foreign fighters in Syria, the work of anti-Islamophobia initiatives, Moroccan-Dutch Muslim youth and their religious experiences, and the rise and developments of 'Salafism' in the Netherlands.

Rune Ellefsen is a postdoctoral research fellow in the 'Radicalisation and resistance' project at the University of Oslo, Norway. He completed his PhD in 2018 at the Department for Criminology and Sociology of Law at Oslo University. Rune's research interests include social movements, conflict processes, the policing of protest, as well as politically motivated crime and violence. His recent research has explored these issues in relation to policies and practices to 'prevent radicalisation and violent extremism' in Norway, Sweden, and England. He is also involved in qualitative research projects about young people's experiences with religious and ethnic discrimination in Norway.

Eda Gemi is a Political Sociologist specialised in governance of migration and integration. She is Associate Professor at the University of New York Tirana, Albania. From 2010 to 2020 she was Research Fellow (project-based) at the Robert Schuman Centre for Advanced Studies of the European University Institute (EUI). In the period 2018–2019 she was Visiting Researcher at the ISR–Institute for Urban and Regional Research of the Austrian Academy of Sciences in Vienna. A Research Fellow at the Hellenic Foundation for European and Foreign Policy (ELIAMEP) in the period 2012–2016, she headed the migration research team and conducted a series of studies on migration. Currently, she serves as the national correspondent for migration in preparing the annual SOPEMI report and representing Greece at OECD Network of International Migration Experts. Dr. Gemi has authored three books on migration, integration and transnationalism, and the EU-Western Balkan migration system. Her monograph (co-authored with Anna Triandafyllidou) *Rethinking Migration and Return in Southeastern Europe: Albanian Mobilities to and from Italy and Greece* is published by Routledge. She has also published many articles in refereed journals (e.g., *International Review of Sociology*), book volumes (e.g., Oxford University Press), and media. She was awarded from London Metropolitan University, UK a PhD in Business and Law with a focus on migration and integration. She holds a Master of Arts in Southeast European Studies from the Faculty of Political Science and Public Administration of University of Athens. Her main areas of research are the governance of migration, social integration, transnationalism, return migration, and political participation.

Vivian Gerrand is Research Fellow at the Alfred Deakin Research Institute for Citizenship and Globalisation, Deakin University, Australia. She coordinates the Addressing Violent Extremism and Radicalisation to Terrorism (AVERT) Research Network. She is also a co-investigator of the EUI-led Horizon 2020 Building Resilience against Violent Extremism and Polarisation (BRaVE) Coordination and Support Action (2019–2021). Her research interests lie in the areas of belonging and migration, image-making and representation, re-imagined citizenship, and resilience to violence and violent extremism. In 2017–2018, she was a Max Weber Fellow in the Global Governance Programme, Robert Schuman Centre for Advanced Studies, at the European University Institute. Vivian completed her PhD at the University of Melbourne on representations of Somali belonging in Italy and Australia. She is the author of *Possible Spaces of Somali Belonging* (Melbourne University Press 2016).

Contributors

Michele Grossman is Professor of Cultural Studies and Research Chair in Diversity and Resilience at the Alfred Deakin Institute for Citizenship and Globalisation at Deakin University, Australia. She is also the Convenor of the Australian-based AVERT (Addressing Violent Extremism and Radicalisation to Terrorism) Research Network and Director of the Collaborative Centre of Excellence for Resilient Communities and Inclusive Societies (CERCIS), an eight-member university and practitioner consortium on social cohesion, community resilience, and violent extremism led by Deakin University. Michele's expertise lies in addressing and countering violent extremism within communities and understanding terrorism in diverse gender and cultural contexts. Her research has had both national and international policy impacts, particularly in relation to developing new approaches and understandings related to community reporting of violent extremism; youth vulnerability and resilience to violent extremism; gender roles in supporting and opposing violent extremism, and the reintegration of child and women returnees from conflict zones. She holds current or recent research grants from a wide range of funding agencies including National Institute of Justice (USA), Public Safety Canada, ESRC-CREST (UK), ANZCTC and Department of Home Affairs (Australia) and others.

Jana Hrckova is a PhD researcher at the Department of Sociology and Social Anthropology at the Central European University, Austria. Her research interests are urban anthropology, environmental anthropology, pollution, Eastern Europe, materiality, and infrastructure. Her doctoral dissertation investigates the entanglement of processes surrounding the air pollution crisis in Warsaw, Poland.

Brian Hughes is the Associate Director of the Polarisation and Extremism Research and Innovation Lab (PERIL) at American University, United States of America. His work pursues evidence-based approaches to intervening in radicalisation processes with a focus on community resilience, non-carceral solutions, and centring the needs of victim-survivors. His research and writing explore the impact of communication technology on political and religious extremism, terrorism, and fringe culture. His writing has addressed the media ecosystem of ISIS, 20th-century precursors of the so-called alt-right, eco-fascism, and accelerationism. This work seeks to identify the affective and material commonalities between extremists of differing ideologies, cultures, times, and places.

Richard McNeil-Willson is a research fellow in the field of terrorism and political violence at the Institute of Security and Global Affairs (ISGA) at Leiden University, Netherlands and Visiting Scholar at King's College, the University of Cambridge, United Kingdom. His work critically examines the interconnections between groups labelled 'extremist' and counter-extremism legislation, as well as the impact of counterterrorism on democratic and human rights. He is also a former Max Weber research fellow at the Robert Schuman Centre for Advanced Studies, at the European University Institute, Florence, Italy, and holds a UK Research Council-funded PhD from the Institute of Arab and Islamic Studies, Exeter University. He has worked on several European Commission projects and has advised the European Commission directly in developing policy responses to far-right violence.

Sheryl Prentice is Senior Research Associate in the Department of Psychology at Lancaster University, United Kingdom, working on the European Commission-funded Building Resilience Against Violent Extremism (BRaVE) project. Previously, Sheryl worked on a range of language analysis projects, particularly in the area of security, including Native Language Influence Detection; Exploring Discursive Representations of EU Maritime Security; Time, Response and Audience Construed Evaluation of Extreme and Counter-Messages; and Understanding the Language of Extremism and its Potential for Predicting Risk. She continues to publish and undertake consultancy work in this area. In addition to work in the field of security, Sheryl has also undertaken language analysis research on present and historical English and Scottish relations, as well as development work on UCREL's automated semantic tagger and corpus approaches to biomedical text analysis.

Francesca Scrinzi is Senior Lecturer in Sociology at the University of Glasgow, United Kingdom. She is currently British Academy Mid-Career Fellow on a project titled 'Gender and the populist radical right in Europe'. In 2012–2014, she researched women and gender relations in populist radical right parties (project titled 'Gendering Activism in Populist Radical Right Parties: A Comparative Study of Women's and Men's Participation in The Northern League (Italy) and The National Front (France)' with an ERC Starting Grant). In 2015–2018, she was Marie Skłodowska-Curie Fellow at the European University Institute (project titled 'Migrant Christianity: Migration, religion, and work in comparative perspective. Evangelical "ethnic churches" in Southern Europe'). Furthermore, she has carried out ethnographic comparative research work on gendered migration and migrant care workers in Italy and France. Among her recent publications are: 'Migrant Masculinities In-between Private and Public Spaces of Reproductive Labour: Asian Porters in Rome' (co-authored with E. Gallo) in *Gender, Place & Culture* (published online on 16 April 2019); 'Gender and women in the Front National discourse and policy. From "mothers of the nation" to "working mothers"?' in *New Formations. A Journal of Culture/Theory/Politics*, 91, (2017); 'Caring for the elderly in the family or in the nation? Gender, women and migrant care labour in the Lega Nord' in *West European Politics* (2017); and *Migration, Masculinities and Reproductive Labour. Men of the Home* co-authored with Ester Gallo, Basingstoke: Palgrave Macmillan (2016).

Martin M. Sjøen is Associate Professor at the Department of Education at the University of Bergen, Norway. He holds a PhD in safety and security studies from the University of Stavanger (2020). Martin's research interests include human security, terrorism research, and transformative education. He is currently working on multiple projects focusing on how different social domains can prevent extremism, violence, and hate crime, as well as scrutinising potential negative outcomes of the continued 'securitisation' of social life.

Paul Taylor is director of the United Kingdom's hub for behavioural and social science for national security (CREST). Commissioned by the ESRC with funding from the UK intelligence community and Home Office, CREST currently supports 143 researchers from 35 UK HEIs and SMEs who have, through their research and engagement activities, added value to training, investigative practices, and policies. Between 2012 and 2019, Paul was the inaugural director of Lancaster University's institute for security research. He helped the institute establish its socio-technical focus, housing staff and students from 10 departments and growing an interdisciplinary strength that defines Lancaster's contribution to initiatives such as the EPSRC-NCSC Academic Centre of Excellence for Cyber Security network and the academic-industry engagement accelerator SPRITE+. Paul's own research in security, safety, and resilience has been supported by £23M of funding from the ESRC, EPSRC, EU, and others. This work is published in computing, linguistics, management, and psychology outlets and has led to several awards, including the EAPL mid-career award. Paul is a full Professor at Lancaster University,

United Kingdom, and the University of Twente, Netherlands, but he works outside of academia too. He helped establish a government research unit between 2006 and 2008 and, for his contribution to police investigations, he received a Commissioner commendation in 2005. He is a member of a number of government science groups, sits on Imperial's Data Science Institute's advisory board, and has served as an editor and board member for the British Psychological Society.

Anna Triandafyllidou holds the Canada Excellence Research Chair in Migration and Integration at Toronto Metropolitan University (formerly Ryerson University), Canada. Her interdisciplinary research focuses on the governance of migration and asylum; nationalism and identity issues; and overall, the contemporary challenges of migration and integration across different world regions. Her authored books include *What is Europe?* (with Ruby Gropas, Second Edition, Routledge, 2022), *Migration and Return in Southeastern Europe* (with E. Gemi, Routledge, 2021), *Migrant Smuggling* (with T. Maroukis, 2012), and *Immigrants and National Identity in Europe* (Routledge 2001). She recently edited a volume on *Migration and Pandemics* (2022). Her recent journal publications have appeared in the *Journal of Ethnic and Migration Studies* (2022), *Comparative Migration Studies* (2021, 2022), *Environment and Planning A: Economy and Society* (2022), *Ethnicities* (2022), *International Migration* (2021), and *Nations and Nationalism* (2020).

Sara K. Thompson is Professor of Criminology at Toronto Metropolitan University, Canada, and Associate Director of the Canadian Network for Research on Terrorism, Security and Society (TSAS). Her recent and ongoing research focuses on urban violence, radicalisation to violence/violent extremism, and the implementation and evaluation of violence prevention programmes and policy. Since 2012, she has been involved as principal investigator on a number of major research projects funded by the Social Sciences & Humanities Research Council of Canada (SSHRC), Public Safety Canada, the Canada Centre for Community Engagement and Prevention of Violence, and Defence Research & Development Canada. Thompson has presented on her research at a range of domestic and international academic and practitioner conferences, and has briefed high-level government, police, and other security officials on issues related to urban violence, terrorism/violent extremism, and programme evaluation. One of the key drivers of her work is the desire to inform effective, legally responsible, and socially engaged violence-prevention policies and programmes.

Zsuzsanna Vidra is a research fellow at the Centre for Policy Studies, Central European University, Hungary, and a senior lecturer at Eötvös Lóránd University (ELTE PPK), Intercultural Psychology and Education, Hungary. She holds a PhD in Sociology from École des Hautes Études en Sciences Sociales, France, an MA in Sociology from ELTE, Hungary, and an MA in Nationalism Studies from the Central European University, Hungary. Her main areas of research are poverty, ethnicity, migration, education, racism, political extremism, and media and minorities. She has published several articles on Roma and non-Roma interethnic relations, educational inequalities, labour market, and social policy issues. She has edited a volume on Roma migration to Canada, and another volume on the far-right and Roma self-mobilisation, and she has co-authored a book on ethnic relations, migration, labour market conditions, and informal economy in marginal rural communities. Her recent work focused on child trafficking and mainstreaming extreme-right discourses, limits of tolerance, as well as Islamophobia in Hungary.

Fabian Virchow is Professor of Social Theory and Theories of Political Action at the University of Applied Sciences Düsseldorf, Germany, where he also directs the Research Unit on Right-Wing Extremism. He has published numerous books and articles on worldview, strategy, and political action of the far right.

Maria Vliek is an associated researcher at the Radboud University Nijmegen, the Netherlands. Her doctoral project at the same university focused on the narratives and experiences of former Muslims in contemporary Europe. She is currently working at the Social and Cultural Planning Office (Sociaal en Cultureel Planbureau) at the Dutch Ministry of Health, Welfare and Sports, where her research projects are primarily concerned with social inequality and participation as well as mechanisms of societal inclusion and exclusion. Her research interests include the anthropology of religion, secularism, and religious conversion. Previously, she has researched identity development among radicalised Muslim youth in Mombasa, Kenya.

Lianne Vostermans is a postdoctoral researcher in the field of Terrorism and Political Violence at the Institute of Security and Global Affairs (ISGA), Leiden University, Netherlands. Her research focuses on (violent) social and political mobilisation, paying particular attention to the interplay between emotions, identity, ideology, religion, organisational networks, and opportunity structures. Lianne obtained her PhD from the Durham Global Security Institute at Durham University (with an ESRC scholarship), holds an MSc in Defence, Development and Diplomacy at Durham University, a PCG in the Psychology of Religion at Cambridge University, and a BA in Liberal Arts and Sciences from University College Utrecht. She was also previously an affiliate at King's College London.

Amy-Louise Watkin is a PhD candidate at Swansea University, United Kingdom, and member of the Cyber Threats Research Centre. She is also a Research Assistant at Dublin City University, Ireland, with the European Commission Horizon 2020-funded project Building Resilience against Violent Extremism and Polarisation (BRaVE).

Michael C. Zeller is an Associate Researcher at the CEU Centre for Policy Studies, working on the 'Building Resilience against Violent Extremism and Polarisation' (BRaVE) project. He is also a doctoral candidate in the Department of Political Science at Central European University, Austria. His dissertation research concerns the demobilisation of far-right demonstration campaigns, particularly the role of counter-mobilisation against the far right. Michael earned a Masters' degrees in political science and in Russian, Central and Eastern European Studies, from Corvinus University of Budapest and the University of Glasgow, respectively.

ACKNOWLEDGEMENTS

This Handbook finds its origins in the conceptual and empirical work developed under the auspices of the Horizon 2020 EU-funded research project BRaVE: Building Resilience against Violent Extremism (contract no. 822189). The project started in January 2019 and we had the opportunity to meet in person once in summer 2019 and after that had to work mostly online as the pandemic prevented us from holding in-person events and meetings. Nonetheless, there have been many opportunities to engage with non-governmental organisations and other stakeholder and experts, beyond, academic, given that this was the project's mandate as a Coordination and Support Action. At the same time, it is important to note that the whole polarisation and violent extremism discourse has evolved during the pandemic, where populist anti-vax mobilisations rose while, for instance, religiously attributed violent extremism was sidelined, at least temporarily. What transpired though through these developments was the importance of both the concept and practice of community resilience as a way of addressing the complex phenomenon of polarisation and the many factors that contribute to it. We hope that this Handbook can serve as a knowledge tool for both researchers and practitioners in this field.

We would like to thank our BRaVE project colleagues for their work and contribution to the book not only as single chapter authors but also in forging our reflections; Diane Shugart for as always skilfully copyediting this manuscript and raising important 'lay person's questions' that helped us clarify some of our arguments.

During the BRaVE project and the writing and edition of this book, Anna has been based in Toronto at Toronto Metropolitan University (formerly Ryerson) while Richard was initially at the European University Institute, in Florence, Italy before moving to the Netherlands to Leiden University. Completing this book has been challenging across countries and time zones and multiple work commitments. A big thanks goes to our families and friends for their tolerance of long working hours, often at weekends and evenings.

Anna Triandafyllidou, Toronto; Richard McNeil-Willson, Leiden
14 September 2022

PART I

Core issues on violent extremism and resilience

PART 1

1
VIOLENT EXTREMISM AND RESILIENCE IN THE 21ST CENTURY

Richard McNeil-Willson, Anna Triandafyllidou, and Vivian Gerrand

Introduction

Europe and the West have grown increasingly polarised in recent years, suffering from financial crises and political instability, the rise of malicious actors and irregular violence, and the creation of new forms of media and social media. Such factors have been pivotal in enabling the spread of new forms of extremism, and there has been growing awareness that there must be a holistic approach in response – a need made even more urgent by the Covid-19 pandemic. By responding to these factors of violent extremism and polarisation through the strengthening of local communities and wider societies, policymakers, practitioners, and civil society groups can combat violent extremism in a way that is led and supported at a grassroots level. This Handbook will offer a means of understanding how this is currently, and can be further, achieved.

This Handbook brings together research conducted throughout Europe and the world to analyse various articulations of violent extremism and consider the impact that such groups and networks have had on the wellbeing of communities and societies. The Handbook will examine different theories, factors, and national case studies of extremism, polarisation, and societal fragmentation, drilling deep into national examples to map trends across Europe, North America, and Australasia to allow for regional and state-level comparative analyses. It will also offer a thorough exploration of resilience – a recent addition to counter-extremism policy and practice – to consider how it has come to play this increasingly central role in articulations of Preventing and Countering Violent Extremism (P/CVE) and where such practices and policies can be shared, developed, problematised, and deployed to further counter violence and polarisation.

By looking at 13 case study countries, we gain insight into regions such as Western and Northern Europe (France, the Netherlands, and the UK), which have often led the discussion on P/CVE in Europe and have developed significant resilience-building programmes countering extremism. It also provides us with the opportunity to explore patterns of extremism and resilience-led responses in European regions not often included in such discussions, such as Southern Europe (Italy and Greece) and Central and Eastern Europe (Germany, Poland, and Hungary), which face different sets of factors and histories that contribute to extremism. These are compared to more global examples, which influence and are influenced by European trends of extremism, in North America (Canada and the USA) and Australasia (Australia and New Zealand) – both of which are dealing with instances of national and transnational violent extremism and developing their own trailblazing resilience programmes.

The book takes a national approach, as well as providing important discussion on terms and processes of extremism and resilience, and aims to inform policy, practitioner, and research efforts in understanding and responding to societal polarisation and its link to violence in the wider world.

This chapter starts with an overview of recent trends in violent extremism and resilience, providing critical context and a conceptual introduction for the Handbook. Briefly tracing the development of violent extremism in the twenty-first century, it highlights key events that have informed this process, such as terrorist attacks, policy changes, and civil society movements or organisations. It also introduces the concept of resilience, providing an overview of its historical development and how it has come to be integrated within these discussions. The chapter concludes with a synopsis of the chapters in this volume, exploring how they contribute to our understanding of resilience and the role it plays within current countering violent extremism (CVE).

Recent trends and approaches

Europe and the West face new and growing threats from violent extremism and polarisation. The context of financial crises and swingeing austerity has provided an important context for violent extremism and polarisation to develop, fuelling existing and new forms of populism and exclusionary identities (Norris and Inglehart 2018; Wodak 2015, 2019). Further interwoven in this setting of increasing inequality are reinvigorated 'racialised' elements in the politics of society – such as problematic elements of counterterrorism or the so-called refugee crisis – which have exacerbated pre-existing societal divisions (Krzyzanowski, Triandafyllidou and Wodak 2018; Kirtsoglou and Tsimouris 2018; McNeil-Willson 2017). Such a context has set the stage for the rise of new radical actors, including several populist and exclusionary groups that take aim at the practice of liberal governance and safety of minority communities (Mudde 2016; Minkenberg 2015). This climate of greater political and societal polarisation has been further linked to new trends in traditional and online media, enabling the spread of more extreme ideas and discourse internationally, as well as phenomena such as 'echo chambers' that reinforce extreme speech and allow for the radicalisation of wider political discourse (O'Callaghan et al. 2014; Conway, Scrivens and Macnair 2019).

Together these socio-economic, cultural, political, and historical factors play important roles in the development of violent extremism across the European continent, requiring further examination and interrogation. What constitutes violent extremism can sometimes be difficult to determine with precision, with the term containing a normative, relational, and context-specific value: one is judged radical or extremist against culturally specific benchmarks, and the term's application is dependent on who is doing the labelling (McNeil-Willson et al. 2019, p. 5). Violent extremism is understood in this Handbook as the use of violent acts, or the threat thereof, by irregular actors in the pursuit of political aims to erode or subvert democratic processes and pluralistic values, often at the expense of minority faith, cultural, or political communities. Polarisation often provides the necessary context for the growth and legitimisation of such recent patterns of violent extremism (McNeil-Willson et al. 2019).

In the context of liberal democratic countries, extremist groups and networks engage in acts of violence as part of an expressed desire to create a homogenous society based on rigid, dogmatic tenets, including the active suppression of political opposition and ethnic and cultural minorities (Mudde 2007; Schmid 2013). Often cherry-picking from religious or nationalist doctrines, such ideologies rely on superficial understandings and interpretations of complex events or beliefs and aim to pit certain groups against others through exclusivist violence.

We can see several constructions of extremisms in recent years developing in Europe and the West: recent Islamically justified attacks in France and the UK, such as the 'Bataclan' attacks in Paris in 2015 or the Manchester Arena bombing in 2017; far-right attacks, such as those in Oslo and Utøya in 2011 or the Christchurch killings in New Zealand in 2019; or misinformation surrounding democratic elections in the USA or the global Covid-19 pandemic, which led to rioting and the storming of the US Capitol Building in 2021. But violent extremism also includes less overtly violent acts that fray the fabric of communities – conspiracy theories heavily laden with anti-Semitism and Islamophobia, ideas hostile to migrants and human rights, or exclusionist and racist political identities – creating a societal context more conducive to extremist violence and polarisation. As such, any response against violent extremism must also account for these less overt but often more insidious articulations of extremism.

In recent years, resilience has emerged as a potentially key means of response. Resilience-based approaches to addressing violent extremism focus on what is keeping people resistant to violence rather than what is making them vulnerable to it. Instead of asking why people are radicalising to violence, the question becomes why aren't more people radicalising (Grossman et al. 2020). Resilience has been cited as the ability of people to face and respond to adversity, and the capacity to draw on a variety of sources of strength and resources to maintain core functioning when met with challenges and situations of strain, stress, or trauma (Kirmayer et al. 2009).

Traditionally associated with individual psychological response mechanisms (Hall and Lamont 2013), researchers have begun to pioneer a way to reframe the burden of resilience as a socio-ecological phenomenon (Mukherjee and Kumar 2017; Ungar 2013). Resilience thus becomes a dynamic process that can be enhanced or diminished by the allocation and negotiation of intersecting contextual factors and social resources (Hunter and Warren 2013; Sippel et al. 2015; Ungar 2008). The social-ecological framework of community resilience pioneered by Ungar et al. (Ungar 2011; Ungar et al. 2007; Masten and Wright 2010) considers resilience as a dynamic, interdependent, multi-system, and multi-level process rather than a fixed set of features or attributes for individuals or groups. It analyses resilience risks and protections as 'opportunity structures' through assessing communities' adaptability and transformative capacity in response to changes, challenges, and adversities – relevant for understanding community resilience strengths and vulnerabilities (Grossman et al. 2020).

A variety of resilience approaches have sprung up across Europe and the West in recent years, aiming to push back against the polarisation that often inspires and enables extremism. Resilience offers an approach to CVE which, in part, aims to address criticism of more 'securitised' counter-extremism measures, critically exploring the role that the allocation of societal resources, racism, structural discrimination, or state militarisation can play in the development of violence, alongside ideological factors of extremism. It helps to shift focus away from a top-down state-led response and towards actions that provide better foundations for communities and grassroots projects to take the lead in strengthening localised systems of support. Research in this area lags behind practice, but several significant projects have been conducted in Melbourne (Grossman, Tahiri and Stephenson 2014), Minnesota (Weine and Ahmed 2012), and Canada (Joosse, Bucerius and Thompson 2015) to identify protective resources that can help mitigate the risk factors for involvement in violent extremism (Grossman et al. 2020). The recent rise of new online spheres and Covid-19 has created further impetus to build communities more resilient to external and internal threats and disruption.

This Handbook seeks to advance our understanding of the different factors of extremism and how these play out in different national case studies. It also aims to analyse how new resilience measures are attempting to respond to these factors of extremism – their successes and limitations – and how they may do so in the future. The first part of the book covers core analytical discussions on theories and factors of violent extremism and resilience, international trends, the use of relevant indicators, and approaches to online resilience, with a special focus on youth. The second part of the volume offers a broad range of 13 case studies that explore the origins of violent extremism in each respective country, the factors that contributed to its rise as well as those that helped build resilience. Specific case studies are discussed in each country chapter with a view of highlighting both country-specific and broader issues. The book thus offers a geographical mapping of instances, groups, and impacts of violent extremism in European and other Western case study countries.

The country cases reviewed in the book cover several sub-regions within Europe – notably Western, Northern, Southern, and Central and Eastern Europe – as well as Australasia and North America with the aim of sharing comparative regional experiences of violent extremism and resilience-building. Each of the identified macro-regions shares some common elements that have shaped both violent extremism trends and policies and practices of P/CVE.

Western Europe has tended to dominate discussion over violent extremism, largely due to its longer history of counterterrorism and greater available counterterror resources and structures. The attacks in Madrid (2004) and London (2005) ushered in the implementation of new counterterrorism measures throughout most of Europe and played a significant role in the subsequent development of early deradicalisation and programmes for countering extremism. That many of the acts of violence in Western Europe since the turn of the century have been carried out by so-called Islamist actors has meant that policy in most of Europe has been orientated towards such a threat. However, this approach has been criticised as obscuring or underplaying the threat posed by far-right extremism, impacting P/CVE in Western Europe and the rest of the continent.

In Northern Europe, concerns about both 'Islamist' and far-right extremism are evident. The 2011 Oslo and Utøya attacks in Norway led to significant attention towards the far-right, and recently concern has also been raised over the rise of far-right groups like the neo-fascist Nordic Resistance Movement. This has resulted in the development of several localised resilience-building projects, for instance the Nordic Safe Cities network. However, Northern Europe has also placed emphasis on responding to 'Islamist' extremism, with Denmark implementing measures such as the Aarhus model to deal with the relatively high number of Danish foreign fighters linked to Syria and Iraq, as well as increasingly focusing policy on Muslim minority communities in Denmark.

Central and Eastern Europe offers a specific set of challenges. A region still grappling with historical legacies of fascism, Eastern Europe has seen a surge in far-right groups with links both East and West. Such movements have gained substantial regional legitimacy and footholds in recent years, enabling the mainstreaming of far-right discourses in countries such as Hungary and Poland (Zeller 2019; McNeil-Willson 2020; Bustikova 2019). The threat that the far-right poses is also increasingly recognised in Germany, where several far-right groups have been proscribed. Several resilience-based programmes have been implemented to share experiences within the region on tackling violent extremism and support youth-led grassroots responses. However, the threat from the far-right is sometimes underplayed, and some resilience-led programmes operate in the region despite – rather than with the support of – governmental measures.

Approaches in Southern Europe have tended towards 'harder' formations of counter-extremism – with preventative measures generally far less developed. In Italy, for instance, extremism has been framed as largely linked to migration and, as such, governments have relied on measures like deportation. However, concerns over recent instances of extremism and the need to keep in step with EU counter-extremism measures have led to the introduction of new programmes – mostly concentrated in prisons and schools – to create resilience through the building of ties to Italian culture (McNeil-Willson 2021). Countries such as Greece have also recently introduced resilience-based measures, particularly in response to the rise and fall of the Neo-Nazi party Golden Dawn.

Finally, Australasia and North America enable a wider comparison of resilience and counter-extremism. Violent extremism has significantly impacted these regions, the most notable being the Christchurch killings in 2019, leading to the Christchurch Call to Action of global social media platforms to target the spread of violent content online. Meanwhile, the impacts of conspiracy and misinformation reverberate throughout these regions, particularly in the fallout from the Trump presidency in the USA, the rampant spread of Covid-19, and an increasingly muscular far-right. However, countries such as Canada and Australia have also led some of the most significant early research and practice into resilience, pioneering new theories and approaches – some of which have since informed or been adopted by European states (Bucci 2020).

We have grouped our country studies in these regions to move beyond the usual Western European focus that has characterised discussions over violent extremism and counter-extremism in recent years (for example, Belgium, France, or the UK). As a result, transnational analysis and practice has suffered due to Western European biases – focus on 'Islamist' terrorism by the European Union, for instance, over and above concerns about far-right terrorism, has led to the far right being largely obscured in European policy until very recently, despite its historical prevalence in Eastern and Central Europe (Weilnböck and Kossack 2019). Our aim, therefore, is to allow for highlighting and comparison between national experiences of violent extremism and resilience-building across the European continent and the wider world. This will provide an illustration of the different ways that countries have struggled with, conceptualised, and responded to violent extremism, the various groups or attacks that have shaped national discourse, and how resilience has been implemented in a variety of different ways. By building on these case studies, the Handbook will provide scope for considering potential future global trends of violent extremism, as well as how we might respond by developing new notions of resilience. As such, the Handbook allows for the exploration of international forms of extremism, their interaction within and between different countries and regions, and how governments and local communities can better respond to such threats.

The Handbook's contents

Methodological note

This book is largely based on analytical and empirical research conducted within the framework of the EU-funded Horizon 2020 project 'Building Resilience against Violent

Extremism and Polarisation' (BRaVE, www.brave-h2020.eu, grant number 822189). The analytical and empirical research for each chapter includes the following, conducted as part of the BRaVE project: research into existing literature and practice into violent extremism and resilience; mapping of hundreds of policies, projects, and institutes countering extremism through resilience-building within European countries; interviews with policymakers and practitioners throughout Europe; and indicators of polarisation and resilience in Europe. As well as providing a deep understanding of current resilience-based approaches towards extremism throughout Europe, the BRaVE project has also been involved in undertaking detailed research into factors of violent extremism and resilience-building, conducting research and workshops that bring together academics, practitioners, and policymakers to understand the role that socio-economic, cultural, political, and network-related factors play. The countries covered in the Handbook go beyond the BRaVE project's selection of case study countries, as we have chosen to include Australia, New Zealand, the USA, and Canada, as well as a few additional countries from Europe, such as Norway, as we felt they would be important to complement our overview of polarisation and resilience trends, policies, and practices.

Core issues on violent extremism and resilience

The second chapter 'Assessing our understanding of (violent) extremism', by Richard McNeil-Willson, provides a critical assessment of current theories of violent extremism, and their links to resilience. Conceptualisations of violent extremism represent a relatively recent addition to discussions of counterterrorism, built on the policy-based need to develop a pre-criminal approach to terrorism by authorities. Although countering extremism is becoming centralised in national policies in recent years, key questions remain: the definition of extremism remains more unstable than that of terrorism, poorly enshrined in national laws; the link between extremism and violence is contested; and, counter-extremism strategies risk conflicting with existing hate crime legislation or stifling freedom of expression and assembly. This chapter offers an overview of current theories of violent extremism, the assumptions upon which elements of these theories do (and do not) rest, and suggestions as to how limitations may be remedied. It suggests firstly that theories of extremism need to better account for the transnational links between violence without lapsing into universalist conceptualisations of 'extremism'; and furthermore, that greater awareness of the political processes involved in both extremism and counter-extremism, including understanding of the role the state potentially plays in both deradicalising and radicalising groups and movements labelled as 'extremist'. It also considers the means by which discussions of resilience can offer a solution, the links between polarisation and extremism, and where these explanations need to be further developed.

This discussion is complemented by Chapter 3 (Michele Grossman), which looks at resilience as a response to violent extremism. Across recent years, resilience has come to be a key feature in P/CVE frameworks within different countries and regions, mobilised by a range of theoretical models and national or multinational policy frameworks to drive policy and practice in strengthening protective factors against extremist violence. Yet despite the enthusiasm with which 'resilience to violent extremism' has been conceptualised and promoted through policy and programming, there remain key questions about the ways in which: first, current concepts of resilience to violent extremism are operationalised; second, how fit for purpose these concepts are in relation to the diversifying ideological and tactical landscape of violent extremist threats; and third, whether the field has paid sufficient attention not only to resilience to violent extremism but also the resilience of violent extremist movements and networks themselves, including the maladaptive resilience that can characterise trajectories of violent radicalisation. This chapter reviews recent developments in relation to these three key questions and proposes further directions for future policy and research on resilience to violent extremism.

Chapter 4 (Sheryl Prentice and Paul Taylor) looks at European trends in polarisation and resilience, exploring how these two phenomena are currently framed and experienced within their socio-economic, historic, cultural, and communication-based contexts via a thematic conceptual analysis of relevant publications and policy documents. It also examines how the popularity of particular conceptualisations of polarisation and resilience have evolved and which of the identified conceptualisations now dominates present academic, practitioner, and governmental understandings. The data is drawn from the European Commission-funded BRaVE project (2019–2021), which sought to gain a deeper understanding of polarisation and resilience across Europe. The project conducted a comprehensive review of various perspectives on these phenomena, including those of academics from multiple disciplines, practitioners, and governments. The findings presented in this chapter suggest a cross-context focus on the themes of group identity, understanding, and (to a certain extent) education – with some contexts foregrounding issues such as the challenges of addressing polarisation in increasingly diverse societies. Moreover, the data suggest that key actors in this space are speaking to differing priorities. The chapter discusses the reasons behind variabilities and shifts in academic, practitioner, and policymaking trends in perceptions and understanding; the real-world impact of observed patterns; and what foci may soon emerge in the discussion and implementation of polarisation and resilience-building in Europe.

In Chapter 5 on young people, radicalisation, and resilience, Vivian Gerrand examines why young people become involved in violent extremist organisations, with the understanding that they most often join to be part of something, that is, for social rather than ideological reasons. Young people today face uncertain future employment prospects in an age of inequality, climate emergency, and a pandemic – all factors that may create a conducive environment for radicalisation. Indeed, some level of radicalisation is no doubt a healthy response to such existential threats, depending on its orientation and articulation. Most young people who are recruited by terrorist organisations are led to believe they are mobilising for a 'just cause' that seeks to uphold human dignity. Socio-ecological studies of resilience understand resilience to be multisystemic and intersectional rather than simply up to the individual. These approaches to resilience help us to appreciate that youth resilience to violence and extremism is deeply contingent upon the extent to which societal structures can provide sufficient resources and opportunities to support the needs and build on the strengths of young people. Drawing on relevant case studies, this chapter explores pathways of prosocial and maladaptive radicalisation/resilience among youth, including the mobilisation of alternative narrative interventions as radical pro-social approaches to addressing, rather than countering, violent extremism.

In the final chapter of the book's first section, Amy-Louise Watkin focuses on online extremism and resilience. While the internet has long been exploited by extremist groups, events such as Brexit, divisive US presidential campaigns, the Covid-19 pandemic, alarmist language over irregular migration to and within Europe, and new terrorist attacks around the world have created a wave of new concerns. The anger and fear generated by such events create ideal conditions for polarisation and extremism to flourish. Further, the ever-evolving ecosystem of social media platforms, file-sharing sites, and messaging services, amongst others, can facilitate this, providing easy access to mass audiences and the tools to spread their message wide and gain support and sympathisers. This chapter begins by providing an overview of online extremism in recent years by examining numerous events such as the 2019 Christchurch attack, the 2020 US Presidential election, the 2021 Capitol Hill Riots, and the Covid-19 pandemic response. There has been enormous pressure on tech platforms to do more to counter polarisation and extremism on their services. The second half of the chapter focuses on tech platforms' responses to these events and the exploitation of their platforms. While much previous scholarly work has focused on debates such as deplatforming, this chapter will focus on resilience-building on these services through the lens of a social capital framework. This is in line with this volume, which explores resilience as a key response to violent extremism and polarisation: specifically, what causes people to be resistant to violence rather than what makes them vulnerable to it.

Country cases

Turning to our country specific chapters, Chapter 7 by Francesca Scrinzi explores the case of France. During the past five years, France has become one of the main targets of so-called jihadist violence and has been the largest producer in Europe of foreign fighters to Islamic State. The country has also seen a surge of anti-Semitic incidents. Indebted to the historical experience of the French New Right, extreme right movements are very active and have recently been bolstered in the context of the 'anti-gender' mobilisations. The country is marked by an important colonial history and long-standing Islamophobia as well as Muslims' substantial social and spatial discrimination; it also hosts an electorally successful radical right populist party. All this can fuel the extreme right but also resentment among Muslims, which can provide fertile ground for 'jihadist' extremism. Since 2015, French governments have repeatedly established a national state of emergency, and prevention policies target people believed to be at risk of radicalisation. Criticism has been levelled at these measures, based on the claim that they jeopardise human rights. Reflecting the distinctive republican relegation of religion to the private sphere, counter-radicalisation policies emphasise the value of *laïcité* and 'French Islam'. Overall, although security measures to protect Jewish sites and organisations have been heightened, the emphasis is put on 'jihadist' extremism as opposed to right-wing extremism.

Chapter 8 investigates the case of the UK. Policy and political debates around violent extremism and counter-extremism policies are exceedingly polarised and contentious in the UK as they have focused mostly on securitisation in recent times, moving away from positive community engagement. Tahir Abbas, Richard McNeil-Willson, and Lianne Vostermans provide a critical overview of the British context, as regards both Muslim communities and far-right groups and reactions to reciprocal violent extremist trends as well as policies and practices aimed at building community resilience. The UK represents an important site of debate around the securitisation process within counter-extremism, largely due to the controversial Prevent programme. As a greater focus on counter-extremism has developed and the securitised lens has expanded, Prevent's strategy has continued to reproduce a neo-colonial racist ideology and embed racialised inequality. As a result of this, debate over CVE has become increasingly polarised and community challenges of counter-extremism more evident – and 'resilience-building' more difficult. Such processes challenge core assumptions about violent extremism and offer lessons for radically reconsidering how policy responses can and should be conducted, in Britain and elsewhere.

Turning to the case of the Netherlands, Maria Vliek and Martijn de Koning trace the origins of the 'Dutch approach' to counterterrorism and extremism by focusing on the interaction between extremist groups, politics, public debate, and the subsequent development of P/CVE policy and legislation. Whilst in the 1970s various groups and violent attacks spurred the government to develop new policies addressing the criminal violations within the existing legal framework, after 9/11 and in response to various (inter)national attacks, it was thought necessary to amend the law in addition to the various preventive policies that were put in place as part of the 'broad approach'. This broad approach was developed to address various factors considered root causes of radicalisation, such as socio-economic or cultural triggers. Unpacking the differences in the development of P/CVE policies, this chapter investigates not only the terrorist attacks that these policies supposedly responded to, but also looks at the groups themselves and their interaction with the public and politics. How do different extremist groups perceive and respond to policies across time? By taking into account various perceptions of the development of P/CVE policy, the chapter offers both a historical overview of policy development and a critical appreciation of different perspectives from both politics as well as extremist groups themselves, on what extremism may entail.

Chapter 10 (Rune Ellefsen and Martin M. Sjøen) focuses on the case of Norway. This country has come under the spotlight during the last decade as it has registered a growing concern with violent extremism and introduced policies to prevent and counter such phenomena. No less than three national action plans have been launched to counter violent extremism. Suffering from an extensive history of right-wing extremism, Norway was once the scene of the relative successful pioneering of European EXIT-programme. However, extremist groups today are more socially complex, and in rethinking how society can strengthen P/CVE programmes through social networks, 'resilience' has emerged as a favoured concept about what might make people resistant to violence and extremism. This chapter provides an overview of recent trends of violent extremism in Norway and the social and political responses to it. The authors emphasise the role of 'resilience' in this context by examining the various P/CVE programmes and initiatives having emerged. Drawing on empirical research from a range of civil society and public sector institutions, the chapter offers a critically informed perspective on how violent extremism can be prevented through community networks. It suggests deemphasising the securitised venues of preventing violent extremism through vigilante surveillance to the advantage of developing trust-based community preventive networks.

Shifting our geographical focus slightly, Chapter 11 (Fabian Virchow) looks at the case of Germany. Violent right-wing extremism has increased in Germany in the last years. Racists and right-wing extremists have answered the growing number of refugees arriving in Germany since 2014 with various forms of violence. Many of these acts were directed against refugees, others selected German citizens of Turkish origin or Jewish faith as targets. Politicians who had campaigned for liberal immigration policies were also violently attacked, including Walther Lübcke, who was assassinated in June 2019. The German government runs and finances numerous programmes and projects against right-wing extremism in its various shapes. They address a wide range of issues – preventive, repressive, and interventionist alike. While right-wing groups are brought to justice if they can be proven to have committed or prepared violent acts, other projects aim at protecting vulnerable populations addressed by right-wing extremists and building resilience against their messages of radicalisation. The chapter critically discusses the different strategies of violent-prone extreme-right groups to recruit and radicalise young people in particular, and the effectiveness of different approaches to counter these attempts and build long-standing resilience in target communities.

Moving further east, Chapter 12 by Zsuzsanna Vidra and Michael C. Zeller examines extremism and counter-extremism in Hungary. First, the chapter looks at the progression of far-right social forces and the trends of resentment and xenophobic attitudes. Then, three phases of the post-socialist era are discussed, each exploring radical and extreme right political actors and movements, their political participation and influence on mainstream politics and the public. In the early years, while far-right political actors and movements proliferated, they remained marginal. With the rise of a new far-right party, Jobbik, in the 2000s, masses of voters were mobilised, and the party became the second strongest political force. Since 2010, Hungary has been marked above all by the political hegemony of Viktor Orbán's Fidesz. The party's turn to illiberalism and populism, and indeed its adoption of extreme positions on issues like immigration and so-called gender ideology, has closed opportunities for other far-right actors. In the final section, the chapter analyses counter-extremism policies and politics, revealing that extant measures are reactive rather than proactive and most of the time can be characterised as legally permissive and weakly implemented. What is more, since 2010 there have been no significant governmental attempts to address radicalisation, far-right activism, and associated criminality.

Chapter 13 (Michael C. Zeller and Jana Hrckova) looks at the case of Poland. The country's transition to democracy was not blighted by violence or intense contestation and was capped by smooth accession to the EU; the national economy developed well (though unequally) over the past three decades, including during the 2008–2009 economic crisis from which Poland emerged largely unscathed; and the ethnic and religious homogeneity of the population portended no danger of inter-group conflict. Yet Poland today is marked by strong polarisation and rising extremism. This chapter unpacks this empirical puzzle. First, it delineates the arc of macro-political developments that brought the populist radical right Law and Justice (PiS) party to power. Then, it identifies and classifies the variants of (violent) extremism in contemporary Poland, many of which have been nurtured or emboldened by PiS. This typological overview is complemented by a detailed examination of one violent extremist actor, the National Radical Camp (ONR). The perils of polarisation and extremism have not gone unchallenged, thus the next section identifies and classifies the types of resilience-building practices existent in Poland. This is complemented by an examination of the activity of the Polish 'Autonomy Foundation'. The final section summarises the diagnosis of polarisation and extremism in Poland, as well as the prognosis suggested by political trends and resilience-building practices.

Turning to Southern Europe, in Chapter 14 Francesca Scrinzi reviews the experience of Italy. A country characterised by a bloody history of left-wing and right-wing terrorism in the 1970s and 1980s, Italy today stands out among other European countries because of the limited incidence of violent extremism. However, the notion of an Italian 'exceptionalism' is being increasingly challenged. So far, the national and linguistic diversity of the Muslim population – a still-limited Muslim second-generation and the absence of urban 'ghettos' afflicted by poverty, unemployment, and crime – has been seen as protecting Italy. Nonetheless, terrorists have used Italy as a logistical platform, and the threat of home-grown 'jihadism' seems to be growing. Similarly, while the security forces consider that the right-wing terrorist threat is limited, the country has witnessed some lone-actor attacks. At the same time, given the intense politicisation of immigration, the influence of the populist radical right in public debates and important fascist historical legacies, Italian grassroots neo-fascist and 'Identitarian' movements are very active. Lagging other countries, Italy lacks a national policy counter- and de-radicalisation policy: preventive work – a pillar of EU approach to fighting terrorism – is still underdeveloped. Preventive policies have only recently been implemented, focusing on prisons and schools, and mainly targeting 'jihadism' rather than the extreme right.

In Chapter 15, Eda Gemi investigates the case of Greece. In October 2020, a landmark court verdict in Greece's highest-profile political trial in decades was met with jubilation after the Neo-Nazi party Golden Dawn was found guilty of running a criminal organisation. Despite the party's fall, the threat of violent extremism in Greece has not receded. Although right-wing extremism is a relatively new phenomenon in Greek politics, its causes are deeply rooted in society and politics. A dual crisis in the 2010s, both financial and humanitarian, provided fertile ground for the rise of political extremism. Indeed, right-wing extremism, hate speech, and violence have largely targeted immigrants and religious minorities. Far-right extremists, in particular, exploit popular fears by propagating views of immigrants and religious 'Others' as 'usurpers', thus advancing a racist and ethnicist rhetoric in public discourse. Three elements have played a crucial role in shaping the trends of extremism and social polarisation in Greece: the political factor, the religious factor, and the media. This chapter offers an overview of recent trends of violent extremism and social polarisation in Greece and assesses some of the resilience-based projects implemented in response.

The volume's last four chapters turn to the Asia Pacific and North America regions. In their chapter on Australia, Michele Grossman and Vivian Gerrand explore how resilience discourse and frameworks have been mobilised within the context of CVE theory, policy, and practice in Australia over two decades. As in many other countries, resilience has been central to the policy landscape of Australia's prevention of violent extremism and radicalisation to terrorism. The historical emphasis in Australian CVE policy on deploying a social-ecological construct of resilience that is enmeshed with creating and sustaining social cohesion as a core tenet of CVE practice reflects Australia's composition and history, particularly since the 1970s, as a multicultural, pluralist democracy with a strong focus on integrating culturally diverse communities. While this approach reflects a range of prosocial aims, its primary focus on ethnocultural minority communities, and Muslim communities in particular, has also been critiqued as undermining the very resilience it purports to build by securitising communities in the name of promoting resilience to violent extremism. The acceleration of diverse forms of extremism in Australia, including far-right violent extremism, now raises questions of how fit for purpose Australian models of CVE resilience may be, and what might need to change as a result.

Chapter 17 (Jacinta Carroll) turns to the case of New Zealand. Had this book been published prior to March 2019, there would perhaps have been no mention of New Zealand. The country had been largely free from the perceived heightened threat from terrorism in the post-9/11 environment. This all changed on 15 March 2019, when 51 people were murdered by a lone terrorist in Christchurch in the worst single act of violence experienced in the country in its modern history. New Zealand's experience of and engagement with violent extremism, however, belies this simple assessment and presents a more complex and nuanced story. As an archetypal and successful small state, New Zealand has been a vocal and engaged participant in multilateral forums and activities to counter violent extremism throughout the post-9/11 era, even through providing combat and humanitarian assistance to military operations to counter terrorism operations in Afghanistan. It also has extensive collaboration with Australia, its ally and closest partner, on domestic, regional, and international approaches to counterterrorism. This contrasts, however, with how violent extremism is understood to directly affect New Zealand: the country's status and national self-perception as a peaceful, liberal, multicultural, and internationalist nation has reinforced the notion of terrorism as primarily a matter of foreign policy concern, leaving domestic responses to CVE as optional and largely neglected. In the wake of the Christchurch attacks, however, New Zealand's government and community have engaged thoughtfully to understand and learn the lessons from that event, while seeking to further reinforce community resilience to violent extremism and terrorism.

In Chapter 18, Sara K. Thompson examines patterns and trends of violent extremism in Canada over time and the current landscape. The chapter reviews groups and attacks that have shaped the national discourse. In the wake of back-to-back extremist attacks in Ottawa and Quebec in October 2014, followed by clusters of young men and women leaving Canada to take up arms overseas with groups like Al Shabaab and Daesh (in 2014 and 2015), the Canadian government began to realise that traditional enforcement-based approaches to national security were not, on their own, sufficient to counter the multidimensional threat posed by transnational and 'home-grown' extremism. Following the lead of other nations, Canada began to develop a host of measures aimed at preventing and intervening in situations where there is actual (or the potential for) radicalisation to violence – which amounted to the birth of P/CVE in this country. (Many argue that as Canada started 'doing' P/CVE in the country later than other nations, this enabled Canadian practitioners to benefit from the previous successes and lessons learnt elsewhere). The chapter briefly reviews the infrastructure that was built to support P/CVE work in Canada and the related national strategy. It also discusses how Canada conceptualises and defines the spectrum of extremist types (ideologically motivated, religiously motivated, politically motivated, and so on). The dual concepts of social polarisation and resilience underpin the bulk of Canadian responses to the threat posed by violent extremism – which is outlined and illustrated with reference to a number of different models of P/CVE programming. In reviewing the Canadian approaches, this chapter discusses the importance of national coordination, particularly in a country as large and geographically diverse as Canada, and the importance of evaluation in the context of P/CVE for developing best practice, avoiding the potential for iatrogenic effects, and most importantly, so that we can grow the international evidence base to better understand what works, for who, and why.

The final chapter in this volume focuses on the USA. Here, Brian Hughes argues that the US radical right has undergone a rapid process of metamorphosis in the first two decades of the twenty-first century. These changes have been intimately connected with larger trends of polarisation in the electorate and media, the so-called culture wars, and a struggle within the US conservative movement between populist, elite, imperial, and ethno-nationalist tendencies, among others. Political violence, from street fighting to lone actor terrorism, has likewise developed according to new conditions overlaid on both the recent past and the very origins of American colonialism. The economic and cultural legacy of White supremacy, the failures of Reconstruction and successes of civil rights, the persistence of Confederate sympathy, and the rise of the White power and militia movements between the 1970s and 1990s have fed a vast reservoir of cultural resources and structural abetment to a radical right that is today organised and imagined through the decentralised networks of digital communication media. Resilience in the USA is typically conceived as either a process of healing for individuals and communities following a terrorist attack or alternatively as bolstering the protective and self-defence capabilities of likely targets of political violence. Resilience, understood within the framework of prevention, is far less common in the USA. This chapter explores the historical and political-economic reasons for such a disparity. It argues that the legacy of White supremacy in the USA, along with key anti-democratic dynamics in its political structures, bias resilience away from the steps necessary to build preventative resilience. It concludes with an overview of prevention programmes and describes the possibility that a more preventative approach may be on the horizon – should federal support for it materialise.

References

Bucci, Nino (2020) Growing far-right threat should spark new approach to extremism, Australian expert says. *The Guardian*, 25 November, section Australian security and counter-terrorism.

Bustikova, Lenka (2019) *Extreme Reactions: Radical Right Mobilization in Eastern Europe*. Cambridge: Cambridge University Press.

Conway, Maura, Scrivens, Ryan and Macnair, Logan (2019) *Right-wing Extremists' Persistent Online Presence: History and Contemporary Trends*. The Hague: International Centre for Counter-Terrorism (ICCT).

Grossman, Michele, Hadfield, Kristin, Jefferies, Philip., Gerrand, Vivian. and Ungar, Michael (2020) Youth resilience to violent extremism: Development and validation of the BRaVE measure. *Terrorism and Political Violence*, 34(3), pp. 468–488.

Grossman, Michele, Tahiri, Hussein and Stephenson, Peta (2014) Harnessing Resilience Capital: An Investigation of Resilience and Cultural Diversity in Countering Violent Extremism. Canberra: Australia-New Zealand Counter-terrorism Committee.

Hall, Peter A. and Lamont, Michele (2013) *Social Resilience in the Neoliberal Era*. Cambridge: Cambridge University Press.

Hunter, Billie, and Warren, Lucie (2013) *Final Report: Investigating Resilience in Midwifery*. Cardiff: Cardiff University.

Joosse, Paul, Bucerius, Sandra M. and Thompson, Sara K. (2015) Narratives and counternarratives: Somali-Canadians on recruitment as foreign fighters to al-Shabaab. *The British Journal of Criminology*, 55, pp. 811–832.

Kirmayer, Laurence, Sedhev, Megha, Whitley, Rob, Dandeneau, Stéphane. and Isaac, Colette (2009) Community resilience: Models, metaphors and measures. *International Journal of Indigenous Health*, 5(1), pp. 63–117.

Kirtsoglou, Elisabeth, and Tsimouris, Giorgos (2018) Migration, crisis, liberalism: The cultural and racial politics of Islamophobia and 'radical alterity'. *Ethnic and Racial Studies*, 41, pp. 1874–1892.

Krzyzanowski, Michal, Trianafyllidou, Anna and Wodak, Ruth (2018) The mediatisation and the politicisation of the 'refugee crisis' in Europe. *Journal of Immigrant & Refugee Studies*, 16, pp. 1–14.

Masten, A.S. and Wright, M.O (2010) Resilience over the lifespan: Developmental perspectives on resistance, recovery and transofmation. In: Reich, John W., Zautra, Alex J. and Hall, John Stuart (eds.), *Handbook of Adult Resilience*. New York: The Guilford Press, pp. 213–237.

McNeil-Willson, Richard (2017) A primer on the impact of Islamic State on counterterrorism legislation. In: Romaniuk, Scott Nicolas, Grice, Francis, Irrera, Daniela and Webb, Stewart (eds.), *The Palgrave Handbook of Global Counterterrorism Policy*. London: Palgrave Macmillan, pp. 909–921.

McNeil-Willson, Richard (2020) *Right-wing extremism in Central and Eastern Europe: context, challenges, latest research results and best practices*. Policy Brief. Madrid: MINDb4ACT, Real Instituto Elcano (ELCANO).

McNeil-Willson, Richard (2021) Understanding the interplay of counter-extremism trends and Muslim communities in Europe. In: Bonino, Stefano and Ricucci, Roberta (eds.), *Islam and Security in the West*. London: Palgrave Macmillan, pp. 163–196.

McNeil-Willson, Richard, Gerrand, Vivian, Scrinzi, Francesca and Triandafyllidou, Anna (2019) *Polarisation, Violent Extremism and Resilience in Europe today: An analytical framework for the BRaVE project*. Concept Paper. Florence: European University Institute.

Minkenberg, Michael (2015) *Transforming the Transformation? The East European Radical Right in the Political Process*. London: Routledge.

Mudde, Cas (2007) *Populist Radical Right Parties in Europe*. Cambridge: Cambridge University Press.

Mudde, Cas (2016) The Study of Populist Radical Right Parties: Towards a Fourth Wave. *C-Rex Working Paper Series*. Oslo: Centre for Research on Extremism (C-REX), University of Oslo.

Mukherjee, Swati, and Kumar, Updesh (2017) Psychological resilience: A conceptual review of theory and research. In: Kumar, Updesh (ed.), *The Routledge International Handbook of Psychosocial Resilience*. London: Routledge, pp. 3–12.

Norris, Pippa and Inglehart, Ronald (2018) *Cultural Backlash: Trump, Brexit and the Rise of Authoritarian Populism*. Cambridge: Cambridge University Press.

O'Callaghan, Derek, Greene, Derek, Conway, Maura, Carthy, Joe and Cunningham, Pádraig (2014) Down the (White) rabbit hole: The extreme right and online recommender systems. *Social Science Computer Review*, 33, pp. 459–478.

Schmid, Alex P. (2013) Radicalisation, de-radicalisation, counter-radicalisation: A conceptual discussion and literature review. *ICCT Research Paper*. The Hague: The International Centre for Counter-Terrorism.

Sippel, Lauren M., Pietrzak, Robert H., Charney, Dennis S., Mayes, Linda C. and Southwick, Steven M. (2015) How does social support enhance resilience in the trauma-exposed individual? *Ecology and Society*, 10(4), DOI: 10.5751/ES-07832-200410

Ungar, Michael (2008) Resilience across cultures. *The British Journal of Social Work*, 38(2), pp. 218–235.

Ungar, Michael (2011) *The Social Ecology of Resilience: A Handbook of Theory and Practice*. New York: Springer.

Ungar, Michael (2013) Resilience, trauma, context and culture. *Trauma, Violence and Abus*, 14(3), pp. 255–266.

Ungar, Michael, Brown, Marion, Liebenberg, Linda, Othman, Rasha, Kwong, Wai Man, Armstrong, Mary and Gilgun, Jane (2007) Unique pathways to resilience across cultures. *Adolescence*, 42, pp. 287–310.

Weilnböck, Harald, and Kossack, Oliver (2019) The EU's 'Islamism' bias and its 'added damage' in Central and Eastern Europe. *OpenDemocracy*, 26 November, section Global Extremes.

Weine, Steven and Ahmed, Osman (2012) *Building Resiliencec to Violent Extremism Amongst Somali-Americans in Minneapolis-St. Paul*. National Consortium for tthe Study of Terrorism and Responses to Terrorism (START), Department of Homeland Security Science and Technology Centre of Excellence.

Wodak, Ruth (2015) *The Politics of Fear*. London: SAGE Publishing.

Wodak, Ruth (2019) Entering the 'post-shame era': the rise of illiberal demcoracy, populism and neo-authoritarianism in Europe. *Global Discourse (Themed Issue: The Limits of EUrope: Identities, Spaces, Values)*, 9, pp. 195–213.

Zeller, Michael C. (2019) Whither Poland? After the 2019 parliamentary elections. *OpenDemocracy*, 27\ October, section Global Extremes.

2
ASSESSING OUR UNDERSTANDING OF (VIOLENT) EXTREMISM

Richard McNeil-Willson

Introduction

This chapter assesses our understanding of (violent) extremism not only through analysis of groups labelled extremist but also through how the label of extremism has been applied by states and stakeholders. In doing so, it considers the state a key actor for understanding processes by which individuals, groups, or milieus engage or disengage in irregular violence, as well as seeking to account for the malleable and politically charged nature of the term and its usage.

How the term '(violent) extremism' is constituted reveals a great amount about our knowledge of the term itself. Significant debate has been had on how best (or whether at all) the term should be definitively defined (S. Jackson 2019a). Scholars have suggested that it has proven consistently difficult to adequately describe, highly contested in its construction, and often problematically used – hinting at several foundational limitations in our understanding of 'extremism' (Lowe 2017). The range of definitional attempts and debates within scholarship, as well as the struggle of states to enshrine any concept of extremism in law, speaks to this problem – with definitions and their legal basis differing wildly across contexts (McNeil-Willson 2021). This has not stopped scholars from attempting to align elements of existing definitions as a means of better understanding extremism, and some have suggested that an agreement on extremism in policy or academia is both possible and advantageous for systemising what we know about the cause of societal polarisation and political violence (Carter 2018, p. 175; Lowe 2017; McNeil-Willson et al. 2019).

To assess our understanding of (violent) extremism, this chapter looks at how extremism is defined and understood through academic, policy, and human and civil rights lenses, respectively. Firstly, it explores the understanding of extremism from scholars and researchers in recent studies to determine the state-of-the-art, key features of debate, and the problems and limitations of recent conceptualisations. This is followed by a critical discussion on how definitions of (violent) extremism have been understood and applied in policy arenas, including exploration of whether and to what extent violent extremism has come to operate as a replacement term for terrorism. Finally, the human and civil rights implications of the operationalisation of (violent) extremism are explored, including concern about its role in the 'pre-criminal' space, the negative impact this has had on freedoms of speech, assembly, and human rights, and the role of the state in legitimising and enabling violence.

Ultimately, I take the position that one cannot understand extremism without simultaneously attempting to understand counter-extremism. The contentious nature of the term itself, the problems with enshrining it in policy and the various human and civil rights questions brought about by attempting to respond to (violent) extremism suggest that the problem of extremism is one enshrined at the heart of the contemporary liberal-democratic state. As the labelling of someone or something 'extremist' represents a political act, it is incumbent on scholars to consider how and why the concept is used, to avoid uncritically adopting state-security narratives – to act, in the words of Schmid and Jongman (1988), not as a 'fireman' to solve problems such as extremism, but as a 'student of combustion', prioritising scholarly understanding over policy cure (Silke 2004). By examining both the groups labelled as 'extremist' and the authorities doing this labelling, we are best placed to assess our understanding of (violent) extremism. This chapter therefore examines extremism by detailing how the term has been understood and applied in a Western academic and policy context. It begins with a discussion on the state-of-the-art, examining how academics have conceptualised and researched extremism and its link to violence. This is followed by an exploration of the ways in which extremism has been applied within various legal and practitioner frameworks, including consideration of whether concern over 'violent extremism' is displacing and replacing that of 'terrorism' in governmental and media language. The chapter then embarks on a critical discussion of how the development of extremism – and subsequent efforts to counter it – has impacted on civil and human rights. And finally, it concludes by considering how some of the problems detailed throughout can be remedied, at least in part, by ensuring that the role the state plays in enabling political violence is brought into the heart of future theories and practice.

Scholarship: state-of-the-art

This first section lays out the state-of-the-art on the concept of '(violent) extremism' within recent scholarship. Extremism and violent extremism are framed throughout this chapter as a bifurcation of the same concept, and therefore examined together – although discussions over their potential differences, overlaps, and iterations are had at a later stage. By examining recent studies on the definitional aspects of extremism, we find some concepts emphasised by several scholars in the quest for a definition. Commonality in definitions of (violent) extremism is found on the following three themes: the construction of *exclusivist in-groups* which sit at odds to out-groups; the use of *anti-democratic and anti-pluralist* ideologies; and the advocating of the use of *force or violence*, largely by non-state actors, or those lacking state legitimacy – sometimes referred to as 'irregular actors'. This section explores key academic debates around these conceptual ideas, considering their possibilities and limitations for understanding (violent) extremism.

One characteristic that has been found by several scholars to be useful in defining extremism is the creation of specific and *exclusivist in-groups* and out-groups, which are framed as operating in direct antagonism with each other. Berger, in his long-view study of extremism across national and historical contexts, describes extremism as 'a spectrum of beliefs in which an in-group's success is inseparable from negative acts against an out-group' (2018, p. 6). The creation of such exclusivist in-groups requires the casting of an external enemy community or communities, whose perceived success results in the diminishing of one's own. This zero-sum framing is used to provide justification for hostile action under the guise of ensuring the survival of one's in-group (Berger 2018 pp. 44–46).

Hellyer and Grossman (2019) also emphasise the central role played by in-/out-group constructions in their analysis of extremism in relation to religion and violence. They suggest that extremism is 'the effort to legitimise and assert superiority and domination of an exclusivist in-group identity over other out-groups in ways that are inseparable from proposing or causing harm to those out-groups' (ibid. p. 12). Grossman et al. (2016) highlight that extremism is linked to a high level of exclusivism, stating that 'exclusivist in-group and out-group dynamics may, but do not necessarily, support trajectories of extremism' (ibid. p. 4). Schmid (2013) also suggests that extremism is a simplified mono-causal and Manichaean interpretation of the world, in which the political and cultural environment is divided into competing communities; whilst Coolsaet (2015) highlights the simplistic '*Us* versus *Them*' narratives often used to promote hatred, intolerance, and violence amongst 'extremist groups' of various stripes.

As well as the construction of competing in-group/out-groups, another possible facet of 'extremism' is the embracing of political beliefs that are *anti-democratic and anti-pluralistic*. Mudde (2014), for instance, argues that extremism exists in opposition to certain widely accepted democratic practices and beliefs that are held in a Western context; extremism is therefore identified by the desire of individuals to overturn standardised democratic norms. Bötticher has described extremism as 'by its very nature, anti-democratic' (2017, p. 75). Carter, meanwhile, conceptualises extremism as encompassing 'authoritarianism, anti-democracy and exclusionary and/or holistic nationalism' (2018, p. 157), and Jupskås and Segers (2020) stress that extremist groups involve 'anti-democratic opposition towards equality'.

This anti-democratic tendency is not just a goal of such groups; it is the means for preventing societal equality of other faith, ethnic, gender, or political communities – and scholars emphasise the promotion of inequality as key to extremism. Lowe, for instance, understands extremism as the vocal or active opposition to 'the legal principle of the law and the existence of a pluralist society', manifested in 'an intolerance of an individual's rights and freedoms, and different faiths and beliefs that encourages discord in society' (2017, p. 927). McNeil-Willson et al. (2019) also consider the targeting of minorities as important, suggesting that violent extremism involves the use of irregular violence 'in the pursuit of political aims to erode democratic processes and pluralistic values, often at the expense of minority faith, cultural, or political communities' (ibid. p. 7). Ultimately, anti-democratic methods are, at least in part, understood as a tactic by which extreme groups seek to remove key civil rights from, and undermine the security of, other communities.

Another consistent idea is *force and violence*, seen as existing in proximity to 'extremist' groups either through their direct engagement in violent acts or their active encouragement thereof. Schmid (2014) has argued that extremism cannot be understood without violence, and that non-violent and violent extremism are equivalent – or 'two sides of the same coin'. Even when violence is neither present nor explicit, some have argued it is inherent in extremism. Berger, for instance, states that whilst violent extremist groups may claim to consider temporary cessation of hostilities, the ideologies of such groups often 'stipulate in various ways that fighting against out-groups must continue until the end of history' (2017). Bötticher echoes this sentiment, concluding that '[e]xtremism is, due to its dogmatism, intolerant and unwilling to compromise' (2017, p. 76). As such, whilst groups may publicly eschew violence or extreme views, it has been suggested that this is only ever strategic and is consistently subjugated to extreme acts and ideologies. Others suggest that violence comes from a desire to create a highly conformist society through the suppression of opposition and the subjugation of minorities (Mudde 2007), extremist groups inevitably acting to reject the rule of law (Schmid 2013).

Whilst these three traits – the construction of *exclusivist in-groups* which sit at odds to outgroups; the use of *anti-democratic and anti-pluralist* ideologies; and, the advocating of the use of *force or violence* by irregular groups – are present across many definitional discussions on '(violent) extremism', there are problems and challenges raised by their inclusion.

The focus on the potential use of *force or violence* in defining extremism is problematic as, in maintaining a definitional split between violent and non-violent forms of extremism, it is uncertain as to whether violence is inherent within 'extremism' unless qualified as 'violent'. Midlarsky (2011, p. 18), for instance, notes several different kinds of extremism, including a significant divergence between violent groups and those that are explicitly anti-democratic but do not envision the use of violence to attain political goals. Lowe (2017) also argues for a strong definitional difference between the two, whilst Khalil (2014) challenges the idea that extremist ideologies are inherently violent – with even some of the most exclusionary ideas often not resulting in violence.

The problem with framing violence or force as, if not a constituent feature of extremism, at least inherently linked, is that it ascribes objectives to actors that may directly conflict with their own actions and statements, essentialising actors as beholden to a literal interpretation of their ideologies. Islamic activist groups labelled as 'extremist', for instance, have often been shown to eschew views that may be central to their official ideologies or texts, evolving in response to their political context (cf. Gunning 2007; McNeil-Willson 2019; Pieri 2015). Meanwhile, attempts to enshrine violence within extremism risks the assumption of certain objectives of such actors – sometimes in direct contradiction to their own actions – and can obscure organisational changes within and amongst such milieus. As Hellyer and Grossman therefore conclude, 'violence *as a constituent feature* of extremist thinking and feeling should not be taken as a given' (2019, p. 10).

The suggestion that extremism is inherently anti-democratic is also questionable. Extremism tends to have a particularly 'anti-social' designation – in contrast to related terms such as, for example, radicalisation, which has a wider variety of normative uses and may be used to refer to instances of 'pro-social' change-making movements. The application of 'extremism', by authorities and commentators, however, tends to always signal something negative or 'anti-social', and has been used against a host of groups that engage directly and indirectly with often legitimate forms of democratic practice. This has included registered political parties (Jupskås and Segers 2020), climate activists (Dodd 2020), social justice movements (McDonald 2009), and a broad swathe of Muslim faith and political groups (Tazamal 2022). Even groups who have found themselves labelled as 'extremist' due to their openly anti-democratic ideologies have sought democratic legitimacy and participation in certain contexts. Activist groups with openly anti-democratic doctrines have been shown to engage in elements of state democracy such as lobbying, political campaigning, and public support of democratic practice in response to changing political contexts (McNeil-Willson 2019; Pieri 2015), as have several far-right groups (Kølvraa 2019). It is thus far from possible to determine extremist groups as consistently 'anti-democratic'.

Finally, the construction of exclusivist in-groups operating in a set of hostile or antagonistic relations is a difficult descriptor, with the potential to obscure power imbalances between communities. For instance, several Muslim activist organisations have been labelled 'extremist' as part of their work seeking to tackle Islamophobia in counterterrorism (Cossé 2021; Dathan 2022). The community or power imbalance that is the target of antagonistic relations may also be lost in this descriptor. Far-right movements, for instance, largely focus on targeting other communities, particularly minorities, through their activism; whilst Muslim or left-wing groups labelled as 'extreme' often engage in actively tackling (state-led) structural racism and Islamophobia. By drawing equivalence between a disparate band of ideologies, the term risks flattening community relations and assuming cumulative processes between milieus that engage with society and power in radically different ways (cf. Macklin and Busher 2018). It also risks misdirecting attention away from similar acts of constructing hostile in-/out-group relations created by governments and authorities – particularly in the increasingly 'populist' political environment of Western Europe (Norris and Inglehart 2018).

Exclusionary ideas and language, so often framed as 'extremist', have often been echoed and adopted by national-level politicians and governments. These are sometimes deployed as part of a security-based narrative that simultaneously decries the threat posed by violent extremism (Winter and Mondon 2020) – the language of counter-extremism interacting with and, in some cases, actively fuelling far-right movements (Aked 2017). Meanwhile, limitations in understanding 'extremism' have led to confusion over how to categorise legitimised state actors who promote 'extreme' narratives or actions. In reference to the 2021 attack on the US Capitol building, for instance, analysts referred to US society as participating in 'mass radicalisation', with 'tens of thousands – if not millions – of individuals' vulnerable to extremist messages from a former head of state (Stanton 2021). Questions thus remain over whether it is appropriate to consider extremism as linked to 'irregular' actors when it can and has operated in step with national governments and media.

There has been concern in a wide range of scholarship that extremism, at least in its application, operates as a politically freighted term used to determine and describe activities that are either not in accordance with norms of the government of the time or to attack political opponents (Berger 2017; Sotlar 2004). McNeil-Willson et al. (2019) raise concern over the term's 'normative, relational, and context-specific value', determining that 'one is judged radical or extremist against culturally specific benchmarks, and this label is dependent on who is doing the labelling' (ibid., p. 5). Whether and how the label of 'extremist' is applied is largely dependent on the government in power, national media, recent events, and the changing political winds. Whilst European governments have attempted to claim the benchmark of 'core values' as a means of tackling extremism – such as democracy, rule of law, minority rights, relative separation of church and state, equality before the law including gender equality or freedom of expression or both – these ideas have been deployed hypocritically, dropped entirely when electorally convenient.

This section has sought to provide an overview of the state-of-the-art surrounding extremism. As 'extremism' is a term often led by and operationalised within policy, the following section explores how (the response to) extremism has been articulated as well as seeking to understand how extremism is seen as being linked to concepts of terrorism, radicalisation, and political violence.

Policy: (violent) extremism and legislative practice

This section explores how the understanding of '(violent) extremism' has developed in a Western policy setting. It notes that most states have failed in attempts to enshrine this concept in law or national penal codes, with (violent) extremism ultimately falling outside of legal frameworks (Lowe 2017). It is thus important to consider how extremism has been understood in policy, the ways in which it has been linked to terrorist-style violence, and how the term is used in government and national media discourse – engaging with evidence that suggests that violent extremism is increasingly being used as a descriptor in place of 'terrorism'.

When assessing what we know of (violent) extremism, it is notable that many liberal-democratic states have failed to develop a legal definition. The UK government, for instance, unsuccessfully attempted to enshrine a definition of extremism in law, something ultimately deemed 'too difficult' and flagged as potentially criminalising a large swathe of views and individuals across British society (Dixon 2019). David Anderson KC, a former reviewer of terrorism legislation for HM Government, dubbed attempted governmental definitions 'broad and ill-defined', whilst evidence from the Commission for Countering Extremism found that many people held a range of views as to what they considered to be extremism (Commission for Countering Extremism 2019). Similarly in the EU, there exists no formal definition of extremism that has been adopted or put forward by the Commission and, where definitions have been made, these have not been integrated into European or Member State law – acting instead as purely advisory terms.

Several national and supranational policy bodies have understood extremism to be the adoption of a set of problematic values that are positioned in opposition to thinly defined 'national', 'European', or 'Western' values – framing extremism as the context in which terrorism happens. The UK government has defined extremism as a set of values that, when adopted, 'create an atmosphere conducive to terrorism and can popularise views which terrorists then exploit' (HM Government, 2021). Such beliefs include 'vocal or active opposition to fundamental British values, including democracy, the rule of law, individual liberty and mutual respect and tolerance of difference faiths and beliefs' – as well as including those who call for the death of UK Armed Forces (ibid.). The EU understands extremism as encompassing a wide range of ideological expressions linked to European values, 'including hate speech, incitement to violence (e.g. terrorist violence) and more generally, messages that go against EU values and create division in our societies' (Burchett, Weyembergh, and Theodorakakou 2022, p. 75); the UK government's Commission for Countering Extremism (CCE) has called extremism a 'rejection of democratic values and principles' as part of a 'mindset that can justify or lead to hate crime or terrorism' (Commission for Countering Extremism 2022). Thus, extremism is considered in this policy setting as providing an ideological context for acts of violence.

This focus on national or European 'values' and its operationalisation in countering extremism has proved to be controversial (Lowe 2017). James's study of British counter-extremism approaches to the far-right finds that 'British Values are positioned within the education system as the antithesis to all forms of extremism' – as well as evidencing that the language and focus of this approach ultimately 'echoes in-group/out-group constructions of (ethno-nationalist) acceptability found within far-right ideologies' (2022, p. 121). Other research has problematised the vague conceptualisation of such national or regional values (Revell and Bryan 2018), the notion that such values should be considered 'national' or 'European' in character (Habib 2018), and further examined the relationship these might have with exclusionary constructions of nationalism emanating from the far right (Aked 2017; Brown, Mondon and Winter 2021; James 2020).

Whilst some governments have framed extremism as value-focused, other states have focused on the role extremism plays in the lead up to specific acts of violence. Canada, for instance, determines violent extremism to refer to individuals who support or commit ideologically motivated violence due to 'extreme political, religious or ideological views' (Public Safety Canada 2009), whilst the FBI has called extremism the 'encouraging, condoning, justifying or supporting the commission of a violent act to achieve political, ideological, religious, social or economic goals' by those who have 'rejected Western cultural values, beliefs and norms' (IACP 2018). Meanwhile, Sweden has determined an extremist to be someone 'deemed repeatedly to have displayed behaviour that does not just accept the use of violence but also supports exercises of ideologically motivated violence to promote something' (Swedish Ministry of Justice 2011). These conceptualisations see extremism as the combination of the rejection of a singular set of national or Western values, as well as a set of complementary and related actions that lead up to an instance of terrorist-style violence. To some extent, this conceptualisation seems to fit within Neumann's definition of 'radicalisation', as 'what goes on before the bomb goes off' (Neumann 2008, p. 4).

Other governments have centred extremism even further within definitions of acts of violence. Norway, for instance, has labelled extremism as 'activities of persons and groups that are willing to use violence in order to achieve political, ideological or religious goals' (Norwegian Government 2014). The Australian government, meanwhile, has conceptualised terrorism as just one form of extremism (Australian Government n.d.). Government documents even categorise groups such as *Euskadi Ta Askatasuna* (ETA) – officially sanctioned by several Western states as a 'terrorist' organisation – as 'ethno-nationalist or separatist *violent extremist* groups', leading to such groups being listing alongside environmental activist movements (Angus 2016).

Such policy definitions and conceptualisations have been criticised as containing phrases that are 'subjective, awkward and opaque' (Lowe 2017, p. 919), and there is consistent confusion over the link between extremism and terrorist-style violence in policy. Whilst the UK government understands extremism as a set of contextual factors and ideologies that have the potential to be drawn upon by terrorist groups (HM Government 2021), the Australian government considers extremism to refer to multiple forms of politically motivated and communal violence, including terrorism. Thus, confusion over policy understanding of extremism is evident in what constitutes the link between so-called 'violent extremism' and 'terrorism'. Research has suggested that these terms have come to be often considered as either intricately connected as part of the same process or as entirely interchangeable, noting the muddying of language in policy and political debate.

In a study of British parliamentary debates between 2010 and 2017, Onursal and Kirkpatrick (2021) observe a recent convergence between the two concepts, with violent and non-violent extremism acting to reproduce the same signifiers and markers as were previously held for terrorism. The authors show that, just as the War on Terror discourse normalised and securitised various legal practices through counterterrorism, so a constructed threat to 'British values' has normalised practices that conflate non-violent political expression with political violence through Preventing and Countering Violent Extremism (P/CVE), as 'extremism has become framed as if it were terrorism undermining wider counterterrorism' (ibid. 2021, p. 1095). This has broader implications for security and civil rights – replacement of the term 'terrorism' with '(violent) extremism' in mainstream political debate has increased the problematisation and securitisation of both violent and non-violent forms of political expression, under the rubric of national security.

Policy documents from several Western contexts show a tendency for slippage between terrorism and extremism. The European Parliament and Commission, for example, make reference in recent policy documents to 'terrorist/extremist' content or actors (Burchett et al. 2022, p. 71). Awan (2013) has found evidence that terms such as terrorism, violent extremism, and radicalisation have often been applied interchangeably in policing and other formations of counterterrorism, whilst Sedgwick (2010) notes confusion around the links between 'radicalisation' and 'extremism' in policy in North America and Northern

European countries. Vandenberg and Hoverd also find that, following the Christchurch mosque attack in 2019 in New Zealand, ideas around 'extremism' and 'violent extremism' appeared with far greater frequency in national agencies (2020, p. 7), with extremism used to explain the motivation for the attack – although this was almost always in a manner that left the connection unexplained.

In the UK context, extremism only entered the political landscape in a significant way after the killing of British soldier Lee Rigby outside Woolwich barracks, London, in 2013. This attack represented one of the first instances of violence being framed as extremist rather than terrorist, with then-Prime Minister David Cameron stating the assault was justified by 'an extremist ideology' that must be confronted 'in all its forms…not just on violent extremism' (UK Parliament 2013). Other events have shaped the narrative towards extremism in the UK and Europe. Greater focus on extremism has appeared in the British press since 2015 following the Trojan Horse hoax, an instance that centred on since-disproven fears that four UK schools in Birmingham, associated with the Park View Education Trust, were attempting to 'Islamicise' children (Holmwood and O'Toole 2017). Despite accusations being debunked as falsified and the legal cases brought against schools and individual teachers collapsing, the event saw the start of new legislation and practice countering extremism. This was crystallised in a new Government Counter Extremism Strategy which included the 2015 Prevent Duty, obligating schools to promote 'fundamental British values' and framing British values as a key bulwark against the development of extremism (Department for Education 2015).

The centralisation of extremism in British media is possible to observe through an examination of articles published on extremism and terrorism. In a study of UK national and local newspapers between 2001 and 2021, a dataset of 1,090,315 articles that make use of the term 'terrorism' (and associated terms, such as terrorist or terrorists) and 'extremism' (and related terms) demonstrates a marked increase in focus on extremism (McNeil-Willson 2024).

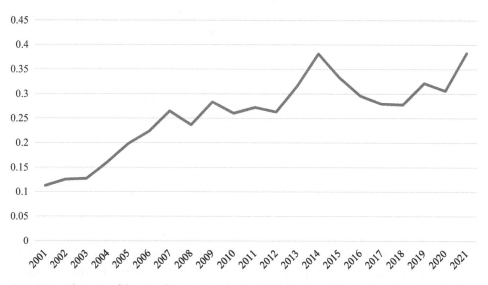

Figure 2.1 The ratio of the use of 'extremism' to 'terrorism' (and associated terms) as mentioned in British media

Source: McNeil-Willson 2024

Comparing use of 'terrorism' and 'extremism' as a ratio, findings suggest that extremism is increasingly being used in relation to – and in many cases, instead of – terrorism in the British media landscape. This data and analysis show that, since 2001, the use of extremism in relation to terrorism has grown significantly, from just over 0.1 uses of extremism per one use of terrorism in 2001 to a high of nearly 0.4 by 2021 – although focus on terrorism is still shown to be more prevalent in the dataset (McNeil-Willson 2024).

This section has offered an overview of policy understandings of (violent) extremism in several Western countries, paying particular attention to case studies mentioned in this handbook on *violent extremism and resilience*. It suggests that many countries face continued problems in operationalising a consistent understanding of extremism, resulting in a range of definitional ideas that are mostly not institutionalised in law due to their broad focus and their potential for criminalising a wide range of legal and democratic activities. This operational confusion has led to extremism being identified in policy as: a contextual or motivating factor for violence; a set of acts in the lead-up to terrorism; and the carrying out of acts of terrorist-style violence. It also found support for existing evidence that violent extremism is increasingly coming to be associated with, and in some instances actively replacing, discussion on terrorism in political and media language. The next and final section will examine (violent) extremism through a human-rights lens, detailing the problems of current counter-extremism approaches, as well as considering the push within discussion to develop a rights-led response to violence that challenges the state securitisation paradigm.

Human rights: undefining 'extremism'

This third section explores how a focus on human and civil rights has challenged notions of extremism and countering extremism, and notes approaches that seek to understand and respond to violence through rights-led paths. Three interrelated trends are particularly problematic in the development of countering extremism through policy. Firstly, the expansion of counter-extremism has led to and enabled the continuation of an overbearing focus on ideology and ideological factors in understanding processes of terrorism and political violence. Secondly, in attempting to 'up-stream' responses to terrorism, a 'pre-criminal' approach has developed – leading to a host of legal activities being cast as causal mechanisms for and indicators of political violence. And thirdly, policy has increasingly come to rely on the language of risk and vulnerabilities in attempting to map the processes of engagement with political violence, uncritically using safeguarding language in a policing and security context.

Counter-extremism programmes have tended to focus on challenging ideology, as the long 'War on Terror' crystallised an early policy consensus that the 'true problem' of terrorism is 'the rise of this theocratic, fascist ideology' which must be challenged through means that 'reassert, classical small-"L" liberal values' (Githens-Mazer and Lambert 2009; Nawaz 2015). Such focus on ideology is predicated on an (often unspoken) reliance on 'conveyor belt' theories of violence, which suppose that engagement with certain ideologies, groups, or content will lead to a process of radicalisation in the direction of acts of terrorist-style violence (Orofino 2019; Qureshi 2014). In this way, the dissemination of extremist ideas is likened to 'a socially transmitted disease' that 'spreads through social contact', as in a pandemic (Berger 2018). This has essentialised engagement in violence, sidelining the role of acts and manifestations in creating paths to violence, the processes that lead to them, and the political context within which this engagement occurs (McNeil-Willson et al. 2019). It has also centralised ideologies of 'hate' within concepts of extremism – extremism framed as the result of an ideological 'hatred' of the West and Western values – which has been used by polarising actors in mainstream media to attack minority communities and entrench societal racism (cf. Cockbain and Tufail 2020).

Alarm has been raised on the impact of this understanding of 'extremism', cited as representing a particular threat to human rights and civil society norms – beyond those already brought about by counterterror law (Lowe 2017). Counterterror legislation already notably diverges from most of the criminal justice system through its use of emergency and preventative powers, and the focus on extremism in controversial approaches such as the UK government's *Prevent* programme has raised concern about the growth of what has been described as the 'pre-criminal' space (Goldberg, Jadhav and Younis 2017). In focusing on 'pre-criminal' acts to counter-extremism, counter-extremism approaches have sought to identify legal activities that could be linked to violence. This has led to criticism that pre-criminal approaches are targeting and degrading human and civil rights (Martini, Ford and Jackson 2020; O'Toole et al. 2016), securitising physical and mental healthcare (Heath-Kelly and Strausz 2017; Younis and Jadhav 2020), imperilling freedom of speech (Faure Walker 2021; Holmwood and O'Toole 2017), and engaging in the widescale racialisation of Muslims and minority communities under a broadening lens of state surveillance and suspicion (Qureshi 2014; Sabir 2022).

Attempts by states to respond to terrorism 'up-stream' (Schneider 2020) or to 'defend further up the field' (Greene 2017) by preventing attacks from happening in the first place are particularly dubious because the further intervention moves from the (potential) act of violence, the wider the lens of suspicion falls, the more individuals and actions become securitised, and the greater the (ab)use of such laws becomes. As seen in its broad variety of approaches and definitions, 'violent extremism encompasses a wider category of manifestations' than terrorism, including various forms of 'ideologically motivated violence' beyond that which has been classed as terrorism (United Nations General Assembly, report A/70/674, para. 4). This expanding of the security lens has seen, in turn, widening instances of 'false positives' – the reporting of individuals to authorities based on counter-extremism concerns arising from limited, often racialised, assumptions around extremism (Aked 2020; Faure Walker 2021) – and has led to the questionable normalisation of the logic of prevention in public sectors such as schools and universities, hospitals, health and support centres, and prisons and reform systems (Kaleem 2021).

It has also led to the introduction of a focus on 'risk' and 'vulnerabilities' towards violence, ushering in a new language centred on 'safeguarding' individuals from extremism. Extremism is increasingly being framed by practitioners as akin to child abuse, gender-based violence, substance-related harm, or sexual abuse – which is evident in the language of counter-extremism programmes and the recent European policy (HM Government 2021). Whilst such language has helped legitimise controversial P/CVE in public sector bodies, such as educational, judicial, and health and social care institutions (Fernandez, Walker and Younis 2018; Heath-Kelly and Strausz 2017; McCulloch and Pickering 2009), it is problematic as counter-extremism differs substantially from other conceptualisations of safeguarding. P/CVE seeks ultimately to 'safeguard' the state from violence perpetrated by the 'radicalised' individual, over and above the wellbeing of the 'victim'; most extremism-based referrals result in individuals being referred away from counter-extremism programmes; whilst actual community support structures have faced radical austerity cuts in recent years (Heath-Kelly and Strausz 2017). It has also led to the intrusion of counter-extremism into places where individuals are susceptible to institutional harm, such as mental health services. The creation of Vulnerability Support Hubs in Britain, a mental health-related project run by UK counterterror police, for instance, has seen police working with mental health professionals to assess individuals suspect of 'extremism', using policing and surveillance practices (Aked, Younis, and Heath-Kelly 2021).

Some have suggested that this expansion of policy and practice towards countering extremism represents, at least in part, a crisis in counterterrorism, reflecting failures in adequately tracing the causes of terrorist-style violence (R. Jackson 2015), whilst the category of P/CVE has been critiqued as 'a catchall category that lacks precision and focus', which 'reflects problematic assumptions about the conditions that promote violent extremism' (Heydemann 2014, p. 1). The operationalisation of counter-extremism has seen instances in which a 'direct link is being made between refugees and multicultural communities and the risk of radicalisation' (Kaleem 2021, p. 6), with 'colour-blind' approaches shown instead to promote a racialised construction of threat, based primarily in a non-White, Muslim identity (Younis and Jadhav 2020). Meanwhile the ever-expanding remit of counter-extremism has seen a failure in the ability 'to draw clear boundaries that distinguish CVE programmes from those of other, well-established fields such as development and poverty alleviation, governance and democratisation, and education' (Heydemann 2014, p. 1), leading to creeping securitisation.

There have, however, been approaches designed to bring human rights perspectives to tackling concerns around extremism. Recent definitions, for instance, have sought to recentre the role of the state in creating the conditions for irregular violence. Sam Jackson (2019a) has sought to shift the definition of extremism onto understanding what it is positioned against, arguing that because extremism is designed to be 'purposefully disruptive political behaviour', it cannot be understood without reference to its specific political context; it is 'activity that aims to change fundamental features of a particular political system (or the ideas that motivate such activity)' (S. Jackson 2019b, p. 4). This sits adjacent to ideas put forward under theories of social movements, which posit that political or 'extremist' violence is better understood as a form of 'contentious politics' – the result of interactions between, on the one hand, movements that seek to challenge aspects of the current status quo, and on the other, authority-led counter actions that seek to repress such challenges (Tilly and Tarrow 2015).

Other studies have sought to account for the state's role in enabling violence, examining how structural racism and inequality can act to fuel processes of violence. Recent studies have suggested that polarisation plays a potentially important role in European instances of political violence. These processes are often driven on the national level by politicians and national media through high levels of segregation, a strong far-right political influence, a lack of state welfare or hate crime legislation, and the spread of polarising mainstream media content – amongst other factors (McNeil-Willson et al. 2019). Other studies have suggested that more attention should be paid to how the state creates and perpetuates social exclusion towards different communities in society, or the impact that legitimising Islamophobia can have in mainstreaming more extreme views and movements (Abbas 2019; Abbas et al. 2022; Winter and Mondon 2020). Such approaches centre the state as key to understanding why irregular or community violence occurs.

New policy definitions of violent extremism that avoid broad and essentialising understandings of extremism may also be useful in developing stronger responses to hate crime, racism, and xenophobia. Work by the European Commission, for instance, to develop an accepted EU definition of Violent Right-Wing Extremism was conducted with the aim of ensuring that Member States and the EU were better able to measure the level of far-right hate crime taking place throughout the bloc. Meanwhile, the utilisation of approaches to understanding and responding to political violence that have been developed outside of the paradigms of counterterrorism and the long 'War on Terror' may be useful in illuminating complex processes of engagement and disengagement with violence (Gunning 2007; Olesen 2009; Wiktorowicz 2004), and potentially offer a way to desecuritise complex processes (see also Grossman in this volume; Gerrand in this volume).

Concluding remarks

This chapter has looked to provide a broad overview of how (violent) extremism is understood through the lenses of academic discussion, policy and practice, and human rights. It finds that our understanding of extremism remains unstable, with definitions poorly enshrined in national laws and increasingly framed as operating in the same space of, and as a signifier for, terrorism. It also raises concerns over how concepts of (violent) extremism can and do draw upon and reinforce crude understandings of the dynamics of violence and its link with ideology, as well as the concerning implications that counter-extremism strategies have for human and civil rights – particularly amongst minority communities. It does, however, suggest that the way forward in this discussion is not around the development of another definitional understanding of extremism, but rather in a practical recentring of the state's role in enabling political violence. We perhaps have more to learn about what (violent) extremism is not by examining groups termed to be 'extremist' but by looking at how the contemporary liberal-democratic state articulates this politically charged term, using theories that challenge the security-first conceptualisation that has so often plagued discussion on extremism.

References

Abbas, T. (2019) *Islamophobia and Radicalisation: A Vicious Cycle*. London: Hurst.
Abbas, T., Vostermans, L., McNeil-Willson, R., Müller, T., Sedgwick, M., Thorleiffson, C., …Walklate, S. (2022) *Radicalisation in North-West Europe: The State of the Art*. The Hague.
Aked, H. (2017) Islamophobia, Counter-extremism and the Counterjihad Movement. In: Massoumi, N., Mills, T. and Miller, D. (eds), *Racism, Social Movements and the State*. London: Pluto Press, pp. 163–185.
Aked, H. (2020) *False Positives: The Prevent counter-extremism policy in healthcare*. London: Medact, www.medact.org/wp-content/uploads/2020/07/MEDACT-False-Positives-WEB.pdf
Aked, H., Younis, T., and Heath-Kelly, C. (2021) *Racism, Mental Health and Pre-crime Policing – The Ethics of Vulnerability Support Hubs*. London: Medact, https://stat.medact.org/uploads/2021/05/Racism_mental_health_pre-crime_policing_Medact_Report_May_2021_ONLINE.pdf
Angus, C. (2016) *Radicalisation and Violent Extremism: Causes and Responses*. Parliament e-brief. Sydney: Parliament of New South Wales, www.parliament.nsw.gov.au/researchpapers/Documents/radicalisation-and-violent-extremism-causes-and-/Radicalisation%20eBrief.pdf
Australian Government (n.d.) *What is Violent Extremism – Important Information for Australian Communities*. Canberra: Living Safe Together, www.livingsafetogether.gov.au/Documents/what-is-violent-extremism.PDF
Awan, I. (2013) Extremism, Radicalisation and Terrorism. In: Awan, I. and Blakemore, B. (eds), *Extremism, Counter-Terrorism and Policing*. London: Ashgate Publishing, pp. 5–20.
Berger, J. M. (2017) Extremist Construction of Identity: How Escalating Demands for Legitimacy Shape and Define In-group and Out-group Dynamics. The Hague: International Centre for Counter-Terrorism (ICCT).
Berger, J.M. (2018) *Extremism*. Cambridge, MA: MIT Press.
Bötticher, A. (2017) Academic consensus definition of radicalism and extremism. *Perspectives on Terrorism*, 11(4), pp. 73–77.

Brown, K., Mondon, A. and Winter, A. (2021) The far right, the mainstream and maintreaming: Towards a heuristic framework. *Journal of Political Ideologies*, DOI: 10.1080/13569317.2021.1949829

Burchett, J., Weyembergh, A. and Theodorakakou, G. (2022) *Counterterrorism policies, measures and tools in the EU: An assessment of the effectiveness of the EU counterterrorism policy*. Brussels: The European Parliament, www.europarl.europa.eu/RegData/etudes/STUD/2022/730 581/IPOL_STU(2022)730581_EN.pdf

Carter, E. (2018) Right-wing extremism/radicalism: Reconstructing the concept. *Journal of Political Ideologies*, 23(2), pp. 157–182.

Cockbain, E. and Tufail, W. (2020) Failing victims, fuelling hate: Challenging the harms of the 'Muslim grooming gangs' narrative. *Race and Class*, 61(3), pp. 3–32.

Commission for Countering Extremism (2019) *Challenging Hateful Extremism*,, https://assets.publish ing.service.gov.uk/government/uploads/system/uploads/attachment_data/file/874101/200320_Challenging_Hateful_Extremism.pdf

Commission for Countering Extremism (2022) *End of Year Report, 2021–2022*, www.gov.uk/governm ent/publications/end-of-year-report-2021-to-2022/end-of-year-report-2021-to-2022-accessible

Coolsaet, R. (2015) *What Drives Europeans to Syria, and to IS? Insights from the Belgium Case*. Egmont Papers. Brussels: Royal Institute for International Relations, www.egmontinstitute.be/what-dri ves-europeans-to-syria-and-to-is-insights-from-the-belgian-case/

Cossé, E. (2021) French Court Confirms Dissolution of Anti-Discrimination Group. *Human Rights Watch*, 27 September, www.hrw.org/news/2021/09/27/french-court-confirms-dissolution-anti-discrimination-group

Dathan, M. (2022) David Cameron takes aim at Muslim critics of anti-terror Prevent programme. *The Times*, 26 April, www.thetimes.co.uk/article/david-cameron-takes-aim-at-muslim-critics-of-anti-terror-prevent-programme-d56jfblb6

Department for Education (2015) The Prevent duty: Departmental advice for schools and childcare providers, https://assets.publishing.service.gov.uk/government/uploads/system/uploads/attachme nt_data/file/439598/prevent-duty-departmental-advice-v6.pdf

Dixon, H. (2019) Extremism definition fails Clarkson test: Government gave up on laws to fight ideology because it's 'too difficult'. *The Telegraph*, 6 April, www.telegraph.co.uk/news/2019/04/ 06/government-abandoned-creating-extremism-laws-difficult-former/

Dodd, V. (2020) Extinction Rebellion could sue police over extremist ideology listing. *The Guardian*, 11 January, www.theguardian.com/environment/2020/jan/11/extinction-rebellion-could-sue-police-listing-extremist-ideology

Faure Walker, R. (2021) *The Emergence of 'Extremism': Exposing the violent discourse and langauge of 'radicalisation'*. London: Bloomsbury.

Fernandez, S., Walker, R. F., and Younis, T. (2018) Focus: The 'Where' of Prevent. *Discover Society*, https://discoversociety.org/2018/06/05/focus-the-where-of-prevent/

Githens-Mazer, J. and Lambert, R. (2009) Quilliam on Prevent: The wrong diagnosis. *The Guardian*, 19 October, www.theguardian.com/commentisfree/belief/2009/oct/19/prevent-quilliam-fou ndation-extremism

Goldberg, D., Jadhav, S., and Younis, T. (2017) Prevent: What is pre-criminal space? *BJPsych Bulletin*, 41(4), pp. 208–211.

Greene, A. (2017) Defining terrorism: One size fits all? *International Comparative Law Quarterly*, 66(2), pp. 411–440.

Grossman, M., Peuker, M., Smith, D. and Dellal, H. (2016) *Stocktake Research Project: A Systematic Literature and Selected Programme Review on Social Cohesion, Community Resilience and Violent Extremism 2011–2015*. Melbourne: Community Resilience Unit, Department of Premier and Cabinet, State of Victoria.

Gunning, J. (2007) *Hamas in Politics: Democracy, Religion, Voilence*. Columbia: Columbia University Press.

Habib, S. (2018) *Learning and Teaching British Values*. London: Palgrave Macmillan.

Heath-Kelly, C. and Strausz, E. (2017) *Counter-terrorism in the NHS: Evaluating Prevent Duty Safeguarding in the NHS*. Coventry: University of Warwick.

Hellyer, H. A. and Grossman, M. (2019) A Framework for Understanding the Relationship between Radicalisation, Religion and Violence. *GREASE project concept paper*.

Heydemann, S. (2014) Countering violent extremism as a field of practice. *Insights*, 1(Spring), p. 1. Washington, DC: US Institute of Peace,, www.usip.org/sites/default/files/Insights-Spring-2014.pdf

HM Government (2021) *Statutory Guidance: Revised Prevent Duty Guidance for England and Wales*. Westminster: Home Office, www.gov.uk/government/publications/prevent-duty-guidance/revised-prevent-duty-guidance-for-england-and-wales.

Holmwood, J. and O'Toole, T. (2017) Prevent: from hearts and minds to muscular liberalism. In: Holmwood, J. and O'Toole, T. (eds), *Countering Extremism in British Schools? The Truth about the Birmingham Trojan Horse Affair*. Bristol: Bristol University Press & Policy Press, pp. 45–65.

IACP (2018) *Awareness Brief: Homegrown Violent Extremism*. Alexandria, VA: The International Association of Chiefs of Police, www.theiacp.org/sites/default/files/2018-07/HomegrownViolentExtremismAwarenessBrief.pdf

Jackson, R. (2015) The epistomological crisis of counterterrorism. *Critical Studies on Terrorism*, 8(1), pp. 33–54.

Jackson, S. (2019a) Non-normative political extremism: Reclaiming a concept's analytical unity. *Terrorism and Political Violence*, 31(2), pp. 244–259.

Jackson, S. (2019b) *A Schema of Right-Wing Extremism in the United States*. The Hague: International Centre for Counter-Terrrorism.

James, N. (2020) *Implementing the Prevent Duty: Conceptualising Threat within Greatear Manchester's Further Education Sector*. PhD Thesis, University of Leeds.

James, N. (2022) Countering far-right threat through Britishness: The Prevent duty in further education. *Critical Studies on Terrorism*, 15(1), pp. 121–142.

Jupskås, A.R. and Segers, I.B. (2020) *What is right-wing extremism?* C-Rex – Centre for Research on Extremism, University of Oslo, www.sv.uio.no/c-rex/english/groups/compendium/what-is-right-wing-extremism.html

Kaleem, A. (2021) The hegemony of Prevent: Turning counter-terrorism policing into common sense. *Critical Studies on Terrorism*, 15(2), pp. 267–289.

Khalil, J. (2014) Radical beliefs and violent actions are not synonymous: How to place the key disjuncture between attitudes and behaviours at the heart of our research into political violence. *Studies in Conflict & Terrorism*, 37, pp. 198–211.

Kølvraa, C. (2019) Embodying 'the Nordic race': imagniaries of Viking heritage in the online communications of the Nordic Resistance Movement. *Patterns of Prejudice*, 53(3), pp. 270–284.

Lowe, D. (2017) Prevent strategies: The problems associated in defining extremism: The case of the United Kingdom. *Studies in Conflict & Terrorism*, 40(11), pp. 917–933, DOI:10.1080/1057610X.2016.1253941

Macklin, G. and Busher, J. (2018) *Understanding 'Reciprocal Radicalisation' as a Component of Wider Conflict Dynamics*. Radicalisation Research [online], www.radicalisationresearch.org/debate/busher-reciprocal-radicalisation-wider-dynamics/

Martini, A., Ford, K. and Jackson, R. (2020) *Encountering Extremism: Theoretical Issues and Local Challenges*. Manchester: Manchester University Press.

McCulloch, J. and Pickering, S. (2009) Pre-crime and counter-terrorism: Imagining future crime in the 'War on Terror'. *The British Journal of Criminology*, 49(5), pp. 628–645.

McDonald, G. (2009) *Extremism in the UK*. London: Royal United Services Institute, https://rusi.org/publication/extremism-uk

McNeil-Willson, R. (2019) *Islamic Activism and the Counterterror State: The Impact of the Securitised Lens on Hizb ut-Tahrir in Britain and Denmark*. PhD Thesis, University of Exeter, Exeter, UK.

McNeil-Willson, R. (2021) Understanding the Interplay of Counter-extremism Trends and Muslim Communities in Europe. In: Bonino, S. and Ricucci, R. (eds), *Islam and Security in the West*. London: Palgrave Macmillan, pp. 163–195.

McNeil-Willson, R (2024), A Tale of Two Threats: The creation of 'Islamism' and the 'Far Right' in UK policy and media. In: Magazzini, T. and Fahmi, G. (eds), *Causes and Consequences of the Governance of Islam and Violent Radicalisation*. Routledge Studies in Extremism and Democracy. Oxfordshire: Routledge, Chapter 11.

McNeil-Willson, R., Gerrand, V., Scrinzi, F. and Triandafyllidou, A. (2019) *Polarisation, Violent Extremism and Resilience in Europe Today: An Analytical Framework for the BRaVE Project (Concept Paper)*. Global Governance, Robert Schuman Centre of Advanced Studies. Florence: European University Institute.

Midlarsky, M.I. (2011) *Origins of Political Extremism: Mass Violence in the Twentieth Century and Beyond*. Cambridge: Cambridge University Press.

Mudde, C. (2007) *Populist Radical Right Parties in Europe*. Cambridge: Cambridge University Press.
Mudde, C. (2014) Introduction: Political Extremism – Concepts, Theories and Democratic Responses. In: Mudde, C. (ed.), *Political Extremism*. Los Angeles: SAGE, pp. xxiii–xxix.
Nawaz, M. (2015) *Radical: My Journey Out of Islamist Extremism*. Washington, DC: The Aspen Institute.
Neumann, P. (2008) Introduction. In Neumann, P. (ed.), *Perspectives on Radicalisation and Political Violence – papers from the first international conference on radicalisation and political violence*. London: International Centre for the Study of Radicalisation and Political Violence, pp. 3–7.
Norris, P. and Inglehart, R. (2018) *Cultural Backlash: Trump, Brexit and the Rise of Authoritarian Populism*. Cambridge: Cambridge University Press.
Norwegian Government (2014) *Action plan against Radicalisation and Violent Extremism*. Oslo, www.regjeringen.no/en/dokumenter/Action-plan-against-Radicalisation-and-Violent-Extremism/id762413/.
O'Toole, T., Meer, N., Nilsson, D., Jones, S.H. and Modood, T. (2016) Governing through prevent? Regulation and contested practice in State-Muslim engagement. *Sociology*, 50(1), pp. 160–177.
Olesen, T. (2009) Social Movement Theory and Radical Islamic Activism. In: Olesen, T. and Khosrokhavar, F. (eds), *Islamism as Social Movement*. Aarhus University: Centre for Studies in Islamism and Radicalisation (CIR), pp. 7–33.
Onursal, R. and Kirkpatrick, D. (2021) Is extremism the 'new' terrorism? The convergence of 'extremism' and 'terrorism' in British parliamentary discourse. *Terrorism and Political Violence*, 33(5), pp. 1094–1116.
Orofino, E. (2019) *Hizb ut-Tahrir and the Caliphate: Why the Groups Is Still Appealing to Muslims in the West*. London: Routledge.
Pieri, Z. (2015) *Tablighi Jamaat and the Quest for the London 'Mega-Mosque': Continuity and Change*. London and New York: Palgrave.
Public Safety Canada (2009) *Research Summary: Assessing the risk of violent extremists*. Ottawa, ON, www.publicsafety.gc.ca/cnt/rsrcs/pblctns/ssng-xtrms/ssng-xtrms-eng.pdf.
Qureshi, A. (2014) PREVENT: creating 'radicals' to strengthen anti-Muslim narratives. *Critical Studies on Terrorism*, 8(1), pp. 181–191.
Revell, L. and Bryan, H. (2018) *Fundamental British Values in Education: Radicalisation, National Identity and Britishness*. Bingley: Emerald Publishing Limited.
Sabir, R. (2022) *The Suspect: counterterrorism, Islam and the security state*. London: Pluto Press.
Schmid, A.P. (2013) *Radicalisation, De-radicalisation, Counter-radicalisation: A Conceptual Discussion and Literature Review*. The Hague: International Centre for Counter-Terrorism (ICCT).
Schmid, A.P. (2014) Violent and non-violent extremism: two sides of the same coin? *ICCT Research Paper 5*. The Hague: International Centre for Counter-Terrorism.
Schmid, A.P. and Jongman, A. (1988) *Political Terrorism: A New Guide to Actors, Concepts, Databases, Theories and Literature*. Amsterdam: North Holland Publishing Company.
Schneider, L. (2020) Dynamics of Securitisation: An Analysis of Universities' Engagement with the Prevent Legislation. In: Gearon, L.F. (ed.), *The Routledge International Handbook of Universities, Security and Intelligence Studies*. Oxford: Routledge, pp. 312–325.
Sedgwick, M. (2010) The concept of radicalisation as a source of confusion. *Terrorism and Political Violence*, 22(4), pp. 479–494.
Silke, A. (2004) The Devil You Know: Continuing Problems with Research on Terrorism. In: Silke, A. (ed.), *Research on Terrorism: Trends, Achievements and Failures*. London: Routledge, pp. 57–71.
Sotlar, A. (2004) Some Problems with a Definition and Perception of Extremism within a Society. In: Mesko, G., Pagon, M. and Dobovsek, B. (eds), *Policing in Central and Eastern Europe: Dilemmas of Contemporary Criminal Justice*. Slovenia: University of Maribor, pp. 1–5
Stanton, Z. (2021) The Problem Isn't Just One Insurrection. It's Mass Radicalisation. *politico.com*, 11 February, www.politico.com/news/magazine/2021/02/11/mass-radicalization-trump-insurrection-468746
Swedish Ministry of Justice. (2011) *Action plan to safeguard democracy against violence-promoting extremism*. Stockholm, www.government.se/contentassets/b94f163a3c5941aebaeb78174ea27a29/action-plan-to-safeguard-democracy-against-violence-promoting-extremism-skr.-20111284
Tazamal, M. (2022) *The Criminalisation of Muslim Civil Society*. Bridge Initiative. Washington, DC: Georgetown University, https://bridge.georgetown.edu/research/the-criminalization-of-muslim-civil-society/.
Tilly, C. and Tarrow, S. (2015) *Contentious Politics* (2nd ed.). Oxford: Oxford University Press.

UK Parliament (2013) EU Council and Woolwich. Hansard, vol. 563, debated 3 June. House of Commons, https://hansard.parliament.uk/Commons/2013-06-03/debates/13060311000002/EUCouncilAndWoolwich?highlight=1235.

Vandenberg, H. and Hoverd, W. (2020) The inconsistent usage of the terms 'extremism' and 'terrorism' around the Christchurch mosque attacks. *National Security Journal*, 2(1), DOI:10.36878/nsj20200201.03

Wiktorowicz, Q. (2004) Introduction: Islamic Activism and Social Movement Theory. In: Wiktorowicz, Q. (ed.), *Islamic Activism: A Social Movement Theory Approach*. Bloomington: Indiana University Press, pp. 1–35.

Winter, A.S. and Mondon, A. (2020) *Reactionary Democracy: How Racism and the Populist Far Right Became Mainstream*. London: Verso Books.

Younis, T. and Jadhav, S. (2020) Islamophobia in the National Health Service: An ethnography or institutional racism in PREVENT's counter-radicalisation policy. *Sociology of Health and Illness*, 42(3), pp. 610–626.

3
RESILIENCE TO VIOLENT EXTREMISM AT THE CROSSROADS

Michele Grossman

Introduction

For more than a decade, resilience has been a key feature of preventing and countering violent extremism (P/CVE) frameworks in different countries and regions, mobilised by a range of theoretical models and national or multinational policy frameworks to drive policy and practice in building resistance to violent extremism at both community and individual levels (Dalgaard-Nielsen and Schack 2016; Grossman et al. 2014, 2016, 2017, 2020; Longstaff et al. 2010; Spalek and Davies 2012; Ungar et al. 2017; Grossman 2021; Weine et al. 2013; Dechesne 2017; McNeil-Willson et al. 2019; Sieckelinck and Gielen 2018; Stephens et al. 2019; Public Safety Canada 2013; GCTF 2012; Global Community Engagement and Resilience Fund 2017).

Yet, despite the enthusiasm with which 'resilience to violent extremism' has been conceptualised and promoted through policy and programming, there remain key questions about the ways in which, first, concepts of resilience to violent extremism have been defined; second, how such concepts are operationalised; third, how fit for purpose these concepts are in relation to the diversifying ideological and tactical landscape of violent extremist threats; and, fourth, whether the field has paid sufficient attention not only to resilience *to* violent extremism but also the resilience *of* violent extremist movements and networks, including the maladaptive resilience that can characterise violent radicalisation trajectories. In the discussion that follows, I will draw on an interrelated series of articles, chapters, and reports I've published in recent years to explore these four questions and propose some further directions for policy and research that can help guide consideration and analysis.

Community resilience to violent extremism at the crossroads

Since its inception, P/CVE has traditionally served as a soft-power adjunct to more security-oriented approaches and logics in reducing the risks and impacts of radicalisation to violence. Its relevance has grown over time in response to dynamic threats and challenges in relation to extremist violence around the world. Whatever its local or regional inflections, P/CVE is animated by the conviction that at least part of our response to threats posed by radicalised violence must be a prosocial response, one that recognises and tries to work at various scales with the human needs, conditions, grievances, conflicts, hopes, and influences that – under certain circumstances – can become channelled into terrorist ideology and action. A primary goal of virtually all P/CVE efforts is to intervene in trajectories of radicalised violence before they reach criminal thresholds so that P/CVE is ultimately premised upon an ethics of pre-terror prevention and interdiction, rather than post-terror response.

Today, however, P/CVE is at something of a crossroads in its philosophical and strategic orientations. There is now broad international acceptance that P/CVE requires durable engagement, not just by law enforcement and security agencies but by communities, civil society actors, researchers, and everyday citizens – an approach that some analysts term as 'whole of society' (Rosand et al. 2018; OSCE 2018; ICRC 2017; GCTF 2012) or 'whole of community' (Los Angeles Interagency Coordination Group 2015; National Academies of Sciences, Engineering and Medicine 2017). This reflects the view that P/CVE has become an essential companion, and sometimes an explicit counterpoint, to harder-edged counterterrorism measures that seek – through legal, intelligence, policing, and technological mechanisms – to prevent, disrupt, and mitigate the planning and impact of terrorist plots and attacks. The UN Security Council's Resolution 2178 (UN Security Council 2014) on reducing the flow of foreign fighters to Syria and Iraq, for example, identified P/CVE as an 'essential element' in addressing beliefs and actions that can lead to radicalised violence, and a broad range of nations on virtually all continents have implemented P/CVE policies and platforms to address multiple violent extremist movements and threats.

Over the last decade, some P/CVE policy paradigms have begun to move from risk-based to needs-based strategic analysis and design. This tends to collapse the boundaries between violent extremist-specific interventions, on the one hand, and more generically oriented prosocial efforts around building resilience to violent extremism and other social harms, as well as strengthening social cohesion, on the other. This shift is partly theory-driven and partly politically driven, responding as it does to the current landscape of escalating rather than moderating tempos of social and cultural polarisation.

Defining 'resilience to violent extremism'

But what do we mean when we talk about 'resilience' to violent extremism? From a policy perspective, the answer can be surprisingly thin, reflecting the ways in which resilience is often deployed as a taken-for-granted term (Grossman 2021) in P/CVE policy and programming. Such policies and programmes often earnestly promote resilience as a key tool of preventing or remediating violent extremism as a social harm, but neither define nor contextualise what 'resilience' means conceptually and how it can be applied empirically as a P/CVE construct. This continues to result in perceptions that 'resilience' is deployed as a 'diffuse and contested concept' (Walklate et al. 2012, p. 190) in ways that can undermine its effectiveness as a prosocial policy and programming tool in P/CVE contexts.

Despite this, however, one of the most consistent seams running through the conceptualisation of resilience to violent extremism over time has been the ways in which resilience to violent extremism is primarily constructed in P/CVE policy and practice as a question of meso-level community strengthening, particularly in relation to social cohesion and social capital (Ellis and Abdi 2017; Weine et al. 2013; Weine and Ahmed 2012; Grossman et al. 2016; 2017; Walklate et al. 2012; Dalgaard-Nielsen and Schack, 2016). While micro-level individual resilience-building to violent extremism (both social-psychological and social-ecological in orientation) has also generated analysis and theory-building (Lösel et al. 2018; Sieckelinck and Gielen 2018; BOUNCE 2018; Stephens et al. 2019; Van Brunt et al. 2017), issues around macro-level societal or systems-level resilience (Grossman 2021; McNeil-Willson et al. 2019) have generally been overlooked (Dechesne 2017).

Both the perception and reality of security-driven logics and political exigencies in relation to resilience to violent extremism theory and programming at various points and in various settings have generated significant critiques over the years (Coaffee and Fussey 2015; Ngyuen 2019; Hardy 2015; Walklate et al. 2012; Stephens et al. 2019; Sieckelinck and Gielen 2018; Grossman 2021). It has also at times driven community discomfort and suspicion regarding resilience-building initiatives as a thinly disguised camouflage for P/CVE efforts focused on the surveillance and securitising of the communities with which they engage (Hardy 2015). Yet, there has also been real interest by governments, policymakers, researchers, practitioners, and communities to think innovatively about how constructs of both individual and community resilience can contribute to effective extremist violence prevention efforts, including a significant amount of analysis and guidance developed through the lens of public health models (Bhui et al. 2012; Challgren et al. 2016; Ellis and Abdi 2017; Harris-Hogan et al. 2016; Weine et al. 2017).

However, by far the most prominent strand of meso-level theory, policy, and programming around building community resilience to violent extremism has been the linking of prosocial resilience to social cohesion, social integration, and social capital (Dalgaard-Nielsen and Schack 2016; Ellis and Abdi 2017; Grossman et al. 2014, 2017, 2020; also Grossman and Gerrand, this volume). In Denmark, for example, resilience to 'militant Islamist' violent extremism has been conceptualised as the capacity to 'leverage social capital' – defined as 'stable trust-based relationships and networks among actors (civil society, local government, local businesses)' – in addition to resilience at the levels of families, peer and social networks (Dalgaard-Nielsen and Schack, 2016, p. 312). Ellis and Abdi (2017) and Grossman et al. (2014, 2017, 2020) draw on the interrelationship between bonding, bridging, and linking social capital in fostering prosocial engagement and partnerships that shape their everyday lives, both horizontally, between inter-cultural 'others', and vertically, between communities and the systems of regulatory and institutional power and governance.

Weine et al. (2013, p. 331) suggest that key social capital dimensions of community resilience to violent extremism include shared problem-solving, safe community spaces for youth, and investment in community-building activities such as 'afterschool programmes, mentoring programmes, community policing [and] opportunities for civic dialogue'; while Lösel et al. (2018) see basic attachment to or integration within society, informal social control, and social bonding as important protective factors linked to the influence of social capital on resilience to violent extremism, alongside a concept of linking capital reflected by attitudes that accept as legitimate the presence and functioning of the law, society, and policing (ibid., p. 98). If the drivers of violent extremism are bound up with social conditions, protections, dynamics, and adversities, then the solutions that seek to prevent or mitigate adversities, redress conditions and dynamics that create vulnerabilities, and strengthen protections must also be socially grounded (Day and Kleinman 2017).

What does the emphasis on linking resilience to social cohesion, social integration, and social capital tell us? At least two issues arise. One issue concerns the blurring of lines between configurations of *community resilience to violent extremism* and *community resilience* more generally. In many respects, there are assumptions that the general protective features of social-ecological resilience (Ungar 2008, 2011; Masten 2014, 2016) – with their emphasis on open, trusting, dynamic, stable, adaptive, and appropriately resourced systems and relationships for individuals, families, and communities – will carry over as protective factors against a broad range of social harms, including violent extremism.

While this may be true, it reprises the question of what we mean specifically by resilience to violent extremism. Are we talking about building resilience by promoting the capacity to resist the appeals of violent extremist narratives, ideologies, and networks, or are we talking about building resilience by addressing the underlying or precursor conditions of material and social disadvantage and marginalisation that are seen to create vulnerabilities that must be mitigated? Constructs of violent extremism engage with both these premises so that intersecting with the idea of building resistance to the legitimation of violence as a solution to individual, social, or political grievances runs the idea that addressing those conditions seen to enable grievances and the legitimation of violence will result in stronger community safety and well-being.

In turn, both these seams of thinking within concepts of building community resilience to violent extremism invite a further question – that of which 'communities', precisely, are the focus of such resilience-building efforts. The resilience-as-social-cohesion model in relation to violent extremism has been driven largely by three trends: first, the meaning of 'community' in resilience to violent extremism discourse as a proxy for Muslim minority communities; second, the concern to mitigate intercultural tensions and hostilities between majority and minority ethnocultural groups, particularly in the West; and, third, by assumptions about Muslim communities as experiencing deficits in both resilience and social capital. As Thomas and Grossman (forthcoming, 2023) argue,

> P/CVE policy and practice frameworks have overwhelmingly identified Muslim communities as their key engagement targets. Until recently, the perception that the key terrorist threat was generated first by Al Qaeda and its global affiliates, then by the emergence of Islamic State, meant that 'community' was most often defined as visibly racialised and often spatially concentrated Muslim minority communities within broader Western societies. ... P/CVE policies have frequently identified that such community capital may need to be further bolstered, particularly amongst socially marginalised Muslim communities, by the further strengthening of domestic civil society (Thomas 2012) and the linking capital conferred by deepening connections with external state organisations (Vermeulen and Bovenkerk 2012).

This trend is well-evidenced in the literature. For example, Ellis and Abdi (2017) suggest that resilience to violent extremism leverages social capital capacities to help resolve identity tensions, remediate disadvantage, and build trust to offset vulnerabilities amongst marginalised or fragile individuals and communities. Yet in some instances, resilience-to-violent-extremism initiatives have been developed that seek to transform identity and subjectivity rather than merely to address structural, material, and social features of marginalisation and disadvantage for Muslim minorities in the West. As Nicole Nguyen argues in her discussion of education and resilience to violent extremism programming in *Suspect Communities* (2019), the development of global citizenship educational programmes in the US aimed to produce culturally diverse students who would become cosmopolitan global citizens in ways that transcended national identities or the pulls of transnational affiliations and loyalties that can be leveraged by terrorist narratives and recruiters. She asserts that the promotion of integrated identities as part of the global citizenship education agenda has countermanded culturally diverse identity-based groups such as those organised by Muslim students in universities, casting pluralism and the accommodation of difference as socially divisive (Keddie 2014).

This is of a piece with several other policy and programme settings that, as Grossman and Gerrand elsewhere in this volume argue in relation to Australia, have defined building resilience to violent extremism largely as a process of building and strengthening social cohesion. The approach of countries such as Canada and Australia to building resilience to violent extremism has been largely congruent with international resilience-building frameworks in emphasising engagement with Muslim communities in particular. This has been balanced, to some extent, by framing the project of building and sustaining social cohesion as a process that must engage not only minority but also majority cultures in fostering intercultural social engagement, empathy, and solidarity as a prophylactic against crises and events that can potentially escalate inter-communal tension and conflict (Multicultural New South Wales 2018). It has involved efforts to continuously promote the prosocial values of pluralism and multiculturalism as normative and, where these are contested or fragile, desirable. However, in countries such as France and Denmark, the price of social cohesion is often articulated in ways that predicate it upon the sacrifice of minority identities and resources in favour of majority cultural norms, regardless of the social realities of pluralism (Sealy and Modood 2019; Meret 2019).

In such settings, then, promoting resilience to violent extremism can become simply another way of advancing an integrationist agenda that seeks to valorise majority culture and subsume minority identities within it. Resilience-building initiatives in these contexts ignore the fact that what majority culture theorists and policymakers might regard as positive resilient adaptation, for example, may not coincide with what minority groups themselves deem to be so (Castro and Murray 2009, p. 377). They identify Muslim minorities themselves as a social problematic and 'Muslim communities' (frequently understood as homogenous rather than heterogenous entities in policy terms) as requiring levels of intervention and support that can occlude recognition or leveraging of resilience assets – what has elsewhere been termed 'resilience capital' (Grossman et al. 2014) – that may already exist within various ethnocultural community contexts.

As noted above, one result of this is that government-initiated community resilience strategies have come to be perceived by some within Muslim communities as securitised proxies for government efforts to conduct surveillance and manage cultural diversity in repressive ways rather than being focused on building genuine community awareness of and resistance to the social harms created by violent extremist ideologies and actions (Hardy 2015; CAIR Minnesota 2016).

More problematically, however, rendering 'resilience to violent extremism' as equivalent to social cohesion and integration gives rise to the tendency to create 'out-group' communities that require integration and strengthening, with little effort made to examine and strengthen the resilience of 'in-group' majority or mainstream society. This tends to elevate the status quo of a society's mainstream norms, values, and behaviours to a level that excludes these from critique or scrutiny in relation to majority-culture individual and systemic resilience to violent extremism (Stephens and Sieckelinck 2020). Such 'norming' of majority culture values and assumptions about resilience and about the consequent perceived resilience deficits of minorities – combined with the failure to explore and address the resilience protections and vulnerabilities of majority cultural groups themselves in relation to violent radicalisation – remains a persistent lacuna in the ways in which 'community resilience to violent extremism' has come to be conceptualised and implemented.

Resilience to violent extremism in a diversifying threat landscape

In effect, resilience to violent extremism models have arguably failed to capitalise on many of the cross-cutting features of systemic resilience-building, such as the relationship between persistence, resistance, recovery, adaptation, and transformation in contexts of adversity (Ungar 2018) that provide alternatives to the legitimation of violence as a means of resolving social and political grievances. This is because they have, in keeping with the field of counter-extremist architecture and policy more broadly, tended to attribute terrorist and violent extremist ideologies and behaviours to *communal identity* structures (e.g., Muslims, Whites, men) rather than to *communal ideological or belief* structures (e.g., Islamist, far-right extremist, incel) (Grossman 2021).

One consequence of how the 'community' in 'community resilience to violent extremism' has generally been constructed as a result – socially disadvantaged or marginalised, ethnoculturally minoritised and in need of 'integration' and 'cohesion' with mainstream society – has been the fractures that such conceptual models reveal when we begin to think about how they apply to the rise in far-right violent extremism that has been steadily mobilising across North America, Western and Northern Europe, and Australasia. Any consideration of how we can build and operationalise models of resilience to violent extremism must now account for the fact that while Islamist-inspired or attributed violent extremism has dominated the policy and political agenda since 9/11, the terrorist landscape is now more complex and diversified in the range of ideologies and movements that require mitigation strategies by governments and civil society.

While this diversification has come to include, for example, threats posed by violent incels (involuntary celibates) (Brzuszkiewicz 2020) and a recent upswing in violent radical conspiracy and sovereign citizen movements, the most coherent and well-organised threats are now resurgent transnational right-wing violent extremist movements (Jones 2018; Hutchinson 2017; Froio and Ganesh 2018). These movements capitalise on the extent to which democracies around the world are increasingly experiencing social and political polarisation, 'a process whereby the normal multiplicity of differences in a society increasingly align along a single dimension and people increasingly perceive and describe politics and society in terms of "Us" versus "Them"' (McCoy et al. 2018, 16).

'Far-right extremism' is an umbrella term that can refer to a range of racially, ethnically, religiously, or gender-based ideological movements or groups (Miller-Idriss 2021) that are xenophobic or exclusivist (Grossman et al. 2016), supremacist, sometimes (but not always) nationalist or authoritarian or both in orientation, valorise the importance of assumed or claimed heritage (particularly in relation to race and to 'homeland') and 'traditional values' (Perliger 2012), reject globalisation, and assert the illegitimacy of established governments or regimes of power (Lauder 2002). They also tend to be more distrustful of others and of political institutions (Bartlett and Littler 2011).

Similarly, Perry and Scrivens (2015, 2019) define far-right extremism as

> a loose movement, characterised by a racially, ethnically and sexually defined nationalism. This nationalism is often framed in terms of White power and is grounded in xenophobic and exclusionary understandings of the perceived threats posed by such groups as people of colour, Jews, immigrants, the LGBTQ community and feminists.
>
> *Perry and Scrivens 2015, p. 5*

This raises the issue not only of what or who 'community resilience to violent extremism' policy and programmes should be targeting when the communities in question are drawn largely from majority groups that are not structurally disadvantaged on the basis of racial, ethnic, or religious identity, but also the more fundamental question of whether a dominant focus on *community* resilience to violent extremism is the right approach to take in P/CVE work with these cohorts.

In one sense, it may well be the right focus if the goal is to build and sustain social cohesion, thereby reducing polarisation (McNeil-Willson et al. 2019). A community resilience approach can help ensure that the resilience protections and vulnerabilities of majority culture groups are a core part of the resilience to violent extremism matrix. This might include a specific focus, in far-right extremist contexts, on promoting understanding and acceptance of culturally diverse 'others' and acknowledging that social cohesion does not mean endless social harmony but, instead, developing meaningful frameworks for managing 'the conflict and tensions that naturally occur in pluralistic modern societies' (Rutter 2015; Ho 2011, cited in Grossman et al. 2016, p. 44).

However, if, as Ragazzi (2016) has argued, the social construct of 'community' develops in part based on responses to 'external forces such as state policies through active social and political interaction as well as internal conflict, producing different or contested versions of communities in the plural' (Thomas and Grossman, forthcoming 2023), then what we are now dealing with are far-right extremist sub-communities formed through these processes for whom the antidote of social cohesion is synonymous with the very so-called ill they are trying to eliminate from the sociopolitical ecosystem.

This means that the 'tautology of how social cohesion is supposed to address' the attitudes and behaviours characterising far-right extremist thinking and behaviour 'if social cohesion is defined as the recognition of diversity and equal opportunity for all members of society' (Grossman et al. 2016, p. 44) remains unresolved. In addition, opportunities for addressing resilience in relation to the diversity of far-right extremists – a diversity that spans multiple and sometimes contradictory ideological coordinates, ethnocultural identities, and geospatial locations, including digital ecosystems – potentially calls for a rethink of how 'community'-bounded models of building resilience to violent extremism may need to be refined or repositioned.

This problem is linked, in turn, to the ways in which the persistence of cultural identity and practice can be both a strength and a weakness in relation to community resilience. Persistence of cultural identity is very important for the maintenance of bonding capital (Putnam 2000) within a social or cultural group. It strengthens a sense of cultural identity, pride, belonging and efficacy, all of which are key features of resilience. It also helps people feel they have a reservoir of cultural knowledge, memory, practice, and values to draw upon in times of adversity or challenge. Persistence of cultural identity can also be a positive influence in relations involving bridging capital (ibid.), where people feel they have something valuable and concrete to share with cultural 'others' from a position of strength, stability, and cultural integrity.

However, in pluralist societies where an exclusivist cultural identity persists and remains rigid and insular – as we see in both Islamist and far-right extremist contexts – rather than adaptable and both outward and inward-facing, it can threaten both the capacity for bridging capital and also that of linking or vertical capital (Szreter and Woolcock 2004). It can also weaken the ability to deal successfully with institutional and governmental frameworks, services, and authorities through refusal to accept or take advantage of available resources and unwillingness to accept legal or social constraints on practice and behaviour.

Another approach to building resilience to violent extremism for these cohorts, therefore, might lie in supplementing 'community' resilience approaches – which may still remain relevant in some settings — by focusing further on individual-level resilience vulnerabilities and protections. Work that considers what individual-level social-psychological resilience characteristics and processes may serve as protective factors in relation to all forms of violent extremism has focused in particular on empathy (Aly et al. 2014; BOUNCE 2018; Lösel et al. 2018; Stephens et al. 2019; Taylor et al. 2017; Van Brunt et al. 2017), self-regulation/self-control and value complexity (Lösel et al. 2018; Sieckelinck and Gielen 2018), self-esteem and assertiveness (BOUNCE 2018), and intercultural tolerance of diversity (Ellis and Abdi 2017).

In addition, resilience characteristics related specifically to right-wing extremists have been identified by Lösel et al. (2018) as the degree to which 'perceived personal discrimination' and 'subjective deprivation', or the negative evaluation of one's own socio-economic status relative to others, are present for an individual (see also McNeil-Willson et al. 2019). Reconsidering what P/CVE resilience models might look like if they grapple with how to engage with individuals' feelings, behaviours, attitudes, and experiences rather than with ethnoculturally defined communities – especially where an ideological paradigm privileges radical individualism over collectivism, for example – might offer new pathways towards building resilience to violence and towards either new or existing resilience resources that are unavailable or overlooked in the social-cohesion-inflected community resilience paradigm.

This is not to say, however, that a focus on individual-resilience building at the micro-level alone will be sufficient or that a focus on community-level social cohesion should be discarded; the social cohesion agenda remains critical because so much of the social influence – in both face-to-face and online settings – that is germane to processes of violent radicalisation across ideologies occurs within socially networked communities through both local and transnational vectors. There is also a strong case to make for macro-level resilience-building that continues to address the structural factors of exclusionary racism and discrimination, unevenly distributed economic opportunities (including for regions or countries undergoing profound change as the result of shifting labour markets or industrial transformations), and competition rather than cooperation in relation to accessing social resources and supports. These macro-level factors are also critically important for strengthening social cohesion and reducing social conflict, and in many ways a resilience-as-social-cohesion model would be even more effective if these macro-level considerations were more prominently identified and embraced.

It is thus possible that incorporating a greater focus on micro-level and macro-level resilience measures, alongside strategies related to meso-level approaches, might effect greater change in relation to far-right extremism than continuing to focus on meso-level community resilience models alone that may not be wholly fit for purpose in these contexts.

This kind of shift would also have to engage with the changing geospatial dynamics of where we need to focus our resilience to violent extremism-building efforts. One historical feature of how building resilience to violent extremism has been conceptualised and operationalised – often unremarked, but increasingly open to contestation as the violent extremist landscape pivots and diversifies – is the dominance of resilience-building to violent extremism policy and programming in urban contexts. This has arisen because violent extremist influence, networks, and mobilisations have been understood largely as a problem in and of densely populated cities (State of Victoria 2015; Coaffee 2006; Coaffee et al. 2008; Sampaio 2017) characterised by attractive high-density population and infrastructure targets for terrorists; geographically concentrated 'vulnerable' ethnocultural communities; the proximity of multiple social networks, contacts, and material resources; and intercultural conflicts in cosmopolitan social environments (Chermak et al. 2013).

Yet a novel feature of far-right extremist activity is the way in which it is now moving beyond cities (while still maintaining an active presence in urban settings across different countries) into rural and regional areas where faltering economies, diminished labour market opportunities, and insufficient infrastructure, social services, and resources can create a range of grievances and sense of disenfranchisement and alienation amongst formerly self-sufficient rural and regional communities, particularly amongst the young. While it is important to avoid conflating the radical right solely with White, working-class communities (Arbuthnot 2021), there is a case to be made for meso-level regional analyses that can reveal greater receptiveness to extreme-right narratives and ideologies as the result of changing economic and social conditions.

For example, subnational regional electoral research conducted in Europe drawing on 'contact' and 'salience of change' hypotheses demonstrates that communities that undergo sudden shifts in economic and employment profiles are more likely to support extreme-right political parties than subnational areas with high levels of immigration who are not struggling economically to the same degree (Georgiadou et al. 2018). Other studies show a correlation between rural regions, increases in unemployment rates, but also higher levels of education (and therefore one kind of social capital) with the radical-right vote across multiple European countries (Stockemer 2017). Right-wing extremists, in particular nationalist and racist groups, are, 'compared with other forms of violent extremism…more widely dispersed across [Australia] – including in regional and rural areas' (ASIO 2021). Violent-extreme right groups now recruit and train in ex-urban regional and rural locations, running 'hate camps' in remote desert areas in the US (Ware 2019), and mounting media spectacles and assaults in rural areas in Australia (McKenzie and Tozer 2021; Tran 2021).

None of this is to say that rural and regional communities are inherently problematic or more likely to produce radical right violent extremists than urban constellations. But from a social-ecological perspective, where such ex-urban communities experience dwindling availability of or access to opportunities, infrastructure, and resources that can help them cope with increasing social and economic adversities and challenges, then the shifting balance this occasions between vulnerabilities and protective factors invites us to look beyond an approach that focuses intensively on cities to think about how we might strengthen resilience at all levels in regional, provincial, and rural communities where extreme-right actors and narratives are making, or attempting to make, their presence felt and actively trying to draw new members into their networks.

When resilience goes bad

As the foregoing discussion suggests, social-ecological resilience is often characterised as an inherently prosocial process, generating and making accessible and culturally meaningful a multi-level, multi-dimensional suite of resources that help strengthen an individual's, community's, or society's ability to adapt and thrive in the context of adversity or challenge.

However, such thriving can, at times, manifest in antisocial rather than prosocial ways. In some contexts, anyone's resilient responses to challenge or adversity can become maladaptive rather than prosocial. This is especially so if the social ecology in which resilience is navigated is itself deficient or struggling with broader vulnerabilities so that the most meaningful resources in one's local environment are those that simultaneously create harms (for self and others) while appearing to offer coping and strengthening mechanisms.

One of the paradoxes this can create is the formation of a 'transactional risk economy' (Grossman 2019), in which the response to environmental stressors that pose risks and create vulnerabilities for a person or group is exchanged for coping strategies that pose new risks and create new vulnerabilities. This is a variety of what Mahdiani and Ungar (2021) term 'the dark side of resilience'. Resilience involves navigating towards available and culturally meaningful resources for coping and thriving in a person's social-ecological environment. If the more powerful of these resources are themselves toxic or harmful, they can produce forms of 'invulnerability' that 'are context-dependent' and may not be perceived as 'positive by institutional leaders like mental health professionals, educators, employers, and government policymakers' (Ungar 2004).

Consider the following hypothetical scenario. We might think of a young person who is struggling with poverty, family dysfunction, and lack of status and self-respect in his life. He has negative experiences with the education and social support systems in his community. He sees other people getting what he considers to be 'handouts' and 'special treatment' while he struggles to meet his basic needs, and feels he is worth less in society's eyes than people who can access and benefit from these resources.

If he joins a violent extremist group focused on anti-immigration or White supremacist ideology, for example, he may find that his access to coping resources increases. For instance, he may be able to access practical resources such as housing or employment through the group; find friends and social networks that make him feel wanted and valued by a new 'family'; feel he is learning and growing through education resources provided as part of the group's recruitment and indoctrination efforts; and find his sense of grievance and victimisation turned into an opportunity for action with meaning and purpose, which allows him to feel better about himself and his place in the world through adopting new forms of agency and identity frames.

It is critical to understand, from this young person's vantage point, that this constitutes a resilient response to his circumstances, reducing some of the vulnerabilities his original environment created. But it is also one that sends him in a high-risk direction for both others and for himself. This includes the risk of harm to others; the risk of arrest, incarceration, and loss of life if he mobilises to violent extremist action; the potential risk of harm *from* the group he joins if he becomes disenchanted and attempts to exit; and, of course, the multi-level risks to community cohesion caused by the violent ideology and actions to which he has committed. Risk and vulnerability in this scenario have thus not been mediated or avoided, but instead are embedded within social-ecological exchanges that may lever a young person out of an initial risk setting but, rather than leading to more prosocial supports, simply swap out one set of risks for another (see Figure 3.1).

This suggests the importance of trying to assess and work with the resilience orientation that those on violent extremist trajectories bring with them as they transit towards radicalised violence. It is not merely about understanding the social-ecological environments in which they operate but drilling down into the resources towards which they can navigate – both antisocial *and* prosocial, and finding ways not only to promote the prosocial but to limit or undermine the availability and navigability of the antisocial or maladaptive. Engaging with the 'dark side' of building resilience to violent extremism means willingness to expand the P/CVE policy and programming remit to include how we might best undermine maladaptive resilience resources as well as foregrounding and strengthening the take-up of prosocial resources. At the moment, policy settings tend to leave this project to counterterrorism rather than P/CVE strategies. It is perhaps time to consider how we might do differently.

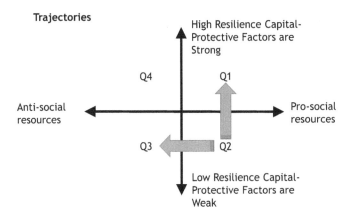

Figure 3.1 Transactional risk economy: prosocial and antisocial resilience

It is also important to recognise that, while we tend to concentrate on the vulnerabilities of those radicalising to violence when engaged in resilience-building programming, they may also be demonstrating their capacity for resilience, even if in maladaptive ways – as the hypothetical scenario above suggests – to address unmet psychological, social, and material needs. Understanding the 'hidden resilience' capacity (Ungar 2004) of individuals who gravitate towards violent extremism and building on these strengths where they exist, rather than solely targeting vulnerabilities, can potentially result in more nuanced and effective programme and treatment options than the 'vulnerability' paradigm alone is likely achieve.

Finally, there is the resilience of violent extremist networks and movements themselves. One of the core features of multi-systemic resilience is openness to new information, the capacity to integrate environmental and systemic shocks, and the initiation of new behaviour regimes as an adaptive response to adversity or stress (Ungar 2018). While the kinds of complex, reciprocal relationships between different political, social, and institutional actors that these elements of resilience speak to are often taken as read in P/CVE contexts, less considered is the way in which the same features hold true for violent extremist movements and organisations themselves. As I've noted elsewhere (Grossman 2021, pp. 307–308), a range of terrorist groups and movements have revealed their capacity over time 'to integrate environmental shocks (for example, financial or territorial losses), initiate new behavioural regimes (for example, shifting from large-scale high-tech attack strategies to small-scale, low-tech domestic attacks; developing new or adapted digital behaviours and strategies), integrate both internal and co-occurring system stressors (for example, internal competitions for movement control; military assaults), and negotiate new resources to accommodate these stressors through complex, reciprocal relationships – by, for example, decentralising a terrorist movement's resource base and creating local franchises in a range of different regional or national locations, increasing transnational resourcing and connectedness, or adopting a 'leaderless' small-group or lone actor model that autonomously generates locally attuned strategy and tactics in different settings.

Recent work by Argentino et al. (2021, p. 3) on terrorist innovation shows that both violent Islamist and far-right violent extremist groups are 'constantly innovating to circumvent the state' and becoming better at 'learning and uptake – that is to say, the means by which innovative processes and technologies are observed and mimicked after their initial point of emergence' across, and not just within, different ideological configurations. This means that the resilience-building project of P/CVE must not only contend with its own multi-systemic system dynamics and complexities, but also continuously adapt to and transform its strategies in relation to the resilience capacity of the violent extremist networks and influences it is attempting to disarm or nullify. This is all the more urgent in light of some of the new intersections, for example, those between conspiracy theory and violent extremism (Rottweiler and Gill 2020) that are reorienting what 'resilience to violent extremism' might mean in the context of such hybrid and swiftly evolving dynamics.

Concluding remarks

At their best, the drivers for P/CVE resilience policy, programming, and strategy are premised on the understanding that potential violent actors in any community – from any political or cultural background – are part of a complex social ecology; that everyday individuals, families, groups, and organisations within this ecology have knowledge, expertise, and shared interests in keeping people safe and well; and that failure to engage meaningfully, respectfully, and authentically with individuals, families, and communities will undermine the effectiveness of this approach.

Efforts to build resilience to violent extremism have taken this emphasis on civil society engagement in various directions. This has included: strategies and programmes focused on building individual and community resistance to and rejection of extremist and exclusivist social influences; addressing structural vulnerabilities to violent extremist influence and ideology; developing counter or alternative messaging strategies to combat violent extremist propaganda; disrupting financing, recruitment, and other enabling mechanisms that fuel capacity for violent action; leveraging awareness and early intervention by families, youth, women, and community groups; diverting people on violent pathways towards prosocial alternatives; and attempting to disengage violent extremist offenders. A dominant theme is that however centralised such initiatives may be in policy or theoretical terms, they require locally based interventions that respond contextually to situated needs, capacities, and dynamics on the ground.

Any intervention that seeks to change either or both thinking and behaviour requires high and also deep thresholds of social and cultural literacy to be successful: you can't change what you don't understand, as the success or failure of public health campaigns, for example, around smoking, seatbelts, and vaccines have repeatedly demonstrated. Like public health challenges, violent extremisms across the ideological and political spectrum are always contextual, always contingent, and always in dynamic interplay with both swiftly and slowly moving undercurrents of social and political flux. Navigating these rapids and narrows to determine the kinds of resilience-building measures that will be most effective in any given context – social, ideological, cultural, spatially or digitally based – calls for sustained learning and interaction between communities, practitioners, and policymakers: what one might call the 'slow resilience' movement. Durable resilience-building takes time.

Yet a number of models for building resilience to violent extremism have, as has P/CVE policy and programming more broadly, approached the need for deep sociocultural literacies more as a question of mastering thinly conceptualised competencies around the beliefs and behaviours of 'others' (even when those 'others' are our neighbours, our children, our friends), rather than as a complex social ecology of interdependent, multi-level factors and actors.

Much of this stems from the originary focus of P/CVE on Muslim diaspora communities, which over time has resulted in a range of negative impacts. These negative impacts include deep suspicion, mistrust, and hostility by communities who feel stigmatised and victimised by cultural or ethnic profile-based community-resilience programming; the lack of a clearly articulated 'better offer' for those seeking to redress real and perceived grievances and injustices; and relatively weaker investment in both the quantum and diversity of resources needed to embed a needs-based rather than risk-based approach.

It has also led to the dilemma of P/CVE resilience-building initiatives remaining primarily focused on finding ways to tackle the resilience capacity of 'them' and not 'us', which has in turn led to reluctance by many state and mainstream civil society actors to locate their own policies and actions as variables within the overall ecology of resilience-building strategies and impacts. At their worst, P/CVE resilience policies and programmes have positioned communities as targets rather than partners; treated sociocultural dispositions as static artefacts rather than dynamic and interdependent processes; and largely ignored or downplayed the impacts and implications of their own roles and behaviours within local P/CVE ecologies.

At their best, however, the P/CVE resilience models most likely to be both effective and sustainable are those that are themselves resilient. If we develop models of resilience to violent extremism that are adaptive (for example, to the emergence of new threats, new resources, and untapped capacities); open to learning and experimentation (for example, incorporating majority-culture and government resilience indicators into the model, learning from and with communities, taking risks in partnerships, and learning from failures or stalled programming); able to absorb systemic shocks (for example, shifts in the profile and tactics of violent extremist actors or the risk appetite of governments); initiate new behavioural regimes (for example, modifying definitions, resources, relationships, and structures in context-dependent resilience programming); and negotiate new resources through complex, reciprocal relationships (for example, through respectful and genuine partnerships with an expanded range of civil society and institutional actors and organisations who may be newly relevant to changing circumstances and contexts), then building resilience to violent extremism may become a more productive and durable prospect in the current landscape.

The American ethnographer George Marcus (1998, pp. 187–188) has called attention to the challenges of describing 'the ways that…positions and norms take shape in diverse, broad and conflicted spaces of social life', going on to say that:

> once we…analytically 'fix' by naming [what we are analysing], we have already circumscribed the space and dimensions of our object of study – we know what we are talking about prematurely. But we can also be sure that our object of study will always exceed its analytic circumscription.

Drawing on Marcus's insights here means conducting our efforts to promote the capacity for prosocial resilience to violent extremism in ways that strive continuously for insight and efficacy, while recognising that such work will always be contingent and partial, particularly as we both anticipate and respond to emergent challenges in the sociopolitical landscape. It also means abandoning the pretence that as practitioners, policymakers, service providers and researchers, we approach such inquiry from a 'transcendent, detached point' rather than as part and parcel of the very terrain in which we seek to intervene.

References

Aly, A., Taylor, E., and Karnovsky, S. (2014) Moral disengagement and building resilience to violent extremism: An education intervention. *Studies in Conflict & Terrorism*, 37(4), pp. 369–385, DOI: 10.1080/1057610X.2014.879379

Arbuthnot, S. (2021) *Can Community Engagement Counter the Radical Right?* Center for the Analysis of the Radical Right (CARR), 24 March, www.radicalrightanalysis.com/author/sean-arbuthnot/

Argentino, M-A., Maher, S., and Winter, C. (2021) *Violent Extremist Innovation: A Cross-Ideological Analysis*. Report for National Counter-Terrorism Innovation, Technology and Education Center. London: International Centre for the Study of Radicalisation, https://icsr.info/wp-content/uploads/2021/12/ICSR-Report-Violent-Extremist-Innovation-A-Cross%E2%80%91Ideological-Analysis.pdf

ASIO (2021) *Australia's Security Environment and Outlook*. Canberra: Australian Security and Intelligence Organisation, www.asio.gov.au/australias-security-environment-and-outlook.html

Bartlett J. and Littler M. (2011) *Inside the EDL: Populist Politics in a Digital Age*. London: DEMOS.

Bhui, K.S., Hicks, M.H., Lashley, M.H., and Jones, E. (2012) A public health approach to understanding and preventing violent radicalization. *BMC Medicine*, 10(16), https://bmcmedicine.biomedcentral.com/articles/10.1186/1741-7015-10-16

BOUNCE (2018) *Resilience Training, Network and Evaluation STRESAVIORA II: Strengthening Resilience against Violent Radicalisation 2015–2018*. Brussels: European Commission with the Egmont Institute.

Brzuszkiewicz, S. (2020) Incel radical milieu and external locus of control. *ICCT Journal Special Edition: Evolutions in Counter-Terrorism, Volume II: Contemporary Developments*. The Hague: International Centre for Counter-Terrorism, pp. 1–21, https://icct.nl/app/uploads/2020/11/Special-Edition-2-1.pdf

Castro, F.G. and Murray, K.E. (2009) Cultural adaption and resilience: Controversies, issues, and emerging models. In: Reich, J., Zautra, A., and Hall, J. (eds.), *Handbook of Adult Resilience*. New York: Guilford Press, pp. 375–403.

Challgren, J., Kenyon, T., Kervick, L., Scudder, S., Walters, M., Whitehead, K., Connor, J., and Flynn, C.R. (2016) *Countering Violent Extremism: Applying the Public Health Model* (*Georgetown Security Studies Review*). Washington, D.C.: Center for Security Studies, Georgetown University, https://georgetownsecuritystudiesreview.org/wp-content/uploads/2016/10/NSCITF-Report-on-Countering-Violent-Extremism.pdf

Chermak, S., Freilich, J., and Suttmoeller, M. (2013) The organisational dynamics of far-right hate groups in the United States: Comparing violent to non-violent organisations. *Studies in Conflict and Terrorism*, 36(3), pp. 193–218, DOI: 10.1080/1057610X.2013.755912

Coaffee, J. (2006) From Counterterrorism to Resilience. *European Legacy*, 11(4), pp. 389–403, DOI:10.1080/10848770600766094

Coaffee, J. and Fussey, P. (2015) Constructing resilience through security and surveillance: The politics, practices and tensions of security-driven resilience. *Security Dialogue*, 46(1), pp. 86–105, DOI:10.1177/0967010614557884

Coaffee, J., Moore, C., Fletcher, D., and Bosher, L. (2008) Resilient design for community safety and terror-resistant cities. *Proceedings of the Institution of Civil Engineers – Municipal Engineer*, 161(2), pp. 103–110, DOI:10.1680/muen.2008.161.2.103

CAIR Minnesota (2016) *Countering Violent Extremism Program (CVE): What You Need to Know*. Council on American-Islamic Relations-Minnesota, www.cairmn.com/index.php/civil-rights/cve-toolkit

Dalgaard-Nielsen, A. and Schack, P. (2016) Community resilience to militant Islamism: Who and what? An explorative study of resilience in three Danish communities. *Democracy and Security*, 12(4), pp. 309–327, DOI: 10.1080/17419166.2016.1236691

Day, J. and Kleinmann, S. (2017) Combating the cult of ISIS: A social approach to countering violent extremism. *The Review of Faith & International Affairs*, 15(3), pp. 14–23, DOI:10.1080/15570274.2017.1354458

Dechesne, M. (2017) The concept of resilience in the context of counterterrorism. In: Kumar, U. (ed.), *The Routledge International Handbook of Psychosocial Resilience*. London and New York: Routledge, pp. 414–423.

Ellis, H.B. and Abdi, S. (2017) Building community resilience to violent extremism through genuine partnerships. *American Psychologist*, 72(3), pp. 289–300, DOI:10.1037/amp0000065

Froio, C. and Ganesh, B. (2018) The transnationalisation of far-right discourse on Twitter. *European Societies*, DOI:10.1080/14616696.2018.1494295

Georgiadou, V., Rori, L., and Roumanias, C. (2018) Mapping the European far right in the 21st century: A meso-level analysis. *Electoral Studies,* 54, pp. 103–115, DOI: 10.1016/j.electstud.2018.05.004

Global Community Engagement and Resilience Fund (2017) *Strategy to Engage Communities and Address the Drivers of Violent Extremism 2017-2020.* Geneva: Global Community Engagement and Resilience Fund, www.gcerf.org/wp-content/uploads/GCERF-Strategy-2017-2020.pdf

GCTF (2012) *Ankara Memorandum on Good Practices for a Multi-Sectoral Approach to Countering Violent Extremism.* Global Counterterrorism Forum, www.thegctf.org/documents/10162/72352/13Sep19_Ankara+Memorandum.pdf

Grossman, M. (2019) Understanding youth resilience to violent extremism: From questions to measurement. Conference presentation. Melbourne: Youth Resilience to Violent Extremism Symposium, CVE Centre, Department of Home Affairs, 10 April.

Grossman, M. (2021) Resilience to violent extremism and terrorism: A multi-systemic analysis. In: Ungar, M. (ed.), *Multisystemic Resilience: Adaptation and Transformation in Changing Contexts.* Oxford: Oxford University Press, pp. 293–317. Open Access: https://oxford.universitypressscholarship.com/view/10.1093/oso/9780190095888.001.0001/oso-9780190095888-chapter-17

Grossman, M., Hadfield, K., Jefferies, P., Gerrand, V., and Ungar, M. (2020) Youth resilience to violent extremism: Development and validation of the BRaVE measure. *Terrorism and Political Violence*, DOI:10.1080/09546553.2019.1705283

Grossman, M., Peucker, M., Smith, D., and Dellal, H. (2016) *Stocktake Research Project: A Systematic Literature and Selected Program Review on Social Cohesion, Community Resilience and Violent Extremism 2011–2015.* Melbourne: Victoria University and Australian Multicultural Foundation.

Grossman, M., Tahiri, H., and Stephenson, P. (2014) *Harnessing Resilience Capital: An Investigation of Resilience and Cultural Diversity in Countering Violent Extremism.* Canberra: Australia-New Zealand Counter-terrorism Committee.

Grossman, M., Ungar, M., Brisson, J., Gerrand, V., Hadfield, K., and Jefferies, P. (2017) *Understanding youth resilience to violent extremism: A standardised research measure. Final research report*. Melbourne and Halifax: Alfred Deakin Institute for Citizenship and Globalisation, Deakin University, and The Resilience Research Centre, Dalhousie University.

Hardy, K. (2015) Resilience in UK counterterrorism. *Theoretical criminology*, 19(1), pp. 77–94, DOI: 10.1177/1362480614542119

Harris-Hogan, S., Barrelle, K., and Zammit, A. (2016) What is countering violent extremism? Exploring CVE policy and practice in Australia. *Behavioral Sciences of Terrorism and Political Aggression*, 8(1), pp. 6–24, DOI: 10.1080/19434472.2015.1104710

Ho, C. (2011) Respecting the presence of others: School micropublics and everyday multiculturalism. *Journal of Intercultural Studies*, 32, pp. 603–619.

Hutchinson, J. (2017) Violent extremism and far-right radicalism in Australia: A psychosocial perspective. *Counter Terrorist Trends and Analyses*, 9(11), pp. 16–19, www.rsis.edu.sg/wp-content/uploads/2017/11/CTTA-November-2017.pdf

ICRC (2017) *Background note and guidance for National Red Cross and Red Crescent societies on 'preventing and countering violent extremism'*. Geneva: International Committee of the Red Cross.

Jones, S.G. (2018) The rise of far-right extremism in the United States. *CSIS Brief*. Washington, DC: Center for Strategic and International Studies, www.csis.org/analysis/rise-far-right-extremism-united-states

Keddie, A. (2014) The politics of Britishness: Multiculturalism, schooling and social cohesion. *British Education Research Journal*, 40(3), pp. 539–554.

Lauder, M.A. (2002) *The Far Rightwing Movement in Southwest Ontario: An Exploration of Issues, Themes, and Variations*. The Guelph and District Multicultural Centre.

Longstaff, P.H., Armstrong, N.J., Perrin, K., Parker, W.M., and Hidek, M.A. (2010) Building resilient communities: A preliminary framework for assessment. *Homeland Security Affairs*, V1(3), Article 6, www.hsaj.org/articles/81

Los Angeles Interagency Coordination Group (2015) *The Los Angeles framework for countering violent extremism*. Los Angeles, www.dhs.gov/publication/los-angeles-framework-countering-violent-terrorism

Lösel, F., King, S., Bender, D., and Jugl, I. (2018) Protective factors against extremism and violent radicalization: A systematic review of research. *International Journal of Developmental Sciences*, 12(9), pp. 1–14, DOI:10.3233/DEV-170241

Mahdiani, H. and Ungar, M. (2021) The dark side of resilience. Adversity and Resilience *Science*, 2, pp. 147–155, https://link.springer.com/article/10.1007/s42844-021-00031-z

Marcus, G. (1998) *Ethnography Through Thick and Thin*. Princeton: Princeton University Press.

Masten, A.S. (2014) Global perspectives on resilience in children and youth. *Child Development*, 85(1), pp. 6–20, DOI: 10.1111/cdev.12205

Masten, A.S. (2016) Resilience in developing systems: The promise of integrated approaches. *European Journal of Developmental Psychology*, 13(3), pp. 297–312, DOI: 10.1080/17405629.2016.1147344

McCoy, J., Rahman, T., and Somer, M. (2018) Polarization and the global crisis of democracy: Common patterns, dynamics, and pernicious consequences for democratic polities. *American Behavioral Scientist*, 62(1), DOI: 10.1177/0002764218759576

McKenzie, N. and Tozer, J. (2021) Neo-Nazis go bush: Grampians gathering highlights rise of Australia's far-right. *Sydney Morning Herald*, 27 January, www.smh.com.au/politics/federal/neo-nazis-go-bush-grampians-gathering-highlights-rise-of-australia-s-far-right-20210127-p56xbf.html

McNeil-Willson, R., Gerrand, V., Scrinzi, F., and Triandafyllidou, A. (2019) *Polarisation, Violent Extremism and Resilience in Europe Today: An Analytical Framework*. Concept paper for BRaVE (Building Resilience Against Violent Extremism and Polarisation, Horizon 2020 Project 822189, http://brave-h2020.eu/repository/D2.1_BRaVE_concept_paper_final_10Dec2019.pdf

Meret, S. (2019) Islam and the Danish-Scandinavian welfare state: A 'Muslims in the West' reaction essay. *The One Percent Problem: Muslims in the West and the Rise of the New Populists*. Brookings Institution Initiative, www.brookings.edu/articles/islam-and-the-danish-scandinavian-welfare-state/

Miller-Idriss, C. (2021) White supremacist extremism and the far right in the U.S. *Political Extremism and Radicalism: Far-Right Groups in America*, Cengage Learning (EMEA) Ltd., www.gale.com/intl/essays/cynthia-miller-idriss-white-supremacist-extremism-far-right-us

Multicultural New South Wales (2018) *COMPACT Program Guidelines*. Sydney: Multicultural New South Wales.

National Academies of Sciences, Engineering and Medicine (2017) *Countering Violent Extremism through Public Health Practice: Proceedings of a Workshop*. Washington, DC: The National Academies Press.

Nguyen, N. (2019) *Suspect Communities: Anti-Muslim Racism and the Domestic War on Terror*. Minneapolis: University of Minnesota Press.

OSCE (2018) *The Role of Civil Society in Preventing and Countering Violent Extremism and Radicalization that Lead to Terrorism: A Guidebook for South-Eastern Europe*. Vienna: Organisation for Security and Co-operation in Europe Secretariat, www.osce.org/secretariat/400241

Perliger, A. (2012) *Challengers from the Sidelines: Understanding America's Far Right*. West Point NY: Combating Terrorism Center.

Perry, B. and Scrivens, R. (2015) *Right-wing Extremism in Canada: An Environmental Scan*, www.researchgate.net/publication/307971749_Right_Wing_Extremism_in_Canada_An_Environmental_Scan_2015/link/593aa39a0f7e9b3317f41358/download

Perry, B. and Scrivens, R. (2019) *Right-Wing Extremism in Canada*. Cham: Palgrave Macmillan (Palgrave Hate Studies), DOI: 10.1007/978-3-030-25169-7

Public Safety Canada (2013) *Building Resilience against Terrorism: Canada's Counter-terrorism Strategy*. Ottawa: Public Safety Canada, www.publicsafety.gc.ca/cnt/rsrcs/pblctns/rslnc-gnst-trrrsm/index-en.aspx

Putnam, R.D. (2000) *Bowling Alone: The Collapse and Revival of American Community*. Princeton: Princeton University Press.

Ragazzi, F. (2016) Suspect community or suspect category? The impact of counter-terrorism as 'policed multiculturalism'. *Journal of Ethnic and Migration Studies*, 42(5), pp. 724–741.

Rosand, E., Winterbotham, E., Jones, M., and Praxl-Tabuchi, F. (2018) *A Roadmap to Progress: The State of Global P/CVE Agenda*. The Prevention Project and Royal United Services Institute.

Rottweiler, B. and Gill, P. (2020) Conspiracy beliefs and violent extremist intentions: The contingent effects of self-efficacy, self-control and law-related morality. *Terrorism and Political Violence*, DOI:10.1080/09546553.2020.1803288

Rutter, J. (2015) *Moving Up and Getting On: Migration, Integration and Social Cohesion in the UK*. Bristol, UK: Policy Press.

Sampaio, A. (2017) Resilience gains ground in counter-terrorism strategies. *Jane's Intelligence Review*, 29(12), pp. 18–21.

Sealy, T. and Modood, T. (2019) *Country Report: France*. GREASE: Radicalisation, Secularism and the Governance of Religion: Bringing Together Asian and European Perspectives. Horizon 2020 Project 770640, http://grease.eui.eu/wp-content/uploads/sites/8/2019/10/France-country-report.pdf

Sieckelinck, S. and Gielen, A-J. (2018) *Protective and promotive factors building resilience against violent radicalisation*. RAN Issue Paper. Brussels: European Commission, Radicalisation Awareness Network, https://pure.uva.nl/ws/files/33181089/ran_paper_protective_factors_042018_en.pdf

Spalek, B. and Davies, L. (2012) Mentoring in relation to violent extremism: A study of role, purpose, and outcomes. *Studies in Conflict & Terrorism*, 35(5), pp. 354–368, DOI: 10.1080/1057610X.2012.666820

State of Victoria (2015) *Strategic Framework to Strengthen Victoria's Social Cohesion and the Resilience of its Communities*. Melbourne: State of Victoria (Department of Premier and Cabinet, www.mav.asn.au/__data/assets/pdf_file/0012/22512/Strategic_Framework_to_Strengthen_Victorias_Social_Cohesion-Dec-2015.pdf

Stephens, W. and Sieckelinck, S. (2020) Being resilient to radicalisation in PVE policy: A critical examination. *Critical Studies on Terrorism*, 13(1), pp. 142–165.

Stephens, W., Sieckelinck, S., and Boutellier, H. (2019) Preventing violent extremism: A review of the literature. *Studies in Conflict & Terrorism*, DOI: 10.1080/1057610X.2018.1543144

Stockemer, D. (2017) The success of radical right-wing parties in Western European regions: New challenging findings. *Journal of Contemporary European Studies*, 25(1), pp. 41–56.

Szreter, S. and Woolcock, M. (2004) Health by association? Social capital, social theory, and the political economy of public health. *International Journal of Epidemiology*, 33, pp. 650–667, DOI: 10.1093/ije/dyh013

Taylor, E.L., Taylor, P.C., Karnovsky, S., Aly, A., and Taylor, N. (2017) 'Beyond Bali': A transformative education approach for developing community resilience to violent extremism. *Asia Pacific Journal of Education*, 37(2), pp. 193–204, DOI: 10.1080/02188791.2016.1240661

Thomas, P. (2012) *Responding to the Threat of Violent Extremism – Failing to Prevent*, London: Bloomsbury Academic.

Thomas, P. and Grossman, M. (forthcoming, 2023) Working with communities to counter radicalisation. In: Busher, J., Marsden, S., and Malkki, L. (eds.), *Routledge Handbook on Radicalisation and Counter-radicalisation*. London: Routledge.

Tran, D. (2021) Two Australian neo-Nazis face court over alleged assault in Cathedral Ranges State Park. *ABC News* (Australian Broadcasting Corporation), 27 October. www.abc.net.au/news/2021-10-27/australian-supremacist-neo-nazi-thomas-sewell-cathedral-ranges/100574050

Ungar, M. (2004) *Nurturing Hidden Resilience in Troubled Youth*. Toronto: University of Toronto Press.

Ungar, M. (2008) Resilience across cultures. *British Journal of Social Work*, 38, pp. 218–235, DOI: 10.1093/bjsw/bcl343

Ungar, M. (2011) The social ecology of resilience: Addressing contextual and cultural ambiguity of a nascent construct. *American Journal of Orthopsychiatry*, 81(1), pp. 1–17, DOI: /10.1111/j.1939-0025.2010.01067.x

Ungar, M. (2018) Systemic resilience: Principles and processes for a science of change in contexts of adversity. *Ecology and Society*, 23(4), 34ff, DOI: 10.5751/ES-10385-230434

Ungar, M., Hadfield, K., Amarasingam, A., Morgan, S., and Grossman, M. (2017) The association between discrimination and violence among Somali Canadian youth. *Journal of Ethnic and Migration Studies*, DOI: 10.1080/1369183X.2017.1374169

UN Security Council (2014) Resolution 2178, www.un.org/en/ga/search/view_doc.asp?symbol=S/RES/2178%20%282014%29

Van Brunt, B., Murphy, M., and Zedginidze, A. (2017) An exploration of the risk, protective, and mobilization factors related to violent extremism in college populations. *Violence and Gender*, 4(3), DOI: 10.1089/vio.2017.0039

Vermeulen, F. and Bovenkerk, F. (2012) *Engaging with Violent Islamic Extremism: Local policies in Western European cities*. The Hague: Forum.

Walklate, S., Mythen, G., and McGarry, R. (2012) States of resilience and the resilient state. *Current Issues in Criminal Justice*, 24 (2), pp. 185–204.

Ware, J. (2019) *Siege: The Atomwaffen Division and Rising Far-Right Terrorism in the United States*. ICCT Policy Brief, July. The Hague: International Centre for Counter-Terrorism, https://icct.nl/app/uploads/2019/07/ICCT-Ware-Siege-July2019.pdf

Weine, S. and Ahmed, O. (2012) *Building Resilience to Violent Extremism Among Somali-Americans in Minneapolis-St. Paul*. National Consortium for the Study of Terrorism and Responses to Terrorism. A Department of Homeland Security Science and Technology Center of Excellence, University of Maryland.

Weine, S., Eisenman, D.P., Kinsler, J., Glik, D.C., and Polutnik, C. (2017) Addressing violent extremism as public health policy and practice. *Behavioral Sciences of Terrorism and Political Aggression*, 9(3), pp. 208–221, DOI: 10.1080/19434472.2016.1198413

Weine, S., Henderson, S., Shanfield, S., Legha, R., and Post, J. (2013) Building community resilience to counter violent extremism. *Democracy and Security*, 9(4), pp. 327–333, DOI: 10.1080/17419166.2013.766131

4
EUROPEAN TRENDS IN POLARISATION AND RESILIENCE

Sheryl Prentice and Paul Taylor

Introduction

The aim of this chapter is to explore concept trends in academic, practitioner, and government writings on polarisation and resilience, as well as to determine how these concepts change over time. We consider the reasons for trends and changes in both the immediate linguistic context of the concepts and their external contexts of occurrence. In other words, we will be looking both inside and outside the text.

The chapter is informed by the work of the 'Building Resilience Against Violent Extremism and Polarisation' project (BRaVE), a European Commission-funded project undertaken by a consortium of research institutions.[1] One of the project's aims was to organise existing knowledge on violent extremism, polarisation, and resilience in a systematic fashion. To this end, BRaVE consortium member Lancaster University compiled a review of literature into polarisation and its associated phenomena. This review included polarisation literature (conceived in the broadest sense) from a range of fields, including, but not limited to, economics, sociology, information technology, linguistics, psychology, and political science. This literature can be roughly categorised into the following contexts:

(1) Socio-economic: relating to financial and welfare factors of polarisation
(2) Historical: relating to state factors and historic conflicts and politics
(3) Cultural: relating to identity and cultural practices
(4) Communication-based: relating to offline and online content and interaction

This chapter uses the abstracts associated with this literature as its input in addition to related entries from the BRaVE project database (BRaVE 2019). The BRaVE project database contains searchable summaries of 696 collated polarisation and resilience policies (98), projects (335), studies (160), and institutional (103) information from ten European states (Belgium, Denmark, Greece, Italy, Poland, Hungary, France, Germany, the Netherlands, and the UK). The information featured in the database was collated by BRaVE consortium members.

DOI: 10.4324/9781003267102-5

We apply a thematic analysis to literature that seeks to understand popular conceptualisations of polarisation and resilience within its socio-economic, historic, cultural, and communication-based contexts. Then we use the dates associated with literature releases to explore how these conceptualisations of polarisation and resilience have changed over time in relation to three sets of users: academics, practitioners (including Non-Governmental Organisations, charities, and grassroots initiatives), and European governments. Finally, we discuss the implications of prevalent framings and the reasons for their occurrence, whilst also considering what trends may emerge around the concepts of polarisation and resilience in the coming years.

It is hoped that this will assist academic researchers, practitioners, and government policymakers alike in gaining insights into how polarisation and resilience in Europe are discussed across a range of contexts, by a variety of actors, at different points in time, thus assisting their understanding of these phenomena and the alternative perspectives towards them. In addition, the chapter aims to highlight how these groups might learn from the findings to reflect on their priorities and to extol the benefits of a more coordinated approach.

Framing of polarisation and resilience

A thematic analysis is used to gain insights into the central concepts present in literature relating to four different contexts of polarisation and resilience discussed in the introduction to this chapter, namely, socio-economic, historic, cultural, and communication-based. The analysis employs a classic corpus linguistic approach, in which one moves from a quantitative overview of one's texts to a more in-depth qualitative study to understand the patterns observed. For a more detailed overview of corpus linguistics as a field and its associated methods, see Kennedy (2014).

To conduct the analysis, the abstracts associated with each of the ~200 literature items were extracted and separated according to one of the four contexts. Each set of abstracts was imported into a separate text document (35,622 words in total). The BRaVE project database was then searched for policies, projects, institutions, and studies associated with the following search terms: 'econom*', 'histor*', 'cultur*', and 'communicat*', respectively. The summaries of studies and objectives of policies, projects, and institutions were extracted, along with their dates, titles, and types (e.g., policy, project). The textual content of summaries and objectives from each search was added to the relevant textual abstract data from the literature items to form four separate corpora.

Each corpus was then run through the corpus software tool Wmatrix (Rayson 2021), where every word in the respective corpus was tagged for its part of speech (e.g., noun, verb) and semantic concept(s). Semantic concepts are derived from the UCREL Semantic Analysis System (USAS); a framework of 21 semantic domains and 232 sub-domains, which describe the meaning or 'sense' of a word. For further details of this system and how it is employed on linguistic data, see Rayson et al. (2004).

Once processed, each corpus was compared to the Informative Writing section of the BNC Sampler corpus in a method known as Key Concept Analysis, which determines whether a concept is significantly more frequent in literature on socio-economic, historic, cultural, or communication-based polarisation and resilience when compared to a general corpus of informative writing. These concepts are referred to as 'key concepts' and are presented in our analyses in the form of clouds. The larger a concept appears within the cloud, the more 'key' it is to a specific type of polarisation and resilience literature (see Rayson 2008 for more information on this method).

Key concepts observed in these clouds were manually grouped into themes. Collocations of key concepts within these themes were derived in order to gain insights into who or what the concept generally referred to. Collocation is a method whereby one measures the co-occurrence of a concept (in this case) and a nearby word. In this case, the span of co-occurrence was set to five words either side of the concept in question and collocation was measured using the mutual information statistic, which indicates the strength of association between a concept and a particular word. Mutual information scores of three or above are generally interpreted as indicating a strong association (see Church and Hanks 1990 for further information). However, whilst this gives one an indication of who or what is being referred to in connection with a concept, it does not tell one why this co-occurrence is present. Therefore, the corpus linguistic method of concordance analysis was used to gain a deeper understanding of how a concept was used in the corpora. This involved viewing a given collocate word in its immediate linguistic context (described as a concordance). Example concordances are provided throughout the sections that follow to illustrate the process. Within these examples, key concept words appear in bold, while collocate terms are underlined.

Socio-economic context

The socio-economic context corpus contains 50 abstracts from the literature review and an additional 45 records from the BRaVE project database (5 institutions, 7 policies, 9 projects, and 24 studies), amounting to 15,792 words. Figure 4.1 presents the results of the thematic analysis of the corpus.

Within the current literature and government and practitioner spheres dealing with the socio-economic contexts of polarisation and resilience, the thematic analysis focuses on the following key areas: Education (e.g., 'Education in general'), Understanding (e.g., 'Knowledge', 'Mental object: Conceptual object', 'Cause & Effect/Connection', 'Investigate, examine, test, search'), Identity (e.g., 'Belonging to a group'), and Comparison (e.g., 'Comparing: Varied', 'Comparing: Different', 'Degree', the latter mainly occurring due to use of the term 'relative' and its derivatives).

Collocates of the concept 'Education in general' include 'preservice' (MI = 9.02), 'achievement' (MI = 7.04), 'multicultural' (MI = 6.51), 'parents' (MI = 6.26), and 'immigrant'

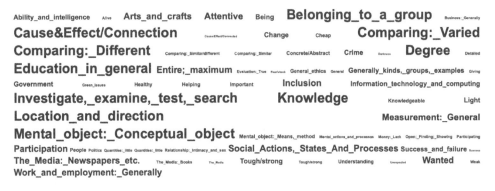

Figure 4.1 Showing a comparison of socio-economic abstracts and objectives with the BNC Informative Writing Sampler

(MI = 6.13). The focus here is on levelling up the gaps that exist in the education of different cultural groups within European societies, for example:

> Principles for **Teaching** and **Learning** in a <u>Multicultural</u> Society contains research-based guidelines for reforming teaching and the **school** in order to increase the **academic** <u>achievement</u> and social development of students from diverse racial, ethnic, cultural, language, and gender groups.
>
> Banks 2015

There is a sense that educational practices are not keeping pace with the increasingly diverse societies of certain European nations, and that this is presenting barriers to achievement in education and development opportunities for minority communities, including immigrants, and parental involvement in child education.

Within the theme of Understanding, collocates of the 'Knowledge' concept include the words 'records' (MI = 8.19), 'survey' (MI = 7.41), and 'analysis' (MI = 5.72), with concordances suggesting a current focus on how the use of data can assist our understanding of socio-economic polarisation and resilience, for example:

> Our <u>analysis</u> of quantitative **data** from service and manufacturing organisations in Ireland confirms that HPWS practices are associated with positive business performance and finds specifically that DEMS practices are positively associated with higher labour productivity and workforce innovation and lower voluntary employee turnover.
>
> Armstrong et al. 2010

> This is the third in a series of annual Integration Monitors that measure migrant integration in four life domains: employment, education, social inclusion and active citizenship…Most indicators are derived from the latest available <u>survey</u> **data** and compare outcomes for Irish and migrant populations in each domain.
>
> McGinnity et al. 2010

The first of these examples explains how data analysis has enabled researchers to observe the positive effects of a Diversity and Equality Management System (DEMS) on productivity and innovation in the workplace, while the second describes how insights from survey data can be used to monitor the integration of migrants into different societal domains when compared to Irish nationals. Meanwhile, the 'Cause&Effect/Connection' concept within the Understanding theme includes the collocate 'business'; for example, 'Even in Silicon Valley, where many leaders tout the need to increase diversity for both <u>business</u> and social justice **reasons**, bread-and-butter tech jobs remain dominated by white men' (Dobbin and Kalev 2016). In a similar way to the Education theme, examples from the Understanding theme further illustrate a pattern of focusing on diverse population challenges.

In relation to the theme of Comparison, collocates of the key concept 'Comparing: Different' include 'horizontal' (MI = 5.52), 'residential' (MI = 5.10), 'racial' (MI = 4.93), 'regional' (MI = 4.78), and 'inequality' (MI = 3.93). Such collocates hint at socio-economic differences due to race (e.g., 'racial') and location (e.g., 'residential' and 'regional'), for example:

This report shows the findings from a field experiment that involved submitting matched job applications from white and ethnic minority applicants to estimate the extent of <u>racial</u> **discrimination** in different areas of the British labour market.

Wood et al. 2009

However, differences are not always interpreted in a negative sense in the literature and database records, as the following example illustrates:

This questions the generally held view that segregation in a multicultural society is undesirable per se and suggests that a one size fits all government policy towards <u>residential</u> **segregation** is insufficiently perceptive.

Brimicombe 2007

In this case, a degree of residential segregation was found to be beneficial for particular minority groups in London (with the exception of Asian-Bangladeshi and Muslim communities – see Brimicombe (2007) for further details). Akin to the observations made in relation to other socio-economic themes, there is a focus in polarisation research and practice on levelling up between different sections of society. However, as the last example demonstrates, this focus or blanket treatment can, on occasion, be to the detriment of positive aspects of difference.

Historic context

The historical context corpus contains 78 abstracts from the polarisation and resilience literature review and a further 54 records from the BRaVE database (7 institutions, 2 policies, 24 projects, and 21 studies). Historical abstracts make up the largest percentage of the literature reviewed (38.42 per cent). The corpus contains 19,383 words.

The key concept analysis presented in Figure 4.2 highlights the themes of Attention (e.g., 'Attentive'), Negative attitudes or behaviours (e.g., 'Crime', 'Dislike', and 'Violent/Angry'), and the State (e.g., 'Government' and 'Politics'). The historical context corpus also bears similarity with the socio-economic context corpus in its prominent references to the themes of Education (e.g., 'Education in general'), Comparison (e.g., 'Comparing: Different' and 'Comparing: Varied'), and Understanding (e.g., 'Cause&Effect/Connection', 'Investigate,

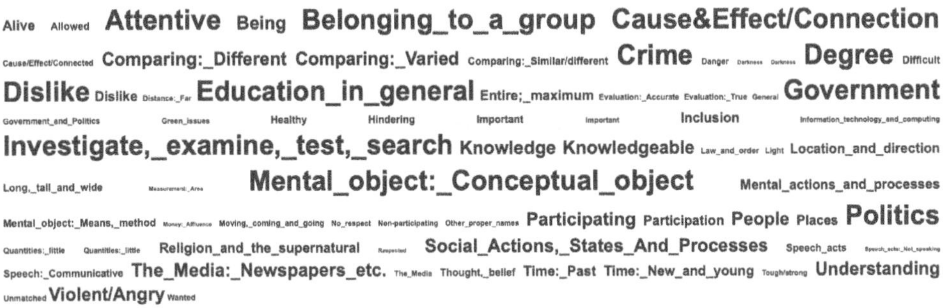

Figure 4.2 Showing a comparison of historic abstracts and objectives with the BNC Informative Writing Sampler

examine, test, search', and 'Mental object: Conceptual object' – in reference to theories and hypotheses).

With respect to Attention, concordance analysis of the key concept 'Attentive' shows that typical words within this concept include 'focus', 'highlight', and 'attention' and their derivatives, which are typically used as a means of attempting to refocus past academic and practitioner understanding on polarising issues such as radicalisation, for example:

> The authors step away from readily available explanations and rethink the notion of the radical. Rather than merely **focusing** on individuals or ideologies, they advocate for a contextual perspective that allows to consider the complex interaction between individuals, groups, and institutions, both at a national and international level.
>
> Clycq et al. 2019

However, other research is attentive to the lack of change or progress and draws parallels between trends of the past and the present, for instance:

> As well as appearing online, the posters and tweets were then combined in an outdoor campaign **highlighting** the similarities between today's tweets and some of the darker times of the past.
>
> Licra 2019

This example refers to discourse on antisemitism.

This brings one to the theme of Negative attitudes and behaviours. The key concept of 'Crime' contains collocates such as 'lone-actor' (MI = 6.87), 'hate' (MI = 6.53), 'victims' (MI = 5.87), 'right-wing' (MI = 4.65), and 'immigrants' (MI = 3.41), reflecting current trends to focus on lone-actor terrorism, hate-crime, right-wing extremism, and immigration. However, immigrants are constructed as victims of crime rather than the perpetrators in efforts to challenge public perceptions of immigrants as a threat, for example,

> To describe and critique the extent and nature of data collection in European Union (EU) Member States on <u>immigrants</u> as <u>victims</u> of **crime**, and to contextualise this situation with regard to wider debates concerning the EU that focuses on <u>immigrants</u> as a **crime** problem.
>
> Goodey 2009

Collocates of the key concept 'Dislike' include 'develop' (MI = 7.23), 'people' (MI 5.44), 'speech' (MI = 5.38), and 'forms' (MI = 5.00). The concept itself is dominated by use of the term 'hate' and its derivates, hence its collocation with the word 'speech'. Whilst this phenomenon has received much attention of late, it is not just a contemporary concern, as examples such as the following demonstrate:

> Since the 1960s, many liberal democracies have instituted laws that penalise **hate** <u>speech</u> and hate crimes in ways that limit the freedom for racists to express themselves.
>
> Bleich 2011

In terms of the State theme, collocates of the 'Government' concept include 'trade' (MI = 10.65), 'evidence' (MI = 6.70), 'vote' (MI = 6.61), 'right' (MI = 6.40), 'general'

(MI = 6.26), 'electoral' (MI = 5.53), 'local' (MI = 5.53), and 'right-wing' (MI = 5.08), while collocates of the 'Politics' concepts include 'number' (MI = 5.98), 'house' (MI = 5.95), 'pedagogical' (MI = 5.63), 'member' (MI = 5.56), and 'minority' (MI = 5.45). The latter appear due to a focus on the lack of minority representation in European politics, for example:

> It argues for the importance of research on this topic, noting the large, established populations of immigrant-origin citizens and their descendants across Western European countries and these minorities' underrepresentation in elected bodies. Current research gaps concern both empirical knowledge and the theoretical conceptualisation of immigrant and ethnic <u>minority</u> **political** involvement.
>
> *Bloemraad and Schönwälder 2013*

With respect to the former concept of 'Government', aside from current concerns surrounding the rise of 'right-wing' influence in governance, a further trend emerges via an in-depth examination of concordance examples: that of the involved citizen, for example:

> Research projects examine the nature and conditions of Roma participation in social, economic, cultural life and in public affairs, encouraging active **citizenship.**
>
> *Tom Lantos Institute 2019*

This trend relates to encouraging the inclusion of minority groups in governance and politics in order to build a sense of 'nation' or 'community'. This links to observations made regarding the 'Politics' concept above.

Cultural context

The cultural context corpus contains 42 abstracts from recent polarisation and resilience papers and an additional 165 records from the BRaVE project database (24 institutions, 19 policies, 87 projects, and 35 studies), amounting to 26,228 words. Therefore, just over a quarter (25.97 per cent) of the 335 projects featured in the database have a cultural slant. This context also accounts for around 20 per cent of the institutions, policies, and academic literature featured (both in the database and the review).

Figure 4.3 presents the results of comparing this corpus with the BNC Informative Written Sampler corpus. Again, the theme of Education is prevalent (as suggested by the concept 'Education in general'), as is the theme of Identity (see 'Belonging to a group', which can also be observed in the key concepts of the historical and socio-economic corpora). Other themes that re-emerge include Understanding (for example, 'Knowledgeable' and 'Mental object: conceptual object', again referring to theories). The presence of this theme across corpora is perhaps not surprising, given the aim of researchers, governments, and practitioners alike in understanding the underlying causes of polarisation and the means of building resilience.

However, the cultural corpus reveals other themes that gain prominence in this context, including Society (e.g., 'Social Actions, States and Processes'), Youth (e.g., 'Time: New and Young'), Assistance (e.g., 'Helping' and 'Hindering'), Art (e.g., 'Arts and crafts'), and a particular focus on difference within the theme of Comparison (e.g., 'Comparing: Different'). The key concept of 'People', like 'Belonging to a group', points to frequent discussions of particular groups of individuals within the literature. A view of the collocates associated with this concept tells us who is generally referred to in the current literature. Groups of

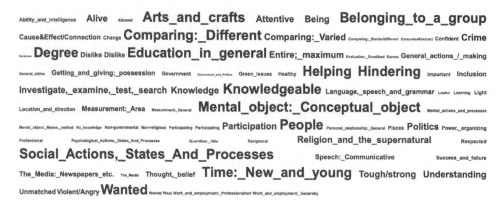

Figure 4.3 Showing a comparison of cultural abstracts and objectives with the BNC Informative Writing Sampler

people include 'kurds' (MI = 7.97), 'immigrant' (MI = 7.58), 'muslim' (MI = 7.19), 'young' (MI = 6.63), and 'migrants' (MI = 6.88).

There is therefore a current focus on specific minority ethnic and religious groups, those migrating to Europe, and the youth (the latter also being reflected in the key concept 'Time: New and Young', whose concordances reflect a continued referral to the 'young' or 'youth'). Collocates of the 'Time: New and Young' concept link with the themes of Assistance (e.g. 'help', MI = 6.78) and Education (e.g. 'education', MI = 4.80), with concordances highlighting the importance of retaining one's cultural identity – for example, 'to raise awareness of the value of maintaining the worlds languages and cultures by promoting and resourcing mother tongue-based education for **young** children' (Ball 2010) – and of offering cultural education to young people so that they may learn about other cultures, for example:

> One of the main objectives of the federal association of cultural education for children and **young** people is to represent the different arts, cultural sectors and fields of cultural education. Its goal is the further development and promotion of cultural education. Cultural education should be socially sensitive, sustainable, accessible to as many people as possible, from the outset and throughout one's life (BKJ 2019, as summarised in the BRaVE Database, BRaVE 2019).

Youth is seen as a critical stage at which to engage people in learning about their own cultures and those of others. Culture and the arts are regarded as an ideal vehicle for fostering inclusion, both within peer groups and between disadvantaged young people and their wider societies:

> The institution aims to reach out to those adolescents which seem most resistant to any of the traditional pedagogical practices and are at risk of turning away from the school system and from civilized society with a focus on cultural and emotional intelligence. The goal is to initiate processes that promote young people's opportunities for long-term social and professional participation, regardless of their origin. The institution wants to increase democratic participation with the youth cultural **art** of 'do-it-yourself' (Cultures Interactive 2019, as summarised in the BRaVE Database, BRaVE 2019).

In such a way, arts and culture are viewed both as a means to develop individuals who have an awareness and understanding of others, whilst also assisting individuals in fulfilling their potential, thereby linking to socio-economic contexts. Within the literature, society is seen to play a crucial role in creating a sense of inclusion and in the prevention of polarising behaviours such as racism, right-wing extremism, and radicalisation (for example, 'the prevention of Racism and intervention in racist incidents'), as evidenced by collocates of the 'Social Actions, States and Processes' concept that include 'intercultural' (MI = 9.15), 'opportunities' (MI = 6.18), 'prevention' (MI = 5.25), and 'intergroup' (MI = 5.13).

However, accommodating a mix of cultures is not viewed as being without its difficulties, as concordances from the 'Comparing: Different' concept suggest, for example:

> While attending to the (re) production of social **difference** and the problematic accounts of anxiety, hierarchy and belonging that fracture the school community, the paper also examines the shared parental commitments and aspirations that underpin the motivations for intercultural dialogue and learning.
>
> *Wilson 2014*

In such examples, tensions are observed between the cultural practices of, for instance, schools and the cultural practices of young people and their families (N.B. this example is taken from a study conducted in the UK). However, as will be discussed in more detail in the next section on communication-based contexts, dialogue is seen as a popular means by which to address such tensions and build more resilient communities, whether these be within an educational setting or elsewhere.

Communication-based context

The communication-based corpus consists of 32 abstracts from the review of relevant literature and a further 55 records from the BRaVE project database (9 institutions, 10 policies, 33 projects, and 3 studies). This amounts to a corpus of 10,485 words. What is notable is the smaller size of this corpus compared to those compiled for other contexts, which may be due to communication-based polarisation and resilience being a somewhat more recent focus of research and practitioner and policy interest. The results of comparing the communication-based corpus with the BNC Informative Written Sampler are provided in Figure 4.4.

One can again observe the prevalence of the themes of Understanding (as instantiated in the key concepts of 'Knowledge' and 'Investigate, examine, test, search'), and Identity

Figure 4.4 Showing a comparison of communication-based abstracts and objectives with the BNC Informative Writing Sampler

(e.g., 'Belonging to a group') observed in the previously discussed contexts. Perhaps understandably, given that the corpus deals with communication, one can observe concepts relating to language use (such as 'Speech: communicative' and 'Language, speech and grammar'). However, other key concepts point to the specific mediums of communication that trend in current literature, including 'Information technology and computing', 'The Media: Newspapers', and the 'The Media' at large. Other foregrounded themes are those of Assistance (see the concept 'Hindering') and the domain of 'Politics'.

The Wmatrix interface provides a summary of corpus content, including words that generally appear in a negative context, words typically appearing in a positive context, common verbs, negative emotion words, and typical roles. These words alone provide some interesting insights into the communication-based context data. Words typically used in a negative context include 'minority', 'new', 'hate', 'young', and 'other'. These words suggest groups of people involved in discussions of communication-based polarisation, including minorities and young people, a focus on hate-based communication, and the 'othering' that is typically a result of such communication (Lumsden and Harmer 2019). Words used in a positive context include 'public', 'groups', 'is', 'are', and 'can', perhaps indicating what the public or particular groups can do or are doing to build resilience towards communication-based forms of polarisation.

Common verbs include 'fact-checking', 'training', 'building', 'understanding', and 'providing'. Use of the word fact-checking may refer to the current phenomenon of 'fake news' and the communication and spread of conspiracy theories. Other verbs point to potential means of building resilience, such as the use of training and facilitating understanding. Negative emotion words – which include 'hate', 'violent', 'hatred', 'violence', and 'concerns' – point to recent debates around the communication of hate and violence, particularly in online contexts. Actors in this context include 'newspapers', 'users', and 'members'. Indeed, collocates of 'The Media' concept include 'role' (MI = 5.36), pointing to the responsibility of media outlets in tackling polarisation and building resilience towards it. The words 'digital' (MI = 5.13) and 'social' (MI = 3.00) indicate that online media in particular are the focus of current research and policy on polarising communication. These appear, in part, due to the relatively recent advent of digital communication platforms such as social media and desires to address the polarising phenomena that such platforms have introduced into societies, such as online trolling and abuse.

However, there is a second way in which the media are referenced in communication-based discussions of polarisation, and that is the need for media organisations and institutions to address the needs of ethnic minorities in their communications. Further collocates of 'The Media' concept include 'ethnic' (MI = 5.25) and 'minority' (MI = 4.85); concordance examples include statements such as the following: 'The key question addressed in this article is whether the media landscape in its new form can maintain its institutional capacity to embrace and serve minority languages, and under what conditions'. Therefore, the media are also seen as playing a role in societal exclusion.

Collocates of the key concept 'Politics' reveal a focus on right-wing extremism and radicalisation, and include 'right-wing' (MI = 5.42), 'free' (MI = 5.42), 'violent' (MI = 4.85), 'protect' (MI = 4.74), 'extreme' (MI = 4.57), 'extremist' (MI = 3.93), and 'radicalisation' (MI = 3.68). Concordance examples highlight the tensions that exist between addressing communication-based polarisation and protecting the rights to freedoms of speech, a factor played on by right-wing advocates, for example:

> On a recent visit to Norway, the legal philosopher Professor Ronald Dworkin, a known prominent advocate of what I will refer here to as '<u>free</u> speech **absolutism**'

or the idea that there should – on the basis of an attempt to universalise US First Amendment understandings which Dworkin can be associated with – be minimal legal regulations of freedom of expression.

Bangstad 2012

Concordances of the key concept 'Hindering' reveal that the most used term in this category is 'prevention' and its derivatives, pointing to efforts to build resilience against communication-based polarisation. These resilience building measures include online disruption (e.g., 'The aim is to undermine the appeal of the extremist propaganda, while also providing credible and positive alternatives to the related narratives', Cicero 2021); holding public figures (including politicians) accountable for the spread of misinformation (e.g., 'fact-checking can help to both dispel misinformation and inhibit political lying', Graves and Cherubini 2016); challenging the support networks of polarising communication (including financial supports, marketing and host platforms); and educating people to recognise and challenge polarising communication (e.g., 'The aim of the project is to impart competences to recognise xenophobic conspiracy theories, right-wing populist statements and other forms of group-related misanthropy, to oppose them argumentatively and to actively oppose the dissemination and establishment of hate culture on the Internet', Federal Education Centre of the Socialist Youth of Germany 2019, as summarised in BRaVE 2019).

So far, we have explored the themes present in literature and BRaVE (2019) database entries relating to various contexts of polarisation and resilience. Broadly, these analyses have revealed that popular themes across multiple contexts include those of Education, Understanding, Identity, and Comparison (particularly of group differences), with cultural contexts further emphasising Society, Youth, and Assistance, communication-based contexts highlighting the role of Technology, Media, and Politics, and historic contexts alluding to Negative attitudes and behaviours, Attention (the need to change areas of focus), and the State.

However, whilst this provides a holistic overview of current trends in research, practice, and policy, it is important to understand how these trends in concept use have shifted over time and why. Research in this area evolves quickly in response to societal changes and events. In order to gain the most up-to-date insights and explore how modern trends might be influenced by those of the past, it is to a discussion of such shifts that the chapter now turns.

Exploring conceptualisations over time

This section will explore how conceptualisations of polarisation and resilience have changed over time within three different sectors: academia, the practitioner sector (such as NGOs, charities, and grassroots initiatives), and the government sector. To do this, 100 records (98 in the case of policies, as this was the maximum available) from the BRaVE database were selected at random from the following categories: policies (representing European government perspectives), projects (representing practitioner perspectives), and studies (representing academic perspectives). The abstracts or objectives associated with the randomly selected records were placed in date order. Sets of abstracts or objectives were then combined into separate text files according to their year of publication (2019, 2018, 2017, 2016, 2015, and pre-2015) to create six diachronic corpora.

As described earlier, each corpus was run through the Wmatrix interface for part-of-speech and semantic processing. Within this interface, one is able to obtain a frequency list of concepts, listing each concept with both its raw and relative frequency of occurrence in each diachronic corpus. The relative frequencies of the top ten most frequently occurring concepts at each time period in academic literature, government policy summaries, and practitioner project summaries were recorded. Relative frequencies were used rather than raw frequencies due to differing corpus sizes. Where a concept did not occur in the top ten concepts for a given year but did occur in the top ten concepts of another year or years, its relative frequency in that given year was obtained for comparison purposes. The respective relative frequencies of concepts at each time point in data representing a random sample of perspectives from academia, governments and practitioners were plotted and are presented in Figures 4.5, 4.6, and 4.7, a discussion of which follows.

Academia

Figure 4.5 presents the results of tracing the relative frequencies of concepts over time in a randomly selected sample of 100 academic article abstracts from the BRaVE project database. Particular concepts have seen general increases in their relative frequency in recent years, including 'Politics' and to a more minimal degree, 'Movement'. As discussed in the thematic analysis, the former concept is most typically associated with right-wing extremism and radicalisation. The time-based analysis shows that these phenomena have received a surge in academic interest in the years 2018 and 2019. 'Movement' may have seen modest increases due to research into migration. Indeed, concordances of the concept reveal a focus on terms such as 'immigration', 'migration', and their variants, for example:

> Largely focusing on Belgium and Sweden, this collection of interdisciplinary research essays attempts to unravel the determinants of peoples preferences regarding **migration** policy, expectations towards **newcomers**, and economic, humanitarian and cultural concerns about **immigration**'s effect on the majority population's life.
>
> *d'Haenens, Joris and Heinderyckx 2019*

Such examples mark an increasing desire within resilience-focused programmes to understand why and how immigration has a polarising effect on European societies. The concept of 'Belonging', which was relatively prevalent in pre-2014 literature, declined in usage up to and including the year of 2017. However, the concept then saw a resurgence in discussion in the year 2018 and, to some extent, 2019. This concept was shown to be key across all contexts of polarisation and resilience, and its resurgent use suggests a renewed perception of the importance of identity to academic understandings of polarisation and the building of resilience.

The concept of 'Religion' whilst comparatively common in 2016 has seen a decline in the years since. This is particularly noticeable in the most recent year for which the database holds records: 2019. Concordance examples of this concept between 2016 and 2019 reveal that this concept is almost exclusively used in relation to the religion of Islam and its Muslim followers. Its decreased usage in academic literature may reflect an increased sensitivity towards the effects that linking a particular religion to polarisation can have on communities. The concept of comparing differences (i.e., 'Comparing: Different') was observed as being typical across multiple contexts of polarisation and resilience discussed earlier. However, an analysis over time reveals that whilst this concept features in academic literature, its use was most popular around the years of 2016 and 2017, and it has seen a drop-off in more recent literature. One potential reason for this observation is the

European trends in polarisation and resilience

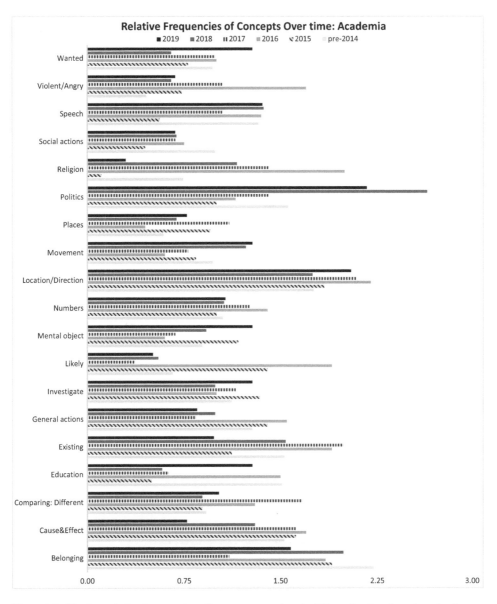

Figure 4.5 Tracing relative frequencies of concepts over time in 100 randomly selected academic article abstracts

desire to move away from an emphasis on differences, which is counter-intuitive to reducing polarisation.

Practitioners

Figure 4.6 presents the results of tracing concepts over time in a random sample of 100 practitioner project summaries. The results show that specific concepts appear more prevalent in practitioner project summaries than in academic literature. These include 'Time: New/

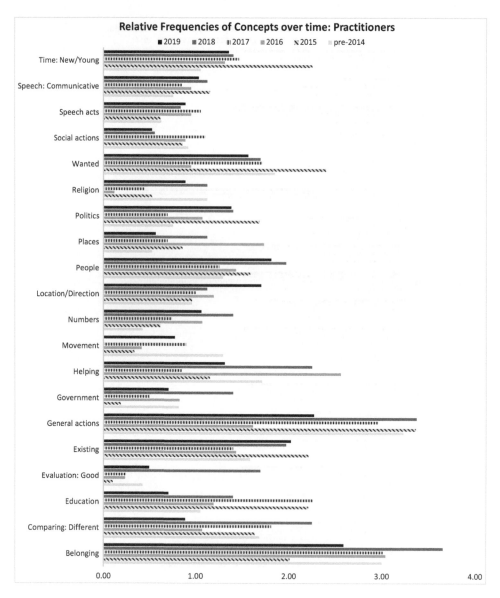

Figure 4.6 Tracing relative frequencies of concepts over time in 100 randomly selected practitioner project objective summaries

'Young', which as described above typically refers to the youth or young people, showing that projects in particular are generally focused on this age group.

Relatedly, the concept 'People' is more commonly referred to in practitioner literature than in academic literature, which is likely due to the more people-centred approach adopted in this context. Indeed, this concept remains relatively stable over time, with a slight increase in recent years. Concordances typically refer to 'young people' or the 'individual', re-affirming a trend to focus on the younger generation in this context, in addition to the importance placed on the personal approach. This concept links to the concept of 'Belonging' in its discussions of identity, for example:

Topics covered include **identity**, love, resilience, positive thinking and seeking help. These themes are dealt with by, among other things, role plays, knowledge transfer, a photo game, a scaffolding game and **group** discussions (My Identity project, NL, summarised by BRaVE 2019).

In a similar way to academic literature, 'Belonging' is a well-used concept over time in practitioner literature – indeed, slightly more so than in an academic context. Examples such as the one given above highlight practitioners' focus on bringing people (particularly, young people) together and providing them with opportunities to bond with others, whilst also supporting the health and well-being of young people. Hence, the concept of 'Helping', which is not observed so readily in an academic context where the focus is more theoretical. Forms of help include 'counselling', 'mediation', and 'services'. The practical nature of practitioner projects may explain its more prevalent usage of the 'General actions' concept when compared to academic literature.

Another concept held in common across the practitioner and academic time-based analyses is 'Education'. Whilst this concept's appearance has been somewhat variable over time in an academic context, with a recent rebound in its popularity in 2019, 'Education' shows a decline in the practitioner context from 2017 to 2019. This is not the only commonly held concept across practitioner and academic contexts that demonstrates a differing trend over time. The concept of 'Politics', for example, does not demonstrate the 2018/2019 surge seen in an academic context. The concept of 'Religion', while typically more often referred to in the academic context has, as described above, demonstrated a fall in use since 2016. However, in a practitioner context, the concept has regained some ground. This appears to be in response to the effects of religious polarisation, which have garnered practitioner efforts to tackle antisemitism and Islamophobia, given an examination of concordance examples of the concept in practitioner project summaries. However, a focus on preventing young Muslims in particular from being drawn into extremism is also retained.

Governments

Figure 4.7 presents the results of tracing concepts over time in a random sample of 100 government policy objective summaries. Particular concepts emerge in the government context that are not so observable in academic or practitioner contexts, for example, 'IT/Computing', whose presence was discussed in the section on communication-based context. Rates of usage of the concept of 'Belonging' in 2019 are considerably lower than rates of usage of this concept in 2015. While current relative frequencies of this concept (r.f. = 1.13 in 2019) are not drastically dissimilar to rates in academic literature (r.f. = 1.58 in 2019), they do demonstrate a more notable difference from the frequency of this concept in current practitioner project summaries (r.f = 2.59 in 2019 and r.f. = 3.65 in 2018). Unlike academic contexts, in which rates of this concept fell and then rose again in 2018/2019 and practitioner contexts which retain relatively high levels of usage of 'Belonging', rates in Government contexts have generally fallen from 2015 to 2019.

The recent surge in reference to the concept 'Numbers', on consultation with concordance examples, appears to be due to pledges of monetary funds to address socio-economic polarisation in particular. This concept also appears due to references to the numbers of articles, numbers, and decrees. Indeed, one notable difference between the most common concepts in government policy objective summaries and the project summaries of practitioners or academic article abstracts is the presence of the concepts 'Law and order' and 'Crime'. The latter

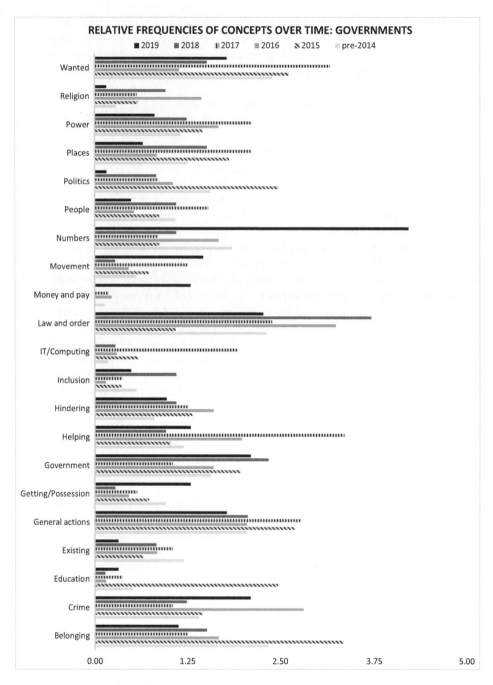

Figure 4.7 Tracing relative frequencies of concepts over time in 100 randomly selected government policy objective summaries

shows two rises, one between 2014 and 2016, before a fall and second rise between 2017 and 2019. The majority of the concordance examples in 2016 and 2019 refer to 'terrorism' or 'terrorist' activity. The concept of 'Law and order' typically maintains relative frequencies of 2.5 or more, with the highest levels recorded in 2018. Concordances in 2018 typically outline laws relating to three matters: counterterrorism, Muslim communities (i.e., restrictions on traditional Islamic dress and 'Islamic religious courts'), and xenophobia; concordances of the peak in 2016 reveal a focus on prisons, policing, and probation.

While the 'Education' concept appears in Figure 4.7, with the exception of the year 2015, rates of the concept are typically half that of practitioner usage. The peak in usage in 2015 can be explained via concordance examples, which suggest this is due to a focus on policies targeting radicalisation in schools and the offering of training and resources to teachers relating to this issue. Interestingly, given that policy documents are being considered here, the concept 'Politics' has demonstrated a general fall in usage over time from its 2015 levels. Concordances of this concept at its peak in 2015 typically refer to 'democracy', 'radicalism', and 'extremism'. The 2015 peak is not completely explained by the aforementioned discussions of the 'Education' concept, which demonstrates a peak in the same year.

Meanwhile, the concept of Power, which was not picked up amongst the top concepts in academic or practitioner contexts, demonstrates a rise to 2017, followed by a fall to 2019. Concordances of this concept in 2017 present discussions of 'control' and 'orders' (such as 'control orders', 'control structures', and 'court orders'), suggesting attempts to crack down on particular social issues. The decline in this concept may be explained by the introduction of 'softer' approaches to tackle these issues, for example, 'The combatting of jihadism through both law and order approaches as well as culturally-based approaches' (Italian Chamber of Deputies 2017, as summarised by BRaVE 2019).

Concluding remarks: future trends and impacts of framing and change

With respect to the framing of polarisation and resilience explored in the thematic analyses, the themes of Identity (in the form of 'Belonging to a group') and Understanding loom large across contexts, as does, to a certain extent, Education (with the exception of communication-based contexts, where this does not feature as prominently). The emphasis placed on grouping individuals is potentially problematic in that it could have the impact of enhancing group divides (see Tunçgenç and Cohen 2016). Given the observation in both socio-economic and cultural contexts that increasingly diverse and intercultural populations pose certain considerations in terms of addressing different forms of polarisation, it is conceivable that future research will seek to understand the precise nature of these challenges and whether a single unified nation approach is ultimately viable, or indeed, conducive to addressing such challenges.

The corpus of communication-based literature examined in this chapter is comparatively smaller than the corpora amassed for other contexts of polarisation and resilience. This suggests that communication-based literature is a less well-established area than, for example, historical or cultural explorations of polarisation and resilience (however, see Watkin, Gerrand and Conway 2022 for an exploration of the various facets involved in building societal resilience to polarising online communications). It is likely that this area will see considerable growth in the coming years as new forms of communication evolve.

Socio-economic research into polarisation and resilience is also a comparatively under-explored area (though see Zeller and Vidra 2021 for an exploration of such issues in the context of illiberal regimes). Current economic pressures left in the wake of the recent Covid-19 outbreak and the manner in which the pandemic has disproportionately affected certain sectors of European communities may well bring discussions of socio-economic forms of polarisation to the fore in the coming months and years (see, for example, McNeil-Wilson 2022 for a discussion of extremism in relation to the Covid-19 pandemic).

The thematic analysis revealed particular preferences, with practitioner projects and government policies showing a leaning towards addressing the cultural contexts of polarisation, while academic literature favours research on a historical perspective. Such leanings could potentially overlook other relevant factors in polarisation and resilience-building that are worthy of research, practice, or policy attention.

This brings one to the time-based analyses. It is notable that academic, practitioner, and government contexts demonstrate some differing trends. Government contexts, for example, place an emphasis on 'Crime' and 'Law and order', which is not apparent amongst the most widely used concepts in academic and practitioner contexts. Likewise, 'Education' generally appears in the context of tackling crime when related to polarisation and resilience-building. This is not the case in academic and practitioner contexts, with academic contexts using this concept in relation to understanding and practitioner contexts using it in the sense of educating or training young people. In addition, the concept of 'Belonging' has typically demonstrated a decline in government contexts, whilst it has regained ground in academia and retained ground in a practitioner context. Foregrounding polarisation as an issue of crime and law and order has potentially polarising consequences itself, in that it speaks to 'curing' polarisation rather than addressing the contextual factors leading to it.

With regard to the practitioner context, a focus on supporting youth or young people in particular may neglect the needs of older generations, who also currently experience the effects of polarisation, or indeed, are party to it. In academia, a comparative lack of 'General actions' and presence of 'Mental objects' when compared to practitioner and government contexts indicates that academia is focused on theory rather than action. Whilst to a degree this is understandable, academics could perhaps do more to highlight actionable outcomes to address polarisation and build resilience on the basis of their findings. Academic literature also demonstrates comparatively high levels of the 'Politics' concept in the years 2018 and 2019, a dominant pattern that is not observed in practitioner or government literature.

Taken together, these findings have a key implication, which is that different groups with an interest in tackling issues of polarisation and violent extremism and of building resilience within and across communities are, to some extent, speaking at cross purposes. This could have an impact on the effectiveness of tackling these societal issues, in that doing so requires a coordinated effort across academic, practitioner, and government contexts – a task that is made difficult when each group expresses differing priorities and at different times.

It is important to caveat the findings presented in this chapter. The observations presented here are based on abstracts or objective summaries, or both. As a consequence, the corpora used are rather small by corpus standards. It is possible that had full article and policy or project documents been used in the analysis that one might observe differing patterns. Nevertheless, the insights provided here give a useful snapshot of the current polarisation and resilience-building landscape by making use of a range of collated sources from various contexts.

Note

1 The BRaVE consortium was led by the European University Institute (EUI) and included the Central European University (CEU), Dublin City University (DCU), Cultures Interactive, A Jewish Contribution to an Inclusive Europe (CEJI), Lancaster University (LU), and ITTI. More information on the project can be found at www.brave-h2020.eu.

References

Armstrong, C., Flood, P.C., Guthrie, J.P., Liu, W., MacCurtain, S. and Mkamwa, T. (2010) The impact of diversity and equality management on firm performance: Beyond high performance work systems. *Human Resource Management*, 49(6), pp. 977–998.

Ball, J. (2010) *Enhancing learning of children from diverse language backgrounds: Mother tongue-based bilingual or multilingual education in early childhood and early primary school years*. Canada: University of Victoria.

Bangstad, S. (2012) Failing to Protect Minorities Against Racist and/or Discriminatory Speech. *Nordic Journal of Human Rights*, 30(4), pp. 484–514.

Banks, J.A. (2015) *Cultural diversity and education*. London: Routledge.

BKJ (2019) *Federal Association of Cultural Education for Children and Young People*, www.bkj.de/

Bleich, E. (2011) The rise of hate speech and hate crime laws in liberal democracies. *Journal of Ethnic and Migration Studies*, 37(6), pp. 917–934.

Bloemraad, I. and Schönwälder, K. (2013) Immigrant and ethnic minority representation in Europe: Conceptual challenges and theoretical approaches. *West European Politics*, 36(3), pp. 564–579.

BRaVE (2019) *Database*. http://brave-h2020.eu/database

Brimicombe, A.J. (2007) Ethnicity, religion, and residential segregation in London: evidence from a computational typology of minority communities. *Environment and Planning B: Planning and Design*, 34(5), pp. 884–904.

Church, K.W. and Hanks, P. (1990) Word association norms, mutual information, and lexicography. *Computational Linguistics*, 16(1), pp. 22–29.

Cicero (2021) *Counter-narrative communication campaign aimed at preventing radicalisation*, www.cicero-project.eu/

Clycq, N., Timmerman, C., Vanheule, D., Van Caudenberg, R. and Ravn, S., eds (2019) *Radicalisation: A marginal phenomenon or a mirror to society?* (Vol. 4). Leuven: Leuven University Press.

Cultures Interactive (2019) *Cultures Interactive: About*, www.cultures-interactive.de/de/

d'Haenens, L., Joris, W. and Heinderyckx, F. (2019) *Images of immigrants and refugees in Western Europe*. Leuven University Press.

Dobbin, F. and Kalev, A. (2016) Why diversity programs fail. *Harvard Business Review*, 94(7), 14.

Federal Education Center of the Socialist Youth of Germany (2019) *#dislike – Counterpoints against hatred in the net*, www.kurt-loewenstein.de/de/bildungsbereiche/projekt-dislike

Goodey, J. (2009) Immigrants as crime victims in the European Union: With special attention to hate crime. In: McDonald, W.F. (ed.), *Immigration, crime and justice*. Bingley: Emerald Group Publishing Limited, pp. 147–161.

Graves, L. and Cherubini, F. (2016) *The rise of fact-checking sites in Europe*. Reuters Institute for the Study of Journalism. Oxford: University of Oxford.

Italian Chamber of Deputies (2017) *Anti-Radicalisation Strategy: Law 3558*, www.camera.it/leg17/126?idDocumento=3558

Kennedy, G. (2014) *An introduction to corpus linguistics*. London: Routledge.

Licra (2019) *AI Campaign*. Available at https://adage.com/creativity/work/licra-post-racism/2171971

Lumsden, K. and Harmer, E., eds (2019) *Online othering: Exploring digital violence and discrimination on the web*. Cham: Springer.

McGinnity, F., Quinn, E., O'Connell, P. and Donnelly, N. (2010) *Annual monitoring report on integration 2010*. Dublin: Economic and Social Research Institute and The Integration Centre.

McNeil-Willson, R. (2022) Understanding the #plandemic: Core framings on Twitter and what this tells us about countering online far right COVID-19 conspiracies. *First Monday*, 27(5), 2 May 2022.

Rayson, P. (2008) From key words to key semantic domains. *International Journal of Corpus Linguistics*, 13(4), pp. 519–549.

Rayson, P. (2021) *Wmatrix*, http://ucrel.lancs.ac.uk/wmatrix/

Rayson, P. Archer, D., Piao, S. and McEnery, T. (2004) The UCREL Semantic Analysis System. In: Guthrie, L., Basili, R., Hajicova, E. and Jelinek, F. (eds), *Proceedings of the Workshop on Beyond Named Entity Recognition Semantic Labelling for NLP Tasks in Association with 4th International Conference on Language Resources and Evaluation, LREC 2004, Lisbon, Portugal, May 25, 2004*. Lisbon: LREC, pp. 7–12.

Tom Lantos Institute. (2019) *Roma Rights and Citizenship Programme*, https://tomlantosinstitute.hu/en/romak-emberi-es-allampolgari-jogai/

Tunçgenç, B. and Cohen, E. (2016) Movement synchrony forges social bonds across group divides. *Frontiers in Psychology*, 7, 27 May 2016.

Watkin, A-L., Gerrand, V. and Conway, M. (2022) Exploring societal resilience to online polarization and extremism. *First Monday*, 27(5), 2 May 2022.

Wilson, H.F. (2014) Multicultural learning: Parent encounters with difference in a Birmingham primary school. *Transactions of the Institute of British Geographers*, 39(1), pp. 102–114.

Wood, M., Hales, J., Purdon, S., Sejersen, T. and Hayllar, O. (2009) A test for racial discrimination in recruitment practice in British cities. *Department for Work and Pensions Research Report*, 607, pp. 1–69.

Zeller, M. and Vidra, Z. (2021) Resilience and resistance in illiberal regimes. *East European Journal of Society and Politics*, 7(4), 1–179.

5
YOUNG PEOPLE, RADICALISATION, AND RESILIENCE

Vivian Gerrand

Introduction

Over the past few years, the demographic of people becoming involved in violent extremist activities has grown younger (Heath 2022; Lowe 2021). It is now more common than previously for adolescents as young as the early teen years to gravitate towards groups that lead them to support or mobilise to action through violent extremist movements and activities. The proportion of minors joining violent extremist groups now encompasses approximately 15 per cent of all cases (Nicholson 2022). Young people today are faced with important challenges such as precarious employment as well as economic and geopolitical instability combined with climate, health, and information crises. These challenges put the resilience of emerging generations to the test (Cahill and Leccardi 2020). Such conditions demand radical, pro-social responses and resources to ensure human survival (Demos 2021). In the absence of such responses and resources, these conditions may also increase the likelihood of violent radicalisation.

Studies of why young people become involved in violent extremist organisations reveal that they most often join to be part of something, that is, for social rather than ideological reasons (Barelle 2014; Cottee 2011; Kruglanski, Bélanger and Gunaratna 2019). Most young people who are recruited by terrorist organisations are led to believe they are mobilising for a just cause. And yet, for most, violent extremism holds little appeal. Instead, faced with the realities of the climate crisis, a collective of young people in the West have formulated a resilient response through taking radical actions that involve civic disruption to draw global attention to the urgent need to stop emitting carbons (Catanzaro and Collin 2021; Collin and Matthews 2021). Their actions have attracted both negative and positive attention from authorities. It is critical to distinguish between those radical action orientations that are pro-social and anti-social. In recent years, some governments have failed to do this. The ways in which extremism has been framed within some Western contexts, for example, has led otherwise pro-social radical action to be cast as 'extremism', as in the case of a UK policing bill that criminalised civil disobedience acts such as the non-violent Black Lives Matter protests and climate activism (Alberro 2021).

Within policy contexts that seek to 'counter' (violent) extremism and terrorism – and have, since the 9/11 terrorist attacks on the World Trade Centre emphasised hard counter-terror measures invoked in the War on Terror, followed by softer preventing and countering violent extremism (P/CVE) de-radicalisation initiatives and controversial counter-narrative campaigns targeting Muslim-background minorities in the West (Jackson 2015) – little attention has been paid to the potential of alternative, radical narratives that may support disengagement from maladaptive radicalisation.

The growing threat of a variety of forms of violent radicalisation, and especially those presented by the diverse affiliations and networks of the global far-right, means that attempts to 'counter' terrorism through targeting cultural and religious minority communities are now challenged by their inability to identify specific cohorts with which to work (Grossman this volume; Thomas and Grossman 2022). The mainstreaming of far-right politics that emerged most notably during the Trump presidency in the US has further complicated the prevention landscape (Brown, Mondona and Winter 2021).

Thinking with multisystemic understandings of resilience, this chapter considers the relationship between young people, radicalisation, and resilience to violent extremism. To begin to address this complex, fast-moving landscape of terrorism, it explores different kinds of radicalisation that highlight radical action as a resilient strategy, albeit not always a prosocial one. It then differentiates between violent and non-violent radicalisation to draw attention to the kinds of resources that can support non-violent, pro-social radical action and community resilience that is alive to where young people are at. It argues for the potential of pro-social radicalisation to be regarded as a form of resilience in the prevention landscape. Conceptualising pro-social resilience as a rejection of exclusivism, the chapter invites us to consider a selection of radical alternative narrative interventions that have emerged from outside the domain of P/CVE practices as valuable precisely for their independent grassroots positioning that responds to the reasons why people are embracing extremism. These responses both address the 'root causes', such as the legitimate grievances that may contribute to driving some towards terrorism, and provide alternative radical, pro-social pathways.

Young people and resilience

Resilience is commonly thought of as the ability to 'bounce back' in situations of adversity. Too often, however, the burden of being resilient has fallen upon the shoulders of individuals or of specific communities (Thomas and Grossman 2022). Within atomised neoliberal societies, this limited view of resilience (Joseph 2013) has allowed governments to shirk responsibility through expectations of community members to be resilient in place of policy settings that would ease adversities. Alternatively, thinking about resilience as a socio-ecological phenomenon (Ungar 2013) unburdens particular individuals (Mukherjee and Kumar 2017) by emphasising resilience as a dynamic process (Hunter and Warren 2013) that can be enhanced or diminished by the allocation and negotiation of intersecting contextual factors and social resources (Sippel et al. 2015; Ungar 2008). Just as there is no single factor involved in trajectories of radicalisation to violent extremism, resilience is formed dynamically, and is a process comprised of multiple push and pull vectors at micro, meso, and macro levels that are context-bound (see Figure 5.2).

Recent studies that emphasise the intersectional (McNeil-Willson et al. 2019) and multisystemic (Ungar 2021) qualities of resilience provide an analytical framing that can help us address resilience deficits that are the consequence of crises such as the Covid-19 pandemic.

Crises threaten domains and resources needed for community resilience. For example, the pandemic has led to widespread job loss, uncertainty, and trauma. It has accentuated global instability and inequalities by producing a financial windfall for billionaires (Kaplan 2021), while government supports distributed in earlier stages of the pandemic have dwindled (Henwood 2021) even though Covid-19's impact on human lives and livelihoods has not. The adversities to which ever-greater numbers are exposed as they struggle with diminished supports continue to test the limits of societal resilience, leading to adaptations that are both pro- and anti-social.

Youth resilience to violent extremism

To understand what might make youth resilient to violent extremism (Grossman et al. 2017; Grossman et al. 2020) scholars of violent radicalisation have long emphasised the need to address the root causes of a minority of young people's involvement in violent extremism. Mobilisation to violence requires a complex interplay of push and pull factors (McCauley and Moskalenko 2008; Vergani et al. 2020), as is illustrated in Figure 5.2. So, too, does resilience to violence. When conceptualised within a socio-ecological framework, resilience is understood to be multisystemic (Grossman 2021; Ungar 2021) and intersectional (McNeil-Willson et al. 2019) rather than simply up to the individual. Resilience to violence is thus deeply contingent upon the extent to which societal structures can provide sufficient resources and opportunities to support the needs and build on the strengths of young people.

A key reason young people become involved in violent extremism is belonging through forms of social capital. Youth resilience against violence, similarly, requires social capital, but social capital alone is unlikely to suffice in supporting youth and community resilience to violent extremism. According to the Australian/Canadian comparative study that pioneered a BRaVE measure of youth resilience to violent extremism, youth are more resilient to violence when they have access to bonding, bridging, and linking social capital, **together with the adoption of non-violent behaviours and a view that violence is unacceptable:**

(1) *Cultural identity and connectedness:* Familiarity with one's own cultural heritage, practices, beliefs, traditions, values, and norms; knowledge of 'mainstream' cultural practices, beliefs, traditions, values, and norms if different from own cultural heritage; having a sense of cultural pride; feeling anchored in one's own cultural beliefs and practices; feeling that one's culture is accepted by the wider community; feeling able to share one's culture with others.;
(2) *Bridging capital:* Trust and confidence in people from other groups; support for and from people from other groups;
(3) *Linking capital:* Trust and confidence in government and authority figures, and in community organisations; the addressing of inequalities to support trust;
(4) *Violence-related behaviours*: Willingness to speak out publicly against violence; willingness to challenge the use of violence by others; acceptance of violence as a legitimate means of resolving conflicts (ethical code of conduct for social media platforms);
(5) *Violence-related beliefs*: Degree to which violence is seen to confer status and respect; degree to which violence is normalised or tolerated for any age group in the community (Grossman et al. 2017; Grossman et al. 2020).

This study was based upon earlier work that sought to understand the resilience of Somali communities to violent extremism undertaken by Grossman, Stephenson and Tahiri (2014) in Melbourne, Australia, by Weine and Ahmed (2012) in Minnesota, US, and by Joosse, Bucerius and Thompson (2015) in Canada. These studies pioneered a framework for researching violent extremism in relation to community resilience, focusing on Muslim minority communities. Weine and Ahmed (Weine 2017; Weine and Ahmed 2012) devised a model, Diminishing Opportunities for Violent Extremism (DOVE), to identify protective resources that can help mitigate the risk factors for involvement in violent extremism. These studies found that having a positive cultural image and identity, including family and community support networks, and access to traditional knowledge, or bonding capital, are key to being resistant to violent extremism.

At the same time, Grossman, Stephenson, and Tahiri (2014) found that bridging capital, 'the capacity to link and interact meaningfully between communities with different backgrounds, values, and belief systems' is just as vital. Flexible, as well as strong, cultural identities are critical, then, in enabling young Somalis to experience healthy cultural identity and belonging – factors that prevent polarisation and socialisation into violent extremism – in their Western contexts. Healthy cultural identities are therefore critical factors in building resilience to polarisation and extremism (ibid.).

To these resources, we might add a worldview that resists exclusivism, that refutes the privileging of *us* over *them* (Grossman et al. 2016). Together with a refusal of complexity, partitioning the world into black-and-white sustains polarisation. This polarisation has served the political aims of far-right and Islamist violent extremist groups who have taken advantage of misunderstandings of Islam perpetuated in dominant media, strategically deploying images that are designed to heighten antagonism towards Muslims to further marginalise Muslim minorities living in West for recruitment purposes (Wignell, Tan and O'Halloran 2017).

Challenging stereotypes through targeted complex image-making and interfaith education initiatives can serve to depolarise such paradigms by enabling interaction of different and culturally diverse members of the community. Should resources not be equitably distributed with adequate communication of their distribution, however, the encounter with such complex cultural identities may be used by nativist and extreme right reactionary positions that mobilise polarising scapegoat narratives such as the 'great replacement' theory and galvanise fear of losing privilege and status within identity structures that have conferred them power over others (Wodak and Rheindorf 2022).

The rise of the anti-egalitarian White supremacist far-right presents a challenge to complex, democratic forms of representation that are in themselves alternative narratives to dominant discursive racialisation. This trend has heightened within a media landscape dominated by vested interests. Arguably, addressing anti-democratic radicalisation when it is occurring at an institutional level is much more challenging than reaching prospective young terrorists. Violent extremist and conspiracy groups recruit people through different forms of social capital, especially bonding and linking capital. They meet people where they are at and become trusted sources of information in an environment in which trust has been eroded. So how might young people be acculturated into valuing democratic non-violence and thereby develop pro-social resilience to violent radicalisation? Violence is most likely to occur when there is a perceived threat or enemy that must be eradicated for one's survival. In the absence of enemies, one has opponents who may be defeated but not destroyed. In a democracy, good conflict between opponents (agonism) is preferred to violent conflict, or antagonism (Mouffe 2013). Violent extremist groups of all kinds rely on the creation of a friend/enemy binary to foster a sense of belonging to an in-group whose survival is contingent upon the annihilation of an out-group (Berger 2017). Where such a binary no longer exists and where there are sufficient resources so that friend/enemy scapegoat narratives mobilised by anti-democratic groups no longer resonate thus difference is not regarded as a threat to one's identity, violence becomes redundant.

The section below on young people and radicalisation explores ways how within a conducive environment – that is, one lacking in sufficient resources – young people are more vulnerable to messaging or unique selling points that offer them something they are missing. Some examples of anti-democratic radicalisation and extremist narratives include the historical example of Nazi Germany as well as the examples of Al-Qaeda, so-called Islamic State (IS), and Al-Shabaab, and those of far-right and incel movements. Each of these groups has succeeded in using social capital at a time of heightened vulnerability to capture young people's attention and radicalise them towards violent action orientation. The next section then turns to some examples of alternative radical narratives and networks that support prosocial resilience through an emphasis on social capital that supports complex cultural identity, empathy, equality of opportunity, and a commitment to non-violence.

Young people and radicalisation

This section provides an overview of the push and pull factors that may contribute to violent radicalisation. It is divided into understanding the conducive environment of vulnerabilities or 'push' factors and the unique selling points that 'pull' people towards violent extremist groups.

Figure 5.1 Meme reflecting intergenerational inequality and diminished prospects for the future

Understanding the conducive environment

A sense of relative deprivation is a key factor that may contribute to radicalisation trajectories. The allocation of societal resources is therefore crucial in determining vulnerability to extremist messaging. The Covid-19 pandemic in particular exposed resource deficits and inequalities that amplified real and perceived deprivation. It also demonstrated anew that violent extremism is a phenomenon with which anyone could become engaged.[1] On the one hand, the multi-scalar intersections of loss – of lives and livelihoods, of opportunities, of trust in institutions – have produced a grievance-rich, traumatised, and traumatising environment. On the other, increased time spent online within in an opaque Web 2.0 environment has led to an infodemic (WHO 2020) and a simultaneous erosion of a public sphere with consequent diminished opportunities for a shared narrative about what was occurring, evident in the proliferation of conspiracy theories at this time. Young people are growing up in this milieu of fragmented messaging (see Figure 5.1). While socio-economic deprivation can but does not necessarily contribute to violent radicalisation (Panayotov 2019), a sense of relative deprivation does (Hun Yu and Haque 2016).

Unique selling points: young people in digital environments and recruitment

This sense of deprivation can be amplified online through social media, which has replaced traditional media and other online media in providing a platform for violent extremist propagandists and aspiring violent extremist sympathisers to promote their ideology and inspire people towards violent action either at home or abroad (Gerrand and Grossman 2022). As the heaviest users of online social media yet with limited psychological maturity (Odaci and Çelik 2016), young people around the world are growing up more immersed than ever in volatile, image-saturated digital spaces. At the outset of the pandemic, youth with the highest degree of connectivity appeared to be the best prepared for the transition to life lived online as the most tech-savvy members of society (Brandtzaeg and Lüders 2021). And yet, while young people engage in online spaces with considerable technical competence, they are also highly vulnerable to manipulation by a range of perspectives, dynamics, and political agendas (Harsin 2015).

In the absence of shared narratives and algorithmic transparency, online environments are in multiple ways conducive to anti-social forms of extremism (Aly et al. 2016) and surveillance (Zuboff 2019). Extended time spent in closed groups with limited exposure to different perspectives, for example, may deepen polarisation (Gerrand 2020). Within such spaces, a minority of young people have become involved in maladaptive forms of resilience (Grossman 2021), such as adhering to far-right and conspiracy groups, radical misogyny, or through religiously inspired or attributed forms of radicalisation.

Radicalisation as resilience

Radicalisation is a contested term when considering young people's resilience to violent extremism (Coolsaet 2016; Neumann 2013; Sedgewick 2010). While the prevention of radicalisation and the term 'de-radicalisation' relate to preventing maladaptive forms of resilience and radicalism (Grossman 2021), their 'radical' etymology reminds us of their pro-social dimensions. Recent studies in fact have theorised *radicalisation as a form of resilience* (Walker 2022; Grossman this volume; 2021). Accordingly, young persons' impulses and

Mapping Violent Radicalisation

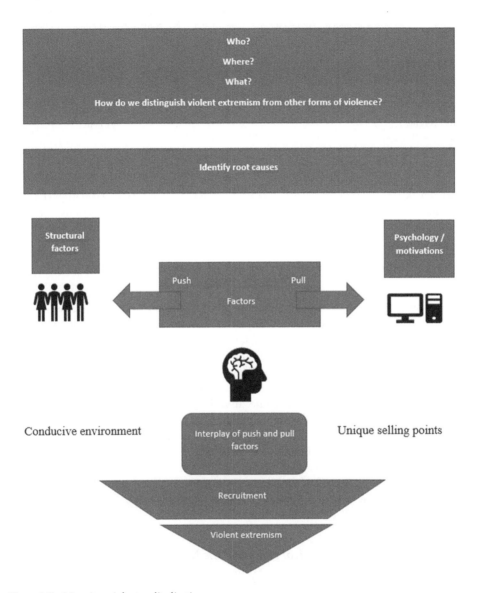

Figure 5.2 Mapping violent radicalisation

desires for radical action may be necessary responses to the urgent interlocking crises of our time (Walker 2022; Gerrand 2022).[2] When young people radicalise, they do so to access social capital resources otherwise unavailable to them. Table 5.1 outlines non-exhaustive examples of both exclusivist and pro-social radical movements.

Social capital is therefore critical to youth resilience but, as discussed in the previous section, it is no guarantee that such resilience will be pro-social. As is clear in Figure 5.2, the process of radicalising to violent extremism is complex and influenced by a range of

Table 5.1 Exclusivist and prosocial radical movements

Radical social movement	Bonding social capital	Bridging social capital	Linking social capital	Violent beliefs upheld	Action-orientation	Democratic intent
AQ, AS, IS	x		x	x	Violent	
Black Lives Matter	x	x	x		Non-violent	x
Climate activism	x	x	x		Non-violent	x
Incel movement	x		x	x	Violent	
Feminism	x	x	x		Non-violent	x
Radical Right/ Nazi	x		x	x	Violent	

factors. The key behavioural and social networks, ideology, and action orientation (Barrelle 2014) are supported by violent extremist propaganda that energises and exploits a sense of grievance and victimhood (RAN 2016).

Radical 'Islamist' movements: Al-Qaeda, Al-Shabaab, Islamic State

Negative stereotyping of Muslim minorities in non-Muslim majority countries produced a lack of belonging that led some young Muslims in the West to look towards alternative communities of belonging. In a minority of cases, such belonging was found in terrorist groups such as Al-Qaeda, Al-Shabaab, and IS (Gerrand 2015). So-called Islamic State, for example, offered a range of resources to lure young Western people to join its ranks: these included offers of adventure, belonging and purpose, status (Roose 2016), redressing injustice, but also material assets such as housing and a spouse. In different ways, these resources appealed to the Muslim minority targets of IS recruitment campaigns who were accustomed to increased suspicion that arose from counterterrorism measures such as the UK 'Prevent' strategy (Hickman et al. 2012; Jarvis and Lister 2013). They appeared to meet young Muslims experiencing discrimination and alienation in their societies with a ready-made community and dignity (Lakomy 2019; Nilan 2017) that were otherwise inaccessible. Joining so-called Islamic State, therefore, was for this minority cohort of youth, a resilient (though destructive and maladaptive) response to discrimination.

The radical right and the Nazi Party

This sense of victimhood and relative deprivation is shared by those on the radical right, though in this case it derives from fear of losing enjoyed status and privilege. The Christchurch killer believed he was acting in the interests of 'the White race', in accordance with White supremacist 'great replacement' ideology (Debney 2019). His fear of losing sovereignty and preparedness to engage in its violent defence motivated him to commit the Christchurch Massacre atrocity and continues to inspire radical right groups who share his worldview (Ali 2021). Historically, the rise of the Nazi Party in Germany was also premised on bonding and linking social capital, offering sense of belonging, purpose, and solidarity to its adherents (Koshar 1986; Satyanath, Voigtländer and Voth 2017). As Paul Mason (2021, pp. 153–154) writes, drawing on Koshar's study:

The Nazis grew most rapidly where there was a strong culture of civic associations: choirs, bands, gymnastic clubs, and organised hiking groups. Critical to each local breakthrough was the Nazis' ability to colonise the social networks of influential people. If a Nazi recruit was a member of the local gym...they would then recruit people in every one of these locations. The more clubs they were in, the more effective they were at recruiting.

Deciding on a common scapegoat, these groups reassured their anxious adherents through a reductive sense-making framework that relied on the elimination of perceived enemies. In Nazi Germany, Jews were blamed for the economic crisis and portrayed as unfairly profiting from it. Aspects of this recruitment strategy are being replicated today by radical right, conspiracy, and violent extremist groups through gyms and anti-vaccine wellness community influencers (Amarasingham and Argentino 2020). In similar vein, such actors provide simple points of reference for those bewildered by the multisystemic crises through which we are living, appearing to address their grievances while undermining public health responses (Dickson 2022).

Radical misogyny: the incel movement

Materials associated with the so-called manosphere, which comprises materials on social networking sites and subreddit forums, promote the narrative that men are victims of women's empowerment. Intersecting with far-right and neo-fascist views, these materials promoting traditionalist gender norms that eschew feminism are often imbued with misogyny (Roose, Flood and Alfano 2020). At the extreme end of the manosphere are incels, men who are unsuccessful at forming relationships with women and who advocate violence against women.

The involuntary celibate (incel) movement has offered succour to isolated, lonely, alienated young men who identify as NEETs – Not in Education, Employment, or Training (Lee Moyer 2020). Housebound and aimless, they have found a narrative and a network via forms of social capital that place them in a zero-sum game in which women's empowerment equals their disempowerment and in which they believe themselves to be genetically disadvantaged in their perceived unattractiveness to women. On the internet, such black-and-white beliefs are readily reinforced, funnelling them towards more extreme materials that encourage anti-social behaviour (Lennings et al. 2010) and violence against women (RAN 2021).

Within digital ecosystems, young people are also promoting non-violent radical perspectives through joining critical anti-racist, class, climate, and feminist movements, exerting social influence through their digital affiliations and identities (Abidin 2016; Leurs and Ponzanesi 2011; Papacharissi 2010). Adherence to such movements enables youths' empowerment while instilling sense of belonging and providing their own radical alternative narratives of inclusive change that support good conflict and democracy (Gerrand 2022). Whether a young person is drawn to an exclusivist or a pro-social group is determined by the resources – vulnerabilities and protective factors – in their lives (Grossman Stephenson and Tahiri 2014; Grossman et al. 2017; Grossman et al. 2020).

Within P/CVE literatures, relatively little focus has been given to the ways in which young people approach digital environments with agency and pro-social radical action orientation. And yet, to understand how to prevent contemporary forms of violent radicalisation, such attention is crucial. The next section highlights three examples that relate, respectively, to multi-faith belonging, anti-racism, and gender equality of how pro-social radical alternative narratives are being developed and disseminated online and offline.

Radical alternative narratives and pro-social resilience

Unlike counter-narratives which, at worst, may reinforce existing paradigms of discrimination and, at best, have limited efficacy (Rosand and Winterbotham 2019; Roy 2018), alternative narratives directly address root causes such as real and perceived grievances as well as the psycho-social needs that may lead to engagement with extremist discourse. They acknowledge the 'kernel of truth' in extremist narratives. They have credible messages and messengers that engage audience as active agents, redirecting rather than deradicalising, are context specific, stand *for* rather than *against* something, are grassroots rather than top-down, and empower (Roose, Gerrand and Akbarzadeh 2021). Online such narratives feature sophisticated multimodal content/representation practices – videos, memes, music, and posts to convey alternative messages to those deployed by extremist influences that meet people where they are at. For this reason, they work at the level of affect and imagination (Appadurai 1990). They may be created or co-created with the target audience, promote ambiguity and agonism (good conflict), inspire critical thinking, work online and offline, shift from 'us and them' to 'we'. Above all they move audiences from either/or black-and-white thinking to both/and appreciation for complexity (see Figures 5.4 and 5.5). Such resilience-building narratives that target 'fence-sitters' are not explicitly C/PVE and complement and contribute to structural change (Gerrand 2022; Roose, Gerrand and Akbarzadeh 2021).

From *either/or* to *both/and*

Rather than being sources of 'de-radicalisation', alternative narrative interventions address the root causes of violent extremist behaviour. Alternative narratives can strengthen resilience or resistance to violent extremism:

- in responding to situations of conflict, they enable good conflict, or **'agonism'** (struggle between adversaries) rather than **'antagonism'** (struggle between enemies) (Mouffe 2013);
- such interventions promote **complex cultural identity** as a source of strength and a resource for belonging and living well together (Gerrand 2022; Weine and Ahmed 2012);
- they rearrange cultural variables and taken-for-granted dualistic understandings of Self and Other, providing alternative and counter-hegemonic forms of identification (Gerrand 2016b; Mouffe 2013).

To a significant degree communities are established via narratives, and narratives can 'do' and 'undo' projects of conviviality, nationhood (Bhabha 1990), and contribute to public discourses about who belongs in a particular community.

Alternative narratives for multifaith belonging

With the understanding that every society is constituted in and through a people's distinctive forms of image-making, the imaging of Muslims as outsiders in Figure 5.3, echoed in much dominant Western media and political discourse, reinforces their experience

Young people, radicalisation, and resilience

Figure 5.3 Either/or antagonistic narratives of incompatibility. French officers police the Burkini ban in France
Source: Vantagenews.com

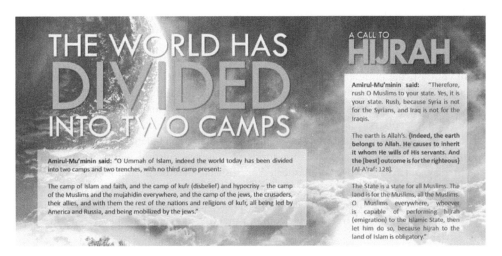

Figure 5.4 Either/or antagonistic narratives of incompatibility. IS propaganda promotes a similar polarising narrative
Source: *Dabiq* Magazine, Issue 1, pp. 10–11)

of disconnection from their homes in the West. The French burkini ban (pictured in Figure 5.3) and *Dabiq* magazine's characterisation of the world as being 'divided into two camps' (Figure 5.4) both uphold the zero-sum narrative that living in the West and practicing Islam are incompatible. Akin to the prohibition of other religious garments in

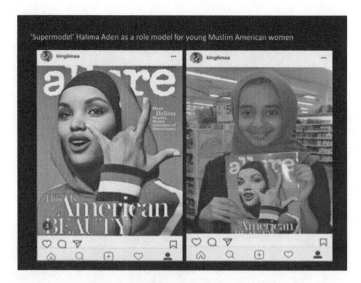

Figure 5.5 Both/and agonistic narratives of belonging. Somali American supermodel Halima Aden: A role model for young Muslim women in the West
Source: Instagram, 2017

France, the burkini ban was intended to enhance the liberties of French women under its policy of *laïcité* (Sealy and Modood 2021). In denying Muslim minority women the opportunity to wear an empowering, innovative garment and reducing their possibilities for belonging (Gerrand 2016a; Taylor 2016), the ban failed to promote liberty and instead served to deepen polarisation. The ensuing sense of antagonism and exclusion is likely to have only increased the vulnerability of some Muslims at the margins to the radicalising forces of violent extremist groups.

In contrast, the popular magazine cover image of American supermodel Halima Aden (Figure 5.5), who has Somali heritage and is a practising Muslim, upholds the alternative narrative that it is possible to be *both* American *and* Muslim, supporting complex cultural identity and depolarisation. Cultural migration studies of belonging have made a critical distinction between fixed notions of belonging and national identity that demand *either* assimilation *or* exclusion, and dynamic forms of complex cultural identity represented in the literary and artistic works of diasporic Somalis that view home and identity as *both* 'in-between understandings' *and* 'where one is' (Carroli and Gerrand 2012; Gerrand and Omar 2015). The effect of this representation of *both/and* belonging is to allow young Muslim American women to feel free and welcome to practise their faith as they see fit, fostering pro-social resilience.

The fact that the image is of a Somali-background American is significant. As a racialised Black and Muslim minority – and one that has survived war and displacement and created new forms of diasporic belonging in the West – Somalis have often been represented in terms of their vulnerability rather than their resilience. This community is thus a key site of exploration for how both vulnerabilities and resilience factors intertwine in complex ways at the levels of both everyday life and specific social challenges, including vulnerability to violent extremism in digital environments. Research, for example, on Somali minority belonging (Gerrand 2016b) and on the arts as cultural and identity resources for Somali youth in Australia (Gerrand and Omar 2015) found that representations of Somali minorities in their multiplicity or distinctiveness allow Somalis to build complex cultural identities based on a sense of potential and to take part in the societies in which they have resettled. If Somali alternative narrative practices can articulate and contribute to a sense of belonging (Gerrand 2016b), they may also arguably contribute to pro-social radicalisation and resilience through complex cultural identity and agonism (Gerrand 2022).

Alternative narratives can be very effectively disseminated online to meet young people where they are at. Social media platforms are sites of bonding and bridging capital on which disparately located people can build strong ties with like-minded others in real time (Williams 2019). They enable reinforcing connections that may support community and youth resilience. Building upon their positive attributes can support pro-social resilience (Gerrand 2022).

Radical alternative narratives for racial equality

Social networking sites gave global reach and visibility to the Black Lives Matter movement in 2020, for example, and contributed to the record turnout of early voters in the US (Olson 2020), a significant proportion of them from marginalised Black communities whose votes were deliberately suppressed in the 2016 election (Sabbagh 2020). Women of colour influencers such as rapper Cardi B and Michelle Obama promoted multimodal messages (Kress 2009) about a democratic future to their respective 77.4 and 44.2 million followers (Gerrand 2020). Pop artist Lizzo's (2020) images and videos of herself dressed in Americana,

Figure 5.6 Representative Ilhan Omar with her then 17-year-old daughter and activist, Isra Hirsi, on the cover of *Teen Vogue*, November 2020 Radical feminist alternative narratives for gender equality: addressing young men and the manosphere

singing 'It's time to vote', were popular on Instagram; the artist used the platform to mobilise her 9.3 million followers to 'take their protest to the ballot box', directing them towards how-to-vote instructions.

These efforts were replicated offline, with Lizzo appearing on the cover of the October issue of *American Vogue* dedicated to 'Hope, Justice and Election 2020' (Asmelash 2020). Somali-background Representative Ilhan Omar with her eldest daughter Isra (Figure 5.6) featured on the cover of the November issue of *Teen Vogue* (Farah 2020). Their photo was captioned: 'Our time is now'.

> I am choosing to participate, to organise, to vote, encourage people – especially young people – to vote, because I want us to be able to use our collective power to get people in office that we can hold accountable.
>
> Ilhan Omar, cited in Farah 2020

Omar is also Somali-American, and to see her empowered in processes of American governance with her daughter is a powerful alternative narrative of what is possible for Black and Muslim minority youth in the US. Akin to the earlier magazine cover of Halima Aden, this showcasing of complex cultural identities contests dominant stereotypes and promotes *both/and* democratic identities in which it is possible to be *both* Muslim *and* American, without contradiction (Gerrand 2016b).

Radical feminist alternative narratives for gender equality: addressing young men and the manosphere

Popular feminist influencer and comic artist Lily O'Farrell's cartoons about sexism began to engage with the nuances of the manosphere in 2021 after she decided to talk to some of the young men who had begun trolling her Instagram social media account. These men had become aware of her account after it was shared in a men's rights subreddit group. Concerned that the group was made up of young men predominantly aged 16–23, O'Farrell (2021b) decided to investigate the movement by joining incel (involuntary celibate) subreddit groups. Following these engagements, the artist produced a series of cartoons on her findings. O'Farrell's 'Everything I've learned about Incels' (2021a) comic is an example of an alternative narrative within this context. Produced after the feminist influencer spent time in incel forums learning about their grievances, the cartoon series illuminates the dynamics of the phenomenon for her largely feminist audience. Instead of demonising and shaming incels, her drawings provide an anatomy of the movement that allows viewers insight into its logics. O'Farrell reveals that at one end of the spectrum are pick-up artists; at the other, 'black-pilled' violently oriented incels who may share NEET, Doomer, and Alt-Right characteristics (Figure 5.7).

O'Farrell powerfully acknowledges the real and perceived grievances of young men in these groups, such as loneliness, body-image insecurities, and lack of mental health support and resources, which incels blamed on women (ibid.). The artist's cartoons expose the root causes of these grievances as being tied to the structures of patriarchy, helping young male viewers on the incel spectrum to see that women are not responsible for, but are instead also victims of, such structures.

The final slide within the series poses the question of what to do about the phenomenon, and advises her 266,000 followers to engage in empathy, to listen to and challenge the assumptions put forward by adherents of the movement. This empathetic analysis and call to

Figure 5.7 'Everything I've learned about Incels.' Vulgadrawings Instagram post, 2021

arms led to significant numbers of young men engaging with O'Farrell, with one young man sharing that he had left the movement and found a girlfriend after his DM (direct messaging) exchange with the artist.

O'Farrell's memes are an example of an alternative narrative intervention that supports good conflict and cultivates bonding, bridging, and linking social capital while encouraging a shift away from 'us and them' to 'we'. O'Farrell's intervention compellingly promotes the radical message that everyone is ultimately diminished by patriarchal power structures. In this sense, her cartoons have the capacity to depolarise and encourage a shift away from violence-based solutions to grievances towards pro-social radical and resilient action.

Concluding remarks

In thinking about resilience, radicalisation, and how these processes shape and are shaped by young people and the global community, it is necessary to consider the kinds of resources

Figure 5.8 'Everything I've learned about Incels.' Vulgadrawings Instagram post, 2021

young people have at their disposal. What kinds of social capital, for example, are available to them? While bonding and linking social capital may be common online in closed groups, bridging social capital – or interaction with others who think differently – may be harder to find. The examples of Muslim minority empowerment and feminist engagements with the manosphere are instances of bridging capital that enable forms of complex cultural identity and agonisms that open new empowering possibilities that do not rely on the creation of an out-group against which an in-group must defend itself.

Alternative narratives that support complex cultural identity and ambiguity contribute to an emerging, albeit contested, body of depolarising content. The process of reconnecting young people via alternative narratives that restore dignity through *both/and* complex imagery is an important symbolic and material step in activating agency that is in direct contrast to the kinds of agency offered by extremist groups that seek to polarise and fortify rigid black-and-white identities. Those engaged in producing such narratives provide crucial bridging capital between generations, cultures, and classes, political perspectives, and wider communities of people, adding to existing societal forms of bonding and linking social capital.

Whilst these creative, grassroots alternative narrative approaches can be highly effective at engaging with young people who are at risk of exposure to extremist content, the conducive environment of push factors including Covid-19 and the algorithmic design of social media platforms present formidable challenges for practitioners to amplify such alternative pro-social radical narratives. In the absence of offline follow-up, we should be cautious in assessing the capabilities of social networking sites to generate more material alternative narrative interventions that are critical to restore the trust and resources in communities experiencing real and perceived resource deficits.

Even so, within a polarised environment, alternative narrative interventions produced by young influencers of all backgrounds can enhance resilience, empathy, and pro-social forms of radical action that are built on an appreciation for complexity. As this chapter has illustrated, such radical alternative narratives can promote forms of radicalisation as resilience through providing sense of belonging and drawing attention towards global inequalities and injustices that may focus and unite youth in critical and pro-social sense of purpose. They thus support young people's capacity to address the injustices that may otherwise drive some to violence. This understanding can support pathways to pro-social radicalisation that are based on solidarity or good conflict with political opponents who may be challenged without being regarded as enemies to be destroyed. By building on the positive attributes of young people's radical action orientation, these interventions provide democratic, radical, and resilient alternatives to the appeal of violent extremist pathways.

Notes

1 A 'silver lining' to this predicament is that it has shifted the attention of authorities away from Muslim communities who were for two decades the primary focus of counter terror and CVE measures in the West (Abdel-Fattah 2021).
2 To encourage young people to appreciate the nuances of class, artist and independent researcher Joshua Citarella seeks to radicalise young people towards pro-social activism that includes a rejection of capitalism. Deploying techniques such as nudging (Walker 2022), Citarella has successfully created a Discord community through his Patreon subscriber account where he delivers critical content one might otherwise find attending a Humanities course at a university.

References

Abdel-Fattah, R. (2021) *Coming of Age in the War on Terror*. Sydney: New South.
Abidin, C. (2016) 'Aren't These Just Young, Rich Women Doing Vain Things Online?': Influencer Selfies as Subversive Frivolity. *Social Media + Society* 2(2), DOI:10.1177/2056305116641342
Alberro, H. (2021) The UK's policing bill will make climate activism illegal – just when it's most needed. *The Conversation*, 7 December.
Ali, K. (2021) 'Unsettling' the Christchurch Massacre Foregrounding Settler Colonialism in Studies of Islamophobia. *Journal of the Contemporary Study of Islam*, 2(2), pp. 87–111.
Aly, A. et al. (2016) *Violent Extremism Online: New Perspectives on Terrorism and the Internet*. Abingdon: Taylor and Francis.
Amarasingham, A. and Argentino, M. (2020) The QAnon Conspiracy Theory: A Security Threat in the Making? *Combating Terrorism Center Sentinel*, July, Vol. 13, p. 7.
Appadurai, A. (1990) Disjuncture and Difference in the Global Cultural Economy. *Theory, Culture, Society*, 7, pp. 295–310.
Asmelash, L. (2020) Lizzo is Vogue's October cover girl. *CNN Style*, 25 September.

Barrelle, K. (2014) Pro-integration: Disengagement from and Life after Extremism. *Behavioural Sciences of Terrorism and Political Aggression*, 7(2), pp. 129–142.

Berger, J.M. (2017) Extremist Construction of Identity: How Escalating Demands for Legitimacy Shape and Define In-Group and Out-Group Dynamics. *Terrorism and Counter-Terrorism Studies*, 8(7), DOI:10.19165/2017.1.07

Bhabha, H. (1990) *Nation and Narration*. London: Routledge.

Brandtzaeg, P.B. and Lüders, M. (2021) Young People's Use and Experience of the Internet during the COVID-10 Lockdown: Well-being and Social Support. *First Monday*, 26(12).

Brown, K., Mondona, A., and Winter, A. (2021) The Far Right, the Mainstream and Mainstreaming: Towards a Heuristic Framework. *Journal of Political Ideologies*, DOI:10.1080/13569317.2021.1949829

Cahill H. and Leccardi, C. (2020) Reframing Resilience. In: Wyn J., Cahill H., Woodman D., Cuervo H., Leccardi C., and Chesters J. (eds), *Youth and the New Adulthood. Perspectives on Children and Young People*, Vol 8. Singapore: Springer, pp. 67–81. DOI:10.1007/978-981-15-3365-5_5

Carroli, P. and Gerrand, V. (2012) *La mia casa è dove sono*: Subjects and Narratives beyond National Borders. *Scritture Migranti: Rivista di scambi interculturali*, 5, pp. 81–104.

Catanzaro, M. and Collin, P. (2021) Kids Communicating Climate Change: Learning from the Visual Language of the SchoolStrike4Climate Protests. *Educational Review*, DOI:10.1080/00131911.2021.1925875

Collin, P. and. Matthews, I. (2021) School Strike 4 climate: Australian Students Renegotiating Citizenship. In: Bessant, J. Mesinas, A.M., and Pickard, S. (eds), *When Students Protest: Secondary and High Schools*. Lanham, MD: Rowman & Littlefield, pp. 125–143.

Coolsaet, R. (2016) 'All Radicalisation is Local.' The Genesis and Drawbacks of an Elusive Concept. Egmont Paper 84, June.

Cottee, S. (2011) Jihadism as a Subcultural Response to Social Strain: Extending Marc Sageman's 'Bunch of Guys' thesis. *Terrorism and Political Violence,* 23(5), pp. 730–751.

Debney, B. (2019) Christchurch, the White Victim Complex and Savage Capitalism. *Counterpunch*, 15 March.

Demos, T.J. (2021) *Beyond the World's End: Arts of Living at the Crossing*. Durham: Duke University Press.

Dickson, E.J. (2022) 'A Menace to Public Health': Doctors Demand Spotify Puts an End to Covid Lies on 'Joe Rogan Experience'. *Rolling Stone*, 12 January.

Farah, S.H. (2020) Representative Ilhan Omar and Isra Hirsi on the Future of Politics and 2020. *Teen Vogue*, 27 October.

Gerrand, V. (2015) Zaky Mallah. A Cautionary Tale of Radicalisation and the Need for Belonging. *The Conversation*, 29 June.

Gerrand, V. (2016a) No Longer Afraid to Come Out of the Locker: Going Berko for Burkinis. *Overland*, 25 August.

Gerrand, V. (2016b) *Possible Spaces of Somali Belonging*. Carlton: Melbourne University Press, Islamic Studies Series.

Gerrand, V. (2020) Can Social Networking Platforms Prevent Violent Extremism and Polarisation? *Open Democracy*, 13 November.

Gerrand, V. (2022) Communicative Channels for Pro-social Resilience in an Age of Polarisation. *First Monday*. 27(5), 2 May, DOI:10.5210/fm.v27i5.12599.

Gerrand, V. and Grossman, M. (2022) Understanding the Experiences of Families of Radicalised Muslim Youth in Australia: Implications for Social Work Practice. In: Robinson, L. and Rafik Gardee, M. (eds), *Radicalisation, Extremism and Social Work Practice*. London: Routledge, pp. 92–111.

Gerrand, V. and Omar, Y. (2015) The Arts as Cultural and Identity Resources for Somali Youth in Australia: Nadia Faragaab's 'Kronologies'.' In: McConnell, C. (ed.), *Hopeful Places: Migration and belonging in an unpredictable era*. Brisbane: Connor Court Publishing, pp. 153–176.

Grossman, M. (2021) Resilience to Violent Extremism and Terrorism: A Multi-systemic Analysis. In: Ungar, M. (ed.), *Multisystemic Resilience: Adaptation and Transformation in Changing Contexts*. Oxford: Oxford University Press, pp. 293–317. Open Access, https://oxford.universitypressscholarship.com/view/10.1093/oso/9780190095888.001.0001/oso-9780190095888-chapter-17

Grossman, M., Hadfield, K., Jefferies, P., Gerrand, V., and Ungar, M. (2020) Youth resilience to violent extremism: Development and validation of the BRaVE measure. *Terrorism and Political Violence*, DOI:10.1080/09546553.2019.1705283

Grossman, M., Peucker, M., Smith, D., and Dellal, H. (2016) *Stocktake Research Report: A Systematic Literature and Selected Program Review on Social Cohesion, Community Resilience and Violent Extremism 2011–2015.* Melbourne: Dept. of Premier and Cabinet, Victoria State Government.

Grossman, M., Stephenson, P., and Tahiri, H. (2014) *Harnessing Resilience Capital: An Investigation of Resilience and Cultural Diversity in Countering Violent Extremism.* CTCU, Victoria Police.

Grossman, M., Ungar, M., Brisson, J. Gerrand, V., Hadfield, K., and Jefferies, P. (2017) *Understanding Youth Resilience to Violent Extremism: A Standardised Research Measure.* Research Report, published November.

Heath, N. (2022) Alt-right groups are targeting young video gamers – and finding a culture where extremist views can flourish. Australian Broadcasting Corporation, 15 July.

Henwood, B. (2021) Who has been hit hardest by the Covid-19 pandemic in Australia? University of New South Wales, Newsroom, 4 October.

Hickman, M.J., Thomas, L., Nickels, H., and Silvestri, S. (2012) Social Cohesion and the Notion of 'Suspect Communities': A Study of the Experiences and Impacts of Being 'Suspect' for Irish Communities and Muslim Communities in Britain. *Critical Studies on Terrorism*, 5(1), pp. 89–106.

Harsin, J. (2015) Regimes of Posttruth, Postpolitics and Attention Economies. *Communication, Culture and Critique*, 8(2), pp. 327–333.

Hun Yu, S. and Haque, O.S. (2016) Vulnerabilities among young Westerners joining ISIS. *Connections. The Brown University Child and Adolescent Behavior Letter*, 32(2), pp. 1–6.

Hunter, B. and Warren, L. (2013) *Final Report: Investigating Resilience in Midwifery.* Cardiff: Cardiff University

Jackson, R. (2015) The Epistemological Crisis of Counter-terrorism. *Critical Studies on Terrorism*, 8(1), pp. 33–54.

Jarvis, L. and Lister, M. (2013) Disconnected Citizenship? The Impacts of Anti-terrorism Policy on Citizenship in the UK. *Political Studies*, 61, pp. 656–675.

Joosse, P., Bucerius, S.M., and Thompson, S.K. (2015) Narratives and Counter-narratives: Somali-Canadians on Recruitment as Foreign Fighters to Al-Shabaab. *British Journal of Criminology*, 55, pp. 811–832.

Joseph, J. (2013) Resilience as Embedded Neoliberalism: A Governmentality Approach. *Resilience*, 1(1), pp. 38–52, DOI:10.1080/21693293.2013.765741

Kaplan, J. (2021) The Number of Billionaires Grew by 13.4% in 2020 – Making the Pandemic a 'Windfall to Billionaire Wealth'. *Business Insider Australia*, 20 September.

Koshar, R.J. (1986) *Social Life, Local Politics, and Nazism: Marburg, 1880–1935.* Chapel Hill and London: The University of North Carolina Press.

Kress, G. (2009) *Multimodality: A Social Semiotic Approach to Contemporary Communication.* London: Routledge.

Kruglanski, A., Bélanger, J., and Gunaratna, R. (2019) *The Three Pillars of Radicalisation: Needs, Narratives, and Networks.* New York: Oxford University Press.

Lakomy, M. (2019) Recruitment and Incitement to Violence in the Islamic State's Online Propaganda: Comparative Analysis of *Dabiq* and *Rumiyah*. *Studies in Conflict and Terrorism*, 44(7), pp. 565–580.

Lee Moyer, A. (2020) *That Feeling When no Girlfriend (TFW NO GF)* [documentary]. Los Angeles: Alex Lee Moyer

Lennings, C.J., Amon, K.L., Brummert, H., and Lennings, N.J. (2010) Grooming for Terror: The Internet and Young People. *Psychiatry, Psychology and Law*, 17(3), pp. 424–437.

Leurs, K. and Ponzanesi, S. (2011) Youthful Digital Diasporas. *Mediated Crossroads*, 14(2). DOI: 10.5204/mcj.324

Lizzo (2020) 'Auntie Sam out here doin what she gotta do to get y'all to vote!' [Instagram], www.instagram.com/p/CGStTlKBknh/

Lowe, P. (2021) Young People and Violent Extremism in the Covid-19 Context. *Counterterrorism Yearbook 2021.* Canberra: Australian Strategic Policy Institute, pp. 101–105.

Mason, P. (2021) *How to Stop Fascism.* London: Allen Lane.

McCauley, C. and Moskalenko, S. (2008) Mechanisms of Political Radicalisation: Pathways Toward Terrorism. *Terrorism and Political Violence*, 20(3), pp. 415–433.

McNeil-Willson, R., Gerrand, V., Scrinzi, F. and Triandafyllidou, A. (2019) Polarisation, Violent Extremism and Resilience in Europe Today: An Analytical Framework for the BRaVE Project (Concept Paper). In. Florence: European University Institute.

Mouffe, C. (2013) *Agonistics. Thinking the World Politically.* London: Verso Books.

Mukherjee, S. and Kumar, U. (2017) Psychological Resilience: A Conceptual Review of Theory and Research. In: Kumar, U. (ed.), *The Routledge International Handbook of Psychosocial Resilience.* London: Routledge, pp. 3–12.

Neumann, P.R. (2013) The Trouble with Radicalisation. *International Affairs,* 89(4), pp. 873–893.

Nicholson, B. (2022) ASIO Chief Flags Alarming Increase in Children Lured to Extremism. Australian Strategic Policy Institute, 11 February.

Nilan, P. (2017) *Muslim Youth in the Diaspora.* Abingdon: Routledge.

Odaci, H and Çelik, C.B. (2016) Does Internet Dependence Affect Young People's Psycho-social Status? Intra-familial and Social Relations, Impulse Control, Coping Ability and Body Image. *Computers in Human Behaviour,* 57, pp. 343–347.

O'Farrell, L. (2021a) Everything I learned about Incels. Vulgadrawings series [Instagram], 19 August, www.instagram.com/p/CSuV-izIU_q/

O'Farrell, L. (2021b) My parents at 30. Me at 30. Vulgamemes post. [Instagram], 28 December, www.instagram.com/p/CYAUftHKr1W/

Olson, E. (2020) Why the 2020 US Presidential Election Has Millions of Americans Waiting in Line for Hours to Vote Early. *ABC News,* 27 October.

Panayotov, B. (2019) Crime and Terror of Social Exclusion: The Case of 13 Imams in Bulgaria. *European Journal of Criminology,* 16(3), pp. 369–387.

Papacharissi, Z, ed. (2010) *A Networked Self: Identity, Community, and Culture on Social Network Sites.* Abingdon: Routledge.

RAN (2021) Incels. A First Scan of the Phenomenon (in the EU) and its Relevance and Challenges for P/CVE. Radicalisation Awareness Network, European Commission.

RAN (2016) Radicalisation Awareness Network (RAN) ISSUE PAPER, The Root Causes of Violent Extremism, RAN Centre of Excellence.

Roose, J.M. (2016) *Political Islam and Masculinity: Muslim Men in the West.* New York: Palgrave.

Roose, J.M, Flood, M., and Alfano, M. (2020) Challenging the use of masculinity as a recruitment mechanism in extremist narratives. Report to Victorian Department of Justice and Community Safety. Melbourne: Deakin University.

Roose, J.M., Gerrand, V., and Akbarzadeh S. (2021) Rapid Evidence Assessment of Alternative Narratives. AVERT Research Network.

Rosand, E. and Winterbotham, E. (2019) Do Counter-narratives Actually Reduce Violent Extremism? Brookings Institution, 20 March, www.brookings.edu/blog/order-from-chaos/2019/03/20/do-counter-narratives-actually-reduce-violent-extremism.

Roy, O. (2018) The power of a narrative, the weakness of a counter-narrative. Paper presented at *The role of image-making in the prevention of violence,* Max Weber Multidisciplinary Workshop, European University Institute, 5 July.

Sabbagh, D. (2020) Trump 2016 Campaign 'Targeted 3.5m Black Americans to Deter Them from Voting'. *The Guardian,* 29 September.

Satyanath, S., Voigtländer, N., and Voth, H.J. (2017) Bowling for Fascism: Social Capital and the Rise of the Nazi Party. *Journal of Political Economy,* 125(2), pp. 478–526.

Sealy, T. and Modood, T. (2021) France: From *laïcité* to *laicism*?' In: Triandafyllidou, A. and Magazzini, T. (eds.), *Routledge Handbook on the Governance of Religious Diversity.* Abingdon: Routledge, pp. 24–34.

Sedgewick, M. (2010) The Concept of Radicalisation as a Source of Confusion. *Terrorism and Political Violence,* 22(4), pp. 479–494.

Sippel, L., Pietrzak, R., Charney, D., Mayes, L., and Southwick, S. (2015) 'How does social support enhance resilience in the trauma-exposed individual?' *Ecology and Society* 20(4), p. 10. DOI:10.5751/ES-07832-200410

Taylor, A. (2016) The Surprising Australian Origin Story of the Burkini. *The Sydney Morning Herald,* 19 August.

Thomas, P. and Grossman, M. (2022) Working with Communities to Counter Radicalisation. In: Busher, J., Marsden, S., and Malkki, L. (eds.), *Routledge Handbook on Radicalisation and Counter-radicalisation.* London: Routledge.

Ungar, M. (2008) Resilience across Cultures. *The British Journal of Social Work,* 38(2), pp. 218–235, DOI:10.1093/bjsw/bcl343

Ungar, M. (2013) Resilience, Trauma, Context and Culture. *Trauma, Violence and Abuse,* 14, pp. 255–266.

Ungar, M., ed. (2021) *Multisystemic Resilience: Adaptation and Transformation in Contexts of Change*. Oxford: Oxford University Press.

Vergani, M., Iqbal, M., Ilbahar, E., and Barton, G. (2020) The Three Ps of Radicalisation: Push, Pull and Personal. A Systematic Scoping Review of the Scientific Evidence about Radicalization into Violent Extremism. *Studies in Conflict and Terrorism*, 43(10), p. 854.

Walker, A. (2022) Joshua Citarella Speaks to Us from the Inescapable Gutter of Art and Tech. *Meme Insider*, no. 67, June.

Weine, S. (2017) Resilience and Countering Violent Extremism. In: Kumar, U. (ed.), *The Routledge International Handbook of Psychosocial Resilience*. Oxon and New York: Routledge.

Weine, S. and Ahmed, O. (2012) *Building Resilience to Violent Extremism Among Somali-Americans in Minneapolis-St. Paul*. National Consortium for the Study of Terrorism and Responses to Terrorism. A Department of Homeland Security Science and Technology Center of Excellence, University of Maryland.

WHO (2020) Managing the Covid-19 Infodemic: Promoting Healthy Behaviours and Mitigating the Harm from Misinformation and Disinformation. Joint statement by WHO, UN, UNICEF, UNDP, UNESCO, UNAIDS, ITU, UN Global Pulse, and IFRC, 23 September. Geneva: World Health Organisation.

Wignell, P., Tan, S., and O'Halloran, K. (2017) Violent Extremism and Iconisation: Commanding Good and Forbidding Evil? *Critical Discourse Studies* 14(1), pp. 1–22.

Williams, J.R. (2019) The Use of Online Social Networking Sites to Nurture and Cultivate Bonding Social Capital. *New Media and Society*, 21(11–12), pp. 2710–2729.

Wodak, R. and Rheindorf, M. (2022) Nativist Gender and Body Politics: A Cross-Sectional and Multimodal Analysis of Discourses in Politics, Popular Culture and the Media. In: Wodak, R. and Rheindorf, M., *Identity Politics Past and Present: Political Discourses from Post-War Austria to the Covid Crisis*. Exeter, UK: University of Exeter Press, pp. 193–224.

Zuboff, Z. (2019) *The Age of Surveillance Capitalism. The Fight for a Human Future at the New Frontier of Power*. New York: Public Affairs.

6
ONLINE EXTREMISM AND RESILIENCE

Amy-Louise Watkin

Introduction

While other scholarly literature has increasingly focused on the role that tech platforms play in furthering polarisation, this chapter is focused on a discussion of platform exploitation by the extreme right and the role that tech platforms can play in building resilience to counter polarisation and extremism on their services. This chapter does so by examining four events (the 2019 Christchurch attack, the 2020 US Presidential election, the 2021 Capitol Hill Riots, and the Covid-19 pandemic) where the extreme right exploited various platforms in attempts to further their own agendas. The chapter also discusses that during this time, these platforms were increasingly coming up against the problem of authority figures (such as world leaders), violating their policies. We have increasingly seen scholarly debates around deplatforming, and platforms taking deplatforming actions against the extreme right and even world leaders. However, this chapter argues that it is worth exploring resilience as a key response to this exploitation of platforms. This chapter uses the lens of a social capital framework to examine some of the actions that platforms have taken thus far. Social capital is the ability to secure benefits or resources through social relationships and memberships in various communities or social networks (Portes 1998). There are three kinds of social capital, and it is crucial that all three are present for the efficient functioning of a liberal democracy (Fukuyama 2001). However, while some attempts to create social capital can be positive, there are also considerations to be had because some attempts to create social capital can have the opposite effect and create, for example, situations of exclusion. This chapter examines a number of relevant examples of platform actions that could create both the positive and negative effects of social capital. It is argued that with these considerations, building resilience could be a key response by platforms in countering polarisation and extremism on their services.

The mid-2000s saw the rise of tech platforms such as Facebook, Twitter, and YouTube. Almost 20 years on, the internet has expanded with hundreds of various-sized tech platforms. In early analysis, the internet was often conceptualised as a separate realm; treated differently from the 'offline world', it was largely framed as a new space that allowed more speech to be heard and more information to be accessed than ever before, therefore allowing greater freedoms (Freedman 2012). These platforms allowed easy access to mass audiences, anonymity, fast flowing information, community-building tools, content repositories, and an array of multimedia services. Many early internet activists were completely against the idea of internet regulation (ibid.), and regulation aimed specifically at social media platforms (regarding hate, extremist, violent extremist, and terrorist content) took a decade to come to fruition. This attitude towards regulation, in combination with the benefits that the platforms brought, created conditions that were conducive to exploitation by those seeking to polarise or recruit to their extremist organisations, making it easier than ever to spread their messages, attract new supporters, build communities, and even plan, incite, undertake, and live-stream attacks (Weimann 2004; Weimann 2010; Wu 2015; BBC 2019).

It is no surprise, then, to learn of the quick uptake of tech platforms by violent extremists and the emergence of a mass of polarising content (Scrivens and Conway 2019). A backward glance at major events of the last decade including the 2016 'Brexit' referendum in the UK, the 2016 and 2020 presidential campaigns in the US, Europe's so-called refugee crisis in 2015–2016, the Covid-19 pandemic since 2020, and a plethora of terrorist attacks globally evidences this (Conway, Scrivens and McNair 2019). While there is considerable research into online violent extremism and the role that the platforms play in polarisation, much less work has considered the role that tech platforms can play in building resilience to counter violent extremism and polarisation on their services. This volume explores resilience as a key response to violent extremism and polarisation. Specifically, what causes people to be resistant to violence, rather than what makes them vulnerable to it (McNeil-Willson et al. 2019; Grossman et al. 2020).

This chapter has two parts. The first provides an overview of online extremism by examining numerous events that have taken place in recent years such as the 2019 Christchurch attack, the 2020 US Presidential election, the 2021 Capitol Hill Riots, and the Covid-19 pandemic response. The second half of the chapter examines tech platforms' responses and resilience-building on these services through the lens of a social capital framework.

Online extremism

The adoption of social media by jihadist groups such as the so-called Islamic State has been subject to significant study for some time now. However, the last five years has seen the spotlight focus on tech platforms and how they can counter the extreme right through their services. Right-wing extremists 'were some of the very first users to engage in online politics and were the earliest adopters of internet technology for violent extremist purposes' (Conway, Scrivens and McNair 2019, p. 2). Extreme right movements have been using social media to their advantage to capitalise on the fear and anger that is often generated by terrorist attacks and the refugee crisis to push their own agendas. They often further benefit from the efforts of foreign influence campaigns that spread disinformation in the same areas of interest (ibid.).

Whilst there have been many incidents instigated by right-wing extremism in recent years, four in particular offer examples of how extremists harnessed the power of tech platforms: the 2019 Christchurch shootings, the 2020 US Presidential election, 2021 Capitol Hill Riots, and the Covid-19 pandemic. This includes disseminating disinformation, misinformation, and conspiracy theories, as well as facilitating radicalisation and the potential for 'real world' extremist mobilisation and violence. However, by demonstrating the power of tech platforms, these examples have since sparked mass discussion about not just the platforms' roles in these events but also their responsibilities towards countering those who use their services to radicalise and spread polarising narratives.

Christchurch attack

On 15 March 2019, a lone gunman walked into two mosques in Christchurch, New Zealand, and killed 50 people. What was particularly notable about this attack was that the shooter had a Go-Pro strapped to his body, enabling a live stream of his attack to be uploaded to Facebook. Facebook's artificial intelligence technology did not flag the live stream and the first user report did not take place until 29 minutes after the live stream had begun, that is, 12 minutes after the live stream had ended, with the live broadcast having approximately 200 views. In short order, the footage went viral, with copies shared on Facebook and other social media sites. In the first 24 hours after the live stream, Facebook removed approximately 1.5 million videos of the attack and had to contend with users editing the footage to circumvent systematic removals (Sonderby 2019). The failure of Facebook's technology to flag the live stream earlier was explained by the company on the Facebook *Newsroom* site:

> AI systems are based on 'training data', which means you need many thousands of examples of content in order to train a system that can detect certain types of text, imagery or video...however, this particular video did not trigger our automatic detection systems. To achieve that we will need to provide our systems with large volumes of data of this specific kind of content, something which is difficult as these events are thankfully rare. Another challenge is to automatically discern this content from visually similar, innocuous content – for example if thousands of videos from live-streamed video games are flagged by our systems, our reviewers could miss the important real-world videos where we could alert first responders to get help on the ground.
>
> *Rosen 2019*

The Christchurch attack appears to have inspired a number of attacks in its aftermath, with other attackers, such as the attacker of a synagogue in Poway, California, the attacker of the El Paso shooting, and more recently the attacker of the Buffalo Shooting in New York claiming Christchurch as their inspiration (Dearden 2019; Gelineau 2019; Bayoumi 2022).

In a survey published a year before the attack, 15 per cent of adults in New Zealand reported having been the target of online hate speech; this included Muslim and Hindu respondents, people with disabilities, and those in the LGBTQ+ community (Pacheco and Melhuish 2018). Three in ten people reported that they had seen online hate speech targeted at someone else, eight in ten believed that more is required of tech platforms to prevent this, and three-quarters supported stricter legislation to stop online hate speech. A comparative Australian study had similar results (Netsafe 2019).

Covid-19 pandemic

The Covid-19 pandemic is the first global health crisis to erupt in the age of social media, leading to lockdowns, national and international travel restrictions, and an unprecedented reliance on the internet – which has brought a new wave of concerns about the role of the internet in society and radicalisation. The *European Union Terrorism and Situation Trend report (TE-SAT) 2020* stated its concern that,

> [L]ockdown measures introduced to combat the spread of Covid-19 could further escalate some of the trends identified in the TE-SAT, given the potential economic

and social impact of the pandemic worldwide. These developments have the potential to further fuel the radicalisation of some individuals, regardless of their ideological persuasion. Activists both on the extreme left and right and those involved in jihadist terrorism attempt to seize the opportunity the pandemic has created to further propagate their aims.

Europol 2020, p. 4

The Covid-19 pandemic was first recorded in Wuhan Provence, China, in late 2019 (Mallapaty 2021). It wasn't long before a spike in hate crimes towards Asian Americans began to be reported around the world (BBC 2021b). This is not the first time that a pandemic has resulted in an increase in hate crimes towards a perceived 'other' based on nationality or ethnicity, however it is believed that much of the stigma stemmed from former US President Donald Trump repeatedly calling it the 'China virus' (Gover, Harper and Langton 2020). An analysis by the news organisation Al Jazeera found more than 10,000 posts on Twitter in March 2020 using the term 'kung-flu', with other variations including 'chop fluey' and 'rice babies' (Macguire 2020). Al Jazeera also reported that there were 72,000 posts on Instagram using 'WuhanVirus' and 10,000 posts using '#KlungFlu', as well as 110 million views on TikTok content tagged '#chinese_coronavirus' (ibid.). In response, social media campaigns seeking to counter anti-Asian hate began to trend, including #WashTheHate and #HateIsAVirus (Gover, Harper and Langton 2020). However, a study of anti-Asian hate by Ziems, Soni, and Kumar (2020), which created a COVID-HATE database containing 30 million tweets, found that only 200,198 tweets contained counter-hate. A key finding revealed that, 'while hateful users are less engaged in the Covid-19 discussions prior to their first anti-Asian tweet, they become more vocal and engaged afterwards compared to counterhate users' (ibid., p. 1). In an attempt to overcome this anti-Asian hate, a decision was made at a global level to change the names of virus variants to Greek alphabetic terms such as the Beta or Delta variant to avoid geographical stigmas (Callaway 2020).

Both jihadist groups and the extreme right took to the internet to exploit the pandemic to further their respective agendas. Findings from a report by the Tony Blair Institute for Global Change (2020) include that the so-called Islamic State celebrated the virus's impact 'on enemy Western militaries' and that Al Qaeda put out narratives that the virus was a plague and punishment against their enemies. The report also found that the prominent neo-Nazi website *Daily Stormer* alleged that the severity of the virus had been exaggerated and the *Infowars* online media outlet had launched a new website called *cantcloseamerica.com* that theorised the virus was created to allow the United Nations and World Health Organisation (both of which they believe to be controlled by China) to instigate lockdowns around the world. Overall, Marone (2022, p. 208) argues that right-wing propaganda used the pandemic to 'challenge authority, to mobilise sympathisers, sometimes even explicitly inciting violence, and to lash out against their usual enemies'.

The pandemic created many issues for tech platforms, notably mass misinformation and disinformation campaigns. The difference between the two is intent: in other words, when content is false but not purposefully intended to deceive, it is misinformation; when it is false and intended to deceive, it is disinformation (Norri-Sederholm et al. 2020). Tech platform services were filled with 'misleading healthcare information, dangerous hoaxes with false claims, conspiracy theories and consumer fraud' from the earliest stages of the pandemic (European Commission 2020) – for instance that drinking bleach could help cure someone or that the virus was created by the global elites to reduce population growth or that the virus was linked to 5G installations.

During the time when tech platforms were feeling pressured to respond to mass misinformation and disinformation on their sites, a consequence of national lockdowns around the world was that many employees had to work from home. This included content moderators, forcing platforms to rely more heavily than ever on artificial intelligence tools to make important decisions on content removals; 'while far more content was flagged and removed for allegedly breaking the companies' rules on what could be posted online, in some areas, dangerous and possibly illegal material was more likely to slip past the machines' (Scott and Kayali 2020). Although these errors are not new, there was an increase during this period in the erroneous removal of activist accounts that were trying to document potential war crimes and human rights violations whilst many pieces of violating content were seen to remain (ibid.). Furthermore, while platforms such as Facebook allow users the opportunity to appeal content removal decisions, during this phase of the pandemic, appeals either took much longer or did not happen at all due to content moderators being sent home for lockdown (ibid.). Although scholars have been discussing the important work done by content moderators for some time now (Gillespie 2018; Roberts 2019; Suzor 2019), the pandemic highlighted the issues with artificial intelligence technology in identifying and removing polarising and violent extremist content and raised the question of whether content moderators were required to be classed as 'essential' workers.

Whilst a range of polarising and extremist content was able to flourish online during the pandemic, the opportunities to carry out physical attacks decreased in countries with strict lockdowns. The ban on large gatherings meant that there were no longer crowded places, such as concerts or other events, that would appeal to an extremist or even terrorist organisation (Marone 2022). Any attacks that were carried out were much smaller in scale than the attacks we saw across Europe in the years before the pandemic, such as the suspected jihadist stabbing attack in Romans-sur-Isére, France, in April 2020 during a Covid lockdown where two people died and five more were injured (ibid.). The only crowded places during national lockdowns were hospitals. The FBI foiled a plan of a right-wing attack on a hospital in the US in 2020, where it was thought that the hospital was not originally going to be the attacker's target, but became the target because of the lockdown (ibid.; BBC 2020). Both jihadist and extreme right-wing groups, however, published requests for any of their followers who contracted Covid-19 to try to spread it to their enemies, for example, by putting their saliva on various places that others are likely to touch, such as on door handles of their enemies' places of worship (ibid.; Daymon and Criezis 2020; Ackerman and Peterson 2020).

2020 US election

On 14 December 2020, the electoral college formalised Joe Biden's election as President of the United States and Kamala Harris as the first female and first Black and Asian American Vice President (BBC 2021a). Chen et al. (2021) collected 67 million tweets between March and August 2020 and identified two main misinformation narratives connected to the 2020 election. The first was the legitimacy of mail-in ballots. The second was the use of face masks relating to Covid. The study found that,

> A large and expansive cluster of politically heterogenous users (both liberal and conservative) advocate for wearing masks and mail-in voting. A small but dense cluster of conservative users pushes misinformation about the inefficiency of masks and potential for voter fraud.
>
> *Ibid.*

In the months leading up to the election, tech platforms were fighting a battle against false narratives, largely put forth by then-incumbent US President Trump that mail-in ballots would result in voter fraud. A poll conducted in September 2020 revealed that nearly one-half of Republican voters believed this narrative (Benkler et al. 2020). According to a BBC article, Trump mentioned rigged elections and voter fraud more than 70 times between April 2020 and the election on the 3 November 2020 (Spring 2020). On 4 November 2020, Trump falsely announced that he had won the election and demanded a stop to vote-counting, again making reference to voter fraud. At the same time, Trump supporters began protesting at ballot-counting locations across several states under the slogan 'Stop the steal', while a 'Stop the Steal' Facebook group mobilised to organise election protests, gaining 361,000 members before Facebook removed it on 5 November 2021 (Horwitz 2021b). Facebook implemented emergency restrictions on such groups. However, when violence failed to materialise in the following days, Facebook began to undo some of the restrictions – a move subsequently criticised, given what unfolded in the days, weeks, and months that followed. After the official announcement of Joe Biden's victory, Trump supporters took to the internet to organise and mobilise for what they called the 'million MAGA march' in Washington, DC, on 14 November 2020 where they turned out in their thousands, with Trump participating in a motorcade drive-by (Holt 2021). The march saw violence between protesters and counter-protesters (ibid.).

The second misinformation narrative found by Chen et al. (2021) was around mask-wearing. Lang, Erikson, and Jing-Schmidt (2021) also investigated online misinformation surrounding mask-wearing and argue that,

> the mask guidelines touched upon a deep-seated tension between government authority and individual liberty, which is a perennial challenge in American political life…mask wearing was politicized in an election year marked by violent partisan vitriol, which was deliberately inflamed by populism and divisive rhetoric and amplified by the media.

Lang, Erikson, and Jing-Schmidt (2021) identified a number of polarising hashtags on Twitter, including #MaskOn vs #MaskOFF; #MasksSaveLives vs #MasksKill; #MasksWork vs #MasksDontWork; and #MaskMandate vs #NoMaskMandate. The authors argued that the polarising rhetoric was magnified by news headlines of the Trump White House's flouting of mask guidelines.

Violating content from the accounts of world leaders has been an increasing issue for tech platforms over the last few years, with former US President Donald Trump providing the most prominent example. While many platforms claim that their policies apply to all users, in September 2021, this was debunked by a *Wall Street Journal* series entitled 'the Facebook files' based on internal Facebook documents. The story revealed a Facebook programme called Cross Check, or also known as XCheck, that appears to have 'given millions of celebrities, politicians and other high-profile users special treatment, a privilege many abuse' (Horwitz 2021a). The *Wall Street Journal* noted that Cross Check

> shields millions of VIP users from the company's normal enforcement process… some users are 'whitelisted' – rendered immune from enforcement actions – while others are allowed to post rule-violating material pending Facebook employee

reviews that often never come. At times, the documents show, XCheck has protected public figures whose posts contain harassment or incitement to violence, violations that would typically lead to sanctions for regular users.

Ibid.

The *Wall Street Journal* also reported an incident noted in the internal documents concerning Trump and a post he made that read 'When the looting starts, the shooting starts'. While such an incitement to violence would typically be removed coming from other, non-VIP users, Facebook CEO Mark Zuckerberg publicly acknowledged that he personally made the decision to leave the post online (ibid.). A further finding was that while XCheck protected many government officials from enforcement actions, it did not protect all of them, meaning that some government officials had an advantage over others in elections.

Facebook's response to the *Wall Street Journal*'s series was that the company had asked the 'independent' Facebook Oversight Board to review the Cross Check system and offer recommendations as to how to improve it. Facebook said that they were specifically seeking recommendations on the criteria used 'to determine what is prioritised for secondary review via cross-check' as well as on managing the programme more generally (Clegg 2021).

Capitol Hill Riots

On the 19 December 2020, Trump posted on Twitter that there would be a 'big protest in DC on January 6th. Be there, will be wild!' (Horton 2020). A number of other tweets and online activities occurred in the run up to 6 January 2021. A pro-Trump attorney and conspiracy theorist, Lin Woods, tweeted that Vice President Mike Pence should be 'executed by firing squad' for not overturning the election result (Holt 2021). Pro-Trump online spaces reportedly contained content that offered advice regarding the use of weapons and how to stay safe while participating in the forthcoming riot (ibid.). The day before the riots, Trump once again tweeted about election fraud, saying, 'I hope the Democrats, and even more importantly, the weak and ineffective RINO section[1] of the Republican party, are looking at the thousands of people pouring into D.C. They won't stand for a landslide election to be stolen' (ibid.).

On 6 January 2021 protesters arrived in the thousands and violently attacked the US Capitol with a range of weapons in an unprecedented event that resulted in five deaths and approximately 200 arrests. According to Hold (2021), the protesters,

> included groups across a spectrum of radicalisation: hyperpartisan pro-Trump activists and media outlets; the neo-fascist Proud boys…; unlawful militias from around the country with a high degree of command and control, including the so-called Three Percenters movement; adherents to the collective delusion of Qanon; individuals identifying with the Boogaloo Bois,…; and ideological fellow travelers of the far-right, who wanted to witness something they believed would be spectacular.

The day's violence was viewed as at least partially a consequence of online disinformation campaigns, conspiracy theories, and their intersection with domestic terrorism (ibid.). It also raised serious questions about tech platform policies regarding authority figures and global leaders.

Private groups on platforms such as Facebook played a significant role in organising the Capitol Hill Riots. The *Wall Street Journal* reported in January 2021 that 'Facebook's own research found that American Facebook Groups became a vector for the rabid partisanship and even calls for violence that inflamed the country after the election' (Horwitz 2021b). According to the *Wall Street Journal*, Facebook's data scientists had been warning that misinformation and calls for violence were commonplace in the majority of the platform's top 'civic' groups, which are thought to reach hundreds of millions of users (ibid.). As a result, after the riots, Facebook took action against QAnon, amongst other groups and movements, as part of what appeared to be an emergency response (ibid.; Rosen and Bickert 2021); the platform also continued the ban on recommending 'civic' or 'health' groups and disabled tools that were thought to facilitate the fast growth of such groups (Horwitz 2021b).

Tech platform responses and building resilience online

In discussing these various landmark events over the last few years, we are able to observe tech platforms' exploitation in efforts to polarise and misinform, not just by average users but also by global leaders, and the serious consequences of propaganda, conspiracy theories, and misinformation. It is therefore not a surprise that tech platforms have received so much attention regarding their responses and perceived responsibilities.

The discussion around tech platform responses and responsibilities has centred on the practice of 'deplatforming' – the removal of a user's account on social media because they have been deemed as breaking the platform's rules. While several studies have shown that deplatforming can make it much more difficult for extremists and terrorists to reach a mass mainstream audience with their propaganda (see Berger and Morgan 2015; Conway et al. 2019; Nouri, Lorenzo-Dus and Watkin 2020), it has also been shown that groups and movements are highly adaptable, using a diverse ecosystem of tech platforms in response to their removal (Frampton et al. 2017; Conway et al. 2019; Nouri, Lorenzo-Dus and Watkin 2020; Macdonald et al. 2019).

This chapter, however, explores the possibility of responses that build on alternative methods to violent extremist content, such as resilience. The author has previously employed the concept of social capital to examine the efforts that tech platforms could undertake to build resilience and discourage polarising and extremist content on their services (Watkin and Conway 2022). It has been argued that social capital is crucial to the efficient functioning of liberal democracies (Fukuyama 2001), and has been defined as the ability to secure benefits or resources through social relationships and memberships in various communities or social networks (Portes 1998). Social capital is dependent on social norms and values, participation in social networks, a culture of trust, norms of reciprocity, and collective action (Putnam 2001; Mignone and O'Neil 2005; Frank and Yasumoto 1998).

There are three types of social capital, all of which are required for a community to be considered as truly resilient (Brisson et al. 2017). The first, 'bonding social capital', is the strongest, and refers to the relationships individuals have with family, friends, or other close social groups, for instance, those with a shared religion (Ali et al. 2019). This social capital contributes to feelings of collective strength and protection from external threats but can also create situations of exclusion with other social groups. 'Bridging social capital', meanwhile, refers to relationships between heterogeneous social groups (ibid.). This can create inter-community connections, trust, harmony, and resources (ibid.; Brisson et al. 2017; Mignone and O'Neil 2005; Fukuyama 2001). Where this social capital is missing, feelings of isolation and disenfranchisement can arise among certain social groups (Brisson et al. 2017).

Finally, 'linking social capital' is the relationship between authority figures or those in power and citizens (Ali et al. 2019). It requires citizens having trust in authority figures and being provided with opportunities to influence policies that affect their communities (Brisson et al. 2017). Social groups that lack linking social capital are likely to be disadvantaged regarding various policy decisions and available interventions (Putnam 2000).

Social capital has been argued to be a neutral resource that creates various actions that can have both positive and negative consequences for communities (Narayan 1999; Coleman 1988). The social capital framework therefore argues that, for a truly resilient community, there must be opportunities to engage positively with in-group networks (bonding social capital), wider heterogeneous networks (bridging social capital), and those in power (linking social capital). The discussion below will explore tech platform responses in relation to the potential building of the three different types of social capital.

Online resilience in response to the Christchurch attack

After the Christchurch attack, the 'Christchurch Call' was established and co-sponsored by President Emmanuel Macron of France and New Zealand's Prime Minister Jacinda Arden (Crothers and O'Brien 2020). 'The call outlines collective, voluntary commitments from Governments and online service providers intended to address the issue of terrorist and violent extremist content online and to prevent the abuse of the internet...' (Christchurch Call 2019). The Call vowed to be consistent with the principles of a free, open, and secure internet, respectful of human rights and freedom of expression, and to promote innovation, economic development, and inclusion. Over 50 governments committed to provide education and digital literacy, enforce applicable laws that prohibit online terrorist and violent extremist content in line with the rule of law and human rights commitments, encourage media outlets to meet ethical standards when reporting attacks, support frameworks and industry standards, join collaborative initiatives, and work towards preventing the exploitation of platforms by terrorist and violent extremist organisations. Ten tech platforms committed to transparent measures regarding the prevention of violent extremism on their services, including increasing transparency around their community standards and terms of service with consideration to human rights and publishing regular transparency reports. They further committed to providing users with complaints and appeals mechanisms regarding content removal, taking greater measures to mitigate the risks of their live-streaming services being exploited, reviewing their algorithms to prevent the amplification of violent extremist content, and joining collaborative initiatives. Both the participating governments and tech platforms agreed to work with civil society organisations to promote community-led efforts, assist research efforts, and cooperate with law enforcement.

While the Christchurch Call proposed several strategies that have the potential to create bridging social capital (e.g., digital literacy and education) and linking social capital (e.g,. increased transparency, complaints and appeals mechanisms), and to undertake neglected commitments in regulatory areas (e.g., assistance to smaller platforms), there are limitations. Perhaps the most notable of these is that the Call is voluntary and therefore provides no regulatory incentives or enforcement measures for either the governments or platforms to fulfil any of their commitments. One of the reasons why so many countries are implementing new regulations and legislation to counter this type of content is because previous voluntary initiatives have not worked sufficiently to counter this content (Yar 2018).

Another, pre-existing collaborative initiative that worked with Facebook in the aftermath of the Christchurch attack is The Global Internet Forum to Counter Terrorism (GIFCT)

(Sonderby 2019). The GIFCT was established in 2017 when Facebook, Twitter, YouTube, and Microsoft joined forces to improve removal of violent extremist and terrorist content from their services. One of the key aspects of the collaboration is the shared database of hashes that they began compiling in 2016 before their formalised collaboration. The database allows those with access to remove already identified violent extremist and terrorist content from their platforms more easily (Facebook 2016). The GIFCT also works to equip civil society organisations with the tools and knowledge required to counter terrorist and violent extremist content (GIFCT 2021). Tactically, it brings key stakeholders together to mitigate the impact of attacks. Finally, GIFCT supports research into understanding and responding to terrorist and violent extremist content via its Global Network on Extremism and Technology (GNET) initiative. The GIFCT became an independent organisation in 2019, headed by an Executive Director, and expanded in 2020 to include an Independent Advisory Council that includes government and civil society representatives, as well as a number of Working Groups to allow various stakeholders to raise and discuss issues.

While this collaboration has been praised for bringing stakeholders together and for sharing tools and best practice, issues have been raised about accountability and the lack of transparency that users have regarding decisions that are made within the GIFCT. There is the further issue that ineffectual measures taken on one platform could quickly become standard across other platforms within the collaborative initiative, with users having little way of knowing whether this is occurring or not (Douek 2020; Llansó 2019). These criticisms could limit the ability to create trust and subsequently linking social capital between users and the platforms.

Online resilience in response to Covid-19

The 'major' platforms responded quickly to Covid-19-related mis- and disinformation, which was expected given their scale, reach, and access to resources. Facebook reported on their *Newsroom* website in January 2020 that they had started,

> showing educational pop-ups connecting people to information from the WHO, the CDC and regional health authorities toward the top of News Feed in countries with reported person-to-person transmissions and in all countries when people search for COVID-19 related information.
>
> *Clegg 2020*

Facebook followed up by launching a Covid-19 Information Centre in March 2020 to provide users with real-time updates from national health authorities and organisations such as the World Health Organisation, for which they also provided free advertisements (ibid.). Facebook reported removing 'posts that make false claims about cures, treatments, the availability of essential services or the location and severity of the outbreak' and that they were working with over 55 fact-checking partners in over 45 languages to try to debunk false claims on their services (ibid.). The tech platform, in addition to other platforms, made headlines when they removed a video that was posted to their site by former US President Trump in which he falsely claimed that children were 'almost immune' to the virus (Hatmaker 2020).

Twitter was similarly quick to launch 'a new dedicated search prompt to ensure that when you come to the service for information about the #coronavirus, you're met with credible authoritative information first' and put a stop to auto-search results that were leading users to content thought to be false (Chu and McDonald 2020). By March 2020, Twitter reported having increased its efforts to 'build partnerships, protect the public conversation, help people find authoritative health information, raise relief funds, and contribute pro bono advertising support to ensure people are getting the right message, from the right source' (Twitter Public Policy 2020).

Furthermore, it wasn't just the well-established 'major' tech platforms that were quick to respond. TikTok, which only launched in 2016, gained an enormous number of global users throughout 2020. They too partnered with the World Health Organisation 'to create an informational page on TikTok that provides trustworthy information, offers tips on staying safe and preventing the spread of the virus, and dispels myths around COVID-19' (TikTok 2020). TikTok has also put labels on all videos identified as being Covid-19-related which direct their viewers to trusted sources of health information (Zhu 2020).

While many of the platforms' responses to this misinformation and disinformation appear to focus on increasing users' ability to easily identify credible from non-credible sources, the platforms do so based on the assumption that the majority of their users are happy to accept that the platforms are well-placed to determine what is and is not reliable, credible content. Such platforms thus operate on the assumption that sufficient linking social capital has already been established.

Online resilience in response to the Capitol Hill Riots

The immediate aftermath of the Capital Hill Riots saw tech platforms taking unprecedented actions against a President of the United States. Both Facebook and Twitter locked former US President Trump's accounts and removed a number of his posts, citing their policies prohibiting the spread of misinformation and the incitement of violence as justifications (Paul 2021). The former US President was active on several platforms, and YouTube removed a video that he had posted in which he expressed love towards the riot protesters (ibid.). The platforms faced ongoing pressure in the riots' aftermath to do more in response. On 8 January 2021, Twitter announced that it had permanently suspended Donald Trump's account, stating that it had done so 'due to the risk of further incitement of violence' (Twitter 2021). A few days later the platform announced that they had decided to suspend 'thousands of accounts that were primarily dedicated to sharing QAnon content' as a result of the violent Capitol Hill Riots, and implemented a provision that tweets labelled for inaccuracy would no longer be able to be liked or retweeted (Twitter Safety 2021).

Facebook also published a blog post on 6 January 2021 stating,

> We believe the risks of allowing President Trump to continue to use our service during this period are simply too great, so we are extending the block we have placed on his Facebook and Instagram accounts indefinitely and for at least the next two weeks.
>
> Rosen and Bickert 2021

A range of other platforms took actions against Trump and content related to the riots in the days that followed, including Snapchat, Twitch, and TikTok (Heater and Hatmaker 2021). This response from platforms was met with some controversy as some commentators questioned tech platforms' power over free expression. Facebook was particularly criticised for imposing an 'indeterminate and standardless penalty of indefinite suspension' (Facebook Oversight Board 2021), which could affect the ability to build linking social capital.

Tech platforms have also sought to implement tools that provide users with more power and control over their own experiences on the platform, such as allowing users to mute, block, or filter certain accounts or types of content and comments. In a survey by the Pew Research Center, 31 per cent of participants reported that they used such tools and settings to reduce how much politics-related content was on their newsfeeds, and 27 per cent said that they had previously blocked/unfriended/unfollowed a fellow user because they shared too much politics-related content. When asked why, 60 per cent of the participants said that they did so because they found that type of content offensive; others' answers included that they disagreed with the content or thought it was abusive or harassing. The survey also found that participants with high levels of online political engagement take an active approach to curating the type of content and accounts that they want to see online (Duggan and Smith 2016).

Such tools and settings allow users to have more of a sense of control over the conversations, overcome the time lag that comes with reporting content, shield themselves from content that they consider harmful to themselves, and create bonding social capital with like-minded others that increases collective strength and protection (Basak et al. 2019; Elder 2019). However, it could also lead to the exclusion of alternative or challenging narratives, curbing opportunities to be exposed to different opinions, perspectives, cultures, and social groups, and eliminating all but the dominant voices supporting that user's worldviews (Elder 2019). Indeed, Elder (ibid.) argues that this is concerning because people can be reluctant to speak up when they perceive their views to be in the minority, which could ultimately skew the conversations that are heard. It has therefore been argued that, overall, such tools and settings allow user experiences to be in constant change and construction that could increase or decrease the creation of social capital (Bozdag 2020).

Another response from tech platforms that could have a similar negative impact on social capital is the tools and powers tech platforms have given to page and group admins. Users who become admins are assumed to be users who are strongly committed to the success of their group or page and have a disproportionate degree of influence over the type of content and conversations that happen within the group or page (Leskovec, Huttenlocher and Kleinberg 2010; Poell et al. 2016). Admins thus have the power to take control of conversations, shield what they may consider harmful or offensive content, and create a space conducive to the creation of bonding social capital. However, once again this risks excluding certain people and groups, and subsequently alternative views and perspectives. These effects are particularly concerning given that during the global pandemic many individuals have increasingly turned to tech platforms for opportunities to socialise and access information (Gerrand 2021).

Another response that many online platforms have developed is the creation and dissemination of various digital-literacy initiatives and resources, such as Facebook's digital literacy library[2] and TikTok's 'Be Informed' series,[3] as well as spreading awareness about a range of social issues and movements (for example, Black Lives Matter, Juneteenth, Pride, Hispanic Heritage Month, International Women's Day). This awareness is spread in a number of ways, including special features, hashtags, filters, and emojis, as well dedicating pages to educational resources, and supporting activists, civil society and social justice organisations to create content for these pages.[4] All of these types of efforts and resources could lead to increased education and exposure on issues that affect other social groups that users may not have been exposed to otherwise, which may have the potential to increase bridging social capital. However, linking social capital must also be present because without user trust in the tech platforms, these resources may not be considered credible or trustworthy, and other users may simply have no interest in reading or engaging with them. Regarding attempts to build trust and transparency (i.e., linking social capital), many of the tech platforms have been making greater effort to explain their policies, enforcement actions, and appeals processes to their users. They also publish transparency reports and create opportunities for users and other stakeholders to participate in consultations and provide feedback on policies. One example being when Twitter sought to expand their hateful conduct policy to also address dehumanising language on their services. Twitter opened this to user feedback by making a survey available to users to comment on how various communities and cultures would be impacted by the policy before it formally became part of the Twitter Rules (Gadde and Harvey 2018). Whilst there are many benefits to transparency reports and such user feedback opportunities, they are also are risks. For example, if platforms omit important pieces of information, are vague with the information that they provide, or fail to implement responses from the user consultations that they run, it will be difficult to build sufficient linking social capital, and this will have a knock-on effect on the above-mentioned attempts to build bridging social capital on their services.

Concluding remarks

There have been several landmark events in recent years that have showcased the dangers that online radicalisation, misinformation, disinformation, conspiracy theories, and extremist content can have. We saw unprecedented levels of coordination amongst the extreme-right with the spread of the Christchurch footage across the internet, and violence and mobilisation with the Capitol Hill Riots. We also saw difficulties with global leaders spreading misinformation and conspiracy theories during the US presidential election campaign. Finally, this chapter discussed the first global pandemic in the social media age. Throughout all of this, there were concerns regarding the protection of free speech, human rights, and public interest issues. Furthermore, the Covid-19 pandemic exposed our reliance on content moderation and tech platforms more generally to counter these problems.

It is important that policymakers and social media platforms explore approaches that move beyond deplatforming and content removal. Extremist groups have integrated a diverse and interconnected ecosystem of tech platforms into their operations (Williams et al. 2021; Frampton et al. 2017; Fisher, Prucha and Winterbotham 2019; Conway Scrivens and McNair 2019; Macdonald et al. 2019). Their content and followers are connected and backed-up across various platforms and accounts. This chapter argues that a deeper exploration of resilience as a key means of response by tech platforms is required. In keeping with this book's theme of exploring resilience and what is keeping people resistant to violence rather than what is making them vulnerable to it, this chapter has put forth the idea of what tech platforms are able to do, and need to consider, to create all three types of social capital.

Given that all three types of social capital are vital for a community to be resilient against violent extremism and polarisation, as well as for the efficient functioning of liberal democracies, this chapter argues that tech platforms must ensure that their services provide opportunities to engage positively with in-group networks (to create bonding social capital), wider heterogeneous networks (to create bridging social capital), and the platforms themselves (to create linking social capital). However, there are several difficulties in doing so. Many of the ways in which tech platforms could attempt to build social capital could result in exclusion and skewing the conversations on their services or rely on users considering the platforms as trustworthy and credible enough to make important decisions on their behalf and supply educative and informative content and resources. This is no doubt a complex and challenging task, in which this chapter is simply a starting point for discussions moving forward.

Acknowledgements

I would like to thank Professor Maura Conway for her helpful feedback during the drafting of this chapter; it is much appreciated.

Notes

1 RINO is an acronym for 'Republican in Name Only', which prior to the Trump administration meant 'someone insufficiently faithful to conservative values'. However, many have argued that Trump changed the term from being measured by conservatism to being measured in one's loyalty to (Trump) himself (see Mair 2021).
2 https://about.fb.com/news/2018/08/digitalliteracylibrary/.
3 https://newsroom.tiktok.com/en-us/tiktoks-be-informed-series-stars-tiktok-creators-to-educate-users-about-media-literacy.
4 Examples of these can be found in the tech platforms' official blog websites or newsrooms. Some examples are here, however, this is not an exhaustive list: https://about.fb.com/news/2022/02/black-history-month/; https://blog.twitter.com/en_us/topics/company/2020/inclusion-and-diversity-report-blacklivesmatter-september-2020; https://newsroom.tiktok.com/en-us/recognizing-juneteenth; https://discord.com/blog/our-stand-on-racial-equality; https://about.fb.com/news/2021/06/forward-with-pride-celebrating-elevating-lgbtq-voices/; https://about.fb.com/news/2020/09/celebrating-latinx-and-hispanic-heritage-month-across-our-apps/; https://blog.twitter.com/en_sea/topics/company/2022/-ownit--celebrating-greatness-this-international-women-s-day.

References

Ackerman, G. and H. Peterson (2020) Terrorism and COVID-19: Actual and potential impacts. *Perspectives on Terrorism*, 14(3), pp. 59–73.

Ali, M., Azab, N., Sorour, M.K. and Dora, M. (2019) Integration v. polarisation among social media users: Perspectives through social capital theory on the recent Egyptian political landscape. *Technological Forecasting and Social Change*, 145(C), pp. 461–473.

Basak, R., Sural, S., Ganguly, N. and Ghosh, S. K. (2019) Online public shaming on Twitter: Detection, analysis, and mitigation. *IEEE Transactions on computational social systems*, 6(2), pp. 208–220.

Bayoumi, M. (2022) The alleged Buffalo shooter was also inspired by Islamaphobia. That's telling. *The Guardian*, 22 May, www.theguardian.com/commentisfree/2022/may/22/buffalo-shooter-islamophobia-replacement-theory

BBC (2019) Facebook: New Zealand attack video viewed 4,000 times. *BBC News*, 19 March, www.bbc.co.uk/news/business-47620519 (accessed 26 May 2020).

BBC (2020) Coronavirus: Man planning to bomb Missouri hospital killed, FBI says. *BBC News*, 26 March, www.bbc.co.uk/news/world-us-canada-52045958 (accessed 9 June 2022).

BBC (2021a) Kamala Harris becomes first female, first black and first Asian-American VP. *BBC News*, 20 January, www.bbc.co.uk/news/world-us-canada-55738741 (accessed 23 September 2021).

BBC (2021b) Covid 'hate crimes' against Asian Americans on rise. *BBC News*, 21 May, www.bbc.co.uk/news/world-us-canada-56218684 (accessed 24 October 2021).

Benkler, Y., Tilton, C., Etling, B., Roberts, H., Clark, J., Faris, R., Kaiser, J. and Schmitt, C. (2020) *Mail-In Voter Fraud: Anatomy of a Disinformation Campaign*. Research Publication No. 6. Cambridge, MA: Berkman Klein Center for Internet & Society, DOI: 10.2139/ssrn.3703701

Berger, J.M. and Morgan, J. (2015) *The ISIS Twitter Census: Defining and describing the population of ISIS supporters on Twitter*. Washington, DC: The Brookings Institution.

Bozdag, C. (2020) Managing Diverse Online Networks in the Context of Polarization: Understanding How We Grow Apart on and through Social Media. *Social Media+ Society*, 6(4), DOI:10.1177/2056305120975713

Brisson, J., Gerrand, V., Hadfield, K. and Jefferies, P. (2017) Understanding Youth Resilience to Violent Extremism: A Standardised Research Measure.

Callaway, E. (2021) Coronavirus variants get Greek names – but will scientists use them? *Nature*, 1 June, www.nature.com/articles/d41586-021-01483-0 (accessed 23 September 2021).

Chen, E., Chang, H., Rao, A., Lerman, K., Cowan, G. and Ferrara, E. (2021) COVID-19 misinformation and the 2020 US presidential election. *The Harvard Kennedy School Misinformation Review*, 1(Special Issue, March), DOI:10.37016/mr-2020-57

Christchurch Call (2019) Christchurch Call: To eliminate terrorist and violent extremist content online, www.christchurchcall.com/

Chu, J. and McDonald, J. (2020) Helping the world find credible information about novel #coronavirus. *Twitter Blog,* https://blog.twitter.com/en_us/topics/company/2020/authoritative-information-about-novel-coronavirus.html (accessed 23 September 2021).

Clegg, N. (2020) Combating COVID-19 misinformation across out apps. Facebook Newsroom, https://about.fb.com/news/2020/03/combating-covid-19-misinformation/ (accessed 23 September 2021).

Clegg, N. (2021) Requesting oversight board guidance on our Cross-Check system. Facebook Newsroom, https://about.fb.com/news/2021/09/requesting-oversight-board-guidance-cross-check-system/ (accessed 3 November 2021).

Coleman, J.S. (1988) Social capital in the creation of human capital. *American Journal of Sociology*, 94, S95–S120.

Conway, M., Scrivens, R. and McNair, L. (2019a) Right-wing extremists' persistent online presence: History and contemporary trends. *The International Centre for Counter-Terrorism – The Hague*, https://icct.nl/wp-content/uploads/2019/11/RWEXOnline-1.pdf

Conway, M., Khawaja, M., Lakhani, S., Reffin, J., Robertson, A. and Weir, D. (2019b) Disrupting Daesh: Measuring takedown of online terrorist material and its impacts. *Studies in Conflict & Terrorism*, 42(1–2), pp. 141–160.

Crothers, C. and O'Brien, T. (2020) The contexts of the Christchurch terror attacks: social science perspectives. *Kōtuitui: New Zealand Journal of Social Sciences Online*, 15(2,1), pp. 247–259.

Daymon, C. and Criezis, M. (2020) Pandemic narratives: pro-Islamic state media and the coronavirus. *CTC Sentinel*, 13(6), pp. 26–32.

Dearden, L. (2019) Revered as a saint by online extremists, how Christchurch shooter inspired copycat terrorists around the world. *The Independent*, 24 August, www.independent.co.uk/news/world/australasia/ brenton-tarrant-christchurch-shooter-attack-el-paso-norway-poway-a9076926.html (accessed 22 September 2021).

Douek, E. (2020) *The Rise of Content Cartels*. Knight First Amendment Institute at Columbia University, 11 February, https://knightcolumbia.org/content/the-rise-of-content-cartels

Duggan, M., and Smith, A. (2016) *The political environment on social media*. Pew Research Center, 25 October, www.pewresearch.org/internet/2016/10/25/the-political-environment-on-social-media/ (accessed 12 January 2021).

Elder, A. (2020) The interpersonal is political: Unfriending to promote civic discourse on social media. *Ethics and Information Technology*, 22(1), pp. 15–24.

European Commission (2020) Tackling coronavirus disinformation, https://ec.europa.eu/info/live-work-travel-eu/coronavirus-response/fighting-disinformation/tackling-coronavirus-disinformation_en (accessed 23 September 2021)

Europol (2020) European Union Terrorism Situation and Trend Report (TE-SAT). The Hague: Europol, www.europol.europa.eu/activities-services/main-reports/european-union-terrorism-situation-and-trend-report-te-sat-2020 (accessed 23 September 2021).

Facebook (2016) Partnering to help curb spread of online terrorist content. Facebook, https://newsroom.fb.com/news/2016/12/partnering-to-help-curb-spread-of-online-terrorist-content/ (accessed September 2021).

Facebook Oversight Board (2021) The Oversight Board upholds former President Trump's suspension and finds that Facebook failed to impose proper penalty, https://oversightboard.com/news/2266 12455899839-oversight-board-upholds-former-president-trump-s-suspension-finds-facebook-failed-to-impose-proper-penalty/ (accessed 3 March 2023).

Fisher, A., Prucha, N. and Winterbotham, E. (2019) Mapping the Jihadist Information Ecosystem: Towards the next generation of disruption capability. *Global Research Network on Terrorism and Technology: Paper No. 6*

Frampton, M., Fisher, A., Prucha, N. and Petraeus, D.H. (2017) *The New Netwar: Countering Extremism Online*. London: Policy Exchange.

Frank, K.A. and Yasumoto, J.Y. (1998) Linking action to social structure within a system: Social capital within and between subgroups. *American Journal of Sociology*, 104(3), pp. 642–686.

Freedman, D. (2012) *Misunderstanding the Internet*. London: Routledge, pp. 95–120.

Fukuyama, F. (2001) Social capital, civil society and development. *Third World Quarterly*, 22(1), pp. 7–20.

Gadde, V. and Harvey, D. (2018) Creating new policies together. *Twitter Blog*, https://blog.twitter.com/en_us/topics/company/2018/Creating-new-policies-together.html (accessed 9 March 2020).

Gelineau, K. (2019) 5 months on, Christchurch attacker influences others. *ABC News*, 6 August, https://abcnews.go.com/International/wireStory/months-christchurch-attacker-inspires-64790853 (accessed 22 September 2021).

Gerrand, V. (2021) Communicative channels for pro-social resilience in an age of polarization. *First Monday*, forthcoming.

GIFCT (2021) Global Internet Forum to Counter Terrorism, www.gifct.org/

Gillespie, T. (2018) *Custodians of the Internet. Platforms, Content Moderation, and the Hidden Decisions That Shape Social Media*. New Haven, CT: Yale University Press.

Gover, A.R., Harper, S.B. and Langton, L. (2020) Anti-Asian hate crime during the COVID-19 pandemic: Exploring the reproduction of inequality. *American Journal of Criminal Justice*, 45(4), pp. 647–667.

Grossman, M., Hadfield, K., Jefferies, P., Gerrand, V. and Ungar, M. (2020) Youth resilience to violent extremism: Development and validation of the BRaVE measure. *Terrorism and Political Violence*, 1–21.

Hatmaker, T. (2020) Facebook just took down a Trump post that claimed kids are immune to COVID-19. *TechCrunch*, 6 August, https://techcrunch.com/2020/08/05/facebook-trump-false-covid-claim-fox-news/?guccounter=1 (accessed 23 September 2021).

Heater, B. and Hatmaker, T. (2021) Twitch disables Trump's channel until the end of his term to 'minimize harm' during transition. *TechCrunch*, 2 January, https://techcrunch.com/2021/01/07/twitch-disables-trumps-channel-over-incendiary-rhetoric/.

Holt, J. (2021) #StopTheSteal: Timeline of social media and extremist activities leading to 1/6 insurrection. *Just Security*, 10 February, www.justsecurity.org/74622/stopthesteal-timeline-of-social-media-and-extremist-activities-leading-to-1-6-insurrection/ (accessed 22 September 2021).

Horton, J. (2020) US election 2020: What legal challenges remain for Trump? *BBC News*, 23 December, www.bbc.co.uk/news/election-us-2020-54724960 (accessed 23 September 2021).

Horwitz, J. (2021a) Facebook says its rules apply to all. Company documents reveal a secret elite that's exempt. *The Wall Street Journal*, 13 September, https://www.wsj.com/articles/facebook-files-xcheck-zuckerberg-elite-rules-11631541353?mod=article_inline#_=_ (accessed 3 November 2021).

Horwitz, J. (2021b) Facebook knew calls for violence plagued 'Groups', now plans overhaul. *The Wall Street Journal*, 31 January, www.wsj.com/articles/facebook-knew-calls-for-violence-plagued-groups-now-plans-overhaul-11612131374?mod=article_inline (accessed 3 November 2021).

Lang, J., Erickson, W.W. and Jing-Schmidt, Z. (2021) # MaskOn!# MaskOff! Digital polarization of mask-wearing in the United States during COVID-19. *PloS One*, 16(4), e0250817.

Leskovec, J., Huttenlocher, D. and Kleinberg, J. (2010) Governance in social media: A case study of the Wikipedia promotion process. *Proceedings of the International AAAI Conference on Web and Social Media*, 4(1), 98–105.

Llansó, E. (2019) Platforms want centralized censorship. That should scare you. *Wired*, 18 April, www.wired.com/story/platforms-centralized-censorship/ (accessed 14 September 2020).

Macdonald, S., Grinnell, D., Kinzel, A., and Lorenzo-Dus, N. (2019) *A Study of Outlinks Contained in Tweets Mentioning 'Rumiyah'*. The Global Research Network on Terrorism and Technology, Paper No. 2.

Macguire, E. (2020) Anti-Asian Hate continues to spread online amid COVID-19 pandemic. *Al Jazeera*, 5 April, www.aljazeera.com/news/2020/4/5/anti-asian-hate-continues-to-spread-online-amid-covid-19-pandemic (accessed 2 November 2021).

Mair, L. (2021) *'RINO' used to mean Donald Trump. Now it means Liz Cheney*. The Washington Post, 11 May. www.washingtonpost.com/outlook/2021/05/11/cheney-trump-stefanik-cruz-hawley-mccarthy/ (accessed 2 November 2021),

Mallapaty, S. (2021) Where did COVID come from? Five mysteries that remain. *Nature,* News Explainer, 26 February, www.nature.com/articles/d41586-021-00502-4.

Marone, F. (2022) Hate in the time of coronavirus: exploring the impact of the COVID-19 pandemic on violent extremism and terrorism in the West. *Security Journal,* 35, pp. 205–222.

McNeil-Willson, R., Gerrand, V., Scrinzi, F. and Triandafyllidou, A. (2019) Polarisation, violent extremism and resilience in Europe today: an analytical framework. BRaVE, D2.1 [Global Governance Programme], [Cultural Pluralism], http://hdl.handle.net/1814/65664 (accessed 9 June 2022).

Mignone, J. and O'Neil, J. (2005) Conceptual understanding of social capital in first nation communities: An illustrative description. *Pimatisiwin: A Journal of Aboriginal & Indigenous Community Health,* 3(2), 8–44.

Narayan, D. (1999) *Bonds and Bridges: Social Capital and Poverty* (Vol. 2167). Washington, DC: World Bank.

Netsafe (2019) *Hate speech online findings from Australia, New Zealand and Europe.* Report. Office of the eSafety Commissioner (Australia), https://apo.org.au/node/276421 (accessed 22 September 2021).

Norri-Sederholm, T., Norvanto, E., Talvitie–Lamberg, K. and Huhtinen, A.M. (2020) Misinformation and Disinformation in Social Media as the Pulse of Finnish National Security. In: Moehlecke de Baseggio E., Schneider O. and Szvircsev Tresch T. (eds), *Social Media and the Armed Forces.* Cham: Springer, pp. 207–225.

Nouri, L., Lorenzo-Dus, N. and Watkin, A.L. (2020) Impacts of radical right groups' movements across Social Media platforms–A case study of changes to Britain First's visual strategy in its removal from Facebook to Gab. *Studies in Conflict & Terrorism: Special Issue,* pp. 1–27.

Pacheco, E. and Melhuish, N.L. (2018) *Online Hate Speech: A Survey on Personal Experiences and Exposure among Adult New Zealanders.* Wellington: Netsafe.

Paul, K. (2021) Twitter and Facebook lock Donald Trump's accounts after video address. *The Guardian,* 7 January, www.theguardian.com/us-news/2021/jan/06/facebook-twitter-youtube-trump-video-supporters-capitol (accessed 23 September 2021).

Poell, T., Abdulla, R., Rieder, B., Woltering, R. and Zack, L. (2016) Protest leadership in the age of social media. *Information, Communication & Society,* 19(7), pp. 994–1014.

Portes, A. (1998) Social capital: Its origins and applications in contemporary sociology. *Annual Review of Sociology,* 24(1), pp. 1–24.

Putnam, R. (2000) *Bowling Alone: The Collapse and Revival of American Community.* New York: Simon and Schuster.

Putnam, R. (2001) Social capital: Measurement and consequences. *Canadian Journal of Policy Research,* 2(1), pp. 41–51.

Roberts, S.T. (2019) Behind the Screen. In *Behind the Screen.* New Haven, CT: Yale University Press, pp. 20–32.

Rosen, G. (2019) Community1 Standards Enforcement Report, November 2019 Edition. *Facebook Newsroom,* https://about.fb.com/news/2019/11/community-standards-enforcement-report-nov-2019/ (accessed 22 December 2019).

Rosen, G. and Bickert, M. (2021) Our response to the violence in Washington. Facebook Newsroom, https://about.fb.com/news/2021/01/responding-to-the-violence-in-washington-dc/ (accessed 3 March 2023).

Scott, M. and Kayali, L. (2020) What happened when humans stopped managing social media content. *Politico,* 21 October, www.politico.eu/article/facebook-content-moderation-automation/ (accessed 3 March 2023).

Scrivens, R. and Conway, M. (2019) The Roles of 'Old' and 'New' Media Tools and Tin the Facilitation of Violent Extremism and Terrorism. In: Leukfeldt, R. and Holt, T.J. (eds), *The Human Factor of Cybercrime.* London: Routledge, pp. 286–309.

Sonderby, C. (2019) Update on New Zealand. Facebook Newsroom, 18 March, https://about.fb.com/news/2019/03/update-on-new-zealand/ (accessed 22 September 2021).

Spring, M. (2020) 'Stop the steal': The deep roots of Trump's 'voter fraud' strategy. *BBC News,* 23 November, www.bbc.co.uk/news/blogs-trending-55009750 (accessed 23 September 2021).

Suzor, N. P. (2019) *Lawless: The Secret Rules that Govern Our Digital Lives.* Cambridge: Cambridge University Press.

TikTok (2020) WHO to livestream on TikTok. TikTok Newsroom, https://newsroom.tiktok.com/en-us/who-to-livestream-on-tiktok (accessed 23 September 2021).

Tony Blair Institute for Global Change (2020) Snapshot: How extremist groups are responding to Covid-19, https://institute.global/sites/default/files/2020-05/Snapshot%203%20COVID19%20V02.pdf (accessed 3 March 2023).

Twitter (2021) Permanent suspension of @realDonaldTrump. *Twitter Blog*, https://blog.twitter.com/en_us/topics/company/2020/suspension.html (accessed 23 September 2021).

Twitter Public Policy (2020) Stepping up our work to protect the public conversation around Covid-19. *Twitter Blog*, https://blog.twitter.com/en_us/topics/company/2020/stepping-up-our-work-to-protect-the-public-conversation-around-covid-19.html (accessed 3 March 2023).

Twitter Safety (2021) An update following the riots in Washington, DC. *Twitter Blog*, https://blog.twitter.com/en_us/topics/company/2021/protecting--the-conversation-following-the-riots-in-washington--.html (accessed 23 September 2021).

Watkin, A. and Conway, M. (2022) Building social capital to counter polarization? An analysis of tech platforms' official blog posts. *First Monday*, 27(5)

Weimann, G. (2004) *WWW.Terror.Net: How Modern Terrorism Uses the Internet: Special Report*. Washington, DC: United States Institute of Peace.

Weimann, G. (2010) Terror on Facebook, Twitter, and Youtube. *The Brown Journal of World Affairs*, 16(2), pp. 45–54.

Williams, H.J., Evans, A.T., Mueller, E.E., Downing, B. and Ryan, J. (2021) *The Online Extremist Ecosystem: Its Evolution and Framework for Separating Extreme from Mainstream*. Santa Monica, CA: The Rand Corporation.

Wu, P. (2015) Impossible to regulate: Social media, terrorists, and the role for the UN. *Chicago Journal of International Law*, 16(1), Article 11, pp. 281–311.

Yar, M. (2018) A failure to regulate? The demands and dilemmas of tackling illegal content and behaviour on social media. *International Journal of Cybersecurity Intelligence & Cybercrime*, 1(1), pp. 5–20.

Zhu, A. (2020) Supporting our global health workers. TikTok Newsroom, https://newsroom.tiktok.com/en-us/supporting-our-global-health-workers (accessed 23 September 2021).

Ziems, C., He, B., Soni, S. and Kumar, S. (2020) Racism is a virus: Anti-Asian hate and counterhate in social media during the Covid-19 crisis. *arXiv preprint arXiv:2005.12423*.

PART II

Country cases

7
FRANCE

Francesca Scrinzi

Over the past decade, France has become one of the main European targets of jihadist violence, being heavily affected by the 'home-grown' terrorism and 'foreign fighters' phenomena. The country has also seen rising activism and visibility of extreme right movements and a surge of anti-Semitic incidents. Indeed, emergent challenges seem instead to point to the growing activism and legitimacy of right-wing extremism: counterterrorism officers recently claimed that, although no operational links were identified between US-based groups and French extremists, groups espousing conspiracy theories such as QAnon are influencing the French extreme right as well as, more broadly, Europe (Barnes 2021).

The French context is marked by an important colonial history and long-standing Islamophobia as well as substantial Muslim social and spatial discrimination. Immigration has been intensely politicised since the 1980s, favouring the emergence of the most successful and long-lived populist radical right party in Europe, the *Front National* (National Front, since 2018, renamed *Rassemblement National*, 'National Gathering' or National Rally). All this can fuel the extreme right but also resentment in the Muslim population, which can provide fertile ground for jihadist extremism.

This chapter will, first, discuss the history and recent developments of both jihadist and right-wing extremism, and second, existing measures aiming at countering terrorism and preventing radicalisation in France: these have disproportionately focused on violent jihadism while right-wing extremism has been marginal both in debates and policy. The discussion will locate these phenomena and policies in the specifics of the French historical, political, and cultural context, shaped by an emphasis on secularism as a 'civil religion'. Since the French Revolution, a long-standing conflict between clerical and anticlerical forces has animated national history: this came to an end at the start of the twentieth century, as republican forces prevailed and secularism was institutionalised. While the Catholic legacy still profoundly shapes arrangements of the 'secular' public sphere, the Church has limited influence on politics and religiosity levels are low. Together with secularism – *laïcité* – the republican values of *liberté*, *égalité*, and *fraternité*, inherited from the French Revolution, are closely associated with nationhood and constitute a powerful source of political legitimacy. The so-called French republican model of integration and citizenship is based on principles of universalism and individualism: 'civic nationalism' requires citizens to compromise their religious faith in public. Citizenship is based on the prescriptive distinction between the public political sphere, which should remain 'neutral', and the private sphere, where the display of religious and cultural specificities is tolerated (Brubaker 1992). Since the 1990s, Islam and *laïcité* became central to debates on EU integration, non-French nationals' voting rights, and the *sans-papiers* movement. Issues of religious and cultural difference increasingly overlapped, as public discourses emphasised the supposedly difficult integration of post-colonial Arab migrants, represented as Muslims rather than as migrants. This narrative targets the migrants' and ethnic minorities' alleged 'communitarianism', or cultural sectarianism, as divisive of the Republic. In the wake of the recent terrorist attacks, *laïcité* has been increasingly regarded, framed, and implemented in an exclusionary manner. Today, an 'ideological laicism' (Sealy and Modood 2021, p. 32) informs the public discourse on terrorism and counter-terrorism. In particular, the 2020 attacks in Conflans and Nice reinforced a 'tough' understanding of *laïcité* and were followed by a crackdown against mosques and Muslim associations. In the same year, President Emmanuel Macron claimed that this principle is key to France's counterterrorism policy, employing warlike language in arguing for a struggle against 'separatism' (Ragazzi 2016).

Jihadist extremism in France

France has been the target of so-called Islamist attacks since the 1990s. At the time of the Civil War fought between the Algerian government and Islamist groups, an airplane hijacking and a series of bombings were perpetrated in Paris and other cities by the Armed Islamic Group in 1993 and 1995. Almost 20 years later, successive attacks have been conducted by jihadist extremists and 'lone wolves', starting in 2012 in Toulouse and Montauban; 2015 witnessed the deadliest attacks on French soil: the shooting at the Charlie Hebdo satirical magazine headquarters and the attacks by gunmen and suicide bombers throughout Paris, all claimed by Islamic State; 2016 saw two further lethal attacks inspired by jihadism. In 2015, it was estimated that almost 2,000 French nationals had travelled to Iraq and Syria, making France the largest source of 'foreign fighters' in Europe (Campelo et al. 2018; Counter-Extremism Project 2021).

The recent wave of terrorist attacks has amplified anxieties around migrant integration and Islam – issues that have been intensely politicised and mediatised for over three decades. In particular, since 2015 fierce debates have developed around the causes of jihadist radicalisation and violence. These have been shaped by prominent scholars whose positions, while not entirely contradictory, have been polarised in public debates. On the one hand, Gilles Kepel's thesis regards cognitive radicalisation as a major root of extremist violence. In this view, while not automatically resulting in jihadism, Salafist ideology is a prerequisite of jihadism (Kepel 20014; 2016). On the other hand, Olivier Roy sees jihadist extremism and violence as partially independent from Salafist practice and ideology: rather than being associated with religion – as a radicalisation of Islam – radicalisation should be seen as a generational revolt of disenfranchised youth – as an 'islamisation of radicalisation' (Roy 2008; 2015). Thus, while Roy offers a more sociological interpretation, inscribing jihadist engagement in the macro-context of secularisation and globalisation, as well as in the individual actors' trajectories (Roy 2004), Kepel presents a more religious and theological vision, while also emphasising the relevance of the global context, referring for instance to the role played by US-led 'global wars' and secret services in Afghanistan (Kepel 2016). Considering Saudi-sponsored Islam as a major player in jihadist radicalisation in France, and regarding this as a phenomenon 'imported' from the Middle East, Kepel's stance has been viewed as an essentialist approach lying in continuity with Samuel Huntington's thesis on the 'clash of civilisations' (Conti 2018). However, some scholars note that Kepel's and Roy's interpretations are compatible, as both authors locate jihadism in global trends and reach the same conclusion 'that Islam is the cover for radicalisation and not its main cause' (Blanc 2020, p. 217). Others point out that the two authors concur on the significance of identity in explaining radicalisation, arguing that that this 'occurs as individuals seek to reconstruct a lost identity in a perceived hostile and confusing world' (Dalgaard-Nielsen 2010, p. 499). Finally, regretting that studies of jihadist radicalisation are not, with rare exceptions (Khosrokhavar 2014), grounded in empirical research, others stress that both Kepel's and Roy's research is largely based on secondary sources such as judiciary profiles and jihadist texts, which introduces a significant bias in understanding the actors' motives (Conti 2018).

It is Kepel's view that seems to have prevailed in the polity, being mobilised by different politicians from the left to the right of the political spectrum (Samaan and Jacobs 2020). Indeed, focusing on the foreign and exogenous ideological roots of radicalisation, Kepel's arguments 'resonate' with dominant framings of immigration and national belonging that have been mainstreamed in French public debates for decades. These focused on overlapping issues of religious and cultural difference, emphasising the supposedly difficult integration of post-colonial Arab migrants, who were increasingly represented as Muslims rather than as migrants. Since then, a 'republican school of thought' (Baubérot 2012, p. 52) has been prominent in French debates on immigration, making *laïcité* an emblem of national identity and targeting the migrants and ethnic minorities for their alleged unwillingness to assimilate. According to Baubérot (2012), this 'new French secularism' should be distinguished from the historical secularism that developed towards the end of nineteenth century. While the latter developed as a response to the clerical threat jeopardising loyalty to the republican nation-state, the former reacts to decolonisation and immigration, and is set in the context of France's declining geopolitical influence in the globalised world. Others mention a contemporary 'republican racism' discourse (Tevanian 2007) functioning through reference to an exclusionary idea of *laïcité*. Such exclusionary framing of secularism has been employed in gendered ways in successive debates on Muslim veiling: issues of secularism were mobilised by representatives of various political forces from left to right, framing Islam as patriarchal and France as the summit of women's freedom. For example, profound divisions emerged in the feminist and antiracist movements around the proposed law banning the wearing of 'conspicuous signs' of religious affiliation in public schools, which was passed in 2004. While antiracist feminists argued that the bill was informed by a 'neo-colonialist' approach targeting Muslim girls, 'republican feminists' supported it as a means to increase gender equality, seeing secularism as the best guarantee for women's emancipation (Scott 2007).

In the deepened political polarisation that followed the 2015 attacks, these discourses crystallised into even more rigid representations of secularism and French liberties threatened by 'communitarianism'. The Charlie Hebdo attacks were seen as targeting the freedom of expression and fundamental French institutional values. Prime Minister Manuel Valls described them as an assault led by 'Islamofascism' against the Republic. In dominant discourses, the threat of 'communitarianism' was associated with the *banlieues*, dilapidated suburbs largely inhabited by racialised people with high unemployment rates and low levels of education (Moran 2017). In 2020, President Emmanuel Macron declared that the Republic should be protected against 'Islamic separatism' and called for building an 'Islam of Enlightenment' (*Islam des Lumières*), free from foreign influences (Sandford 2020). In 2021, the Minister of Higher Education and Research, Frédérique Vidal aligned with these framings of secularism, declaring that '*islamo-gauchisme*[1]' (Islamo-leftism) is a gangrene of French society (Le Monde 2021). As the state emphasised the institutional and legal integration of Islam, Muslim organisations have appeared divided. While the French Council of the Muslim Faith (*Conseil français du culte musulman*, CFCM), the umbrella organisation for Muslim groups, signed the anti-extremism charter championed by President Emmanuel Macron in 2021, three Islamic organisations, including two catering for French of Turkish origins, rejected it (Arslan 2021). Divisions among French Muslims were exacerbated by the wider international context: severe diplomatic tensions emerged between France and Turkey when President Erdogan criticised Macron's policy against violent Jihadism (France24 2021).

In 2022, it was decided that CFCM, undermined by this internal dissent, would be replaced with a grassroots-style Forum of the Islam of France (FORIF) (RFI 2022).

This emphasis in public debates on the 'foreign' ideological roots of radicalisation indirectly served to downplay socio-economic issues (Samaan and Jacobs 2020). Instead, recent scholarship has pointed to socio-economic drivers of jihadist radicalisation in France, linking it with the economic deprivation, political exclusion, discrimination, and stigmatisation affecting Muslims (Kaya 2021). France is home to an important Muslim population, which prevalently originates from northern Africa, is on average much younger than the overall population, and is mainly concentrated in highly urbanised areas: 8.6 per cent of the population is of Islamic faith (Dell'Isola 2021). Many Muslim migrants came to France from the former colonies of Algeria, Morocco, and Tunisia in the 1950s and 1960s, recruited to work in the expanding national economy; subsequently, since the 1970s, Muslims have arrived from Turkey and western Africa. While French Muslims display an important ethnic and linguistic diversity, most are Sunni (Andre et al. 2015). Although today Islam represents the second religion in the country, a historically established unequal treatment of 'new' religions, including Islam, persists (Blanc 2020). Most Muslims are employed in low-skilled industrial jobs and are affected by higher level of unemployment compared to the overall population (Dell'Isola 2021). In 2005, riots broke out in the *banlieues* surrounding Paris and other cities: these did not express any political or religious claims but represented a protest against the poor living conditions in the suburbs and discrimination experienced in the wider society (Moran 2017).

As discussed, the *banlieues* have been increasingly represented in public debates as examples of failed republican integration and, more recently, as 'hotbeds' of radicalisation. Indeed, they are characterised by high levels of crime and young local inhabitants are over-represented among prison inmates, particularly those of Muslim background. However, empirical research demonstrated that it is the prison institutions that play an active role in the spiral of the radicalisation process: this is seen as a co-production between extremist organisations and their opponents, particularly in the prison context: 'a "fundamentalist" version of secularism might encourage the violent radicalisation of people who, otherwise, would stick to Islamic fundamentalism' (Khroshovar 2014).

Right-wing extremism in France

Similar to the discussion on processes of jihadism in France, this section argues that issues of religion and secularism are important and recurrent elements shaping historical and contemporary developments of French right-wing extremism. Since the French Revolution this has included monarchists, traditionalist Catholics, and those nostalgic of colonialism, particularly French Algeria (Betz 2018). Alongside republican nationalism, which is rooted in the Revolution, an anti-egalitarian and anti-republican radical nationalism has periodically emerged. In the nineteenth century, this was embodied by different movements such as the Boulangist nationalist movement, hostile to the parliamentary regime: theoretician Maurice Barrès discarded the universalist republican concept of the nation inherited by the French Revolution to support a conservative and deterministic view of society. Similarly, Charles Maurras's monarchist *Action française* supported the restoration of the Bourbon monarchy and, after the 1905 law separating Church and State, of Catholicism as the state religion. It advocated the return to a pre-Revolutionary social order, seeing Church and family as the primordial organic structures underpinning authority and hierarchy in society (Goodliffe 2012). Catholicism provided a key rhetorical basis for reasserting the social and moral order promoted by these movements (Passmore 2000). Later, under Marshall Pétain's Vichy regime (whose leading cadre had Maurrassian and integralist Catholic affiliations), nationalism was centred on the idealisation of the French peasant community and its rural virtues. After World War II, a similar idealised representation of the people was espoused by the Poujadist movement, a populist anti-tax movement representing the petty bourgeoisie and upholding conservative Catholic values such as the traditional family (Winock 1994). While several strands of French right-wing extremism have thus relied on the nexus between nation and Catholicism, mobilising religion as a symbol of the nation, others sat on the opposite edge of the secularist cleavage. Starting in the 1970s, right-wing intellectuals of the New Right, gathered in the groups GRECE and *Club de l'Horloge*, elaborated new repertoires to express anti-egalitarian racist views by emphasising the need for preserving cultural differences and drawing on anti-Christianism as a structuring element of a new right-wing paganism (Mammone 2015).

As discussed, immigration has been increasingly politicised in France since the 1980s in the context of decolonisation, economic restructuring, and, later on, EU integration. Different actors beyond the extreme right have played a role in establishing a political climate of 'moral panic' around immigration and Islam. The populist radical right party FN (*Front national*), founded and led by Jean-Marie Le Pen, formerly a Poujadist politician, emerged and grew electorally in the 1980s and 1990s, successfully framing immigration as the social problem *par excellence* (Rydgren 2004). The 2002–2005 period was dominated by the political and mediatic figure of Nicolas Sarkozy, then leader of the conservative party UMP (*Union pour un Mouvement Populaire*). The conservative right radicalised its positions on immigration and 'law and order' to win back the voters attracted by FN hard-line anti-immigration discourses, powerfully contributing to the mainstreaming of xenophobic ideas (Carvalho 2014). More recently, Marine Le Pen took over from her father as leader of the FN in 2011, defeating her opponent Bruno Gollnisch, who represented the conservative Catholic fringe. With the declared objective of transforming the FN into a mainstream party with a vocation to govern, she has appropriated a republican repertoire at odds with the historical anti-egalitarian extreme right. Seeking to enlarge electoral support and build a more respectable public image, the 'second FN' (Wieviorka 2012, p. 35) presents itself as the defender of republican unity against 'communitarianism' and the 'Islamisation' of France. However, despite Le Pen's efforts to 'de-demonise' her party, a substantial continuity can be observed in terms of the FN ideology, electorate, and organisation (Mayer 2018). Rather than disappearing, anti-Semitism in the FN discourse has moved from being overt to being covert: while taking a distance from historical anti-Semitism and fascism, Marine Le Pen attacks all 'communitarian associations', including the main French Jewish community and Jewish student organisations, stigmatising them based on 'republicanised' grounds. Further, while some of the most radical members have been expelled, the FN retains connections with extreme right organisations.

Beyond party politics, various extreme right movements that adopt street politics are active in France. Such non-party actors include *Les Identitaires* (The Identitarians), which rallies for so-called French patriots, attacking Islam and globalisation. This movement, initially called *Bloc Identitaire* (Identitarian Block), emerged at the start of the 2000s as an ethno-regionalist formation including groups of the extreme right subcultures such as sport associations and music bands. It targeted youth by organising community-building activities like concerts and excursions (Bouron 2015). Further non-party actors are active on the extreme right, such as *Civitas* (Civitas Institute), gathering traditionalist Catholic associations calling for a greater role of religion in society and politics; and the secularist and Islamophobic *Riposte Laïque* (Secular Counter-attack). These groups have been bolstered in the context of the 'anti-gender' mobilisations that developed in 2012 to counter the proposed law on same-sex marriage. The most active movement has been *La Manif Pour Tous* (The Demonstration for All), which gathers traditionalist Catholic groups opposing gender+ equality. Further, in the context of the so-called refugee crisis, some extreme right groups have staged confrontational and spectacular actions to exert pressure on policymakers. At this time, in public debates, concerns around the management of the migrants stranded by the North Sea near Calais combined with anxieties around jihadist terrorism. The Identitarians have presented themselves as offering answers to French citizens concerned by the 'Calais' jungle', while *Civitas* and *Riposte Laïque* accused the media of silencing the truth about immigration and Islamisation, allegedly covered up by the national and EU corrupt élites (Castelli Gattinara 2018; Castelli Gattinara and Froio 2021). More recently, in the context of the pandemic, both the radical right and the extreme right have exploited the anti-vaccine movement, mobilising around the so-called sanitary dictatorship. Since 2020, both the *Patriotes* (Patriots) party, led by Florian Philippot, formerly a key FN representative, and Jacline Mouraud, former leading activist of the Yellow Vests, a populist grassroots movement protesting for economic justice since 2018, have joined demonstrations against the sanitary pass. Marine Le Pen too has attacked the government's Covid restrictions, claiming that the measures are an attack on citizens' liberties. As in other European countries, the anti-vaxer movement is radicalised by the extreme right: demonstrators displayed yellow stars as a reference to the Stars of David that Jews were forced to wear under Nazism. In recent years, the royalist extreme right has also benefited from greater visibility and activism. In particular, *Action Française*, founded in the late nineteenth century, maintains its support of a traditional hereditary and anti-parliamentary monarchy and is strongly Eurosceptic: this organisation has been active in southern France, where its members attacked left-wingers demonstrating against labour reform. In 2017, ten people linked to *Action Française* were arrested in relation to a plot to attack mosques, migrants, and politicians (RFI 2017). Finally, there is evidence that the harsh counterterrorism measures implemented in the past few years have crystallised existing anti-Muslim sentiments, leading to a significant increase of hate incidents since 2015 (Bartolucci 2017). In the same years, a surge of anti-Semitic incidents was observed. Reports of the Interior ministry indicated for instance that anti-Semitic incidents jumped by 74 per cent in 2018 to 541, up from 311 in 2017. This is partly related to violent jihadism: several victims of 'lone wolf' attacks were Jewish (Counter-Extremism Project 2021).

The activism and visibility of these non-party extreme right actors should be located in the wider context of the mainstreaming of anti-immigration politics and the FN 'informal co-optation' (Carvalho 2014) by the conservative right. Besides ideological continuities, there are organisational linkages between the electoral and protest arenas. For instance, *Génération Identitaire* (Identity Generation), the youth organisation of the Identitarians – which was dissolved in 2021 for inciting hate and violence – endorsed

Marine Le Pen in the 2017 presidential elections, and some movement activists have been included in local FN electoral lists. This indicates that growing right-wing extremism lies in some continuity with ideologies diffused in the broader society and political arena. In the French context, this is importantly linked to the widespread use of exclusionary framings of secularism across the political spectrum, in both the electoral and protest arenas. This represents a crucial resource for the right-wing extremists in their attempts to secure legitimacy and normalise their ideas (Froio 2018).

Countering and preventing violent extremism: French policies and practices

France has a well-established counterterrorism approach, targeting both extremist violent behaviour and cognitive radicalisation: it mainly focuses on surveillance, repression, and prosecution (Hellmuth 2015). In line with the state's centralised nature, French policies deploy a stringent top-down approach, relying on the close relationship between anti-terrorism investigating judges (*juges d'instruction*) and the domestic intelligence service, and giving significant coercive and intrusive powers to the police (Schwarzenbach 2018). This had been initially developed as a response to the attacks by Islamist groups in the 1980s and 1990s. Indeed, this security-oriented approach has been credited for the fact that the country was not affected by any major terrorist attacks between 1986 and 2012 (Bartolucci 2017). Several adaptations of the legislation were made after 9/11, in 2006, and subsequently triggered by successive attacks on French soil in 2012, 2014, and 2015. The 2014 law introduced new measures against 'foreign fighters', 'lone wolves', and internet recruitment. Since the 2015 attacks, a prolonged national state of emergency has been established as the authorities reinforced counterterrorism legislation. Today, the French counterterrorism apparatus is quite exceptional in the European context and has indeed been likened to the US approach (Hellmuth 2015). French legislation has been described as 'draconian' (Foley 2013, p. 316), criminalising the intention to commit a crime. After 2015, the country has combined this security-centred policy with a 'war on terror' through military interventions in Syria, Mali, and Iraq: French governments have argued that the fight against jihadism abroad was necessary to prevent terrorist attacks on national soil, and President Emmanuel Macron has named counterterrorism as his primary foreign policy goal (Samaan and Jacobs 2020).

These counterterrorism measures have led to criticism. First, this is based on the claim that they jeopardise human rights. For example, Amnesty International expressed concern about the prolonged state of emergency and contended that massive repression in the Paris *banlieues*, for instance through raids on Muslim-owned business and mosques, may abet home-grown radicalisation (Mucha 2017). These concerns have been echoed by scholars, arguing that the repressive measures heavily targeting the population of northern African background risk alienating the Muslim communities whose cooperation is key to fighting terrorism (Bartolucci 2017). Others criticised the reliance on detention without charges, the mass arrests of suspects, and the pervasive surveillance, expressing concerns that this could result in a banalisation of exceptional procedures (Bigo 2002). Finally, concern arose in relation to other fundamental rights beyond privacy and the right to a fair trial, such as the freedom of expression. Following the Charlie Hebdo attacks, 54 people were arrested on the grounds of 'apology of terrorism', including the comedian Dieudonné, who said in a Facebook post that he sympathised with one of the Paris gunmen.

Centred on security and repressive measures, French counterterrorism policies have a poor track record in preventing radicalisation or facilitating the disengagement of radicalised individuals (Moran 2017). It is only recently, in 2014, and more importantly in the wake of the 2015 attacks, that French governments, drawing on the experience of other European countries such as Germany and the UK, have turned to implementing 'softer' measures, targeting people believed to be at risk of falling for extremism ideologies, particularly in prisons and schools, as well as local-level programmes of vocational training, family and psychological counselling, and civic education (Quivooij 2016). For instance, the pilot project by the Ministry of Justice 'AMAL' ('hope' in Arabic) aimed at preventing jihadi recidivism in prisons through a series of individual and group conversations. Further initiatives have included a national phone hotline and the internet portal 'Stop-jihadism' addressing the families of 'at-risk' individuals to provide advice, support, and an opportunity to notify the authorities (Hellmuth 2015). Actions implemented to prevent and counter radicalisation are coordinated at the national level by the Inter-Ministerial Committee for the Prevention of Delinquency and Radicalisation, which devises actions, provides training for civil servants, and advises local-level actors (Schwarzenbach 2018). In addition, French authorities have sought to promote a 'French Islam'. In 2015, the *Instance de dialogue avec l'Islam de France* (Instance of Dialogue with French Islam), a formal dialogue between representatives of the French government and Muslim communities, was set up. Finally, a hallmark of French counter-radicalisation efforts is the launch, in 2016, of the first of a series of 'Centres for Prevention, Integration and Citizenship', with the objective of de-radicalising and reintegrating individuals convicted of jihadist terrorism. However, the programme was halted following a parliamentary commission declaring it a failure (Benbassa and Troendlé 2017).

Reflecting the Republican model of integration, French counter-radicalisation policies emphasise the value of *laïcité* and generally avoid any discussion of or reference to religious issues: differing from other European countries, 'France has either neglected the role of religion in the field of de-radicalisation or understood religious deradicalisation as a "neutralisation" of religion' (Schwarzenbach 2018, p. 116). Moreover, French policies carefully omit any measures that disproportionately target religious minorities; instead, most actions are addressed to the whole population, with a view to enhancing awareness of republican values among all citizens, irrespective of their religious and ethnic background. In a similar vein, the *Instance de dialogue avec l'Islam de France* appears quite exceptional in the overall action of French governments (Hellmuth 2015). Resilience-building initiatives based on interfaith dialogue have been developed, whose impact however is limited by their small size and grassroots level nature (Magazzini 2020).

Criticism has been levelled at this approach in relation to various aspects. Experts and scholars have advocated the need for a greater involvement of Muslim élites in counter-radicalisation efforts, as mediators but also in more active roles. Similarly, they have claimed that counter-radicalisation measures should directly engage with religious and theological issues (Conesa 2014; Hellmuth 2015). This was also stressed by a report produced by a former French government official, claiming that 'the presence of theological aspects in the jihadist movement shows that there is need for a theological counter-discourse' (Pietrasanta 2015). More specifically, the role of imams in prisons has received growing public scrutiny, as the authorities increasingly call upon moderate Muslim religious leaders to oppose the influence of radicalised inmates acting as imams. Experts have called for improving the training, status, and legitimacy of Muslim prison chaplains as well as for an increase in their ranks. Issues arise regarding the imams' qualification: there is no formal education for Muslim spiritual leaders, and prison imams are volunteers in precarious working conditions, which in turn makes it difficult to attract viable candidates (Mucha 2017). Related to this, experts have tackled the use of theological arguments in counter- or de-radicalisation programmes and the need for improving the management of the diverse 'profiles' of individuals considered at risk of radicalisation, which include converts and women: due to their different social positioning and experiences, it is unlikely that the same theological arguments will appeal to them. Indeed, it is a subject of great debate as to which target groups and at which stages of the (de)radicalisation process might certain theological arguments be most effective. Moreover, different schools of Islamic thought could be mobilised to counter the Salafi-jihadist ideology (Kudlacek 2020).

Finally, further policy recommendations include implementing a systematic scientific evaluation of the successes and weaknesses of existing actions, with a view to identifying 'good practices' and sustaining a comprehensive national-level policy of counter-radicalisation: current recommendations, mainly following the EU approach, do not go beyond providing a legal framework. Drawing on the example of other countries such as Germany, the experts also call for a greater involvement of local actors and NGOs, for instance Muslim associations and organisations providing psychological support services (Kudlacek 2020; Schwarzenbach 2018).

Concluding remarks

Located in a context marked by high political and ideological polarisation, French jihadist and right-wing extremism as well as counterterrorism and counter-radicalisation policies are significantly shaped by the distinctive republican model of integration and its relegation of religion to the private sphere. The French security-oriented counterterrorism approach, which is well-established due to its being implemented and strengthened in the last two decades in response to the terrorist attacks of the 1990s, faces the challenge of reconciling security with dignity and human rights. Instead, counter-radicalisation policies are still 'vague, improvised, and sporadic' (Hellmuth 2015, p. 31) and public debate on resilience is almost absent. The efficacy of those recent resilience-building initiatives that attempted to address issues of socio-economic deprivation and of ethno-religious inequalities, has to some extent been limited by a security-led character which has been forced upon preventive actions (Magazzini 2020). Most importantly, prevention programmes are silent about religious issues in countering and preventing radicalisation and therefore 'hampered by divisions over the role of Islam': debates are likely to continue regarding this 'bone of contention' of counter-radicalisation strategy (Quivooij 2016, p. ii).

Whether an approach that avoids targeting specific ethnic and religious communities is fairer and more effective than those adopted in other countries such as Germany or the UK has been questioned (Schwarzenbach 2018). On the one hand, as it has been argued in other national contexts too, counterterrorism and counter-radicalisation policies may fuel extremism rather than counter it, as 'the fight against radicalisation may produce discriminatory narratives and practices that increase feelings of stigmatisation and injustice and reinforce a culture of mistrust and suspicion' (Conti 2020, p. 3, Khosrokhavar 2014). While promoting shared experiences and feelings of national belonging has a great potential in countering polarisation and extremism, this effort can be jeopardised by a distorted and exclusionary use of *laïcité* rather than as a democratic and inclusive principle (Quivooij 2016). It is also necessary to shift public debate through reframing issues of immigration and radicalisation, as political and ideological polarisation benefits both jihadist and right-wing extremists by alienating the Muslim population and mainstreaming xenophobic views: greater attention should be given to issues such as labour, tax, or pension reforms to also expose that the supposedly 'civilisational' and religious divide is indeed defined by socio-economic grievances (Mucha 2017).

On the other hand, various interventions support the view that the historical inclusive secularism and 'colour-blind values', as opposed to its derogatory contemporary uses, 'could act as a counterbalancing protective factor' against jihadist radicalisation and that they should not be hastily dismissed as a resource to counter intolerance and racism; these also point 'that secular criticism of religion, and Islam in particular, does not correlate with anti-Muslim prejudice' (Adam-Troian 2021, pp. 52–53). These interventions focus in particular on the school as an environment where critical thinking can be promoted among the younger generations, based on principles of rationality and argumentation, for instance around issues of disinformation and conspiracy theories. Indeed, the Charlie Hebdo attacks, and more recently Samuel Paty's murder, exposed the difficulties that teachers face in managing discussions around such issues as well as on *laïcité* and freedom of speech, showing the need for training programmes to engage in these difficult conversations (James 2020).

Future steps in countering radicalisation in France should also consider that, so far, radicalisation research and policymaking has disproportionately focused on jihadist extremism. Further debate and initiatives targeting right-wing extremism are needed in the context of the rising threat coming from these groups, including, as discussed, in relation to the role played by dominant understandings and practices of secularism in this country.

Note

1 An expression coined to attack those (left-wing) actors who criticise the mainstreaming of Islamophobia or support identity politics and antiracist claims, and to accuse them of abdicating the defence of democratic secularism or colluding with jihadist extremists.

References

Adam-Troian, Jais (2021) The French (non) connection: A closer look at the role of secularism and socio-educational disparities on domestic Islamist radicalization in France. *Journal for Deradicalization*, 24, pp. 39–66.
Andre Virginie, Mansouri, Fethi and Lobo, Michele (2015) A fragmented discourse of religious leadership in France: Muslim youth between citizenship and radicalization. *Journal of Muslim Minority Affairs*, 35(2), pp. 296–313.
Arslan, Berna Zengin (2021) Reforming Islam or reforming laïcité? Institutional and legal integration of Islam in France. *Berkley Forum*, 4 June, https://berkleycenter.georgetown.edu/responses/reforming-islam-or-reforming-laicite-institutional-and-legal-integration-of-islam-in-france
Barnes, Julian E. (2021) U.S. Antigovernment Groups Are Influencing the French Far Right, *The New York Times*, 13 October, www.nytimes.com/2021/10/13/us/politics/france-far-right-extremists-qanon.html
Bartolucci, Valentina (2017) The Perils and Prospects of the French Approach to Counterterrorism. In: Romaniuk et al. (eds), *The Palgrave Handbook of Global Counterterrorism Policy*. London: Palgrave Macmillan, pp. 437–458.
Baubérot, Jean (2012) The Evolution of French Secularism. In: Ghosh, Ranjan (ed.), *Making Sense of the Secular*. New York and Abingdon: Routledge, pp. 44–55
Benbassa, Esther and Troendlé, Catherine (2017) Désendoctrinement, désembrigadement et réinsertion des djihadistes en France et en Europe. Sénat, www.senat.fr/rap/r16-633/r16-633.html
Betz, Hans-Georg (2018) The Radical Right and Populism. In: Rydgren, Jens (ed.), *The Oxford Handbook of the Radical Right*. Oxford University Press, DOI: 10.1093/oxfordhb/9780190274559.013.5
Bigo, Didier (2002) L'impact des mesures anti-terroristes sur l'équilibre entre liberté et sécurité et sur la cohésion sociale en France. In: Bribosia, E and Weyembergh, A. (eds), *La lutte contre le terrorisme et les droits fondamentaux*. Brussels: Nemesis/Bruylant, pp. 221–227

Blanc, Maurice (2020) The Place of Islam Within a Secular France and Europe: How to Avoid the Traps of the So-Called Islamic Extremism? In: Blanc, M., Droeber, J. and Storrie, T. (eds), *Citizenship and Religion: A Fundamental Challenge for Democracy*. Cham: Palgrave Macmillan, pp. 203–230.

Bouron, Samuel (2015) 'Un militantisme à deux faces', *Agone*, 54, pp. 45–72.

Brubaker, Rogers (1992) *Citizenship and Nationhood in France and Germany*. Cambridge, MA: Harvard University Press.

Campelo, Nicolas et al. (2018) Joining the Islamic State from France between 2014 and 2016: an observational follow-up study. *Palgrave Communications*, 4, p. 137.

Carvalho, João (2014) *Impact of Extreme Right Parties on Immigration Policy*. London and New York: Routledge.

Castelli Gattinara, Pietro (2018) Europeans, Shut the Borders! Anti-refugee Mobilisation in Italy and France. In: della Porta, Donatella (ed.), *Solidarity Mobilizations in the 'Refugee Crisis*. Cham: Palgrave Macmillan, pp. 271–297.

Castelli Gattinara, Pietro and Caterina Froio (2021) Politicising Europe on the far right: Anti-EU mobilization across the party and non-party sector in France. *Social Movement Studies*, 21(1-2), pp. 199–215.

Conesa, Pierre (2014) *Quelle politique de contre-radicalisation en France?* Paris: Fondation d'aide aux victims du terrorisme (FAVT).

Conti, Bartolomeo (2018) Une radicalisation religieuse? Politique, religion et subjectivité dans les processus de radicalisation. Paris: Centre d' études des mouvements sociaux (CEMS) Ecole des Hautes Etudes en Sciences Sociales, https://halshs.archives-ouvertes.fr/halshs-03089691/document

Conti, Bartolomeo (2020) Case studies of interactive radicalisation. France, DARE – Dialogue About Radicalisation and Equality, European Union's H2020 research and innovation programme, grant agreement no. 693221.

Counter-Extremism Project (2021) France: Extremism and Terrorism, www.counterextremism.com/countries/france

Dalgaard-Nielsen, Anja (2010) Violent radicalisation in Europe: What we know and what we do not know. *Studies in Conflict and Terrorism*, 33(9), pp. 797–814.

Dell'Isola, Davide (2021) Discrimination against Muslims, the role of networks and terrorist attacks in Western Europe: The cases of United Kingdom, France, and Italy. *Italian Political Science Review/Rivista Italiana di Scienza Politica*, 52, pp. 1–16.

Foley, Frank (2013) *Countering Terrorism in Britain and France: Institutions, Norms and the Shadow of the Past*. Cambridge: Cambridge University Press.

France24 (2021) French Muslim groups at odds over Macron's anti-extremism charter. *France24.com*, Europe, 21 January, www.france24.com/en/europe/20210121-french-muslim-groups-at-odds-over-macron-s-anti-extremism-charter.

Froio, Caterina (2018) Race, religion, or culture? Framing Islam between racism and neo-racism in the online network of the French far right. *Perspectives on Politics*, 16(3), pp. 696–709.

Goodliffe, Gabriel (2012) *The Resurgence of the Radical Right in France*. New York: Cambridge University Press.

Hellmuth, Dorle (2015) Countering jihadi radicals and foreign fighters in the United States and France: très similaire. *Journal for Deradicalization*, 4, pp. 1–43.

James, Johnathan (2020) Teaching anti-terrorism: how France and England use schools to counter radicalisation, *The Conversation*, 1 December, https://theconversation.com/teaching-anti-terrorism-how-france-and-england-use-schools-to-counter-radicalisation-150921.

Kaya, Ayhan (2021) Islamist and nativist reactionary radicalisation in Europe. *Politics and Governance*, 9(3), pp. 204–214.

Kepel, Gilles (2014) *Fitna: Guerre au coeur de l'islam*. Paris: Gallimard.

Kepel, Gilles (2016) *Terreur dans l'Hexagone: Genèse du djihad français*. Paris: Gallimard.

Khosrokhavar, Farhad (2014) *Radicalisation*. Paris: Editions de la Maison des sciences de l'homme.

Kudlacek, Dominic (2020) Prevention of radicalisation in selected European countries A comprehensive report of the state of the art in counter-radicalisation, report PERICLES Policy recommendation and im-proved communication tools for law enforcement and security agencies preventing violent radicalisation, https://radical.hypotheses.org/files/2017/11/Pericles-D1.1-Findings-Report.pdf.

Le Monde (2021) Frédérique Vidal, une ministre de l'enseignement supérieur dans la tourmente. *LeMonde.fr,* 19 February, www.lemonde.fr/societe/article/2021/02/19/frederique-vidal-le-bon-petit-soldat-dans-la-tourmente_6070542_3224.html.

Magazzini, Tina (2020) *Radicalisation and Resilience Case Study France*, GREASE – Resilience, Religion and Radicalisation, http://grease.eui.eu/wp-content/uploads/sites/8/2021/01/WP4-Report_France.pdf.

Mammone, Andrea (2015) *Transnational Neofascism in France and Italy.* Cambridge: Cambridge University Press.

Mayer, Nonna (2018) The Radical Right in France. In: Rydgren, Jens (ed.), *The Oxford Handbook of the Radical Right.* Oxford University Press (Oxford Hanbooks Online), DOI: 10.1093/oxfordhb/9780190274559.013.22

Moran, Matthew (2017) Terrorism and the banlieues: The Charlie Hebdo attacks in context. *Modern & Contemporary France,* 25(3), pp. 315–332.

Mucha, Witold (2017) Polarization, stigmatization, radicalization. Counterterrorism and homeland security in France and Germany. *Journal for Deradicalization,* 10, pp. 230–254.

Passmore, Kevin (2000) Femininity and the Right: From moral order to moral order. *Modern & Contemporary France,* (1), pp. 55–69.

Pietrasanta Sébastian (2015) La déradicalisation, outil de lutte contre le terrorisme. Rapporteur du projet de loi relatif à la lutte contre le terrorisme, www.vie-publique.fr/sites/default/files/rapport/pdf/154000455.pdf.

Quivooij, Romain (2016) *The French Counter-radicalisation Strategy.* RSIS Working Paper, No. 301. Singapore: Nanyang Technological University

Ragazzi, Francesco (2016) Suspect community or suspect category? The impact of counter-terrorism as 'policed multiculturalism'. *Journal of Ethnic and Migration Studies,* 42(5), pp. 724–741.

RFI (2017) French far-right plot to attack mosques, migrants, politicians uncovered. *RFI.fr,* France, 18 October, www.rfi.fr/en/france/20171018-french-far-right-plot-attack-mosques-migrants-politicians-uncovered

RFI (2022) France dumps Muslim advisory council that is 'under foreign influence. *RFI.fr,* France, 1 February, www.rfi.fr/en/france/20220201-france-dumps-muslim-advisory-council-under-foreign-influence-cfcm-islam-darmanin

Rydgren, Jens (2004) *The Populist Challenge: Political Protest and Ethno-Nationalist Mobilization in France.* New York: Berghahn Books.

Roy, Olivier (2004) *Globalised Islam.* London: Hurst.

Roy, Oliver (2008) *La Sainte Ignorance. Le temps de la religion sans culture.* Paris: Seuil

Roy, Oivier (2015) Le djihadisme est une révolte nihiliste. Le Monde, 25 November.

Samaan, Jean-Loup and Jacobs, Andreas (2020) Countering jihadist terrorism: A comparative analysis of French and German experiences. *Terrorism and Political Violence,* 32(2), pp. 401–415.

Sandford, Alasdair (2020) Macron and Islam: What has the French president actually said to outrage the Muslim world? *Euronews,* 2 November, www.euronews.com/2020/11/02/macron-and-islam-what-has-the-french-president-actually-said-to-outrage-the-muslim-world.

Schwarzenbach, Anina (2018) Fighting the 'Threat from Within': France and Its Counter-Radicalization Strategy. In: Vidino, Lorenzo (ed.), *De-Radicalization in the Mediterranean. Comparing Challenges and Approaches.* Milan: Ledizioni LediPublishing, pp. 21–33.

Scott, Joan Wallach (2007) *The Politics of the Veil.* Princeton: Princeton University Press.

Sealy, Thomas and Modood, Tariq (2021) France: From Laïcité to Laicism? In: Triandafyllidou, Anna and Magazzini, Tina (eds), *Routledge Handbook on the Governance of Religious Diversity.* Abingdon: Routledge, 24–34.

Tevanian, Pierre (2007) *La République du mépris: les métamorphoses du racisme dans la France des années Sarkozy.* Paris: La Découverte.

Wieviorka, Michel (2012) *Le Front national entre extrémisme, populisme et démocratie.* Paris: Éditions de la maison des sciences de l'homme.

Winock, Michael (1994) *Histoire de l'extreme droite en France.* Paris: Editions Seuil.

8
UNITED KINGDOM

Tahir Abbas, Richard McNeil-Willson, and Lianne Vostermans

Introduction

In the UK, globalisation, localisation, economic inequality, and social polarisation (Ali 2015), as well as the growth of populist and nationalist movements, have all generated new trends in violent extremism (Bieber 2018). Recent years have seen instances of religiously justified terrorist attacks in the UK, with several linked to the rise and decline of Islamic State. This period has also witnessed a relative increase in far-right extremism and some concern about its impact on local communities and wider society. However, while much academic and policy-oriented scholarship in the UK and elsewhere has focused on the potential solutions to violent extremism, these approaches have been programmatic, responding to predetermined policy directives that converge on objectives that are less concerned with the long-term needs and desires of local communities and more preoccupied with short-term national or international security priorities (Abbas 2021a).

It is perhaps particularly difficult to adequately assess both violent extremism and resilience within the British context. Discussions around extremism are exceedingly polarised and contentious, whilst the UK government's counterterror and counter-extremism programme has, since its centralisation within the Home Office, increasingly moved away from positive community engagement, subsumed in a mire of securitisation stemming from suspect practices and the obscuring of counterterror funding (Birt 2019). Meanwhile, a charged environment associated with reporting extremism has produced judgements and actions laced with racial stereotyping – with public sector workers such as teachers, lecturers, prison officers, doctors, and mental healthcare practitioners legally obliged to report signs of perceived extremism. Widespread concerns from British communities, faith groups, and human rights bodies about the suitability and impact that UK Countering Violent Extremism (CVE) approaches have on community trust and engagement, furthermore, have either been ignored or rebuffed by UK politicians and *Prevent* practitioners as 'enabling terrorism', smeared as 'Islamist agitators and their ideological bedfellows' (Dathan 2022; Baldét 2020). In the UK context, therefore, it is particularly difficult to extricate any 'extremism' from the pervadingly political lens of counter-extremism and entirely questionable as to whether conditions even allow for programmes to build community 'resilience' in light of the political contestation that continues to swirl around British CVE.

The landscape of violent extremism in the UK cannot, therefore, be adequately assessed without concurrent recognition of UK counter-extremism policies, due to both the high levels of politicisation and contestation towards British CVE – perhaps far more so than in other European countries (Mathews and McNeil-Willson 2021). One indicator of this contestation is how successive UK governments have tended to modulate the framing of counter-extremism approaches between the naked prioritisation of so-called Islamist extremism – which problematises Muslim political activism and frames an accused lack of integration as a core mechanism within violent extremism – and approaches that aim to also identify and respond to far-right, 'other', or 'mixed' forms of extremism. The nature of the UK Home Office's counter-extremism *Prevent* programme has seen an already highly politicised and reactive set of policies further caught in the choppy political headwinds of successive Conservative governments. And despite significant political change in Britain since the launch of the Prevent programme and CONTEST strategy in 2003, deep structural problems remain entrenched within an approach that fails not only to find adequate responses to terrorism, but actively advances racial inequalities.

This chapter will look at recent patterns of violent extremism and counter-extremism in Britain under the long shadow of the ongoing War on Terror. It will detail recent patterns of violent extremism in Britain, before deconstructing the historical and social structures that lead to the patterns of extremism and counter-extremism within a UK context, the impact this has had on the normalisation of Islamophobia, and what implications this has for 'resilience-building' against community violence. The Western academy and policy, often led by the UK (Kundnani and Hayes 2012), has constructed a set of industries dealing with radicalisation, deradicalisation, and CVE – yet they are still unable to grapple with questions of cause and effect, diverting attention away from deeper historical and structural challenges that do or do not affect people and their routes to violence (Silva 2018). Britain represents an important case study, one of the first states to adopt widescale counterterror and counter-extremism approaches, and a potential weathervane of how responses to violent extremism may develop – or unravel – in future years.

Patterns of violent extremism and CVE in Britain

Discussions in Britain on the threat of violent extremism have tended to modulate between concern over 'Islamist extremism' and worries about a resurgent European far right. Blunter iterations of countering extremism, designed and implemented in the nascent years of the War on Terror, were openly focused on Muslim communities – such as the Metropolitan Police's Muslim Contact Unit, which centred intelligence gathering operations on Muslim communities in London between 2002 and at least 2008. The UK government's Prevent programme was also built on assumptions of extremism as emanating from Britain's Muslim minorities, with counterterror funding initially allocated to councils and police based on the proportion of Muslim minorities present in each area. However, growing concern about far-right violence – enhanced following the 2019 Christchurch shooting in New Zealand in which the attacker referenced several far-right tropes from the UK – coupled with consistent damning criticism of Prevent as highly Islamophobic, helped to shift discussion, at least in part, towards incorporating some response to far-right violence.

Debate over where the threat of violent extremism comes from, and what form it takes, continues from within HM Government and the Home Office. In 2018, Assistant Commissioner Neil Basu, the national police lead for counterterrorism, stated that 80 per cent of counterterror investigations were connected to what he termed the 'Islamist Jihadist threat' (Perry 2021); whilst a Home Office report stated that, of the 220 people in custody at the time for terrorism-connected offences in Britain, 'the vast majority (70%) were categorised as holding Islamist-extremist views' (Home Office 2021). Meanwhile, the long-delayed government-led Independent Review into Prevent – implemented into law with the 2019 Counterterror and Border Security Bill and subsequently boycotted by many human rights and community groups – has been used by more reactionary elements within and around the government to force the focus back onto Islamically justified forms of violent extremism; the highly controversial review suggesting that, despite recent high profile acts of far-right violence in the West, there is too much focus on far-right extremism, and that its definition has become so broad as to include 'mildly controversial or provocative forms of mainstream, right-wing-leaning commentary' (Elgot and Dodd 2022).

In recent years, the UK government and security services have sought to highlight the changing nature of Islamically justified violent extremism. Whilst the rise of groups like al-Qaeda and Islamic State has traditionally dominated concerns, attacks since the fall of Islamic State have tended to be carried out by individuals with limited planning and a high level of response to opportunity for casual violence. This includes the 2019 London Bridge attack by a prisoner from an offender-rehabilitation programme conference in Fishmongers' Hall, the 2020 Reading stabbings in a public park, the 2021 murder of MP David Amess at his constituency surgery, and a botched attack on Liverpool Women's Hospital in the same year. All involved rudimentary or homemade weaponry, with knives used as the main form of violence, and hint at declining opportunities for larger networks to conduct more significant attacks.

There has also been new focus on the role that prisons may play in violent extremism as sites of radicalisation by authorities. In 2022, the UK government announced an expansion of laws and practices to 'clamp down' on terrorist activities in gaols in England and Wales, seeking to 'isolate more of the most radical terrorists in separation centres'. This also involved an attack on human rights legislation, with the then Justice Secretary Dominic Raab stating that the government 'will prevent terrorists using the Human Rights Act to claim a "right to socialise" in prison' and will not allow 'cultural and religious sensitivities to deter us from nipping in the bud early signs of terrorist risk' (Ministry of Justice 2022). In general, we see a coordinated approach by the UK government to move the dial of counter-extremism back towards Muslims as particularly at risk with regard to violent extremism.

This has, however, taken place in broader societal concern over the rise of far-right violence in Britain. This perceived threat of the far-right has largely centred on diffuse activist organisations, as well as the spread of violent content online – reflecting what is now a highly fragmented far-right scene in the UK. Unlike in many other European states, official far-right parties have failed to make much headway in British electoral politics, partly due to the restrictive First Past the Post system of democratic representation. However, there are conditions specific to the national context that have been cited as enabling far-right activism and ideologies to thrive, including: significant and growing levels of economic and social inequality, political polarisation (Duffy et al. 2019), and the legitimisation of far-right tropes and policies from national government and media. As such, the UK represents an interesting case of how the far-right may represent a present threat to communities and wider society, whilst simultaneously being limited to a low profile, at least in terms of the presence of parties officially classified as such.

Far-right violence has been recognised as a potential threat in recent years, with warnings about right-wing extremism and terrorism entering into the UK Home Office documentation lexicon from the 2011 Prevent Strategy onwards (HM Government 2011). Since then, government counterterror approaches have stressed dangers over a 'far-right ecosystem' that particularly targets young people through social media and online gaming forums (Adams and Weale 2022). As well as growing focus on identifying and reporting far-right extremism in the UK – borne out to some extent in Prevent statistics, which show a broad (but still highly under-representative) increase in far-right referrals – there has also been a number of far-right groups legally proscribed under the Terrorism Act 2000.

Much of the current far-right scene in the UK has grown out of the ruins of more traditional fascist and far-right parties. The British National Party (BNP), for instance, scored some successes in the early years of the twenty-first century, reaching an electoral high for the British far-right following the election of two MEPs in the European Parliament, a seat in the London Assembly, and several counsellors in Barking, Dewsbury, and Burnley. However, internal schisms, the public leaking of membership lists, and an increase in public scrutiny on the BNP following its success, led to a swift decline into irrelevance from 2009 onwards. Britain First, another British pro-fascist party, which split from the BNP in 2011, has been unable to make any electoral gains, even struggling with correct processes for registration via the Electoral Commission. It has been able to glean some fringe support via direct actions (or 'invasions') against mosques and refugee centres. However, this has meant its political activism has largely been constrained to a limited social media presence, and it has been inept in its attempts to establish any kind of recognisable political party structure. Meanwhile, the United Kingdom Independence Party (UKIP), which was at least partly responsible for forcing the issue of the 2016 Brexit referendum onto the British public, has since flirted with increasingly far-right policies and openly Islamophobic rhetoric, although this has coincided with a sharp decline in their pre-referendum electoral gains.

Ultimately, Britain does not seem to offer a success story for openly far-right political parties, although there have been some limited opportunities for activist-centred organisations that eschew traditional politics. These have often taken aim at Muslim minorities in the UK, self-styling themselves as part of a 'counter-jihad' movement, or as acting in protection of White British majority communities (Lee 2016). The English Defence League (EDL), for instance, gained some notoriety by organising rallies against British Muslim communities (Fekete 2017; Pearson 2019), whilst ideological successors such as Pegida UK (2017) or the For Britain Movement (2017–2022) have also used anti-Muslim public activism as a means of gaining publicity. Many of these groups have been heavily centred on a few key individuals, such as Paul Golding, Jayda Fransen, Anne Marie Waters, or Tommy Robinson of the EDL. However, as many such actors have struggled for respectability (and have even become embroiled in successive court cases), their decline has coincided with a decline in their respective movement organisations. Bans against the social media presence of some of these organisations on mainstream platforms, as well as the prevention of their means to raise funds via online fundraising platforms, have also scuppered serious far-right activism. More recent networks that have sought to replace them, however, are slicker in their output and less centralised in their organisation.

One such network is the Identitarian movement. This movement gained prominence following the launch in autumn 2012 of the French *Génération Identitaire*, a group that attacked concepts of multiculturalism by drawing on neo-fascist frames of 'land', 'blood', and 'identity' whilst encouraging irregular forms of street activism (Murdoch and Mulhall 2019, p. 6). Generation Identity offers a highly racialised ideology, which calls for 'ethnopluralism' and the protection of cultural and biological heritage, pushing the 'great replacement' theory of mass migration (Obaidi et al. 2021; Ekman 2022). Since its public emergence, Identitarian movement organisations have been established in countries including Germany, Austria, the

Nordic states, Britain, and Ireland, as well as North America, Russia, South America, and Australia (Zuquete 2018). One of the largest is Generation Identity, active in 2019 in nine European countries and with 63 regional branches (Murdoch and Mulhall 2019, p. 6). It has also been brought under international examination following revelations that the 2019 Christchurch attacker had donated €1,500 to the organisation prior to his attack on New Zealand mosques.

The British context again seems to present a mixed case study of the far-right. Generation Identity was unable to establish a significant foothold in Britain and Ireland, and has since collapsed following splits in the movement, accusations of antisemitism, and anti-racist infiltration (Hope Not Hate 2019). Its possible ideological successor, Patriotic Alternative, founded by neo-Nazi Mark Collett, has attracted some limited support. Such groups have, however, been effective in using guerrilla activism, engaging in acts such as public leafletting and stickering, the unveiling of banners at historic sites, and conducting short bursts of public activism such as its 'White Lives Matter' campaign which, in 2022, coincided with the UN's International Day of the World's Indigenous Peoples. Such tactics have also been recently embraced by British Neo-Nazi networks that have also used stickers, fliers, and banners as a decentralised, cost effective, and impactful means of spreading their views (McNeil-Willson 2020).

There has thus broadly been a decline of far-right parties and only very limited support for protest movements in Britain. The far-right have found themselves further constrained due to the proscribing of groups such as National Action and several of its various aliases, such as Scottish Dawn, NS313 (National Socialist Anti-Capitalist Action), and System Resistance Network. What remains is a more atomised far-right – one that often uses online spaces in place of public platforms and that often seems to have less clear set of ideologies and objectives. New concerns around the far-right have been raised in response to violence from individuals linked to networks around 'Involuntary Celibate' (or 'incel') movements, following a 2021 fatal shooting in Plymouth, as well as the intersections between the Covid-19 pandemic and far-right violent extremism. This has focused on the role that misinformation and conspiracy theories have come to play in far-right activism. Research, however, has challenged the link assumed by UK counterterror practitioners between far-right groups, conspiracy, and misinformation (McNeil-Willson 2020). Whilst the Covid-19 pandemic has seemed to give rise to irregular movements that spread false information rooted in historically racist, anti-migrant tropes (O'Donnell 2019; McNeil-Willson 2022), the oft-assumed link between misinformation and extremism within CVE is unclear and may arguably represent a continuation of the 'creep' of counter-extremism further into societal spaces.

Ultimately, the threat posed by both the far-right and so-called Islamist extremism in Britain cannot be adequately assessed without accounting for its relationship with national governmental and media actors. Whilst counter-extremism programmes such as Prevent have been continuously criticised as targeting Muslims, encouraging Islamophobic stereotyping, and entrenching widespread structural inequality along racial lines (Fernandez, Walker and Younis 2018), its limited approach to the far right has taken place in a wider political context, led by national media and government, that has sought to mainstream racist far-right tropes against migrants and minorities (Winter and Mondon 2020). Where official far-right parties have struggled in mainstream politics, far-right policies and narratives have thrived. Adopted by an increasingly reactionary Conservative Party throughout its time in government, far-right or far-right-adjacent narratives have fed into a racial inequality that has greatly negatively impacted on community cohesion. It is thus important to further examine these community issues and the position that CVE plays within it.

The UK context of (countering) violent extremism

When the 2001 attacks in the US and the London bombings in 2005 occurred, the 'rules of the game changed', to paraphrase then-Prime Minister Tony Blair in a Downing Street speech in the immediate wake of the terrorist attacks (Abbas 2005, 2011). This focus has had serious consequences for Muslim minorities in the Global North and Muslim majorities in the Global South. Today, we have seen the securitisation of Muslims because of the standardisation of Islamophobia. For example, legislation that restricts Muslim women's cultural and religious expression, minaret bans in Europe; cartoons mocking significant Muslim religious symbols for the sake of mockery, and digital surveillance – whether online or through the eyes of face-recognition cameras everywhere – have all become the new normal (Cesari 2012). The 'War on Terror' has normalised society's securitisation and legitimised the existence of Islamophobia. This has enhanced rather than decreased the risk of radicalisation.

CVE, and its antecedent, 'deradicalisation', has put the cart before the horse. The key premise of such CVE – particularly evident in the Prevent programme – is that Islamist radicalisation and violent extremism appear from inside the faith (Qureshi 2018). Individual or group actors lose agency because of such a methodological framework, whose motivations may have more to do with network-related factors, or their views and experiences of pursuing justice, recognition, or having no choice but to respond to violence with violence (Dawson 2018; Roy 2017). Rather than perceiving violence as caused by abuses of power by people, governments, or corporate interests, radicalisation is framed as a result of those who adhere to a religion or ideology that is considered authoritarian at best – that is, rigid, dogmatic, uncompromising, and promoting violence (Elshimi 2018).

This misperception of radicalisation actively encourages Islamophobia, which in turn increases polarisation and radicalisation (Abbas 2019). Previously, state authorities had continued to look to religion for answers, such as delegitimising certain interpretations, reframing jihadism as ideas in Islamic poetry, using strategic communications (i.e., alternative narratives), or combating online content to deal with harm before it occurs – all with little measurable impact and with a significant potential for negative side effects (Hemmingsen and Castro 2017). Counter-narratives are still deployed in the contemporary CVE landscape (albeit not always named as such) and online interventions that deal with harm before it occurs are developing exponentially. While both commitment and investment are essential, their impact has been restricted due to the nature of the content (Glazzard 2017). Most Muslims in Britain confront a variety of legitimate societal pressures, but many are motivated to engage in violence due to a lack of perceived options rather than a desire to do so borne out of a specific choice (Kaufman 2006).

While ideologues are dangerous and have a plethora of tools at their disposal, they are uncommon in comparison to the average young men and women who join extremist organisations for local causes but project their goals internationally. Supporting extremist organisations is an expression of agency. There have been reports of far-right organisations paying jobless, aimless, and dissatisfied young men to pose as actors to spread far-right ideologies and ideas. It was no different for the young Britons who joined the Islamic State in Iraq or Syria (Roy 2017). The impact of a class system that embeds inequities into elite discourses may lead to a variety of struggles against the dominant interests of capital, something even more relevant considering the prominent function of class in the UK and further worsened by various far-right and 'Islamist' radicalised groups who perceive and instrumentalise high levels of inequality (Franc and Pavlović 2018).

The global financial crisis of 2008 and the subsequent hollowing out of welfare and support structures through swingeing austerity measures by successive British governments have impacted markedly on post-industrial urban areas already blighted by problems of poverty, social exclusion, and inadequate institutional infrastructure. Research has suggested links between marginalisation and engagement with extreme movements, as declining opportunities have been successfully framed by divisive political actors through a racialised lens – of majority communities losing out to minorities (Abbas 2019). Many far-right organisations posit that people from a non-British background are trying to 'colonise' or 'take over' British society, with local political, social, or economic problems projected onto 'out groups', who often become receptacles for other tensions or perceived grievances (Allen 2011). The UK's slumping levels of social mobility and the centralisation of debate on immigration and identity since the Brexit referendum has meant that societal inequality has stoked far-right sentiment and become tied to the securitisation of Muslim minorities in Britain. However, it is also important to recognise that government policy plays a key role in both deradicalising *and radicalising* politics, and so it is integral that we examine the prevailing CVE policy agenda and the Prevent programme in the following sections.

A protracted policy development landscape

The prevailing CVE policy agenda, particularly evident within the Prevent programme, has taken specific people's experiences and constructed a public narrative around the idea that an ideological awakening occurs among young (males) who are concerned about their identity and belonging. This generalisation, however, overstates the role of ideology as the sole pull factor. It fails to adequately investigate the driving forces that lead people towards engagement with violent extremism, such as their history or personal life concerns, as well as the larger social and political frameworks in which identities and actions are formed, such as community polarisation (McNeil-Willson et al. 2019, pp. 18–19). It is indeed troubling that there are young people who seek violent solutions by perusing the internet and finding substance in problematically framed narratives. At the same time, we must recognise that it takes a significant amount of possible effort and commitment for a person to arrive at this scenario; otherwise, we would see more of it. As a result, there are always trigger points that operate on a variety of individual and structural levels that aid in connecting the intersection of push and pull forces into causal mechanisms to create instances of violence and contention (cf. Boykoff 2007) – with research ongoing in this area.[1]

In the current atmosphere, there is comparable anxiety about the return of foreign fighter families – that is, widows and orphaned children of deceased foreign militants from the former Islamic State in Iraq and Syria. There is a human element to what we need to do as a policy to aid returning foreign soldiers and their children in Britain. But part of the confusion and immobility in terms of direction stems from a specific presumption about what prompted these people to leave, which is amplified by the belief that they were broken individuals before they left (Pokalova 2020). It is critical to recognise that ideology was not always the driving force, a virulent ideological perspective appearing as people become dissatisfied with their lives in the British setting and feel driven to take ownership of grand narratives that are appealing owing to black-and-white thinking and practise.

One case in point relates to Shamima Begum, a British-born girl of a Bengali-origin family who joined Islamic State at the age of 15. In 2019, while in a camp of former Islamic State members, she was stripped of her British citizenship, resulting in a legal challenge. In October 2021, the Supreme Court ruled that she could neither return to the UK to appeal the verdict, nor have a fair and effective appeal while held in a Syrian refugee camp. She thus cannot return to the UK to contest her denaturalisation, nor can she face terrorist charges in a British court of law (BBC News 2021). Irrespective of the actions of Begum, the current state response towards her case has far wider implications on British society, citizenship, and discussions around extremism. British-born young people from minority or family migrant backgrounds now face greater instability and vulnerability, holding what is, in effect, a 'second-class citizenship' (Masters and Regilme 2020). Counterterror procedures already accused of targeting minorities have degraded further the legal status of minorities through this act, legitimising both feelings of resentment and unease amongst many minority communities in Britain, as well as far-right hate speech and racialised tropes that frame Muslims and migrants as a security threat (Murphy 2021).

As a result of over-securitisation brought about through this and other counterterror legislation, the UK government perpetuates a set of racist processes that link strong borders against migration, integration, and the overt support of a narrowly defined set of 'British values' as key to national security (James 2022). One of the most notable processes through which this securitisation process plays out is the UK's Prevent programme, to which further analysis in relation to violent extremism and resilience is now conducted.

The trouble with 'Prevent'

Since its start, 'Prevent' has received varying degrees of criticism from actors who argue that its mission is ineffective and divisive as a response to violent extremism (Archer 2009). The UK government evaluated its counterterrorism strategy in 2011, which was first created in private in 2003 but then publicly in 2006 following the events of 7 July 2005, and from which evolved the language of the Prevent agenda. In this reappraisal, countering ideology was considered critical in the fight against terrorism. Furthermore, the legal mandate of Prevent was enlarged to emphasise its collaboration with other organisations such as health, education, and social services. A youth component was also incorporated into the policy content (HM Government 2011). In effect, the UK government expanded its counter-terrorist strategy to include not only terrorism but also extremist ideology (Richards 2011). As a result, even while the strategy highlighted a substantial conflation between social cohesion and counterterrorism, Prevent re-emphasised the dominant assumption that individuals are on a direct road towards violent extremism as the fundamental concern. Allegations were made that they were exclusive, not inclusive, in their approach to life in society (Edwards 2016). This led to even more differences between them.

The 2011 review had two policy consequences. First, communities confronted with extreme Islamist narratives were required to create resilience. Second, it established a specific policing, security, and intelligence mandate to engage in overt and covert counterterrorism measures as part of a communication and information battle. This was implemented to mitigate the anxiety felt amongst communities and local government around their new obligations for implementing specific counter measures. Such unease was further compounded by the shifting of Prevent from the Department of Community and Local Government to the more centralised Home Office. While there are actions conducted by organisations such as Connect Justice that show that these initiatives have an anecdotal influence, there is limited independent evidence to say that strategic communications have any effect at all on CVE. It also emphasises the importance of fostering community trust – a task failed by a contested Prevent model that has specifically been highly problematic for state-Muslim engagement (O'Toole et al. 2016), due to the targeting of Muslim communities and the allocation of budgets based on the residential concentration levels of British Muslims (Murray et al. 2015).

The perniciousness of Prevent is patent (Awan 2014). The murky lines that give rise to the politicisation of radicalisation from above, the repercussions of placing too much emphasis on 'Muslimness' (Heath-Kelly 2017), and the structural drivers of radicalisation from below are all blurred by the 'at risk' versus 'risky' dichotomy (Lakhani 2012). In an ironic twist, the elimination of ethnic inequities from the mainstream vocabulary of variety and difference has resulted in ethnicity and religiosity being given special weight in the counterterrorism sphere (Lewis and Craig 2014). Attempts to distinguish between social cohesion and counterterrorism exacerbate uncertainty among politicians and civil officials, eventually leading to political and policy stalemate. This has fed the flames of far-right sentiment based on anti-immigration, anti-religion, and anti-multiculturalism conceptualisations – a 'Muslim paranoia narrative', which is frequently the perspective taken by numerous governments when making counter-extremism, deradicalisation, or CVE policy development decisions (Aistrope 2016).

Such approaches have ultimately led to an increase in violence against Muslims following terrorist attacks throughout the world (Hanes and Machin 2014; Awan and Zempi 2016), where Islamophobia is becoming an increasingly acceptable institutionalised norm (Warsi 2017). In this charged and poisonous environment, relations between the state and British Muslim communities are constrained and reduced to a top-down system of design and delivery that is regarded as ideological in design and implementation by those affected as well as those providing it (Thomas 2012).

The mentoring system known as 'Channel' is another major worry with Prevent (Qureshi 2015). It employs a one-to-one method to supposedly educate, encourage, and inspire vulnerable young people away from the paths of violent extremism (Powers 2015). The UK government claims that this approach prevented several young individuals from becoming foreign fighters for Islamic State. It is, however, unable to grant access to original files or even anonymised case material about specific individuals or groups. Other counterterrorism agencies throughout the world have taken interest in replicating the Channel model, including those in France and Germany, with Denmark pushing its unique mentorship technique, known as the 'Aarhus model' (McNeil-Willson 2017; Bertelsen, 2015). However, it is not clear if mentoring is the main factor or if a specific mechanism for deradicalisation from Islamist extremism happens because of Channel or other systems like it.

This area requires research into at least three separate strands that must be considered. First, given the importance of this strategy for state–community relations, it is vital to evaluate Prevent externally from the government. Second, given the current period's fissures and the lack of any systematic examination of them, the nature of these state–community ties needs to be better understood. Finally, there is an urgent need to pay special attention to the viewpoints of British Muslims. What groups perceive as specific and critical to help strengthen connections, thereby boosting community confidence while acknowledging resource needs, ensures that government and policymakers are better prepared to bridge these critical communication and engagement gaps.

Concluding remarks: resilience-building in the shadow of Prevent

Even though the terminology has changed, the 'War on Terror' is still ongoing. However, the rise of the far-right, alt-right, and groups like the incels in recent years has brought fresh concerns to the CVE milieu. Apprehensions about radicalisation and violent extremism will remain relevant, not because they are religious in nature, but because they allude to socioeconomic poverty and inequality. Inequalities have widened in the UK over the last two decades, accelerating under economic decline, austerity, and the fallout from the Covid-19 pandemic to the point where critical measures for social mobility are poor in comparison to the rest of Europe (Social Mobility Commission 2021, p. xv). Such inequities – exacerbated by the political language and replicated by the media – worsen societal divisions, resulting in the continual framing of Muslims, minorities, and migration as a perpetual threat (Kundnani 2014). Political events in Britain such as the Brexit referendum and a series of reactionary right-wing governments, have enabled the normalisation of a framing that British (majority) liberties, freedoms, values, and norms are threatened by the very existence of these (minority) 'others'. All this flows from a racist, neoliberal, and secular rationale, with acute Islamophobia as its most visible result. Some may be radicalised by this Islamophobia, feeding into a cycle of violence and repression.

With the growth of far-right violence, the UK government continues to debate whether existing CVE programmes are adequate to meet the problems posed by this type of extremism, or indeed whether CVE should even focus on the far-right. The difficulty in this discussion is that it transforms the policy problem from one facing a minority (Muslims) to one posed by a majority group (Anglo-Saxon). This raises a slew of political issues. It calls into question the link between CVE and counterterrorism, which has stymied engagement with Muslims. Is the 'White majority' now in danger of becoming radicalised? Is the majority population now to be 'securitised'? Why not, if not? Should CVE work be mainstreamed into government departments such that it becomes an everyday occurrence rather than something separate and distinct from, say, concerns about schoolchildren's safeguarding? What about renaming the concept itself? This is a dynamic landscape, but the reality of the far-right threat has caused the UK government a dilemma – either to reconsider their CVE and counterterrorism tactics or revert to early approaches that overtly target Muslim communities.

The context and result of this is an increasingly convergent distrust towards Prevent from Muslim and other faith groups, local community groups, and human rights bodies in an already charged political discussion over extremism. The proposals emanating from the UK government, senior ministers, and the official Prevent Review – which play up the threat of 'Islamist extremism', downplay concern about the far-right, and attack (particularly Muslim) organisations, communities, and individuals that question the UK's counter-extremism approach – ultimately foments distrust towards authorities and the political system, and entrenches religious and racial inequalities. Community 'resilience-building', a term increasingly evident in government and counter-extremism rhetoric, is thus hobbled within a UK context, partly due to declining levels of what Grossman et al. (2020) call 'linking capital' – vertical trust and confidence from communities towards national authorities and politics because of the actions of government.

The 'War on Terror' began over 20 years ago, and while the rhetoric has changed, the notion of a never-ending battle against terror and terrorism in Europe and across the Global North and Global South, in general, remains largely unquestioned (Abbas 2021b). Today's terrorism is confronted with many more conundrums, particularly from the far-right and alt-right, as well as conversations on social exclusion, mental health, and new ideologies. But Islamophobia has persisted, worsened by the 'War on Terror', and fuelled by well-projected, widely held racialist and culturalist stereotypes about Muslims from social media, mainstream media, and governmental politics in the UK (Abbas 2019). There is a need to advocate a critical, grounded, and community-directed approach that extends beyond the simplistic concept that those who engage in violent extremism are distinct from the rest of society. Violence takes place in a social and political environment and should be approached as such.

Ultimately, the UK case shows we need a new way of thinking about violent extremism and CVE that investigates these challenges in a broader social context, addressing concerns at the individual level and supporting communities, to achieve a richer and more honest picture of what goes wrong (and right). It is important to remain wary of the impact 'Prevent' continues to have, with a significant movement in Britain proposing its complete disestablishment as an actively harmful policy approach. If we continue to focus on the most pressing challenges where there is an orthodoxy for ending violent extremism, the 'War on Terror' will repeat its failures. But new focuses may allow a new generation to escape the problems of the old. Whilst the UK may have led in the development and spreading of CVE, greater attention to and recognition of the problems caused by it – such as racial inequality, Islamophobia, and community polarisation – may provide a chance for radically rethinking policy responses to violent extremism in Britain and elsewhere.

Note

1 The DRIVE project has received its funding from the European Union's H2020 Research and Innovation Actions programme under grant agreement No 959200. DRIVE explores the role of social exclusion in far-right and Islamist radicalisation in north-west Europe, led by Leiden University Institute of Security and Global Affairs in The Hague. Further details at www.driveproject.eu/

References

Abbas, Tahir, ed. (2005) *Muslim Britain: Communities under Press*. London and New York: Zed Books.
Abbas, Tahir (2011) *Islamic Radicalism and Multicultural Politics: The British Experience*. London and New York: Routledge.
Abbas, Tahir (2019) *Islamophobia and Radicalisation: A Vicious Cycle*. London and New York: Hurst and Oxford University Press.
Abbas, Tahir (2021a) *Countering Violent Extremism: The International Deradicalization Agenda*. London: Bloomsbury Academic.
Abbas, Tahir (2021b) Reflection: the 'war on terror', Islamophobia and radicalisation twenty years on. *Critical Studies on Terrorism* 14(4), pp. 402–404.
Adams, Richard and Weale, Sally (2022) Revealed: UK children being ensnared by 'far-right ecosystem' online. *The Guardian*, 3 August, www.theguardian.com/politics/2022/aug/03/revealed-uk-children-ensnared-far-right-ecosystem-online
Aistrope, Tim (2016) Social media and counterterrorism strategy. *Australian Journal of International Affairs* 70(3), pp. 121–138.
Ali, Tariq (2015) *The Extreme Centre: A Warning*. London and New York: Verso Books.
Allen, Chris (2011) Opposing Islamification or Promoting Islamophobia? Understanding the English Defence League. *Patterns of Prejudice*, 45, pp. 279–294.
Archer, Toby (2009) Welcome to the Umma: The British state and its Muslim citizens since 9/11. *Cooperation and Conflict* 44(3), pp. 329–347.
Awan, Imran (2014) Operation 'Trojan horse': Islamophobia or extremism? *Political Insight* 5(2), pp. 38–39.
Awan, Imran and Zempi, Irene (2016) The affinity between online and offline anti-Muslim hate crime: Dynamics and impacts. *Aggression and Violent Behavior,* 27, pp. 1–8.
Baldét, Will (2020) Why have we let Islamist agitators dominate the counter-terrorism discourse? *CAPX*, 28 October, https://capx.co/why-have-we-let-islamist-agitators-dominate-the-counter-terrorism-discourse/.
BBC News (2021) Shamima Begum cannot return to UK, Supreme Court rules. *BBC: UK News*, 26 February, www.bbc.com/news/uk-56209007

Bertelsen, Preben (2015) Danish preventive measures and de-radicalization strategies: The Aarhus model. *Panorama: Insights into Asian and European Affairs*, 1, pp. 241–253.
Bieber, Florian (2018) Is nationalism on the rise? Assessing global trends. *Ethnopolitics* 17(5), pp. 519–540.
Birt, Yahya (2019) Astroturfing and the rise of the Secular Security State in Britain. *Medium*, 17 August.
Boykoff, Jules (2007) Limiting dissent: The mechanisms of state repression in the USA. *Social Movement Studies* 6(3), pp. 281–310.
Cesari, Jocelyn (2012) Securitization of Islam in Europe. *Die Welt des Islams*, 52(3/4), pp. 430–449.
Dathan, Matt (2022) David Cameron takes aim at Muslim critics of anti-terror Prevent programme. Home Affairs Section, *The Times*, 26 April.
Dawson, Lorne (2018) Debating the role of religion in the motivation of religious terrorism. *Nordic Journal of Religion and Society*, 31(2), pp. 98–117.
Duffy, Bobby, Hewlett, Kirstie, McCrae, Julian and Hall, John (2019) Divided Britain? Polarisation and Fragmentation trends in the UK. *The Policy Institute, King's College London* www.kcl.ac.uk/policy-institute/assets/divided-britain.pdf
Edwards, Phil (2016) Closure through resilience: The case of prevent. *Studies in Conflict & Terrorism* 39(4), pp. 292–307.
Ekman, Matthias (2022) The great replacement: strategic mainstreaming of far-right conspiracy claims. *Convergence: The International Journal of Research in New Media Technologies*, DOI: 10.1177/13548565221091983
Elgot, Jessica and Dodd, Vikram (2022) Leaked Prevent review attacks 'double standards' on far right and Islamists. UK News, *The Guardian*, 16 May, www.theguardian.com/uk-news/2022/may/16/leaked-prevent-review-attacks-double-standards-on-rightwingers-and-islamists
Elshimi, M.S. (2018) *De-radicalisation in the UK Prevent Strategy: Security, Identity and Religion*. London: Routledge
Fekete, Liz (2017) *Europe's Fault Lines: Racism and the Rise of the Right*. London: Verso Books.
Fernandez, Shereen, Faure Walker, Rob and Younis, Tarek (2018) Focus: The 'Where' of Prevent. *Discover Society*, 5 June, https://archive.discoversociety.org/2018/06/05/focus-the-where-of-prevent/
Franc, Renata and Pavlović, Tomislav (2018) Systematic Review of Quantitative Studies on Inequality and Radicalisation. DARE Project.
Glazzard, Andrew (2017) Losing the Plot: Narrative, Counter-Narrative and Violent Extremism, *International Centre for Counter-Terrorism – The Hague*.
Grossman, Michele, Hadfield, Kristin, Jefferies, Philip, Gerrand, Vivian and Ungar, Michael (2020) Youth resilience to violent extremism: Development and validation of the BRaVE Measure. *Terrorism and Political Violence*, 34(3), pp. 468–488.
Hanes, Emma and Machin, Stephen (2014) Hate crime in the wake of terror attacks: Evidence from 7/7 and 9/11. *Journal of Contemporary Criminal Justice*, 30(3), pp. 247–267.
Heath-Kelly, Charlotte (2017) The geography of pre-criminal space: epidemiological imaginations of radicalisation risk in the UK Prevent Strategy, 2007–2017. *Critical Studies on Terrorism* 10(2), pp. 297–319.
Hemmingsen, Ann-Sophie and Castro, Karin Ingrid (2017) *The Trouble with Counter-Narratives*. Copenhagen: DIIS report 2017:1.
HM Government (2011) Prevent Strategy. Policy paper. Westminster: Home Office, www.gov.uk/government/publications/prevent-strategy-2011
Home Office (2021) Operation of police powers under the Terrorism Act 2000 and subsequent legislation: Arrests, outcomes, and stop and search, Great Britain, quarterly update to June 2021, www.gov.uk/government/statistics/operation-of-police-powers-under-the-terrorism-act-2000-quarerly-update-to-june-2021.
Hope Not Hate (2019) Generation Identity United Kingdom and Ireland: The Runt of the Litter, https://hopenothate.org.uk/generation-identity-united-kingdom-and-ireland-the-runt-of-the-litter/.
James. Natalie (2022) Countering far-right threat through Britishness: The Prevent duty in further education. *Critical Studies on Terrorism*, 15(1), pp. 121–142.
Kaufman, Stuart J. (2006) Symbolic politics or rational choice? Testing theories of extreme ethnic violence. *International Security*, 30(4), pp. 45–86.

Kundnani, Arun (2014) *The Muslims Are Coming! Islamophobia, Extremism and the Domestic War on Terror.* London and New York: Verso Books.

Kundnani, Arun and Hayes, Ben (2012) *The Globalisation of Countering Violent Extremism policies: Undermining Human Rights, Instrumentalising Civil Society.* Amsterdam: Transnational Institute.

Lakhani, Suraj (2012) Preventing violent extremism: Perceptions of policy from grassroots and communities. *The Howard Journal of Criminal Justice*, 51(2), pp. 190–206.

Lee, Benjamin (2016) Why we fight: Understanding the counter-Jihad movement. *Religion Compass*, 10, pp. 257–265.

Lewis, Hannah and Craig, Gary (2014) 'Multiculturalism is never talked about': Community cohesion and local policy contradictions in England. *Policy & Politics*, 42(1), pp. 21–38.

Mathews, Priya Sara and McNeil-Willson, Richard (2021) Repressive Security and Civil Society in France. In: Romaniuk, Scott N. and Thaddues Njoku, Emeka (eds), *Counter-Terrorism and Civil Society: International Challenges Since 9/11.* Manchester: Manchester University Press: Manchester, pp. 125–142.

McNeil-Willson, Richard (2017) Between Trust and Oppression: Contemporary Counter-Terror Politics in Denmark. In: Romaniuk, S.N., Grice, F., Irrera, D. and Webb, S. (eds), *The Palgrave Handbook of Global Counterterrorism Policy.* London: Palgrave MacMillan UK, pp. 419–435.

McNeil-Willson, Richard, Gerrand, Vivian, Scrinzi, Francesca and Triandafyllidou, Anna (2019) *Polarisation, Violent Extremism and Resilience in Europe today: An analytical framework for the BRaVE project (Concept Paper).* Florence: European University Institute.

Master, Mercedes and Regilme, Salvador Santino F. (2020) Human rights and British citizenship: The case of Shamima Begum as citizen to homo sacer. *Journal of Human Rights Practice*, 12(2), pp. 341–363.

McNeil-Willson, Richard (2020) *Framing in Times of Crisis: Responses to Covid-19 amongst Far-Right Movements and Organisations.* The Hague: International Centre for Counter-Terrorism.

McNeil-Willson, Richard (2022) #plandemic: Online resilience for countering Far Right Covid-19 conspiracies. *First Monday*, 27(5), DOI:10.5210/fm.v27i5.12614

Ministry of Justice (2022) New drive to tackle terrorism in prisons. Press release, 27 April, www.gov.uk/government/news/new-drive-to-tackle-terrorism-in-prisons

Murdoch, Simon and Mulhall, Joe (2019) *From Banners to Bullets: The International Identitarian Movement.* London: Hope Not Hate, https://hopenothate.org.uk/wp-content/uploads/2019/08/Identitarianism-Report.pdf

Murphy, Alexander (2021) Political rhetoric and hate speech in the case of Shamima Begum. *Religions*, 12(10), pp. 834–851.

Murray, Alex, Mueller-Johnson, Katrin and Sherman, Lawrence W. (2015) Evidence-based policing of UK Muslim communities: Linking confidence in the police with area vulnerability to violent extremism. *International Criminal Justice Review*, 25(1), pp. 64–79.

O'Donnell, S. Jonathon (2019) Antisemitism under erasure: Christian Zionist anti-globalism and the refusal of cohabitation. *Ethnic and Racial Studies*, 44(1), pp. 39–57.

O'Toole, Theresa, Meer, Nasar, Nilsson DeHanas, Daniel, Jones, Stephen H. and Modood, Tariq (2016) Governing through Prevent? Regulation and contested practice in state-Muslim engagement. *Sociology*, 50(1), pp. 160–177.

Obaidi, Milan, Kunst, Jonas, Ozer, Simon and Kimel, Sasha Y. (2021) The 'Great Replacement' conspiracy: How the perceived ousting of Whites can evoke violent extremism and Islamophobia. *Group Processes & Intergroup Relations*, DOI:10.1177/13684302211028293

Pearson, Elizabeth (2019) Extremism and toxic masculinity: The man question re-posed. *International Affairs*, 95(6), pp. 1251–1270.

Perry, Damon L. (2021) Islamist terrorism remains a threat to Britain 20 years after 9/11. *Policy Exchange*, 15 September, https://policyexchange.org.uk/islamist-terrorism-remains-a-threat-to-britain-20-years-after-9-11/.

Pokalova, Elena (2020) *Returning Islamist Foreign Fighters: Threats and Challenges to the West.* Cham: Palgrave-Macmillan.

Powers, Samuel (2015) Expanding the paradigm: Countering violent extremism in Britain and the need for a youth centric community-based approach. *Journal of Terrorism Research*, 6(1), DOI:10.15664/jtr.1074

Qureshi, Asim (2015) PREVENT: Creating 'radicals' to strengthen anti-Muslim narratives. *Critical Studies on Terrorism*, 8(1), pp. 181–191.

Qureshi, Fahid (2018) The Prevent Strategy and the UK 'War on Terror': Embedding infrastructures of surveillance in Muslim communities. *Palgrave Communications*, 4(1), pp. 1–17.

Richards, Anthony (2011) The problem with 'radicalization': The remit of 'Prevent' and the need to refocus on terrorism in the UK. *International Affairs*, 87(1), pp. 143–152.

Roy, Olivier (2017) *Jihad and Death: The Global Appeal of Islamic State*. London: C Hurst & Co Publishers Limited.

Silva, Derek M.D. (2018) 'Radicalisation: The journey of a concept', revisited. *Institute of Race Relations*, 59(4), pp. 34–53.

Social Mobility Commission (2021) *State of the nation 2021: Social mobility and the pandemic*. Westminster: HM Government.

Thomas, Paul (2012) *Responding to the Threat of Violent Extremism: Failing to Prevent*. London: Bloomsbury Academic.

Warsi, Sayeeda (2017) *The Enemy Within: A Tale of Muslim Britain*. London: Penguin UK.

Winter, Aaron S. and Mondon, Aurelien (2020) *Reactionary Democracy: How Racism and the Populist Far Right Became Mainstream*. London: Verso Books.

Zuquete, Jose Pedro (2018) Introduction. In: Zuquete, Jose Pedro (ed.) *The Identitarians: The Movement against Globalism and Islam in Europe*, Indiana: University of Notre Dame Press, pp. 1–6.

9
THE NETHERLANDS

Maria Vliek and Martijn de Koning

Introduction

The Netherlands had no explicit approach to countering terrorism until the early 1970s. Nor was any legislation aimed at countering terrorism passed by Dutch governments in the 1970s, 1980s, or 1990s; only targeted policy was formulated. The various hostage situations, 'violent political actions', and other damages to life and capital were chiefly a concern for the justice department and the police (De Graaf 2010). There were, however, significant events that led to a response often dubbed 'The Dutch Approach': policy aimed at preventing violence within the existing legislative framework. These developments have been relevant to post-9/11 counterterrorism efforts (Rasser 2005) and the emergence of the 'broad approach' – that is, policy and legislation designed to both prevent and repress radicalisation and terrorist activities. In this chapter we outline the emergence of these particular approaches by looking at events that triggered debates and policies across four periods spanning five decades: (1) the 1970s and 1980s, (2) the 1990s, (3) the early 2000s, and (4) the 2010s until 2020. We show how policies slowly but gradually extended the idea of what security pertains to in reaction to violent events. What is often left out in these analyses of Dutch policies are the interactions between governmental bodies and those groups labelled by the government as extremist. As such, preventing and countering violent extremism (P/CVE) policies and evaluations of them tend to reinforce the rather mechanical idea of the state engineering society through countering the extremists whereby the extremists are mostly passive consumers of the policies aimed against them. Following della Porta's (2006) work, we analyse the reciprocity between the government and extremists through, among other things, injustice frames, by looking at two different groups: a network of Dutch war volunteers in Syria and the far right Islamophobic network of Pegida.

Political violence and the 'Dutch Approach': the 1970s and 1980s

After Indonesia declared its independence from the Dutch colonisers in 1945 and the demobilisation of the Royal Netherlands East Indies Army (KNIL) troops in 1950, the Indonesian government refused to let the Moluccan soldiers demobilise.[1] In 1950, South Moluccan rebels also unilaterally declared a fully independent Republic of South Maluku (RMS). The

Dutch government decided to bring the Moluccan soldiers who fought for the Dutch during the independence wars to the Netherlands. The soldiers and their families were placed in former concentration camps left behind by the German occupier after the second world war. The Dutch government's silence on the issue of the Moluccan families living in these camps for decades caused a growing number of second-generation Moluccans to feel that only violence would effect change.

On 31 August 1970, 33 South Moluccans entered and forcibly occupied the residence of the Indonesian ambassador in protest to the anticipated visit of the Indonesian president the next day. One police officer was shot dead and 35 people were taken hostage. Eventually, the RMS president in-exile negotiated with the hostage-takers and they surrendered the following day. At the time of the occupation, no policy was in place and decisions were made ad hoc. Slow negotiations and the intervention of a Moluccan eventually ended the situation. Maartje van der Woude (2010) identifies this approach as the blueprint for the strategy against terrorism that was subsequently developed. The hostage-takers were jailed for one year (ANP 2020; Rasser 2005). The Dutch government considered the attack a 'one-off' incident and did not undertake any action or formulate any policy to anticipate future violent attacks (Rasser 2005). However, the government did order a major raid on a Moluccan camp in October 1970 to arrest those involved in the occupation of the embassy: 'Although the government achieved its stated goals justifying the raid, the extreme military action was ill conceived. The move only served to further alienate the Moluccan population' (ibid., p. 484). During this time, there was a lot of talk *about* but never *with* the Moluccans. In addition, the role of the national security services, the Binnenlandse Veiligheidsdienst (BVD), was questioned, but not what had led to the attack – that is, the attackers' grievances which helped bolster radical elements (Van der Woude 2010).

Although the Moluccan raid did not prompt the formulation of a comprehensive counterterrorism policy, from September 1971 onwards, police directors, the BVD head, and attorney generals met regularly (De Graaf 2010).[2] Furthermore, after the bombing of gas installations at Ommen and Ravenstein by suspected Palestinian commandos in February 1972, a high ranking police officer was installed as national terrorism expert, sending the clear message that terrorism was seen as a criminal offence that could be prevented, traced, and punished as such (ibid.). But again, no actual policy or legislation was formulated, nor did attacks by the Maoist urban guerrilla movement 'Rode Jeugd' (Red Youth) throughout the early 1970s alter this.

The hostage crisis at the 1972 Olympics in Munich, however, touched off debate in the Netherlands (and worldwide) on the state of security at airports and, in general, as to whether the country was prepared for such acts of terrorism. Again, this was primarily determined as a task for the police and the justice department. The first national strategy for counterterrorism was presented in February 1973 by Prime Minister Barend Biesheuvel. This two-page *Terreurbrief*[3] (terror letter), as it was called, requested the formation of a close-combat unit and sharpshooter units. Furthermore, a role for the army was envisioned in the event of any hostage situation and the elite special forces units Bijzondere Bijstandseenheid (BBE) were created. All measures could be taken within the existing legal framework; there was no mention of implementing special counterterrorism legislation. According to De Graaf (ibid.), this approach was once again a blueprint for subsequent policy. Van der Woude (2010) notes: 'By placing terrorism under the criminal penal code, political control was achievable by way of the hierarchy of the judiciary' (p. 147, our translation).

One major point of contestation of the *Terreurbrief* was that it was wholly unclear what would be classified as 'terrorism'. Therefore, the policy lines which were to counter '*verschijnselen van terroristische aard*' (phenomena of terrorist nature) could be applied without any judicial backing. Furthermore, it had not been specified when the BBEs should or could be deployed. Terrorism was now classified as a criminal offence, making counterterrorism primarily a police task (ibid.).

After the first 'action' by the Moluccan youth in 1970, the Dutch government failed to keep their promise to the RMS government in Indonesia. On the contrary, the brute force used by police in evicting Moluccan camps and houses caused unrest. Furthermore, as De Graaf (2010) notes, there were various occasions when Dutch politicians spoke of the pointlessness of the RMS case for independence – and, adding insult to injury, Queen Juliana stated in a speech that Suriname, another former Dutch colony, had the right of self-determination. Since the Moluccans felt wholly disadvantaged by the Dutch government, talking was no longer thought to be sufficient. Demant et al. (2008) spoke to former RMS members who explicitly referred to the Dutch government's communication and the consequences this had for the processes of radicalisation among the South Moluccan youth. One of them stated:

> If only they had listened to us or had taken us seriously, that would have taken away a great deal of the fuss and unrest. But instead, these feelings were actually fuelled by statements such as 'What they want is irrational, a dream'.
>
> Demant et al. 2008, p. 38

During two subsequent attacks by South Moluccans in December 1975, the government pursued a strategy of negotiations rather than violent interference, which was later internationally termed 'The Dutch Approach' (Rasser 2005; Van der Woude 2010). It should be noted that what later became known as the 'broad approach' was already being implemented in the government's reconciliation efforts with the South Moluccan community: officials now realised the importance of addressing the grievances that the Moluccans had in order to prevent – and suppress – feelings of hate and discontent (Van der Woude 2010, p. 153).

In the 1970s, various violent interventions were discussed in terms of 'countering terrorism'. Although the intensity around the South Moluccan cause had eased, in Left circles, the focus was on the trial of the Red Army Faction (RAF) in Stuttgart, with demonstrations against the supposed rise of a police state in West Germany. The protests were blunted somewhat after an RAF member shot dead a Dutch policeman during an arrest operation (De Graaf 2010). A harder line was drawn in 1977 by the new 'Van Agt' government after a primary school hostage situation by the South Moluccans. One final attack in 1978 by Moluccan terrorists on a provincial government building saw officials order a Marine unit to storm the building after only 28 hours. Despite the new government building claiming they would implement stricter antiterrorism legislation, with no further hostage situations, terrorism disappeared from the political agenda (ibid., p. 47): internationally, '[p]artially because of that, the "myth" of the little repressive and liberal "Dutch Approach" lived on'.

The 'Dutch Approach' is generally understood as a 'hands off' approach to counterterrorism, supposedly used in the Netherlands during the 1970s to ward off terrorist threats such as those posed by Palestinian youths, Moluccan terrorists, and Rode Jeugd actions. However, De Graaf categorically states that this is a misunderstanding. It is not that the Dutch Approach was 'hands off', rather, the national government never formulated any legislation in and by which policy could have been defined. This meant that terrorism was seen as a criminal offence against which the judiciary and police were the primary weapons.

Furthermore, the establishment of the BBEs without any judicial underpinnings suggested they could operate with minimal legal or political control.

During the early 1980s, political attention for terrorism had subsided as the Centrale Recherche Informatiedienst (Central Police Intelligence Service) stated in 1985 that the Netherlands at that time did not have any dealings with terrorism (Klerks 1989). This is not to say that political violence did not occur during this period. There were shootings connected to the colonial past involving attacks by Surinamese and Moluccan people. In addition, there were bombings and arson attacks by anti-nuclear or anti-Apartheid protestors (Fijnaut 1992). From 1985 onward, the 'actions' of the Revolutionaire Anti Racistische Actie (RaRa) became a matter of great concern for the Dutch authorities. Unlike in the Moluccan case, it was hard to arrest the perpetrators or prevent any violent actions without thorough intelligence work (Klerks 1989). After a series of attacks in 1985–1986 on the facilities of large corporations, including Shell and Makro, the Landelijk Coördinatie Team (LCT, National Coordination Team) was set up to direct intelligence efforts against the RaRa (Van der Woude 2010). In spite of this, the judicial department found great difficulty in convicting any of their members due to the lack of evidence they were able to present against them. Van der Woude (2010) notes that during this time, the terminology used by the authorities shied away from 'terrorism' and rather used the term 'violent political activism'.

The rise and fall of the 'political centre parties' such as 'de Centrum Partij' Centrum Democraten, and CP'86 in the 1980s and 1990s is interesting since they were considered 'extreme right' yet despite members' violent actions against people of colour and immigrants, were not regarded as terrorist threats. Demant et al. (2008) analysed the decline and limited success of these parties, concluding that they remained on the political margins chiefly due to the lack of parliamentary interaction and judicial measures against their members as well as no coverage in the press. Furthermore, there were various anti-fascist actions during their meetings that were largely condoned by the authorities. Nonetheless, it should be noted that these parties were never part of the terrorism discourse or classified as 'violent political actions' like the RaRa. With regards to the far-right political parties, no anti-terrorism legislation was passed nor were any preventive or counter-radicalisation policies implemented.

1990s: security, democratic order, and social cohesion

Several events in the 1990s were important precursors to the 'broad approach' that emerged in the subsequent decade. In 1992, the security service, BVD, published a domestic security update. The report stated that one of the possible side effects of migration from southern European and North African countries could be the 'progressive radicalisation or fundamentalisation of Muslim communities in foreign parts', and that conflicts from the countries of origin could be transferred to the Netherlands with violence as a potential outcome (De Koning 2020). The BVD emphasised the need for 'integral security care'.[4]

The BVD report was released amidst a broad political debate on immigration, Islam, and integration (De Koning 2016). Noting a spate of violent incidents against migrants, from arson to explosives attacks, the BVD's 1992 annual report emphasised its commitment to work for the safety of migrants in the Netherlands.[5] The monitoring of violent and non-violent racist actions, however, was inconsistent and, in general, such actions were depoliticised, with any connection to racism denied (Witte and Scheepmaker 2012).[6]

In a 1998 report on 'political Islam in the Netherlands', the BVD warned against political Islam gaining influence through Dutch mosques and funding from Islamic foundations abroad.[7] The report signalled a trend connecting the security question with an alleged lack of integration and, subsequently, grievances as an indicator for potential future violence'.[8] Throughout the 1990s and early 2000s, the question of security was to include integration and social cohesion and thereby partly foregrounded as a matter of care (instead of only repression). It also made a nuanced distinction between different forms of political violence and applied a narrow definition of terrorism (Fadil and de Koning 2019). Attention to the radical left remained marginal, but several far-right political parties were on the radar as extremist, such as the nationalist Centre Democrats, the Neo-Nazi Nederlandse Volksunie (NVU), and the nationalist Voorpost organisation, but this did not result in their inclusion in counter-radicalisation policies.

2000–2010: Salafism and the proliferation of the 'broad approach'

The September 11, 2001, attacks in the US were seen by politicians and policymakers as a wake-up call for new and more compelling anti-terrorism measures. This perspective is also underpinned, however, by ideological factors related to existing racialising ideas about a 'clash of civilisations' between Islam and the West (De Koning 2016). These perspectives merged with the perceived need to break taboos in the debate about multiculturalism, migration, and Islam (Prins 2002) and the rise of populist leaders such as Pim Fortuyn and later Geert Wilders with his Freedom Party. Both blamed the 'political elite' for being politically correct and lax against the looming threat of creeping Islamisation. As such, 9/11 became an event that contributed heavily to furthering the problematisation of Muslims in debates and policies (Dooremalen 2021; but see also Vanparys, Jacobs and Torrekens 2013). In response to 9/11, a comprehensive policy against terrorism was devised, the *Actieplan Terrorismebestrijding en Veiligheid* (Actionplan Counterterrorism and Security), which included a mixture of preventive and repressive measures facilitating strong immigration and financial controls and new anti-terrorism legislation (Den Boer 2007). This later came to be known as the 'broad approach'.

In May 2002, a week before the national elections, Pim Fortuyn, leader of the Lijst Pim Fortuyn (LPF) party was murdered by a left-wing animal rights activist citing Fortuyn's rhetoric on Muslims (Buijs 2009). This attack led only to a recommendation to increase the staff of the Algemene Inlichtingen en Veiligheidsdienst (AIVD), the intelligence service that succeeded the BVD (Den Boer 2007). Attempts by two Dutch youths to join the violent struggles in Kashmir in 2002 (which resulted in the deaths of both before they actually joined the fighting), triggered debates about home-grown radicalisation. This intensified after the Madrid attacks in 2004 and the murder of controversial filmmaker Theo van Gogh by a member of the 'Hofstad Network'[9] later that same year. Slowly but gradually a more compelling and far-reaching counter-radicalisation policy was considered as a response to concerns about radicalisation and violence. However, this also led to concerns about the instrumentalisation of these events and the subsequent potential for stigmatising Muslims by political parties such as Wilders's Freedom Party (De Koning, Becker and Roex 2020).

Notwithstanding such concerns, the attacks of 2001 and 2004 have been instrumental in a huge expansion and diversification of state powers to strengthen the rule of law (and the state's use of force in its support). This raised questions about human security and equality before the law but without many consequences (see, for example, Bolhuis and Van Wijk 2020). In 2004, after the Madrid attacks, the Nationale Coördinator Terrorisme en Veiligheid (NCTV, National Coordinator for Counter-Terrorism and Security) was established, followed by a new prison regime for terrorists; administrative measures such as the potential for stripping citizenship in instances when suspects have dual nationality;

changes in the penal code; travel and area bans; financial surveillance; extending the period of temporary custody; and pre-emptive community engagement (Manjikian 2017; Van der Heide and Kearney 2020; Van der Heide and Schuurman 2018). A resilience and integration policy was also formulated in 2005, followed by a more long-term approach in 2007 with the Action Plan on Polarisation and Radicalisation 2007–2011. With these plans, the broad approach envisioned by the AIVD security service materialised: repression of radicalisation and violence, on the one hand, and prevention and awareness-raising, on the other.

Focus on the far-right took a back seat in AIVD policy, which increased the emphasis on Islam – and Salafi Islam in particular. The security service's risk assessment zoomed in on the belief that the Salafi ideology (and its variants) was in and of itself intolerant, anti-Western, anti-integrationist, and anti-democratic. Combined with other factors seen as potential breeding grounds – for instance, marginalisation, identity crisis, social isolation, or personal problems – the teachings of Salafi preachers could lure young Muslims into radical convictions about how society ought to be, thus rejecting the authority and the legitimacy of the Dutch state institutions. An active struggle against society and, ultimately, involvement in 'radical Islamic violent activities' could then be the result (De Koning 2020; Fadil and de Koning 2019).

A crucial part of the 'broad approach' is the early risk assessment and management by identifying risk factors among segments of the population that may indicate a potential for political violence in an undefined future. Within these discourses of counter-radicalisation, ideas about risk, as Lupton (2006, p. 13) argues, produce symbolic boundaries and legitimise the management of risk to facilitate social cohesion and democracy. Risk assessment, then, is based upon a combination of abstract factors that must be made legible and tangible, for example, by attaching them to phenomena such as 'Salafism' and 'jihadism' (and identifying them as such). Selected indicators of risk are phenomena (such as Salafi/Jihadi ideologies and acts) threatening particular moral principles directly or indirectly (the breeding ground approach within counter-radicalisation) and are seen as unevenly distributed between population subsets (O'Malley 2016). Furthermore, as radicalisation is considered a process rather than a static situation, risks are often related to specific stages in a person's development leading up to a potential for political violence by foregrounding 'pathways', 'journeys', 'drivers', 'breeding grounds', and so on (Mythen, Walklate and Peatfield 2016). This takes into account not only Islam and Islamic movements, ideologies, and key doctrinal themes such as 'jihad', 'umma', and 'hijra' but also socio-emotional factors, personal circumstances, and networks that may provide protective or accelerating incentives. Such an approach is often likened to a 'conveyor belt' or 'slippery slope' analysis (Mythen 2020; Walklate and Mythen 2014). However, this analogy misses some of the ambiguities in risk assessment that make the link between Islam, Salafism, and violence less straightforward in policies than it appears in such critiques. For example, although Islam – and therefore Muslim communities – by definition are part of the counter-radicalisation surveillance against jihadists (and therefore a necessary part of it), it is never a sufficient condition to label an individual at risk. Salafism, however, (and by extension jihadism as it is seen as part of Salafism) is a necessary *and* sufficient condition to label someone as a risk or at-risk, but the type of intervention depends on other factors as well.

2010–2020: war volunteers, risk, and the integral approach

In the throes of global financial crisis in 2008 and 2009, the tone of the debate and the warnings by security services became less alarmist. However, around 2010, the emergence of militant networks among Muslim communities led to the fear that this would again fuel processes of radicalisation. With a stream of people from these networks going to Syria in 2012 and 2013 to join the violent struggles against the al-Assad government, the threat level was raised, and a new counter-radicalisation policy took shape between 2014–2016 (De Koning et al. 2020). Several new laws were announced and implemented, again pertaining to the penal code and administrative law. The main rationale behind almost all legislation after 9/11 and 2004 stems from the idea of serious threats to the state, democratic order, and society, and can be seen as the product of and reproducing a culture of control with the Dutch state as its main protector (Van der Woude 2010).

Some of these laws had been part of a 2014 NCTV programme to target jihadism as a response to the phenomenon of the Dutch transnational war volunteers (often dubbed foreign fighters or *Syriëganger*, Syria-goer or Syria-traveller) and political pressure. The *Actieprogramma Integrale Aanpak Jihadisme* (Action-programme Integral Approach Jihadism) outlined 38 measures (some pre-existing) aimed at reducing the risks emerging from people travelling to conflict zones, including interventions against potential travelling; tackling radicalisation and social tensions early on; fighting radicalising online content inciting hatred and violence; and information sharing and (international) cooperation. The programme shows a mix typical of the broad approach: criminal and administrative law, care and prevention, surveillance, and ideological monitoring. Additional local measures also included changes in the urban landscapes such as blocking access to particular public squares and streets through concrete blocks and other (in-)visible barriers.[10]

The new laws and measures were implemented against the background of political debates in which Islam and migration were increasingly connected to violence and hence seen as opposites of and endangering security, Dutch identity, and the rule of law (De Goede 2008; Manjikian 2017; Roggeband and Vliegenthart 2007; Van Meeteren and Van Oostendorp 2019; Van Munster and Aradau 2008). The continuing intertwinement of security and migration at the national (Engbersen and Broeders 2011; Groenendijk 2008) and EU levels (Luedtke 2008), together with law enforcement agencies' ever-expanding technological capabilities and (restricted) use of secret information in trials, amplify the risk of ethnic profiling. This has received some attention in academic studies but little in political debates (Van Ark (née Grozdanova) and Renckens 2020; Van der Leun and Van der Woude 2011; Wesseling and De Goede 2018).

Such expansion of state powers stands in sharp contrast to the waning attention to the far-right after 2001, even though (or perhaps because) it had acquired a strong position in Dutch politics (in particular Wilders's Freedom Party). This was accompanied by a growing visibility of far-right militant groups – but not by definition a growing membership of such groups (Linden 2009; Sterkenburg 2021). This started changing after the attack in Norway by Anders Breivik and the 2016 attack on a Dutch mosque for which the perpetrators were convicted of arson with terrorist intent. It was not until 2018, however, that the far-right was the focus of assessment reports by the NCTV (2018) and AIVD (2018). In both, with some minor differences, the far-right is regarded as a phenomenon of organisations or loosely coupled networks and, increasingly, 'lone actors'. The reports signal an increase in violence, arson, and vandalism in particular aimed against Muslims and their institutions but also Jews and Black people, and involving symbols that are viewed by the far-right (and abroad) as symbols of 'Dutchness'.

At the same time, the growing focus on the far-right is accompanied by significant changes in the definitions of extremism used by the AIVD. While previously organisations were considered a threat to democratic order by the anti-democratic goals they pursue or by the non-democratic goals they deploy or both, after 2018 the use of non-democratic methods no longer appeared to be a necessary condition. Rather, a distinction is made between violent and non-violent methods. Non-violent organisations are considered to be operating within the framework of democratic rule of law and therefore are not part of the working sphere of the AIVD (2018, p. 4). As in the 1990s, there is no sustained reflection on how various forms of racism intersect with the ideas of the far-right. Several academic researchers have noted how the far-right's ideas and discourse have been mainstreamed due to political leaders taking over far-right talking points and terminology on Islam and migration, as well as interaction on social media making particular ideas and phrasings more common and acceptable (Akkerman, Lange and Rooduijn 2016; Hainsworth 2016; Houtum and Bueno Lacy 2017; Vieten 2016). This also works the other way around: the far-right adjusting to the political mainstream by taking over topics and discourses from mainstream parties, for example, talking about Islam as an ideology (Klandermans and Mayer 2005; Linden 2009; Van Donselaar 1991). This circularity points to an important element that needs to be taken into account in our analyses of extremism: interaction.

The interactive construction of the extremists – Vignette 1: jihadism

In her work on social movements, violence, and the state, Donatella della Porta (2006) analysed the interaction between, for example, the police and protesters, and above all, saw it as reciprocal. When the police use more force, so do protesters and vice versa, and with the decrease in repression, the demonstrations also decrease. According to della Porta, this interaction is further characterised by the creation of myths and martyrdom and 'injustice frames', or the fuelling of a feeling of absolute injustice. Inspired by this work, we want to draw attention to these dynamics of reciprocity between public authorities and the groups involved by paying attention to the reappropriation of particular themes and tropes, injustice frames, the bolstering of deviant attitudes, and the role of victimisation in two brief vignettes based upon earlier research (Vliek and De Koning 2020).

The issue of the Dutch war volunteers in Syria triggered many debates, reinvigorated old policies, and gave rise to new ones. Particularly important has been the Integral Action Programme Jihadism published in 2014. Shortly after, two videos appeared online from Syria: Islam and jihad, part 1 and part 2.[11] Both videos were made and distributed by Muhajiri Shààm, one of the many names adopted by Abdelkarim el Atrach, a Dutch jihadist who had left the Netherlands for Syria in 2013 and already known by 2014 for disseminating a video message in which he criticised the Dutch government and called on 'brothers' to take action against the Dutch and American authorities in response to the US air strikes on a Jabhat al-Nusra base.[12] Three of El Atrach's friends were killed during that attack. Sometime before the release of both videos, El Atrach had been placed on the Dutch national terrorism watchlist.

In the two videos, he claims that Islam and jihad are inextricably linked (part 1) and sets his sights on the Action Programme (part 2). He saw the programme as part of 'a diabolical plan' to stop jihad. He describes mobilising civilians to help track down and report possible war volunteers as well as using experts in educational institutions to monitor people with jihadist ideas or the establishment of new 'jihadist' centres as elements of a cunning plan to draw in citizens:

> They even go so far as to use the Muslim community in fighting jihad…This is where the red line is drawn…That infidels help each other in fighting jihad is still

understandable…But that they even want to go so far as to want to use Muslims in this false cunning crusade is very distasteful. And dangerously misleading.

In this way, he adds, Muslims are 'used as a human shield against the other Muslims' and notes that the Action Programme is cleverly packaged as a fight against 'an extremist group'.

Here El Atrach re-appropriates common tropes in policies and debates aimed at jihadists or at Muslims in general such as 'human shield' and the term 'extremist' to reveal what he sees as a ploy against all Muslims. He urges viewers to side with the fighters in Syria and against the Dutch government that sends fighter jets to bomb Muslims and restricts the freedom of Muslims – which he regards as hypocritical. His advice to Muslims is to completely distance themselves from any cooperation with the Dutch government. El Atrach's statement aligns with what della Porta (2006) calls secondary deviancy, that is, those using clandestine violence in the face of what they see as injustice are actually strengthened in their deviant attitudes and practices as a response to being targeted. And El Atrach goes one step further, using the injustice frame to mobilise others: government policies directed against jihadists are presented as an incentive to 'persevere' and remain 'steadfast'. Going against policy in public videos and taking a stand was, in addition to being a form of recruitment, also intended as a demonstration of one's own steadfastness (De Koning, Becker and Roex 2020). El Atrach was killed in Syria in 2015.

No right to demonstrate? – Vignette 2: far-right protest

Edwin Wagensveld, frontman of far-right group Pegida Nederland, is adamant about operating within the confines of the law, arguing that it is the only way he can demonstrate the government's 'double standard'. Challenging the various policies aimed at the far-right is a very explicit method to highlight his group's views. Despite their pledge for non-violent ways of protest and demonstration, Pegida Nederland is consistently classified as 'extremist' in various reports by the security and intelligence services, as well as in other policy documents.

In the summer of 2019, Eindhoven's mayor banned a series of planned demonstrations by Pegida Nederland where they intended to hand out pork chops at the Al-Fourqaan mosque during Ramadan. Their first march was interrupted by Muslim youth who clashed with the police, and subsequent events were forbidden by the mayor in anticipation of further disturbances. Another demonstration was eventually allowed, but only at a designated area away from the mosque. However, there was a brief confrontation when Pegida showed up at the Al-Fourqaan mosque, with counter-protesters throwing eggs and stones. Eventually a total ban on demonstrations around mosques within Eindhoven was enforced. This ban has been challenged by Pegida Nederland in the courts, a move that eventually led to the measure being revoked.

Wagensveld explained how the state was actively restricting his right to demonstrate. With the help of repressive measures during protests, such as short detentions and threats of persecution as well as bans on protesting in the first place, he reckons the (local) government tries to silence him. He finds it hypocritical that left-wing protests or Muslim activists' marches, for which local authorities have not received prior notification are allowed to take place, but that his properly organised demonstrations are not. He perceives the restriction of his fundamental right to demonstrate in the name of keeping the peace as anti-democratic, unjust, inconsistent, and a confirmation of the repressive policies currently in place. By using the courts to show the government they are in the wrong, he demonstrates the problematic behaviour he wishes to challenge.

Pegida Nederland regularly uses the courts (and often wins) to prove their point (Vliek and De Koning 2020). Despite their distrust towards 'the system', they use the law's power. This ambivalent relationship with government, in which they use state policy against itself, gives their message even more strength, especially in the eyes of their followers.

Perception, and interaction

These two vignettes show that policy is not merely a one-way measure taken against groups or individuals that effect the government's intended outcome or change. Rather, policies are also subject to how these groups or individuals perceive policy and the governing bodies that formulate measures. These policies thus tend to form, shape, and alter the ways in which people take action and respond. Indeed, previous research has shown the importance of those perceptions and the meanings given to them as well as to the actions of groups and individuals (Vliek and De Koning 2020). Recurring themes are trust in the government and the importance of an individual approach. How groups interact with the government as well as with and through the policies targeting them is crucial in our understanding of extremism and policymaking. The history of how the Dutch government has formulated legislation and policy in relation to various 'events' such as terrorist attacks and protest demonstrations has shown that, for example, the lack of interaction actually exacerbated the feelings of distrust and anger among the Moluccans. The brief descriptions and short examples of interactions of extremist groups and government agencies in more recent years show how groups and individuals may actually be fuelled by the policies aimed at them.

Concluding remarks

The Dutch Approach has often been regarded as a 'hands off' approach to counterterrorism. However, the actual 'Dutch Approach' during the 1970s and 1980s was rather one that responded to violent political events (and not so much to non-violent extremism) as a criminal offence and not as separate policy. Police and special forces held considerable power – if the authorities were willing to deploy them. In response to violent attacks in the US, Spain, and the assassination of film director Theo van Gogh, along with fears about home-grown radicalisation among Dutch Muslim communities, this lack of policymaking and legislation would change after 2004. Already prior to 2001, in response to perceived foreign threats coming from, among others, political Islam, the definition of what constituted a threat to security was extended to include risks to social cohesion and anti-integrationist tendencies. The increasing focus on Islam as a risk factor to social cohesion emerged throughout the 1990s but even more so after 2001. This meant that the P/CVE policies were no longer (only) devised as a response to clandestine political violence but were also a response to what was regarded as Salafist/jihadist extremist tendencies. The September 11 attacks in the US and 2004 Madrid bombings led to a compelling P/CVE strategy, encompassing preventive measures that could pertain to care but also to penal and administrative legal measures and changes in immigration and integration policies (as also happened to a lesser extent in the 1970s). This comprehensive approach to legislation and policy has been referred to as the 'broad approach' against terrorism. The focus on racist political extremism and violence almost disappeared from the radar in the Netherlands until around 2018. The potential adverse effects of these policies regarding the rule of law, stigmatisation, racialisation, and Islamophobia have been addressed in debates and by policymakers but have not impacted very strongly on laws and practice yet.

The preventive aspect of the broad approach has often been regarded as the soft side of P/CVE measures. This, however, can be questioned as it puts considerable subsets of the Muslim populations under scrutiny and may also include the use of penal law (De Graaf 2019). The distinction between a soft (preventive) and hard (repressive) approach is important as it draws in perspectives and practices of care and community work, but the distinction should not be overestimated. Prevention is still part of repression and may lead to prosecution by the Netherlands Prosecution Service (for example by focusing on preparatory acts of terrorism) in particular because extremism and terrorism seem to become conflated in the case of Muslims (Van De Weert and Eijkman 2021). Furthermore, it could also lead to care practices being ruled by principles of risk assessment and surveillance focused on security (Ragazzi 2016; Van De Weert and Eijkman 2019).

As we have shown, for example, in the case of the Moluccan activists, the focus on extremism and political violence tends to hide the grievances of those violent and nonviolent extremists behind ideas about deviancy and public order with the state as the central actor deciding what is labelled extremism and what is not. However, as our vignettes have shown, there is a reciprocal interaction between the government and state institutions, on the one hand, and the groups labelled extremists (in any fashion), on the other. Therefore, to understand these dynamics it is important to include in our analysis the individuals and groups targeted by the policy: their histories, aspirations, and ideas about identity and subjectivity; in other words, the reflexive work that takes place in relation to, anticipation of, and response to government policy. In that sense, the Dutch case exemplifies the case that the P/CVE policies of state institutions are just as much political instruments as the violent and non-violent actions of the extremists, informing and shaping the sociopolitical context as active players and having consequences for much larger subsections of the population.

Notes

1 For a more elaborate elucidation on the particulars of the Dutch occupation, the Indonesian independence wars, and the role of the Moluccans, see Rasser (2005) or Penders (2001).
2 It should be noted, however, that the BVD was not given a terrorism department until 1985.
3 Handelingen II, 1972-1973, 12.000, nr. 11.
4 TK (1990/1991) 22463, nr. 1 Verslag van de vaste Commissie voor de inlichtingen- en veiligheidsdiensten over haar werkzaamheden (Juli 1990-Juli 1991), p. 20.
5 BVD, Jaarverslag 1992 (The Hague, Ministry of the Interior 1993), pp. 2–12 and pp. 15–16.
6 Ibid., pp. 15–16
7 BVD, *De politieke Islam in Nederland* (The Hague: Ministry of the Interior 1998), p. 20.
8 BVD, *Jaarverslag 1999* (The Hague: Ministry of the Interior 2000), p. 15.
9 On the 'Hofstad Network', an Islamist group composed of Dutch citizens, see Schuurman, Eijkman, and Bakker 2014.
10 Het Parool, Amsterdam treft extra maatregelen tegen terrorisme (Amsterdam takes extra measures against terrorism, 20 October 2017, www.parool.nl/nieuws/amsterdam-treft-extra-maatregelen-tegen-terrorisme~b4642ea4
11 Videos archived by M. de Koning.
12 El Atrach features in a JN propaganda documentary against ISIS ('The Glorious'). In this video it is mentioned he died because of injuries sustained in battle.

References

AIVD (2018) *Rechtsextremisme in Nederland. Een fenomeen in beweging*. The Hague: General Intelligence and Security Service.

Akkerman, T., de Lange, S.L. d.and Rooduijn, M., eds. (2016) *Radical Right-Wing Populist Parties in Western Europe: Into the Mainstream?* New York: Routledge.

ANP (2020) 18 verdachten rellen rond Pegida-demo Eindhoven voor de rechter. *De Telegraaf*, 4 September. Retrieved from www.telegraaf.nl/nieuws/495634930/18-verdachten-rellen-rond-pegida-demo-eindhoven-voor-de-rechter?utm_source=twitter&utm_medium=social&utm_campaign=seeding-telegraaf

Bolhuis, M.P. and Van Wijk, J. (2020) Citizenship Deprivation as a Counterterrorism Measure in Europe; Possible Follow-Up Scenarios, Human Rights Infringements and the Effect on Counterterrorism. *European Journal of Migration and Law*, 22(3), pp. 338–365, DOI:10.1163/15718166-12340079

Buijs, F.J. (2009) Muslims in the Netherlands: Social and Political Developments after 9/11. *Journal of Ethnic and Migration Studies*, 35(3), pp. 421–438, DOI:10.1080/13691830802704590

De Goede, M. (2008) The Politics of Preemption and the War on Terror in Europe. *European Journal of International Relations*, 14(1), pp. 161–185, DOI:10.1177/1354066107087764

De Graaf, B. (2010) *Theater van de angst. De strijd tegen terrorisme in Nederland, Duitsland, Italië en Amerika.* Amsterdam: Boom.

De Graaf, B. (2019) Foreign Fighters on Trial: Sentencing Risk, 2013–2017. In: Fadil, N., De Koning, M. and Ragazzi, F. (eds), *Radicalization in Belgium and the Netherlands – Critical Perspectives on Violence and Security.* London and New York: IB Tauris, pp. 97–130.

De Koning, M. (2016) 'You Need to Present a Counter-Message': The Racialisation of Dutch Muslims and Anti-Islamophobia Initiatives. *Journal of Muslims in Europe,* 5(2), pp. 170–189, DOI:10.1163/22117954-12341325

De Koning, M. (2020) The Racialisation of Danger: Patterns and Ambiguities in the Relation between Islam, Security and Secularism in the Netherlands. *Patterns of Prejudice*, 54(1-2), pp. 123–135, DOI:10.1080/0031322x.2019.1705011

De Koning, M., Becker, C. and Roex, I. (2020) *Islamic Militant Activism in Belgium, the Netherlands and Germany – 'Islands in A Sea of Disbelief'.* London: Palgrave.

della Porta, D. (2006) *Social Movements, Political Violence, and the State: A Comparative Analysis of Italy and Germany.* Cambridge: Cambridge University Press.

Demant, F., Slootman, M., Buijs, F. and Tillie, J.N. (2008) *Decline and Disengagement: An Analysis of Processes of Deradicalisation.* Amsterdam: IMES.

Den Boer, M. (2007) Wake-up Call for the Lowlands: Dutch Counterterrorism from a Comparative Perspective. *Cambridge Review of International Affairs*, 20(2), pp. 285–302, DOI:10.1080/09557570701414658

Dooremalen, T. (2021) How Happenings Do (Not) Turn into Events: A Typology and An Application to the Case of 9/11 in the American and Dutch Public Spheres. *The British Journal of Sociology*, 72(3), pp. 725–741, DOI:10.1111/1468-4446.12847

Engbersen, G. and Broeders, D. (2011) Fortress Europe and the Dutch Donjon: Securitization, Internal Migration Policy and Irregular Migrants' Counter Moves. In: Truong, T.-D. and Gasper, D. (eds), *Transnational Migration and Human Security. The Migration-Development-Security Nexus.* Berlin: Springer, pp. 81–89.

Fadil, N. and de Koning, M. (2019) Turning 'Radicalisation' into Science. Ambivalent Translations into the Dutch (speaking) Academic field. In: Fadil, N., De Koning, M. and Ragazzi, F. (eds), *Radicalization in Belgium and the Netherlands. Critical Perspectives on Violence and Security.* London: IB Tauris, pp. 53–81.

Fijnaut, C. (1992) Political Violence and the Police Response in the Netherlands. *Conflict Quarterly*, 12(4), 55–66.

Groenendijk, K. (2008) La Nouvelle Politique d'intégration (NPI) aux Pays-Bas depuis 2002. *Cultures & Conflits* 69, pp. 113–129, DOI:10.4000/conflits.10832

Hainsworth, P. (2016) *The Politics of the Extreme Right: From the Margins to the Mainstream*: London: Bloomsbury Publishing.

Houtum, H.V. and Bueno Lacy, R. (2017) The Political Extreme as the New Normal: The Cases of Brexit, the French State of Emergency and Dutch Islamophobia. *Fennia – International Journal of Geography*, 195(1), 85, DOI:10.11143/fennia.64568

Klandermans, B. and Mayer, N. (2005) *Extreme Right Activists in Europe: Through the Magnifying Glass*: London: Routledge.

Klerks, P. (1989) *Terrorismebestrijding in Nederland 1970–1988.* Amsterdam: Ravijn.

Linden, A. (2009) *Besmet: Levenslopen en motieven van extreem-rechtse activisten in Nederland.* Amsterdam: Vrije Universiteit Amsterdam.

Luedtke, A. (2008) Fortifying Fortress Europe? The Effect of September 11 on EU Immigration Policy. In: Givens, T., Freeman, G.P. and Leal, D.L. (eds), *Immigration Policy and Security. U.S., European, and Commonwealth Perspectives.* New York: Routledge, pp. 138–155.

Lupton, D. (2006) Sociology and Risk. In: Mythen, G. and Walklate, S. (eds), *Beyond the Risk Society: Critical Reflections on Risk and Human Security.* Maidenhead: Open University Press, pp. 11–24.

Manjikian, M. (2017) Walking a Thin Line: The Netherland's Counterterrorism Challenge. In: Romaniuk, S.N., Grice, F., Irrera, D. and Webb, S. (eds), *The Palgrave Handbook of Global Counterterrorism Policy.* London: Palgrave Macmillan, pp. 371–392.

Mythen, G. (2020) Against the Odds? Unraveling the Paradoxes of Risk Prevention in Counter-Radicalization Strategy. In: Pratt, J. and Anderson, J. (eds), *Criminal Justice, Risk and the Revolt against Uncertainty.* Cham: Springer International Publishing, pp. 167–189.

Mythen, G., Walklate, S. and Peatfield, E.-J. (2016) Assembling and Deconstructing Radicalisation in PREVENT: A Case of Policy-based Evidence Making? *Critical Social Policy*, 37(2), pp. 180–201, DOI:10.1177/0261018316683463

NCTV (2018) *De golfbewegingen van rechts-extremistisch geweld in West-Europa – Aard, ernst en omvang van de rechts-extremistische dreiging in West-Europa, inclusief Nederland.* The Hague: National Coordinator for Counterterrorism and Security.

O'Malley, P. (2016) Risk, Law, and Security. In: Crichton, J., Candlin, C.N. and Firkins, A.S. (eds.), *Communicating Risk.* London: Palgrave Macmillan, pp. 85–102.

Penders, C.L.M. (2001) *The West New Guinea Debacle. Dutch Decolonisation and Indonesia 1945–1962.* Leiden: KITLV Press.

Prins, B. (2002) The Nerve to Break Taboos: New Realism in the Dutch Discourse on Multiculturalism. *Journal of International Migration and Integration/Revue de l'integration et de la migration internationale*, 3(3-4), pp. 363–379, DOI:10.1007/s12134-002-1020-9

Ragazzi, F. (2016) Suspect Community or Suspect Category? The Impact of Counter-Terrorism as 'Policed Multiculturalism' *Journal of Ethnic and Migration Studies*, 42(5), pp. 724–741, DOI:10.1080/1369183x.2015.1121807

Rasser, M. (2005) The Dutch Response to Moluccan Terrorism, 1970–1978. *Studies in Conflict and Terrorism*, 28(6), pp. 4814–4892.

Roggeband, C. and Vliegenthart, R. (2007) Divergent Framing: The Public Debate on Migration in the Dutch Parliament and Media, 1995–2004. *West European Politics*, 30(3), pp. 524–548, DOI:10.1080/01402380701276352

Schuurman, B., Eijkman, Q., and Bakker, E. (2014) The Hofstadgroup Revisited: Questioning its Status as a 'Quintessential' Homegrown Jihadist Network. *Terrorism and Political Violence*, 27(5), pp. 906–925, DOI:10.1080/09546553.2013.873719

Sterkenburg, N. (2021) *Van actie tot zelfverwezenlijking: routes van toetreding tot radicaal- en extreemrechts.* Leiden: Leiden University.

Van Ark (née Grozdanova), R. and Renckens, C. (2020) The Normalisation of Secrecy in the United Kingdom and the Netherlands: Individuals, the Courts and the Counter-Terrorism Framework. In: Paulussen, C. and Scheinin, M. (eds), *Human Dignity and Human Security in Times of Terrorism.* The Hague: T.M.C. Asser Press, pp. 333–365.

Van De Weert, A. and Eijkman, Q.A.M. (2019) Subjectivity in detection of radicalisation and violent extremism: a youth worker's perspective. *Behavioral Sciences of Terrorism and Political Aggression*, 11(3), pp. 191–214, DOI:10.1080/19434472.2018.1457069

Van De Weert, A. and Eijkman, Q.A.M. (2021) In Every Artery of Society? How Dutch Community Police Officers Perceive Their Role in Early Detection of Violent Extremism among Youth. *Policing: A Journal of Policy and Practice*, 15(2), pp. 1144–1157, DOI:10.1093/police/paaa038

Van der Heide, L. and Kearney, O. (2020) *The Dutch Approach to Extremist Offenders.* The Hague: International Centre for Counterterrorism.

Van der Heide, L. and Schuurman, B. (2018) Reintegrating Terrorists in the Netherlands: Evaluating the Dutch approach. *Journal for Deradicalisation*, 17, pp. 196–239, DOI:10.1080/1057610x.2017.1311111

Van der Leun, J.P. and Van der Woude, M.A.H. (2011) Ethnic Profiling in the Netherlands? A Reflection on Expanding Preventive Powers, Ethnic Profiling and a Changing Social and Political Context. *Policing and Society*, 21(4), pp. 444–455, DOI:10.1080/10439463.2011.610194

Van der Woude, M. (2010) *Wetgeving in een Veiligheidscultuur. Totstandkoming van antiterrorismewetgeving in Nederland bezien vanuit maatschappelijke en (rechts)politieke context*. PhD thesis, Boom Juridische Uitgevers, The Hague.

Van Donselaar, J. (1991) *Fout na de oorlog: fascistische en racistische organisaties in Nederland, 1950–1990*. Amsterdam: B. Bakker.

Van Meeteren, M.J. and Van Oostendorp, L.N. (2019) Are Muslims in the Netherlands constructed as a 'suspect community'? An analysis of Dutch political discourse on terrorism in 2004–2015. *Crime, Law and Social Change*, 71(5), pp. 525–540, DOI:10.1007/s10611-018-9802-y

Van Munster, R. and Aradau, C. (2008) Taming the Future: The Dispositif of Risk in the War on Terror. In: Amoore, L. and De Goede, M. (eds), *Risk and the War on Terror*. London: Routledge, pp. 23–40.

Vanparys, N., Jacobs, D. and Torrekens, C. (2013) The Impact of Dramatic Events on Public Debate Concerning Accommodation of Islam in Europe. *Ethnicities*, 13(2), pp. 209–228, DOI:10.1177/1468796812470899

Vieten, U.M. (2016) Far Right Populism and Women: The Normalisation of Gendered Anti-Muslim Racism and Gendered Culturalism in the Netherlands. *Journal of Intercultural Studies*, 37(6), pp. 621–636, DOI:10.1080/07256868.2016.1235024

Vliek, M. and De Koning, M. (2020) *Beleidsinstrumenten en extremistische wereldbeelden – Een verkennend rapport*. Radboud University [online] hdl.handle.net/20.500.12832/3020.

Walklate, S. and Mythen, G. (2014) *Contradictions of Terrorism: Security, Risk and Resilience*. London: Routledge.

Wesseling, M. and De Goede, M. (2018) *Counter-Terrorism Financing Policies in The Netherlands. Effectiveness and Effects (2013–2016)*. Amsterdam: Amsterdam Institute for Social Science Research.

Witte, R. and Scheepmaker, M. (2012) De bestrijding van etnische discriminatie: van speerpunt tot non-issue? *Justitiele Verkenningen*, 38(6), pp. 107–126.

10
NORWAY

Rune Ellefsen and Martin M. Sjøen

Introduction

Violent extremism has emerged as one of the most urgent threats to human security across Europe (European Security Strategy 2009). Extremism and political instability are exacerbated by populist narratives that risk undermining liberal democracy. Together, these challenges lead to growing demands for policies to counter threats to social and cultural well-being. The management of terrorism in particular has raised new questions about what makes people resistant to violence (Jore 2020a). The global 'War on Terror' is predicated upon the idea that violent extremism and terrorism cannot be prevented through traditional policing or military force alone (Aly, Balbi and Jacques 2015). New approaches to preventing extreme forms of violence therefore focus on strengthening the psychological and social capacity and capability that may keep people resistant to violence.

It is in this context that the notion of 'resilience' has found traction, with the international discourse on preventing violent extremism adopting it as the favoured aim (Stephens, Sieckelinck and Boutellier 2021). This might partly be a response to criticism of policies to prevent and counter violent extremism (P/CVE) for their securitisation of the social domain: resilience-building involves seemingly less problematic preventative approaches (Amery 2019; Wimelius et al. 2018). As a response to violent extremism, resilience may have some merit because it focuses on strengths rather than deficiencies by asking what makes individuals resilient rather than who is vulnerable to extreme violence. Exploring dimensions, processes, and pathways of individual and collective resilience may thus be a far more promising approach than the hegemonic top-down agendas that have dominated security politics since the 9/11 attacks (Aly, Balbi and Jacques 2015; Dalgaard-Nielsen and Schack 2016).

A variety of resilience policies and approaches targeting both individuals and communities, usually labelled as 'preventing' or 'countering violent extremism', have been developed across Europe. This policy field was pioneered in the United Kingdom, where it is now a statutory duty for several public sector services to have due regard to the need to prevent people from being drawn into terrorism (Home Office 2015). Research, however, has lagged practice on these matters, perhaps because of the way P/CVE approaches are being oriented by policy (Jore 2020b). Norway represents a particularly important case study of violent

DOI: 10.4324/9781003267102-12

This chapter has been made available under a CC-BY-NC-ND license.

extremism because of how much right-wing extremism it has suffered, alongside the relatively high number of Muslim foreign fighters who travelled from Norway to the Middle East (Lia and Nesser 2016).

Seeking to synthesise developments over recent decades, this chapter provides an overview of the emergence of violent extremist milieus in Norway and societal responses. We also explore challenges and different agendas in P/CVE approaches that aim to build resilience. Taking the example of the increased securitisation of P/CVE, we find a certain discrepancy between how resilience appears in security discourse versus P/CVE practice. We argue for deemphasising security-oriented P/CVE strategies that rely on intelligence and law enforcement actors in favour of facilitating social transformation as part of a pro-social approach to resilience.

Being resilient to violent extremism

The concept of resilience is based on the recognition that it is possible to overcome, if not improve, social and psychological conditions after adversity. Despite its current popularity, the notion of resilience is rife with contradictions and ambiguities since it has been widely used in both the natural and social sciences for many years (Jore 2020b). According to Grossman (2021), close analysis reveals that the notion of resilience varies greatly in content and meaning; Jore (2020c, p. 352) goes as far as to claim that resilience has been used to cover all psychosocial, physical, and technical factors related to violent extremism and terrorism and therefore explains very little. In short, critical scrutiny must be exercised in deciding the analytical precision of this all-encompassing conceptualisation of resilience.

A central tenet across much of the literature is that approaches to resilience focus on what makes people resistant to violence rather than on what makes them vulnerable to it. Psychological traits such as critical thinking and moral traits such as empathy and democratic values are often considered essential elements of resilience against violence (Stephens and Sieckelinck 2021). Resilience can thus be seen as a variety of strengths and resources enabling core functioning to be maintained when there are challenges arising from radicalisation and violent extremism. Resilience tends to be portrayed as an individual capacity – which means there is a need to focus on socio-ecological approaches to resilience. This 'pro-social' resilience involves the assumption that it is more reasonable to explore social contexts in which resilience can be demonstrated rather than seeking resilient individuals (Stephens and Sieckelinck 2020). Empirical research in the Nordic countries give credence to the notion of pro-social resilience to be seen in the key roles played by social agents such as family (Ellefsen and Sandberg 2022; Mohamed and Sandberg 2019), local communities (Dalgaard-Nielsen and Schack 2016), and other civil society actors like religious groups (Haugstvedt and Sjøen 2021).

In relation to pro-social resilience, Stephens and Sieckelinck (2020) explicate the need to focus on how social factors can block or mitigate the threat of violent extremism. They use the phrase 'resilience as connection', a conceptualisation that echoes an *a priori* idea that sees the main locus of resilience as being in social environments. All definitions of resilience concern social entities – be they individuals, organisations, or local communities – and their abilities to tolerate, absorb, cope with, and adjust to threats of various kinds (Keck and Sakdapolrak 2013, p. 8). Social approaches to resilience can also involve a form of democratisation, which may guide the process of societal and political transformation. Such transformation may provide an alternative to the individualised and vulnerability-oriented perspective on resilience that aligns with a performative post-modern society, where individuals who do not conform to the ideal images of citizens can be made subject to control and surveillance. The notion of community resilience is, however, sometimes criticised for offering a depoliticised and decontextualised understanding of violent extremism by shifting the responsibility from structural challenges to individuals and communities (Stephens and Sieckelinck 2021). To meet this criticism, the prevention of violent extremism should entail building capacity not only to counter extremist ideas, but also to empower individuals and communities to take action to address their grievances. We therefore propose to differentiate between a security-oriented approach to resilience in which security actors become a 'potent driver and shaper of contemporary resilience practices' (Coaffee and Fussey 2015, p. 87) and a pro-social approach, which is less security-driven and acknowledges the importance of social transformation and the democratisation of communities for the purpose of P/CVE work.

Norway: shifting extremist trends and responses

There are great differences between extremist milieus and responses to them in the period from 1990[1] to 2009 and between 2010 and the time of this publication. We use this temporal division to point out key developments determining the characteristics of contemporary P/CVE.

In the first period (1990–2009), the far-right landscape largely centred on localised racist youth gangs, Neo-Nazi skinhead groups, anti-immigration organisations, and a few small ethno-nationalist parties (Bjørgo 1999; Bjørgo and Carlsson 1999; Fangen 2001). There were racist gangs and Neo-Nazi skinheads in several communities in eastern and southern Norway. These milieus triggered the mobilisation of militant antifascist activists and broader civic engagement across local communities. There were violent attacks by right-wing extremists, targeting mainly immigrants of colour and anti-racists (Bjørgo and Gjelsvik 2018). The right-wing extremist milieu consisted largely of adolescents with troubled backgrounds and low socio-economic status. There were various responses to the phenomenon of right-wing extremism, which was usually depicted as a problem of youth gangs and youth crime (Bjørgo and Gjelsvik 2018).

Serious violent attacks by right-wing extremists forced local communities and government to acknowledge the need to change their understanding of these events and their response to them. In 1991, attacks by anti-immigrant and neo-Nazi activists on anti-racist demonstrators in the city of Brummundal became the catalyst that led the municipality to initiate measures to be carried out by a network of parents, civil society organisations, municipal actors, and local police. These responses were part of 'Action Plan Brummundal', which later became a model for other local communities and municipal governments with similar challenges (Fangen and Carlsson 2013). In later years this model – which combined targeted efforts by preventive police with interventions by voluntary organisations, parents, and the district administration – also helped dissolve right-wing extremist milieus in Oslo, Vennesla, and Kristiansand (Carlsson 1995; Carlsson and Lippe 1997). Organisations established by concerned parents, mentoring projects, and initiatives by civil society organisations like the local church also played key roles. Experience gained from these community network responses led to the launch of the pioneering EXIT project in 1997 by Tore Bjørgo[2] and other scholars (Carlsson and Haaland 2004; Bjørgo, Donselaar and Grunenberg 2009). However, local communities often failed to provide support for those who fell victim to right-wing extremist attacks (Bjørgo and Gjelsvik 2018, p. 58), and there has been little research into the role played by civic mobilisations against racism in dissolving right-wing extremist milieus and building community solidarity.

During the 1990s, right-wing extremist violence attracted much public attention and various counter-responses. The most violence-prone groups had their heyday from the late 1990s to the early 2000s when there was a series of serious violent attacks involving the use of firearms and bombs (Fangen 2001; Ravndal 2018). After three Neo-Nazis killed 15-year-old Benjamin Hermansen in Oslo in 2001, there was a massive counter-mobilisation against racism throughout the country. The youth's murder triggered a backlash that marked the demise of the form of right-wing extremism typical of this period.

There is extensive research on the years from 1991 to 2001, which is the period of greatest right-wing extremist activity between 1991 and 2009 (Bjørgo and Gjelsvik 2018; Fangen 2001). The period from 2005 to 2009, however, attracted much less public and scholarly attention (Bjørgo and Gjelsvik 2018) despite the emergence of new milieus with different characteristics from their subcultural Neo-Nazi predecessors.

At the beginning of our second period (2010–2021), it was primarily militant Islamist milieus that attracted the attention of scholars, security services, municipalities, and local communities as objects of concern. In 2010, the government introduced the first national Action Plan to prevent radicalisation and violent extremism.

The country's attention abruptly turned towards right-wing extremism and radical anti-Islamic milieus in 2011, following the 22 July terrorist attacks near government offices in Oslo and on the Labour Party's youth camp at Utøya that killed 77 people – the worst carnage in Norway's modern history. This was a turning point in policy, triggering a wave of changes in the national security apparatus and the introduction of laws to increase the ability of the security services, police, and correctional services to monitor, prosecute, and punish terrorist acts, including their planning and preparation (Sandvik, Ikdahl and Lohne 2021). It was Norway's first major lone-actor terrorist attack; the perpetrator published a manifesto citing widespread anti-Muslim conspiracy theories that motivated the attack and led to his selection of targets (Hemmingby and Bjørgo 2015). This lone-actor attack subsequently inspired similar incidents in other countries including the 2016 Munich shooting in Germany and the 2019 Christchurch Mosque shootings in New Zealand (Berntzen and Ravndal 2021).

National attention shifted back towards militant Islamists when they began to be more active in 2012 and 2013. Security concerns grew when people started travelling to Syria and recruiting others to go too. The rising numbers of travellers to Syria to become foreign fighters (at least one hundred) was high, considering Norway's relatively small Muslim population (Lia and Nesser 2016), which led to great national security concern about militant Islamist activist milieus. This resulted in another substantial wave of counter-responses by the Norwegian government.

In 2014, the second national Action Plan against violent extremism was launched with a much greater impact than the first. It was more specific about the course of action that should be taken and required greater emphasis on implementing multi-agency measures and cross-sectoral collaborations as well as efforts to educate frontline personnel and practitioners about radicalisation and violent extremism (Ellefsen 2021). Between 2012 and 2015, the emergent policy arena of radicalisation and violent extremism prevention was rapidly marked out as the police, regional agencies, and municipalities established designated positions to work on P/CVE and contact points where possible radicalisation and extremism could be reported. Those tasked with engaging in P/CVE work would now include municipal agencies like schools, childcare services, social services, outreach workers, and the local police together with civil society actors and religious communities as well as regional and national agencies.

Even after ISIS collapsed in 2016, militant Islamism remained a core issue for law enforcement agencies and municipalities primarily because of concern over returnees from Syria. By 2019, however, the militant Islamist milieu in Norway was greatly reduced due to more cohesive security policies and stricter legal frameworks at the national level, and the security services were starting to express concern about a rise in right-wing extremism in Norway and Europe (Bjørgo and Ravndal 2019). That same year, a right-wing lone-actor terrorist killed one person before unsuccessfully attacking a mosque on Oslo's outskirts as worshippers managed to overpower and disarm the terrorist. This attack, and similar ones in other countries by persons expressing right-wing extremist views, drew greater attention to this type of threat and the potential for single individuals to become radicalised and plan attacks with the internet as their main source of inspiration, without being physically engaged in an extremist milieu (PST 2020).

Despite militant Islamists taking up much attention in this second period spanning 2010 to the present day, important developments have occurred in the broader right-wing extremist milieu, which differs substantially from what it was like before 2010. The Neo-Nazi Norwegian Resistance Movement, for instance, re-emerged in 2011 and became the Norwegian chapter of the Nordic Resistance Movement (Bjørgo and Gjelsvik 2018), with greater visibility and presence online and offline after 2015 (Ravndal 2021). The right-wing extremist landscape of this period has some ideological similarities to that of the earlier period (Wilhelmsen 2021), but certain changes are important for understanding the groups, platforms used for mobilisation, and individuals involved (Ravndal 2020). This period is marked by stronger anti-Islamic ideology and more frequent actions targeting Muslims, although anti-Semitism is still recorded as being widespread (Berntzen 2019; Fangen and Nilsen 2020).

With the Neo-Nazi skinhead subculture having dissolved in the wake of Benjamin Hermansen's murder in 2001, right-wing extremist activity shifted focus, with the internet providing a new and important arena for the growth of these milieus (Haanshuus and Jupskås 2017). Internet and social media platforms have provided easy access to these groups and opportunities for them to disseminate propaganda (Conway, Scrivens and McNair 2019). Responses such as police online patrols have thus been introduced, and increased attention is paid to the internet's role in radicalisation. A shift towards online activity by organised milieus also seems to be related to the lower number of violent attacks by right-wing extremist groups in this period. Nonetheless, the lone-actor attacks in 2001 and 2011 caused more deaths, serious injuries, and negative societal ramifications than any others in the post-war period.

Like those recently engaged in militant Islamism, people in right-wing extremist milieus are now older than their counterparts in the earlier period (PST 2016, 2019). They are not mainly adolescents, generally being in their mid- or late twenties (Dalgaard-Nielsen and Lund 2019). They are still, however, largely characterised by their low socio-economic status. Members of one far-right anti-Islamic organisation – 'Stop Islamisation of Norway' – are, however, distinctly more better-off than those linked directly to violent extremism, and 75 per cent of the group's members are over the age of 50 (Tranøy 2020).

The anti-Islamic propaganda of the current groups and of other non-violent groups of the far right seems to resonate with a more widespread hostility towards Muslims, and the public debate has seen a growing normalisation of far-right viewpoints. These tendencies reflect a growing polarisation between sections of the population that is causing broader societal concern. Today, violent extremism is also influenced more strongly and rapidly by trends and influences from across the globe through easy access to the internet and globalisation (Grossman 2021).

These changing characteristics and the increased complexity of extremist milieus continue to be decisive for how P/CVE evolves. For example, the increased age of those engaging with extremist milieus reduce the available opportunities for responses; when individuals are over the age of legal adulthood (18 years) most non-coercive P/CVE initiatives require the voluntary consent of the target person. Consent is often challenging or impossible to attain, thus potentially leaving out many of the available soft types of intervention involving actors outside the criminal justice system. Also, the shift of much extremist activity from offline to online arenas – and the increased importance of online communities for individual radicalisation – calls for new types of P/CVE response. So far, a majority of P/CVE responses to these phenomena rely on increased online surveillance and content moderation, while efforts to build pro-social resilience in this area seems to be lagging behind and thus calls for innovative efforts. The changes of extremist milieus we have outlined trigger a simultaneous shift in what P/CVE responses are possible and appropriate. The rapid phase at which changes currently occur in extremist milieus, their online presence, and preferred tactics is thus a major challenge in itself.

Resilience in the Norwegian P/CVE policy discourse

Resilience-based P/CVE models have seemingly become more prominent in contemporary P/CVE policy in Norway, although existing societal crime prevention models lent themselves towards pro-social resilience approaches in the past. For instance, during the 1990s, counterterrorism policies were regarded as a controversial and unnecessary element in a democratic society, and Norwegian governments were reluctant to put them in place (Jore 2016). However, since 2008, following the surge in Islamist terrorism on the European continent that began in the mid-2000s, the idea of a Norwegian policy on preventing violent extremism started to gain traction and led to the 2010 Action Plan. As noted above, Norway had by then been severely affected by violent extremism, but the phenomenon was considered a local problem rather than a national security threat, and responses were tailored accordingly. In the last ten years, Norwegian governments have launched three national Action Plans for preventing violent extremism (in 2010, 2014, and 2020), while also encouraging the creation of at least 36 municipal P/CVE policies and guidelines (Jore 2020a).

According to Lid et al. (2016), the Norwegian P/CVE approach is based on a societal crime prevention model that is grounded in the ideals and values of a democratic welfare state. Like the other Scandinavian countries, Norway has a long-established system of community policing, along with a very liberal criminal justice system (Vindino and Branden 2012). Even the Norwegian police and criminal care system is said to differ from that of many other countries in its wide use of soft resilience measures, which include building trust, dialogue, and being present in the community and building close relations with it. Yet the concept of 'resilience' is not often invoked in the domain of Norwegian P/CVE policy and is rarely mentioned in political documents.

In the Action Plan of 2010, one of few mentions of 'resilience' can be found in the claim that P/CVE approaches should 'increase the resilience of communities to violent extremism, and [...] address the grievances which ideologues are exploiting' (p. 12). Resistance is also referred to here:

> [A] strong democratic culture is an aim in itself for the whole of Norwegian society, but can also help strengthen the individual's resistance to violent extremist ideology and thereby have a preventive effect in this field.
>
> *Action Plan 2010, p. 32*

These sentiments may reflect a form of pro-social resilience with the emphasis on strengthening democratic capacity and capability to prevent violent extremism. However, the document is characterised by a content in which vulnerable individuals should be protected, rather than exploring what is keeping people resistant to violence:

> Whether a person ends up as a criminal with a substance abuse problem, or as a violent extremist, usually happens by chance and depends on 'who gets to you first'. The common denominator is vulnerability, and therefore good preventive measures will usually be general measures.
>
> *Action Plan 2010, p. 8*

The vulnerability perspective is frequently criticised for its close association with a security-driven perspective on violent extremism (Kundnani 2014). This conceptualisation of vulnerability is, nevertheless, a consistent feature of the Norwegian P/CVE policy domain. However, a discursive change can be seen in the national Action Plans of 2014 and 2020, as the concepts of 'resilience' and 'resistance' against violent extremism are absent from what seems to be more security-oriented policies. It should be noted that these policy documents underline the importance of creating a safe and inclusive society for everyone, yet a reconfiguration of the security rhetoric can be seen in the frequent use of the word 'combat' to describe P/CVE approaches in Norway (Action Plan 2014). There are, for instance, statements claiming that the 'Norwegian government wants to combat radicalisation and violent extremism more effectively' (p. 5). Furthermore, the 2014 Action Plan argues that it is of great importance to base P/CVE efforts 'to combat radicalisation and violent extremism on the same basic principles as the general prevention of crime' (p. 13). One could certainly question the merit of 'combat' in a policy that aims to prevent conflict, particularly as Norwegian police and the correctional service have been characterised by their soft rather than hard preventive approaches. This policy document even equates 'combat' and 'dialogue', as efforts to prevent extremism are said to require 'support of dialogue and preventative efforts to combat radicalisation' (p. 21).

Based on these observations and readings of other policy documents, it seems that the concept of resilience features indirectly in Norwegian policy discourse via claims about preventing violent extremism through democracy and social welfare. Thus, while P/CVE policy is a continuation of counterterrorism in Norway (Jore 2020a), prevention is still sometimes used in parts with a meaning that corresponds to how pro-social resilience is understood in the scholarly literature (cf. Grossman 2021). For instance, counterterrorism was once a centralised task of the state, but now we see it transferred from the state to all sectors of society, with a focus on early intervention and prevention of 'home-grown' radicalisation. There is increased attention to social resilience, as shown by the 2021 white paper on societal security in which there are 45 references to resilience; the government's stated aim, for example, is to 'further develop societal resilience through increased emphasis on preventive work' (White Paper 2021, p. 15, authors' translation). Democratic resilience to violent extremism has even found its way into the revised national curriculum (Sjøen and

Mattsson 2022). Contemporary P/CVE approaches in Norway are thus to a great extent embedded in localised prevention efforts where there are existing networks for collaborative work against various forms of crime (Ellefsen 2021).

While resilience seems to be neither precisely defined nor conceptualised in Norwegian P/CVE policy discourse, our analysis indicates there has been a change from top-down security-oriented measures towards more localised pro-social approaches to preventing violent extremism. However, other developments seem to be taking P/CVE in a more security-oriented direction, which we examine in the next section.

Resilience in Norwegian practice

Between the earlier (1990–2009) and later (2010–2021) periods, the phenomenon that was to be countered changed from being understood as a youth problem to being one associated with violent extremism. The public discourse about what amounted to violent extremism and terrorism has also changed substantially across the two periods (Husabø 2018). The dominant labelling of the phenomena in question also impacts our understanding of the appropriate and legitimate measures of response to it (Fangen and Kolås 2016). While terrorism and the societal attempts to prevent terrorism were once viewed as unnecessary and a threat to civil liberties, preventing extreme forms of violence is now perceived as a necessity and a societal obligation (Jore 2016).

Changes in criminal, administrative, and other areas of law have also extended the powers available to the police, security services, and state administration to intervene at earlier stages and to utilise a wider array of interventions, surveillance, and preventive intelligence-gathering. The changed societal responses to extremism since the 1990s raise important questions about contemporary P/CVE approaches; below, we look closely at examples of the increased securitisation to be observed in P/CVE practice and its implications.

In the 1990s, local initiatives to disengage people from extremist milieus developed into the first EXIT project in Europe. What seems unique to that period was the new model of local community collaboration between private, civil, local municipal actors, and the police in using a variety of largely soft preventive and pro-social measures against extremism. This model seemingly inspired today's P/CVE policy and is still reflected in it. In 2012, a comparison of Norway with other European countries found that 'more weight has so far been put on preventive measures than on repressive measures' in Norway's P/CVE approach (Vindino and Branden 2012). Scholars have also argued that the strategies implemented most successfully in many Norwegian municipalities are precisely the soft forms of social intervention that aim to disengage right-wing extremists and reintegrate them into their local communities (Fangen and Carlsson 2013).

It remains to be assessed whether the soft measures and social interventions identified as core traits of Norway's P/CVE approach – which overlaps with what we term a pro-social approach to resilience – are changing, and whether the predominance of such measures is being reduced in favour of harder ones, that is, more control and closer surveillance. Based on empirical research by ourselves and others, we argue that Norwegian P/CVE practice has in some ways moved away from being mainly soft and pro-social oriented.

For instance, the first P/CVE Action Plan (2010, p. 5) stressed the importance of preventing violent extremism mainly through the winning of 'hearts and minds' – in recognition of the role of democratic values as a bulwark against violent extremism. However, in the most recent addition to policy in this area, we see indications of an emphasis on societal vigilant surveillance: there are frequent mentions of the need for the public to report suspicious activity to law enforcement agencies (Action Plan 2020, p. 5). This would suggest that pro-social P/CVE strategies are being challenged by the expansion of security-based social control measures to prevent extremism, which as mentioned has been a dominant characteristic of the War on Terror (Kundnani 2014).

After the 22 July 2011 terrorist attacks, and in the wake of extraordinary security threats related to global jihadism between 2013 and 2016, the local P/CVE approach seemed to be accompanied by a parallel increase in security-oriented efforts and harder measures. In contrast to the soft measures we described as characteristic of early preventive strategies, the white paper published after the 22 July attacks declared the need for new initiatives that were more focused on control and surveillance than on integration and education (Fangen and Carlsson 2013, p. 347; White Paper 2012). Scholars and civil society actors in European countries with more developed P/CVE arenas have already pointed to many of the issues that arise from an excessively security-driven approach to building resilience (Kundnani 2014).

Since 2014, P/CVE policy has featured a related specialisation within the police, with new positions designated in each police district ('radicalisation contacts') to gather intelligence as well as monitor and handle concerns reported by the general public and public services about individuals who may be becoming radicalised. An earlier investigation of P/CVE collaborations across Norwegian municipalities reported concerns about this specialisation and the ever-greater and more central role this gave the police in preventive networks where they collaborated with other municipal actors outside the criminal justice field (Lid et al. 2016). The specialised role of the police was seen to influence its relationship with the municipality in a way that led more of the preventative work to be channelled to the police or security services, taking it away from other more socially oriented agencies. This also led the police to take on a more extensive role in following up with people linked to radicalisation or extremist milieus than might be desirable (ibid., pp. 233–234; Nybø 2020). As such, there has been a securitisation of community-based approaches towards the prevention of violence.

Increased specialisation and the building of competence across other municipal actors has the potential for reversing this trend and making P/CVE practice less security-driven and less reliant upon police and law enforcement agencies. Even if municipal actors outside the criminal justice system take on a more prominent role in P/CVE, close involvement with the police and security service, including exchanges of intelligence, might lead to these municipal actors being less trusted if they were perceived as an extension of state security (Lid et al. 2016; Kruse 2019). Such challenges manifest, for example, when law enforcement and intelligence actors seek to become directly involved with the families of radicalised individuals or with peers that have strong social ties with them. When state security agencies seek to 'engage with the family and peers close to a target person, they risk undermining that person's trusting relation' to them – which effective informal intervention depends on – if they are seen as collaborating closely with the police or secret service (Ellefsen and Sandberg 2022).

The above examples demonstrate some of the challenges of the Norwegian P/CVE approach that has become perhaps too oriented towards tackling risk and where criminal justice actors are too dominant in cross-sectoral preventive networks. There has been little public debate about these issues or scholarly attention to them in Norway, perhaps because of the short history of national P/CVE practice and the relatively low level of imminent threats of large-scale terrorist attacks. Scholars have also suggested that when Norwegian counterterrorism evolved into a policy to prevent radicalisation and violent extremism, critical investigation seemed absent. This is presumably because the discourse on preventing violent extremism 'fits the values of the welfare state that Norwegian society is based on' and because P/CVE practice is 'portrayed as a form of caregiving and safeguarding of vulnerable individuals', which aligns with how many local municipal agencies and civil society organisations understand their role in the Norwegian welfare state (Jore 2020a, p. 194). In 2020, the aim of preventing terrorism through education was even made part of the core curriculum in Norway, with surprisingly little criticism or debate among educational scholars and practitioners (Sjøen and Mattsson 2022). Although the curricular description extends from how democratic citizenship is seen as a protective factor against terrorism, accompanying the securitisation of curricular activities are political expectations on educators to use their classrooms to detect future terrorists and report potential violent crimes that have not yet been committed. Hence, the education–security nexus is characterised by a discursive struggle where pro-social logics and security-oriented logics are co-existing, competing, and mixed in educational policy documents.

A pro-social approach to resilience

While the work of the police and security services is clearly necessary in P/CVE and counterterrorism, we have identified some of the challenges their involvement might create, particularly in cross-sectoral preventive efforts. The challenges of securitised P/CVE approaches make it worthwhile to further explore what a pro-social approach to resilience might entail, with its somewhat different agenda. Grossman (2021, p. 310) argues that a core feature of such an approach is that it recognises the relevance of 'aspects of resilient systems drawn from outside an immediate concern with social or political violence', which might include social capital and connectedness, as well as 'the strength of social support and development systems such as the education, health, social welfare, and human rights sectors'. The strand of literature that emphasises social capital as key for community resilience has also influenced the perception of resilience in the context of P/CVE – not only by taking a less securitised, more pro-social approach to preventing violent extremism, but also by inspiring an agenda that diverges from the security-driven resilience approaches seen abroad that have been criticised for targeting entire communities as suspect, vulnerable, or deficient (Grossman 2021; Kundnani 2014).

Pro-social P/CVE initiatives have, for example, included youth mentoring programmes designed to develop resilience by using team sports to address issues of identity, belonging, and cultural isolation amongst young Muslim men (Johns, Grossman and McDonald 2014). A Norwegian study demonstrated the decisive role of friends and parents in disrupting radicalisation of close friends or relatives without the need of involving the police (Ellefsen and Sandberg 2022), and thus underlining the importance of trusting relations as a basis for pro-social efforts by civil society actors. Another example from Norway is the 'deep debate' initiative developed by the municipality of Fredrikstad that provides middle and high school students a platform for discussing controversial societal issues. The initiative is a cooperation between local and regional education services, the municipality, and Fredrikstad Literature House, and it confronts complicated issues such as extremism, ethics, and foreign policy (Nordic Safe Cities 2021).

Norwegian schools have the task of educating students in values like democracy and assisting them to develop multicultural understanding, with the underlying assumption that such education 'in citizenship itself' helps make pupils resistant to radicalisation (Fangen and Carlsson 2013, p. 340). Education about diverse religious and non-religious values in schools may assist in 'addressing religious vilification, discrimination and interreligious tensions' and even help build 'religious literacy and social inclusion' among adolescents, and thereby provide pupils with resources that strengthen individual and collective resilience (Halafoff, Lam and Bouma 2019, p. 381). Scholars have pointed out the risks of undermining the positive influence of such democratic spaces for debate, dialogue, and learning in schools and universities. If teachers are required to report any sign of radicalisation or expression of radical viewpoints to the police, this security-driven obligation may disrupt teachers' efforts to build trusting relations with their pupils (Sjøen and Mattsson 2022). Important pro-social efforts for building community resilience may thus be undermined.

Local political participation and civic activism may also play important roles in a pro-social approach to building community resilience. When communities mobilise popular support for, and public expressions of, anti-racism they demonstrate that racism is unacceptable. For members of minority groups such bottom-up community mobilisation might counter potential alienation and even provide some protection from extremist milieus. This was seemingly the case in Brummundal, which racists and Neo-Nazis made a hostile place for immigrants; this hostility was then countered by local anti-racist mobilisation (Fangen and Carlsson 2013). Scholarship on anti-racist pro-social action has also pointed out the great policy potential of 'bystander anti-racism' – action taken by ordinary community members in response to racist incidents (Nelson, Dun and Paradies 2011).

Informal everyday initiatives are important components of a pro-social approach that uses trusting social relations to resist violent extremism and build resilience to it. Some studies of experiences of interventions against radicalisation revealed that young Norwegian Muslims found their peers and family to be most important for preventing radicalisation into violent extremism (Ellefsen and Sandberg 2022; Mohamed and Sandberg 2019). While Muslim communities have been the primary target of top-down measures to prevent violent extremism (Winsvold, Mjelde and Loga 2019), local people also mount their own bottom-up resistance to religious extremism, including religious counter-narratives to jihadism that might help fend off jihadist propaganda among Muslims (Sandberg and Colvin 2020; Haugstvedt and Sjøen 2021). Such bottom-up efforts, along with the others described above, are all important parts of a multi-level pro-social approach to resilience.

Concluding remarks

In this chapter we have explored developments in Norwegian extremist milieus between 1990 and 2021 and responses to them. Our aim has been to capture the changing characteristics of P/CVE policy and practice in Norway and relate them to a discussion about resilience and what makes people resistant to violence. The historical changes we describe in P/CVE policy and practice are related to different perceptions of resilience, where we show the difference between security-oriented and pro-social approaches. We found that the concept of resilience rarely figures in Norwegian P/CVE policy documents, although it often appears in recent policy documents on general societal security. The discourse on resilience in P/CVE policy, however, expresses certain logics that align with a pro-social approach to resilience, and the discourse emphasises the need to strengthen protective factors in communities to prevent radicalisation and violent extremism. At the same time, the discourse also involves security-oriented aims and measures, and these have become more pronounced in recent years. Simultaneously, contemporary P/CVE practices have visibly become increasingly securitised during the last decade by a greater focus on surveillance and the establishment of society-wide structures for reporting signs of radicalisation and violent extremism to the authorities. We argue that this 'softer' form of surveillance in Norwegian P/CVE approaches represents the social legitimation of preventive actors being watchful observers for the central state.

While Norwegian P/CVE policy and practice seek to combine measures and actors across sectors in preventative efforts outside the realms of criminal justice and security, both of these seem to have become more influenced by security concerns. Law enforcement and intelligence actors increasingly have influence and brokerage roles in local multi-agency preventive practice, while security concerns and monitoring are becoming more prominent in policy. These developments have taken P/CVE in a more securitised direction than was the case in the 1990s, and we have outlined some of the dilemmas that result from this. The increased orientation towards security might, as we have demonstrated, be counterproductive for certain pro-social efforts to build community resilience. We have briefly described what a pro-social approach to resilience might entail, suggesting an agenda less dominated by security concerns and security actors.

Recognising the social factors in resilience, we emphasise the need to build individual and collective ability to reject extremist narratives to reduce mobilisation into extremist movements. However, Norwegian communities could also be empowered to build resilience by encouraging criticism of oppressive ideologies and social grievances. Until recently, this approach has scarcely been explored, as the focus on vulnerability in the security-oriented discourse on resilience tends to divert attention from structural reasons for people joining extremist groups. If structural explanations are not addressed properly, however, involvement in extremist movements will persist, while pro-social resilience may make it possible to explore political and structural reasons that create space and opportunity for democratic transformation (Stephens and Sieckelinck 2020).

Because a securitised approach to resilience and P/CVE has become more dominant in Norway, it is important to avoid disrupting local community-led, pro-social efforts that have existed and been developed since the 1990s. Particularly, the strong emphasis of central government on an early warning system based on extensive surveillance and reporting of perceived radicalisation risks creating barriers for building trust and social networks across social, political, and religious groups in communities. This is one of the reasons we suggest deemphasising securitised P/CVE approaches in favour of developing pro-social forms of resilience to violent extremism in Norway.

Notes

1 There were also right-wing extremist milieus before the 1990s but because of space limitations we start our description in 1990. Some of the tendencies and groups of the 1990s were, however, established in the 1980s or were continuations of what started then (see Bjørgo 1997; Fangen 1999).
2 Bjørgo is currently the director of the Centre for Research on Extremism (C-REX) in Norway.

References

Action Plan (2010) *Action Plan against Radicalisation and Violent Extremism*. Oslo: Norwegian Ministry of Justice and Public Security.
Action Plan (2014) *Action Plan against Radicalisation and Violent Extremism*. Oslo: Norwegian Ministry of Justice and Public Security.
Action Plan (2020) *Action Plan against Radicalisation and Violent Extremism*. Oslo: Norwegian Ministry of Justice and Public Security.
Aly, A., Balbi, A.M. and Jacques, C. (2015) Rethinking Countering Violent Extremism: Implementing the Role of Civil Society. *Journal of Policing, Intelligence and Counter Terrorism*, 10(1), pp. 3–13, DOI:10.1080/18335330.2015.1028772

Amery, F. (2019) Resilience in British Social Policy: Depoliticising Risk and Regulating Deviance. *Politics*, 39(3), pp. 363–378, DOI:10.1177/0263395718777920

Berntzen, L.E. (2019) *Liberal Roots of Far Right Activism: The Anti-Islamic Movement in the 21st Century*. Abingdon and New York: Routledge.

Berntzen, L.E. and Ravndal, J.A. (2021) Monster or Hero? Far-right Responses to Anders Behring Breivik and the July 22, 2011, Terrorist Attacks. *Perspectives on Terrorism*, 15(3), pp. 37–59.

Bjørgo, T. (1997) *Racist and Right-Wing Violence in Scandinavia: Patterns, Perpetrators, and Responses*. Oslo: Tano Aschehoug.

Bjørgo, T. and Carlsson, Y. (1999) *Violence, Racism, and Youth Gangs: Prevention and Intervention*. Oslo: Tano Aschehoug.

Bjørgo, T., Donselaar, J.V. and Grunenberg, S. (2009) Exit from Right-Wing Extremist Groups: Lessons from Disengagement Programmes in Norway, Sweden and Germany. In: Bjørgo, T. and Horgan, J. (eds.), *Leaving Terrorism Behind: Individual and Collective Disengagement*. New York: Routledge, pp. 135–151.

Bjørgo, T. and Gjelsvik, I.M. (2018) *Right-Wing Extremism in Norway: Development trends, conspiracy theories and prevention strategies*. PHS Research, 4.

Bjørgo, T. and Ravndal, J.A. (2019) *Extreme-Right Violence and Terrorism: Concepts, Patterns, and Responses*. ICCT Policy Brief, International Centre for Counter-Terrorism, DOI:10.19165/2019.1.08

Carlsson, Y. (1995) *Action plan Brummundal – Did it Yield Results? Combating Xenophobic Violence in the Local Community*. Report. Oslo: Norwegian Institute for Urban and Regional Research.

Carlsson, Y. and Haaland, T. (2004) *Violent Youth Groups – Intervention on a Municipality Level. Report from Kristiansand 2001–2004*. Report. Oslo: Norwegian Institute for Urban and Regional Research.

Carlsson, Y. and Lippe, H.V.L. (1997) *The Industrial area and Racism: The Development and Dismantling of Xenophobic Youth Environment in Vennesla 1991–1996*. Report Oslo: Norwegian Institute for Urban and Regional Research.

Coaffee, J. and Fussey, P. (2015) Constructing Resilience through Security and Surveillance: The Politics, Practices and Tensions of Security-Driven Resilience. *Security Dialogue*, 46(1), pp. 86–105.

Conway, M., Scrivens, R., and McNair, L. (2019) *Right-Wing Extremists' Persistent Online Presence: History and Contemporary Trends*. Policy Report. The Hague: International Centre for Counter-terrorism.

Dalgaard-Nielsen, A. and Lund, L. (2019) *Safe in a Time of Terror*. Copenhagen: Lindhardt Ringhof.

Dalgaard-Nielsen, A. and Schack, P. (2016) Community Resilience to Militant Islamism: Who and What? An Explorative Study of Resilience in Three Danish Communities. *Democracy and Security*, 12(4), pp. 309–327, DOI: 10.1080/17419166.2016.1236691

Ellefsen, R. (2021) Prevention of Radicalization as an Emergent Field of Plural Policing in Norway: The Accelerating Role of Militant Islamists. *Nordic Journal of Studies in Policing*, 1(8), pp. 1–23, DOI:10.18261/issn.2703-7045-2021-01-03

Ellefsen, R. and Sandberg, S. (2022) Everyday Prevention of Radicalization: The Impacts of Family, Peer, and Police Intervention. *Studies in Conflict and Terrorism*, DOI: 10.1080/1057610X.2022.2037185

European Security Strategy (2009) *A Secure Europe in a Better World*. Council of the European Union. Belgium: DGF-Communication/Publications.

Fangen, K. (1999) *Pride and Power – A Sociological Interpretation of the Norwegian Radical Nationalist Underground Movement*. PhD thesis. University of Oslo, Norway.

Fangen, K. (2001) *A Book about Neo-Nazis*. Oslo: Universitetsforlaget.

Fangen, K. and Carlsson, Y. (2013) Right-Wing Extremism in Norway: Prevention and Intervention. In: Melzer, R. and Serafin, S. (eds.), *Right-Wing Extremism in Europe: Country Analyses, Counter-Strategies and Labor-Market Oriented Exit Strategies*. Berlin: Friedrich Ebert Stiftung, pp. 327–358.

Fangen, K. and Kolås, Å. (2016) The 'Syria traveller': Reintegration or Legal Sanctioning? *Critical Studies on Terrorism*, 9(3), pp. 414–432, DOI:10.1080/17539153.2016.1192260

Fangen, K. and Nilsen, M.R. (2020) Variations Within the Norwegian Far Right: From Neo Nazism to Anti-Islamism. *Journal of Political Ideologies*, 26(3), pp. 278–297, DOI:10.1080/13569317.2020.1796347

Grossman, M. (2021) Resilience to Violent Extremism and Terrorism: A Multisystemi Analysis. In: Ungar, M. (ed.), *Multisystemic Resilience*. New-York: Oxford University Press, pp. 293–317.

Haanshuus, B.P. and Jupskås A.R. (2017) Right Click! An Analysis of the Far Right on Social Media in Norway. *Tidsskrift for Samfunnsforskning*, 58(2), pp. 145–165, DOI:10.18261/issn.1504- 291X-2017-02-01

Halafoff, A., Lam, K. and Bouma, G. (2019) Worldviews Education: Cosmopolitan Peacebuilding and Preventing Violent Extremism. *Journal of Beliefs & Values*, 40(3), pp. 381–395, DOI: 10.1080/13617672.2019.1600113

Haugstvedt, H. and Sjøen, M.M. (2021) Exploring Youths' Willingness to Engage with Civil Society and Public Sector Institutions: The Untapped Potential of Religious Communities in Preventing Violent Extremism. *Democracy and Security*, 17(4), pp. 337–355, DOI: 10.1080/17419166.2021.1950383

Hemmingby, C. and Bjørgo, T. (2015) *The Dynamics of a Terrorist Targeting Process: Anders B. Breivik and the 22 July Attacks in Norway*. London: Palgrave Macmillan.

Home Office (2015) *Counterterrorism and Security Act 2015*. United Kingdom Parliament, c.6, February. London: TSO.

Husabø, E.J. (2018) *Terrorism in Norwegian Criminal Law. An Analysis of Penal Code Chapter 18*. Bergen: Fagbokforlaget.

Johns, A., Grossman, M. and McDonald, K. (2014) 'More Than a Game': The Impact of Sport-Based Youth Mentoring Schemes on Developing Resilience toward Violent Extremism. *Social Inclusion*, 2(2), pp. 57–70, DOI:10.17645/si.v2i2.167

Jore, S.H. (2016) Norwegian Media Substantiation of Counterterrorism Measures. *Journal of Risk Research*, 19(1), pp. 101–118, DOI: 10.1080/13669877.2014.961507

Jore, S.H. (2020a) Countering Radicalisation in Norwegian Terrorism Policy. A Welfare State Approach to Societal Security. In: Larsson, S. and Rhinard, M. (eds.), *Nordic Societal Security Convergence and Divergence*. London and New York: Routledge, pp. 179–198.

Jore, S.H. (2020b) Is Resilience a Favourable Concept in Terrorism Research? The Multifaceted Discourses of Resilience in the Academic Literature. *Critical Studies on Terrorism*, 13(2), pp. 337–357, DOI:10.1080/17539153.2020.1733788

Jore, S.H. (2020c) Is Resilience a Good Concept in Terrorism Research? A Conceptual Adequacy Analysis of Terrorism Resilience. *Studies in Conflict & Terrorism*, DOI: 10.1080/1057610X.2020.1738681

Keck, M. and Sakdapolrak, P. (2013) What Is Social Resilience? Lessons Learned and Ways Forward. *Erkunde*, 67(1), pp. 5–19.

Kruse, E.L. (2019) *Giving Me a Problematic Life Was Not Right. A Qualitative Study of Being the Target of Radicalisation Concern*. Master's thesis, Østfold University College, Norway.

Kundnani, A. (2014) *The Muslims are Coming! Islamophobia, Extremism, and the Domestic War on Terror*. London: Verso Books.

Lia, B. and Nesser, P. (2016) Jihadism in Norway: A Typology of Militant Networks in a Peripheral European Country. *Perspectives on Terrorism*, 10(6), pp. 121–134.

Lid, S., Winsvold, M., Søholt, S., Hansen, S.J., Heierstad, G. and Klausen, J.E. (2016) *Preventing Radicalisation and Violent Extremism: What Is the Role of the Municipality?* Norwegian Institute for Urban and Regional Research Report 2016/12.

Mohamed, I.A.A. and Sandberg, S. (2019) I Cannot Watch my Sisters Walk Into the Trap. Ung Muslims as Preventers. In: Lid, S. and Heierstad, G. (eds.), *Preventing Radicalisation and Violent Extremism*. Oslo: Gyldendal Akademisk, pp. 199–222.

Nelson, J.K., Dunn, K.M. and Paradies, Y. (2011) Bystander Anti-Racism: A Review of the Literature. *Analyses of Social Issues and Public Policy*, 11(1), pp. 263–284, DOI: 10.1111/j.1530-2415.2011.01274.x

Nordic Safe Cities (2021) *Fredrikstad, Norway*, https://nordicsafecities.org/member-cities/fredrikstad.

Nybø, T.K. (2020) *When Good Intentions Make Matters Worse – The Unintended Side Effects and Negative Consequences of Measures to Prevent Radicalisation and Violent Extremism*. Master's thesis. University of Oslo, Norway.

PST (2016) *Theme Report: What Background do People who Frequent Extreme Islamist Circles in Norway Have Before They are Radicalised?* The Norwegian Police Security Service, External report 16/03327.

PST (2019) *Theme Report: What Background Do People Have in 'Extreme-Right Environments in Norway?* The Norwegian Police Security Service, 17/12585-16.

PST (2020) *Police Security Service's Threat Assessment 2020*. Norwegian Police Security Service.

Ravndal, J.A. (2018) Right-wing Terrorism and Militancy in the Nordic Countries: A Comparative Case Study. *Terrorism and Political Violence*, 30(5), pp. 772–792, DOI: 10.1080/09546553.2018.1445888

Ravndal, J.A. (2020) From Treason to 'Trolling' – the Development in the Norwegian Right Wing Extremist Threat Picture from 1945 to 2019. *Nytt Norsk Tidsskrift*, 37(4), pp. 355–368, DOI:10.18261/issn.1504-3053-2020-04-06

Ravndal, J.A. (2021) From Bombs to Books, and Back Again? Mapping Strategies of Right-Wing Revolutionary Resistance. *Studies in Conflict & Terrorism*, DOI:10.1080/1057610X.2021.1907897

Sandberg, S. and Colvin, S. (2020) 'ISIS Is Not Islam': Epistemic Injustice, Everyday Religion, and Young Muslims' Narrative Resistance. *The British Journal of Criminology*, 60(6), pp. 1585–1605, DOI:10.1093/bjc/azaa035

Sandvik, K.B., Ikdahl, I. and Lohne, K. (2021) Law after July 22, 2011: Survivors, Reconstruction and Memory. *Norsk Sosiologisk Tidsskrift*, 5(3), pp. 28–45, DOI:10.18261/issn.2535-2512-2021-03-03

Sjøen, M.M. and Mattsson, C. (2022) Depoliticising political violence: State-centric and individualised discourses in the Norwegian counterterrorism policy field. Scandinavian Journal of Educational Research, DOI: https://doi.org/10.1080/00313831.2022.2114543

Stephens, W., Sieckelinck, S. and Boutellier, H. (2021) Preventing Violent Extremism: A Review of the Literature. *Studies in Conflict & Terrorism*, 44(4), pp. 346–361, DOI: 10.1080/1057610X.2018.1543144

Stephens, W. and Sieckelinck, S. (2020) Being Resilient to Radicalisation in PVE Policy: A Critical Examination. *Critical Studies on Terrorism*, 13(1), pp. 142–165, DOI: 10.1080/17539153.2019.1658415

Stephens, W. and Sieckelinck, S. (2021) Resiliences to Radicalization: Four Key Perspectives. *International Journal of Law, Crime and Justice*, 66, pp. 1–14, DOI:10.1016/j.ijlcj.2021.100486

Tranøy, H.P.R. (2020) *Activists Against Islam: An Empirical Study of the Members of SIAN*. Master's thesis, University of Oslo, Norway.

Vindino, L. and Branden, J. (2012) *Countering Radicalization in Europe*. Policy report. London: International Centre for the Study of Radicalisation and Political Violence.

Winsvold, M., Mjelde, H. and Loga, J. (2019) What Should be Prevented, and How? Muslim Faith Communities View on Their Role in Preventing Radicalisation and Violent Extremism. In: Lid, S. and Heierstad, G. (eds.), *Preventing Radicalisation and Violent Extremism*. Oslo: Gyldendal Akademisk, pp. 115–132.

White Paper (2012) *The Gjørv Report*. Report of the 22 July Commission.

White Paper (2021) *Societal Safety in an Unsafe World*. Oslo: Ministry of Justice and Public Security.

Wilhelmsen, F. (2021) From New Order to the Millennium of White Power: Norwegian Fascism Between Party Politics and Lone-Actor Terrorism. *Politics, Religion & Ideology*, 22(1), pp. 17–39, DOI:10.1080/21567689.2021.1877669

Wimelius, M.E., Kinsman, J., Strandh, V. and Ghazinour, M. (2018) What is Local Resilience Against Radicalization and How can it be Promoted? A Multidisciplinary Literature Review. *Studies in Conflict & Terrorism*, DOI: 10.1080/1057610X.2018.1531532

11
GERMANY

Fabian Virchow

As the successor state to German Nazism, right-wing extremist tendencies, occurrences, and events in Germany are registered with particular attention in neighbouring European countries, but also within Germany. During the last seven decades, there have been lots of different activities of right-wing extremist protagonists: parties seeking to gain influence in parliament, right-wing extremist think tanks and cultural organisations, but also a variety of violent actors aiming to intimidate and drive out particular social groups whom they regard as enemies of the idea of a Voelkish nation. For a long time, the Federal Republic of Germany relied on three main approaches to combat right-wing extremism: banning the corresponding associations or setting limits with criminal law, social work, and civic education. Only in the last 20 years have further approaches been added to strengthen the resilience of society.

Resilience is a concept fed by various academic perspectives and has a wide range of concretisations (Ungar 2021); particular conceptualisations of resilience have become part of counterterrorism strategies (Hardy 2015), supplementing risk-focused approaches on extremism and radicalisation by strengthening the idea of protective factors (Stephens, Sieckelinck and Boutellier 2021). Stephens and Sieckelinck (2021) have identified four key perspectives regarding resilience against radicalisation, which they describe as critique and transform, environmental conditions, maintain status-quo, and individual traits.

Lösel et al.'s (2018) systematic review of studies dealing with risk factors and protective factors identified several having a positive protective impact on the level of the individual, the family, the school, the peer, and the community/society. A near-consensus has been reached that successfully combating right-wing violence and extremism needs a more proactive and preventive approach rather than reacting. In addition, there is a strong tendency to also address structural causes of violent extremism, including intolerance, governance failures, and political, economic, and social marginalisation. In fact, concepts of resilience now go well beyond the original approach of post-event resilience (Boese et al 2021; Grossman 2021; Merkel and Lührmann 2021). Referring to the issue of resilience from a sociological perspective, Blum et al. (2016, p. 170) have emphasised that there are three different dimensions of resilience: capacities to cope with a particular disruptive event in the short term aimed at maintaining or restoring the assumed status quo ante; in a medium- to long-term perspective; adaptive capacities refer to adapting to new contextual conditions within a certain framework and, in doing so, secure the existence of the resilient unit; and, transformative capacities that make sure that the resilient units are able to change comprehensively and in the long term.

In the first decades of the Federal Republic, a dogmatic anti-communist consensus had a strong impact. With 9/11, the focus shifted strongly to jihadist violence, with the launch of extensive research, prevention, and repression measures. In the meantime, however – not least because of a series of serious right-wing extremist acts of violence that claimed a relevant number of victims – the security authorities and large sections of politics and the public have come to realise that the most significant threat to democracy and social cohesion comes from right-wing extremism.

Following the overall perspective of this handbook, violent right-wing extremism is understood as the use of violent acts, or the threat thereof, by irregular actors in pursuit of political aims to erode or subvert democratic processes and pluralistic values, often at the expense of minority faith, cultural, or political communities (McNeil-Willson et al. 2019). Depending on the particular political situation in a country as well as the strategy and tactical decisions of violent right-wing actors, acts of right-wing violence pursue one or more instrumental objectives: intimidating, driving out, or punishing social groups or outstanding individuals, but also escalating the overall situation, mobilising supporters, or distracting by false flag operations (Virchow 2021b.) This analytical perspective must be taken into account in the development and implementation of measures to strengthen resilience, as must be the impact of right-wing extremist violence on those affected by that violence and their resources for empowerment.

More fundamentally, resilience should go beyond the realm of violent action. Democratic resilience can be understood as the ability of a community to have democracy (as a form of organising political decisions, state structures, and everyday cultural processes) be accepted in situations of social and political crises as well as in processes of transformation by a majority of the population (Klie 2020).

This chapter is organised as follows. It starts with an overview of historical trends of right-wing extremism and its violent expressions. Next, the three most important approaches of counter-extremism are briefly outlined in historical perspective. Subsequently, the interactional dynamic between right-wing extremism and socio-economic, cultural, political, and network-related factors are discussed. The chapter ends with some considerations of most recent challenges.

Right-wing violence and its contexts

Researchers on right-wing terrorism in the Federal Republic of Germany disagree whether it begins in the late 1960s with the emergence of numerous small groups that appeared alongside the National Democratic Party (NPD) or can already be identified in the early 1950s. The latter focuses on the anti-communist Bund Deutscher Jugend (BDJ) and its sub-organisation Technischer Dienst (TD). The BDJ attracted attention through violent demonstrations and the singing of Hitler Youth songs. At the same time, TD members received weapons training and practiced covert communication. The BDJ and TD were finally banned in Hesse in early 1953; police found lists with the names of 40 people – mostly high-ranking politicians from the Social Democratic Party – who were to be 'put out of action' on 'Day X'.

Right-wing groups in the late 1960s and early 1970s violently attacked meetings, individuals, and infrastructure of left-wing groups, but also stockpiled weapons and explosives, and sought to disrupt the policy of détente with the German Democratic Republic and the recognition of the German-Polish border. In the 1970s, massive extreme right violence targeted synagogues and tried to intimidate state representatives pushing forward education about the Nazi crimes (Benz 1984; Kopke 2014; Steinke 2020); several groups made efforts to force Rudolf Hess's release from prison in Berlin-Spandau (Virchow 2020). The highest number of fatalities of right-wing violence, to that time, was in 1980 due to the attack on the Munich Oktoberfest, the double murder of a Jewish author and his wife in Erlangen, and a shootout with police officers. In addition, an arson attack killed two refugees from Vietnam. In the early 1980s, Neo-Nazis carried out attacks with explosives against U.S. soldiers in hopes to create a situation of fear and insecurity that would lead to the withdrawal of US forces from Germany. Racist skinheads murdered several immigrants from Turkey (Koehler 2016; Gräfe 2017; Virchow and Puls 2023).

Regarding right-wing street-level violence, the unification of the two German states led to an all-time high in the early 1990s (Borchers 1992; Kleffner and Spangenberg 2016; Heitmeyer et al. 2020). Especially in rural regions, where the democratic parties had only formed weak structures since 1990 and there were few leisure activities for young people, right-wing extremists were able to gain ground. The violence they perpetrated confronted young people with the dilemma of moving away to escape the violence or joining the right-wing groups so as not to become victims. With a growing number of asylum seekers from the war-ridden Balkan countries, the number of racist acts of violence increased across the country. Pogrom-like assaults in cities such as Rostock, Mannheim, and Hoyerswerda (Prenzel 2012; Wowtscherk 2014), but also nightly arsons and brutal attacks against homeless people resulted in dozens being murdered and an incalculable number of injured and traumatised people.

The majority of political parties gave in to mass racist violence and restricted the basic right to asylum in 1993 as a consequence. The number of right-wing violent acts has declined since that year, thus the right-wing scene showed that demands can be enforced with violence. More systematic attempts to threaten immigrants and those perceived by rightists of not belonging to the German society followed in the 2000s; the *Freikorps Havelland*, for example, repeatedly set fire to Vietnamese-run food trucks to ruin them economically and force them out. From 2000 to 2006, the group National-Socialist Underground (NSU) killed nine men at short range out of racist motives and detonated several bombs, including a nail bomb in the Keupstraße in Cologne in April 2004, injuring 22 people, most of them seriously.

Since 2014, we've seen a considerable increase in the number of people fleeing to Europe. After an initial phase of civic engagement and a 'welcoming culture', uncertainty and scepticism determined many people's attitudes towards the refugees. The extreme right in Germany has since gained new mobilisation capacity around the issues of asylum and Islam; headline-grabbing campaigns and actions by PEGIDA (Virchow 2016) and the Hooligans Against Salafists (HoGeSa) found their continuation in thousands of gatherings across the Federal Republic, mostly organised by local groups but connected by the demand for a restrictive asylum and refugee policy.

In Germany, the 2010s also mark the progressive erosion of the demarcation between 'angry citizens' and extreme right-wing agitators who mobilise for a 'national uprising', which they justify as an act of self-defence, with reference to the alleged necessity of 'saving the Occident' and the 'protection of the people and the homeland' (Korsch 2020). Previously, right-wing extremists had generally kept to themselves with their public manifestations; now, for the first time, they were able to attract to their rallies larger numbers of citizens who had certain racist views but were not right-wing extremists. In the summer of 2015, numerous anti-Muslim and anti-immigration blog entries made visible how the growing number of refugees coming to Europe – and Germany – was perceived as an impending or incipient 'apocalyptic crisis' (Mathias 2017). Because racist and exclusionary nationalist thinking makes immigration and the permanent presence of immigrants an existential threat, it already contains the justification for the use of violence (Piatkowska et al. 2020). Although regularly dressed up as 'self-defence', but by no means coincidentally, racially motivated violence escalated in Germany in the mid-2010s.

This practice of violence is characterised by the dissolution of boundaries: its scope has expanded many times over since 2014 (Benček and Strasheim 2016); the use of explosives has increased; and the violence is also directed against people who are seen by the attackers as representatives of a liberal asylum policy. Among the most prominent cases are the attempted murder of the current mayor of Cologne, Henriette Reker, and the murder of the district president of Kassel, Walter Lübcke, who was shot dead by a Neo-Nazi on 1 June 2019.

The racist and antisemitic terrorist attacks in Hanau and in Halle are also part of the escalation of right-wing violence since the 2010s. From 2017 onwards, right-wing acts of violence number around 1,000 per year – although it is unknown how many additional cases go unrecorded. Although several violent groups such as the Oldschool Society or the Freital Vigilante Group have been uncovered and prosecuted (Philippsberg 2021), many of the corresponding crimes have not been solved.

Banning extreme right groups, doing social work

After the military victory over Nazism in 1945, re-education aimed at pushing back antisemitic and racist attitudes, deradicalising the Nazi regime's huge numbers of ardent followers, and building solid endorsement and support for democratic institutions and processes. While the Conservative, Liberal, and Social Democratic parties were able to integrate large numbers of former Nazis, others remained outside the democratic system and ran an array of parties and associations – some openly, others shielded from the broader public.

For more than 70 years, one way of combating right-wing extremist groups has been to ban selected organisations. This means that their assets are confiscated, their activities may not be continued, and the group's symbols may no longer be displayed in public. For Berlin, a different procedure applied until 1990 due to Special Allied Rights (Laue 1993). Since 1951, there have been more than 100 such bans; in the 1950s they were often directed against organisations that openly called for a return of Nazism (Will 2017) and against groups seeking to organise and recruit youth. In view of the electoral successes of the Nationaldemokratische Partei Deutschlands (National-Democratic Party of Germany, NPD) in the second half of the 1960s, there was also intensive discussion about banning it; two attempts to do so in twenty-first century failed, however (Kliegel and Roßbach 2020).

Since the 1980s, bans have been directed primarily against violence-oriented groups and those openly referring to the Nazi regime and sharing its worldview. The effect of such bans may hardly be measurable in singular cases, as the individuals who belonged to a banned group might continue to work in politically similar groups or found a new group with a comparable orientation. In some cases, bans have in fact severely limited the scope of action of the extreme right (Botsch et al. 2013). The main effect of such bans – as well as other criminal law statutes prohibiting, for instance, the Hitler salute, displaying the swastika and other Nazi symbols in public, or wearing uniforms at rallies (Rösing 2004) – and the restriction of the right to demonstrate under the so-called Wunsiedel ruling of the Federal Constitutional Court (Fohrbeck 2015) might be viewed in their cumulative message as a demarcation of what is seen as an unacceptable political strand hostile to democracy and human rights.

The disappearance of right-wing extremist parties from parliaments in the post-war period was long associated with the expectation that the problem of right-wing extremism would be solved by means of integration into democratic parties, economic prosperity, and the eventual passing of the unrepentant Nazi adherents who had been politically socialised by the Nazi regime. Yet, in the late 1960s, the NPD successfully campaigned in several states and narrowly missed entering the national parliament in 1969. The 1970s saw a renewed interest in the Nazi regime in the media and in political debates; numerous books aimed at a broader public recorded high sales figures. At the same time, social workers drew attention to the appearance of Neo-Nazi youth groups. The expectation that young people who had grown up in the democratic Federal Republic of Germany would no longer be responsive to extreme right-wing ideology proved false. In 1981, the SINUS study attracted considerable attention with its finding that 13 per cent of the electorate in the Federal Republic of Germany held a right-wing extremist worldview (Greiffenhagen 1981).

Not least because of social workers' warnings, social science research turned its attention to this phenomenon. Among the early attempts to explain this development was educationalist Wilhelm Heitmeyer's so-called disintegration approach. For Heitmeyer (1987, 1992) right-wing extremism and its promises of clear orientation in the form of hierarchies, self-valorisation, and violence as an expression of power was attractive for young people due to processes of individualisation and disintegration in modern capitalist societies. The pressure arising from the erosion of traditional social and political milieus is particularly noticeable in adolescence, a life phases already marked by struggle to overcome challenges and crises (ibid.).

Although one objection to the disintegration approach was that young people who do not belong to the so-called losers of modernisation also hold right-wing extremist attitudes, thus pointing to the importance of ideological convictions and the offers of extreme right-wing organisations. The disintegration approach nevertheless emerged as the central frame of reference for social work action. In practice, the concept of 'accepting youth work' became widespread (Krafeld et al. 1993). The concept's main perspective was to focus on problems young people face (e.g. a lack of vocational qualification or unemployment) instead of on the problems they create. The assumption was that the reduction in right-wing violence would also serve (re)integration into society and reduce the attractiveness of right-wing extremist ideology and action.

The emphasis on violence prevention was also key in the Action Programme against Aggression and Violence (AgAG) run by the Federal Ministry of Youth since 1992 as a reaction to the wave of racist violence in the early 1990s. The programme aimed to develop regular structures of youth work in the East German states and to reduce youth violence overall through youth welfare. However, right-wing violence was not understood as a political expression, but as a provocation and cry for help from a misunderstood and neglected youth. The goal was therefore to get the youth 'off the streets'. Accordingly, young people with an affinity for the right and right-wing extremists were also given opportunities to participate in youth clubs. Young people holding racist and antisemitic worldviews or hating homeless people were not confronted with counternarratives but left to their ideological dispositions. In this respect, social work almost exclusively offered support to former or future perpetrators, especially young men with extreme right-wing attitudes, but not to social groups affected by racism and right-wing violence. This was a consequence of an approach that did not take the political dimension of right-wing violence seriously enough, but merely as a problematic result of unsatisfactory interpersonal relationships, lack of recognition, or the inability to cope with problems (ZDK 1999).

In today's social work and childhood education (Gewalt Akademie Villigst 2016; Amadeu Antonio Stiftung 2018), there are numerous theory-based approaches and practice-tested action paradigms in the critical confrontation with the various expressions of right-wing extremism and ideologies of inequality (Pingel and Rieker 2002; Baer et al. 2014; Rahner 2021). The idea that disintegrated, educationally disadvantaged young men in particular should be addressed has meanwhile given way to a much more differentiated perspective and more diverse social work practice. Young men are still addressed but are now also invited to critically engage with ideas and concepts of masculinity – a substantial change compared to the late 1980s and early 1990s (Hechler and Stuve 2015). In view of the different styles of upbringing (authoritative, indifferent, controlling) and ways of connecting (Becker 2008), social work must consider the different ways in which the family deals with an already existing right-wing orientation of a child, as well as the degree of ideological agreement between parents and adolescents, and finally the dynamics of conflict and parental intervention strategies. In special cases where children grow up in right-wing extremist families and are consistently isolated from other influences and experiences, such as in the case of Voelkisch settlers who follow a lifestyle framed by racist criteria and is concentrated in closed rural communities (Schmidt 2014), the question of endangering the welfare of the child can also become relevant. Of course, not every institution can carry out such demanding professional work with parents; however, a municipal educational counselling service, for example, should also have knowledge of the referral structures.

In recent times, welfare organisations in Germany have clearly positioned themselves as important actors in the field of social work against racism, antisemitism, and right-wing extremism. This is often based on an understanding of social work as a human rights profession. According to Borrmann (2006, p. 204), social work is a 'profession and discipline…that tries to uncover human rights violations, to support people whose rights have been violated and to fight for a society that can guarantee the realisation of human rights for its members'. In many cases, members of vulnerable groups are the addressees of social work. Since social work is also a science and agency of normalisation, it requires critical reflection on the socially effective notions of normality. If, for example, social work with young right-wing extremist men also addresses their idealisations of soldierly masculinity and their heteronormative and biologistic gender constructions, it must be remembered that social structures continue to be determined by male dominance beyond these specific interpretations. Similarly, in the critical confrontation with social Darwinist ideas, which may be linked to practices of discrimination or violence against the homeless or the long-term unemployed, it should also be considered that productivist paradigms (à la only those who are productive should be allowed to participate in the goods produced) are widely shared in society (Virchow 2023).

Educating people, counselling, supporting victims

Since the start of the twenty-first century, the narrow focus on (male) youths from right-wing extremist scenes has been overcome and there is now a strong differentiation of measures and approaches on the basis of a systematic distinction between primary, secondary, and tertiary prevention. Supported by the federal programme Tolerance for Diversity and Democracy, opportunities for civic education in and out of school were offered on a large scale within the framework of primary or universal prevention to strengthen the population's overall resilience against radical right-wing appeals.

Primary prevention aims to prevent people from turning to the extreme right-wing milieu or ideology (Virchow 2022b). There is no specific target group; it is aimed at everyone, regardless of age and education. These offers seek to counteract the spread of racist, antisemitic, and misogynist attitudes and worldviews by strengthening democratic values and behaviour oriented towards the principle of equality of human rights. Under different names – anti-discrimination work, democracy education, or critical race theory – primary prevention promotes a self-confident approach to diversity, tolerance of ambiguity, and resilience to the above-mentioned ways of thinking and acting.

In the context of secondary prevention, there is a variety of approaches that target individuals and small groups differently depending on how much they are affected by racist, antisemitic, and misogynist worldviews or how deeply they are already involved in extreme right-wing milieus (Virchow 2022a). For example, it can make a significant difference whether the addressee occasionally represents elements of racist or antisemitic ideology or whether they have been active in corresponding scenes for a long time and participate in the dissemination of propaganda, for example. In Germany, a broad range of NGOs as well as state-funded projects are active in this field offering advice and support (Virchow 2014).[1]

In contrast, tertiary prevention focuses strongly on distancing and exit processes as well as on deradicalisation measures for activists of extreme right-wing milieus and organisations. There are numerous exit programmes in Germany (www.bag-ausstieg.de/). They share their experiences intensively and have developed comprehensive quality standards for their work (Jende 2015; Buchheit et al. 2016; Glaser 2017; Bundesarbeitsgemeinschaft 2019). To be effective, they presuppose that people are willing to break away from the right-wing extremist context. Only the state-run exit programmes pro-actively contact activists, mostly in cases of Neo-Nazis in prison. Part of tertiary prevention is also the support of relatives and close caregivers. A recent evaluation of these programmes has proven that 'exit and distancing work is increasingly developing into a special field of social work with its own professional standards' (Figlestahler and Schau 2021, p. 6).

Over the last two decades, a broad landscape of counselling agencies has developed, funded by the federal states or by the federal government. On the one hand, there is a nationwide network of mobile counselling support points against right-wing extremism (Mobile Beratung gegen Rechtsextremismus/MBR or MBT, www.bundesverband-mobile-beratung.de/). They monitor right-wing extremist activities, publish analyses (e.g., on anti-feminist elements in far-right ideology and on far-right interventions in environmental issues), but mainly offer support on request to a broad range of protagonists confronted by extreme right-wing activities and seeking help and advice. Demand for such kind of support comes from the education sector, public administration, individuals, and sport clubs, among many others.

There is also a nation-wide network of institutions supporting victims of right-wing harassment and violence (https://verband-brg.de/). People who are threatened, insulted, or attacked as a result of right-wing extremist, racist, or misanthropic motives receive support from the counselling service. Those affected receive a protected space to talk about what they have experienced; they also receive advice on legal issues and support in dealing with the police and authorities, as well as help in dealing with the material consequences of the acts of hate speech and hate crime. The free, confidential, and partisan work is often also aimed at empowering those who have been attacked and injured. A recent evaluation of the work of the associations offering specialised victim counselling has confirmed that there is a consensus in the professional discourse that effective support work should focus on the micro, meso, and macro levels in view of the effects of right-wing racist and antisemitic violence. This includes a focus on interventions at the local level thereby taking the spatial dimension seriously (Davolio and Drilling 2008) and as key for counselling and support work (Haase 2021). Such an approach tries to engage relevant community leaders in problem-solving. This might include the attempt to change the discourses and practices in the local handling of right-wing violence, but also to strengthen the perspectives of those affected in the public discourse and promote their participation. Social transformation processes are thus stimulated or supported. Such local interventions represent a practical realisation of solidarity, empowerment, and community orientation, going beyond an individualising perspective.

Primary and secondary prevention against right-wing extremism and ideologies of inequality also have a place in schools and in the profile of school social workers. This applies to youth welfare offices and their facilities for outreach work for youths (Möller and Schuhmacher 2014). Where extreme right-wing actors aim to establish socio-spatial dominance and to restrict human rights-based action and fundamental rights by threatening or exercising violence, democratic actors – 'be they public authorities, municipal administrations, child and youth welfare institutions or civil society projects – must be oriented accordingly and act appropriately' (Milbradt 2020, p. 55). The aforementioned MBRs (Mobile Beratung gegen Rechtsextremismus) support such action with their community work approach (Bringt 2021).

On the local level, a growing number of cities – funded by state and federal money – have developed and implemented local strategies to prevent the spread of racist, antisemitic, and extreme right-wing ideology, but also to strengthen democratic participation and involvement of (mostly) young people. Programmes such as NRWeltoffen often involve a broad range of state actors and civil society protagonists. However, their immediate impact is hard to measure.

Concluding remarks: complex interactions

Despite all these efforts, opinion surveys show that a relevant share of the German population still holds attitudes hostile towards immigrants, people of Muslim faith, long-term unemployed, Roma people, and other groups. When it comes to a right-wing extremist worldview, the results of the attitude research show significant changes in agreement with the overall index of right-wing extremist orientation over the course of the 2010s. The proportion of the population with a pronounced extreme right-wing attitude initially rose from 8.2 per cent in 2010 to 9 per cent in 2012, only to level off to between two and three per cent in subsequent years. For the period 2020–2021, depending on the study, this figure is between 4.3 and 8 per cent of the population (Vehrkamp 2021; Decker and Brähler 2020). When it comes to more focused surveys, such as those measuring attitudes towards Roma people, some 45 per cent hold negative ways of thinking. The level of related acts of violence is also still high. In 2021, police authorities registered 1,024 cases of right-wing violence (Bundesministerium des Innern 2022). However, a significant number of cases goes unreported.

Although there is empirical evidence that attitudes hostile to particular groups such as migrants, Muslims, or the long-term unemployed are higher than average in economically disadvantaged regions (Quent 2012; Quent and Schulz 2015), there are hardly any programmes consistently addressing this particular constellation. On the individual level, there is no linear connection between economic, social, or political deprivation and holding extreme right-wing attitudes (Poli and Arun 2019; Strom et al. 2020). More relevant is the experience of perceived deprivation and discrimination that is not measured along objective figures, but which refers to the subjective perception of disadvantage in terms of economic situation, but also sociocultural participation (ibid.).

There is an ongoing public debate as well as a growing number of actions and efforts by a variety of actors to promote cultural diversity, for instance along the lines of origin or ethnicity or sexual preference. Compared to one or two decades ago, when the conservative Christian Democratic Party lobbied heavily against the idea that today's Germany is a country of immigration, there has been significant progress in accepting the reality. In this party, too, Muslims can now occupy prominent positions and its ministers are open about their homosexuality.

However, there is a notable minority opposing society's liberalisation and diversification. This poses a challenge to the efforts to the development of an equal rights society. Those who are against such a development see the Alternative for Germany (AfD) party in particular as their representative. AfD follows an authoritarian, racist, and nationalistic political course (Wiegel 2022) and in March 2021 was classified by the Federal Office for the Protection of the Constitution as a suspected case for constitutional illegality. The party is continuously running political attacks on social work organisations and projects that feel committed to human rights, especially with regard to religious, cultural, and sexual diversity, but also with regard to children's rights or pro-choice politics. The AfD and its allies not only demand budget cuts, but also spread defamatory statements to discredit particularly committed actors. Such attacks affect singular projects initially but are aimed at human rights-oriented social work as a whole (Haase et al. 2020; Gille et al. 2022).

The extreme right is versatile in terms of its structures, tactics, and arguments. Today, it often uses youth-cultural approaches (Virchow 2021a), is extensively active in digital public spheres, and comes across as pop-cultural or tries to sow confusion by using vocabulary commonly understood as 'left-wing'. Extreme right groups also frequently present themselves as 'caretakers' – in a form that can be misunderstood as social work. They also use degree programmes in social work/social pedagogy to inculcate children and young people in a racial-nationalist sense (Gille et al. 2022). Accordingly, social work must resist such attempts and further develop its concepts. This should include, to take just one example, offering critical race theory a place in the curriculum.

Digital media have become an important place for hate speech, including death threats against specific individuals. Social media platforms and messaging services have been used as a tool of communication for assembling violent crowds and organising racist and White supremacist hate groups. While there are a growing number of activities of disruption, diversion, and counter-messaging – as well as legal prosecutions resulting in convictions – this is hardly sufficient to control the massive number of hate messages spread every day. This is illustrated by AfD's success in running candidates in every major election from 2014 to 2021, which has further polarised society and politics.

In a recently published article, Somer et al. (2021) referred to the issue of polarisation in way that understands this as a deliberate strategy by some actors. They define 'pernicious polarisation' as the 'division of society into mutual distrustful Us versus Them camps in which political identity becomes a social identity' (ibid., pp. 929–930) and argue that this is a major threat for democracy. In the German context, this became visible regarding the rallies, threats of violence, but also acts of lethal violence on the part of people who saw government action to contain the pandemic – including vaccination – as a conspiracy and illegitimate action (Virchow and Häusler 2020). Following a range of conspiracy narratives, they fundamentally distrust every action taken by the government, but also media coverage explaining the decisions behind these actions.

Indeed, this creates new challenges for resilience-oriented approaches (Klafki 2020; Meléndez and Rovira Kaltwasser 2021). While those groups pose as defenders of democracy, they actually aim at restricting public debate, threaten politicians elected by fair and open elections, and blame particular groups (often Jewish people) to be the beneficiaries of the 'conspiracy'. Like more traditional right-wing extremists, they exploit and fuel discontent and misinformation to gain influence. Both groups should be addressed by a strategy of resilience that 'balances targeted sanctions against radicals with attempts to persuade moderate followers, and [that] has the aim of decreasing the salience of antipluralists' narratives by means of democratic (voter) mobilisation' (Lührmann 2021, p. 1017).

In Germany there is a broad range of state-run and civil society-run projects covering preventive measures aimed at strengthening tolerance of ambiguity; these programmes are often funded by the Federal Agency for Civic Education, which in 2012 established its own department on issues of extremism. Also relevant are trajectories of action with a stronger interventionist approach that take place in fields like social work, in schools, or in the penal system. Germany's federal structure means that, in addition to the federal government, the 16 federal states (as well as numerous municipalities) offer programmes to combat racism and antisemitism. This may sometimes seem to create confusion but this also offers numerous opportunities for involvement by citizens and grassroots groups. With an extreme right-wing party in parliament, polarisation has deepened in society and strengthening resilience against violent actions by extreme-right protagonists remains an ongoing task.

The naïve notion of 1950s that economic satisfaction and the gradual death of the Nazi generation would almost automatically make the problem of right-wing extremism insignificant has now been debunked. Right-wing extremism has proven itself capable of change in many ways and, with the AfD party, is currently organisationally stronger than at any time in the history of post-war Germany. At the same time, however, the diverse programmes and activities aimed at countering right-wing extremism are a clear indication of increased resilience.

Note

1 See also www.demokratie-leben.de/das-programm/ueber-demokratie-leben/modellprojekte; www.bpb.de/veranstaltungen/ reihen/qualifiziert-handeln/; www.amadeu-antonio-stiftung.de/.

References

Amadeu Antonio Stiftung (2018) *Ene, meine, muh – und raus bist du! Ungleichwertigkeit und frühkindliche Pädagogik*. Berlin: AAS.

Baer, Silke, Möller, Kurt and Wiechmann, Peter (2014) *Verantwortlich Handeln: Praxis der Sozialen Arbeit mit rechtsextrem orientierten und gefährdeten Jugendlichen*. Opladen/Berlin/Toronto: Verlag Barbara Budrich.

Becker, Reiner (2008) *Ein normales Familienleben. Interaktion und Kommunikation zwischen ‚rechten' Jugendlichen und ihren Eltern*. Schwalbach/Ts.: Wochenschau-Verlag.

Benček, David, and Strasheim, Julia (2016) Refugees Welcome? A Dataset on Anti-refugee Violence in Germany. *Research and Politics*, 3(4), pp. 1–11.
Benz, Wolfgang, ed. (1984) *Rechtsextremismus in der Bundesrepublik*. Frankfurt/Main: Fischer.
Blum, Sabine, Endreß, Martin, Kaufmann, Stefan and Rampp, Benjamin (2016) Soziologische Perspektiven. In: Wink, Rüdiger (ed.), *Multidisziplinäre Perspektiven der Resilienzforschung*. Wiesbaden: Springer, pp. 151–177.
Boese, Vanessa A., Edgell, A.B., Hellmeier, S., Maerz, S.F. and Lindberg, S.I. (2021) How Democracies Prevail: Democratic Resilience as a Two-Ptage process. *Democratization*, 28, pp. 885–907.
Borchers, Andreas (1992) *Neue Nazis im Osten*. Weinheim/Basel: Beltz quadriga.
Borrmann, Stefan (2006) *Soziale Arbeit mit rechten Jugendcliquen*. Wiesbaden: VS.
Botsch, Gideon, Kopke, Christoph and Virchow, Fabian (2013) Banning Extreme Right-Wing Associations in the Federal Republic of Germany. In: Melzer, Ralf and Serafin, Sebastian (eds), *Right-Wing Extremism in Europe. Country Analyses, Counter-Strategies and Labor-Market Oriented Exit Strategies*. Berlin: FES, pp. 255–279.
Bringt, Friedemann (2021) *Umkämpfte Zivilgesellschaft: mit menschenrechtsorientierter Gemeinwesenarbeit gegen Ideologien der Ungleichwertigkeit?* Opladen/Berlin/Toronto: Budrich.
Buchheit, Frank, Küpper, B., Möller, K. and Neuscheler, F. (2016) Was nützt Ausstiegshilfe? Zur Evaluation des Aussteigerprogramms für Rechtsextremisten NRW. *Demokratie gegen Menschenfeindlichkeit*, 1(2), pp. 21–36.
Bundesarbeitsgemeinschaft 'Einstieg zum Ausstieg' e.V., ed. (2019) *Qualitätsstandards in der Ausstiegsberatung*. Jena.
Bundesministerium des Innern und für Heimat/Bundeskriminalamt (2022) *Politisch motivierte Kriminalität im Jahr 2021. Bundesweite Fallzahlen*. Berlin: BMI.
Davolio, Miryam Eser, and Drilling, Matthias (2008) *Gemeinden antworten auf Rechtsextremismus*. Bern/Stuttgart/Wien: Haupt.
Decker, Oliver, and Brähler, Elmar (2020) *Autoritäre Dynamiken: Alte Ressentiments – neue Radikalität*. Gießen: Psychosozial-Verlag.
Figlestahler, Carmen, and Schau, Katja (2021) *Entwicklungen, Handlungspraxen und Herausforderungen im Feld der Ausstiegs- und Distanzierungsarbeit. Wissenschaftliche Begleitung Handlungsbereich Land im Bundesprogramm "Demokratie leben!" in der Förderphase 2020 bis 2024*. München: DJI.
Fohrbeck, Till (2015) *Wunsiedel: Billigung, Verherrlichung, Rechtfertigung. Das Verbot nazistischer Meinungen in Deutschland und den USA*. Berlin: Duncker & Humblot.
Gewalt Akademie Villigst, and Mobile Beratung gegen Rechtsextremismus im Regierungsbezirk Arnsberg (2016) *Rassismuskritische Arbeit mit Kindern*. Schwerte: Amt für Jugendarbeit der EKvW.
Gille, Christoph, Jagusch, Birgit and Chehata, Yasmine, eds (2022) *Die extreme Rechte in der Sozialen Arbeit. Grundlagen – Arbeitsfelder – Handlungsmöglichkeiten*. Weinheim/Basel: BeltzJuventa.
Glaser, Michaela (2017) Disengagement and Deradicalisation Work with Girls and Young Women – Experiences from Germany. In: Köttig, M., Bitzan, R. and Petö, A. (eds), *Gender and Far Right Politics in Europe*. Cham: Palgrave Macmillan, pp. 337–349.
Gräfe, Sebastian (2017) *Rechtsterrorismus in der Bundesrepublik Deutschland*. Baden-Baden: Nomos.
Greiffenhagen, Martin (1981) *5 Millionen Deutsche: „Wir sollten wieder einen Führer haben …". Die SINUS-Studie über rechtsextremistische Einstellungen bei den Deutschen*. Reinbek bei Hamburg: Rowohlt.
Grossman, Michelle (2021) Resilience to Violent Extremism and Terrorism. A Multisystemic Analysis. In: Ungar, Michael (ed.), *Multisystemic resilience: adaptation and transformation in contexts of change*. New York: Oxford University Press, pp. 293–317.
Haase, Katrin (2021) *Entwicklungen und Herausforderungen im Feld der Beratung von Betroffenen rechter, rassistischer und antisemitischer Gewalt. Wissenschaftliche Begleitung Handlungsbereich Land im Bundesprogramm „Demokratie leben!" in der Förderphase 2020 bis 2024*. München: DJI.
Haase, Katrin, Nebe, Gesine and Zaft, Matthias, eds. (2020) *Rechtspopulismus – Verunsicherungen der Sozialen Arbeit*. Weinheim/Basel: BeltzJuventa.
Hardy, Keiran (2015) Resilience in UK Counterterrorism. *Theoretical Criminology*, 19, pp. 77–94.
Hechler, Andreas, and Stuve, Olaf, eds (2015) *Geschlechterreflektierte Pädagogik gegen Rechts*. Opladen/Berlin/Toronto: Budrich.
Heitmeyer, Wilhelm (1987) *Rechtsextremistische Orientierungen bei Jugendlichen*. Weinheim/München: Juventa.
Heitmeyer, Wilhelm et al. (1992) *Die Bielefelder Rechtsextremismus-Studie*. Weinheim/München: Juventa.
Heitmeyer, Wilhelm, Freiheit, Manuela and Sitzer, Peter, eds (2020) *Signaturen der Bedrohung*. Berlin: Suhrkamp.

Jende, Sebastian (2015) *Qualität in der Ausstiegsberatung*. Jena.
Klafki, Anika (2020) Resilienz des Grundgesetzes im Zeitalter des Populismus. *Kritische Vierteljahresschrift für Gesetzgebung und Rechtswissenschaft*, 103, pp. 113–127.
Kleffner, Heike, and Spangenberg, Anna, eds (2016) *Generation Hoyerswerda. Das Netzwerk militanter Neonazis in Brandenburg*. Berlin: Be.Bra Verlag.
Klie, Thomas (2020) *Demokratische Resilienz*. Freiburg: EHF.
Kliegel, Thomas, and Roßbach, Matthias, eds. (2020) *Das NPD-Verbotsverfahren*. Tübingen: Mohr.
Koehler, Daniel (2016) *Right-wing Terrorism in the 21st Century*. Abingdon: Routledge.
Kopke, Christoph, ed. (2014) *Angriffe auf die Erinnerung an die nationalsozialistischen Verbrechen*. Berlin. Metropol.
Korsch, Felix (2020) Deutschland ist Abendland'. Anmerkungen zu Ideengeschichte und Wiederkehr eines Kampfbegriffs. In: Burschel, Friedrich (ed.) *Das faschistische Jahrhundert*. Berlin: RLS, pp. 39–110.
Krafeld, Franz Josef, Möller, Kurt and Müller, Andrea (1993) *Jugendarbeit in rechten Szenen*. Bremen: Edition Temmen.
Laue, Sabine (1993) *Die NPD unter dem Viermächtestatus Berlins – Verhandlungsmasse zwischen den Großmächten*. Egelsbach/Köln/New York: Verlag Hänsel-Hohenhausen.
Lösel, Friedrich, Kinga, Sonja, Bender, Doris and Jugl, Irina (2018) Protective Factors Against Extremism and Violent Radicalization: A Systematic Review of Research. *International Journal of Developmental Science*, 2, pp. 89–102.
Lührmann, Anna (2021) Disrupting the Autocratization Sequence: Towards Democratic Resilience. *Democratization*, 28, pp. 1017–1039.
Mathias, Alexa (2017) Von "Parasiten" und anderen "Schädlingen". Feinddiskreditierung rechtspopulistischer und rechtsextremer Bewegungen in Deutschland. *Linguistik online*, 82(3), pp. 79–94.
McNeil-Willson, Richard, Gerrand, V., Scrinzi, F. and Triandafyllidou, A. (2019) Polarisation, Violent Extremism and Resilience in Europe today: An analytical framework for the BRaVE project. Concept Paper. Florence: EUI.
Meléndez, Carlos, and Rovira Kaltwasser, Cristóbal (2021) Negative Partisanship towards the Populist Radical Right and Democratic Resilience in Western Europe. *Democratization*, 28, pp. 949–969.
Merkel, Wolfgang, and Lührmann, Anna (2021) Resilience of Democracies: Responses to Illiberal and Authoritarian Challenges. *Democratization*, 28, pp. 869–884.
Milbradt, Björn (2020) Sozialräumliche Präventionsansätze gegen Rechtsextremismus: Phänomene, Strategien und Herausforderungen. *Archiv für Wissenschaft und Praxis der sozialen Arbeit*, 51(2), pp. 54–62.
Möller, Kurt, and Schuhmacher, Nils (2014) *Soziale und pädagogische Arbeit mit rechtsextrem affinen Jugendlichen*. Berlin: BIK Netz.
Philippsberg, Robert (2021) Rechtsterroristische Gruppen in Deutschland nach dem NSU. *Zeitschrift für Rechtsextremismusforschung*, 1(1), pp. 147–166.
Piatkowska, Sylwia J., Hövermann, Andreas and Yang, Tse-Chuan (2020) Immigration Influx as a Trigger for Right-Wing Crime: A Temporal Analysis of Hate Crimes in Germany in the Light of the 'Refugee Crisis'. *British Journal of Criminology*, 60(3), pp. 620–641.
Pingel, Andrea, and Rieker, Peter (2002) *Pädagogik mit rechtsextrem orientierten Jugendlichen*. Leipzig: DJI.
Poli, Alexandra, and Arun, Onur (2019) *Report on the Meta-Ethnographic Synthesis of Qualitative Studies on Inequality and Youth Radicalisation*. Manchester: DARE.
Prenzel, Thomas (2012) *20 Jahre Rostock-Lichtenhagen. Kontext, Dimensionen und Folgen der rassistischen Gewalt*. Rostock: Universität Rostock, Institut für Politik- und Verwaltungswissenschaften.
Quent, Matthias (2012) *Mehrebenenanalyse rechtsextremer Einstellungen. Ursachen und Verbreitung in unterschiedlichen sozioökonomischen Regionen Hessens und Thüringens*. Magdeburg: Meine Verlag.
Quent, Matthias, and Schulz, Peter (2015) *Rechtsextremismus in lokalen Kontexten*. Wiesbaden: Springer VS.
Rahner, Judith (2021) *Praxishandbuch Resilienz in der Jugendarbeit. Widerstandsfähigkeit gegen Extremismus und Ideologien der Ungleichwertigkeit*. Weinheim/Basel: BeltzJuventa.
Rösing, Jenny (2004) *Kleidung als Gefahr? Das Uniformverbot im Versammlungsrecht*. Baden-Baden: Nomos.
Schmidt, Anna (2014) *Völkische Siedler/innen im ländlichen Raum*. Berlin: AAS.
Somer, Murat, McCoy, Jennifer L. and Luke, Russell E. (2021) Pernicious Polarization, Autocratization and Opposition Strategies. *Democratization*, 28, pp. 929–948.

Steinke, Ronen (2020) *Terror gegen Juden. Wie antisemitische Gewalt erstarkt und der Staat versagt.* Berlin: Berlin Verlag.
Stephens, William, and Sieckelinck, Stijn (2021) Resiliences to Radicalisation: Four Key Perspectives. *International Journal of Law, Crime and Justice*, 66, p. 100486.
Stephens, William, Sieckelinck, Stijn and Boutellier, Hans (2021) Preventing Violent Extremism: A Review of the Literature. *Studies in Conflict & Terrorism*, 44, pp. 346–361.
Storm, Ingrid, Pavlovic, Tomislav and Franc, Renata (2020) *Report on the Relationship between Inequality and Youth Radicalisation from Existing European Survey Datasets.* Manchester: DARE.
Ungar, Michael (2021) Modeling Multisystemic Resilience. Connecting Biological, Psychological, Social, and Ecological Adaptation in Contexts of Adversity. In: Ungar, Michael (ed.), *Multisystemic resilience: adaptation and transformation in contexts of change.* New York: Oxford University Press, pp. 6–34.
Vehrkamp, Robert (2021) *Zukunft der Demokratie. Rechtsextreme Einstellungen der Wählerinnen vor der Bundestagswahl 2021.* Gütersloh.
Virchow, Fabian (2014) Schlag Nach! – Ein ausgewählter Überblick über Handreichungen und Ratgeber für den Umgang mit extrem rechten Aktivitäten und Einstellungen. *Forum Kriminalprävention*, 1/2014, pp. 2–7.
Virchow, Fabián (2016) PEGIDA: Understanding the Emergence and Essence of Nativist Protest in Dresden. *Journal of Intercultural Studies*, 37, pp. 541–555.
Virchow, Fabian (2020) *Nicht nur der NSU – Eine kleine Geschichte des Rechtsterrorismus in Deutschland.* Erfurt: Landeszentrale für politische Bildung Thüringen.
Virchow, Fabian (2021a) RechtsRock: die 'Weiße Internationale'. *Die Tonkunst. Magazin für klassische Musik und Musikwissenschaft*, 15, pp. 131–137.
Virchow, Fabian (2021b) Einschüchtern und Vertreiben, Bestrafen und Eskalieren. Instrumentelle Zielsetzungen rechtsterroristischen Handelns. *Soziale Probleme*, 32, pp. 131–149.
Virchow, Fabian (2022a) Radikale Milieus, Gruppendynamiken und bewegungsförmige Anrufungen als Faktoren der Hinwendung und Radikalisierung in der Jugendphase. In: Milbradt, B., Frank, A. Greuel, F. and Herding, M. (eds), *Handbuch Radikalisierung im Jugendalter.* Opladen/Berlin/Toronto: Budrich, pp. 233–245.
Virchow, Fabian (2022b) Rechtsextremismus. In: van Rießen, Anne and Bleck, Christian (eds), *Handlungsfelder und Addressierungen der Sozialen Arbeit.* Stuttgart: Kohlhammer.
Virchow, Fabian (2023) Versuch über den Produktivismus. Das produktivistische Paradigma als ein Kernelement rechtspopulistischer und extrem rechter Weltanschauung. In: Botsch, G., Burschel, F., Kopke, C. and Korsch, F. (eds.), Rechte Ränder. Faschismus, Gesellschaft und Staat.. Berlin: Verbrecher Verlag, pp. 153–172.
Virchow, Fabian, and Häusler, Alexander (2020) Pandemie-Leugnung und extreme Rechte in Nordrhein-Westfalen. Düsseldorf/Bonn: HSD/CoRE. CoRE-NRW-Kurzgutachten 3. Available at CoRE_Kurzgutachten3_201123_Pandemie_und_extreme_Rechte.pdf (forena.de)
Virchow, Fabian, and Puls, Hendrik, eds (2023). *Rechtsterrorismus in Deutschland – Historische Perspektiven.* Wiesbaden: VS.
Wiegel, Gerd (2022) *Brandreden. Die AfD im Bundestag.* Köln: PapyRossa.
Will, Martin (2017) *Ephorale Verfassung.* Tübingen: Mohr.
Wowtscherk, Christoph (2014) *Was wird, wenn die Zeitbombe hochgeht?* Göttingen: V & R unipress.
ZDK (1999) *Keine Akzeptanz von Intoleranz. Grenzen der akzeptierenden Jugendsozialarbeit mit rechtsextremen Jugendlichen.* Berlin: Zentrum Demokratische Kultur.

12
HUNGARY

Zsuzsanna Vidra and Michael C. Zeller

Introduction

The inauguration in 2010 of an illiberal and, in several respects, far-right regime has attracted considerable interest and consternation. Yet renewed attention to the extremity of Hungarian politics typically focuses on the regime of Viktor Orbán and obscures both the historical development that elevated it and the right-wing extremist social forces that comfortably coexist with it.

This chapter illuminates several important features in the case of Hungary. First, the resurgence of right-wing extremism after the transition from socialism was bolstered by a deep well of discriminatory and exclusionary attitudes among the Hungarian populace, as well as by economic grievances that abounded in the 1990s. Attitudinal disposition remains an important explanatory factor for the successes of Hungary's far-right. Second, Hungary's post-socialist politics are marked by a steady ascendancy of far-right social forces. Though specific actors rose and fell and changed their ideological position, some moderating and others radicalising, the rise of the Hungarian far-right has mostly been consistent: from re-emergence of far-right organisations in the 1990s to political ascendancy in the late 2000s, and finally to the present phase where far-right actors control state and governmental power. And third, an important condition and outcome of this development is that Hungarian state actors have no impactful counter-extremism strategy. Laws and policies meant to curtail extremism, though enacted, are judicially interpreted with a tolerant regard for the far-right and seldom applied by law enforcement agencies. What is more, since 2010 the illiberal regime has both fostered the far-right in the public sphere and hindered the efforts of civil society actors to implement counter-extremism projects and programmes.

The chapter consists of three parts. The first summarises a few important points of historical context and elaborates the attitudinal trends among Hungary's citizenry that help to identify the base of support for far-right actors. The second part distinguishes the three phases of development for the far-right in Hungary's post-socialist politics. In particular, we trace the (often complementary) evolution of radical and extreme right forces – but underscoring the fuzzy real-world distinction between these forces. The third part focuses on counter-extremism action in Hungary, and why it has so evidently failed.

Historical context of Hungary's far-right

The establishment of the modern Hungarian nation-state is in many ways a story of assimilation: incorporating a multi-ethnic population into the Hungarian Kingdom, part of the Austro-Hungarian empire. Though itself at times suppressed and subject to imperial authority in Vienna, the authorities of the Hungarian Kingdom were also internal colonisers imposing Hungarian predominance in many spheres. A Hungarian identity emerged that represented simultaneously a coloniser's pretence of cultural superiority and a thrall's resentment for a history of subjugation and oppression. Feelings of superiority and inferiority together form core aspects of Hungarian national identity (Erős 2019).

The past century has deepened this stamp of identity, most especially through three climacterics. First, the end of the Great War spelled the end of the Austro-Hungarian Empire; with the 1920 Treaty of Trianon the country lost almost three-quarters of its size and saw significant numbers of ethnic Hungarians displaced outside the newly constricted borders of Hungary. Irredentist aspirations led the inter-war Hungarian regime to ally with Nazi Germany. Nevertheless, late in the war, March 1944, Wehrmacht forces occupied Hungary and installed a government of the Arrow Cross Party (*Nyilaskeresztes Párt*), a National Socialist party and arguably the progenitor of Hungary's modern far-right. Following the Second World War, Hungary found itself still subject to foreign domination by the Soviet Union. The socialist era lasted over four decades and reverberates through contemporary political culture. Taken together, historical factors in Hungary resound with grievance, stemming primarily from foreign domination as well as from interethnic conflict. A prevalence in Hungarian attitudes towards resentment of foreign influence and xenophobia partially reflect these historical factors.

Attitudes

Hungarian attitudes lean to the right. This fact emerges from a wide range of surveys – not to mention the evidence of elections. The World Value Survey (WVS) (Keller 2013) characterises Hungary as situated at the margins of Western Christian culture, a generally closed, inward-looking society. What is more, the WVS reveals low levels of social and institutional trust. Democratic institutions suffer from a conspicuous lack of trust, which accords with low support for democracy and civil society participation. At the same time, a quarter of the population favours authoritarian views and political rhetoric (Gimes et.al. 2009; Juhász et al. 2014). These features of Hungarian attitudes go some way towards explaining how right-wing extremists and their political messages can resonate with some segments of society.

Civic, inclusionary conceptions of Hungarian identity, essential for a democracy with a multi-ethnic population, clash with persistent ethno-national conceptions that are more amenable to far-right discourses. The historical factors that buttress Hungarian ethno-nationalism, chiefly past occupation and foreign domination, also favourably incline many to the contradictory melange of, on the one hand, heightened nationalism and, on the other, collective victimhood and scapegoating (Erős 2019). Far-right narratives that cast Hungarians as a great ethnic nation and implicitly or explicitly exclude minorities, their rights, and multiculturalism generally resonate among a significant proportion of the citizenry.

Two groups have a particularly long history of persecution in Hungary: Roma and Jews. During the socialist era, the state officially suppressed racism against the Roma and, similarly, antisemitism did not manifest itself openly because it was considered a component of fascist ideology. Notwithstanding strong state control, in everyday interactions incidents of racism, hate speech, and other manifestations of interethnic hatred persisted. Enduring mechanisms of institutional racism, such as marking Roma ethnicity in school and criminal records, also remained in place (Dunajeva 2018). After a long historical period without free speech and free press, the new democratic system introduced both, and allowed the re-emergence of open racism and antisemitism.

The psychosocial aspects of prejudice against Roma and Jews, deeply rooted in Hungarian society, are equally and contrastingly premised on socio-economic and cultural factors. Most Roma belong to the lower socio-economic strata of society. This real material position goes hand-in-hand with conceptions of Roma as an underclass, outcasts, pariahs. And their disadvantaged and excluded position is often turned back on them: 'Roma are lazy; they depend on welfare while honest Hungarians work hard.' Such welfare chauvinism and vilification of Roma is common (Kende et.al. 2021). Jews, on the other hand, are conceived of as an upper class, connivers, manipulators. The longstanding image of Jews as obscenely wealthy and possessing socio-economic reigns of power has considerable purchase in Hungary. Across various indicators between one-quarter and one-third of Hungarian respondents express agreement with tropes of antisemitic prejudice: 'there is a secret Jewish conspiracy that determines political and economic processes' (36 per cent fully or partially agreed); 'the number of Jews in certain fields of employment should be restricted' (23 per cent fully or partially agreed); 'the Jews are more prone to using unethical means to achieve their goals than others' (30 per cent fully or partially agreed). Antisemitism in Hungary is rife and pervasive – and growing (Félix et.al. 2020).

Both anti-Roma racism and antisemitism stem from fears of losing socio-economic positions and of losing status. Such fears, typically more pronounced in less stable societies such as Hungary, where scars of the transition from socialism remain, make people more susceptible to discourses that blame other social groups. The widespread anti-Roma and antisemitic sentiment offers fertile ground for extremist actors as well as political actors using explicitly or implicitly racist messages to mobilise support (Munk 2007; Székelyi et al. 2001). Roma are cast as indolent and stupid idlers scrounging off state money; Jews are represented as the rich and powerful and influential, depriving Hungarians of food through conspiratorial machinations. These longstanding distortions remain potent among Hungarian society, and actors playing on them abound.

Added to antiziganism and antisemitism, new antipathies have arisen and indeed been wantonly stirred up in Hungary. Foremost among these new group-focused enmities (Zick et al. 2008) are anti-Muslim, anti-migrant, and anti-LGBTQ attitudes. Whereas radical right political parties, such as Jobbik, preserved and espoused antiziganistic and antisemitic discourses, under Fidesz and Viktor Orbán the government itself is the fountainhead of hate against migrant (sometimes also labelled as Muslim) and LGBTQ individuals.

To be sure, these new hostilities are not ginned up solely by political actors; in European comparison, Hungarians are among the most unaccepting towards foreigners (Bernát et al. 2013; Kende and Krekó 2020). Yet the pull of political opportunism is not hard to detect in recent swells of xenophobia and homophobia. Anti-immigrant and Islamophobic attitudes increased amid the refugee crisis in 2015 after the government launched a fierce anti-migrant campaign. Immigrants and Muslims, often used interchangeably, are cast as invasive foreigners whose culture, especially religious practice or heritage, is incompatible with Hungarian national identity (Vidra 2017). By the same token, the government has targeted LGBTQ individuals and communities in recent years with homophobic rhetoric but also with legislation that confines homosexual rights and relegates them to second-class citizens. In large part, this surge of activity is part of a transnational counter-mobilisation against the 'Istanbul Convention' (officially, the Council of Europe Convention on preventing and combating violence against women and domestic violence), which right-wing, conservative, and religious actors frequently lambaste as promoting 'gender ideology' (Krizsán and Roggeband 2021). The Hungarian government has not implemented the Istanbul Convention – though Hungary is a signatory – which means some protections for LGBTQ individuals enshrined in the Convention are not being instituted. Moreover, the government in 2021 passed an 'anti-LGBT propaganda' law (officially, the 'Amendments to the Child Protection Act, the Family Protection Act, the Act on Business Advertising Activity, the Media Act and the Public Education Act') resembling Russian legislation passed in 2013 that has been used to suppress LGBTQ activism and persecute individuals.

Taken together, the old and enduring prejudicial attitudes towards Roma and Jews and the new and wilfully incited hatred towards Muslims, migrants, and LGBTQ mean that radical and extremist right-wing actors have many areas in which their stridently exclusionary rhetoric, and sometimes violence, would be warmly received by a sizeable audience. As we explain in the following sections, extremist actors in the three phases of post-socialist Hungarian politics have used and further incited these attitudes.

The far-right in Hungary

Young democracy phase, 1990-2002, far-right re-emergence

A prerequisite for the re-emergence of far-right social forces was the lifting of socialist suppression. Fortunately for the far-right, freedoms of speech and assembly represented the most fundamental values of the new democratic regime; they simultaneously offered legitimation and served to delegitimise the old socialist regime (Szőcs 1998). Effectively countering resurgent far-right extremism would have meant to address the limits of these fundamental values. The democratic regime did not take up this task of nuance. No legislative measures were made at the outset to address far-right, and consequently extremist, actors who enjoyed much freedom to mobilise and campaign.

Next, to mobilise and campaign effectively Hungary's revived far-right needed a receptive audience. As described above, sizeable chunks of the population hold attitudes agreeable to far-right exclusionary nationalist discourses. Added to this, the regime change unleashed economic instability and hardships. The inclination of many towards far-right discourses and, bearing in mind that deprivation and threat perceptions reinforce far-right preferences (Lucassen and Lubbers 2012; Onraet, Van Hiel and Cornelis 2013), heightened socio-economic grievances benefited far-right actors.

Onto this scene of new freedoms and favourable grievances emerged a panoply of far-right political parties and militant and skinhead groups. The common distinction between radical and extremist actors is useful to differentiate Hungary's far-right during its early democratic period[1]: radical right-wing actors accept democracy but reject many of its *liberal* components, typically in favour of privileging (ethnic) majorities to the cost of minorities; extreme right-wing actors reject democratic precepts based on free elections.

The most significant radical right-wing actor was the Hungarian Justice and Life Party (*Magyar Igazság és Élet Pártja*, MIÉP). It was founded in 1993 when István Csurka quit the then ruling moderate right-wing Hungarian Democratic Forum party after accusing its leader, Prime Minister József Antall, of being an agent of foreign interests. Under Csurka's leadership MIÉP became the representation of folkish and strident nationalism, antisemitism, and anti-establishment postures. The party won national representation only once, in 1998, garnering a small share of seats from 5.5 per cent of the vote. Nevertheless, MIÉP played an important role in the regeneration of far-right electoral politics in Hungary.

The extreme right-wing scene consisted of a smattering of small neo-fascist or Neo-Nazi political parties and movement organisations. In the early 1990s a trio of organisations emerged: the World-National People's Power Party (*Világnemzeti Népuralmista Pártot*, VNP) led by Albert Szabó, the Hungarian National Front (*Magyar Nemzeti Arcvonal*, MNA) led by István Györkös, and the Association of Those Persecuted by Communism (*Kommunizmus Üldözötteinek Szövetsége*, KÜSZ). These organisations succeeded in mobilising a few hundred young skinheads for rallies espousing elements of Nazism or Szálasi's Hungarism. In 1994, they merged to form the Hungarian Hungarist Movement (*Magyar Hungarista Mozgalom*, MHM), but only existed for a matter of weeks before the Supreme Court imposed a statutory ban for their open antisemitism (Szőcs 1998). Yet this prohibition did not prevent Szabó from reorganising under a new entity, the Hungarian Welfare Association (*Magyar Népjóléti Szövetség*, MNSZ). While the impact of these extremist organisations at the time was minimal – though Szőcs's (ibid., p. 1103) speculation in 1998 that Szabó might 'qualify for the role of the Hungarian [Jean-Marie] Le Pen or [Gianfranco] Fin' attests to the potential ascribed to the extremist movement – they succeeded in re-mobilising right-wing extremist activists in Hungary.

In the early years of post-socialist Hungarian politics, far-right social forces re-emerged and formed organisational infrastructure. Though their factionalisation prevented them from becoming a major political force, they succeeded in raising old grievances, such as the idea of revising the Treaty of Trianon, and criticising growing socio-economic inequalities. Subsequent iterations of Hungary's organised far-right built on the foundations established in this period.

Left-liberal rise and fall phase, 2002–2010, far-right ascendancy

In the 2002 elections MIÉP also lost all its seats, leaving Hungary's far-right without any parliamentary representation. But ultimately of much greater importance was that a coalition led by the Hungarian Socialist Party came to power, supplanting the Fidesz government led by Viktor Orbán. It would be swept out of office in 2010, but not before triggering a new burst of far-right organising and activism, the effects of which endure now.

The first term of the Hungarian Socialist Party government was rather uneventful. The country continued in the direction of Western integration, having joined NATO in 1999 and acceding to the EU in 2004, but the government made no great strides. This torpor may not have posed a problem if not for a fateful leak. In 2006, shortly after being re-elected, the socialist prime minister delivered a speech in front of the inner circles of the party, notorious now as the *Őszödi beszéd* ('Öszöd speech'), in which he admitted that their victory was partly a result of the deception about the government's achievements, that in reality the government had done 'nothing for four years' and had 'lied morning, noon, and night' to get re-elected. The speech was leaked to the media and the resultant outrage led to weeks of violent street riots. Far-right actors were often organisers for the protests, but they were allegedly supported by Fidesz and other centre-right actors. (Szabó (2008) argues that the riots were 'postmodern,' with an eclectic array of participants with different motivations, objectives, etc.) The rioters demanded the prime minister's resignation, but to no avail. Still, the riots represented a political instability that provided an opportunity for the far-right to build group cohesion and burnish its public reputation (Mikecz 2015) – both typical objectives of far-right demonstration politics (Virchow 2007; Zeller 2021).

Among the protesters and rioters, members and supporters of a young political party were prominently represented. A youth association oriented towards the folkish radical right ideology of MIÉP had been founded in 1999 and registered as a political party in 2003: Movement for a Better Hungary (*Jobbik Magyarországért Mozgalom*), or just 'Jobbik.' The second half of the 2000s witnessed the rise of this party from obscurity to notoriety as one of Europe's largest radical right parties.

Beyond the Öszöd speech scandal, two factors were key to the surge in far-right support (cf. Karácsony and Róna 2011; Varga 2014; Mareš and Havlík 2016). First, economic growth and socio-economic welfare stagnated in Hungary in the latter half of the 2000s – and then declined sharply with the onset of the Great Recession. The Hungarian government, thoroughly delegitimised by scandal, was scarcely able to cope with this economic pressure. Voter preferences reflected frustration with the government: between 2002 and 2009, anti-establishment sentiments among voters changed from 12 per cent to 46 per cent (Juhász et al. 2014). Second, tensions surrounding Hungary's Roma communities became a focus of public debate. A particular event helped to draw this focus: in 2006, in the village of Olaszliszka, a Hungarian man was murdered by a mob of Roma after the man had accidentally hit a Roma girl with his car. (The girl was not seriously injured.)

Jobbik used the case to draw public attention to what party figures called 'gypsy criminality.' The phrase denoted the supposed criminal tendencies of Roma people, depicted in Jobbik's narratives as born criminals and blameworthy for the country's social and economic hardships. Jobbik's stance emboldened a network of extreme right-wing actors with varyingly close connection to the party. The biggest of these groups was the Hungarian Guard Traditionalist and Cultural Association founded in 2007. The Hungarian Guard functioned as a sort of paramilitary group and organised marches through Roma communities, torchlit processions reminiscent of marches by Nazi brownshirts. During these demonstrations, Guard leaders and Jobbik representatives delivered anti-Roma hate speeches to phalanxes of uniformed members as well as the community members, the 'neighbours' of the local Roma people. Although the Guard was proscribed by court order in 2009 (Halasz 2009; Pirro 2018) a successor organisation (i.e., the 'Hungarian Guard Foundation') and other groups – such as the Outlaw Army, the Pax Hungarica Movement, the Sixty-Four Counties Youth Movement, and the Our Homeland Movement (see below) – continued to menace and attack Roma communities. Between 2008 and 2009 extreme-right militants committed a series of racist murders (Halasz 2009), killing six and injuring several more. After the perpetrators were caught, it was revealed during their trial that they had sought to retaliate against Roma crimes, echoing narratives about 'gypsy crime,' and that they had selected their attack locations based on where the Hungarian Guard had organised marches.

The extreme right was not the only sector stimulated by Jobbik's anti-Roma rhetoric. Important parts of the mainstream political elite, instead of rejecting Jobbik's racist narratives, adopted and reinforced this perspective. The concept of 'gypsy crime' was taken up and used by politicians and the media. Jobbik successfully radicalised the mainstream (Minkenberg 2017). Having won support with its anti-Roma campaign, Jobbik gained upwards of 14 per cent of the vote in both the 2009 European parliamentary elections and the 2010 national legislative elections, making it the third strongest party in Hungary.

At the end of the left-liberal phase of Hungary's post-socialist politics, the far-right was on the rise. Though the folkish radicalism of MIÉP had disappeared, the cultural infrastructure they established enabled a new generation of the radical right to build their movement into a political force (Mikecz 2015). A rich subculture, organised on a network of websites and connected to 'national rock music,' provided reliable mobilising structures for Jobbik (Pirro and Róna 2019) and offered belonging and a sense of identity to a cohort of young people (Feischmidt and Pualy 2017).

Illiberal phase, 2010–present, far-right in power

Following the catastrophic second term of the Hungarian Socialist Party government, the 2010 elections swept Fidesz into power with a two-thirds majority. The decade since this climacteric witnessed the steady entrenchment of the Fidesz government, shearing away liberal protections in favour of Orbán's illiberal democracy. Simultaneously, the collapse of Hungary's political left-wing and concomitant swing of votes to Fidesz and Jobbik[2] generated a new political dynamic: competition for right-wing voters and marginalisation of the political left.

Whereas Hungary's left receded in 2010, Jobbik surged, signalling to Fidesz a new centre of political competition – on its right flank. Consequently, Fidesz has turned (more) towards far-right discourse, narratives, and indeed policies. Four areas are representative of this shift. First, Fidesz has instituted a new politics of memory, namely, memorialising the interwar authoritarian regime of Miklós Horthy, absolving Hungary of culpability for the Holocaust, and condemning the socialist regime. In the country's new basic law – passed in 2011 with the support of only the government's MPs – there are several historical allusions, one of the most important being the assertion that Hungary lost its sovereignty between 1944 and 1990, lumping together the Nazi and Soviet occupations and entirety of the socialist era, and implicitly denying any Hungarian culpability for the Holocaust. Perhaps the clearest symbols of this historical memory agenda have been erected by the government in concrete, steel, and bronze. The 'Memorial for Victims of the German Occupation' unveiled in central Budapest in 2014 evokes a victimised Hungary set upon by a German imperial eagle (Mikecz 2021); in 2019, a memorial to Imre Nagy, a liberal socialist leader killed by pro-Soviet forces in the aftermath of the failed 1956 revolution, was moved from Martyr's Square in Budapest in order to restore a monument from the Horthy era commemorating victims of the 1919 Hungarian Soviet Republic; and since Fidesz came to power, monuments of Horthy have been installed in Kenderes (2012), Kereki (2012), Budapest (2013), Budapest (2017), Bodaszőlő (2018), Csókakő (2019), Hajdúbagos (2021), and Kiskunfélegyháza (2021). Moreover, these examples are only an important selection of the Orbán regime's memory politics, which commemorate a far-right authoritarian and give form and legitimation to far-right narratives.

Second, seizing the opportunity presented by the refugee crisis in 2015–2016, Fidesz contrived a new threatening out-group: migrants. Whereas Jobbik had previously banged the drum for action against 'gypsy crime,' and benefited from their monopoly of anti-Roma sentiment (Karácsony and Róna 2011), Fidesz representatives were quick to take control of the narrative around refugees and migrants seeking transit through Hungary. The government initiated a vociferous anti-migrant campaign that positioned Hungary as saviour of Europe. In the name of Hungarian and Christian values, no migrants, and especially not Muslim migrants, would be allowed into the country (Szalai and Gőbl 2015; Vidra 2017). This was no empty rhetoric; a fence was completed on parts of Hungary's southern border in September 2015.

Third, Fidesz and Orbán frequently paired their anti-migrant campaign with attacks against the Hungarian-born financier George Soros using antisemitic tropes. While Orbán fostered close ties with Israel's former (until 2021) Prime Minister Benjamin Netanyahu and supported some funding for Hungary's Jewish community, he has also repeatedly described Soros as a creeping, insidious presence in Hungarian and indeed global politics. Government-funded placards have frequently used images of the nonagenarian financier's smiling face and implored Hungarians to be aware of 'the Soros plan,' 'not to let Soros have the last laugh,' and to 'stop Soros.' In 2018, the government passed so-called Stop Soros legislation that criminalised providing certain assistance to illegal immigrants. And the government effectively evicted the Open Society Foundation and the Central European University – both funded by endowments created in part by Soros.

Fourth, the Orbán regime has ostentatiously taken a stance against certain rights for LGBTQ persons and against so-called 'gender ideology.'[3] In recent years, the government has banned university programmes on gender studies, eliminated recognition for transgender individuals, and refused to ratify the Istanbul Convention (Krizsán and Roggeband 2021) – all actions supposedly taken to protect Hungary from the threat of gender ideology. Furthermore, Fidesz passed in 2021 an anti-LGBTQ law – it shares many features with legislation proposed by Jobbik in 2012 and with the gay propaganda law passed in Russia in 2013 – that banned activities supposedly promoting homosexuality to minors and restricted sexual education in schools to groups and individuals registered by the state.

With these four issue areas Fidesz moved into the far-right ideological space previously represented by Jobbik; consequently, Jobbik changed its political profile, recasting itself as a centre-right party (Bálint et al. 2020). But this provoked factionalisation within the party. More extreme Jobbik members, led by László Toroczkai, resigned and founded in 2018 the Our Homeland Movement (*Mi Hazánk Mozgalom*) party. Toroczkai is totemic for Hungary's right-wing extremists. As a young adult, he was a member of MIÉP. In 2001, he founded the Sixty-Four Counties Youth Movement (*Hatvannégy Vármegye Ifjúsági Mozgalom*, HVIM), an irredentist organisation promoting Hungarian nationalism in the territories of the former Kingdom of Hungary; HVIM has been linked to political violence, and Toroczkai is banned from entering Serbia or Slovakia in part because of his activities with HVIM. He participated in the 2006 riots after the Öszöd speech and subsequently supported Jobbik through his role as leader of the HVIM. Since 2013, as mayor of the southern-border village of Ásotthalom, Toroczkai has advocated for the construction of a border fence and used militia forces to perpetrate human rights abuses against migrants, imposed bans on Islamic religious practices (later ruled unconstitutional) and on homosexual behaviour, and founded a new paramilitary organisation (*Nemzeti Légió*) modelled on the Hungarian Guard. Yet Fidesz's shift to the far-right has left little political space for Toroczkai, his Our Homeland party, and likeminded extremists. The government's rhetoric and policies are in many instances aligned with the Hungary's extreme right.

The current phase of Hungary's post-socialist politics, which began in 2010, is marked by the hegemony of Fidesz. Since entering government, the party and Prime Minister Orbán have moved resolutely to stifle political competition on its right flank – to great effect.

Countering the far right in Hungary

Hungary, like most states, upholds the justification to confront the *extreme* right, but not the *radical* right. Legal provisions exist that enable the state to proscribe extremist actors, ban extremist demonstration activity, and punish hate crimes (see Table 12.1). However, 'exist' is nearly all these legal provisions do; courts have typically interpreted them permissively and police agencies have enforced them rarely.

Table 12.1 Legal infrastructure relevant to right-wing extremist activity

Law	Relevant provisions
Basic Law (the constitutional law of Hungary)	• Article VIII – right of assembly • Article IX, §4 and 5 – limitations to free speech
Act on the right of association[a]	• Article 2, §2 – associations cannot be used to commit or encourage criminal offenses or limit others' rights or liberties • Article 2, §3 – armed associations are not permitted
Penal Code[b]	• §215 – Violation against freedom of conscience and religion • §216 – Violence against a member of the community • §222 – Harassment • §254 – Attempt to overturn constitutional order by force • §255 – Conspiracy against constitutional order • §332 – Incitement against a community • §333 – Open denial of Nazi crimes and Communist crimes • §335 – Use of symbols of totalitarianism • §338 – Threat of public endangerment • §339 – Public nuisance • §340 – Disorderly conduct • §351 – Abuse of the right of association • §352 – Unlawful activities concerning the pursuit of public security
Act on the right of assembly[c]	• §9(1)(c) – prohibiting paramilitary or otherwise intimidating clothing • §13 – grounds for prohibiting an assembly (broadly including public endangerment or infringing others' rights or freedoms) • §14 – special prohibitions against denying, doubting, trivialising, or justifying crimes of Nazi or Communist regimes

Notes:
a Available in translation at: www.legislationline.org/documents/id/5353
b Available in translation at: www.legislationline.org/download/id/5619/file/HUngary_Criminal_Code_of_2012_en.pdf
c Available in translation at: www.ilo.org/dyn/natlex/docs/ELECTRONIC/109320/135572/F458116280/LV_english.pdf

This laxity has only become more pronounced since the installation of Orbán's illiberal regime. Indeed, the concept of counter extremism measures may seem problematic in a regime where a form of extremism is the central political position represented by the ruling party (cf. McNeil-Willson 2021). This has led to the vilification of several liberal civil society organisations, limiting their resources and sometimes imperilling their very existence.

The upshot for counter-extremism is that, effectively, there is not much in Hungary. Below, we discuss the evolution of legal provisions aimed to curb right-wing extremism and also explain how they have failed to disrupt extremist organisation and activity. Given the failure of state actors to address right-wing extremism, civil society actors have often engaged in this work – though, as we explain, the illiberal regime's actions have impaired this activity.

State counter-extremism: permissive legal interpretation and weak enforcement

The Hungarian state's legal infrastructure has evolved reactively, responding to challenges posed by right-wing extremism. However, while it includes tools that can curb extremist activity, the judiciary and law enforcement agencies have shown reticence, or else wilful lethargy, to apply them. Given that, Hungary's counter-extremism amounts in most instances to considering whether the non-application of certain laws is cynical or apathetic.

Hungarian law allows courts to ban extremist symbols, organisations, and activities. The existence and application of these limitations was not without controversy. Whereas Western European countries had created proscription powers to counter extremism after the history of interwar and war-time fascist parties, where actors within open societies gained power and suppressed internal dissent, countries in the former Eastern Bloc had emerged from regimes where a foreign power suppressed independent political activity. Nevertheless, Hungary's first post-socialist government enacted in 1993 the Act on the Use of Totalitarian Symbols (currently, §335 of the Penal Code), which forbids public displays of 'the swastika, the insignia of the SS, the arrow cross, the sickle and hammer, and the five-pointed red star.' Szőcs (1998, p. 1108) describes how the main effect of this enactment, though it arose amid concerns about *right*-wing extremists, was to strip the walls of a bar in Budapest that was decorated in communist paraphernalia. Even if police had been intent on applying the law to right-wing extremists, those extremists were generally quick to use other totalitarian symbols that were not one of the handful listed (ibid.).

The power to ban extremist organisations (i.e., through the Association Act as well as section 351 of the Penal Code) has been used to no greater effect. Hungary's Supreme Court ruled in 1994 that the Hungarian Hungarist Movement (MHM) was illegal (Szőcs 1998). But the judiciary's fecklessness and the extremists' minor adaptation set the pattern for future proceedings against the right-wing extremist organisations. The Constitutional Court issued a statement on 24 June 1994, shortly after the ban order, asserting that freedom of expression is protected even when insulting or disconcerting; though strictly correct and seemingly innocuous, the statement was interpreted as a repudiation of the MHM ban. Meanwhile, even before being banned by the court, the MHM had regrouped as a new organisation (ibid.). Yet state authorities pursued no further action against it.

Since that episode, only three organisational bans have been imposed in Hungary. In 2005, the Blood and Honour Cultural Association (*Vér és Becsület Kulturális Egyesület*), a Hungarian branch of the transnational Neo-Nazi music organisation, was banned for violations of the Penal Code and Association Act but re-formed and continued to operate as the Homeland Unity Movement (*Hazáért Egység Mozgalom*). In 2009, the Hungarian Guard, the paramilitary group connected to Jobbik, was banned but re-formed and continued to operate as the New Hungarian Guard and the Association for a Better Future. And in 2014, the Association for a Better Future was banned but immediately re-formed as the Hungarian Defence Movement and continued its activities. Proscription of Hungarian right-wing extremist organisations has been made into a minor bureaucratic formality with no significant force or effect on extremist organisational activity.

The continuity of right-wing extremist activity, often heedless of organisational bans, is on display in several demonstration campaigns, especially in two instances. In 1997, the Hungarian National Front (MNA) organised a march for the 'Day of Honour,' commemorating the attempt by Hungarian and German Waffen-SS soldiers in February 1945 to break out of encirclement by Soviet forces (Virchow 2013). The event has been held every year since, later organised by Blood and Honour and its descendant organisations. From its inception, the campaign trivialised the crimes of the Nazi regime and violated several Penal Code provisions. By 2009 the event – organised not by the Blood and Honour Cultural Association, banned in 2005, but by Blood and Honour Hungaria – had as many as 2,000 participants. In 2019 and 2020, police departments initially prohibited parts of the event, but court rulings overturned these decisions. With the Day of Honour campaign, as in other examples, state authorities have shied away from consistently and resolutely enforcing laws meant to curb right-wing extremist activity.

Similarly, right-wing extremist organisations and paramilitary groups in the late-2000s initiated demonstration campaigns intended to confront so-called 'gypsy criminality.' Spurred on, and in some instances directed, by Jobbik, these demonstrations intimidated Roma communities around Hungary, as apparently this was their aim. Indeed, their threatening character was the main justification for banning the Hungarian Guard – though, as mentioned above, this decision proved only a minor disruption of the group and its activities. What is more, the demonstrations did more than intimidate and threaten; terrorist activity, the perpetrators having connections to far-right groups, resulted in six deaths, multiple injuries, and property damage. Yet the peak of tensions emerged in 2011 when paramilitaries 'invaded' the town of Gyöngyöspata (Feischmidt and Szombati 2012). They conducted nightly patrols, harassed Roma residents, and stoked interethnic tensions – all at the behest of some ethnic Hungarians in the town and with minimal interference from the police. These anti-Roma campaigns prompted the government to amend the Penal Code in 2011 to forbid threatening members of ethnic, national, or religious minorities. However, a variety of laws already prohibited the type of activities seen in Gyöngyöspata. What remains is the problem of enforcement.

In recent years, the government has adopted new policies, including a protocol that entered into force in 2019 on hate crimes for the police and prosecutors, and modified provisions to enable charges for hateful offences. However, law enforcement actors have seldom received training on these new provisions; when they have, it was typically conducted by non-governmental organisations.

Non-government responses

The Hungarian state's deficiencies in addressing right-wing extremism have often spurred non-governmental actors to take up the charge. Broadly, non-governmental counter-extremism activities come in three categories: political mobilisation, anti-racist activism, and contribution to policymaking.

Political mobilisation constituted one of the most crucial civil society responses to the rising far-right threat in the 1990s. The Democratic Charter movement, founded in 1992, problematised the issue that right-wing extremism existed within the right-wing ruling coalition. The movement successfully generated mass mobilisation, whereas preceding anti-racist mobilisation had been limited to a small circle of liberal intellectuals (Szőcs 1998). The mid-2000s saw another important phase in political mobilisation against the far-right, though it was not as extensive or impactful. Demonstrations and activities seeking to counter the Hungarian Guard were organised by Roma and human rights groups. They organised themselves to meet the members of the Hungarian Guard when marching through villages and staging hate demonstrations. Generally, though, counter-mobilisation was sporadic and failed to mobilise large numbers of people. On some occasions, clashes erupted between the far-right and the anti-racist groups – though these disturbances of public order never prompted serious state sanctions against far-right demonstrations (cf. Zeller 2022).

Some civil society actors have also pursued broader programmes of anti-racist activism. A handful of organisations implement projects to counter anti-gypsy, antisemitic, and anti-LGBTQ attitudes. The inauguration of Orbán's illiberal government brought forth political pressure on several of these organisations that received funding from foreign sources. The government did not have an anti-extremism strategy, but the fact that organisations active in the field received financial support from abroad made them suspicious to the regime. The political climate was unfavourable to some of the organisations not only because of the political pressure, but also because of the government's political position that embraced and endorsed extremism in its rhetoric and certain policies. The Working Group Against Hate Crimes (GYEM) was an alliance of four civil rights organisations working on anti-discrimination. In their 2021 report, they asserted that

> it is our experience that almost no effective anti-racism measures and legal strategies have been implemented, we can say quite the opposite: the central government has largely contributed to racism being highly accepted within our society and in the course of public communication.
>
> GYEM 2021, p. 3

The government's direct attacks as well as its contribution to mainstreaming and elevating racist and exclusionary rhetoric has curtailed the capacity of independent anti-racist activism.

Civil society actors are even stymied when they attempt to work with state institutions. A review of the implementation of anti-racism projects (Kende et.al. 2018) found that state institutions are closed off and refuse dialogue with civil organisations. This characterises the post-2010 period. For NGOs, it was not possible to establish contacts with government ministries and state institutions. Part of the government's application of political pressure on civil society includes depriving them of any influence on policymaking and implementation. Concomitant to political attacks on civil society is the marginalisation of academic expertise. Prior to the illiberal regime, there had always been various forms of collaboration between academia, civil society, and certain policy fields relevant on ethnic and minority discrimination and integration. These collaborations ceased to exist with the establishment of the illiberal regime. In general, the government tends to ignore or even be hostile to expert knowledge; many of the issues related to anti-racism and anti-discrimination, or fields relevant to building resilience against extremism, have been labelled a leftist-liberal ideology. The only niche where collaboration between academic research, civil society operations, and policymakers has been possible is in municipalities where opposition parties came into power in the 2019 local elections.

Concluding remarks

Through the three phases of Hungary's post-socialist politics there was a steady progression of far-right social forces. Notwithstanding the evolution of actors in this scene, parties and social movement organisations mobilising, demobilising, and shifting to represent different ideologies, the rise of the Hungarian far-right has been fairly consistent. In the 1990s, Hungary's far-right re-emerged and created a network of organisations – these foundations still underlie the contemporary far-right scene – but was marginalised politically. In the late 2000s, the far-right movement emerged and mobilised masses; a far-right party attracted a large constituency of voters. Their impact on the public sphere, however, was even more remarkable. Through marches and media campaigns, they succeeded in mainstreaming racist anti-Roma discourses and agenda-setting far-right issues. This was the phase of far-right ascendancy. Since 2010 the thrust of Jobbik and several far-right movement organisations has been blunted through the Orbán regime's appropriation of far-right rhetoric and policies.

Hungarian government counter-extremism policies and practices typically have been reactive rather than proactive and have suffered from permissive legal interpretation and weak enforcement. This characterises earlier phases of Hungary's post-socialist politics and indeed accurately describes the pattern under the current political system, dominated by Fidesz. Looking back, the Fidesz government's actions to address extremist mobilisations were trivial. Looking forward, the government has adopted few measures to address how individuals are exposed to extremist views online and has created no de-radicalisation programme that would help individuals exit extremist activism. Any decrease in recent extremist activity is likely attributable to 'problem depletion' (cf. Davenport 2015), whereby Fidesz's ideological shift to the far-right has sapped the mobilising potential of right-wing extremists.

Notes

1 Szőcs (1998) offers a bespoke three-fold typology of extremist actors during this period in Hungary – namely, hangover parties, neo-fascist nostalgia parties, and imitative Neo-Nazis –but it is fitted to the conditions of the 1990s. To clarify the development of the far-right throughout the phases of post-socialist Hungarian politics we prefer the radical/extreme distinction, which offers more consistent analytical leverage. A noteworthy alternative conception of sub-types of the far right is Minkenberg's (2013) four-fold typology, though his 'religious-fundamentalist right' type is insignificant in Hungary.
2 In 2006, right-wing parties won no more than 50 per cent of the vote. In 2010, that became nearly 70 per cent: Fidesz won upwards of 52 per cent and Jobbik upwards of 16 per cent. The pattern held in 2014: nearly 45 per cent for Fidesz and over 20 per cent for Jobbik; and in 2018, more than 49 per cent for Fidesz and 19 per cent for Jobbik.
3 'Gender ideology' is a floating signifier commonly used by conservative or parochial actors to refer to a range of facts and postulates, including that abortion should be legal, that there is a need for campaigns against gender-based violence, that homosexuals should be allowed to marry and adopt, and that gender is non-binary. Some opponents of 'gender ideology' equate it with totalitarian ideologies.

References

Bálint, K., Hunyadi, B., László, R. and Molnár, C. (2020) *Minél Jobbra, Minél Jobban: A magyar (szélső) jobb 100 évvel Trianon után*. Budapest: Political Capital.
Bernát, A., Juhász, A., Krekó, P. and Molnár, C. (2013) *The Roots of Radicalism and Anti-Roma Attitudes on the Far Right*, www.tarki. hu/en/news/2013/items/20130305_bernat_ juhasz_kreko_molnar. pdf
Davenport, C. (2015) *How Social Movements Die*. Cambridge: Cambridge University Press.
Dunajeva, J. (2018) Negotiating Identity and Belonging after Regime Change: Hungarian Society and Roma in Post-Communist Hungary. In: Lebedeva, N., Dimitrova, R. and Berry, J. (eds), *Changing Values and Identities in the Post-Communist World*. Cham: Springer, pp. 349–364.
Erős, F. (2019) Migránsok, menekültek, idegenek. Társadalomlélektani megfontolások és kérdések a menekültválságról. *IMÁGÓ Budapest*, 8, pp. 24–37.
Feischmidt, M. and Pulay, G. (2017) 'Rocking the nation': The popular culture of neo-nationalism. *Nations and Nationalism*, 23(2): pp. 309–326.
Feischmidt, M. and Szombati, K. (2012) GYÖNGYÖSPATA 2011. The laboratory of the Hungarian Far-Right. A case study of political mobilization and interethnic conflict, http://pdc.ceu.hu/archive/00006555/01/Ecopolis_Gyongyospata2012.pdf

Félix, A., Galgóczi, E., Hann, E. and Róna, D. (2020) *Antiszemita incidensek. Jelentés 2019–2020.* MAZSIHISZ, https://mazsihisz.hu/files/public/filecache/ma__medialibrary_media/656/7656/antiszemita_incidensek_2019-2020_hun%20FINAL.pdf

Gimes, G., Juhász, A., Kiss, K. and Krekó, P. (2009) *Látlelet 2009 – a szélsőjobboldal megerősödésének okai,* www.politicalcapital.hu/pc-admin/source/documents/20091028_PC_Latlelet_2009.pdf

GYEM (2021) Contribution to EP study on racism, https://gyuloletellen.hu/sites/default/files/gyem_contribution_to_ep_study_on_racism_3.pdf

Halasz, K. (2009) The Rise of the Radical Right in Europe and the Case of Hungary: 'Gypsy crime' Defines National Identity? *Development,* 52(4), pp. 490–494.

Juhász, A., Krekó, P. and Molnár, C. (2014) A szélsőjobboldal iránti társadalmi kereslet változása Magyarországon. *Socio. hu,* 25–55.

Karácsony, G. and Róna, D. (2011) The Secret of Jobbik. Reasons Behind the Rise of the Hungarian Radical Right. *Journal of East European & Asian Studies,* 2(1), pp. 61–92.

Keller, T. (2013) *Értékek.* TÁRKI Társadalomkutatási Intézet, www.tarki.hu/hu/research/gazdkult/2013/2013_zarotanulmany_gazd_kultura.pdf

Kende, A., Nyúl, B., Hadarics, M., Veszna, W. and Hunyadi, B. (2018) Antigypsyism and Antisemitism in Hungary. Summary of the final report, https://politicalcapital.hu/pc-admin/source/documents/EVZ_Antigypsyism%20Antisemitism_final%20report_%20summary_180228.pdf

Kende, A., Hadarics, M., Bigazzi, S., Boza, M., Kunst, J. R., Lantos, N.A., Lášticová, B., Minescu, A., Pivetti, M. and Urbiola, A. (2021) The Last Acceptable Prejudice in Europe? Anti-Gypsyism as the Obstacle to Roma Inclusion. *Group Processes & Intergroup Relations,* 24(3), pp. 388–410.

Kende, A. and Krekó, P. (2020) Xenophobia, Prejudice, and Right-Wing Populism in East-Central Europe. *Current Opinion in Behavioural Sciences,* 34, pp. 29–33.

Krizsán, A. and Roggeband, C. (2021) *Politicizing Gender and Democracy in the Context of the Istanbul Convention.* Cham: Palgrave Pivot.

Lucassen, G. and Lubbers, M. (2012) Who Fears What? Explaining Far-Right-Wing Preference in Europe by Distinguishing Perceived Cultural and Economic Ethnic Threats. *Comparative Political Studies,* 45(5), pp. 547–574.

Mareš, M. and Havlík, V. (2016) Jobbik's successes. An analysis of its success in the comparative context of the V4 countries. *Communist and Post-Communist Studies,* 49(4), pp. 323–333.

McNeil-Willson, R. (2021) Resilience against Counterterrorism? The Repression and Response of Crimean Muslim Activism against Russian Counterterrorism and Counter-extremism. *Intersections. East European Journal of Society and Politics,* 7(4), pp. 154–173.

Mikecz, D. (2015) Changing Movements, Evolving Parties. *Intersections. East European Journal of Society and Politics,* 1(3), pp. 101–119.

Mikecz, D. (2021) The Living Memorial Movement: Building Resilience based on Grief. *Intersections. East European Journal of Society and Politics,* 7(4), pp. 70–84.

Minkenberg, M. (2013) The European Radical Right and Xenophobia in West and East: Trends, Patterns and Challenges. In: Melzer, R. and Serafin, S. (eds), *Right-Wing Extremism in Europe. Country Analyses, Counter-Strategies and Labor-Market Oriented Exit Strategies.* Berlin: Friedrich Ebert Stiftung Forum Berlin, pp. 9–34.

Minkenberg, M. (2017) The Rise of the Radical Right in Eastern Europe: Between Mainstreaming and Radicalization. *Georgetown Journal of International Affairs,* 18(1), pp. 27–35.

Munk, V. (2007) 'Play to Me Gypsy!' How Roma Stars' Image Change in Hungarian Media. In: Kallioniemi, K., Kärki, K., Mäkelä, J. and Salmi, H. (eds), *History of Stardom Reconsidered.* Turku: International Institute for Popular Culture.

Onraet, E., Van Hiel, A. and Cornelis, I. (2013) Threat and Right-Wing Attitudes: A Cross-National Approach. *Political Psychology,* 34(5), pp. 791–803.

Pirro, A.L. (2018) Lo and Behold: Jobbik and the Crafting of a New Hungarian Far Right. In: Caiani, M. and Císar, O. (eds), *Radical Right Movement Parties in Europe.* Abingdon: Routledge, pp. 151–167.

Pirro, A.L. and Róna, D. (2019) Far-Right Activism in Hungary: Youth Participation in Jobbik and its Network. *European Societies,* 21(4), pp. 603–626.

Szabó, M. (2008) Globális kommunikáció, civil társadalom, tiltakozás [Global communication, civil society, protest]. *Fordulat,* 1, pp. 96–116, http://fordulat.net/pdf/1/szabo.pdf

Szalai, A. and Gőbl, G. (2015) *Securitizing Migration in Contemporary Hungary.* CEU Centre or EU Enlargement Studies Working paper, November 2015, https://cens.ceu.edu/sites/cens.ceu.edu/files/attachment/event/573/szalaigoblmigrationpaper.final.pdf

Székelyi, M., Örkény, A. and Csepeli, G. (2001) Romakép a mai magyar társadalomban [Roma image in today's Hungarian society]. *Szociológiai Szemle*, 3, pp. 19–46.
Szőcs, L. (1998) A Tale of the Unexpected: The Extreme Right vis-à-vis Democracy in Post-communist Hungary. *Ethnic and Racial Studies*, 21(6), pp. 1096–1115.
Varga, M. (2014) Hungary's 'Anti-Capitalist' Far-Right: Jobbik and the Hungarian Guard. *Nationalities Papers*, 42(5), pp. 791–807.
Vidra, Z. (2017) Dominant Islamophobic Narratives: Hungary. *Centre for Ethnicity and Racism Studies*, 1–36, https://cps.ceu.edu/sites/cps.ceu.edu/files/attachment/publication/2923/cps-working-paper-countering-islamophobia-dominant-islamophobic-narratives-hungary-2017_0.pdf
Virchow, F. (2007) 'Capturing the Streets': Demonstration Marches as a Political Instrument of the Extreme Right in Contemporary Germany. In: Reiss, M. (ed.), *'The Street as Stage': Protest Marches and Public Rallies since the Nineteenth Century*. Oxford: Oxford University Press, pp. 295–310.
Virchow, F. (2013) Creating a European (neo-Nazi) movement by joint political action? In: Mammone, A., Godin, E. and Jenkins, B. (eds), *Varieties of Right-Wing Extremism in Europe*. London: Routledge, pp. 197–214.
Zeller, M.C. (2021) Patterns of Demobilization: A Qualitative Comparative Analysis (QCA) of Far-Right Demonstration Campaigns. *Mobilization: An International Quarterly*, 26(3), pp. 267–284.
Zeller, M.C. (2022) Demobilising Far-Right Demonstration Campaigns: Coercive Counter-Mobilisation, State Social Control, and the Demobilisation of the Hess Gedenkmarsch Campaign. *Social Movement Studies*, 21(3), pp. 372–390.
Zick, A., Wolf, C., Küpper, B., Davidov, E., Schmidt, P. and Heitmeyer, W. (2008) The Syndrome of Group-Focused Enmity: The Interrelation of Prejudices Tested with Multiple Cross-Sectional and Panel Data. *Journal of Social Issues*, 64(2), pp. 363–383.

13
POLAND

Michael C. Zeller and Jana Hrckova

Introduction

Since the collapse of the communist regime, Poland has presented an unlikely case for the related afflictions of polarisation and violent extremism. The transformation towards democracy was not blighted by violence or intense contestation and was capped by smooth accession to the EU; the national economy developed well (though unequally) over the past three decades, including during the 2008–2009 economic crisis from which Poland emerged largely unscathed; and the ethnic and religious homogeneity of the population portended no danger of inter-group conflict. Yet Poland today is marked by strong polarisation and rising extremism (Cipek and Lacković 2019; Prentice 2020; Hrckova and Zeller 2021; Khmilevska 2021; Taylor and Prentice 2021).

Polarisation in contemporary Poland can arguably be traced back to 2005. Following a collapse in support for the incumbent government (due to high unemployment, spending cuts, and corruption scandals), there were elections in which two opposition parties were the primary contenders: the Law and Justice (*Prawo i Sprawiedliwość*, PiS) party and Civic Platform (*Platforma Obywatelska*), later Civic Coalition (*Koalicja Obywatelska*). PiS won the 2005 elections. In the aftermath, Civic Platform seemingly decided to take a starkly, absolutely oppositional stance to PiS in all things. This sequence of events set a pattern that has continued since: harsh oppositional rhetoric and polarisation driven by these two major camps. The current PiS arguably represents the apotheosis of that development.

Within the context generated by the current PiS regime, tension between two broad sets of social forces is striking. On the one hand, variants of radicalism and extremism have proliferated and grown stronger in recent years. Though the PiS government has occasionally taken steps to distance itself from extremism, several far-right actors have taken encouragement or even received active support from PiS. On the other hand, actors that accumulate or enact liberal democratic-oriented social resilience seek to mitigate the effects of radical and extremist actors. This chapter dilates on these counterpoised social forces in Poland. First, it uses a conceptualisation of variants of radicalism and extremism to identify Poland's most prominent radical and extremist actors. This typological overview is complemented by a detailed examination of one violent extremist actor, the National Radical Camp (*Obóz Narodowo-Radykalny*, ONR).

Yet the perils of polarisation and extremism have not gone unchallenged, so the next section examines actions affecting liberal democratic-oriented social resilience. We specify this form of resilience, which should be read alongside other conceptions. Broadly, resilience simply refers to an ability to cope with adversity and strains. Within social science, therefore, the concept has been used to refer to everything from institutional resilience (e.g., Merkel and Lührmann 2021) to individual resilience against radicalising pressures (e.g., Grossman et al. 2017). Within an illiberal regime like Poland, actions broadly accumulate, enact, or corrode this social resilience. To illustrate this conceptualisation, we look closely at the activity of *Fundacja Autonomia* (Autonomy Foundation). We posit that under the PiS regime, resilience-building activities are often organised *despite*, not *with*, the national government. This represents a unique shift within the region where, at least on a declaratory level, governments remain supportive of measures promoting equality and supporting societal acceptance. In Poland, this has ceased to be the case in several areas. We conclude with a synthesising discussion on the tension of opposed social forces in Poland, and what it suggests for the future of Polish socio-politics.

Polish variants of radicalism and extremism

Political extremism in Poland is marked by several right-wing variants and no major left-wing or Islamic actors. Two contextual factors help to account for this uneven distribution. First, as in most of the Eastern Bloc, Poland's transformation from socialism in the late 1980s and early 1990s coincided with reinvigorated nationalism in the public sphere; an unsurprising development since Soviet domination typically entailed repressing nationalism. The establishment of democracy also meant the restoration of national sovereignty and resurgence of institutions and actors closely connected with Polish national identity, not least the Catholic Church. It would be highly misleading to insinuate that resurgent nationalism was inherently menacing. Most of it was benign. However, swells within this wave represented more radical, extreme nationalism and related ideologies. The post-socialist era has witnessed the Catholic Church, confined to naves and pulpits during Soviet domination, intervening with great and growing frequency in politics. Promoting a radical social conservatism that relegates certain minorities has at times been the aim and effect of this political intervention. The early 1990s also saw the re-formation of extremist organisations, such as the fascist National Radical Camp. Thus, the origins of Poland's contemporary right-wing radicalism and extremism[1] is to be located in the years surrounding the transformation from socialism.

Second, whereas Western European countries typically face some difficulties from other ideological stripes of extremism, Poland is devoid of significant left-wing and Islamically justified extremism. For the absence of left-wing extremism, the cause is likely also rooted in the transformation from socialism. As nationalism and right-wing extremism advanced, left-wing extremism, often tarnished by ideological proximity to the socialist regime, receded. The absence of Islamically justified extremism is at least in part a factor of Poland's demographics: Muslims are a vanishingly small portion of Poland's religious adherents, with no signs of significant growth. The only significant extremism in Poland therefore emanates from the ideologically right wing – but there is variation within that set.

Before turning our attention to the varying stripes of Poland's right-wing radical and extremist scene, it is worth mentioning that Preventing and Countering Violent Extremism policy in Poland is in several instances shaped by diffusion from Western European policies (Levchuk 2021). Much of the Act on Anti-Terrorist Actions (enacted in 2016) and the PiS government's National Anti-Terrorism Programme and National Security Strategy develop a framework lifted from other contexts for dealing with foreign-based, Islam-inspired terrorism – yet such threats are virtually non-existent in Poland. These policies could be applied to counter the existing right-wing extremism, however, the PiS government has not shown significant activity in this direction.

Right-wing extremism in Poland is diverse, so it helps to establish the different strains therein. Minkenberg (1998) identifies radicalisation of inclusionary and exclusionary criteria of belonging as the characteristic distinguishing variants of the radical right. Though all their redefinitions of belonging reject 'modernisation' or 'post-industrial society' (ibid., p. 29), right-wing radicals' priorities of inclusion and exclusion vary and reveal divisions within the right-wing scene. Based principally on the posture towards historical far-right movements and ideologies, engagement in violence, and, referring to Heitmeyer's (2002) theory of 'group-focused enmity', antagonism to particular groups, Minkenberg (2013, pp. 12–13) discerns four variants of the radical right:

(1) an *autocratic-fascist right*, usually involving racism or ethnocentrism and inspired by right-wing dictatorships of the interwar period;
(2) a *racist or ethno-centrist – but non-fascist – right*, usually employing 'ethnopluralist' arguments for the incompatibility of cultures and ethnicities while denying the existence of a 'natural hierarchy';
(3) a *populist-authoritarian right*, organised around a strong and charismatic leader, with an authoritarian structure and a diffuse nationalist or xenophobic ideology; and,
(4) a *religious-fundamentalist right*, in which nationalism or xenophobia merge with religious rigidity, resulting in the defence of a religiously framed conception of national 'purity'.

All four of these variants are present and active in Poland (see Table 13.1). Indeed, some of them wield state power or otherwise exercise considerable social influence.

The most conspicuous of these in Poland is the *populist-authoritarian right* epitomised by the ruling Law and Justice party (Mudde 2019). The party is still led – indeed, dominated – by one of its co-founders, Jarosław Kaczyński, who acts as an éminence grise within the government. PiS representatives have often given voice to nationalism and xenophobia, but their most consistent rhetoric excludes and dehumanises LGBTQ individuals. MPs like Przemysław Czarnek argue, 'Let's stop listening to these idiocies about human rights. These people are not equal with normal people' (Walker 2020). President Andrzej Duda referred to 'LGBT ideology' during his 2020 election campaign, asserting it was worse than communism (BBC 2020). And the Minister of Defence referred to equality marches as 'parades of sodomites' (Chrzczonowicz 2018). What is more, state action sometimes buttresses this political rhetoric. For example, for displaying an image of the Virgin Mary with a rainbow halo (the so-called Our Lady of Equality action) three activists were detained and charged with 'offending religious feelings' (i.e., Article 196 of the Polish Penal Code) by the Ministry of the Interior and Administration. Though the accused were found not guilty in March 2021, that charges were brought at all may have a deterring effect on LGBTQ advocates. PiS and its governmental partners embody the populist-authoritarian right variant. But it is striking that these actors are closely connected to and supportive of other strains of right-wing extremism.

The *religious-fundamentalist right* in Poland consists of many members of the Catholic Church hierarchy and aligned advocacy groups like Ordo Iuris. Particularly on social policy, the Church hierarchy exercises considerable influence on political affairs (Żuk and Żuk

Table 13.1 Variants of right-wing radicalism/extremism and contemporary Polish examples

Right-wing variant	Contemporary Polish examples
autocratic-fascist right	• National Radical Camp (*Obóz Narodowo-Radykalny*) • Pride and Modernity (*Duma i Nowoczesność*) • National Revival of Poland (*Narodowe Odrodzenie Polski*) • All-Polish Youth (*Młodzież Wszechpolska*)
racist/ethno-centrist right	• Zadruga & the Niklot Association for Tradition and Culture (*Stowarzyszenie na rzecz Tradycji i Kultury 'Niklot'*) • National Movement (*Ruch Narodowy*) • Independence March Association (*Stowarzyszenie Marsz Niepodległości*)
populist-authoritarian right	• Law and Justice party (*Prawo i Sprawiedliwość*) • Kukiz'15 party • United Poland party (*Solidarna Polska*)
religious-fundamentalist right	• Polish Episcopal Conference • Ordo Iuris • Fr Piotr Skarga Christian Culture Association (*Stowarzyszenie Kultury Chrześcijańskiej im. ks. Piotra Skargi*) • Centre of Life and Family (*Centrum Życia i Rodziny*)

2019). Most conspicuously, Church prelates insist on strict adherence to Catholic dogma on women's rights (especially abortion) and LGBTQ issues. Both are often lumped together as 'gender ideology', which, according to the Church, threatens to 'subordinate society to ideological postulates' (Polish Episcopal Conference 2020, p. 9, par. 33). Church opposition to women's rights protections has been matched by PiS governmental actions: instituting strict limitations on abortion and withdrawing from the Istanbul Convention that aims to reduce violence against women (Krizsán and Roggeband 2021). Concurrently, the Church hierarchy has given its official position on LGBTQ issues, declaring it unnatural and calling for 'clinics to help people wishing to regain their sexual health and natural sexual orientation' (Polish Episcopal Conference 2020, p. 11, par. 38). And while the Church explicitly rejects violence against LGBTQ individuals (ibid., p. 8, par. 29), the rhetoric of its conservative bishops has often stoked rather than stifled homophobic violence. For example, ahead of a 2019 equality march in the eastern city of Białystok, the resident bishop, Tadeusz Wojda, called such LGBTQ demonstrations a 'blasphemy against God' and a foreign imposition on the region (Santora and Berendt 2019). The demonstration was met by thousands of strident and violent counter-protesters (Hrckova and Zeller 2021), including many gathered on the steps of Białystok's cathedral. Moreover, beyond the actions of its episcopacy, the Church advances its fundamentalist agenda through advocacy groups, especially Ordo Iuris. This think tank produces draft legislation in an attempt to enshrine Church dogma in law. Ordo Iuris is responsible for several proposals on abortion restriction as well as the legislative template used by many local councils in 2019 and 2020 to declare 'LGBT-free zones'. Together, the populist-authoritarian right and religious-fundamentalist right are the most powerful variants of radicalism/extremism in Poland.

The variegated range of actors comprising the *racist/ethno-centrist right* and *autocratic-fascist right* typically embody the most violent variants of radicalism and extremism in Poland. As denoted in Minkenberg's classification, these two variants share characteristics of racism or ethnocentrism. Unsurprisingly then, these types of groups often collaborate, as when marches are organised for Independence Day and sponsored by both the Independence March Association and the National Radical Camp. The distinguishing feature – though of little consequence – is affiliation with or endorsement of fascist movements and governance. In Poland, the National Radical Camp, the National Revival of Poland, and the All-Polish Youth take their names and foundational tenets from interwar fascist movements; and Pride and Modernity infamously celebrated Hitler's birthday in 2017 (for which it was dissolved by court order in 2019). The violent extremism manifested by these organisations deserves closer inspection, particularly because the PiS government has occasionally encouraged and elevated it. The next section therefore unpacks the case of the National Radical Camp.

National Radical Camp

The National Radical Camp (*Obóz Narodowo-Radykalny*, ONR) is an avowedly fascist organisation. If some members or even leading activists have trepidation about openly admitting it, no matter: a four-year defamation lawsuit concluded in early 2021 confirming the accuracy of that label. The judge in the initial 2019 decision, upheld in subsequent appeals, said matter-of-factly, if somewhat wryly, 'you only have yourself to blame. You refer to the pre-war organisation, which was an openly fascist organisation; you use the same symbols and names' (Dembińska 2019). ONR's contemporary expression dates to the early 1990s, when it reappeared with roughly the same ideology as its predecessor – ethno-nationalist, authoritarian, fiercely Catholic – combined with distinct antipathy to the EU and NATO. Its membership is disproportionately young, often casting themselves as dutiful patriots working to preserve Poland's traditional culture (Kajta 2017). And whereas right-wing extremist movements in other countries are frequently stimulated by dissatisfaction, in Poland ONR members and other young nationalists more often become engaged as part of 'their search for what they see as more solid, clear, and unambiguous foundations of social order' (Mrozowicki and Kajta 2021).

Like many social movement organisations, the ONR's activities are diverse. It produces and disseminates ideological tracts and promotional materials, organises summer camps and educational activities, and sporadically performs volunteer community service. Yet, as with many right-wing extremist groups, its most conspicuous collective actions are demonstrations (Płatek and Płucienniczak 2016). Two campaigns are particularly noteworthy: firstly, in the mid-2000s the ONR mobilised a series of demonstrations in the southern town of Myślenice commemorating a 1936 antisemitic insurrection, akin to the Kristallnacht (Wyborcza.pl 2008). Secondly, since 2005 – and in coordination with other nationalist groups since 2008 – the ONR organises Independence Day marches in Warsaw on 11 November. In recent years it has become known as the largest far-right gathering in Europe, with participation at times exceeding 100,000. Participants, prominently including ONR members, shout racist slogans (Pankowski and Kormak 2013; Wiącek 2019), maraud and vandalise, and attack LGBTQ and other oppositional symbols (BBC 2013; Ciobanu 2020; Pankowski and Kormak 2013, p. 166).

For existing theory on social movements and the far right, the current circumstances of the ONR are somewhat puzzling. Typically, as several cross-national studies have found (Koopmans and Rucht 1995; Minkenberg 2019), where radical right parties are strong, movement mobilisation is correspondingly weak. Right-wing governments or even merely prominent political representation, so the thinking goes, mollifies right-wing social forces. Not so in Poland, where far-right movement strength has grown in parallel with the ascendancy of PiS. Minkenberg (2019) identifies this complementarity as distinctive of Eastern Europe – though right-wing party and movement strength is perhaps nowhere greater than in Poland.

Furthermore, the ONR thrives in Poland without a major ethnic scapegoat (Bustikova and Kitschelt 2010, p. 40). Poland is an overwhelmingly homogenous society; ethnic Poles comprise upwards of 95 per cent of the population. Yet anti-immigration messages and opposition to 'Islamisation' have been recurrent themes at ONR protests, not least at the Independence Day marches where chants ring out about keeping Poland 'all White' (Taylor 2017).

The PiS regime has created an environment that by turns condones and encourages right-wing extremism, fortifying the ONR. At the most basic level, the ONR remains a lawful entity; it is not banned. There have been numerous attempts to ban the ONR – in fact, one local ban was applied in 2009 (Zeller and Vaughan 2021), but was easily circumvented – yet PiS representatives have repeatedly stymied these efforts. The latest application, filed in 2018, was rejected by the state prosecutor's office, which asserted after four years of gathering evidence that none of the ONR's activities promoted fascism or totalitarianism, nor incited nationality-based hatred (Drożdżak 2022). Thus, there are no grounds to ban it. This outcome is clearly in line with the expressed preference of the PiS government (Uhlig 2018).

Yet the leeway granted the ONR goes further than allowing it to operate. Several court rulings and law enforcement (in)action suggest permissiveness towards right-wing extremism. For example, in 2017, amid ongoing disputes about PiS's judiciary reforms, six Polish MEPs (from the PO party) voted in favour of a European Parliament resolution that declared the changes to the judiciary violated the fundamental values of the EU. In response, the ONR, along with two other right-wing extremist organisations, organised a symbolic protest in Katowice: they declared the six MPs 'traitors' and hung their portraits from gallows. Though the Minister of Justice announced an inquiry (Gotev 2017), ultimately no charges were brought against the protesters.

The most symbolic permissiveness is in allowing the ONR's symbols. In 2010, Polish police began using a handbook that identified symbols associated with hate crimes ('Hate Crimes: Supporting Material for Training'). Included was the ONR's *falanga* (meaning 'phalanx') symbol: a stylised arm holding a sword, typically in white on a green field. It is omnipresent at ONR demonstrations, where protesters often wear distinctive green armbands and form phalanxes of ONR flag-bearers. However, following complaints from a right-wing MP (Andruszkiewicz 2016), the Ministry of the Interior and Administration withdrew the handbook from its training materials. These and a spate of other judicial and law enforcement episodes give credence to the notion that the ONR, despite its transparent antipathy to the constitutional order, is a legitimate civil society actor.

At times, PiS has gone beyond permissiveness, actively encouraging ONR activism and enrolling it in positions of authority. Three instances exemplify this worrying practice. First, PiS representatives actively support the ONR's ultra-nationalist Independence Day demonstrations. Three PiS MPs were represented on the organising committee for the 2012 event (Pankowski and Kormak 2013, p. 165). While the government has sometimes distanced itself from the excesses of the demonstrations, such as when participants clashed with police and counter-protesters, PiS has in the main defended the annual event as an admirable expression of patriotism.

Second, PiS has shown its willingness to elevate leaders from the ONR. Consider the case of Tomasz Greniuch, ONR leader in Opole throughout the 2000s. He initiated the Myślenice demonstration campaign mentioned above. Naturally, ascent to this leadership position came only after many years of activism in Poland's right-wing extremist scene (Witkowski 2019). In 2019, PiS named Greniuch the head of the Opole office of the Institute of National Remembrance (*Instytut Pamięci Narodowej*, IPN), an institution tasked with investigating Nazi and communist crimes in Poland. In early February 2021, he was promoted to the head of the IPN's Wrocław office. Renewed complaints within Poland and criticism from Israel and other foreign representatives, especially after pictures emerged of him giving fascist salutes during ONR demonstrations, forced Greniuch to resign his post (Day 2021). Given his long activism with the ONR, that Greniuch rose to that position – that he was even hired by the IPN – attests to the PiS regime's endorsement of right-wing extremism.

Third, PiS indulges ONR militancy. Government representatives mooted the idea of incorporating the ONR into the Territorial Defence Force, making it part of Poland's official armed forces. When it was re-formed in 2016, both the PiS spokesman for the Ministry of National Defence, Bartłomiej Misiewicz, and a PiS senator on the parliament's defence committee, Michał Wojtkiewicz, suggested ONR members could enlist in the armed forces – despite prohibitions against political activism by members of the military (Kuraś 2016). Furthermore, in response to a series of women's rights protests in 2020, the ONR announced through its website (on 27 October 2020) the creation of 'national brigades' to protect Polish society and religious facilities. These units explicitly aimed to create 'political soldiers' to 'defend national and Catholic values through direct action'.

Its origins and history, its avowed ideology, its members and activities all attest to the right-wing extremism represented by the ONR. Support from PiS has imbued the ONR with unprecedented vitality, making it a more menacing social force. In part, this is the result of direct support, but more commonly it is indirect permissiveness that allows the ONR to operate freely despite its contravention of constitutional and criminal laws. The ONR and other right-wing groups comprise, along with Poland's Catholic institutions, the pillars of right-wing civil society. Notwithstanding tensions between the ONR and the Church (e.g., PolsatNews 2016), and ONR members' occasional criticism of PiS, the communion between nationalism and conservative Catholicism is the ideological core of the PiS regime (Kotwas and Kubik 2019). It embodies the PiS agenda of regime change and new elite formation (Pobłocki 2021).

Polish social resilience practices

Defined as 'the ability of people to face and respond to adversity, and the capacity to draw on various sources of strength and social resources to adapt and cope with challenges and situations of strain, stress, or trauma' (McNeil-Willson et al. 2019, p. 19), resilience is, many in Poland would claim, a national characteristic. A commonplace saying, *Polak potrafi*, could be translated as 'Poles can do' or 'Poles will find a way/find a solution', used both in a positive and a negative sense, and is an inherent part of the country's auto-stereotype. And while the saying often refers to hustling or bricolage activities, it also alludes to the nation's collective ability to cope with larger historical shifts, be it years under socialism or turbulent times of post-socialist transformation. Here, too, we focus on resilience as a collective capacity – 'social resilience', not a characteristic ascribed to an individual (Ungar 2013).

In this manner, it is possible to trace larger processes that shape responses to radicalism and violent extremism in the society as a whole. And just as importantly, resilience and resilience-building can be presented as ever-changing and historically grounded processes, not just reactions to the recent developments in the country. This section examines the various resilience-building practices responding to societal polarisation and violent extremism. It refers to the broad categorisation of actions affecting liberal democratic-oriented social resilience within illiberal regimes, namely *accumulating*, *enacting*, and *corroding* (Zeller and Vidra 2021). Moving from the gloomy picture painted by the preceding sections, our focus on resilience should raise hopes that 'Poles finding a way' extends even to meeting the challenges posed by the ONR and other variants of radicalism and extremism.

Comprehending social resilience involves appreciating a vast array of practices that defy neat categorisation. Actions beyond numbering are dynamic and multifaceted in their enhancement of resilience within the society, stretching from societal infrastructure such as accessible education and local community communication all the way to specific interventions in the field of inclusion and anti-discrimination. In practice, some of these paradoxically may fuel both resilience and polarisation, depending on the context (Bonanno 2005). For example, active membership in a religious community – in Poland, predominantly in the Catholic Church – can foster greater solidarity and interconnectedness; at the same time, Polish clerical rhetoric can be exclusionary and oftentimes harmful. Similarly, a sense of belonging may be crucial for building an open, rooted community (be it in a region or at a football stadium) but may also become a vehicle of hate towards outsiders who do not belong to the given group. And just as importantly, there is a range of factors that may play a role in the processes of accumulating, enacting, or corroding social resilience: equality of opportunity, supportive environment, sufficient resources, a sense of belonging, social cohesion, democratic media reporting, and pro-social messaging (McNeil-Willson et al. 2019, p. 22).

Here, we approach the conundrum of conceptualising social resilience by referring to the impact of practices within an illiberal regime. Poland, governed by a coalition of populist-authoritarian right parties (see Table 13.1), fits the bill of a country facing the polarising throes of illiberalisation. In this context, practices may accumulate or enact a social resilience that is liberal-democratic in orientation – or corrode it.

Practices help to *accumulate* social resilience when they 'enhance the liberal democratic esprit of a group and enhance its ability to cope with illiberal attacks' (Zeller and Vidra 2021, p. 6). A range of collective actions and shared activities may become a vital capacity-building mechanism. In particular, groups stigmatised by illiberal rhetoric and policy are in the greatest need of social resilience. The PiS regime routinely targets the LGBTQ community, which has had to rely on certain ameliorative practices. For example, the LGBTQ 'equality marches' have become a means for protesters to replenish a sense of social resilience: by participating – reaffirming their connection to a community and openly expressing their identity – protesters are more capable of withstanding the intermittent pressures of growing illiberalism (Hrckova and Zeller 2021). Such practices build up reserves of social resilience that enable groups to absorb shocks and strains without despairing.

Social resilience is *enacted* when actions directly counter illiberal attacks, drawing on the accumulated resources and oftentimes hidden capacities. The most striking examples in Poland are recent waves of counter-mobilisation against government actions to limit abortion. During a series of so-called Black Protests, hundreds of thousands of people marched in the streets in support of reproductive rights, generating immense (if for now ineffectual) pressure on the government, while creating a strong sense of togetherness among the protesters. Enacting social resilience – 'putting up a good fight' as in the case of the Black Protests – thus does not necessarily lead to immediate changes. Nevertheless, direct actions such as protests, litigation, and electoral politics activities show that standing up to the illiberal challenges is possible using all the social resources available.

Yet the accumulation and enaction of liberal democratic social resilience exists in dynamic tension with actions that *corrode* it, often perpetrated by radical or extremist actors. Zeller and Vidra (2021, p. 6) write, 'For many institutions and vulnerable communities, illiberal regimes are a threat, straining the resiliencies to cope with non-recognition or vilification by governing actors and their supporters'. The PiS regime's policies have consistently eroded judicial independence and constraints on governmental power. Obviously, this corrodes Poland's institutional resilience to illiberalism, but it also strips away judicial protections to vulnerable groups. Grabowska-Moroz and Wójcik (2021) chart how the deteriorating rule of law in Poland parallels vilification of the LGBTQ community; the former enables the latter. At the same time, the corrosive actions rarely remain without a response and often provoke robust counter-movements.

To illustrate the empirical manifestations of practices that accumulate social resilience, the following section looks closely at the work of the Autonomy Foundation.

Fundacja Autonomia

Fundacja Autonomia (Autonomy Foundation) is a Polish non-governmental organisation that focuses on activities fighting against violence and discrimination, with special emphasis on women's and gender issues: 'Autonomia is active so that every girl and every woman can be safe, brave, can decide about herself, develop and shape the world together with others'. *Fundacja Autonomia*'s activities combat systemic causes of inequalities, discrimination, and violence; in recent years, its work has been forced to cope with PiS policies promoting traditional gender patterns and relations and which reject efforts to reduce gender- and sexuality-based violence.

The 'Girls' Power Centres' project exemplifies the organisation's work to accumulate social resilience. The centres aim to create a safe space for girls and women to explore their skills, power, enhance their 'courage', set their own boundaries, learn how to cooperate with others, and how to get rid of feelings of shame and hopelessness. Participation in the activities of the centre is free, guided by the principle of solidarity and sharing within the community. It is ensured that the women have a say in the centre and that all can take part in it regardless of their socio-economic situation.

The centres' activities must be understood in the context of recent backsliding in women's rights in Poland. The attack on reproductive rights followed by a further expansion of what was already one of the strictest abortion bans in Europe has been accompanied by controversial statements on the role of women in the Polish society. For example, the Minister of Science and Education expressed his disapproval of women who prioritise their career and postpone having children until a later age, as they cannot have that many when older, 'as destined by the Lord' (Piekarczyk 2020). Similarly, the education reforms prepared by his Ministry set out a goal to shape 'womanly virtues' in schoolgirls (Sitnicka 2021). Amid the conservative shift that openly nudges women to take on their traditional role as mothers, ideally focusing on family life, the Girls' Power Centres aspire to provide space for women's development. Through activities linked to sexual education, no-means-no campaigns, and violence-prevention programmes, the centres also step in to fill the gaps within the national education system and provide a counterbalance to the government's messaging.

However, it is exactly the encounters with the national education system that have proven tricky under the PiS government. *Fundacja Autonomia* experienced this first-hand in 2016, when the Ministry of Family and Social Policy suddenly and unilaterally decided to cancel a citizen initiative contract with the organisation, citing irregularities in the project's facilitation. The project in question was focused on prevention of gender-based violence and consisted of a series of workshops (including at schools). The decision was announced after a wave of attacks from the right-wing media that accused the *Fundacja Autonomia* of promoting a 'LGBTQ subculture' followed by a sudden and highly irregular 'monitoring' action taken by the Ministry. Eventually, the proceedings were halted, which importantly meant that the organisers did not need to refund the money already spent; however, the organisation has never been officially cleared of wrongdoing and the unusual steps taken by the Ministry have not been subject to investigation.

The actions against *Fundacja Autonomia* stoked concerns within the NGO sector, especially among initiatives dealing with gender-related issues. Many interpreted the Ministry decision as a thinly veiled attempt to intimidate the NGOs dealing with topics that do not chime with the PiS agenda. One of the characteristics of the non-governmental sector in the region is that the organisations often heavily rely on state and state-governed funding (Guasti 2016, p. 9). Without dwelling on the reasons for such an arrangement, it is evident that one of its implications is that non-state actors and their programming can be vulnerable to the whims of the ruling power; many organisations have already experienced difficulties in obtaining government grants. Additionally, as organisations often rely on a project-based funding calendar, sudden withdrawals of sponsor-funding can lead to serious financial problems and even to their complete shutdown. Experience from other fields suggests this approach might have become the go-to play of the government: in 2018, the Ministry of Culture and National Heritage decided not to provide funding for a range of cultural and political journals/platforms that have often been critical of PiS.

The state thus not only vacated space in anti-discrimination and violence prevention education, but actively participates in limiting the scope of the activities of those NGOs that take on such topics. This constitutes a crucial shift in the Polish landscape. It would be wrong to claim that gender-based violence or discriminatory practices were not an issue under the series of liberal governments preceding the current PiS regime. However, the 'division of labour' with the government providing funding to a range of non-state actors and giving them a free hand in their activities seems to have reached its end. In order to continue in their activities, *Fundacja Autonomia* and other NGOs need to learn how to operate without relying on any kind of state support.

Concluding remarks

This chapter portrays Poland as a country gripped by illiberalisation, both spurred by and providing further encouragement of radical and extremist actors, but also possessed of sources of social resilience. After years of the populist-authoritarian Law and Justice government, Polish society seems to be as polarised as ever, witnessing rising right-wing extremism with a quiet nod from the powerful Catholic Church. Laws and policies to counter violent extremism are often configured around foreign and Islam-inspired terrorist threats; they are seldom applied to curb and reduce far-right threats. At the same time, the presence of resilience-building actors and practices is strong, challenging the status quo and acting as a counterpart to insurgent right-wing extremism. The chapter provides two main contributions: a classification and an analysis of the extremist variants in Poland with a deep dive on ONR, an autocratic-fascist right-wing group, and an analysis of social resilience practices with a special focus on *Fundacja Autonomia*, an organisation combatting discrimination.

Following Minkenberg (2013), right-wing radicalism and extremism in Poland can be divided into four variants: autocratic-fascist right, racist or ethnocentrist right,

Table 13.2 Social resilience processes

Type of processes	Examples
Accumulating social resilience	LGBTQ parades and equality marches, women's empowerment trainings
Enacting social resilience	Black Protests, political organising, litigation
Corroding social resilience	Hate speech, attacks on independent judiciary

populist-authoritarian right, and religious-fundamentalist right. Using the ONR as a case study of the autocratic-fascist right, the chapter demonstrates how the PiS government not only tolerates but also directly and indirectly supports extremist groups. The government's support is evidenced by participation in some of ONR's activities and militaristic performances as well as willingness to nominate ONR activists into official positions.

The chapter further uses the concept of social resilience to examine practices resisting the extremist right in Poland. Taking on Zeller and Vidra's (2021) proposal to analyse resilience through the lens of whether processes contribute to accumulating and enacting resilience or, on the contrary, work towards corroding it, the section provides examples of the various social resilience activities in Poland (see Table 13.2). *Fundacja Autonomia* is used as a case study here, illustrating that accumulating resilience is a long and situated process. The Foundation's activities are not only a response to recent developments in the country, but also a long-term project aimed at empowering inhabitants in a conservative society – and building capacities that can be drawn upon when needed. Such projects become all the more important when state-based initiatives to counter extremism and support liberal democratic society are (at best) lacking or (at worst) intentionally undermined.

Polarisation within Polish society has grown in recent years. Yet, as we have shown elsewhere using the example of the LGBTQ marches, the stark divides and accompanying conflict can eventually deliver growing levels of acceptance of differences within the society (Hrckova and Zeller 2021). Countering the rise of right-wing extremism and illiberalisation through oftentimes slow and painstaking resilience-building can feel like an uphill battle; yet, just as polarising topics revealed and fostered some extremist undercurrents in Polish society, so too have they spurred mobilisations of civic and democratic forces.

Note

1 Here and below – as with our invocation of Minkenberg's variants – we refer to radicalism and extremism together. Research on the far-right generally makes a conceptual distinction between these two, but the empirical manifestations are often less clear. So it is, we assert, in contemporary Poland. Given the sometimes anti-democratic and universally illiberal postures of actors discussed in this section, it is appropriate to label these groups extreme.

References

Andruszkiewicz, A. (2016) Interpelacja nr 1305. Sejm Archiwum, 24 February, www.sejm.gov.pl/sejm8.nsf/InterpelacjaTresc.xsp?key=0D27D481.

BBC (2013) Clashes mar Poland independence march. *BBC News*, Europe, 11 November, www.bbc.com/news/world-europe-24902058

BBC (2020) Polish election: Andrzej Duda says LGBT 'ideology' worse than communism. *BBC News*, Europe, 14 June, www.bbc.com/news/world-europe-53039864

Bonanno, G.A. (2005) Resilience in the Face of Potential Trauma. *Current Directions in Psychological Science*, 14(3), pp. 135–138.

Bustikova, L. and Kitschelt, H.P. (2010) The radical right in post-communist in Europe: Comparative perspectives on legacies and party competition. In: Minkenberg, M. (ed.), *Historical Legacies and the Radical Right in Post-War Central and Eastern Europe*. Stuttgart: Ibidem Verlag, pp. 29–62.

Chrzczonowicz, M. (2018) Błaszczak: „Parada sodomitów", „nie po Bożemu", „nienormalni". Minister powinien iść na terapię. *OKO.press*, 13 August, https://oko.press/blaszczak-parada-sodomitow-nie-po-bozemu-nienormalni-minister-powinien-isc-na-terapie/

Ciobanu, C. (2020) Ugly scenes as far right control Poland's Independence Day march. *Balkan Insight*, 11 November, https://balkaninsight.com/2020/11/11/ugly-scenes-as-far-right-control-polands-independence-day-march/

Cipek, T. and Lacković, S. (2019) Civil Society and the Rise of the Radical Right in Poland. *Politička misao: časopis za politologiju*, 56(3-4), pp. 153–176.

Day, M. (2021) Polish WW2 War Crimes Historian Quits over Nazi Salute Pictures. *The Telegraph*, 22 February, www.telegraph.co.uk/news/2021/02/22/polish-ww2-war-crimes-historian-quits-out cry-nazi-salute-pictures/

Dembińska, A. (2019) Koniec bitwy o słowa. *Portel.pl*., 22 March, www.portel.pl/wiadomosci/kon iec-bitwy-o-slowa/110751

Drożdżak, A. (2022) Prokuratura Regionalna w Krakowie nie wystąpi o delegalizację prawicowego Stowarzyszenia ONR. *Gazeta Krakowska*, 19 January, https://gazetakrakowska.pl/prokuratura-regionalna-w-krakowie-nie-wystapi-o-delegalizacje-prawicowego-stowarzyszenia-onr/ar/c1-16005045

Guasti, P. (2016) Development of citizen participation in Central and Eastern Europe after the EU enlargement and economic crises. *Communist and Post-Communist Studies*, 49(3), pp. 219–231.

Gotev, G. (2017) Poland probes pictures of MEPs 'on gallows' at far-right demonstration. *Euractiv*, 28 November, www.euractiv.com/section/central-europe/news/poland-probes-pictures-of-meps-on-gallows-at-far-right-demonstration/

Grabowska-Moroz, B., and Wójcik, A. (2021) Reframing LGBT rights advocacy in the context of the rule of law backsliding: The case of Poland. *Intersections. East European Journal of Society and Politics*, 7(4), pp. 85–103.

Grossman, M., Ungar, M., Brisson, J., Gerrand, V., Hadfield, K. and Jefferies, P. (2017) *Understanding Youth Resilience to Violent Extremism: A Standardised Research Measure*. Final Research Report. Melbourne: Alfred Deakin Institute for Citizenship and Globalisation.

Heitmeyer, W. (2002) Gruppenbezogene Menschenfeindlichkeit. Die theoretische Konzeption und erste empirische Ergebnisse. In: Heitmeyer, W. (ed.), *Deutsche Zustände, Folge 1* (German Conditions, Vol. 1). Frankfurt a.M.: Suhrkamp, pp. 15–36.

Hrckova, J. and Zeller, M. C. (2021) The everyday abnormal and the quest for normalcy: How Polish equality marches build protester resilience. *Intersections. EEJSP*, 7(4), pp. 104–123.

Kajta, J. (2017) Discursive strategies of Polish nationalists in the construction of the Other. *Intersections. East European Journal of Society and Politics*, 3(3), pp. 88–107.

Khmilevska, P. (2021) The structure of the Eurosceptic movement in Poland–political and civil far-right extremists. *Rocznik Integracji Europejskiej*, 15, pp. 233–247.

Koopmans, R. and Rucht, D. (1995) *Social Movement Mobilization Under Right and Left Governments: A Look at Four West European Countries*. Berlin: Social Science Centre (WZB), https://citeseerx.ist.psu.edu/viewdoc/download?doi=10.1.1.376.5982&rep=rep1&type=pdf

Kotwas, M. and Kubik, J. (2019) Symbolic thickening of public culture and the rise of right-wing populism in Poland. *East European Politics and Societies*, 33(2), pp. 435–471.

Krizsán, A and Roggeband, C. (2021) *Politicizing Gender and Democracy in the Context of the Istanbul Convention*. Cham: Palgrave Pivot.

Kuraś, B. (2016) Faszyzujący ONR chce być pod bronią u Macierewicza. MON światopogląd nie przeszkadza. *Wyborcza.pl.*, 22 April, https://wyborcza.pl/7,75398,19957672,faszyzujacy-onr-chce-byc-pod-bronia-u-macierewicza-mon-swiatopoglad.html

Levchuk, O. (2021) Legal and institutional aspects of combatting Radicalism and terrorism in Poland. *Przegląd Geopolityczny,* 37, pp. 132–140.

McNeil-Willson, R., Gerrand, V., Scrinzi, F. and Triandafyllidou, A. (2019) Polarisation, violent extremism and resilience in Europe today: an analytical framework. BRaVE, 2019/D2.1

Merkel, W. and Lührmann, A. (2021) Resilience of democracies: Responses to illiberal and authoritarian challenges. *Democratization*, 28(5), pp. 869–884.
Minkenberg, M. (1998) *Die neue radikale Rechte im Vergleich: USA. Frankreich, Deutschland* . Berlin: Springer-Verlag.
Minkenberg, M. (2013) The European Radical Right and Xenophobia in West and East: Trends, Patterns and Challenges. In: Melzer, R. and Serafin, S. (eds), *Right-Wing Extremism in Europe. Country Analyses, Counter-Strategies and Labor-Market Oriented Exit Strategies*. Berlin: Friedrich Ebert Stiftung Forum Berlin, pp. 9–34.
Minkenberg, M. (2019) Between party and movement: conceptual and empirical considerations of the radical right's organizational boundaries and mobilization processes. *European Societies*, 21(4), pp. 463–486.
Mrozowicki, A. and Kajta, J. (2021) Young people, precarious employment and nationalism in Poland: Exploring the (missing) links. *European Review*, 29(4), pp. 470–483.
Mudde, C. (2019) *The Far Right Today*. Hoboken, NJ: John Wiley & Sons.
Pankowski, R. and Kormak, M. (2013) Radical Nationalism in Poland: From Theory to Practice. In: Melzer, R. and Serafin, S. (eds), *Right-Wing Extremism in Europe. Country Analyses, Counter-Strategies and Labor-Market Oriented Exit Strategies*. Berlin: Friedrich Ebert Stiftung Forum Berlin, pp. 157–168.
Piekarczyk, D. (2020) Przyszły minister edukacji i nauki pochodzi z Goszczanowa. *sieradz.naszemiasto.pl*, 5 October, https://sieradz.naszemiasto.pl/przyszly-minister-edukacji-i-nauki-pochodzi-z-goszczanowa/ar/c1-7929761
Płatek, D. and Płucienniczak, P. (2016) Civil society and extreme-right collective action in Poland 1990–2013. *Revue detudes comparatives Est-Ouest*, 4, pp. 117–146.
Pobłocki, K. (2021) Suburbanization of the self: Religious revival and sociospatial fragmentation in contemporary Poland. *International Journal of Urban and Regional Research*, 45(1), pp. 39–60.
Polish Episcopal Conference (2020) The position of the Polish Episcopal Conference on the LGBT+ issue [Stanowisko Konferencji Episkopatu Polski w kwestii LGBT+], https://info.wiara.pl/files/20/08/28/609063_ZDfi_EpiskopatuPolskiwkwestiiLGBT.pdf
PolsatNews (2016) ONR nie dołączy do obrony terytorialnej. 'Działamy na polu ideowo-wychowawczym, nie paramilitarnym. *PolsatNew's.pl*., 25 April, www.polsatnews.pl/wiadomosc/2016-04-25/onr-nie-dolaczy-do-obrony-terytorialnej-dzialamy-na-polu-ideowo-wychowawczym-nie-paramilitarnym/
Prentice, S. (2020) Why does measuring polarisation matter? *Open Democracy*, 16 July, www.opendemocracy.net/en/global-extremes/why-does-measuring-polarisation-matter/
Santora, M. and Berendt, J. (2019) Anti-Gay Brutality in a Polish Town Blamed on Poisonous Propaganda. *The New York Times*, 27 July, www.nytimes.com/2019/07/27/world/europe/gay-pride-march-poland-violence.html
Sitnicka, D. (2021) Odkryliśmy, co to są cnoty niewieście. Czarnek chce kobiety bogobojnej, która doskonale przędzie. *OKO.press*, 21 July, https://oko.press/odkrylismy-co-to-sa-cnoty-niewiescie-czarnek-chce-kobiety-bogobojnej-ktora-doskonale-przedzie/
Taylor, M. (2017) 'White Europe': 60,000 Nationalists March on Poland's Independence Day. *The Guardian*, 12 November, www.theguardian.com/world/2017/nov/12/white-europe-60000-nationalists-march-on-polands-independence-day
Taylor, P. and Prentice, S. (2021) Polarisation Indicators. Building Resilience against Violent Extremism and Polarisation (BRaVE) Project, http://brave-h2020.eu/toolkit
Uhlig, D. (2018) Wicepremier Gliński: Rząd nie chce delegalizować ONR. *Wyborcza.pl*., 28 February, https://wyborcza.pl/7,75398,23080169,wicepremier-glinski-rzad-nie-chce-delegalizowac-onr.html
Ungar, M. (2013) Resilience, trauma context and culture, *Trauma, Violence and Abuse*, 14(3), pp. 255–266.
Walker, S. (2020) Polish president scales down homophobic rhetoric as election nears. *The Guardian*, 19 June, www.theguardian.com/world/2020/jun/19/polish-president-scales-down-homophobic-rhetoric-poland-election-nears-andrzej-duda
Wiącek, E. (2019) The rhetoric of the 'march of independence' in Poland (2010–2017) as the answer for the policy of multiculturalism in EU and the refugee crisis. *Politeja*, 61, pp. 149–166.
Witkowski, P. (2019) Z ONR do Instytutu Pamięci Narodowej – czyli cała kariera Tomasza Greniucha. *OKO.press*, 11 November, https://oko.press/cala-kariera-tomasza-greniucha/

Wyborcza.pl. (2008) ONR-owcy skazani za hajlowanie. *Wyborcza.pl.*, 4 December, https://opole.wyborcza.pl/opole/7,35086,6024418,onr-owcy-skazani-za-hajlowanie.html

Zeller, M.C. and Vaughan, M. (2021) *Proscribed Right-Wing Extremist Organisations.* Centre for the Analysis of the Radical Right, www.radicalrightanalysis.com/resources/proscribed-right-wing-extremist-organisations.

Zeller, M.C. and Vidra, Z. (2021) Illiberalism, polarisation, social resilience, and resistance: Concepts in dynamic tension. *Intersections. East European Journal of Society and Politics*, 7(4), pp. 1–12.

Żuk, P. and Żuk, P. (2019) Dangerous liaisons between the Catholic Church and State: The religious and political alliance of the nationalist right with the conservative Church in Poland. *Journal of Contemporary Central and Eastern Europe*, 27(203), pp. 191–212.

14
ITALY

Francesca Scrinzi

Italy stands out among other European countries because – so far – it has not been affected by the same levels of ideological radicalisation and experienced limited incidence of right-wing as well as jihadist extremist violence. This has contributed to the notion of an 'Italian exceptionalism' in the matter of violent extremism (Groppi 2017, p. 20). Yet in Italy political polarisation around immigration is intense, fuelling anxieties around migrants' integration and anti-Muslim hostility among the population; in turn, this may aggravate the Muslim population's discrimination and frustration. The financial crisis and austerity policies and, more recently, the pandemic lockdown measures have also increased socio-economic inequalities in Italian society. These material and subjective insecurities can provide both right-wing and violent jihadist actors with greater opportunities to appeal to new recruits and normalise their ideologies. In addition, as noted by Lorenzo Vidino (2018), who, in 2016, was appointed by the Italian government to chair the first research committee on violent jihadist radicalisation and extremism, the country is close to conflict areas in the Middle East and North Africa and receives an important inflow of migrants coming from Muslim majority countries. These characteristics, combined with the fact that Italy – particularly the city of Rome, representing the cradle of Christianity – constitutes a symbolic target for violent jihadists could be regarded as facilitating a surge of radicalisation.

This 'exceptionalism' also conflicts with the country's bloody history of left-wing and right-wing terrorism in the 1970s and 1980s, the so-called *Anni di piombo* (Years of Lead). At that time, in the context of the Cold War, Italy was also affected by a series of terrorist incidents perpetrated by separatist as well as by nationalist Palestinian organisations. Since the 1990s, Italy has faced new challenges, which include right-wing extremism (Marone 2017a). However, Italian public and political debates as well as scholarship on radicalisation and on resilience are still in their infancy.

This chapter takes stock of existing academic studies and experts' contributions to discuss violent jihadist or so-called Islamist as well as right-wing violent and ideological radicalisation in Italy. It then examines existing measures and initiatives to counter and prevent these phenomena. The discussion covers relevant legislation, policies, and debates and is set against the Italian context of historical legacies of extremism and national formations of ethnicity and religion.

Violent jihadist extremism in Italy

As mentioned, Italy has yet to experience a large-scale jihadist terrorist attack. The number of Italian 'foreign fighters' is very small compared with those produced by older European immigration countries such as Belgium or France. 'Home-grown' violent jihadism, a longstanding phenomenon elsewhere, has eventually emerged in Italy too, but on a significantly smaller scale. Scholars concur in identifying the demographics of the Muslim population as the main factor protecting Italy from this threat (Beccaro and Bonino 2019; Groppi 2020; Vidino 2014). First, Muslims are not the largest group of migrants living in Italy: in 2021, most migrants came from Christian majority countries, representing 56 per cent of all foreign residents, while Muslims comprised 27 per cent of the migrant population (Caritas/Fondazione Migrantes 2021). Immigration is a more recent phenomenon than in other European countries: Muslim immigration to Italy began between the 1980s and the 1990s as a male-dominated mobility from northern African countries, mainly driven by economic motives. Today, these migrants are still in the process of settling in and securing a livelihood, thus being less vulnerable to the sense of alienation and lack of purpose that may accompany radicalisation. Instead, 'second-' and 'third-generation' Muslims, who tend to be more prone to the appeals of extremist preachers, are still numerically limited. While a recent survey indicates that most Muslims look at Italy favourably (Groppi 2020), other quantitative studies suggest not only significant levels of socio-economic exclusion of Muslims (FRA 2018) but also high levels of perceived discrimination among this population (EU-Midis II 2017).

Vidino (2014) argues that the experience of discrimination and a failing socio-economic integration – although important – are not key drivers in the Italian 'home-grown' violent jihadists' radicalisation compared with other countries. Second, unlike France or the UK, Italy is marked by the substantial absence of urban 'ghettos' afflicted by poverty, unemployment, and crime, and predominantly inhabited by Muslim migrants or people of Muslim background. The majority of Italian Muslims live in either Rome or northern Italy, scattered across different towns and regions, largely in Lombardy and Veneto, which are the most dynamic economic areas in the country: this spatial distribution has contributed to preventing the formation of so-called 'hotbeds' of radicalisation. Third, the great national and linguistic diversity of the Muslim population functions as a 'prophylactic against the rooting of the trans-national ideology' (Beccaro and Bonino 2019, p. 14) of violent jihadism: Muslims living in Italy come from 48 different countries, mostly Morocco, Albania, Bangladesh, and Pakistan (Guolo 2018). Finally, according to some scholars and counterterrorism experts, another factor protecting Italy from a surge of so-called 'Islamist' radicalisation similar to that experienced by other European countries is the experience and effectiveness of its legislation and security forces in fighting domestic and international terrorism. This was developed during the bloody history of left-wing and right-wing terrorism in the 1970s and 1980s, and has enabled counterterrorism forces and tools to adapt swiftly to new threats emerging at the end of the Cold War (Groppi 2020).

However, the notion of an 'Italian exceptionalism' is challenged by many scholars (Groppi 2020; Vidino 2014). The considerations made above should not lead to thinking Italy is immune from 'home-grown' jihadist radicalisation and terrorism. The country is indeed recognised as a crossroads of renowned terrorists, who have often used it as a logistical platform to organise attacks elsewhere, gathering intelligence and resources or benefiting from it as a transit point. While the threat is deemed to be relatively low, there is evidence that it is increasing as the country has gradually shifted 'from representing a safe haven for foreigner combatants to being the incubator of home-grown jihadists and "lone-wolves"' (Maniscalco

2019, p. 68). Following Italian support of US military interventions in Afghanistan in 2001 and in Iraq in 2003 as part of the 'War on Terror', several 'lone-wolf' terrorist plots have been thwarted, and the police have made various arrests in violent jihadist networks. One of these, originated in Brescia, for instance, threatened Pope Bergoglio and was dismantled in 2015. In 2018, it was established that 130 individuals linked to Italy due to their citizenship or residence permit had travelled to the territories controlled by the Islamic States and al-Qaeda (Beccaro and Bonino 2019). Cominetti (2018) suggests that while the Italian mosques operate less often as sites of propaganda and recruitment than in other European countries, the main hubs for radicalisation are the prisons and the internet. The online violent jihadist community is rather small but active. Indeed, Islamic State developed Italian language social media propaganda for the purpose of recruitment (Groppi 2020). As for prison institutions, these are considered the main physical places of radicalisation in Italy. Cominetti (2018) states that the number of detainees at risk of radicalisation is high when compared to the number of those convicted because of terrorism. All this indicates that although they remain limited, both violent jihadist threats and ideological radicalisation are on the rise.

Ongoing demographic changes, combined with the Muslims' persisting social, juridical, and economic marginalisation may reinforce these trends. The first relatively large 'second generation' of Muslim migrants is coming of age but is still mostly excluded from citizenship. Currently, Italian citizenship is largely based on *ius sanguinis* (right of blood): applying for naturalisation is a lengthy process. Those migrants' children who were born in Italy can apply within one year after coming of age and must provide evidence of uninterrupted residence in the country since their birth. Further, the law does not automatically give citizenship to those born on Italian soil unless at least one of their parents is Italian. This means that many migrants who have lived in the country for years can't become Italian citizens.

Starting in 2015, the criteria for the attribution of citizenship have been the object of heated public and political debates: countered by the populist radical right party *Lega nord* (LN) (now *La Lega*), the so-called *ius soli* – the right to citizenship based on birth – has been framed as increasing the threat of terrorism. The proposed reform of the Nationality Law, based on *ius soli*, has faced several amendments and opposition, and eventually wasn't passed (Tintori 2018). Among counterterrorism officers and experts, those supporting the law claim that it would enhance the sense of national belonging among second-generation migrants, thus helping prevent radicalisation. Instead, others suggest that implementing looser criteria for the attribution of citizenship would narrow the scope of action of the Italian authorities, which are allowed to expel non-citizens from the country through an administrative decree, based on national security grounds: these 'preventive expulsions', introduced in the late 1990s against illegal immigration, represent one important tool of Italian counterterrorism policy (Cominetti 2018). Indeed, it is recognised that such 'fast-track' deportations can prevent or de-stabilise extremist networks. It should be noted, however, that independently from the issue of more open criteria for granting citizenship, the emerging 'home-grown' violent jihadism poses a challenge to the Italian authorities' use of deportations as a major counterterrorism tool since Italian nationals can't be deported (Marone 2017b).

The Muslims' marginalisation in Italy is further enhanced by the persistent juridical invisibility of this faith as well as the lack of comprehensive national-level policies supporting migrants' integration. Despite 20 years of negotiations between Muslim organisations and the Italian state, Islam is not yet acknowledged as an official religion – something which is likely to constitute a drive for jihadist radicalisation (Cominetti 2018). This is partly linked to the difficulty for Muslims to find a unifying institutional voice in their dialogue with Italian authorities: Islam is plural by definition. However, the weak secularisation of Italian society and politics play an important role in maintaining Islam as well as other confessions in a minority juridical status. It was only in 1984 that the Lateran Treaty, signed between Mussolini and the Roman Catholic Church in 1929 and establishing Catholicism as the state religion, was revised, repealing the principle of the Catholic religion as the sole religion of the Italian state. The new Treaty however maintains a series of privileges for the Catholic Church, including fiscal advantages and the teaching of religion in public schools. There are only a few mosques in the country, while most believers practice in more or less formalised prayer rooms. The issue of building mosques has raised fierce controversies and has been faced with the opposition of political forces from the left to right of the political spectrum (Triandafyllidou 2002). This lack of recognition makes it difficult to identify institutional interlocutors for the purpose of anti-radicalisation measures (Dell'Isola 2021). Furthermore, migrants' integration policies are still limited and often delegated to local entities, often supported by the (Catholic) third sector and volunteer associations. This is in line with the nature of Italian immigration policy, which has long functioned based on emergencies and law decrees. Italian authorities have not promptly responded to the shifting status of the country from an emigration country to an immigration country in the 1970s. Indeed, until the late 1980s, Italy did not conceive itself as a receiving country, and a *laissez-faire* institutional approach dominated; policies on immigration have been applied on an ad hoc basis in a juridical vacuum, leaving room for application based on the discretion of the police (Barbulescu 2019). Although violent jihadist threats remain limited in Italy, all this can fuel resentment among Muslim believers and provide a fertile ground for ideological radicalisation.

Right-wing extremism in Italy

As exemplified by the debates on *ius soli*, immigration has been intensely politicised for over 20 years in Italy. In the decade that followed 9/11, Islam and the association between national identity and Christianity were prominent in Italian public and political debates. These have been heavily marked by the significant influence of the Catholic Church, which has often regarded Islam as a challenge to the 'Christian roots' of the nation. Cousin and Vitale (2014) argue that, at this time, Italian Islamophobia was grounded in an intellectual enterprise involving Church representatives and the right-wing political élites, including the conservative right and the populist radical right. While generally the Catholic Church has voiced the need for supporting all migrants irrespectively of their origins and faith, overtly countering anti-immigration positions, in the 2000s some conservative Catholic representatives have intervened in public debates on multiculturalism, aiming to reassert the connection between Catholicism and national belonging and the superiority of Christian values over the allegedly growing cultural relativism. Thus the Church approach oscillates between, on the one hand, a 'Christian moral universalism' (Dorangricchia and Itçaina 2005), a position that has recently become radically pro-migrant position under Pope Francis, and, on the other, an ambivalent approach inspired by a principle of 'selective solidarity' (Garau 2010, p. 168), whereby the immigration of non-Muslim, and particularly Christian, individuals should be favoured. In so doing, over the 2000s the Catholic hierarchies attempted to retrieve a position in the public sphere that had been weakening due to the growing distance of the Italian population from the Catholic doctrine and to the increasing migration-driven religious diversity (Garelli 2013). The decade witnessed a spectacular electoral and ideological growth of the populist radical right party LN, which has been a member of successive centre-right coalition governments led by Silvio Berlusconi. The LN has managed to impose immigration/identity issues on the national political agenda, associating them with 'law and order', based on an aggressive xenophobic propaganda. After 9/11, the party has radicalised its anti-immigration discourse, specifically targeting Muslim migrants and framing immigration as a 'clash of civilisations' through references to Catholicism as a symbol of the nation (Biorcio 2010).

While in power, this populist radical right party heavily influenced immigration policies by forcing mainstream parties to adjust towards stricter positions on the issue. These did little to keep down the anti-immigration rhetoric of their ally, contributing instead to legitimating it, and to further polarising political conflict (Carvalho 2014). In this context, the media have also played a major role in securitising immigration (Dal Lago 1999). Political and ideological polarisation around immigration has reached another peak with the so-called refugee crisis of 2015, as Italy serves as one of the main points of entry into Europe for migrants and refugees, and has been particularly active in migrants' rescue operations in the Mediterranean Sea. At this time, debates are focused on the public costs of these operations and on the refugees' integration as well as on managing the Mediterranean borders. Anti-immigration sentiments are widespread in the country: according to the Pew Research Center, in 2016 a majority of Italians tended to associate the refugees' arrival with terrorism (Hackett 2017).

The 'refugee crisis' has provided favourable opportunities for extreme right politics. Over the past few years, Italy has witnessed a surge of extreme right mobilisation by neo-fascist groups such as *CasaPound Italia*, which organised local-level anti-refugee protests (Castelli Gattinara and Froio 2019). Another neo-fascist organisation, *Forza Nuova*, lobbies to implement migrants' deportations while the Italian Generation Identity movement has organised anti-refugee ship missions in the Mediterranean. These rather active Italian grassroots neo-fascist and 'identitarian' groups claim their origins in Italian Fascism or are indebted to the historical experience of the French New Right (Mammone 2008). As far as *CasaPound Italia* is concerned, this group benefits from significant media visibility and, starting in 2014, has run in local elections based on an alliance with the LN. This unprecedented electoral alliance has meant, for the LN – traditionally an ethno-regionalist formation – dismissing its original secessionist agenda and embracing a fundamentalist, nationalist, and Eurosceptic rhetoric. For *CasaPound Italia*, this alliance enabled tackling issues until then only marginally mobilised by the organisation, including immigration. This hybridisation has enhanced the normalisation of extreme right politics in Italy (Castelli Gattinara and Froio 2019) and further polarised society.

Italian extreme right politics have also recently been bolstered in the context of the so-called anti-gender mobilisations opposing gender+ equality policies, LGBTQ+ rights, and reproductive rights. The ideological connection between the anti-gender movement and the extreme right relies in their simultaneous targeting of the 'gender ideology', conceived as an essential threat to the supposedly 'natural' complementary of the sexes and 'human anthropology' itself, and Islam as a threat to the national identity, thus conflating Italian-ness with the 'natural' heterosexual family. Anti-gender actors, which include conservative Catholics and family associations besides the extreme right and the populist radical right, sometimes employ an anti-Muslim rhetoric, blaming the Italian 'demographic winter' and emphasising that, while Italian women are no longer interested in having babies, the demographics of Muslim migrants is burgeoning. For instance, in 2015, representatives of the Catholic Church and of the 'theo-con' milieu gathered to affirm that the 'moral decadence' of society is the result of the rejection of its Christian roots and, at the same time, of the rampant 'Islamisation' of Europe (Garbagnoli 2018).

More recently, since 2020, extreme right groups have capitalised on the pandemic and Covid-19 restrictions by politicising them. They have benefited from growing visibility and activism in the context of the mobilisations against lockdown measures, vaccinations, and the so-called sanitary dictatorship. As in other European countries, the extreme right diffuses anti-Semitic conspiracy theories accusing pharmaceutical companies and the 'Jewish globalist élites' of scheming to spread the virus in order to generate profits. The national and EU political élites are also blamed for their supposedly 'liberticidal' policies. In Novara, in 2021, protesters against the Green Pass – the certificate confirming its holder's full vaccination –dressed in uniforms similar to those worn by Nazi concentration camp inmates. Besides targeting the élites in such populist fashion, the so-called no-vax extreme right also mobilises traditional xenophobic arguments, blaming migrants and ethnic minorities, particularly the Chinese communities, for the spread of Covid-19. Anti-immigration parties such as the *Lega* and the neo-fascist party *Fratelli d'Italia* (Brothers of Italy), whose agenda on immigration was marginalised during the pandemic, have similarly framed the lockdown by targeting both the racialised 'Others' and the political élites, arguing for instance that the citizens' access to medical services is hindered by the allegedly too generous migrants' integration policies (de Ghantuz Cubbe 2021). These protests have led to some violent episodes. In 2021, a union headquarters and a hospital emergency room were attacked in Rome during a demonstration against the decision to make the Green Pass mandatory for all workers. Following this, representatives of the Democratic Party and of the Five Star Movement called to dissolve and ban the neo-fascist organisations involved.

While these mobilisations may take the form of confrontational street politics, these extreme right groups do not officially endorse violence, even if this 'remains an important corollary to political activism and opposition and is never fully rejected' (Castelli Gattinara and Froio 2014, p. 162). Indeed, so far, Italy has been characterised by high levels of extreme right mobilisation while experiencing a relatively low incidence of right-wing extremist violence. In 2014, a neo-fascist plot to attack migrants and left-wing politicians was uncovered and thwarted. In 2021, the police dismantled a right-wing extremist group that was allegedly plotting to bomb a NATO base. The country has witnessed a few lone-actor attacks, one of which was fatal. In 2011 in Florence, Gianluca Casseri, a *CasaPound Italia* activist, shot and killed two Senegalese migrants and wounded another three before killing himself. In 2018, in Macerata, Luca Traini, a member and former local candidate of the LN party, shot and wounded six African migrants, claiming this as a revenge for the murder of an Italian girl by another migrant. Lone-actor radicalisation has been limited, first, by the legacy of the 'Years of Lead', which saw the neo-fascist armed spontaneity of the 1970s repressed by the authorities and, second, by the presence of options for collective violence offered by the Italian extreme right movement where these actions serve as 'initiation rites' for young recruits. The horizontality and disaggregation characteristic of extreme right movements in the US and in some European countries is absent from the Italian context, as violence remains controlled within the movements (Castelli Gattinara et al. 2018). Nonetheless, several unpunished incidents of xenophobic violence have occurred in recent years. Investigative research reports indicate that in 2013 over 50 'punitive expeditions' against migrants were organised. These actions could be seen as anticipating a new emergence of extreme right 'lone-wolves' violence. Indeed, the police forces warn that the threat of right-wing violent extremism is increasing, with radicalisation being largely based on social media (Europol 2019).

Preventing and countering violent extremism: Italian policies and practices

As mentioned, Italy has a long history of fighting both domestic and international terrorism: such experience has enabled the country to promptly adapt its legislation to 'new' terrorist threats and particularly the so-called Islamist radicalisation. Current Italian counterterrorism legislation includes Decree Law n. 347 (2001), which promotes international cooperation, and Decree Law n. 155 (2005), facilitating the detention of suspects and expediting the deportation of those non-citizens who demonstrate extremist sentiments. Further legislation defined recruitment and training for the purpose of terrorism as a crime (n. 134/2005) and increased punishment for instigation to and apology of terrorism (n. 7/2005). In addition, in the wake of the January 2015 terrorist attacks in Paris, Law 43/2015 punishes 'lone-wolf' terrorists and 'foreign fighters' (Jacobs et al. 2021). The Italian counterterrorism landscape includes the Antiterrorism Strategic Analysis Committee (*Comitato di Analisi Strategica Antiterrorismo*, CASA), which was established by the Ministry of the Interior in 2003 to centralise intelligence and share information, and to coordinate operations against jihadist actors. Overall, the Italian counterterrorism strategy is largely based on repressive measures and particularly, as mentioned, on the administrative deportation of non-nationals. Priority is given to the criminal justice system as Italian authorities have ample powers to conduct lengthy surveillance operations and pre-emptive raids (Beccaro and Bonino 2019).

Such 'fast-track' deportations have been criticised based, on the one hand, on juridical and human rights grounds, and, on the other, on pragmatic concerns. First, administrative expulsions are a discretionary act of the executive and are exempt from the procedural guarantees associated with criminal prosecution. Second, administrative deportations may be counterproductive in terms of counterterrorism efficacy: they can in fact unwillingly intensify individual feelings of frustration and anger as well as violent jihadist groups' narrative of victimhood and persecution. However, thus far the massive use of this measure has not generated much political and public debate (Marone 2017b).

While national security forces and legislation are well equipped to fight domestic and international terrorism, Italy lags other European countries with regard to prevention and the promotion of resilience. Preventive work – a pillar of the EU approach to fighting terrorism – is still underdeveloped, and the country lacks a comprehensive national policy to counter radicalisation. As mentioned, in 2016, an 'Antiterrorism Research Committee on Radicalisation and Jihadi Extremism' was established to provide policy recommendations. The committee advised that Italy align its policy with most European countries by implementing preventive measures including interreligious dialogue and resilience-building activities. It advised that initiatives are implemented to promote resilience at the macro, meso, and micro levels, implementing inclusive counter-narratives, local communities' 'positive engagement', and individual resilience. Work by the committee informed the bill 'Measures aimed at preventing radicalisation and jihadist extremism', proposed in 2016 by MPs Andrea Manciulli and Stefano Dambruoso. The bill targeted key areas of prevention such as prisons, schools, and the internet, and included measures for rehabilitating radicalised individuals based on a multi-stakeholder approach involving government, local authorities, and civil society organisations such as social and cultural associations and religious communities. The proposed bill also established a National Centre on Radicalisation (*Centro nazionale sulla radicalizzazione*, CRAD), which, supported by a series of Regional Coordination Centres (*Centri di coordinamento regionali sulla radicalizzazione*, CCR), should coordinate the implementation of these counter-radicalisation and prevention activities. The text was approved by

Parliament in June 2017 but before it had a chance to be voted on by the Senate was halted by a government change (Vidino 2018).

Despite this policy vacuum, some spontaneous and experimental initiatives have been taken in prisons and schools by local administrations and civil society organisations such as the Catholic *Comunità di Sant'Egidio* and *Caritas* and the Waldensian Church as well as secular politicised and non-politicised NGOs (Cominetti 2018). These include, for instance, training for imams and prison employees. Furthermore, in some cases, Italian courts, at the request of prosecutors, included rehabilitation provisions in convictions of individuals accused of terrorism-related charges. In 2018, the Ministry of Education introduced compulsory civic education programmes in public schools to provide an opportunity to engage youth and their families around issues of digital literacy, including radicalisation and resilience-building. However, no clear legislation or guidelines exist yet to support these initiatives, which are largely driven by the creativity and willingness of individual NGOs, administrators, and magistrates (Jacobs et al. 2021; Vidino 2018). Additional limitations of these 'spontaneous' and random initiatives are that they mainly target violent jihadism while neglecting right-wing extremism, despite authorities' warnings that the latter threat is increasing; moreover, overall, they tend to disregard the internet, a major hub of radicalisation in the country (Cominetti 2018).

Italy thus needs to further develop its preventive approach to radicalisation and violent extremism. Scholars and experts indicate two main avenues to pursue. First, it is necessary to develop appropriate juridical tools to deal with radicalisation. The concept of radicalisation has been adopted by the Ministry of Justice since 2010 for the purpose of monitoring activities in prisons (Berardinelli and Guglieminetti 2018). According to the experts, it would be necessary to attach such definition of radicalisation to existing counterterrorism legislation while avoiding linking it to any specific religions and setting violent action as the threshold for intervention (Groppi 2020). Second, as mentioned, the lack of formal recognition of Italian Islam makes it difficult to identify reliable institutional interlocutors for the purpose of implementing prevention actions. Yet Muslim leaders can be further supported in playing a greater role in countering radicalisation and condemning terrorist violence. Some progress has been recently made in this direction. While a constitutional *Intesa* with the Italian state is still missing, in 2017 a 'National agreement for an Italian Islam' (*'Patto Nazionale per un Islam Italiano'*) was signed between the Italian government and a series of associations including the largest Muslim NGO, UCOII – Union of the Muslim Communities in Italy (*Unione delle Comunità Islamiche in Italia*), allegedly representing 70 per cent of all Muslims living in Italy. The agreement emphasises the rejection of all forms of violence and terrorism and the centrality of Islamic NGOs in countering religious extremism, and points to the major role of trained imams as key moderators in implementing resilience in Italy (Cominetti 2018).

Although the 'National agreement for an Italian Islam' represents an important step towards more solid preventive policies, the relevance and visibility of issues of radicalisation, prevention, and resilience remain very limited in Italian public and political debates (Guglielminetti 2018). While many counterterrorism officials, such as the police forces, are dissatisfied with the existing approach and consider it urgent to further develop the existing normative structure and prevention activities, this is not among politicians' priorities. This may be due to the high political instability characterising the country, which induces policymakers to abstain from focusing on issues that are not perceived as an emergency. Indeed, because of the lack of a large radicalisation problem or significant terrorist attacks, radicalisation prevention is not considered an urgent matter requiring immediate intervention: as a result, Lorenzo Vidino (2018, p. 19) observes 'a disconnect between the needs of the Italian counterterrorism community and the policymaking community' on this issue.

Concluding remarks

Scholars as well as experts and counterterrorism officers indicate that 'Italian exceptionalism' is being challenged by increasing levels of radicalisation and violent extremist threats. Marked by an imbalance in favour of repressive measures and heavily relying on the criminal justice system, Italy has not yet developed full-fledged counter-radicalisation, prevention, and resilience-building policies, relying on one-off or emergency interventions as opposed to a long-term comprehensive strategy (Marone 2017a). Today, the negative socio-economic impact of the lockdown, combined with persistent lack of recognition of Italian Islam and rising levels of Islamophobia, can provide fertile ground for both jihadist and right-wing violent extremism. In particular, the lockdown measures have boosted the internet activity of preachers of violent extremism, but online resilience-building initiatives are still underdeveloped.

While policymakers currently devote little attention to issues of preventing and countering radicalisation and violent extremism, efforts have been deployed by Italian civil society in partnership with local and national authorities. In this respect, the extensive network of volunteering and third-sector organisations constitutes a significant resource that can be directed towards this. To this end, it is necessary to raise awareness of these issues both among the stakeholders and the general public. In this context, various 'second generation' Muslim associations have intervened in the public sphere by organising anti-radicalisation initiatives (Del Re 2018). Some debate has been sparked by one-off initiatives of ideological rehabilitation around issues of secularism and religious freedom, principles which, according to some, should be regarded as the foundation of such programmes (Vidino 2018). Given the weak secularisation of Italian society and politics, and the relevance of Catholicism in defining nationhood, these are likely to become controversial issues in future debates on counter-radicalisation. These recent developments indicate that the Italian public debate is evolving in line with other European contexts. At this time, the joint efforts of scholars, practitioners, and counterterrorism officials are key to nourishing an informed conversation around thorny and potentially controversial issues.

References

Barbulescu, Roxana (2019) *Migrant Integration in a Changing Europe: Immigrants, European Citizens, and Co-ethnics in Italy and Spain*. Notre Dame: University of Notre Dame Press.

Beccaro, Andrea and Bonino, Stefano (2019) Terrorism and Counterterrorism: Italian Exceptionalism and Its Limits. *Studies in Conflict & Terrorism* 1(18), pp. 1–18.

Berardinelli, Diletta and Guglielminetti, Luca (2018) *Preventing Violent Radicalisation: The Italian Case Paradox*. International conference Multidisciplinary perspectives in the quasi-coercive treatment of offenders, 13–14 September, Timisoara, Romania.

Biorcio, Roberto (2010) *La rivincita del Nord*. Rome-Bari: Laterza.

Caritas Italiana/Fondazione Migrantes (2021) *Dossier Statistico Immigrazione*. Rome: Anterem.

Carvalho, João (2014) *Impact of Extreme Right Parties on Immigration Policy*. London and New York: Routledge.

Castelli Gattinara, Pietro and Froio, Caterina (2014) Discourse and Practice of Violence in the Italian Extreme Right: Frames, Symbols, and Identity-building in CasaPound Italia. *International Journal of Conflict and Violence* 8(1), pp. 154–170.

Castelli Gattinara, Pietro and Froio, Caterina (2019) Getting 'Right' into the News: Grassroots Far-right Mand Media Coverage in Italy and France. *Comparative European Politics* 17(5), pp. 738–758.

Castelli Gattinara, Pietro, O'Connor, Francis and Lindekilde, Lasse (2018) Italy, No Country for Acting Alone? Lone Actor Radicalisation in the Neo-Fascist Milieu. *Perspectives on Terrorism* 12(6), pp. 136–149.

Cominetti, Valentina (2018) *The Italian Approach to De-radicalization.* ICT International Institute for Counter-terrorism, Herzliya, Israel.

Cousin, Bruno and Vitale, Tommaso (2014) Le magistère intellectuel islamophobe d'Oriana Fallaci. *Sociologie* 1(5), pp. 61–79.

de Ghantuz Cubbe, Giovanni (2021) How the Italian radical right has framed immigration during the pandemic. *LSE blog*, https://blogs.lse.ac.uk/europpblog/2021/09/06/how-the-italian-radical-right-has-framed-immigration-during-the-pandemic/

Dal Lago, Alessandro (1999) *Non-persone: l'esclusione dei migranti in una società globale.* Milan: Feltrinelli.

Del Re, Emanuela (2018) Giovani, musulmani, europei: Ritratto dei nostri anti-jihadisti. *Limes*, 7 February, www.limesonline.com/cartaceo/giovani-musulmani-europei-ritratto-dei-nostri-anti-jihadisti?prv=true

Dell'Isola, Davide (2021) Discrimination against Muslims, the Role of Networks and Terrorist Attacks in Western Europe: The Cases of United Kingdom, France, and Italy. *Italian Political Science Review/Rivista Italiana di Scienza Politica*, 52, 1–16.

Dorangricchia, Anna and Itçaina, Xabier (2005) Le répertoire de l'hospitalité. In: Ritaine, É. (ed.), *L'Europe du Sud face à l'immigration.* Paris: Presses Universitaires de France, pp. 185–222.

Europol (2019) Terrorism Situation and Trend Report. European Union Agency for Law Enforcement Cooperation, www.europol.europa.eu/activities-services/main-reports/terrorism-situation-and-trend-report-2019-te-sat

EU-Midis II (2017) *Second European Minorities and Discriminations Survey. Muslims, Selected Findings.* Luxembourg: EU Agency for Fundamental Rights.

FRA (2018) *Seconda indagine su minoranze e discriminazioni nell'Unione europea. Musulmani: una selezione di risultati.* European Union Agency for Fundamental Rights. Luxembourg: Publications Office of the European Union.

Garau, Eva (2010) The Catholic Church, Universal Truth and the Debate on National Identity and Immigration. In: Mammone, Andrea and Veltri, Giuseppe A. (eds), *Italy Today: The Sick Man of Europe.* Abingdon and New York: Routledge, pp. 158–169.

Garbagnoli, Sara (2018) Italy as a Lighthouse. Anti-gender Protests between the "Anthropological Question" and National Identity. In: Kuhar, Roman and Paternotte, David (eds), *Anti-Gender Campaigns in Europe. Mobilizing against Equality.* Lanham, MD: Rowman and Littlefield, pp. 151–174.

Garelli, Franco (2013) Catholiques, politique et culture. Le cas Italien. *Social Compass* 60(3), pp. 332–347.

Groppi, Michele (2017) The Terror Threat to Italy: How Italian Exceptionalism is Rapidly Diminishing. *CTC Sentinel* 10(5), pp. 20–28.

Groppi, Michele (2020) Islamist Radicalisation in Italy: Just A Myth? *Journal of Policing, Intelligence and Counter Terrorism* 15(2), pp. 117–135.

Guglieminetti, Luca (2018) Il ritardo italiano nella prevenzione della radicalizzazione: la resilienza. *Quaderni di Benvenuti in Italia* 12, pp. 53–63, https://benvenutiinitalia.it/wp-content/uploads/2018/07/quaderno12DEF.pdf

Guolo, Renzo (2018) *Jihadisti d'Italia: la radicalizzazione islamista nel nostro Paese.* Milan: Guerini e Associati.

Hackett, Conrad (2017) *5 Facts about the Muslim Population in Europe.* Pew Research Center, www.pewresearch.org/fact-tank/2017/11/29/5-facts-about-the-muslim-population-in-europe/

Jacobs, Gabriele, et al. (2021) *International Security Management: New Solutions to Complexity.* Cham: Springer.

Mammone, Andrea (2008) The Transnational Reaction to 1968: Neo-fascist Fronts and Political Cultures in France and Italy. *Contemporary European History* 17(2), pp. 213–236.

Maniscalco, Maria Luisa (2019) Italy and the Preventing Radicalisation and Terrorism Policy. In: Maniscalco, Maria Luisa and Rosato, Valeria (eds), *Preventing Radicalisation and Terrorism in Europe: A Comparative Analysis of Policies.* Newcastle Upon Tyne: Cambridge Scholars Publishing, pp. 64–91.

Marone, Francesco (2017a) The Italian Way of Counterterrorism: From a Consolidated Experience to an Integrated Approach. In: Romaniuk, Scott Nicholas et al. (eds), *The Palgrave Handbook of Global Counterterrorism Policy*. Palgrave Macmillan UK, pp. 479–494.

Marone, Francesco (2017b) The Use of Deportation in Counter-Terrorism: Insights from the Italian Case. *International Centre for Counter-Terrorism*, https://icct.nl/publication/the-use-of-deportation-in-counter-terrorism-insights-from-the-italian-case/

Tintori, Guido (2018) *Ius soli* the Italian Way. The Long and Winding Road to Reform the Citizenship Law. *Contemporary Italian Politics* 10(4), pp. 434–450.

Triandafyllidou, Anna (2002) Religious Diversity and Multiculturalism in Southern Europe: The Italian Mosque Debate. *Sociological Research Online* 7(1), pp. 76–91.

Vidino, Lorenzo (2014) *Home-Grown Jihadism in Italy: Birth, Development and Radicalization Dynamics*. Milan: ISPI.

Vidino, Lorenzo (2018) Italy's Lack of CVE Strategy and Initiatives. In: Vidono, Lorenzo (ed.), *De-radicalization in the Mediterranean. Comparing Challenges and Approaches*. Milan: ISPI/Ledizioni, pp. 13–20.

15
GREECE

Eda Gemi

Introduction

In October 2020, a landmark court verdict in Greece's highest-profile political trial in decades was met with jubilation after judges found the Neo-Nazi Golden Dawn party guilty of running a criminal organisation, with its leaders sent in prison.

The optimism emerging from the end of Greece's economic tutelage in 2018 notwithstanding, the country is back in the eye of the storm as it is undergoing a triple crisis: economic, humanitarian (in the form of migration and refugee crisis), and health as a result of the Covid-19 pandemic. This situation has provided a breeding ground for political extremism, wherefore right-wing extremism, hate speech, and violence have largely targeted immigrants and religious minorities. Far-right extremists, in particular, exploit popular fears by propagating views of immigrants and religious 'Others' as undesirable and 'usurpers', thus advancing a racist, ethnicist, and often anti-Islamic rhetoric in public discourse. In addition, Greece's inability to govern migration and promote social integration appears to have paved the way for domestic far-right, Neo-Nazi, and ultra-nationalist movements to take the lead in mainstreaming their political agenda. This was seen in the 2015 parliamentary elections, when Golden Dawn polled third despite its leadership's arrests and an ongoing trial. Even today, despite the party's disbandment, the threat of violent extremism in Greece has not receded as the far-right is regrouping under a constellation of populist politicians and fringe new parties who have filled Golden Dawn's place in parliament.

This chapter aims to map the phenomena of violent extremism and social polarisation in Greece in the 2010s that were largely triggered by the debt crisis and refugee influx.[1] The underlying assumption is that these institutions have shaped the public discourse by reproducing mainstream views, attitudes, behaviours, and practices that could be assigned to a culture of institutional intolerance, discrimination, and Islamophobia. Here, Islamophobia is understood as anti-Islam and anti-Muslim public perceptions which, in the case of Greece, take the form of cultural racism interwoven with xenophobia and anti-immigrant sentiments (Huseyinoglu, 2015). Such attitudes are embedded in mainstream national identity discourse and institutional structure such as the political system and the Orthodox Church.

This chapter is divided into three parts. The first describes the backdrop to the general trends of violent extremism and social polarisation by particularly focusing on two types of institutions, namely political and religious. The second assesses resilience-based projects that have been implemented in response. Finally, the concluding remarks summarise key findings that point to a typological paradigm of violent extremism and social polarisation fuelled by the political and religious actors characterising the Greek case.

Trends of violent extremism and social polarisation

Historically, Greek national identity has been closely entwined with Christian Orthodoxy, which projects itself as the true guardian of the Greek 'ethnos' and traditions. At the same time, the existential 'national anxiety' of the Greek state, imbued with highly conflictual 'spirit' of the late nationalism and refuelled by geopolitical rivalries in the Balkan Peninsula, found expression in a dominant national discourse of almost 'mythical' ethno-cultural and ethno-religious homogeneity (Gemi 2020; Magazzini and Triandafyllidou 2021). This in turn left little space for ethnic and religious minorities, particularly Muslims, to have their own presence and voice in public life. In fact, as Greek national identity has been historically constructed in opposition to the religious and Muslim 'Other', Muslim populations belonging either to the 'Old Islam' or 'New Islam' communities[2] have been historically identified with Turks and Turkey.

Against that backdrop, this dominant discourse took a new course in the early 1990s when Greece's even closer integration into the EU was associated with further recognition of the Muslim minority of Thrace and the accommodation of the religious 'Other' that monopolised public debate following the unprecedented arrival of relatively large immigrant populations, triggered mostly by the fall of the Iron Curtain (Hatziprokopiou and Evergeti 2014; Tsitselikis 2012; Gemi 2020).[3] In response, Greece struggled, on the one hand, to improve the socio-economic status and overall integration of its native Muslim minorities, while also dealing with a mass influx of migrants initially from neighbouring Albania (mostly of Muslim faith) but also from other Balkan and Eastern European countries, and subsequently from Asia and Africa (Gemi 2020; Magazzini and Triandafyllidou 2021). Significantly, despite a large number of 'Muslim' immigrants entering from Albania, this population is traditionally known for their tendency to refrain from public practice of Islam, including in their limited institutional claims for mosques and religious education (Triandafyllidou 2015). Immigrants from Asia, on the other hand, were mainly male workers with families who remained in their home countries of origin, posing, therefore, little challenge (if any) or seeking public visibility for their children's integration in the education system or women wearing veils as symbols of Islamic tradition (Lazarescu and Broersma 2010). Notwithstanding these characteristics of 'new' Islam, their religious affiliation had been constantly instrumentalised not only by the far-right forces but also by mainstream parties and conservative social actors (Magazzini and Triandafyllidou 2021; Triandafyllidou 2015).

The 2000s marked the period when frustration with the political system – dominated by clientelist-style politics – in conjunction with growing nationalist and xenophobic sentiments produced a new wave of 'ethno-populism' (Andreadis et. al. 2018). The head-on collision of the Orthodox Church with the Greek state over the removal of religious affiliation from identity cards and the arrival on the political scene of newly emerging nationalist, anti-Muslim, and anti-immigrant political parties are illustrative examples of Greek Orthodox synergy with the right-wing of the political spectrum (Lagos et. al. 2021, p. 12). The Popular Orthodox Rally (LAOS) was the first parliamentary political force that reconciled the anti-immigrant discourse with the traditional anti-Muslim and anti-Turkish nationalism articulated by the Orthodox Church within the contemporary far-right political agenda. However, the more significant spark that institutionalised racism and violent extremism as the cornerstone of its Neo-Nazi ideology was the political factorisation of Golden Dawn.

The 2009–2018 economic crises and successive austerity measures have had profound social and political consequences, plunging the Greek economy into a deep recession which, in turn, led to the de-legitimisation of the two mainstream ruling parties: the centre-left PASOK and the centre-right New Democracy. Against this gloomy background, the failure to govern immigration and establish an effective integration mechanism for 'old' and 'new' migrants and asylum seekers was exacerbated by a further intensification of the securitisation of migration policies and anti-immigrant rhetoric in public discourse, using migrants as 'scapegoats' for societal inequalities.

Nationalist discourse was further polarised with the re-emergence of the historic confrontation regarding the name 'Macedonia' between Greece and the former Yugoslav republic. The dispute was formally resolved under the landmark agreement reached between Athens and Skopje in June 2018 on North Macedonia as the neighbouring state's name. This triggered a violent nationalist backlash from the far-right and mainstream actors in the political spectrum (such as New Democracy), as well as the Orthodox Church, with national protests against the Prespa Agreement and defamatory accusations of treason against the left-wing Syriza government (Lagos et. al. 2021, p. 10). Indicative of this sentiment are successive surveys in which some 70 per cent of Greeks were opposed to the agreement (Smith 2019).

Furthermore, the recent migration and so-called refugee crisis from the Middle East has further exacerbated the anti-immigrant and Islamophobic public rhetoric which, along with severe economic repercussions, has created fertile ground for the far-right. This particular situation is also visible when observing the increase in anti-Semitic and Islamophobic discourse, legitimising domestic violent political and religious extremism and reconfiguring the new 'map' of social polarisation in Greece. The Special Eurobarometer in 2015 corroborated this change, showing the category of 'ethnic origin' concentrating 70 per cent of respondents who believe discrimination is widespread in Greece.

A year later, the EU MIDIS II survey (2016) found that 23 per cent of respondents believe that the discrimination on the basis of religion or religious belief is fairly widespread in Greece. Even more revealing are the findings of a very recent study showing the existence of widespread Islamophobic and anti-Muslim ideas and attitudes among Greek Orthodox youth (see Lagos et. al. 2021). These attitudes are rooted in the mainstream Greek Orthodox national identity and resonate in the right-wing ideological triptych 'Fatherland-Religion-Family' (Lagos et. al. 2021; Gemi 2020). Within this new configuration of 'political religion' (Smith 2003, p. 24), the historical anti-Muslim (or anti-Turk or both) nationalism is fused with the contemporary syndrome of 'victimisation' about alleged injustices and unfair treatment by EU partners regarding economic and financial crisis, management of the refugee/migration crisis, and secularisation.

The Covid-19 pandemic found Greece dealing with another acute crisis at its borders. On 28 February 2020, Turkey opened the border for refugees heading to Europe, with hundreds of people gathered at the Evros River, a natural land border between the two countries. The Greek government called this move an 'asymmetric threat' (Kathimerini 2020). On 9 September 2020, a few days after several people at the Moria Camp on Lesvos tested positive for Covid-19, fires erupted, razing the camp and leaving more than 12,000 refugees and migrants homeless. Several reports have since stressed the link between the rise in xenophobic trends and racist behaviour and the overcrowding of refugees over a long period of time on the Greek islands (RVRN 2018).

According to the Racist Violence Recording Network's (RVRN) 2020 annual report there was an increase in incidents of racist violence particularly against refugees, migrants, and human rights defenders who were targeted due to their affiliation with these vulnerable groups (RVRN 2021). This is mostly attributed to the institutional targeting of refugees and migrants through official speeches by political representatives at the central and local levels, as well through the national media. The portrayal of refugees and migrants as a threat to national sovereignty, especially in early 2020, has been instrumental in exonerating racist violence and intensifying a sense of impunity among attackers (RVRN 2021, p. 5). What is even more alarming is that those reproducing racist and Islamophobic discourses are not penalised for their hate-motivated speech (Huseyinoglu and Sakellariou 2018, p. 287). The UN Commission on Human Rights in its Final Observations on Greece's second periodic report[4] (CCPR 2015) noted that the lack of trust in the authorities and the absence of an effective complaint mechanism result in few racism complaints being filed and that penalties imposed were not sufficient to discourage or prevent discrimination. The issue of racist violence in Greece has been also addressed by the European Court of Human Rights (ECHR) in the cases of *Sakir v. Greece*[5] and *Gjikondi and others v. Greece*.[6] The former concerns the authorities' failure to conduct an effective investigation into a violent attack against an immigrant that resulted in injury;[7] the latter, the failure to investigate possible racist motives behind the murder of a foreigner (NAPRI 2020, p. 11).[8]

The period 2019–2021 saw a significant increase in reports and testimonies about irregular forced returns (pushbacks) at Greece's sea and land borders, creating space for racist trends and behaviours (Stevis-Gridneff 2021). Human rights groups, along with mounting evidence gathered by migrants and reporters, found that Greek authorities routinely round up and expel migrants without permitting them to complete asylum requests, often in an indiscriminate and violent way. Greek authorities have also been accused of pushing back migrants crossing the Aegean Sea in flimsy dinghies, sometimes disabling the engines and leaving the migrants to drift back into Turkish waters. These incidents, together with a similar standoff between Greece and Turkey in 2020 with asylum seekers caught in the middle, has laid bare a growing gulf between European laws and norms in treating asylum seekers and the reality on the ground.

The Covid-19 pandemic and the raft of restrictions on individual freedoms have painted a new reality in which racism and social polarisation have taken on new dimensions. As such, migrants, refugees, and asylum seekers are perceived as a real threat to public health, a point further illustrated in the documented acts of organised racist violence in Reception and Identification Centres on Aegean islands but also on the mainland where accommodation sites for asylum seekers are located (RVRN 2021, p. 21). Even more worrying is that in some cases police appear to refrain from rescuing or protecting the victims, with some instances of police even contributing to their harassment (RVRN 2021). It is therefore perhaps no coincidence that in 2019 asylum seekers, refugees, and migrants comprised the majority of victims in incidents involving law enforcement officials or civil servants (RVRN 2020, p. 10). At the same time, concerns grew about public health and xenophobia-fuelled protests in the form of occupations of public schools organised by pupils' parents, often with the support of far-right activists who opposed the enrolment of migrant and refugee children (Lagos et. al. 2021, p. 18).

These anti-immigrant attitudes and the lack of tolerance towards diversity is corroborated by a series of surveys and studies where most respondents (over 51 per cent) believed that immigration is ultimately 'bad for Greece, costing the welfare state and draining resources that could be spent on Greeks' (Dixon et. al. 2019, p. 9). Moreover, the findings of a Pew

Research Center survey (2019), point to 62 per cent of Greek respondents stating that they opposed diversity in the country. In fact, attitudes in Greece about diversity are the most negative among the countries surveyed. Whilst most respondents agreed that Greece has become less homogenous in recent years, only 17 per cent viewed this favourably and 62 per cent did not. What is even more striking is that 67 per cent of Greek respondents reported feeling discomfort in being asked to work or live alongside a 'Muslim person'.

In view of global and European concerns about the threat of terrorism and trends in radicalisation, there are no documented cases or signs of home-grown (Islamically justified) religious radicalisation and extremism in Greece (Skleparis 2017). However, Greece has been described as a crossroads for violent extremist militants trying to reach Syria and Iraq from Europe, as well as for fighters attempting to return home (Mantzikos 2016). ISIS's infiltration of fighters into Europe through Greece raised concerns about the country becoming an 'entry gate' for jihadists. An on-site evaluation of Greek sea and land border sites by EU inspectors revealed

> serious deficiencies in the carrying out of external border control by Greece, in particular due to the lack of appropriate identification and registration of irregular migrants at the islands, of sufficient staff, and of sufficient equipment for verifying identity documents.
>
> *CEU 2016*

Whilst there is less well-documented evidence on this matter, the absence of Islamic radicalisation in Greece could be explained by several reasons such as the level of 'improvised' (bottom-up) inclusion of migrants into Greek society or the fact that Greece does not constitute a significantly important target as it is not seen as a key player in the 'War on Terror'. As regards the former, according to a key informant, this is mostly attributed to the level of self-organisation of Muslim communities and the control that the Muslim leaders in Greece, in collaboration with the national intelligence service EYP, exert over Muslim communities of migrant background. Although Greece does not display evidence of being under threat from home-grown 'Islamist' terrorism, many have raised concerns over the inhumane conditions at the reception and detention centres that could have the potential for encouraging radicalisation and extremism (BBC News 2016).

Political extremism

Recent successive crises in Greece have provided a fertile ground for the rise of political extremism. Although the overall phenomenon is neither new nor unique in Greek politics, it has been ideologically and politically institutionalised over the past two decades.

LAOS represents the first example of a right-wing response to the challenges that Greek Orthodox identity and national ideology was facing at the turn of the twenty-first century.[9] With strong connections to the Church of Greece, military, and police, LAOS emphasised law and order and the ideology of 'Fatherland-Religion-Family' through xenophobic discourse emphasising the supposed danger of Greece's 'Islamification' (Lagos et. al. 2021, p. 13).[10] Having said that, it is not fortuitous that three top LAOS members are now in the New Democracy cabinet.

With its decline, the void left by LAOS was filled by Golden Dawn. It emerged on the broader political landscape after the 2012 parliamentary elections, amidst the collapse of the two ruling parties dominating Greek politics since the mid-1970s. It was against the backdrop of the Greek debt crisis that the mobilisation of far-right anti-systemic, anti-Left, and anti-immigrant forces became openly and particularly violent. Golden Dawn cemented far-right political extremism in Greece by imbuing it with Neo-Nazi ideological authoritarianism, racism, Islamophobia, and overt violence. In its political manifesto, Golden Dawn's key goal is to eliminate all political divisions and for the nation to undergo 'catharsis' from 'outsiders' or external enemies – notably immigrants, but also 'foreign loan sharks, contractors, and media owners' (Halikiopoulou and Vasilopoulou 2015). In its attempt to unmask the 'insiders' or the 'enemy-within', it also portrayed communists as internationalists that seek the annihilation of the Greek nation.[11]

In an attempt to strengthen the alliance with the Greek-Orthodox Church – following in the footsteps of LAOS – Golden Dawn also played a leading role in a dispute over the construction of an official mosque in Athens. After years of delay, in 2015, the then left-wing government passed an amendment to existing legislation finalising the technical issues for the mosque's construction. This triggered furious debates in parliament, with Golden Dawn and other anti-Muslim MPs stating that 'Greece will become Islamised' and that 'Muslims are against the Western way of life'.[12] After a plea for annulment by which the constitutionality of provisions relating to the mosque's location were contested, the Council of State (2014) ruled that the law is in full compliance with the Constitution. In response, in September 2018, Golden Dawn supporters held a protest in front of the mosque, objecting to its construction and chanting 'whoever does not want Greece and its religion should go to Asia' (US State Department 2019, p. 10). Islamophobia, under the mantle of Turcophobia, was also manifested many times in parliament. On 6 March 2018, at the meeting of the Commission of Foreign Policy and Defence, Ilias Kassidiaris, Golden Dawn's vocal parliamentary 'frontman', caused a serious incident when he attacked fellow MP Mustafa Mustafa, who hails from the Muslim minority of Thrace, by shouting 'the agent (of Turkey) must go out. The Turk must leave [the Commission]' (Bokas 2018).

Golden Dawn was not entirely alone in its ideo-political struggle, however, as there have been allegations made against the Greek police of collaborating with (or in the best-case scenario, openly tolerating) Golden Dawn. In January 2013, the Council of Europe Commissioner for Human Rights Nils Muižnieks stated:

> I am deeply concerned with the impunity enjoyed by the perpetrators of racist attacks in Greece. Very few have been led to justice and even fewer have been condemned…The police does not do its job as it should: abuse of authority, excessive use of force, collaboration with Golden Dawn'.[13]

Similarly, in early 2011, Belgium and Greece were both convicted for inhuman practices, after the refoulement of an Afghan seeking asylum in Greece, on the grounds of the Dublin II Regulation. The ECHR held unanimously that there has been a violation by Greece of Article 3 of the Convention because of the applicant's conditions of detention,[14] and the case was seen as constituting a 'thermometer' of the culture of each state's police services (Christopoulos et. al. 2014, p. 59).[15] Furthermore, in March 2017, the ECHR issued a landmark judgment vindicating a group of migrant strawberry pickers who, five years earlier, had been shot at by employers for asking for their wages after months of unpaid labour, holding that the Greek state should pay damages for having 'failed in its obligations to prevent the situation of human trafficking' (Smith 2017).

Ironically, even Greece's mainstream parties didn't hesitate to adopt elements of Golden Dawn's political discourse for electioneering purposes. This is exemplified by New

Democracy leader and later prime minister Antonis Samaras who, during his party's campaign, stated that 'today Greece has become the epicentre of illegal immigrants. We need to reoccupy our cities where drug trafficking, illegal trade, prostitution, and diseases abound' (Naftemporiki 2012). Similarly, Andreas Loverdos, the socialist Minister of Health at the time, appeared to endorse the public vilification of allegedly irregular migrants and HIV-positive women arrested for prostitution:

> HIV-positive prostitutes need to be expelled, in order to stop posing a threat to Greek families...Illegal prostitution is a great problem in Athens and is related to the HIV-virus contagion...the transmission is done by the illegal [female prostitutes] immigrant through the Greek [male] client to the Greek family.
>
> *Fyntanidou 2012*

Soon after it was revealed that most of the 'illegal female prostitutes' whose identities, photos, and private medical records had been made public were not immigrants but Greek citizens. In response, in his Report on Greece, the Commissioner for Human Rights of the Council of Europe, Nils Muižnieks, stated that he 'regrets that rhetoric stigmatising migrants has often been used in Greek politics, including by high-level politicians'.[16]

In September 2020, in a landmark verdict in Greece's highest-profile political trial, an Athens court found the Neo-Nazi party Golden Dawn guilty of running a criminal organisation 'dressed in the mantle of a political party' (CNN Greece, 2020). The indictment had come after a public uproar over the murder of left-wing activist Pavlos Fyssas in September 2013, with charges brought against 65 people including the party's leadership and several sitting MPs. Even with the trial underway since April, in the September 2015 elections, the Neo-Nazi party polled third, taking almost 7 per cent of the national vote and winning 17 seats in the Greek parliament.

Whilst Golden Dawn has since faded from the national political scene, failing to make the 3 per cent threshold for entry into parliament, the story of political extremism in times of crisis has not come to an end. Another ultra-nationalist but less violent right-wing party *Elliniki Lysi* (Greek Solution) has taken its place in Parliament, winning 3.7 per cent of the vote and 10 seats in the 300-member chamber in the 2019 national elections.

A few days after taking office in July 2019, the centre-right party of New Democracy suspended the Ministry of Migration Policy responsible for managing issues of reception, asylum, and integration (Vithoulkas 2019). In response, on 18 July 2019, ten human rights organisations expressed strong opposition to what they called an institutional setback, signalled by the abolition of the Ministry of Migration Policy and the transfer of its competences to the Ministry of Citizen's Protection. Their statement noted that the 'the failure of all repressive policies at times, only result in increased xenophobic perceptions in society and abuse democratic institutions and the rule of law'.[17] Meantime, the Minister of Labour and Social Affairs revoked the relevant circulars on the issue of social insurance numbers (AMKA) to beneficiaries of international protection and asylum seekers. In practice, this meant that all asylum seekers who were unable to get an AMKA and those who arrived after the decision was published had restricted access to various public services, including, among others, the Greek healthcare system, legal employment, or the means to enrol their children in local schools. Both the UNHCR and Greek Ombudsman sounded the alarm over newcomers' lack of access to healthcare and social services.[18] Following the eruption of tension on the Greek-Turkish land borders on 2 March 2020, the Greek authorities issued an Emergency Legislative Order by which access to the asylum procedure was suspended for persons entering the country in March 2020. The Asylum Service, the Regional Asylum Offices (RAO), and the Autonomous Asylum Units (AAU) also suspended the reception of immigrants between March and May 2020. During this period, applications for international protection were not registered, interviews were not conducted, and appeals were not recorded. Finally, amid mounting evidence[19] of systematic pushbacks, Prime Minister Kyriakos Mitsotakis, in an attempt to refute allegations of inhumane and illegal practices in expelling migrants without due process, described his migration policy as 'tough, but fair' (Stevis-Gridneff 2021).

To conclude, political extremism itself, as well as tolerance vis-à-vis hate speech and violence, has been exacerbated by the Greek economic crisis and so-called refugee crisis. But it is overly simplistic to state that the rise in political extremism and violence is solely the result of economic crisis or concerns over migration or both. It is rather the product of an overall crisis of democracy and its representative institutions in Greece.

Religion extremism

In Greece, there is no separation between the State and the Church, and religion has played a fundamental role in defining national identity. National ideology and the Orthodox Church have historically shaped the membership status in the Greek nation. The attachment to the Orthodox Church as a core element of national identity formation makes it difficult to separate ethnicity from religion. It is not a coincidence that, in a recent survey by the Pew Research Center (2018), three-quarters of Greeks consider being Orthodox Christian integral to being Greek, while nearly nine out of ten believe Greek culture is superior to others (2018, p. 6). Such historical and political legacies have forged a genuine model of religious governance whereby the Greek Orthodox confession has an especially prominent place in the public sphere under the status of the 'prevailing religion' (Article 3 of Greek Constitution). The privileged position of the Orthodox Church as a national institution is embedded in the legal order, whereas it enjoys, among other things, the right to have a say to the activities of all 'known religions'[20] and other state affairs such as the curriculum and textbooks for the class on religious education and morning prayer in Greek schools. The most telling example is that the education ministry is also the ministry of 'religious affairs'. It is not a coincidence that until 2019, Athens did not have an official mosque. The attempts of different centre-left governments to build one were vehemently opposed by the Orthodox Church, supported by conservatives and far-right political forces (Kirtsoglou and Tsimouris 2018, p. 1881; Triandafyllidou and Gropas 2009).

In terms of religious governance, Greece offers a model that represents a combination of majoritarian religion/nationalism enshrined in its Constitution. At the same time, the Greek Constitution provides for freedom of religious conscience as inviolable, and enjoyment of civil rights and liberties does not depend on the individual's religious beliefs but recognising Orthodoxy as the 'prevailing religion' (Gemi 2020). In fact, the majoritarian religion is seen by the state as a public good and is complemented by a weak institutional accommodation of religious diversity (Maggazini and Triandafyllidou 2021, p. 14).

In making full use of their privileges, high-ranking Orthodox Church officials have shown a trend of speaking out on any political matter. In this way they claim special space within political discourse by consciously upholding an ultra-right political orientation (Christopoulos et. al. 2014, p. 6). For example, Archbishop Anthimos of Thessaloniki stated in church, regarding a previous government's immigration plan, that 'if it is enforced, the country will turn Black, we will be filled with Al-Qaeda Annexes', adding that 'you cannot bring 700,000 Muslims into the country and make them Greek without asking the Church' (To Vima 2010). Archbishop Amvrosios of Kalavryta has expressed similar views, commenting that the arrival and presence of Muslim migrants is a great danger for Greece, as 'the city will be full of minarets and mosques'.[21]

The Archbishop of Piraeus Seraphim denounced the oath of the Muslim Turkish Minority deputies in the Greek parliament over the Quran as a disgrace to, and betrayal of, Greece and the Greek Orthodox faith, adding that the Ottomans had enslaved, raped, and massacred Greek Orthodox peoples for 400 years (Millet News 2019). This was the latest in a string of such statements over the years, for example, describing Muhammad as a 'false prophet' and Islam as 'aggressive, and by the criminal acts of Islamists it is proven that it remains like this today' after a Janaury 2011 attack on Christian Copts in Egypt;[22] or, when Muslims gathered in Kotzia Square in September 2010 to celebrate the end of Ramadan, railing that

> the concession of the centre of Athens for the performance of religious rituals of a religion other than the dominant religion according to the Constitution is unacceptable behaviour which afflicts the dominant religious faith of the State... Islam is a heavy delusion and its religious faith is not the revelation of the living God, but a flawed human construction that bears no relation to the truth of the Creator of the Universe, revealed in the Old Testament.[23]

Another instance of inciteful statements was the targeting of the Chytirio theatre in Athens over its staging of Terrence McNally's *Corpus Christi* in 2012. Chytirio found itself under siege for several weeks as protestors, including clergy and Golden Dawn members, assaulted actors and audiences entering the theatre. Meanwhile, 'religious citizens' filed three motions for provisional protective measures, demanding the cancellation of the play because it portrayed Jesus and the apostles as gay (Christopoulos et. al. 2014, p. 56).

Some bishops have openly stood by Golden Dawn. In 2012, at an event marking the communist defeat at Grammos and Vitsi during the Civil War, the Bishop of Dryinoupolis, Pogoniani and Konitsa used the warmest words for Golden Dawn, calling them 'lads in black shirts, the good fighting lads', and closed his speech with the wish that they soon replace these black shirts with blue and white ones – the colours of the Greek flag.[24]

It's worth noting that the Church never explicitly condemned Pavlos Fyssas's murder by Golden Dawn.[25] Nor has the Holy Synod of the Orthodox Church ever punished or strongly disapproved of Islamophobic statements and announcements (Sakellariou 2016, p. 214). Even Archbishop Ieronymos of Greece, the leader of the Greek Orthodox Church and a 'moderate', in a November 2016 interview on Skai TV referred to some 'centres that want to deprive the country from Greek values' and commented, that 'the existence of Muslims is not the "best" for Greece'.[26]

Resilience-based projects

The rise of extremism and social polarisation has led the Greek state, along with a number of institutional and NGO actors, to take a series of initiatives at the legal, institutional, academic, and grassroots levels.

The legislative foundation for the adoption and implementation of the national plan of action to prevent violent extremism involves a specific legal framework. To start with, in October 2013, a Public Prosecutor for acts of racist violence was appointed. In the same year, parliament changed the rules for the public financing of political parties, which can be suspended if 10 per cent of its MPs are found guilty of involvement in a criminal organisation or acts of terrorism (such as the case of Golden Dawn).

In 2014, Law 4285/2014[27] on Combating Race Discrimination was adopted to counter certain forms of racism and xenophobia in the frame of penal law. It included special provisions on criminal prosecution against acts of racist violence and hate speech through verbal, media, digital or any other means. In 2016, a new law (L.4375/2016)[28] established the Directorate for Social Inclusion with the responsibility of creating and operating an electronic platform to support interfaith dialogue aimed at preventing radicalisation and fundamentalism. In the same year, Law 4411/2016 provided for ratification of the Council of Europe Convention on Cybercrime and its Additional Protocol on the criminalisation of acts of a racist and xenophobic nature committed through Computer Systems. Finally, in 2018, under Law 4557/2018 measures were introduced for the prevention and suppression of the legalisation of proceeds of crime and terrorist financing.

In terms of institutional settings, in 2012, the Ministry of Public Order and Citizen's Protection established the Departments and Offices for Combating Racist Violence within the Hellenic Police to monitor and tackle racist violence. The Ministry of Justice's General Secretariat for Justice and Human Rights was tasked with coordinating the action plan against extremism and radicalisation. It also oversees the National Council Against Racism and Intolerance (NCRI) established by Law 4356/2015 as a collective advisory body. The Council has, inter alia, the responsibility of drafting the National Action Plan against Racism and Intolerance.[29] Finally, the Greek National Commission for Human Rights (GNCHR),[30] as an independent advisory body to the Greek state on human rights issues, is responsible for monitoring developments in human rights protection. Under a joint initiative with the UNHCR, the Greek Commission established the RVRN,[31] which since 2011 has published annual reports on incidents of racist violence and extremism in Greece.

Additionally, there are several ongoing programmes and projects addressing the phenomena of radicalisation and extremism. One is RADICALISAcTION,[32] whose goal is to raise awareness, empower and strengthen the staff of law enforcement agencies, and support the fight against radicalisation leading to violent extremism and terrorism. Another, 'A Radical Model of Resilience for Young Minds', focuses on the forms of social polarisation caused by the adoption and spread of extremist ideologies.[33]

There are also grassroots initiatives run entirely by civil society actors that focus on preventing religiously inspired violent radicalisation and violent extremism. In 2015, Golden Dawn Watch[34] was launched by a group of NGOs and local actors[35] aimed at making public all information concerning Golden Dawn's actions and to illuminate all aspects of the trial and keep Golden Dawn and its actions under the spotlight of public attention. The Observatory to Prevent Extremist Violence (OPEV) is another active platform of civil society organisations from across the Euro-Mediterranean Region aiming to bring a constructive contribution to prevent violent extremism.

The Mixed Jury Court of Athens set a legal precedent with Decision no. 398/2014, ruling that the murder of Pakistani national Sh. Luqman by two young militants of Golden Dawn in January 2013 constitutes a criminal offence motivated by hatred. This was the first time in Greece's history that a racist motive has been identified in a trial.[36] This was followed by the Piraeus court's ruling against four Greek citizens accused of beating Egyptian worker W. Taleb in November 2012 on the island of Salamina. The four men were found guilty and sentenced to 13 years and two months in prison.[37] In February 2015, another Greek citizen was sentenced to six months in prison (with a three-year suspension) for a verbal racist attack against a Nigerian doctor at a public hospital in Kozani.[38] This process culminated in October 2020 when a landmark court verdict found the Neo-Nazi party Golden Dawn guilty of running a criminal organisation.

These positive developments have certainly contributed to a different sociopolitical climate that is more respectful of migrants' fundamental rights and that condemns racial violence and hate speech. According to the World Population Review's Freedom Index, in 2019 Greece's score (51/60) slightly improved by three points between 2017 and 2019. However, despite the legal and institutional reforms, initiatives and projects on extremism and social polarisation seem to be short-lived. That is, most programmes in Greece are implemented on a temporary basis, which means that such interventions cannot successfully address the issue in the long run. What is the most concerning issue, though, is the ineffectiveness of policy implementation which in fact, reflects the lack of political will to face the challenges of modernity.

Concluding remarks

This chapter shed light on the phenomena of violent extremism and social polarisation in Greece since 2010. It investigated the development of these phenomena in two fields, notably the political and religious, that appear to have played a key role in those trends. As shown in this chapter, these institutions and their respective protagonists of public life have shaped the public discourse by reproducing views, attitudes, behaviours, and practices that are inscribed in the culture and legacy of institutional intolerance, discrimination, and Islamophobia. Moreover, such attitudes are embedded in mainstream national identity discourse and institutional structure such as the political system and the Orthodox Church. Saying this, radicalisation and Islamophobia manifest themselves primarily at the discursive level (hate speech) and to a lesser extent in forms of physical violence.

Evidence suggests a gradual rise in racist violence in the country since 2010, peaking in 2015 in the aftermath of the 'refugee crisis'. The largest increase was observed between 2011 and 2012, a period when the far-right extremist party Golden Dawn established itself in the Greek political arena. Since 2014, the characteristics of racist violence in Greece began to change, becoming 'milder' (i.e., verbal abuse) – a development that might be related to the prosecution of Golden Dawn's MPs and leadership, its electoral collapse in the 2019 national polls, and the closure of its offices in Athens and Piraeus by the authorities. Nevertheless, there are more incidents and violent attacks against migrants and other communities (such as LGBTQ), with perpetrators remaining unidentified. This has commonly happened even for those reproducing hate speech and Islamophobic discourses, such as mainstream political figures and senior Orthodox clergy, who have not been penalised for their hate-motivated speech. In fact, for very long period, judicial authorities and police tended to remain indifferent with regards to hate crimes or other types of abuse and exploitation against vulnerable immigrants.

Initiatives and projects on extremism and social polarisation seem to be short-lived. Most programmes in Greece are implemented on a temporary basis, which means that such interventions cannot successfully address the issue in the long term. However, the most concerning issue is the ineffectiveness of policy implementation that denotes the lack of political will to address the political challenges of modernity.

In conclusion, recent developments have marked a highly conservative shift that is not reflected in laws, but rather in the non-application of laws. Whilst the legal context has been modernised, the mentality and the public attitudes have not been updated in the same way.

Notes

1 Retracing the historical and ideological roots of the violent extremism in Greece is beyond scope of this chapter.
2 'Old Islam' refers to the Muslim minority living in Thrace to distinguish it from those (mostly immigrants) who have recently settled in Greece and compose the 'New Islam'.
3 The Muslim population consists of two legal categories. The first is Greek citizens who belong to the traditional religious minority of Thrace, namely the 'Old Islam' (Tsitselikis, 2012, p. 535). The second includes foreigners, mostly immigrants, who have the legal status of aliens ('New Islam').
4 On the implementation of the International Covenant on Civil and Political Rights, published on 5 November 2015.
5 Application no. 48475/09.
6 Application no. 17249/10.
7 The Court found that the authorities had failed to investigate the possible racist motive for this attack, breaching as such the procedural part of Article 3 of the ECHR.
8 In violation of the procedural part of Article 2 right to life of the ECHR.
9 LAOS was formed in 2000 after a number of politicians and party officials left the mainstream right-wing New Democracy party as result of the latter's turn to more centre-right positions and policies.
10 LAOS entered the Greek parliament in 2007 but in 2012 collapsed electorally as a consequence of the party's support for the harsh austerity policies that were imposed in the context of the economic crisis.
11 http://xryshayghvp.blogspot.com/2014/01/
12 Parliament Proceedings, 24 June 2015, Session ΞB [62], 71.
13 https://www.refworld.org/publisher,COECHR,,GRC,516e76bb4,0.html
14 https://hudoc.echr.coe.int/fre#{%22itemid%22:[%22001-103050%22]}, p. 89.
15 https://hudoc.echr.coe.int/fre#{%22itemid%22:[%22001-103050%22]}
16 Report by Nils Muižnieks Commissioner for Human Rights of the Council of Europe, https://rm.coe.int/report-by-nils-muiznieks-council-of-europe-commissioner-for-human-righ/16806db715
17 See: http://asylum-campaign.blogspot.com/
18 See: https://data2.unhcr.org/en/documents/download/71039
19 www.borderviolence.eu/15638-2/
20 The term 'known religion' is referred to in Article 13, paragraph 2 of the Greek Constitution. According to the Council of State and the Supreme Court, it denotes any religion that is public, with no secret rituals or dogmas, which do not constitute an unlawful union, or a fictitious association or organisation with illegal aims, and its purpose must not negatively affect public order or morals.
21 http://mkka.blogspot.gr/2015/04/blog-post_22.html
22 For details see, https://islamforgreeks.org/2011/01/10/refuting-serafim/
23 www.impantokratoros.gr/9FB97297.el.aspx
24 http://enthemata.wordpress.com/2012/09/02/bournazos-33/
25 www.ecclesia.gr/greek/holysynod/holysynod.asp?id=1706&what_sub=d_typou; also, www.ecclesia.gr/greek/holysynod/holysynod.asp?id=1722&what_sub=d_typou
26 For details, see www.keeptalkinggreece.com/2016/11/02/archbishop-ieronymos-shocks-those-who-thought-he-was-a-progressive-spiritual-leader/
27 www.ministryofjustice.gr/site/LinkClick.aspx?fileticket=Ik2xQr3jIkg%3D&tabid=132
28 "On the Organization and Operation of the Asylum Service, the Appeals Authority, the Reception and Identification Service, the establishment of the General Secretariat for Reception, the Transposition into the Greek legislation of the provisions of Directive 2013/32/EC". Available from: www.refworld.org/docid/573ad4cb4.html
29 Hellenic Republic, Ministry of Justice, National Action Plan Against Racism and Intolerance 2020–2023, December 2020, p. 4.
30 GNCHR is an independent advisory body to the Greek State, see www.nchr.gr/index.php
31 www.nchr.gr/en/racist-violence-recording-network.html
32 https://radicalisaction.gr/en/
33 https://armourproject.eu/

34 https://goldendawnwatch.org/
35 Hellenic League for Human Rights: the Greek Observatory against Fascism and Racist Speech in the Media; the Antifascist League of Athens and Piraeus, and the City of Athens Migrants' Integration Council.
36 www.unhcr.gr/1againstracism/en/comment-the-recognition-of-racist-motive-in-the-case-ofshehzad-luqmans-murder/
37 www.unhcr.gr/1againstracism/en/four-convicted-for-attack-on-egyptian-walid-taleb/
38 http://greece.greekreporter.com/2015/02/26/nigerian-doctor-victim-of-racist-attack-in-norther ngreece/

References

Andreadis, I., Stavrakakis, Y. and Demertzis, N. (2018) Populism, Ethnic Nationalism and Xenophobia. Science and Society. *Review of Political and Ethics Theory*, 37, pp. 11–40.
BBC News (2016, 9 March) Migrant Crisis: Macedonia Shuts Balkan Route, www.bbc.com/news/world-europe-35763101
Bokas, C. (2018) Tension with Golden Dawn Members in Parliament; the session was interrupted. *Proto Thema*, 6 March, www.protothema.gr/politics/article/767477/kekleismenon-ton-thuron-o-kotzias-enimeronei-tin-epitropi-exoterikon-upotheseon/ [in Greek].
CCPR (2015) Concluding observations on the second periodic report of Greece. International Covenant on Civil and Political Rights. United Nations, https://tbinternet.ohchr.org/_layouts/15/treatybodyexternal/Download.aspx?symbolno=CCPR%2fC%2fGRC%2fCO%2f2&Lang=en
CEU (2016) Outcome of Proceedings: Council Implementing Decision setting out a Recommendation on addressing the serious deficiencies identified in the 2015 evaluation of the application of the Schengen acquis in the field of management of the external borders by Greece. Brussels: Council of the European Union, 12 February, https://data.consilium.europa.eu/doc/document/ST-5985-2016-INIT/en/pdf
Christopoulos, D., Kousouris, D., Papadatos-Anagnostopoulos, D., Papapantoleon, C. and Sakelariou, A. (2014) *Mapping Ultra-Right Extremism, Xenophobia and Racismm within the Greek State Apparatus*. Brussels: Rosa Luxemburg Stiftung.
CNN Greece (2020) Golden Dawn trial: Time for mitigating circumstances; Countdown to sentences, www.cnn.gr/politiki/story/237679/diki-xrysis-aygis-h-ora-ton-elafryntikon-antistrofi-metrisi-gia-tis-poines
Council of State (2014) Decision Number 2399/2014. Council of State Decision on Mosque. Courtesy and non-official translation from the Ministry of Education and Religious Affairs, www.minedu.gov.gr/publications/docs2015/Council_of_State_decision_on_Mosque.pdf
Dixon, T., Hawkins, S., Juan-Torres, M. and Kimaram, A. (2019) Attitudes Towards National Identity, Immigration and Refugees in Greece, www.moreincommon.com/media/ltinlcnc/0535-more-in-common-greece-report_final-4_web_lr.pdf
Eurobarometer (2015) Discrimination in the EU in 2015. Special Eurobarometer 437, https://op.europa.eu/en/publication-detail/-/publication/d629b6d1-6d05-11e5-9317-01aa75ed71a1
Fyntanidou, E. (2012) A. Loverdos: Criminalise thhe sexual act without precaution. To Vima, 2 May, www.tovima.gr/2012/05/02/society/a-loberdos-na-poinikopoiithei-i-seksoyaliki-praksi-xwris-profylaksi/ [in Greek].
Gemi, E. (2020) The 'Prevailing Religion' and the Governance of Diversity in Greece. In: Triandafyllidou, A. and Magazzini, T. (eds), *Routledge Handbook on the Governance of Religious Diversity Routledge*.
Halikiopoulou, D. and Vasilopoulou, S. (2015) The Rise of the Golden Dawn in Greece. In: Charalambous, G. (ed.), *The European Far-Right: Historical and Contemporary Perspectives, Report 2/2015*. PRIO Cyprus and Centre Friedrich-Ebert-Stiftung, pp. 23–28.
Hatziprokopiou, P. and Evergeti, V. (2014) Negotiating Ethnic and Religious Diversity in Greek Urban Spaces. *Social and Cultural Geography*, 15(6), pp. 603–626.
Huseyinoglu, A. (2015) Questioning Islamophobia in the Context of Greece. *IRCICA Journal*, Special Issue, III(6), pp. 65–96.
Huseyinoglu, A. and Sakellariou, A. (2018) Islamophobia in Greece: National Report 2018. In: Bayraklı, E. and Hafez, F. (eds), *European Islamophobia Report 2018*. Istanbul: SETA, pp. 407–434.

Kathimerini (2020, 12 March) Mitsotakis tells EU's Johansson Greece, Europe are facing 'asymmetric threat', www.ekathimerini.com/news/250557/mitsotakis-tells-eus-johansson-greece-europe-are-facing-asymmetric-threat/

Kirtsoglou, E. and Tsimouris, G. (2018) Migration, Crisis, Liberalism: The Cultural and Racial Politics of Islamophobia and 'Radical Alterity' in Modern Greece. *Ethnic and Racial Studies*, 41(10), pp. 1874–1892.

Lagos, E., Deligiannidis, E., Serbis, G., Gavrielatos, A. and Malanos, S. (2021) Young people's trajectories through anti-Islam(ist) and extreme right milieus: Country Level Report Greece. Young Orthodox Greeks with Islamophobic/anti-Muslim views and attitudes. Country-level report: Greece. DARE (Dialogue about Radicalisation and Equality) and Panteion University of Social and Political Sciences, www.dare-h2020.org/uploads/1/2/1/7/12176018/d7.1_greece.pdf

Lazarescu, D. and Broersma, F. (2010) New Migrational Routes: Pakistanis and Bangladeshis in Greece. In Triandafyllidou, A. and Maroukis, Th. (eds), *Migration in 21st-Centure Greece*. Athens: Kritiki, pp. 381–440 [in Greek].

Magazzini, T. and Triandafyllidou, A. (2021) *State-Religion Relations in Southern and South-eastern Europe: Between Secularism and Majoritarian Nationalism*. European Consortium for Political Research (ECPR), https://ecpr.eu/Events/Event/PaperDetails/58822

Mantzikos, I. (2016) The Greek Gateway to Jihad. *CTC Sentinel*, 9(6), pp. 16–19.

Millet News (2019, 26 July) Hate Speech by Metropolitan Seraphim the hater of Turks and Islam, www.milletnews.com/view.php?id=547

Naftemporiki (2012, 29 March) Samaras: 'We Need to Reoccupy Our Cities', www.naftemporiki.gr/story/387960/a-samaras-prepei-na-anakataloume-tis-poleis-mas [in Greek].

NAPRI (2020) National Action Plan against Racism and Intolerance 2020–2023. Ministry of Justice, Hellenic Republic, https://moj.gov.gr/wp-content/uploads/2021/03/NAPRI-en.pdf

Pew Research Center (2018) Eastern and Western Europeans Differ on Importance of Religion, Views of Minorities, and Key Social Issues, www.pewresearch.org/religion/2018/10/29/eastern-and-western-europeans-differ-on-importance-of-religion-views-of-minorities-and-key-social-issues/

Pew Research Center (2019) Views of Diversity by Country, www.pewresearch.org/global/2019/04/22/how-people-around-the-world-view-diversity-in-their-countries/

RVRN (2018) *Racist Violence Recording Network Annual Report 2017: Greece,* http://rvrn.org/wp-content/uploads/2018/03/Report_2017eng.pdf

RVRN (2020) *Racist Violence Recording Network Annual Report 2019: Greece.,* http://rvrn.org/2020/06/annual-report-2019/

RVRN (2021) Racist Violence Recording Network: Annual Report 2020, Greece, www.unhcr.org/gr/wp-content/uploads/sites/10/2021/05/ENG_ETHSIA_EKTHESH.pdf

Sakellariou, A. (2016) Islamophobia in Greece: National Report 2015. In: Bayrakli, E. and Hafez, F. (eds), *European Islamophobia Report*. Istanbul: SETA, pp. 201–221

Skleparis, D. (2017) Explaining the absence of Islamist terrorist attacks and radicalisation in Greece. ELIAMEP Public Debate: 'Let's Talk About Security', www.eliamep.gr/en/γιατί-το-ισλαμικό-κράτος-δεν-έχει-πλήξ/

Smith, A.D. (2003) *Chosen Peoples: Sacred Sources of National Identity*. Oxford: Oxford University Press.

Smith, H. (2017) Bangladeshi Fruit Pickers Shot at by Greek Farmers Win Human Rights Case. *The Guardian*, 30 March, www.theguardian.com/world/2017/mar/30/bangladeshi-strawberry-pickers-shot-at-by-greek-farmers-win-european-rights-case

Smith, H. (2019) Thousands of Greeks Protest over Name Change for Macedonia. *The Guardian*, 20 January, www.theguardian.com/world/2019/jan/20/thousands-of-greeks-protest-over-name-change-for-macedonia

Stevis-Gridneff, M. (2021) E.U. Interpreter Says Greece Expelled Him to Turkey in Migrant Roundup. *The New York Times*, 1 December, www.nytimes.com/2021/12/01/world/europe/greece-migrants-interpreter-expelled.html

To Vima (2010) Bartholomew and Jerome on the side of the immigrants, www.tovima.gr/2010/02/02/politics/bartholomaios-kai-ierwnymos-sto-pleyro-twn-metanastwn/ [in Greek].

Triandafyllidou, A. (2015) European Muslims: Caught between Local Integration Challenges and Global Terrorism Discourses. Istituto Affari Internazionali (IAI), Working Papers 15.

Triandafyllidou, A. and Gropas, R. (2009) Constructing Difference: The Mosque Debates in Greece. *Journal of Ethnic and Migration Studies*, 35(6), pp. 957–975

Tsitselikis, K. (2012) *Old and New Islam in Greece: From Historical Minorities to Immigrant Newcomers*. Leiden: Martinus Nijhoff Publishers
US Department of State (2019) *2018 Report on International Religious Freedom: Greece*, www.state.gov/wp-content/uploads/2019/05/GREECE-2018-INTERNATIONAL-RELIGIOUS-FREEDOM-REPORT.pdf
Vithoulkas, D. (2019) How the New Ministry of Citizen Protection Is Formed – Its Additional Responsibilities. *To Vima*, 9 July, www.tovima.gr/2019/07/09/society/pos-diamorfonetai-to-neo-ypourgeio-prostasias-tou-politi-oi-epipleon-armodiotites-tou/ [in Greek].

16
AUSTRALIA

Michele Grossman and Vivian Gerrand

Introduction

While Australia has had a relatively low level of successfully executed terrorist attacks compared to Europe and North America, this has been offset by the number of effectively disrupted plots that, had they been carried out, would have seen a number of sophisticated and large-scale attacks carried out in the two decades since 9/11. Generally speaking, the majority of both plots and attacks on Australian soil have been attributed by terrorist actors to Islamist-related ideologies and movements, largely but not exclusively affiliated with Al-Qaeda and Islamic State (IS). Australia also contributed a significant number per capita of foreign fighters to Syria and Iraq during the peak of IS activity around recruiting for its so-called caliphate from 2014 to 2018 (Farrall 2019). A much smaller number of identified far-right extremist plots have also been detected, although the threat of far-right extremism is now accelerating rapidly in Australia (ASIO 2021, 2022). A core element of the Australian policy response to the threat of violent extremism since 2006 has been to concentrate its countering violent extremism (CVE) framework on building community resilience to violent extremism (Grossman 2021; Abdi and Ellis 2017), with a strong focus on social cohesion and intercultural bridging capital in Australia's modern democratic pluralist and multicultural society. The 'resilience' in this context has generally been understood as a form of resistance to the appeals of violent extremist ideology, while 'community' has largely been conceptualised as Australian Muslim communities, with varying impacts – including sustained negative backlash from targeted communities – and effectiveness over time. 'Resilience' to violent extremism has also drawn discursively in Australia on broader concepts of Australian resilience to crises, disasters, and challenges, for example in relation to bushfires, floods, and, most recently, the Covid-19 pandemic.

However, while the thrust of resilience discourse in relation to natural disasters has been to prime communities for self-reliance rather than government intervention when facing such challenges, the national security context of CVE has meant that government has been far less willing to yield control of resilience policy and programming to communities themselves, or to enter into sustainable community partnerships that involve genuine co-production and power sharing. The result has been both successes and failures in Australian CVE policy on building resilience to violent extremism, creating the opportunity for a revised approach as

Australia confronts a series of new and emerging challenges related to changes in the violent extremist landscape, including the rise in online extremism and polarisation, the uptick in lone actor plots and attacks, and the resurgence of far-right violent extremist movements with transnational affiliations.

In the discussion that follows, we examine first, the history and dynamics of violent extremism in Australia before turning to how both 'resilience' and 'violent extremism' have been conceptualised and then enacted and resourced in policy and programming over time at both Federal and State/Territory levels. We then use the insights drawn from a standardised measure of resilience to violent extremism developed in Australia and Canada (the BRaVE, or Building Resilience to Violent Extremism, measure (Grossman et al. 2017, 2020)) to assess through a brief case study how well one of Australia's most robust state-based resilience to violent extremism initiatives, the COMPACT programme, aligns with the evidence base developed by BRaVE. Finally, we offer a critique of existing Australian approaches to building resilience to violent extremism and map out key current and emerging challenges that provide opportunities for resetting the ways in which Australia conceptualises and applies resilience frameworks to the threat of terrorism, including the balance between building individual versus community resilience; what we mean by 'communities', and whether there is a need to develop parallel approaches to building resilience to *violence* and to *extremism* rather than, as has been the case to date, focusing on *violent extremism* alone.

Violent extremism in Australia: history and dynamics

In historical terms, radicalisation to violence in Australia has been at very low levels. Before 9/11, most Australian terrorist or violent extremist plots and attacks tended to be motivated by non-religious sociopolitical ideologies or ethnic sectarianism, confined largely to attacks on foreign or domestic government embassies or agencies. While a small proportion of Australians either trained for or became foreign fighters linked to various international or regional terrorist groups and movements in countries including Afghanistan, Pakistan, and Lebanon in the late 1990s to early 2000s (Zammit 2015), the domestic growth of explicitly extremist political movements and threats allied to violent jihadist transnational networks did not really emerge in Australia until the early to mid-2000s.

Following 9/11, however, a number of terror-related investigations and cases led to multiple arrests, prosecutions, and convictions of Australians linked to major Al-Qaeda-inspired plots on Australian soil, including cells uncovered by major counterterrorism operations: Pendennis in 2005 and Neath in 2009 (Schuurman et al. 2014; Zammit 2012). The rise of IS in 2014 witnessed a surge in the number of Australians travelling to conflict zones in Syria and Iraq following the IS declaration of a physical caliphate in the region. Informal estimates put the flow of Australian foreign fighters to Iraq and Syria at approximately 150–165 (Kozaki 2017), as well as about half the number again of women, children, and families who either made their own way independently overseas or who travelled with spouses or other relatives.

In this sense, then, 'resilience to violent extremism' as an Australian policy discourse has been framed from its inception as a response to what was perceived as a threat from those designated as 'cultural Others' to mainstream Australia – that is, members of Islamic diaspora communities – who required better integration and support to reduce their vulnerability to transnationally circulating violent extremist narratives and mobilisation. In tandem with this, there was also a renewed focus on the importance of strengthening social cohesion through cross-cultural and cross-faith understanding and exchange, and on the annual measurement of social cohesion attitudes across the national population through mechanisms such as the Scanlon Foundation's Mapping Social Cohesion surveys and reports, produced annually since 2007 and a major source of evidence-based guidance for Australian social cohesion policy.[1]

The rationale for this approach has frequently been linked to the range of both successfully executed and disrupted terrorist attacks in Australia, almost all of which, both before and after the rise of IS in 2014, have been developed or conducted by lone actors or small cell groups who have attributed their actions to violent jihadist ideologies. These include executed attacks in Paramatta, an outer Sydney suburb, resulting in the murder of a NSW Police accountant in 2015;[2] the Endeavour Hills attack on two police officers in 2014;[3] the Brighton siege in 2017;[4] the Mill Park attack in 2018;[5] and the Bourke Street attack, also in 2018[6] – all attributed by their perpetrators to Islamist-based movements or ideologies. Major disrupted plots include the ANZAC Day plot in 2015,[7] the Christmas Day plot in 2016,[8] the New Year's Day plot in 2017,[9] the Mother's Day plot in 2015,[10] and the Etihad Airways plot in 2017,[11] which would have been Australia's most serious attack had it been successful, and – the sole publicly disclosed example linked to far-right extremism – the plot to bomb trade union and left-wing-linked organisational premises by far-right actor Philip Galea in 2016.[12]

All of these planned or executed plots have fallen under Australia's counterterrorism and CVE policies and programmes, which have been designed to improve community safety and to focus on preventing the development and uptake of radicalised ideologies that support political and social violence. An important part of any country's policy environment on violent radicalisation lies in how it defines the terms and parameters of its approach, which is then used to develop and justify particular policy settings. Australia uses the following definitions of *violent extremism, radicalisation*, and *countering violent extremism* in setting its policy and programme directions. While in the 2015 counterterrorism strategy (*Australia's Counter-Terrorism Strategy: Strengthening Our Resilience*, Council of Australian Governments 2015), resilience was foregrounded in the strategy's title, the updated 2022 Strategy[13] now references 'safeguarding' in its title (*Safeguarding our Community Together*) as a guiding principle, in a clear echo of the UK's Prevent strategy.

The 2022 Strategy defines 'violent extremism' as 'a willingness to use unlawful violence, or support the use of violence by others, to promote a political, ideological or religious goal' (p. 8). By contrast, the Australian Department of Home Affairs' Living Safe Together fact sheet on violent extremism[14] offers a definition with a more explicit focus on action and behaviour, rather than 'willingness' or 'support' alone:

> **Violent extremism** is the beliefs and **actions** of people who support or use violence to achieve ideological, religious, or political goals. This includes terrorism and other forms of politically motivated and communal violence. All forms of violent extremism seek change through fear and intimidation rather than through peaceful means. If a person or group decides that fear, terror, and violence are justified to achieve ideological, political, or social change, **and then acts accordingly**, this is violent extremism [emphasis added].

These slight changes in emphasis across policy definitions of violent extremism here participate in broader debates that have revolved around whether CVE is really about combatting the 'violent' in violent extremism or about tackling 'extremist' values and beliefs, which some people have argued lead inexorably to violent action (Schmid 2014).

Essentially, this debate hinges on whether we see violent extremism as a structural or existential threat. Australian CVE has historically tended to focus on addressing the *behavioural* dimensions of violent extremism, placing strong emphasis on balancing freedom of thought and speech (including extremist ideas and speech) against the risk or threat of violent action, while countries that see extremism as an ideological and existential threat in its own right have tended to zero in more explicitly on its **ideological** dimensions, as does France and, in more recent years, the UK, for example, through the UK's Commission to Counter Extremism, set up in 2017 following the Manchester Arena bombing but explicitly distancing itself from 'terrorism' or policy frameworks such as Prevent, set up to deal with radicalisation to violence (www.gov.uk/government/organisations/commission-for-countering-extremism/about).

Over time, however, and as the 2022 Strategy's language demonstrates, Australia's approach to CVE has moderated to some extent, becoming more expansive in its efforts to deal with the underlying extremist beliefs and influences that can lead someone to radicalise to violence. For example, a 2019 review of Australia's CVE framework found that it is characterised by a commitment to 'strengthening Australian's resilience to radicalisation and assisting individuals in disengaging from violent extremist influences and beliefs' (Lauland et al. 2019, p. 15), suggesting that the previous focus on behavioural elements at the expense of ideological coordinates has now moved more explicitly towards addressing underlying 'influences and beliefs'.

This shift has been occasioned by three developments over the last few years in the landscape of Australian (violent) extremism: the rise of social media and its role in promoting hatred, violence, and extremist ideas across the ideological spectrum; the emergence and intensification of organised far-right extremism; and the diversification of violent extremist movements, narratives, and threats in Australia, which have now moved well beyond those posed largely by violent jihadist-associated movements to encompass White supremacism, incel and misogynistic extremism, sovereign citizen movements, and anti-vaccination/anti-government movements. In 2021, the ASIO (Australian Security Intelligence Organisation) Director-General's Annual Threat Assessment for Australia[15] focused in part on how the intensification of online 'extreme right-wing propaganda used COVID to portray governments as oppressors, and globalisation, multiculturalism and democracy as flawed and failing', noting that investigations into far-right extremism in Australia (which ASIO since 2021 terms 'ideologically motivated violent extremism', or IMVE, in contrast to 'religiously motivated violent extremism') have grown 'from around one-third of our priority counter-terrorism caseload, to around 40 per cent. This reflects a growing international trend'.

The 2021 Threat Assessment went on to say that:

> Today's ideological extremist is more likely to be motivated by a social or economic grievance than national socialism. More often than not, they are young, well-educated, articulate, and middle class and not easily identified ... overwhelmingly male ... more widely dispersed across the country, including in regional and rural areas [and also] more reactive to world events, such as COVID, the Black Lives Matter movement, and the recent American Presidential election. COVID has reinforced extremist beliefs and narratives about societal collapse and a race war. As a consequence, we are seeing extremists seeking to acquire weapons for self-defence, as well as stockpiling ammunition and provisions.

In 2022, the ASIO Annual Threat Assessment[16] continued some of the themes from 2021 but placed more emphasis on the impacts of the Covid-19 pandemic, the online environment, and the diversification of extremist ideological confluences:

> Online radicalisation is nothing new, but Covid-19 sent it into overdrive. Isolated individuals spent more time online, exposed to extremist messaging, misinformation and conspiracy theories ... More time in those online environments – without some of the circuit breakers of everyday life, like family and community engagement, school and work – created more extremists. And in some cases, it accelerated extremists' progression on the radicalisation pathway towards violence ... The behaviours we are seeing in response to COVID lockdowns and vaccinations are not specifically left or right wing. They are a cocktail of views, fears, frustrations and conspiracies. Individuals who hold these views, and are willing to support violence to further them, are best and most accurately described as ideologically motivated violent extremists ... The individuals involved [are] driven by a diverse range of grievances, including anti-vaccination agendas, conspiracy theories and anti-government sovereign citizen beliefs.

Notably, the 2022 Threat Assessment went on to comment:

> ASIO does not have any issue with people who have opinions they want to express. This is a critical part of a vibrant democracy. We do not – and cannot – investigate peaceful protest or dissent. Our concern is where opinions tip into the promotion of violence, or actual acts of violence.

As we can see, the distinction between violent behaviours versus free speech – even if extremist or hateful in nature – remains a core element of Australia's conceptualisation of extremism and the threats that it poses from a counterterrorism perspective. However, Australian CVE, while heavily inflected by a counterterrorism focus, exceeds this in its explicit linkage between CVE and enhancing social cohesion – and this is where the focus on building social-ecologically informed resilience to violent extremism comes into its own in Australian policy and practice contexts.

Australian conceptualisations of building resilience to violent extremism

As Grossman (2021) has argued, 'resilience to violent extremism' has variously been conceptualised in P/CVE contexts as *resistance* (to violent extremist ideologies, narratives, and propaganda), *prevention* (building social cohesion and multicultural understanding to forestall narratives of polarisation, conflict, and division), *adaptation* (to develop broader social acceptance of measures focused on community safety), and *recovery* (restoring systemic social and infrastructure stability in the aftermath of a terrorist attack). However, in Australia as well as internationally, the most common conceptualisation of resilience to violent extremism is aligned with the prevention of and resistance to violent extremist beliefs and actions.

While some of the international literature focuses on building the resilience of individuals to violent extremism (Aly et al. 2014; BOUNCE 2018; Lösel et al. 2018; Stephens et al. 2021; Taylor et al. 2017; van Brunt et al. 2017; Sieckelinck and Gielen 2018), the broader policy discourse in Australia has focused more often on developing *community-level* resilience to violent extremism. As Grossman (2021, pp. 299–300) has noted, this reflects four international trends in the way that the field has evolved in its thinking about resilience over time that also resonate in Australian contexts:

1. The extent to which terrorist and violent extremist trajectories themselves have been conceptualised as group-level rather than individual-level processes, involving an understanding of individuals who radicalise to violence as embedded within group-level socio-ideological processes and networks of various kinds and to various degrees.
2. Following from this, the extent to which social-ecological paradigms of resilience, which stress the complex interdependency between individuals and their collective social systems, have resonated most strongly in P/CVE thinking and programming to date.
3. The responsiveness of CT and P/CVE scholars to the needs of policymakers and security agencies, which have been interested in what building collective resilience to social harms such as violent extremism might look like in terms of programming, planning, and resourcing by governments.
4. The problematic tendency to attribute terrorist and violent extremist ideologies and behaviours to *communal identity* structures (e.g. Muslims, Whites, men) rather than to *communal ideological or belief* structures (e.g. right-wing, Islamist, ecological, misogynist).

From a social-ecological standpoint, community resilience in Australia is understood as a set of *processes* rather than a fixed set of traits or characteristics. These processes are multidimensional and best understood as part of a community's social ecology, with a range of individual, social, cultural, and environmental factors influencing resilience protections, vulnerabilities, and risks. Recognising that resilience cannot develop without the presence of both adaptive functioning *and* exposure to risk or adversity, the dialectical relationship between vulnerability and resilience, and between resilience and the availability of and capacity to navigate successfully toward culturally meaningful resources (Ungar 2008, 2011), is essential for an understanding of the social conditions and dynamics that can spur or threaten resilience to violent extremism, as also for resilience more generally.

In practice, however, the ways in which community-level resilience to violent extremism constructs have been operationalised in Australia have become problematised because of their tendency to over-securitise Muslim communities, creating significant sense of stigma and community backlash from within Australian Muslim communities around the country (Hardy 2015; Bull and Rane 2019; Abdel-Fattah 2020). One of the key impacts of this has been to impede the systematic development and sustaining of long-term meaningful government–community partnerships (Ellis and Abdi 2017) in Australia that are critical to successful resilience-building in the context of violent extremism, with many peak Australian Muslim community groups and organisations unwilling to engage with policies or programmes that are badged as 'CVE'. Nevertheless, some important policy and programming outcomes have been achieved despite what are by now widely acknowledged errors in earlier policy iterations relating to Australian Muslim communities, and despite critiques of low investment in Australian CVE programming relative to counterterrorism operations and legislation (Hardy 2018).

National policy and programming

Australian policy focuses on promoting resilience to violent extremism as part of a broader effort to create more generally resilient communities that can successfully manage a range of twenty-first-century social-ecological dynamics, challenges, and transformations (Grossman et al. 2016). For example, the 2010 Counter-Terrorism White Paper (Australian Government 2010) outlined 'resilience' as one of the key pillars of the country's counterterrorism strategy and gave an overview of the radicalisation process undergone by individuals before taking part in terrorist acts, as well as discussing the importance of family and community in CVE. The White Paper stated that it would counter violent extremism by:

- building on Australia's history of inclusion, multiculturalism, and respect for cultural diversity to maintain a society that is resilient to the hate-based and divisive narratives that fuel terrorism;
- working with the Australian community through a cooperative national approach to lessen the appeal of violent extremism and support alternative pathways for those at risk and working internationally to support this (ibid., p. 65).

This emphasis on resilience has been successively reiterated and strengthened since the 2010 White Paper, beginning with Australia's first national CVE framework in 2011 (Council of Australian Governments 2015, p. 30). The national CVE framework sought to build resilience to extremism by taking proactive measures to promote inclusion and by mobilising communities against extremism. This strengthened focus on resilience superseded older terrorism plans such the 2007 National Action Plan, which made only a single passing reference to resilience in its conception of counterterrorism and CVE (Ministerial Council on Immigration and Multicultural Affairs 2007, p. 10).

In 2015, the Government launched an updated version of the National CVE Framework (Department of Prime Minister and Cabinet 2015) which, while focusing on more targeted identification and intervention with persons deemed to be at risk of radicalising to violence, maintained its focus on community resilience and social cohesion, as its four key objectives suggest:

(1) identify and divert violent extremists and provide them with disengagement options;
(2) identify and support at-risk individuals;
(3) **support community resilience and build cohesion** [emphasis added];
(4) achieve effective communications which challenge extremist messages and support alternatives.

Both earlier and later versions of this Framework and the policies that underwrite it have provided targeted funding and grants that explicitly reference resilience. These include the Building Community Resilience Grants Program (2010–2013), superseded in 2015 by the current 'Living Safe Together' framework, which funded local community partners, beginning with the pilot Building Community Resilience (BCR) Youth Mentoring programme in 2010 and ultimately extending across 59 projects that were designed to support young people's rejection of socially divisive radicalised narratives and encourage pro-social community engagement and participation.

Thus, 'building resilience to violent extremism' has since its inception been inextricably bound up in Australia's federated policy approaches, which operate at both national and State/Territory government levels, to addressing radicalisation to violence with a focus on concepts of social cohesion and harmoniously diverse communities. Successive policy documents at both Federal and State/Territory tiers of government have either framed resilience to radicalisation as dependent on how successfully Australia is managing to maintain and strengthen its national and local social cohesion, or alternatively suggested that social cohesion is dependent on the capacity for social and community resilience. As RAND's review of CVE programs in Australia, the US, and Europe notes:

> Australia's national CVE Centre was established in 2010 as a result of a counterterrorism white paper that acknowledged the risk of homegrown terrorism and highlighted the importance of building a strong and resilient community to resist violent extremism and terrorism (McClelland 2010; Australian Government 2010). The vision of the CVE Centre is to reduce the risk of homegrown terrorism by strengthening Australians' resilience to radicalisation [that includes] building strength in diversity and social participation, which focuses on the societal drivers that can lead to disengagement and isolation.
>
> Lauland et al. 2019, p. 15

State-based policy and programming

This emphasis has been mirrored at State level by policies in Victoria and New South Wales (NSW), the nation's two most populous States that have faced the most significant number of challenges and plots in relation to radicalised individuals and groups across the ideological spectrum. Both States have a long-standing focus on building resilience to violent extremism that formulates this in relation to social cohesion, social justice, and community harmony.

In NSW, for example, an Acil Allen Consulting (2019) evaluation of the integrated, multi-agency NSW CVE Program identified seven programmatic elements that focus explicitly on resilience-building across NSW Government agencies including Multicultural New South Wales, Department of Education, Department of Premier and Cabinet, and Department of Communities and Justice. These are both recent and current initiatives such as the COMPACT programme led by Multicultural NSW – discussed in greater detail below – which since 2016 has partnered with community groups to provide pro-social youth and other engagement programmes that focus strongly on resilience-building and social cohesion.

Similarly, the Victorian State Government has contributed support to programmes such as the Australian Multicultural Foundation's (2013) long-established *Community Awareness Training: Building Resilience in the Community* CVE-focused toolkit and training programme, and in 2015 developed a *Strategic Framework to Strengthen Victoria's Social Cohesion and the Resilience of its Communities*[17] through a ministerial taskforce focused on social cohesion, community resilience, and preventing violent extremism. The Framework encompassed specific emphasis on the importance of social cohesion in its key principles, including the ways in which 'prevention relies on strong, trusting community relationships and therefore should not be securitised' and that 'social cohesion should not be used as a "cover story" for efforts to prevent extremism' (State of Victoria 2017, p. 28).

The Victorian Strategic Framework supported, amongst other programme outcomes, a four-year virtual research programme, the Research Institute on Social Cohesion (RIOSC) from 2015 to 2018, with significant involvement from community and civil society organisations in programme development and participation. Following its conclusion, the Victorian Government funded the establishment of the independent Centre for Resilient and Inclusive Societies (CRIS)[18] in 2019, a five-year funding scheme supporting a consortium of eight university, community, and industry partners to advance and build on the work of the foundation RIOSC programme through streams researching the interconnectedness of anti-racism and social belonging, youth digital well-being and social activism, resilience to social harms including violent extremism, and the dynamics of violent radicalisation. The Victorian Government has also funded a series of locally based Community Support Group networks that operate through community–government partnerships to build young people's resilience to a range of challenges. Funded by government, they are delivered by community organisations such as the Australian Multicultural Foundation[19] and the Centre for Multicultural Youth.[20]

However, while the Commonwealth policies have deployed but not specifically defined what they mean by resilience (other than by packaging it with social cohesion), both the Victorian and NSW policy frameworks do explicitly define resilience to violent radicalisation, similarly connecting resilience to social cohesion and community solidarity in times of crisis. For instance, the Victorian Framework articulates resilience in social-ecological, multisystemic terms, drawing on the definition developed by the Rockefeller Foundation's global 100 Resilient Cities programme, which 'defines resilience as the capacity of individuals, communities, institutions, businesses, and systems to survive, adapt and grow no matter what kinds of chronic stresses and acute shocks they experience' (State of Victoria 2015, p. 2) and asserts that:

> Connected communities are resilient communities because they are ready to look after each other in times of crisis, whether that be a flood, a bushfire or an incident of violent extremism. They function reliably and well when under stress; successfully adapt; are self-reliant; and have high levels of social support, social cohesion and social capacity. These social support systems include neighbourhood; family and kinship networks; intergenerational supports; good links between communities, institutions and services; and mutual self-help groups.
>
> *Ibid.*

The NSW COMPACT programme defines resilience similarly, noting that community resilience is 'a whole of society approach ... where "resilience" means proactively building and maintaining strong, responsive and collaborative networks that operate across communities and sectors, and that can mobilise to respond to challenges and threats, resolve conflicts and actively promote social cohesion'.[21] The COMPACT framework argues that:

> Our resilience in the face of hate and extremism can be measured by the way we respond to this threat as a unified, inclusive and democratic society ... But we cannot take our social cohesion for granted [and] the task of strengthening community resilience and safeguarding social cohesion, now and into the future, will require a concerted effort across all sections of our society.[22]

But how effective have these frameworks been, what kinds of resilience to violent extremism do they promote and achieve, and how well do they align with the research evidence base for the factors that meaningfully inform an understanding of resilience to violent extremism from social-ecological perspectives? In the next section, we examine the NSW COMPACT programme through the lens of Australian–Canadian research that developed a five-factor, strengths-based measure for youth resilience to violent extremism, the BRaVE (Grossman et al. 2017, 2020).

From theory to practice: building pro-social resilience with young people

The *Youth Resilience to Violent Extremism* study (Grossman et al. 2017), led in Australia and involving comparative data from both Australia and Canada, understands resilience to be a social-ecological process that can be enhanced or diminished by intersecting resources and systems (Grossman et al. 2017, 2020). This study built on the qualitative data and analysis of two earlier pieces of research – the Australian *Harnessing Resilience Capital* study (Grossman et al. 2014) and the similarly strengths-based 2015 Canadian study on *Barriers to Violent Radicalization: Understanding Pathways to Resilience among Canadian Youth*)[23] funded by Public Safety Canada's Kanishka project (Grossman et al. 2017).

The study's emphasis on resources required to support young people's resistance to violent extremist influences draws directly on the socio-ecological framework that attends to the nuances of local context in resilience processes, arguing that resilience factors and features cannot be isolated from their context-dependent circumstances without risking a misunderstanding of the processual dimensions of the social ecology of resilience as it is lived in real time and place (Grossman et al. 2017).

The contexts of Australia and Canada were chosen for the comparative study for their culturally diverse urban demographics and similar policies of official multiculturalism. The international research team developed a survey in consultation with Australian and Canadian community-based local advisory groups to ensure that questions were tailored to their respective contexts and to ensure strong face validity. These were then trialled in partnership with community organisations with 475 young people aged 18–30 in Australia (n= 200) and Canada (n=275).

The standardised measure addressing these aspects was designed as a toolkit to enable communities and agencies to 'develop effective and meaningful youth-focused policies and programmes' that can identify both existing resilience assets possessed by youth and vulnerabilities that may be in need of redress, as well as being used in programming contexts to determine 'baseline and post-intervention measures of resilience to violent extremism for young people' (Grossman et al. 2017). The five validated factors of the measure (Grossman et al. 2017, 2020) are:

(1) **Cultural identity and connectedness**: Familiarity with one's own cultural heritage, practices, beliefs, traditions, values and norms (can involve more than one culture); knowledge of 'mainstream' cultural practices, beliefs, traditions, values and norms if different from own cultural heritage; having a sense of cultural pride; feeling anchored in one's own cultural beliefs and practices; feeling that one's culture is accepted by the wider community; feeling able to share one's culture with others.
(2) **Bridging capital**: Trust and confidence in people from other groups; support for and from people from other groups; strength of ties to people outside one's group; having the skills, knowledge, and confidence to connect with other groups; valuing inter-group harmony; active engagement with people from other groups.
(3) **Linking capital**: Trust and confidence in government and authority figures; trust in community organisations; having the skills, knowledge, and resources to make use of

institutions and organisations outside one's local community; ability to contribute to or influence policy and decision-making relating to one's own community.
(4) **Violence-related behaviours**: Willingness to speak out publicly against violence; willingness to challenge the use of violence by others; acceptance of violence as a legitimate means of resolving conflicts.
(5) **Violence-related beliefs**: Degree to which violence is seen to confer status and respect; degree to which violence is normalised or well tolerated for any age group in the community.

The combination of the first three factors represents complex cultural identity: the ability to maintain one's cultural identity and connectedness with an in-group (bonding) whilst relating and adapting to different cultures in wider society (bridging) and linking with trusted authority figures and institutions. The latter two factors relate to violent behaviours and beliefs. Where violence is seen as an acceptable way to resolve conflict, there is greater vulnerability to violent extremism. Viewing violence as unacceptable, conversely, is protective and reduces the risk of violent extremism.

We now review the NSW COMPACT programme to see the extent to which these factors have been addressed by a key Australian government–community building-resilience-to-violent-extremism programme.

COMPACT background

Developed by the state government agency Multicultural NSW and first launched in 2015, COMPACT is a whole-of-society, community-targeted CVE programme with a suite of elements that aim to 'strengthen community resilience and safeguard social cohesion … in an uncertain world'.[24] The initiative is strongly inflected by its youth-focused design and delivery. Developed by the NSW government in consultation with community stakeholders at the height of foreign fighter travel and IS outreach and activity in Australia, COMPACT seeks to address violent extremism by building on what it describes as the resilient community response to the Lindt Café siege[25] in Sydney (the capital of NSW) in 2014, which saw local communities in NSW uniting against fear and division in a commitment to counter violent extremism. The programme was then expanded 'as part of a $47 million package of NSW Government CVE measures announced in November 2015' (Wise et al. 2018).

Since its inception, COMPACT has brought together over 60 community-based entities, including schools, universities, community organisations, charities, non-governmental organisations, police, and government agencies. COMPACT's emphasis in framing community resilience as a social cohesion project aligns with the broader Australian CVE policy context outlined earlier in this chapter, as is clear from the way in which it mobilises different forms of resilience capital outlined in the BRaVE measure through its investment in community-based resources.

COMPACT's four pillars focus on preparedness, prevention, response, and recovery align with Grossman's (2021) conceptual pillars of multisystemic resilience as 'resistance, prevention, adaptation, and recovery' (Figure 16.1). The programme's four pillars are designed to:

1. Proactively build and maintain strong, secure, networked, responsive and aware communities (Preparedness).
2. Develop networked communities with the will and capacity to support prevention or intervention programmes (Prevention).

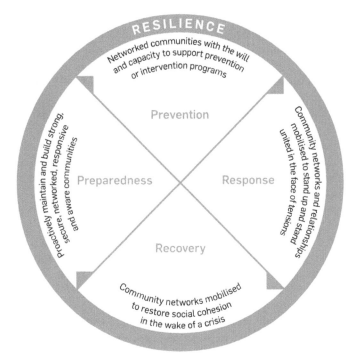

Figure 16.1 COMPACT Resilience-based model
Source: Multicultural NSW, COMPACT Alliance Summit Booklet, 2018

3. Mobilise community networks and relationships to stand up and stand united in the face of tensions brought about by extremist hate and violence (Response).
4. Enable and motivate community partners to support each other and maintain or restore social cohesion in the wake of an incident or crisis brought about by extremist hate and violence (Recovery).

A key element of COMPACT is the opportunities it offers for both bridging and linking capital through its funding of community groups and organisations to resource resilience-building through an annual community grants scheme, which aims to strengthen young people's resistance to hateful and violent extremist narratives and influences by building their awareness of the strengths of multicultural social cohesion and harmony, and to equip them to address and resolve tensions generated by violent extremist conflicts and narratives both domestically and in relation to overseas events.

Since 2016, the programme has funded multi-year community organisation grants of two to three years' duration that support locally based youth-oriented projects. These projects have included the Youth Leadership Program, Celebrating Stories of Strength, Community Action for Preventing Extremism (CAPE) NSW, Community Resilience Engaging Solutions Together (CREST), In League In Harmony, The Sydney 2020 Youth Challenge, Youth Led Social Cohesion, and Youth Off The Streets Case Management (Wise et al. 2018). These initiatives promote complex cultural identity and pride in cultural heritage (BRaVE Factor 1) by working with culturally and linguistically diverse young people who are viewed as part of the solution, rather than positioned as a problem. According to an independent external evaluation, in its first two years, the programme reached over 20,000 young people from 300 schools in addition to youth and community centres (ibid.). Critically, the grants scheme has included funding for programmes that deal not just with Islamist-attributed or inspired violent extremism, but also with nationalist and racist-derived violent extremism, for example, by funding CAPE, a project delivered by community organisation All Together Now that focused on far-right extremist diversion and disengagement.

The COMPACT model fosters a collaborative approach in alignment with Australia's National CVE Framework to addressing violent extremism through its establishment of the COMPACT Alliance group, which brings together relevant stakeholders to fortify organisational relationships and create a network of best practice community-resilience practitioners. The Alliance has cultivated bridging and linking capital (BRaVE Factors 2 and 3) through 'cross-sector engagement between government and community organisations', with 'Alliance partners … involved in a range of initiatives … including working with a number of CVE training, communications and intervention programs' (ibid.).

Evaluations of the COMPACT programme demonstrate its success in building community resilience and social cohesion since its inception through its flexible multi-year funding model and partnership approach. Surveys conducted with participant stakeholders found that 66 per cent of respondents increased their acceptance of and respect for others, or bridging capital (ibid.; Acil Allen Consulting 2019). Enhanced belonging and participation in civic and community life, including increased school attendance and willingness to adopt leadership and volunteering positions, were further positive outcomes that demonstrate the programme's capacity to generate linking social capital (Wise et al. 2018). COMPACT has thus been instrumental in supporting protective factors that enable resilience to violent extremism; its programmes have clearly resulted in high levels of bridging and linking social capital amongst its stakeholders.

However, in a rapidly evolving prevention landscape in which terrorist actors are increasingly 'from majority rather than minority ethnic/faith backgrounds' (Thomas and Grossman, forthcoming), challenges remain in relation to how 'communities' are conceptualised and which community groups are solicited for participation in resilience-building initiatives when, as Thomas and Grossman (forthcoming) contend, the meanings of 'communities' are shifting away from ethnocultural and toward 'mainstreaming' categories of CVE community partners.

Moreover, due to its targeting of young culturally and linguistically diverse sectors of the community, COMPACT potentially stigmatises and 'responsibilises' ethnocultural minorities (ibid.) based on the assumption that they are at particular risk of violent radicalisation or best placed to address such radicalisation within their communities. As Thomas and Grossman (ibid.) argue:

> Targeting specific identity-based communities for P/CVE resilience-building initiatives assumes a deficit of resilience in these communities, rather than an effort to map existing resilience assets that can be drawn on in developing genuine partnerships in relation to counter-radicalisation efforts.

The COMPACT programme of resilience-based interventions moreover relies on competitive grants-based funding for operation. The limitations of this model should not be underestimated. While these programmes intend to promote whole-of-society interventions, they risk missing out on resource-poor sections of the community and thereby neglect to provide the opportunity for cultivating linking capital amongst such sections of the community who will be disadvantaged by their inability to participate in a grants application process that is both time-consuming and reliant upon significant literacy levels.

Finally, there is little evidence that programmes such as COMPACT directly address violent-related beliefs and behaviours. The primary focus of COMPACT on fostering bridging and linking capital and emphasising cultural connectedness and sense of pride in cultural heritage is of a piece with many Australian CVE initiatives that slot comfortably into contemporary policy objectives around social cohesion, but that fail to engage with the ways in which violent extremist narratives and appeals legitimise and valorise violence as an instrument for redressing perceived grievances and injustices. In this sense, such programmes leave intact a central divide between CVE – conceptualised as resilience not so much to violent extremism as to social division and conflict – and CT, or counterterrorism, which deals with the potential for violent acts that cross the criminal threshold. It speaks to a concept of resilience as prevention of and resistance to violent extremism that stops short of explicitly focusing on the prevention of and resistance to *violence* as a legitimate instrument of conflict resolution.

Concluding remarks

Our analysis above raises the question of whether we need to consider a shift from 'building resilience to violent extremism' to a slightly differently pitched framework that runs along two integrated tracks: building resilience to *violence* (whether extremist or not), on the one hand, and building resilience to *extremism* (whether violent or not), on the other. This is not an easy project for any national government to pursue, particularly in the context of social policy settings that value pluralism, freedom of speech, and freedom of thought and association. Yet the current form taken by the social cohesion effort on its own is unlikely to meaningfully address the current landscape of harmful extremisms in Australia, as the continuing escalation in far-right extremism despite years of social cohesion policy and programming attests. Previous iterations of resilience-as-social-cohesion, as we have seen, have tended to focus more on the integration of and perceived 'deficits' in resilience on the part of cultural minority 'Others', in ways that backfired by significantly alienating many Australian Muslim communities (and particularly young people within these communities). Future social cohesion efforts will need to incorporate broader aspects of social cohesion, such as addressing economic and employment precarity, climate change, integrity failures, and other structural inequalities and challenges, for example, uneven resourcing of or access to services and support resources.

Australia now faces more recent challenges that come not only from the threat of polarisation and violence already promoted by violent extremist jihadist movements, although these continue to play a dynamic role in the Australian violent extremist landscape. As our foregoing discussion indicates, Australian communities are now experiencing higher levels of far-right extremist mobilisation than previously seen. The social cohesion focus of resilience-building remains critical, but it needs now to aim squarely at addressing not merely sense of belonging and inclusion for minority cultures, but also the ethnically and racially based supremacism of far-right movements gaining strength within majority-culture communities, as well as their sense of grievance and perceptions of structural inequalities.

This is a complex challenge, because – while all violent extremist groups are skilled at retailing 'victim' narratives that position them as unjustly treated or oppressed by an existing sociopolitical status quo – the problem is really not one of too *little* equality, but too *much* equality for those who don't agree with their worldview. Violent extremist networks, far from seeking equal treatment for themselves and others, wish to reinstate hierarchies of power, status, and privilege in which they have primacy, setting the rules and terms for the sociopolitical order and imposing their values and criteria for belonging or exclusion across entire societies. Whatever their ideological differences, violent extremist movements share a hostility to democracy and pluralism – and in this sense, we may need to think about what 'resilience to violent extremism' might benefit from if the comparatively harder political edge of resilience to anti-democratic norms is introduced into the paradigm.

It has also, arguably, become evident that the ways in which Covid-19 has recently radicalised portions of the Australian population toward support for far-right narratives and conspiracies – including a minority for whom violence has become legitimised – is an outcome of the relative lack of exposure to sustained adversity. This is so because, ironically, many majority-culture communities have been shielded from chronic adversity by Australia's high levels of mainstream economic and social capital, whereas many minority-culture communities are all too familiar with the experience of chronic hardships.

The experience of state-mandated lockdowns, rules around social access based on vaccination status, and the precarious employment and economic circumstances driven by the pandemic meant that many Australians unfamiliar with hardships around freedom of movement, secure income, and discrimination or exclusion (here, in relation to vaccine status) experienced for the first time what many minority communities in Australia have endured repeatedly either domestically or (for refugee-background communities) in their countries of origin. If, as Luthar et al. (2003, p. 543) have argued, 'exposure to significant threat or severe adversity' is a 'critical condition' for developing resilience, then the pandemic has revealed that many Australians are more vulnerable to developing maladaptive coping responses – including adherence to extremist explanatory frameworks – as a response to exposure to adversity than was previously recognised.

This means that the 'social cohesion' elements of resilience to violent extremism cannot simply be drawn together in a one-size-fits-all template that focuses on integrating minority communities and promoting sense of belonging and equality of opportunity and resources. As both research and programming has shown, a significant resilience outcome for the programmes we've examined here has been the painstaking building of trust relations and positive interactions between communities and government agencies that is so essential to the linking capital dimensions of building resilience to violent extremism.

Moreover, in a rapidly evolving prevention landscape such as Australia in which terrorist actors are increasingly 'from majority rather than minority ethnic/faith backgrounds' (Thomas and Grossman, forthcoming), and where polarisation and inter-community tensions are on the rise, we need a better understanding of how the meanings and identities of 'communities' have shifted away from geographically sited, ethnoculturally defined 'communities' towards new models of both spatially and digitally connected communities of interest, with corresponding implications for how social-ecological models of resilience can be enacted in these spaces.

In either case, ongoing policy and resource investment that strengthens social justice and equality of opportunity is needed alongside investment in community cohesion to sustain community resilience into the future. Alongside this, renewed attention and investment in building *individual*-level resilience for young people – which may help counter the trend in lone actor threats that is now a significant part of the Australian violent extremism risk landscape – through education, family-focused and community-based programming that enhances the access to and meaningful navigation of resources that support pro-social coping will be an important and much-needed complement to existing community-level resilience frameworks.

Notes

1. https://scanloninstitute.org.au/research/mapping-social-cohesion
2. www.sbs.com.au/news/article/curtis-cheng-murder-fourth-man-guilty-of-plotting-2015-parramatta-terror-attack/52pekyq7j
3. www.coronerscourt.vic.gov.au/sites/default/files/2018-12/ahmadnumanhaider_491714.pdf
4. www.theage.com.au/national/victoria/coroner-to-examine-state-s-monitoring-of-2017-brighton-siege-shooter-20190719-p528s1.html
5. www.abc.net.au/news/2019-06-05/bangladeshi-homestay-guest-sentenced-for-engaging-in-terror-act/11180560
6. www.theage.com.au/national/victoria/premeditated-coroner-rules-2018-bourke-street-attack-an-act-of-terrorism-20210628-p584su.html
7. www.abc.net.au/news/2016-06-30/sevdet-besim-pleads-guilty-anzac-day-terror-plot/7557574
8. www.theguardian.com/australia-news/2019/nov/29/three-men-jailed-for-28-and-16-years-over-christmas-terror-plot-on-melbournes-federation-square#:~:text=Two%20men%20will%20spend%20at,on%20Christmas%20Day%20in%202016x
9. www.dw.com/en/police-foil-melbourne-new-years-eve-terror-plot/a-41556787
10. www.theage.com.au/national/victoria/victeen-jailed-over-melbourne-terror-plot-20161207-gt5y8s.html
11. www.theguardian.com/australia-news/2019/dec/17/sydney-khayat-brothers-jailed-over-plot-to-blow-up-etihad-plane-with-meat-grinder-bomb
12. www.cdpp.gov.au/case-reports/phillip-galea-jailed-terrorist-offences
13. www.nationalsecurity.gov.au/what-australia-is-doing-subsite/Files/safeguarding-community-together-ct-strategy-22.pdf
14. www.livingsafetogether.gov.au/Documents/what-is-violent-extremism.PDF
15. www.asio.gov.au/publications/speeches-and-statements/director-generals-annual-threat-assessment-2021.html
16. www.asio.gov.au/publications/speeches-and-statements/director-generals-annual-threat-assessment-2022.html
17. www.mav.asn.au/__data/assets/pdf_file/0012/22512/Strategic_Framework_to_Strengthen_Victorias_Social_Cohesion-Dec-2015.pdf
18. www.crisconsortium.org
19. https://amf.net.au/entry/northern-community-support-group-csg-project/
20. www.cmy.net.au/young-people-community/community-connections/community-support-groups/
21. https://multicultural.nsw.gov.au/compact/program-level-outcomes-a-whole-of-society-resilience-based-approach
22. https://multicultural.nsw.gov.au/compact/the-compact-story
23. https://resilienceresearch.org/barriers/
24. https://multicultural.nsw.gov.au/compact/the-compact-story
25. www.abc.net.au/news/2015-12-15/martin-place-siege-what-we-do-and-do-not-know/7021524?nw=0&r=ImageProxy

References

Abdel-Fattah, R. (2020) Countering violent extremism, governmentality and Australian Muslim youth as 'becoming terrorist'. *Journal of Sociology*, 56(3), pp. 372–387, DOI:10.1177/1440783319842666

Acil Allen Consulting (2019) *NSW Countering Violent Extremism Program Evaluation: Final Report*, www.cveevaluation.nsw.gov.au/__data/assets/pdf_file/0006/771963/ACIL-Allen-NSW-CVE-Evaluation-Final-Report-October-2019.pdf

Aly, A., E. Taylor and S. Karnovsky (2014) Moral disengagement and building resilience to violent extremism: an education intervention. *Studies in Conflict & Terrorism*, 37(4), pp. 369–385, DOI:10.1080/1057610X.2014.879379

ASIO (Australian Security and Intelligence Organisation) (2021) *Director-General's Annual Threat Assessment*. https://www.asio.gov.au/resources/speeches-and-statements/director-generals-annual-threat-assessment-2021

ASIO (Australian Security and Intelligence Organisation) (2022) *Director-General's Annual Threat Assessment*. https://www.asio.gov.au/resources/speeches-and-statements/director-generals-annual-threat-assessment-2022

Australian Government (2010) *Counter-Terrorism White Paper: Securing Australia, Protecting Our Community*, www.dst.defence.gov.au/sites/default/files/basic_pages/documents/counter-terrorism-white-paper.pdf

Australian Multicultural Foundation (2013) *Community Awareness Training: Building Resilience in the Community*, https://amf.net.au/entry/community-awareness-training-manual-building-resilience-in-the-community/

BOUNCE (2018) *Resilience Training, Network and Evaluation STRESAVIORA II (Strengthening Resilience against Violent Radicalisation 2015–2018*. Brussels: European Commission with the Egmont Institute, https://arktos.be/en/ondersteuning/bounce

Bull, M. and H. Rane (2019) Beyond faith: social marginalisation and the prevention of radicalisation among young Muslim Australians. *Critical Studies on Terrorism*, 12(2), pp. 273–297, DOI: 10.1080/17539153.2018.1496781

Council of Australian Governments (2015) *Australia's Counter-Terrorism Strategy: Strengthening Our Resilience*. Canberra: Council of Australian Governments, https://apo.org.au/node/56121

Department of Prime Minister and Cabinet (2015). *Review of the Commonwealth's Counter Terrorism Arrangements*. Canberra: Department of Prime Minister and Cabinet, https://apo.org.au/node/53179

Ellis, H.B. and Abdi, S. (2017) Building community resilience to violent extremism through genuine partnerships. *American Psychologist*, 72(3), pp. 289–300, DOI:10.1037/amp0000065

Farrall, L. (2019) The fall of the ISIS 'caliphate'. *Parliamentary Library Briefing Book 2019*. Canberra: Parliamentary Library of Australia, www.aph.gov.au/About_Parliament/Parliamentary_Departments/Parliamentary_Library/pubs/BriefingBook46p/ISISCaliphate

Grossman, M. (2021) Resilience to violent extremism and terrorism: A multisystemic analysis. In: Ungar, M. (ed.) *Multisystemic Resilience. Adaptation and Transformation in Contexts of Change*. Oxford: Oxford University Press, pp. 293–317. Open Access, DOI:10.1093/oso/9780190095888.003.0017

Grossman, M., Tahiri, H. and Stephenson, P. (2014) *Harnessing Resilience Capital: An Investigation of Resilience and Cultural Diversity in Countering Violent Extremism*. Canberra: Countering Violent Extremism Subcommittee, Australia-New Zealand Counter-Terrorism Committee.

Grossman, M. Peucker, M., Smith, D. and Dellal, H. (2016) *Stocktake Research Project: A Systematic Literature and Selected Programme Review on Social Cohesion, Community Resilience and Violent Extremism 2011–2015*. Melbourne: State of Victoria. Open Access, www.researchgate.net/publication/318381446_Stocktake_Research_Project_A_systematic_literature_and_selected_program_review_on_social_cohesion_community_resilience_and_violent_extremism_2011-2015

Grossman, M., Hadfield, K. Jefferies, P., Gerrand, V. and Ungar, M. (2020) Youth resilience to violent extremism: Development and validation of the BRaVE measure. *Terrorism and Political Violence*, DOI:10.1080/09546553.2019.1705283

Grossman, M., Ungar, M., Brisson, J., Gerrand, V., Hadfield, K. and Jefferies, P. (2017) *Understanding Youth Resilience to Violent Extremism: A Standardised Research Measure*. Final Report for Department of Home Affairs, Canberra. Melbourne: Alfred Deakin Institute for Citizenship and Globalisation, Deakin University, https://static1.squarespace.com/static/5aebdc1dcc8fedda5a5815bb/t/5b20c64d70a6adcf82c304dd/1528874577754/Understanding+Youth+Resilience+to+Violent+Extremism+-+the+BRAVE-14+Standardised+Measure.pdf

Hardy, K. (2018) How the Australian Government Is Failing on Countering Violent Extremism, *The Conversation*, 16 October, https://theconversation.com/how-the-australian-government-is-failing-on-countering-violent-extremism-104565

Hardy, K. (2015) Resilience in UK counterterrorism. *Theoretical Criminology*, 19(1), pp. 77–94, DOI:10.1177/1362480614542119

Kozaki, D. (2017) Islamic State: Families of Australian fighters pose security conundrum for authorities. *ABC News*, 12 September, www.abc.net.au/news/2017-09-12/what-to-do-with-australian-islamic-state-family-members/8895730

Lauland, A., Moroney, J.D.P., Rivers, J.G., Bellasio, J. and Cameron, K. (2019) *Countering Violent Extremism in Australia and Abroad: A Framework for Characterising CVE Programs in Australia, the United States and Europe*. Canberra and Santa Monica: RAND Corporation, www.rand.org/pubs/research_reports/RR2168.html

Lösel, F., King, S., Bender, D. and Jugl, I. (2018) Protective factors against extremism and violent radicalization: a systematic review of research. *International Journal of Developmental Science*, 12(1–2), pp. 89–102, DOI:10.3233/DEV-170241

Luthar, S., Cicchetti, D. and Becker, B. (2003) The construct of resilience: a critical evaluation and guidelines for future work. *Child Development*, 71(3), pp. 543–562, DOI:10.1111/1467-8624.00164

McClelland, R. (2010) Budget 2010: Countering Violent Extremism in Our Community. Attorney-General's Department, 11 May. Media release, https://parlinfo.aph.gov.au/parlInfo/search/display/display.w3p;query=Id:%22media/pressrel/L4PW6%22

Ministerial Council on Immigration and Multicultural Affairs (2007) *A National Action Plan to Build on Social Cohesion, Harmony and Security*. Canberra, https://library.bsl.org.au/jspui/bitstream/1/1350/1/National-Action-Plan-2007.pdf

Schuurman, B., Harris-Hogan, S., Zammit, A. and Lentini, P. (2014) Operation Pendennis: A case study of an Australian terror plot. *Perspectives on Terrorism*, 8(4), pp. 91–99, www.jstor.org/stable/26297199

Sieckelinck, S. and Gielen, A-J. (2018) *Protective and Promotive Factors Building Resilience Against Violent Radicalisation*. Radicalisation Awareness Network (RAN) Issue Paper, https://ec.europa.eu/home-affairs/sites/homeaffairs/files/what-wedo/networks/radicalisation_awareness_network/ranpapers/docs/ran_paper_protective_factors_042018_en.pdf

State of Victoria (2015) *Strategic Framework to Strengthen Victoria's Social Cohesion and the Resilience of its Communities*. Melbourne: State of Victoria, www.mav.asn.au/__data/assets/pdf_file/0012/22512/Strategic_Framework_to_Strengthen_Victorias_Social_Cohesion-Dec-2015.pdf

State of Victoria (2017) *Expert Panel on Terrorism and Violent Extremism Prevention and Response Powers. Report 2*. Melbourne: State of Victoria (Department of Premier and Cabinet), www.vic.gov.au/expert-panel-terrorism-report-2

Schmid, A.P. (2014) *Violent and non-violent extremism: Two sides of the same coin?* The Hague: The International Centre for Counter-Terrorism, 5(5), DOI:10.19165/2014.1.05

Stephens, W., Sieckelinck, S. and Boutellier, H. (2021) Preventing violent extremism: A review of the literature. *Studies in Conflict & Terrorism*, 44(4), pp. 346–361, DOI:10.1080/1057610X.2018.1543144

Taylor, E.L., Taylor, P.C., Karnovsky, S., Aly, A. and Taylor, N. (2017) 'Beyond Bali': a transformative education approach for developing community resilience to violent extremism. *Asia Pacific Journal of Education*, 37(2), pp. 193–204, www.researchgate.net/publication/306014416_Beyond_Bali_A_transformative_education_approach_for_developing_community_resilience_to_violent_extremism

Thomas, P. and Grossman, M. (forthcoming) Working with communities to counter radicalisation. In: Busher, J., Marsden S. and Malkki, L. (eds) *Routledge Handbook on Radicalisation and Countering Radicalisation*. London: Routledge.

Ungar, M. (2008) Resilience across cultures. *The British Journal of Social Work*, 38(2), pp. 218–235, DOI: 10.1093/bjsw/bcl343

Ungar, M. (2011) The social ecology of resilience: Addressing contextual and cultural ambiguity of a nascent construct. *American Journal of Orthopsychiatry*, 81(1), pp. 1–17, DOI:10.1111/j.1939-0025.2010.01067.x

Van Brunt, B., Murphy, M. and Zedginidze, A. (2017) An exploration of the risk, protective, and mobilization factors related to violent extremism in college populations. *Violence and Gender*, 24(3), pp. 81–101, DOI:10.1089/vio.2017.0039

Wise, P., Roberts, S. Formosa, J. and Chan, A. (2018) *Evaluation of the COMPACT Program*. Prepared by Urbis for NSW Department of Premier and Cabinet. Final Report, https://multicultural.nsw.gov.au/files/COMPACT_Evaluation%20Report_Final_010219a.pdf

Zammit, A. (2012) The Holsworthy Barracks Plot: A Case Study of An Al-Shabab Support Network in Australia. *CTC Sentinel* 5(6) [online], https://ctc.usma.edu/the-holsworthy-barracks-plot-a-case-study-of-an-al-shabab-support-network-in-australia/

Zammit, A. (2015) *Australian Foreign Fighters: Risks and Responses*. Sydney: Lowy Institute, www.lowyinstitute.org/publications/australian-foreign-fighters-risks-and-responses.

17
NEW ZEALAND

Jacinta Carroll

Introduction

New Zealand is a successful small state: multilateralist in outlook and inclusive in identity, it is stable and relatively free from violence. Until 2019 it had not experienced a designated terrorist attack, and its terrorism threat alert level was assessed as 'very low'. The right-wing-extremist motivated attack in Christchurch on 15 March 2019 was broadly perceived as an aberration: a terrorist attack in the most unlikely of places. This perception, however, belies the more complex story of New Zealand's experience of violent extremism and responses to it.

This chapter provides an overview of New Zealand's experience of, and engagement with, violent extremism in the past two decades. It introduces New Zealand's political culture and social identity for context, then explores the concepts of violent extremism and terrorism as they relate to New Zealand. I argue that there is a disconnect between New Zealand's appreciation of the threat in the foreign versus domestic environments that has hindered its ability to effectively counter terrorism. This chapter examines how New Zealand has postured to engage with and respond to terrorism as an intelligent and active international player, and how – despite limited declaratory policies and programmes to counter violent extremism – its immediate political and societal response to the Christchurch attack provides an exemplar of resilience and social cohesion.

The 2019 Christchurch terrorist attack was a 'focusing event' for New Zealand. The *Royal Commission of Inquiry into the Terrorist Attacks on Christchurch Mosques on 15 March 2019* was established on 8 April 2019 to examine the events surrounding the Christchurch terrorist attacks (RCIC 2020). With its special powers of inquiry, nothing was off-limits to the Royal Commission. This has resulted in the most comprehensive review into New Zealand's counterterrorism approach to date and a valuable source of information on the country's experience of and response to violent extremism.

A small state with impact

Despite a small population of around five million people and relative geographic isolation in the South-West Pacific, New Zealand has a strong heritage of being actively engaged in the world politically, militarily, and socially. As a British dominion, it provided substantial contributions to both the First and Second World Wars, and was a founding member of the United Nations in 1945. After full political independence from Great Britain in 1947, it became an ally of the United States of America (US) and Australia through the 1951 Australia, New Zealand and United States (ANZUS) Treaty, and later made military contributions to the Korean and Vietnam Wars. New Zealand's close bilateral relationship with Australia has been a salient feature of its international engagement, with 'ANZAC' elements serving together since the First World War. Its military and security cooperation with traditional 'Anglo-sphere' partners has continued into the contemporary era of global terrorism, including through the Five Eyes security arrangement.

Since the 1980s New Zealand has chosen a more independent foreign policy path, demonstrating a consciously 'small state' approach to international relations (Brady 2019). In 1984 it declared the country nuclear-free – refusing to allow US nuclear-powered vessels or aircraft to enter – and was consequently suspended from the ANZUS Treaty by the US. The treaty remains an umbrella agreement for Australia's bilateral security alliances with, respectively, New Zealand and the US. While rapprochement with the US has ensued to a relatively normalised bilateral security and military arrangement – excluding nuclear capabilities – through the 2010 Wellington and 2012 Washington Declarations, New Zealand retains its independence as a core element of foreign policy (Graham 2021), which it is unlikely to cede unless forced (Ayson 2017).

Thorhallsson (2019) argues that while small states are traditionally seen as weak, New Zealand along with Iceland demonstrate that small states can leverage multilateral institutions and alliances to their benefit. While small states rely on the protection of larger states and organisations to survive, engaging in a smart and nuanced way can see small states thrive in the complex global security and economic environment.

New Zealand's approach to counterterrorism has followed the small state dictum, characterised by a strong moral voice and being a reliable multilateral supporter. It has consistently supported UN Security Council Resolutions (UNSCR) and General Assembly calls to counter terrorism and violent extremism, while also contributing to US and later NATO-led counterterrorism activities in Afghanistan. New Zealand's contributions demonstrate an astute and successful balance between being – and being seen as – an effective multilateralist and contributor to the global community, while ensuring these commitments are within its means.

Despite its sustained involvement in global counterterrorism activities, New Zealand remains relatively low profile with global terrorist actors. Before 2019's Christchurch attack, it was rarely mentioned as a target in terrorist propaganda. By comparison, its close neighbour and regular partner in counterterrorism activities, Australia has – along with the US and the United Kingdom (UK) – regularly featured as a target of ISIS propaganda. Battersby (2018) describes New Zealand's balancing act on international counterterrorism as 'managing to do enough to be positively noticed by friends as a contributor, but apparently not enough to be noticed negatively by those who could be enemies'.

In his analysis of British and French approaches to counterterrorism policy, Foley (2013) usefully applied constructivist, institutional, and organisational theoretical frameworks to understand the factors that shape state approaches to counterterrorism. Societal or constructivist norms are features that characterise and describe a community including history, identity, and behaviour. Institutional norms refer to government policy and practice, while organisational norms are the routine behaviour of those agencies that are – or should be – involved in countering terrorism activities. The following exploration of New Zealand society, politics, and agencies involved in countering terrorism will also address the societal, institutional, and organisational norms at play in New Zealand's conception of, and response to, violent extremism.

Identity and culture: super-diverse or multicultural?

New Zealand's politics and national identity are historically drawn from a combination of British settler society and local Māori culture. Spoonley (2015) describes the evolution of New Zealand society since British settlement as parallel activities of colonisation of an indigenous people and development of a nation through mass immigration. The 1840 *Te Tiriti O Waitangi*, Treaty of Waitangi, between British representatives and certain Māori chiefs provides a foundation document for the way that New Zealand sees itself and how Māori rights and culture are respected. While the terms of the original Treaty are contested, it has been critically reviewed and reimagined to support New Zealand as a bicultural country, bringing to the fore principles generally described as partnership, protection, and acting honestly and in good faith (Morrison and Huygens 2019). All government agencies are required to be guided by the principles of *Te Tiriti O Waitangi*.

Recent immigration has further diversified New Zealand's population and society. Migrants are predominantly from the South-West Pacific, adjacent to New Zealand, and the UK, but increasingly represent a broader range of source countries (Stats NZ 2018). Spoonley (2015) assesses that this dramatic increase in migration from diverse sources means New Zealand can be categorised as a recently 'super-diverse' community. Despite its strong bicultural foundations and increasingly diverse population, New Zealand does not have a dedicated multicultural policy or strategy articulating a vision of support and engagement for newer settlers (RCIC 2020). This contrasts with Canada and Australia that approach multiculturalism as a declared policy of proactive support to maintain cultural diversity (Metz et al. 2016). In New Zealand, migrants are provided with support services through the Office of Ethnic Affairs to assist living in New Zealand society, but these are mainly transactional, suggesting an integration rather than multicultural approach (RCIC 2020). The Christchurch Royal Commission found that public policy had not adjusted to the rapid changes in New Zealand's demography and its 'super-diverse' community, and the country did not even have reliable data on ethnic and religious diversity (ibid.).

Representatives of New Zealand's Muslim community testified to the Royal Commission that their concerns about being increasingly targeted by hate crimes and violence were not considered by authorities due to a lack of communication channels with authorities (ibid.). In 2018, 1.2 per cent of the national population identified as Muslim, with the vast majority – around 75–80 per cent – born overseas and ethnically diverse (Stats NZ 2018). The Royal Commission identified the need for a more sophisticated and effective approach to engaging with New Zealand's diverse migrant communities, including a cross-agency multicultural strategy (RCIC 2020).

A considered and comprehensive multiculturalism policy can help engender resilience to violent extremism. A 2016 report by the United Nations Security Council Counter-Terrorism Committee found that strong multicultural societies such as Australia and Canada were most effective in addressing violent extremism with affected communities due to established communication and support mechanisms (UNCTC 2016). Grossman et al. (2020) identified five sources of 'capital' within such communities that can be drawn upon to resolve grievances and engender resilience to violent extremism. These factors describe relations between – and actions by – government, the affected community, and broader society. The five sources of capital are:

- Cultural identity and connectedness
- Bridging capital
- Linking capital
- Violence-related behaviours, and
- Violence-related beliefs

The BRaVE methodology, developed by Grossman et al. (2020), assesses individual resilience to violent extremism by measuring their identification and relationship with these factors in the broader community. This research indicates a strong and positive relationship between a comprehensive and declaratory multicultural policy as part of a functioning liberal democracy and the five sources of capital.

Politics and diversity: 'towards a better democracy'

New Zealand is a strong and consultative liberal democracy. It is also categorised as one of the safest and most peaceful countries in the world, with very low levels of violence, and is consistently rated by the Institute for Economics and Peace's *Global Peace Index* as the second most peaceful country in the world (IEP 2021). This indicates that there are effective means of peaceful political representation and that resolving matters with violence is a cultural aberration. This correlates with Grossman et al.'s (2020) categorisation of sources of capital in resilience against violent extremism. New Zealand's highly diverse representative democracy (Hunt 2021) provides the basis for linking capital – the relationship between communities and government – while the normative place of violence in New Zealand society effectively counters tolerance of violence-related beliefs and behaviours.

New Zealand's progress towards independence during the twentieth century occurred in an orderly, unhurried manner: by negotiation and procedure rather than revolution. This resonates with the evolution of New Zealand's approach to politics, which can be characterised as balanced, broadly centrist, and increasingly diverse.

While New Zealand progressed peacefully towards greater political representation, an increasing diffusion of power would ultimately constrain the government's legislative responses to terrorism. For most of the twentieth-century New Zealand had a first-past-the-post or majority vote electoral system, with government alternating between the conservative National Party and the left Labour Party. In 1996 New Zealand changed to a mixed-member proportional electoral system to provide greater diversity of parties and elected representatives and move 'towards a better democracy' (Hunt 2021). Increased diversity has also seen a more dynamic approach to governing and legislating, as the major parties must negotiate with minor parties and sometimes require a coalition to form government. While the National Party and Labour have continued to lead government, this is often as a minority government in coalition with parties more to the left or right or promoting Māori rights. This has limited the government's ability to pass legislation.

In the two decades from 9/11 to 2021 and New Zealand's increased focus on counter-terrorism, the country had minority governments for all but two years, with neither major party holding a majority. In that time, only three major pieces of counterterrorism legislation were passed (Ip 2021) and getting cross-party support for these consumed significant political capital (Battersby and Ball 2019). Counterterrorism legislation is discussed further below.

Violent extremism in New Zealand: 'terrorism where terrorism is not'

While New Zealand is a predominantly peaceful country, and apparently far-removed from the threat of global terrorism, it has nonetheless experienced both internationally inspired and home-grown terrorism.

Rapoport (2004, 2013) identified four 'waves' of terrorism, where popular radical ideologies have caused violence. These are anarchist, anti-colonialist, new left or socialist, and religious fundamentalist. Rapoport recently added far-right ideology as a fifth wave (2021). While this approach is primarily historical, with each wave described as dominant for 30 to 40 years, it has utility for categorising contemporaneous movements. Of the five ideological movements identified by Rapoport, four can be found in New Zealand's recent and current experience of ideologically based extremism: anti-colonialism in Māori and Black power violent extremist movements; new left in the protests of the 1970s and 1980s and environmental violent extremists of the 2000s; and the current faith-motivated and right-wing movements. The addition of a local anti-colonialist extremist movement is a feature of a settler society, contrasting, for example, with the terrorism environment in Europe. New Zealand's terrorism threat environment can be characterised as small but complex, with a variety of concurrent threats and some crossover with non-violent political movements and criminality.

The 1970s saw violent extremist movements motivated by left- and right-wing groups, environmental and Māori activism, and in support of overseas terrorist groups. Some left-wing anti-war protests in the 1970s against New Zealand's involvement in the Vietnam War involved violence, including a bombing. As in Australia, in the 1990s and 2000s, some New Zealanders were convicted of financially supporting the Liberation Tigers of Tamil Eelam and the Palestine Liberation Organisation, which were then designated terrorist groups (Battersby and Ball 2019). While a small number of Australians joined al-Qaeda and other terrorist groups in the 1990s and 2000s, there is little evidence of New Zealanders doing so.

The global pull of ISIS also reached New Zealand; while numbers were small, ISIS had supporters in New Zealand, and some travelled to the Middle East to join the group. In 2015, Rebecca Kitteridge, Director-General of Security and Head of the New Zealand Secret Intelligence Service (NZSIS), stated that the agency estimated that six to 12 New Zealanders had travelled to the Middle East as foreign fighters, including some who had been residing in Australia (Battersby 2018). Kitteridge said counterterrorism authorities were investigating another 30 to 40 people in New Zealand who were assessed to be radicalised to support Islamist violent extremism, now officially referred to in New Zealand as Faith-Based Violent Extremism.

Right-wing extremist groups have been an ongoing presence in the terrorism landscape since the 1990s but have varied in size and ideology. White supremacist groups such as the National Front have also experienced divisions and in-fighting. Like in Australia, since 2001, the size, form, and capability of right-wing extremist groups have been significantly influenced by overseas events and the rise of Islamist extremism (Peucker and Smith 2018; Carroll 2016). The 2005 London bombings inspired right-wing-motivated vandalisation of an Auckland mosque, while the rise of ISIS from 2014 became a focus for discussion and capability-building within some groups and an opportunity to connect with overseas extremists (Battersby and Ball 2019). Right-wing extremist groups and their members in New Zealand also have strong links to organised crimes; this crossover has contributed to tension over whether to deal with them as a national security or criminal threat.

A survey by Battersby and Ball (2019) of security practitioners identified a high level of awareness in the 2000s of right-wing terrorism and the increasing threat. Survey participants expressed frustration that they were unable to investigate and prosecute right-wing terrorism, feeling 'fettered' and concerned with a general complacency in New Zealand society about the terrorist threat. Both police and victims saw right-wing-extremist-motivated hate crimes as being linked to terrorism, with the potential for escalation, but this was neither recognised in law nor the subject of dialogue between affected communities and officials (RCIC 2020).

The Christchurch attack

On Friday 15 March 2019, an Australian far-right extremist undertook two consecutive firearms attacks during Friday prayers at the Al-Noor Mosque and the Linwood Islamic Centre in Christchurch, New Zealand. Some 290 people were in attendance at both venues: 51 people were killed and 40 injured in around 36 minutes. The attacker stated in a prepared manifesto that these were politically motivated attacks against Muslims (Koziol 2019). He live-streamed his actions on Facebook (Sonderby 2019). The attacker would later testify that he chose to conduct his attack in New Zealand, rather than Australia, as its more permissive firearms environment allowed him to obtain semi-automatic weapons (RCIC 2020). In response to the attack, New Zealand's terrorist threat level was raised from 'low' to 'high' but reduced to 'medium' a month later, on 17 April 2019, where it has remained (NZSIS 2019).

A global actor against terrorism

New Zealand's experience of, and response to, terrorism can be conceived in four phases:

(1) Global War on Terrorism (GWOT), 2001–2004
(2) International stabilisation, 2004–2014
(3) Domestic refocus, 2015–2019
(4) Prevention and resilience, 2019 onwards

The GWOT phase from 2001 to 2004 saw New Zealand participate as part of the international response to what was seen as a transnational threat. The second phase, from approximately 2004 to 2014, is New Zealand's international stabilisation phase, when it provided relatively substantial contributions to international efforts to counter terrorism through multilateral forums as well as stabilisation operations in Afghanistan. The third phase, from around 2014 to 2019, can be described as a domestic refocus as the country gradually reduced its international commitments, confining its modest counterterrorism efforts mostly to domestic policy in what was seen as a benign environment.

These first three phases broadly align with international approaches to counterterrorism in the post-9/11 era, with New Zealand playing its part as a member of the international community to deal with a global threat. The fourth phase commenced in 2019 with the shocking attacks in Christchurch and continues with a refocusing on prevention and resilience at home.

GWOT and international stabilisation

Like many other countries, New Zealand responded to the 9/11 attacks with an immediate focus on the existential threat of global Islamist terrorism and a commitment to international efforts to counter terrorism.

In this first internationalist GWOT phase, New Zealand was part of the US-led coalition that conducted counterterrorism operations in Afghanistan from late 2001 in response to 9/11. Importantly in terms of New Zealand's foreign policy posture, the Afghanistan operations were supported by UNSCRs. New Zealand continued to provide combat and combat support elements, including special forces and airlift capability, until 2004. The government also actively supported multilateral efforts to counter terrorism, primarily through UN efforts, such as co-sponsoring terrorist group designations and supporting UNSCRs on terrorist sanctions and financing, and it maintains an ongoing commitment to these diplomatic efforts (MFAT n.d.).

New Zealand continued to focus its main counterterrorism efforts overseas and through the UN and other multilateral forums. In 2003–2004 its commitments in Afghanistan transitioned to the combined security-humanitarian construct of Provincial Reconstruction Teams under the NATO-led International Security Assistance Force. New Zealand's contribution to international efforts in Afghanistan lasted around 20 years, with the last New Zealand Defence Force elements withdrawing in May 2021 as the international community ceased military involvement.

International recalibration and domestic refocus

While in 2014 the conflict of the Arab Spring and the violent rise of ISIS turned global security attention back to the Middle East, New Zealand looked closer to home. With stabilisation operations in Afghanistan appearing to progress well, New Zealand started drawing down its contribution. Even as the country progressed its – ultimately successful – campaign for a seat on the United Nations Security Council, then Prime Minister John Key was non-committal on engaging in other theatres of counterterrorism operations. This was primarily due to domestic pressure: despite his government's robust approach to international security, counterterrorism combat operations were not generally supported by the broader New Zealand polity and society which, as Ayson (2014) observed, 'mistakenly treated Afghanistan as a large peacekeeping mission'. New Zealand would go on to commit a military training team to the Australian-led Task Force Taji in Iraq in 2015, but not directly support operations against ISIS.

There remained much to be done at home. In October 2014, Prime Minister Key publicly announced New Zealand's terrorist threat level had increased – due primarily to the rise of ISIS – from 'very low' to 'low', while also announcing major reviews of New Zealand's counterterrorism laws.

The Key government was committed to working with partners – particularly Australia – to remain up to date on both the threat and how to deal with it. Australia is New Zealand's closest neighbour, its main security and defence partner, and only formal ally; the two countries have a high degree of cooperation across security and defence, and both are members of the Five Eyes international security arrangement.

The Trans-Tasman approach

New Zealand was an invited observer to Australia's highest-level counterterrorism body for some years. The National Counter Terrorism Committee (NCTC) was established in 2001 as part of Australia's response to 9/11 and brought Australia's national government together with its state and territory governments to ensure a coordinated and cooperative approach to counter terrorism across the various jurisdictions. In 2012, New Zealand's involvement in this arrangement was formalised, 'to encourage closer strategic dialogue on matters of bilateral interest' and the grouping renamed the Australia-New Zealand Counter-Terrorism Committee, ANZCTC (COAG 2012). As a full member of the ANZCTC, New Zealand was privy to the environmental updates, policy development, and working group activities of the Committee; it was not, however, required to maintain the same capabilities that were required of the Australian jurisdictions as part of Australia's national counterterrorism response, or to comply with decisions and directions of the Committee unless 'explicitly stated' (COAG 2012).

This meant that although New Zealand was not involved in global counterterrorism activities such as operations against ISIS in Iraq and Syria to the same extent as Australia – and did not face the same 'high' domestic threat – it had information on the threat and efforts to counter the threat from its Australian colleagues. New Zealand also participated in consultations and ANZCTC working groups to develop legislation, policies, and guidelines to counter terrorism, including the Mass Gatherings Advisory Group that produced *Australia's Strategy for Protecting Crowded Places from Terrorism* and accompanying guidelines in 2018, the year before the Christchurch attack (ANZCTC 2017).

The work of the NCTC and later ANZCTC was not confined to policy and exercises, but actively engaged in security for major events. The NCTC was formed the year after Sydney hosted the Olympic Games, enabling members to draw experience and lessons from this very successful event. The intergovernmental grouping was integrally involved in counterterrorism preparations around other major events including the 2006 Melbourne and 2014 Gold Coast Commonwealth Games, the 2007 meeting of the Asia-Pacific Economic Cooperation Forum, and the 2003 Rugby World jointly hosted with Australia. The NCTC and ANZCTC also sponsored skills development and training for members, and conducted a regular programme of counterterrorism desktop and field exercises.

Despite New Zealand's high and ongoing level of policy and practical involvement in an intergovernmental organisation focused on terrorism and countering terrorism, by 2019 there was little evidence of the country's almost 20-year participation translating into counterterrorism preparedness at home. This is underscored by the otherwise comprehensive Royal Commission report which, apparently reflecting testimony from officials, refers to the ANZCTC only as a training provider (RCIC 2020). While the access was there, it appeared difficult for New Zealand's institutions to break out of the prevailing view that terrorism was not a problem for New Zealand.

There were some attempts to craft appropriate national policies and programmes to counter violent extremism, but these had little visible or practical impact. A 2005 *Counter Terrorism Plan* captured New Zealand's official position on counterterrorism, including its risk management framework, coordination mechanism, and the roles of intelligence and legislation in countering terrorism, but this was an internal rather than a public document. The 2013 review, *Counter-Terrorism: a review of the New Zealand CT landscape*, confirmed that New Zealand did not have 'an overarching policy document describing our national approach to counterterrorism', with agencies left to decide what activities they engaged in (ibid.). The Royal Commission found that the need for a counterterrorism strategy had been highlighted in this and a number of other reviews, including another in 2013 on national security and intelligence, and that as of 2020 there were still no formalised arrangements to direct, manage, report, or evaluate New Zealand's counterterrorism approach. As of 2019, it found that the only contemporary document on the counterterrorism effort was a two-page *Counter-Terrorism Strategic Framework* that articulated New Zealand's counterterrorism system but did not set strategic direction or 'assign leadership or responsibility'.

In 2015 Cabinet approved a proposal to institute a social cohesion programme to lower the risk of violent extremism arising from 'at-risk' communities (ibid.). Informed by similar initiatives in Australia, Canada, and the UK, the package sought to rebalance counter-terrorism 'response' options with prevention and resilience measures that engaged directly with the communities considered at most risk of radicalisation to violent extremism. The initial approval was later withdrawn due to funding as well as concern about the sensitivities of engaging with New Zealand's mostly migrant Muslim community on the topic of violent extremism. The Christchurch Royal Commission would later criticise Cabinet's decision as an 'abrogation' of government responsibility (ibid.).

Through the three phases covering 2001 to 2019, New Zealand could be described as having an engaged but selective approach to countering violent extremism.

As a good global citizen and savvy small state actor, New Zealand lent its voice and moral support to condemning terrorism, taking reasonable and considered action as part of the multinational community such as a significant contribution to Afghanistan for around 20 years. Through the ANZCTC, it maintained awareness of the threat as well as best-practice efforts to counter violent extremism, but followed an exceptionalist approach, electing to prioritise resources elsewhere.

This is consistent with Ayson's (2017) description of New Zealand's longstanding foreign policy approach of independent multilateralism – what White (2011) refers to as 'unarmed neutrality' – and relying largely on Australia as its first line of defence. From the small state theory approach, this was a reasonable stance for a relatively small country in dealing with what was seen to be a distant, and highly improbable, threat. Until, of course, it wasn't.

Counterterrorism legislation: when terrorism isn't terrorism

Consistent with New Zealand's internationalist outlook, most of its counterterrorism legislation was initiated as part of broader international responses. At the time of the 9/11 attacks, a draft bill in support of international counterterrorism financing conventions was already before Parliament and under committee review. The attacks saw a dramatic reconsideration and redrafting of the original bill, with the *Terrorism Suppression Act 2002* (TSA) proposed in the immediate aftermath of the 2001 attacks and enacted the following year.

While passage of the TSA meant New Zealand technically had counterterrorism legislation, putting this into practice would prove problematic. An enduring dilemma of counterterrorism law is its tension with criminal law (Williams 2011). Whereas criminal law is focused predominantly on prosecuting after an act of actual or intended harm has occurred, counterterrorism laws are generally preventative, aiming to protect the community from harm. This creates a further tension between individual civil rights and the rights of the broader community (McGarrity and Blackbourn 2016). As a common law country, New Zealand may be usefully informed by British, Australian, and Canadian legislation and judiciary as it considers how to navigate its legislative and policy responses to terrorism.

Unlike these countries, however, New Zealand's TSA had a very narrow definition of types of terrorist acts, did not clearly and broadly define terrorist acts as political violence, and did not include preparatory acts to commit a terrorist attack as a crime, thus severely limiting its utility. If a person can be deemed a terrorist and prosecuted under terrorism legislation only after a violent attack has occurred, this might already be covered, and perhaps more easily and effectively addressed, under existing criminal law. Ip (2021) argues there was reluctance to use the TSA since the criminal code already covered violent acts, was familiar to both police and the courts, and had established proofs that were easier to comprehend and work through. Further, Ip argues that justice could be seen to be served as the criminal code already supported the sentencing purposes of incapacitation and retribution. The utility of the TSA is further constrained as prosecution under the Act can only occur with the consent of the Attorney-General and, while in practice this has been handled by the Solicitor General, this sets a high bar.

Behind this was an enduring sense amongst legislators and the public that terrorism would never hit New Zealand, so any law was unlikely to be used. Birkland (2014) argues that a 'focusing event' is required to shift the presumption away from the status quo towards a new policy. While New Zealand experienced a number of violent extremist events after the TSA was enacted, until the 2019 Christchurch attacks none were of the level of a 'focusing event' that would shift perceptions; even then, the exceptionalist narrative of Christchurch being a 'one-off' event would prove hard to dislodge.

The provisions of the TSA were tested in 2007 in relation to Operation Eight, when a two-year police investigation into a group of environmentalist and Māori activists came to a head with a disruption operation and 17 arrests. The group was planning to undertake violent extremist attacks, including political assassination, and terrorism charges were laid under the TSA. The then-Solicitor General, David Collins, elected not to prosecute under the TSA, describing the laws as 'incoherent and unworkable' (Collins 2007) and stating he was,

> ...unable to authorise the prosecutions that have been sought under the Terrorism Suppression Act. There is insufficient evidence to establish to the very high standard required that a group or entity was planning or preparing to commit a terrorist act, as that term is defined in the legislation.

While minor amendments were subsequently made to the definition of terrorist acts, the TSA remained unattractive to prosecutors. It would be another 14 years – and just under 20 years since the law was enacted – before it would be used. In 2021, in the wake of another successful terrorist attack, the TSA was hurriedly amended to classify as crimes any preparatory acts to undertake a terrorist attack.

The Operation Eight matter demonstrated the ineffectiveness of the TSA: New Zealand's counterterrorism laws could not be used to prosecute a major planned terrorist attack. Operation Eight also reinforced another important aspect of New Zealand's experience of terrorism: it labelled domestic terrorism as something other than terrorism (Battersby and Ball 2019). If politically motivated violence was just another form of crime, New Zealand didn't appear to have a terrorist threat.

The next significant counterterrorism legislation was the 2014 *The Foreign Fighters Act*, enacted at the height of ISIS's so-called caliphate in Iraq and Syria and its accompanying call for foreign fighter support. The legislation was drafted to fulfil New Zealand's international obligations under UNSCR 2178 to limit the movement of foreign fighters and enable prosecution of foreign fighters and their enablers (UNSC 2014).

Organisational approaches: 'nobody's job'

Foley (2013) observes that organisational norms of day-to-day work priorities and practice shape how agencies engage in counterterrorism activities, sometimes despite government guidance and direction on strategy, roles, and responsibilities. For New Zealand, neither strategy nor agency roles are clear.

While a small number of New Zealand government agencies are involved in counter-terrorism, cross-agency leadership and coordination is not clear. Like other countries, New Zealand recognises different roles in countering terrorism across areas including response, prevention, and recovery. The government *Counter-Terrorism Playbook* identifies four 'Rs': reduction, readiness, response, and recovery. The Christchurch Royal Commission found that, while the New Zealand Police was the lead in responding to any counter-terrorism incident, it was not clear who was responsible for the four 'Rs' and how this framework should be applied (RCIC 2020). NZSIS is responsible for intelligence collection and assessment of terrorism and other threats, while the Department of Prime Minister and Cabinet is responsible for coordinating advice to Cabinet. No agency was identified as responsible for New Zealand's counterterrorism strategy, work programme, or coordination. Counterterrorism tasks, therefore, appeared to fit in around the existing roles, workload, and priorities of agencies.

Prevention and resilience: New Zealand responds to Christchurch

Policy development and research into counterterrorism has progressed from focusing primarily on 'response' to preventing and addressing violent extremism, and building resilience to terrorism through social cohesion. While New Zealand's policy approach to counter-terrorism in the domestic environment was flawed and incomplete, lacking strategy or a joined-up approach, in the aftermath of the Christchurch attack the innate resilience and cohesion of New Zealand society provided a masterclass on effectively addressing violent extremism (Carroll 2019). Grossman et al.'s (2020) five sources of capital in building resilience provide a useful reference point to illustrate a healthy and resilient community.

As discussed above, linking capital describes community trust and confidence in government (ibid.). After the Christchurch attack, the engagement between the Al-Noor Mosque and Linwood Islamic Centre communities and the New Zealand authorities presented as respectful and truly representative. For a representative democratic government such as New Zealand's, this accords with the principles of responsible government. The consistent narrative at public events in New Zealand in the aftermath of the attack was of support by the broader New Zealand community for the small minority Muslim community. Significantly in relation to linking capital, this political bond was publicly and enthusiastically affirmed by Christchurch's Muslim community leadership. In response to an initial surprise *haka* by local schoolboys at the emergency welfare centre set up for the local Muslim community, local community member Mohammed Daud Kahn stated (Dole and Ford 2019),

> We are very fortunate to be here in New Zealand with people…who understand our culture and our religion…This event has scarred us but it's also brought us closer together.

In a speech to Parliament on 17 March 2019, Prime Minister Jacinda Ardern emphasised connectedness. She said of the victims, 'They were New Zealanders. They are us'. (Ardern 2019). Ardern extended this to describe a shared and supported journey together into the future,

> We cannot know your grief but we can walk with you at every stage. We can and will surround you with *aroha* [love], *manaakitanga* [extending love and support], and all that makes us us.

Apparently instinctively, Prime Minister Ardern reached out to Christchurch's Muslim community, and the gesture was reciprocated. Underlining this approach, the potentially divisive issue of the citizenship status of those who were killed, injured, and survived the attack was not part of official messaging until a month later when, in a further linking gesture, the government announced that special arrangements were being introduced to allow survivors to apply for permanent residency.

Additional factors of capital in building resilience to violent extremism (Grossman et al. 2020) are how violence-related behaviours and views are treated. 'Calling out' violence is a critical element of addressing violent extremism. Community norms combined with effective law enforcement mean that New Zealand has low incidence and low societal acceptance of violence-related behaviour (IEP 2021). Terrorist violence can, however, create escalatory and divisive rhetoric, including violence-related or comparatively harsh responses.

Official responses to the Christchurch attacks were strong, with government leaders and New Zealand Police immediately labelling them as terrorist acts and denouncing the violence (Carroll 2020). While authorities imposed some temporary security restrictions in the hours and days after the Christchurch attacks – including security for mosques – these were quickly lifted after it became apparent that there was only one attacker and no apparent copycat attacks. Within days, national legislation was introduced to amend firearms regulations by outlawing semi-automatic weapons, and it received cross-party support with little pushback from firearms owners and dealers (Lyons 2019). Further legislation in July 2019 established a national firearms register, imposed tighter restrictions on obtaining firearms licences, and banned foreigners from purchasing firearms in New Zealand. Prime Minister Ardern named the attacker once and affirmed he would not be named again, setting a standard followed by policymakers and media alike in managing publicity around the individual. Further undermining extremist propaganda, New Zealand's leaders consciously avoided engaging in the right-wing extremist narrative of reasons for the attack, choosing instead to focus on community and intercultural messaging.

New Zealand authorities immediately acted to remove the online video of the shootings and the attacker's manifesto, working closely with media companies including Facebook – the original broadcast site – and were able to quickly remove the video from easy online access as well as actively remove ongoing downloads. Members of the public were asked to not view or share the video. This work later grew into the 'Christchurch Call for Action', co-sponsored by New Zealand and France, which enlisted countries and major communications companies to work together to limit terrorist access to social media (New Zealand Government n.d.). The Christchurch Call remains a signature element of New Zealand's approach to countering violent extremism.

In a wide-ranging report, the Royal Commission into the Christchurch attacks found that there was little that authorities could have done to identify and stop the attacker beforehand (RCIC 2020). But they identified gaps in New Zealand's approach to countering violent extremism and areas for improvement. These included the need for a comprehensive review of counterterrorism legislation, which it found to be 'woefully inadequate' and outdated. Significantly, the Royal Commission found that while there had some recent progress in addressing New Zealand's counterterrorism policy, this was piecemeal and disjointed, with no overall responsibility or stewardship for counterterrorism legislation or policy. The country needed a clear, shared, and coordinated strategic approach to countering terrorism, including the ability to identify emerging threats. It recommended creating a new national security and intelligence agency to provide comprehensive strategic policy advice, develop a counterterrorism strategy, and administer relevant national security legislation.

While the Royal Commission's Terms of Reference did not include social cohesion, resilience, or countering violent extremism, after hearing from witnesses, the Commissioners decided that these issues also required serious consideration. They recommended the government lead an 'honest and transparent discussion', engaging and consulting with all parts of the community – particularly Muslim members – and provide public-facing policy on social cohesion and countering terrorism. Overall, the Royal Commission report noted that New Zealand was regarded as having 'a high level of social cohesion, but underlying vulnerabilities and issues remain that are yet to be fully addressed'.

Concluding remarks and future challenges

On 3 September 2021 a Sri Lankan ISIS supporter committed a terrorist attack at a supermarket in Auckland, stabbing and injuring eight people. The attacker had been in prison following his conviction on other terrorism offences and was under surveillance at the time of the attack; he was shot dead by police at the scene.

A year earlier, the perpetrator had faced court in a case that once again highlighted the problem of New Zealand's laws not including preparing for terrorist attacks as offences. With the memory of Christchurch still fresh, legislators were spurred into action. Their draft amendment bill was before Parliament at the time of the 2021 Auckland attack and its passage was fast-tracked.

The Auckland attack is a stark reminder that violent extremism remains a threat to New Zealand, and that the country still needs to do more to deal with the threat at home. From its existing multilateral and bilateral counterterrorism relationships, particularly with Australia, New Zealand has access to leading research, intelligence, policy, and practice to support its deliberations on the way ahead. Key policy gaps that need to be addressed as a priority are well-known from previous reviews as well as the findings of the Royal Commission. These include the need for a comprehensive counterterrorism strategy and to establish a counterterrorism work programme and priority-setting mechanism, confirm agency roles, responsibilities and coordination, regularise reporting and evaluation, and embed stakeholder consultation (RCIC 2020). A surprising finding from the Royal Commission was how little public discussion and debate occurred on approaches to countering violent extremism, given New Zealand's open democracy and active media. Public consultation and political negotiations can be challenging but are essential to developing informed and inclusive policy.

New Zealand is in a comparatively strong position to progress these changes. While other countries are trying to build social cohesion and resilience to violent extremism, New Zealand's reaction to the Christchurch attack showed that it has already achieved this most elusive of tasks (Carroll 2019). Ungar (2008) defines resilience as being evident 'in the context of exposure to significant adversity'; that is, resilience is apparent only when it is tested. New Zealand's compassionate and considered response to the Christchurch attack also garnered support at home and abroad, and the recommendations of the Royal Commission gives impetus to multiparty political support for any proposed legislative and policy changes.

The practicalities of change can be worked through if there is the will. Here, however, New Zealand faces a conceptual dilemma: how to invest in and progress long-term and multifaceted projects to counter violent extremism if terrorism continues to be seen as an occasional aberration rather than an existential threat?

New Zealand's status as a bicultural country provides a firm foundation for ongoing social cohesion. The principles of *Te Tiriti O Waitangi* and its policy focus on equity, consultation, and accountability could provide the basis for a successful multicultural policy and shepherd New Zealand's increasingly diverse community into a resilient future.

The events of 15 March 2019 in New Zealand showed that terrorism can strike anywhere, even in places that appear peaceful, safe, and remote from the threat of violent extremism. Closer examination shows that New Zealand has experienced terrorism more than is popularly understood by both the public and officials: a mismatch in comprehending the impact of terrorism that reinforced a relatively immature approach to counterterrorism at home. This contrasts with the country's relatively high level of international engagement and collaboration on countering violent extremism, including deep practical engagement with Australia.

New Zealand is well placed to effectively counter violent extremism. It has survived a major terrorist attack in a position of strength and unity, and has the benefit of a powerful and far-reaching independent inquiry in the Christchurch Royal Commission. It is in good international standing and, through the Christchurch Call to Action, contributions to Afghanistan, and ongoing UN work, has close and effective working relations with many governments, multilateral organisations, and businesses. New Zealand's special relationship with Australia, further supported by the Five Eyes security arrangement, means that it also has access to high-quality support in understanding both the threat and the best policy, programmatic, and operational responses. As a small state with many competing priorities, however, the challenge will be how to get the balance right.

Developing and maintaining a counterterrorism strategy and supporting programme of work to guide the efforts of the various agencies and civil society members is a crucial starting point for success. While it is difficult to talk publicly about security and to engage with diverse stakeholders, this is essential if New Zealand is to be best-placed to understand the ongoing threat and to mobilise its polity, institutions, and society to work together to counter it. The Royal Commission has demonstrated the need for an effective strategy, improved prioritisation and coordination, and greater community consultation. But this will not be possible without a change in how New Zealanders perceive the threat of terrorism.

Perhaps the most powerful lesson from the Christchurch terrorist attack is that, while societies cannot stop violent extremism, they can control its impact – should they choose to take on the responsibility.

References

Ardern, Rt Hon. J. (2019) Ministerial statements: Mosques terror attacks – Christchurch. *New Zealand Parliament Hansard (Debates)*, 19 March, www.parliament.nz/en/pb/hansard-debates/rhr/combined/HansDeb_20190319_20190319_08

Australia-New Zealand Counter-Terrorism Committee (2017) Australia's strategy for protecting crowded places from terrorism, www.nationalsecurity.gov.au/australias-strategy-protecting-crowded-places-terrorism.pdf

Ayson, R. (2014) New Zealand's weeks of risk aversion on ISIS. *The Strategist*, 4 November, www.aspistrategist.org.au/new-zealands-weeks-of-risk-aversion-on-isis/

Ayson, R. (2017) Will the Ardern government transform New Zealand's foreign and defence policies? *The Strategist*, 27 October, www.aspistrategist.org.au/will-the-ardern-government-transform-new-zealands-foreign-and-defence-policies/

Battersby, J. (2018) Terrorism where terror is not: Australian and New Zealand terrorism compared. *Studies in Conflict & Terrorism*, 41(1), pp. 59–76.

Battersby, J. and Ball, R. (2019) Christchurch in the context of New Zealand terrorism and right-wing extremism. *Journal of Policing, Intelligence and Counter Terrorism*, 14(3), pp. 191–207.

Birkland, T.A. (2014) 'The world changed today': Agenda-setting and policy change in the wake of the September 11 terrorist attacks 21. *Review of Policy Research*, 21(2), pp. 179–200.

Brady, A.M. (2019) Small can be huge: New Zealand foreign policy in an era of global uncertainty. In: Brady, A.M. (ed.), *Small States and the Changing Global Order*. The World of Small States, vol 6. Cham: Springer.

Carroll, J. (2016) Australia's experience of Daesh-linked and directed extremism. In: Gunaratna, R., Gorawantschy, B., Sarmah, M. and Rueppel, P. (eds), *Panorama: Countering Daesh Extremism*. Bonn: Konrad Adenauer Stiftung, www.kas.de/en/web/politikdialog-asien/laenderberichte/detail/-/content/countering-daesh-extremism-european-and-asian-responses1

Carroll, J. (2019) Dignity, inclusiveness and the power to change: The aftermath of the Christchurch attack. *The Strategist*, 20 March,www.aspistrategist.org.au/dignity-inclusiveness-and-the-power-to-change-the-aftermath-of-the-christchurch-attack/

Carroll, J. (2020) The Christchurch terrorist attack – one year on. *The Strategist*, 18 March, www.aspistrategist.org.au/the-christchurch-terrorist-attack-one-year-on/

Collins, D. (2007) Media statement: Decision of the Solicitor-General in relation to the prosecution of people under the Terrorism Suppression Act 2002 ('Operation 8'), 8 November, https://img.scoop.co.nz/media/pdfs/0711/SolGenTerror.pdf

Council of Australian Governments (2012) *Variation to the Intergovernmental Agreement on Australia's National Counter-Terrorism Arrangements*, 8 September, https://federation.gov.au/sites/default/files/about/agreements/ANZCTC%20Variation%20-%20signed.pdf

Dole, N. and Ford, M. (2019) Christchurch schoolboys perform haka in show of respect for attack victims. *ABC News*, 18 March, www.abc.net.au/news/2019-03-18/teens-perform-haka-to-show-respect-to-christchurch-victims/10912140

Foley, F. (2013) *Countering Terrorism in Britain and France*. Cambridge: Cambridge University Press.

Graham, K. (2021) ANZUS at 70: How does New Zealand view the treaty today? *Australian Outlook*, 18 September, www.internationalaffairs.org.au/australianoutlook/anzus-at-70-how-does-new-zealand-view-the-treaty-today/

Grossman, M. Hadfield, K., Jefferies, P., Gerrand, V. and Ungar, M. (2020) Youth resilience to violent extremism: Development and validation of the BRAVE-14 measure. *Terrorism and Political Violence*, 34(3), pp. 468–488, DOI:10.1080/09546553.2019.1705283

Hunt, E. (2021) 'Diversity dilemma': World's most inclusive parliament still faces battle for change. *The Guardian*, 8 February, www.theguardian.com/world/2021/feb/08/diversity-dilemma-worlds-most-inclusive-parliament-still-faces-battle-for-change-new-zealand

Institute for Economics and Peace (2021) *Global Peace Index 2021*, www.visionofhumanity.org

Ip, J. (2021) Law's response to New Zealand's 'darkest of days'. *Common Law World Review*, 50(1), pp. 21–37, DOI:10.1177/1473779521989340

Koziol, M. (2019) Christchurch shooter's manifesto reveals an obsession with white supremacy over Muslims. *The Sydney Morning Herald*, 15 March, www.smh.com.au/world/oceania/christchurch-shooter-s-manifesto-reveals-an-obsession-with-white-supremacy-over-muslims-20190315-p514ko.html

Lyons, K. (2019) New Zealand brings in sweeping gun law changes in wake of Christchurch attacks. *The Guardian Online*, 21 March, www.theguardian.com/world/2019/mar/21/new-zealand-brings-in-sweeping-gun-law-changes-in-wake-of-christchurch-attacks

McGarrity, N. and Blackbourn, J. (2016) Anti-terrorism laws and human rights. In: Weber, L., Fishwick, E. and Marmo, M. (eds), *The Routledge International Handbook of Criminology and Human Rights*. Routledge International Handbooks. New York: Routledge, pp.136–145.

Metz, I., Ng, E., Cornelius, N., Hoobler, J. and Nkomo, S. (2016) A comparative review of multiculturalism in Australia, Canada, the United Kingdom, the United States and South Africa. In: Klarsfeld, A., Ng, E., Booysen, L., Christiansen, L. and Kuvaas, Bård, B. (eds.), *Research Handbook of International and Comparative Perspectives on Diversity Management*. Cheltenham, UK: Edward Elgar Publishing, pp. 131–170.

Morrison, S. and Huygens, Ingrid L. M. (2019) Explainer: The significance of the Treaty of Waitangi. *The Conversation*, 6 February, https://theconversation.com/explainer-the-significance-of-the-treaty-of-waitangi-110982

New Zealand Foreign Affairs and Trade (n.d.). *Counter Terrorism*, www.mfat.govt.nz/en/peace-rights-and-security/international-security/international-security/

New Zealand Ministry for Culture and Heritage (n.d.) Crime timeline. *New Zealand History*, https://nzhistory.govt.nz/culture/nz-crime-timeline

New Zealand Government (n.d.) Christchurch call to eliminate terrorist and violent extremist content online, www.christchurchcall.com

New Zealand Security Intelligence Service (NZSIS) (n.d.) National terrorism threat level, www.nzsis.govt.nz/our-work/counter-terrorism/national-terrorism-threat-level/

Peucker, M., and Smith, D. (2019) Conclusion: Making sense of the far-right in Australia. In: Peucker, M., and Smith, D. (eds), *The Far-Right in Contemporary Australia*. Palgrave Macmillan, Singapore, DOI:10.1007/978-981-13-8351-9_10

Rapoport, D.C. (2004) The four waves of modern terrorism. In: Cronin, A.K. and Ludes, J.M. (eds), *Attacking terrorism: Elements of a grand strategy*. Washington, DC: Georgetown University Press, pp. 46–73.

Rapoport, D.C. (2013) The four waves of modern terror: International dimensions and consequences. In: Hanhimäki, J.M. and Blumenau, B. (eds), *An International History of Terrorism: Western and Non-Western Experiences*. London: Routledge.

Rapoport, D.C. (2021) The Capitol attack and the 5th terrorism wave. *Terrorism and Political Violence*, 33(5), pp. 912–916.

RCIC (2020) The Royal Commission of inquiry into the terrorist attacks on Christchurch mosques on 15 March 2019, *Ko tō tātou kāinga tēnei Report: Royal Commission of Inquiry into the terrorist attacks on Christchurch masjidain on 15 March 2019*, https://christchurchattack.royalcommission.nz/the-report/

Sonderby, C. (2019) Update on New Zealand. *Facebook*, 18 March, https://about.fb.com/news/2019/03/update-on-new-zealand/

Spoonley, P. (2015) New diversity, old anxieties in New Zealand: The complex identity politics and engagement of a settler society. *Ethnic and Racial Studies*, 38(4), pp. 650–661.

Stats NZ (2018) 2018 Census Ethnic Group Summaries, www.stats.govt.nz/tools/2018-census-ethnic-group-summaries/

Thorhallsson, B. (2019) Small states and the changing global order: What small state theory can offer New Zealand foreign policymaking. In: Brady, A.M. (ed.), *Small States and the Changing Global Order*. The World of Small States, vol 6. Cham: Springer, pp. 379–395.

Ungar, M. (2008) Putting resilience theory into action: Five principles for intervention. *Resilience in Action*. Toronto: University of Toronto Press, pp. 17–36, DOI:10.3138/9781442688995-003

United Nations Security Council (2014) *Security Council Resolution 2178 (2014)*, 24 September, https://documents-dds-ny.un.org/doc/UNDOC/GEN/N14/547/98/PDF/N1454798.pdf

United Nations Security Council Counter-Terrorism Committee Executive Directorate (2016), *Implementation of Security Council Resolution 2178 (2014) by States affected by foreign terrorist fighters*

White, H. (2011) New Zealand's strategic options in the Asian century: An Australian view. *Security Challenges*, 7(1), pp. 45–60.

Williams, G. (2011) A decade of Australian anti-terror laws. *Melbourne University Law Review*, 35(3), pp. 1136–1176.

18
CANADA

Sara K. Thompson

Introduction

Canada has a long history of extremist violence, though it differs from many other Western nations in that these incidents have been fewer and, with the exception of the Air India bombing in 1985 that killed 329 people, generally less lethal (MacLeod 2011; Littlewood, Thompson and Dawson 2020). Nevertheless, violent extremism in Canada is more common than is generally perceived; Tishler et al. (2020) show that Canada faced more than 1,846 incidents of this violence between 1960 and 2015, both at home and abroad. These figures, scholars have argued, chafe against the country's international reputation as a 'peaceable kingdom' (Charters 2008; See 2018).

The predominant organisations and ideologies that have shaped extremist violence in Canada have shifted over time and across regions (Charters 2008; Tishler et al. 2020). In the 1960s and 1970s, there were surges in extremist activity committed by the Sons of Freedom in British Columbia and the Front de Liberation du Quebec (FLQ) in Quebec (religiously motivated and politically motivated radical groups, respectively), followed by a decline in incidents by the mid-1970s, which scholars generally attribute to the 'subsequent demise' of these movements (Tishler et al. 2020, p. 29). There were upticks in incidents associated with various factions of international extremism that used Canada as a base for addressing foreign grievances in the 1980s, and subsequent increases in the 2000s related to threats and incidents associated with environmental and what is often and problematically (see Purwanto & Fenton, 2022; Hakim, 2016) called jihadi-inspired extremism (Berube and Ducol 2020; Joosse 2017; Tishler et al. 2020). Environmental extremism in this period was concentrated in Ontario and along the British Columbia/Alberta border, with 11 incidents occurring over a five-year period (2005–2009). In Ontario, the Earth Liberation Front perpetrated three arson attacks against targeted businesses and construction sites, while the remaining eight incidents involved attacks in Canada's western provinces perpetrated by unidentified 'eco-terrorists' and targeting the oil and gas industry, usually with explosives (Tishler et al. 2020). So-called jihadi extremism in the period 2000–2015, on the other hand, involved different manifestations of 'homegrown extremism': Canadian citizens radicalising to violence and leaving Canada to take up arms with extremist groups in other countries (see, for example, Dawson and Amarasingam 2020), and attacks on Canadian soil perpetrated by Canadian citizens (for example, the October 2014 vehicle ramming attack that injured one and killed a second Canadian soldier in Saint-Jean-sur-Richelieu, Quebec, followed by the killing of Corporal Nathan Cirillo as he stood on ceremonial sentry duty at the Canadian National War Memorial in Ottawa, Ontario, two days later). The post-2000 period also evidenced increases in forms of ideologically motivated extremist activity (defined below), which is diverse in its manifestations and remains among the more salient threats to national security in Canada today (CSIS 2022; Perry and Scrivens 2016, 2019).

More recently, though the long-term effects of the Covid-19 pandemic on extremist violence in Canada remain to be seen, there is widespread concern in many nations that the pandemic has already increased the threat of extremist violence and has made counterterrorism and P/CVE work more challenging (United Nations 2022; see also McNeil-Willson in this volume; Gerrand in this volume). Indeed, a recent public report prepared by the Canadian Security Intelligence Service (CSIS 2022, p. 7) argues that the 'continued impact of the Covid-19 pandemic has reinforced the unpredictability of the current [threat] environment', which includes manifestations of ideologically motivated violent extremism (IMVE) – a category that spans xenophobic violence (i.e., racially motivated and ethno-nationalist violence), identity-driven violence (including misogyny, incel and anti-LGBTQ violence), anti-authority violence (anti-government/ anti-law enforcement and anarchist violence), and other grievance-driven and ideologically motivated forms of extremist violence (CSIS 2022). Additional current national security threats facing Canada are extremist travellers – colloquially known as 'foreign fighters' – who left Canada to take up arms in conflict zones overseas; some have survived and returned home, often with young families in tow. International terrorism, most notably that which involves groups like Al-Qaida and Daesh, also continues to pose a threat to Canada (CSIS 2022).

And finally, a series of complex grievances related to the Covid-19 pandemic and associated government-imposed restrictions have taken root, most notably in the form of protests of varying size and intensity across the country – though the extent to which these movements involve a pronounced extremist element remains to be determined. The convoys and related protests and demonstrations that occurred across the country since the pandemic began exemplify the variegated – but ultimately related – anti-vax, anti-government grievances, fuelled by misinformation and disinformation that are driving discontent in some segments of the Canadian population.

As the pandemic spread across Canada, Asian communities experienced surges in hate crime victimisation; in 2020, there was a 301 percent increase in police-reported hate crimes against East and Southeast Asian Canadians, compared to the previous year (Wang and Moreau 2022). And finally, 'shifting power structures posing new and complex challenges to the international rules-based order' further complicate the existing threat landscape – with recent and notable examples including the fall of Afghanistan to the Taliban in August 2021 and the Russian invasion of Ukraine in February 2022 (CSIS 2022, p. 7). More than ever before, the threat landscape in Canada is heterogeneous and complex, consisting variously of established and organised groups, cells, so-called lone wolves, and disorganised, loosely affiliated entities espousing a spectrum of belief systems that are disseminated and bolstered in face-to-face and online relationships and contexts (Littlewood et al. 2020).

This chapter proceeds in six sections. The first provides an overview of the social impacts of extremist violence, followed by a discussion of some of the documented harms that stem from Canada's traditional and disproportionate reliance on reactive, enforcement-based approaches for responding to this violence. Next, the chapter examines what is currently known about polarisation in Canada and how evidence of increasing polarisation, coupled with concerns about the complex threat landscape described above, prompted a 'felt need' to expand the national security apparatus to include a host of prevention/intervention-based programmes and activities. This is followed by an overview of select intervention-based P/CVE programming that is currently operational in different parts of the country. The chapter concludes with some final thoughts on the value of lessons learned in other nations for the development of P/CVE programming in Canada, emerging evidence that speaks to the shifting nature of some extremist categories among some clients of this programming, and the value of integrating an evidence-based ethos to support the development of robust and adaptive P/CVE programming capable of attending to a breadth of existing, emerging, and evolving security threats.

Social impacts

The social impacts of violent extremism are well documented at various levels of analysis, affecting individuals, their families, the broader community, and society more generally (see, for example, Ahmad 2020; Bhadi 2003; Jacoby 2016). These include physical harm experienced by those who are directly victimised by or who otherwise experience a violent extremist event, along with emotional and psychological impacts, such as post-traumatic stress disorder, stress, depression, anxiety, and fear (Lee and Lemyre 2009; Norris 2005). Research also demonstrates that experiencing extremist violence can elicit specific behavioural responses that involve avoiding exposure to certain activities, places or people perceived to be potentially high risk (Eisenman et al. 2006; Fischoff et al. 2004; Goodwin et al. 2005; Huddy et al. 2002).

There are also documented social impacts that stem from traditional (i.e., legislative, disruption- and enforcement-based) approaches for preventing and responding to extremist violence in Canada (see, for example, Ahmad 2020; Millett and Ahmad 2021; Lenard and Nagra 2020; Jiwani 2021). As in other nations, hastily implemented and sweeping legislation in the wake of 9/11, and again following the October 2014 attacks in Saint-Jean-sur-Richelieu, Quebec, and in Ottawa, Ontario, has caused disproportionate harm to Muslim communities in Canada (Ahmad 2020; Forcese and Roach 2015a, 2015b; Roach 2018). Research highlights a series of backlash effects stemming from this legislation and from more general narratives that draw explicit and stereotypical connections between Muslim communities and extremist violence, including increased surveillance, racial profiling, and the suspension of civil liberties (Bhadi 2003; Ellis and Abdi 2017; Jacoby 2016). Muslim Canadians have also experienced significant increases in hate crime victimisation since 9/11, highlighting one within a broader nexus of possible relationships that may exist between terrorist violence and hate crime. This is illustrative of research that suggests hate crime is sometimes perpetrated in response to acts of terrorism as a form of vicarious retribution against innocent members of the group thought to be responsible for the terrorist act. (Benier 2016; Kara and Merali 2020; Mills et al. 2017).

In addition to spikes in hate-motivated crimes, there have also been recent and high-profile incidents of extremist violence against Muslim Canadians. For example, in January 2017, an armed White nationalist and ardent Trump supporter went on a shooting rampage at an Islamic Cultural Centre in Sainte-Foy, Quebec, killing six and injuring 19; in June 2021, a 20-year-old White man rammed his pick-up truck into a Muslim-Pakistani Canadian family who were out for an evening walk, killing four and orphaning a young boy. Such incidents can contribute to feelings of fear and alienation, which can operate to shape the Muslim Canadian experience of well-being, belonging (Lenard and Bagra, 2020; Rousseau et al. 2011).

Canada's proximity to the US raises additional concerns about the potential that deeply polarising populist politics and related narratives, which are disseminated by media and regularly consumed in Canada, will exacerbate existing polarisation, divisions, and grievances therein (McLay and Ramos 2021). There is a related concern about so-called contagion effects related to recent spates of mass casualty attacks in the US, some of which appear to be motivated by White supremacist extremist ideology and belief systems, which many worry will provide fodder for copycat violence in Canada as well (Brown 2022).

Polarisation in Canada

There is evidence to support concerns about polarisation in Canada and its negative effects. While the US is often treated as 'ground zero for political polarisation, Canada does not appear to be experiencing polarisation to nearly the same degree' (McLay and Ramos 2021, p. 2). Nevertheless, polarising rhetoric and division that have attended the rise of populist politics in other nations are present in Canada as well, though for the most part, attempts to import far-right politics into Canadian electoral politics have not been altogether successful. Nevertheless, many Canadians continue to express deep concern over the potential that incendiary, US-style populism might take root, and some Canadian scholars have articulated concern about growth within and the proliferation of right-wing groups in recent years, along with concerns about the potential for extremist violence perpetrated by members of some of these groups (Parent and Ellis 2014; Perry and Scrivens 2018).

At the same time, other Canadian scholarship raises questions about the extent to which these groups (or members thereof) are violent in their orientation (see, for example, Tetrault 2021, 2022), arguing that extremism tends to be assumed based on scholarship from other nations rather than being empirically demonstrated in the Canadian context. This ethnographic research, which examined right-wing groups and politics in Alberta, demonstrated that the leadership and members of many of these groups fetishise law enforcement and eschew violence, at least in part to help to secure the legitimacy of and help to 'grow' the broader movement. Simply put: more research is required to gain a fulsome understanding of the nature of right-wing groups in Canada and the potential security threats they may pose.

An as-yet small Canadian research literature suggests that there is regional variation in terms of the forms of polarisation that manifest in Canada and their prevalence across regions (Banting and Soroka 2020; McLay and Ramos 2021). For example, Canada's western provinces have long been described as hotbeds for ultra-conservative and populist politics, political affiliations that are, in large part, premised upon and facilitated by various forms of political and ideological polarisation (Quan 2016). By comparison, in Canada's Atlantic provinces – which are disproportionately White, rural, and economically depressed – polarisation is comparatively 'rare and unlikely' (McLay and Ramos 2021, p. 10), though there appears to be a 'tiny proportion [who] hold very conservative views, and they may also be highly engaged on contentious matters and in polarising debates, especially on immigration and tolerance for socio-cultural diversity in Canada' (ibid.). That polarisation is not more pronounced in Atlantic Canada, a region that is disproportionately rural and White provides 'an important counterexample to common arguments made about political attitudes endemic in rural, White locales in North America', and highlights the need for more research in 'understudied ... Canadian provinces' (ibid., p. 2). Indeed, the bulk of Canadian scholarship on these issues has focused on the western provinces (most notably Alberta) or on

Quebec, with a particular emphasis on the distinct political cultures in those provinces (see, for example, Sayers and Stewart 2013; Banting and Soroka 2020). More research is needed to gain a comprehensive understanding of the existence and extent of polarisation in other Canadian provinces and territories, particularly of late.

Regional differences notwithstanding, some research points to signs of increasing political polarisation in Canada since at least the 1980s (Cochrane 2015; McLay and Ramos 2021), with evidence suggesting that Canadian politics 'may be experiencing a "flattening" of multiple political dimensions onto a single liberal-conservative dimension, similar to the bifurcation observed in two-party systems like the US' (McLay and Ramos 2021, p. 4; see also Hare and Poole 2014). Other cross-national research that examined political polarisation in the context of the Covid-19 pandemic in Canada, the US, and the UK found that Canada and the US were more alike than they were different in terms of levels of political polarisation, though there was 'some evidence' that this polarisation is greater in the US context (Pennycook et al. 2022, p. 761). Further, political polarisation appears to have increased exponentially between March and December 2020 in all three nations, most especially in the US (Pennycook et al. 2022). It was in this broader context of increasing polarisation, particularly over the last decade, accompanied by a progressively heterogeneous and complex threat landscape, that a felt need to expand the national security apparatus in Canada to include prevention and intervention activities came to the fore. This paved the way for the introduction and implementation of various approaches to P/CVE, selected examples of which will be discussed below.

The response

To respond to the threat landscape described above, Canada, like many countries around the world, sought to enhance its national security apparatus, traditionally reactive and enforcement-based in nature, to include a host of measures aimed at preventing and intervening in situations involving actual or suspected radicalisation to violence. This concept has been widely adopted among academics and practitioners for understanding varied and non-linear pathways to extremist violence (Borum 2011; Bjorgo and Horgan 2009; McCauley and Moskalenko, 2008). Relative to other nations, however, the advent and implementation of P/CVE programming in Canada got off to a 'slow start' (Roach 2018, p. 596), largely due to a lack of political will on the part of then Prime Minister Stephen Harper's Conservative government. Though Harper's government passed legislation (Bill C-51) containing sprawling new counterterrorism powers in the wake of October 2014 attacks in Saint-Jean-sur-Richelieu and Ottawa, this legislation did not contain any measures aimed at addressing the root causes of extremist violence (Roach and Forcese 2015). In a broader international context that evidenced increasing concern about extremist violence emanating from *within* rights-based, multicultural societies, this omission was significant. Indeed, the mid-2000s saw the proliferation of prevention/intervention-based approaches in many nations that were aimed at understanding and addressing so-called 'homegrown' terroristic and extremist violence that occurs after a process of radicalisation to violence (Brouillette-Alarie et al. 2022).

Canada's comparatively slow start to 'doing P/CVE' did, however, provide opportunities to learn from successes and mistakes in other nations (Kubicek and King 2021; Roach 2018). In early 2012, the government published its first counterterrorism strategy, which was composed of four strands: prevent, detect, deny, and respond. The prevent strand represented the first time the Canadian government publicly communicated its aim to 'prevent individuals from turning to terrorism ... [by addressing] the factors that may motivate individuals to engage in terrorist activities and building resilience to withstand violent extremist ideologies and challenge those who espouse them' (Kubicek and King 2021, p. 185). It was, however, not until 2015 that the prevent strand was operationalised and P/CVE programming began to be implemented in Canada – a development facilitated by the emergence of political will on the part of all three national parties to 'prioritise community outreach and counter-radicalisation' (Kubicek and King 2021, p. 188). This set the stage for the design and implementation of the Office of Community Outreach and Counter-radicalisation Coordinator, later renamed as the Canada Centre for Community Engagement and Prevention of Violence (hereafter the Canada Centre). In 2015, the Prime Minister mandated the Minister of Public Safety Canada to develop the Canada Centre; the 2016 Budget allocated $35 million over five years, with an additional and ongoing $10 million per year to establish the Canada Centre and support its work (Canada Centre 2018).

Officially launched in 2017 and housed at Public Safety Canada headquarters in Ottawa, the Canada Centre is composed of a group of professionals with varied expertise; as a centre of excellence, the Canada Centre provides national leadership and coordination on Canada's P/CVE efforts. (ibid.). The Government of Canada, Public Safety Canada, and the Canada Centre have all made clear public statements that they are concerned with all forms of violent extremism. The spectrum of extremist types is organised into the following typology (CSIS 2019):

Ideologically Motivated Violent Extremism (IMVE). There are four general categories of IMVE:
- Xenophobic and/or racially motivated violence
- Anti-authority violence: anti-government violence, violence against law enforcement, anarchist violence
- Identity-driven violence: violent misogyny, anti-LGBTQ2S violence
- Other grievance-driven and ideologically motivated violence: violence committed by individuals with no association to an organised group or external organisation.

*Politically Motivated Violent Extremism (PMVE)***:** the use of violence to create political systems or instil new structures or norms within existing systems.

Religiously motivated violent extremism (RMVE): the use of violence as part of a spiritual confliction against a perceived immoral system.

The Canada Centre's mandate is four-fold: it provides national leadership and coordination on Canada's efforts to prevent and counter extremist violence, including providing policy guidance (the Canada Centre developed the *National Strategy on Countering Radicalisation to Violence*); it promotes coordination and collaboration with a range of actors (all levels of government, communities and community organisations, front-line workers and practitioners, academics, and police) to respond to local realities and prevent radicalisation to violence; it funds, plans, and coordinates research and mobilises evidence to reach front-line workers and practitioners working to prevent radicalisation to violence; and, it provides targeted programming and funding earmarked for P/CVE initiatives in Canada (Public Safety Canada 2022).

It is important to note that the Canada Centre does not design, implement or oversee P/CVE programming, nor is it involved in case management. Instead, it concentrates its efforts on providing support to front-line practitioners and researchers. In the wake of a cross-country 'road trip' that involved extensive engagement and consultation with diverse stakeholders, in 2018, the Canada Centre published its National Strategy on Countering Radicalisation to Violence.

National Strategy on Countering Radicalisation to Violence

The National Strategy on Countering Radicalisation to Violence specifies the federal government's approach to preventing and intervening in cases of suspected or actual radicalisation to violence (Canada Centre 2018). Intended to be a nimble framework that guides prevention- and intervention-based activities and that can be tailored to local specificities and emerging threats, the National Strategy has three main purposes. First, to raise awareness by providing a series of online informational supports on what is currently known about radicalisation to violence and the destructive and harmful behaviours involved. These supports are produced and disseminated by the Canada Centre to better position frontline practitioners and community members to prevent radicalisation to violence. Second, to outline the Government of Canada's approach to preventing and countering radicalisation to violence through efforts that fall within three broad categories: early prevention (akin to primary prevention in the public health framework), at-risk prevention (secondary prevention), and disengagement (tertiary prevention) from violent ideologies. In addition to preventing radicalisation to violence, the National Strategy also recognises that there is increasing concern about expressions of hate and intolerance in the online and public spheres, and is premised on notions of increasing individual and group resilience to all forms of extremist and hate-motivated violence. Third, following extensive consultation with stakeholders, the public and international experts, the Canada Centre identified three priorities that provide a focus for their activities and investments over the short term, with an eye toward building collective capacity to 'do' P/CVE work in Canada (Canada Centre 2018). These are building, sharing, and using knowledge; addressing radicalisation to violence in the online space; and, supporting interventions with training, funding, and capacity-building within and between multi-agency programs.

The third priority has seen considerable funding earmarked for the development, operation, and evaluation of intervention-based P/CVE programming in Canada. The next section provides an overview of select intervention models currently operational in Canada, disaggregated into three main categories: police co-led situation tables (built into existing violence prevention programming or created as standalone P/CVE-specific models), social polarisation teams, and other multi-agency programming models. All the programming described below is primarily or fully funded by Public Safety Canada's Community Resilience Fund. It is important to note that currently most jurisdictions within Canadian provinces and territories do not have operational P/CVE intervention programming; the models discussed here therefore currently take on 'out of catchment' and sometimes 'out of province/territory' clients as a stop-gap measure.

Examples of select intervention-based P/CVE programming in Canada

Though often implied more than explicitly specified, the dual concepts of polarisation and resilience underpin P/CVE programming in Canada. For example, a central function of the National Strategy on Countering Radicalised Violence is to 'build resilience against violent extremism, as well as to build capacity to intervene with individuals who are at risk of – or who already are – radicalising to violence' (Canada Centre 2018). Doing so requires addressing the root causes of this violence, which includes efforts to mitigate polarisation's social impacts. Given Canada's enormous geographic size and significant regional variation, adopting a 'one-size-fits-all' approach to P/CVE would preclude the ability to tailor this programming to local contexts, which research shows is imperative to understanding and addressing different manifestations of extremist violence (Rosand 2021; Lowndes and Thorp 2010; Sommers 2019). As such, Canada's approach to P/CVE programming involves prioritising the development of programming that emerges from context-specific local needs (see, for example, Canada Centre 2018; Thompson and Leroux 2022). As the following examples illustrate, intervention-based P/CVE programming in Canada is diverse, at different stages of development, and involves different combinations of government and non-government stakeholders and partners (Kubicek and King 2021; Thompson and Leroux 2022).

Police co-led situation tables

The Canadian situation table model is characterised by multi-agency response teams of representatives from local police services, social and human service agencies, schools, representatives from the Correctional Service of Canada, housing, health, and other locally relevant community partners. The collaborative process involves regular meetings wherein deidentified 'situations' (i.e., individuals referred to the tables) are introduced by representatives of participating agencies. Situations that meet the inclusion criterion of 'acutely elevated risk' (AER) – meaning that they are at imminent risk of victimisation, the perpetration of harm, or both – are then accepted by the table. Participating agencies with the requisite scope and expertise to provide supports work together to design and deploy an intervention, whose initial element is intended to take place within 24–48 hours of an AER designation.

Canadian situation tables attend to a variety of risk categories (or combinations thereof), including: addictions and mental health issues, criminal victimisation and offending, poor physical health or self-care, lack of social and family support, need for parenting support/parent–child conflict, frequent truancy, inadequate housing, poverty, negative peer and family associations, unemployment, anti-social negative behaviour, and inability to meet basic needs (Bhayani and Thompson 2016; Nilson 2014). Recently, radicalisation to violence was added to the existing list of harms addressed by the FOCUS Toronto (Furthering Our Communities by United Services) suite of situation tables and became the sole focus of Calgary's ReDirect situation table. FOCUS Toronto and Calgary's ReDirect therefore offer examples of two common approaches to implementing P/CVE programming discussed in the research literature: FOCUS Toronto leveraged a pre-existing community violence prevention programme to 'layer-in' a P/CVE mandate, whereas ReDirect was implemented as a standalone, P/CVE-specific programme (Thompson and Leroux, 2022). More detail on both models is provided below.

FOCUS Toronto. FOCUS is a joint initiative of the City of Toronto, the United Way of Greater Toronto, and the Toronto Police Service (TPS) to address community safety and well-being issues across the city. To date, FOCUS Toronto has implemented six tables in different areas of the city. The guiding principle underpinning its approach to P/CVE is that radicalisation to violence is more alike than it is different from other forms of community violence, and consequently can be addressed through more general violence prevention/intervention efforts (Thompson and Leroux 2020, 2022). Between 25 and 55 human and social service agency representatives meet at each of the six situation tables on a weekly basis; deidentified P/CVE 'situations' are referred by the TPS and involved community partners. At the weekly meetings, referred cases are assessed by the table, and only cases meeting the AER inclusion criteria are accepted for P/CVE interventions. It is important to note that

FOCUS Toronto deals with early-stage radicalisation-to-violence and individuals who may be vulnerable to becoming radicalised in the so-called pre-criminal space – i.e., before any related criminality has taken place. FOCUS Toronto does not work with clients in the criminal and post-criminal space, and it does not engage in 'deradicalisation'/disengagement or reintegration-type activities.

Radicalisation to violence is one of a series of potential harms that the FOCUS Toronto situation tables attend to. Following the provision of extensive upskilling and training opportunities to partner agencies affiliated with FOCUS Toronto, the P/CVE function was 'layered in' to FOCUS Toronto table operations in 2015. Between 2017 and 2019, the FOCUS Toronto model was subject to a third-party formative evaluation to provide feedback to stakeholders about programme functioning and some short-term outcomes (also known as proximal outcomes) as well as ensure the programme is operating as intended and that the intended outcomes align with programme activities in such a way as to reasonably expect change on the intended metrics (Graham 2018; Thompson and Leroux 2020, 2022; Yarbrough et al. 2011).

ReDirect. Calgary's ReDirect is a joint initiative spearheaded by the Calgary Police Service and four foundation partners: Calgary Neighbourhoods, the Calgary School Board, Calgary Separate Schools Division (Catholic), and Alberta Health Services. It is a 'programme that works to prevent radicalisation to violence through community education and awareness, as well as prevention and intervention' (ReDirect 2022). ReDirect was introduced in September 2015 as a 'technology pilot', with an eye toward evaluating its impact, strengths and weaknesses prior to full implementation and further growth. Between 2018 and 2020, the Redirect model underwent an independent formative evaluation (the ReDirect evaluation was part of a broader programme of research that involved a formative evaluation of the much larger FOCUS Toronto model as well), which resulted in a re-launching of the initiative in 2020 (Thompson and Leroux, 2020, 2022). Later that year – and following the implementation of the recommendations that stemmed from the evaluation – ReDirect expanded its activities to include some tertiary disengagement-type interventions with individuals 'already adopting extreme beliefs that condone violence, to help them get on a better path' (ReDirect 2022).

Social polarisation teams

Some Canadian jurisdictions have P/CVE programming in the form of social polarisation teams – i.e., networks of mental health practitioners based in local and integrated health and social service centres who specialise in interventions to counter radicalisation to violence. This section provides an overview of two such teams: the Research and Action on Social Polarisation (RASP) team from Montreal, Quebec, and the Estimated Time of Arrival (ETA) programme in Toronto, Ontario.

RASP. The RASP team brings together an interdisciplinary group of researchers and partners to collaborate and 'align knowledge production and local issues in a co-construction process to ensure a thorough understanding and actions that reflect the systemic aspect of violent radicalisation' (CPNPREV 2022). This involves interdisciplinary collaboration in four 'complementary areas of action' – prevention, training, intervention, and research – 'in order to think about [radicalisation to violence] … and respond to it from an ecosystemic perspective' (SHERPA 2022). RASP is but one initiative undertaken by SHERPA University Institute, a research and training centre affiliated with Montreal West Island Integrated University Health and Social Services Centres.

The Polarisation Clinical Team received a mandate from the Quebec Ministry of Health and Social Services in 2015 in the wake of public alarm over a cluster of Montreal students who radicalised and left Canada to take up arms with so-called jihadi groups abroad (Kubicek and King 2021). Today, however, the clinic sees clients whose radicalisation is drawn from a range of social, political, or religious influences (SHERPA 2022). The team includes social workers, psychiatrists, and child psychiatrists with expertise in social polarisation issues and radicalisation leading to violence. Team members do not try to challenge clients' particular ideologies/belief systems; instead, they try to identify and work to address the root causes that fuelled them (ibid.). Treatment options can include counselling, therapy and/or medication, depending on clients' needs. In addition to conducting initial assessments, the clinical team also provides follow-up support, including assistance with education or employment reintegration, along with training for healthcare professionals, community groups, and schools (ibid.).

ETA Toronto. The ETA Toronto programme is another example of social polarisation teams. It is designed and implemented by Yorktown Family Services (YFS), a fully accredited community service agency composed of an integrated services site offering rapid access to multiple mental health, primary health, and social service programmes for youth and young adults (Yorktown Family Services 2022). In 2019, YFS received funding through Public Safety Canada's Community Resilience Fund to outreach, engage, and provide biopsychosocial interventions for youth and young adults involved with, or on the pathway toward, various forms of extremist violence (i.e., extremist and hate-motivated violence). ETA's current catchment area covers all of Toronto and surrounding areas, although the programme has taken service requests from other jurisdictions given the current dearth of intervention supports therein.

ETA uses a variety of evidence-based and evidence-informed psychosocial interactions to engage with clients throughout the continuum of care, including intervention modalities that help facilitate stabilisation of mental health symptoms that may lead to violence, such as impulsivity/emotional dysregulation (Cognitive Behavioural Therapy /Dialectical Behaviour Therapy), trauma (Trauma Focused-Cognitive Behavioural Therapy), oppression created through macro or micro causes (Narrative Therapy), engagement and reducing violence (Motivational Interviewing), engaging with family conflict (Family Systems Therapy), and systems navigation (Intensive Case Management) (ibid.).

In addition to intervention activities, ETA is involved in creating and disseminating informational supports to assist schools and health professionals to inculcate critical thinking and digital media literacy skills among the clients they work with (ibid.). To date, ETA has also provided training and informational supports intended to build knowledge and service capacity related to P/CVE interventions to over 40 organisations and over 1,200 frontline practitioners.

Other approaches to doing P/CVE in Canada

In addition to situation tables and social polarisation teams, P/CVE programming in Canada involves additional collaborative approaches tailored to the local context in which they operate. The Organisation for the Prevention of Violence (OPV) in Edmonton, Alberta, and the Canadian Practitioner's Network for the Prevention of Radicalisation and Extremist Violence (CPN-PREV) are notable examples.

The OPV. The OPV is composed of a diverse group of practitioners and academics with expertise in P/CVE and other forms of violence and risk reduction in Edmonton, Alberta

(OPV 2022a). Its current programming is designed to fill existing gaps in human and social service provision in the Edmonton area by working with individuals in the so-called pre-criminal space – i.e., before any criminality related to their radicalisation has occurred (OPV 2022b). Acknowledging that 'effective P/CVE programming must recognise and include the concerns, inputs, and leadership of impacted communities', and that '[P]/CVE is most effective when it engenders a multi-sectoral response that includes impacted community groups' (ibid.), the OPV purposefully built in a community-facing approach that includes and involves a host of community-based and practitioner partners in all aspects of programme design and operationalisation.

The OPV's activities are varied and involve the development and dissemination of informational supports on a variety of issues related to P/CVE, hate crime, and extremist violence in Alberta. For example, The Resiliency Project, a collaborative initiative involving the City of Edmonton, the Edmonton Police Service, and the OPV, works with the public to prevent and counter violent extremism through awareness, education, and research (OPV 2022c). This is accomplished via a series of webinars that examine the context of hate and extremist violence in Alberta, as well as the resources available to support people affected by these issues.

A second programme involves the design of a 'community-centric P/CVE pilot programme' in Edmonton that combines local knowledge and expertise with best practices gleaned from relevant Canadian and international research literatures. Launched in April 2019, this pilot project – called the Evolve Program – is an interdisciplinary intervention that provides 'direct support to individuals involved in hate or extremism, their affected family or friends, as well as victims of hate incidents' (ibid.). Currently operational, Evolve's multi-disciplinary team, which includes a forensic psychologist, social workers, and 'specialised mentors' – there are currently three such mentors, two former members of the far-right movement in Canada and an Islamic scholar – provide counselling, trauma-informed care, mentorship, and tailored social supports to clients and their families who are 'looking to disengage from extremist and/or hate-motivated groups' (ibid.). Evolve's intervention activities involve the assessment of needs, risk and protective factors, intervention design and delivery, and the provision of programming and supports via an array of in-house and community partners. Available supports and services include personal and family counselling, religious counselling, mentorship, advocacy, crisis management, addiction support, and assistance with basic needs.

Evolve also provides programming and tailored supports for individuals who have been victimised by hate crimes or incidents (i.e., expressions of hate that do not meet the threshold for laying criminal charges). In so doing, Evolve provides much needed support for victims of hate in a broader climate that is seeing exponential increases in the perpetration of hate crime. The programme is confidential, voluntary, offered at no cost, and independent from government and police. It is slated for evaluation as part of its specified programme activities.

CPN-PREV. The intervention-based P/CVE programming discussed above was operationalised in different local contexts and regions of Canada's vast geography. The P/CVE communities in Canada are generally much smaller and more geographically dispersed than in other nations due in large part to Canada's enormous size and the fact that '[extremism] is a smaller issue in Canada than in its allied countries' (Kubicek and King 2021, p. 183). CPN-PREV was created to mitigate these and other issues, bolster the collaborative capacity of Canadian P/CVE practitioners and programming, and expand and improve access to evidence-based resources tailored to Canadian practitioners (CPN-PREV 2022).

CPN-PREV is an evidence-based and practitioner-centred network established to 'support best practices and collaboration among intervention teams through sustained knowledge mobilisation between researchers, practitioners, policymakers, and various community sectors' (ibid.). It engages in activities in six core areas:

(1) Mapping: CPN-PREV created a living, Canada-wide, interactive map of training, prevention, and intervention-focused P/CVE initiatives, periodically updated as P/CVE programming continues to evolve (cpnprev.ca/the-interactive-map).
(2) Awareness: CPN-PREV gathers, produces, and disseminates informational supports that can be used to improve popular and practitioner understandings of the 'complex and quickly evolving contexts of violent radicalisation, while promoting a non-stigmatising approach' (ibid).
(3) Best Practices: CPN-PREV generates a series of evidence-based best practice guidelines and informational supports on issues related to risk assessment, case management, and P/CVE prevention/intervention activities.
(4) Outreach: CPN-PREV works to bolster collaborative resource development 'by and for practitioners across multiple sectors and disciplines, through capacity building', which is accomplished by engaging and connecting existing Canadian assets doing P/CVE intervention work in areas of high need.
(5) Training: CPN-PREV also creates and provides training modules for practitioners from diverse sectors that are tailored to their specific needs and contexts. Further, CPN-PREV supports local implementation and field tests existing training programmes, toolkits, and other prevention/intervention activities.
(6) Resources: CPN-PREV engages in a 'continuous knowledge mobilisation process including diverse sets of outputs and activities' that are tailored to Canadian practitioners – including generating systematic reviews on exposure to extremist online content leading to violent radicalisation; trajectories and shift markers in and out of violent radicalisation; outcomes of intervention programmes and the balance of their respective benefits and harms; and reliability, validity, and outcomes of screening/assessment measures/tools and the balance of their benefits and harms (ibid.).

Concluding remarks

Compared to other nations, P/CVE programming in Canada is in its relative infancy, with a preponderance of this programming implemented post-2015. This comparatively late start to 'doing P/CVE' enabled practitioners and policymakers in Canada to incorporate lessons learned in other jurisdictions into the design and operation of this programming.

One such lesson involved avoiding P/CVE programming that targets specific communities; the research literature includes numerous cautionary tales related to international P/CVE programming in this regard (see, for example, Lenard and Nagra 2020; Shanaah and Heath-Kelly 2022). In response, the Canadian P/CVE prevention/intervention programming discussed above was specifically developed to work with clients espousing a broad swath of ideologies and belief systems, including a host of subtypes that fall under the banner of IMVE, politically motivated violent extremism (PMVE), and religiously motivated violent extremism (RMVE) (Thompson and Leroux 2020). There is, however, emerging evidence of recent growth in idiosyncratic grievance-driven violence that falls outside these categories (Yorktown Family Services 2022; Thompson and Leroux 2020). For example, some P/CVE practitioners have reported 'ideology switching' wherein an individual tries out different ideologies/belief systems, sometimes switching from one to another and sometimes blending aspects of different grievances and ideologies/belief systems into a hybrid extremism category. These and other shifts in the nature of radicalisation to violence underscore the importance of ensuring that P/CVE programming in Canada is appropriately nimble, adaptive, and able to receive and incorporate into their programme activities new empirical and practice-based evidence on the nature and trajectories of radicalised violence. This leads to the second key lesson learned in other jurisdictions: the importance of incorporating researchers and evidence-based approaches in support of P/CVE policy and practice (Kubicek and King 2021).

One way to integrate an evidence-based ethos to support the development of robust and efficacious P/CVE programming is by conducting evaluations at different stages of programme evolution (Thompson and Leroux 2020, 2022). To date, as discussed above, the FOCUS Toronto and Calgary ReDirect models have been subject to early, formative evaluations, and the other models discussed above are slated for evaluation as well. Indeed, evaluation is built into the very design of programme activities; Public Safety Canada will not fund programming that does not have a specified evaluative component at the design stage. Robust evaluation is critical in the context of violence prevention/intervention programming, given the extensive interdisciplinary literature that highlights the potential for iatrogenic effects (or unintended consequences) that cause rather than repair harm (Welsh et al. 2020; Boxer et al. 2005) but also and more generally in order to better understand what works (or does not), for who, and why (or why not).

Ultimately, programme efficacy can be assessed using an impact or outcome evaluation – though the low base rate associated with P/CVE programming precludes the possibility of evaluation until the programme has been operational for some time. In the interim, early formative/developmental and process evaluations can assist programme stakeholders to ensure that their programming is on track, thereby increasing the likelihood that subsequent outcome or impact evaluations demonstrate the efficacy of this programming over the longer term.

References

Ahmad, F. (2020) The Securitization of Muslim Civil Society in Canada. In: Silva, D.M.D. and Deflem, M. (eds), *Radicalization and Counter-radicalization*. Bingley, UK: Emerald Publishing Limited, pp. 115–133.

Banting, K. and Soroka, S. (2020) A Distinctive Culture? The Sources of Public Support for Immigration in Canada, 1980–2019. *Canadian Journal of Political Science,* 53(4), pp. 821–838.

Benier, K. (2016) Global Terrorism Events and Ensuing Hate Incidents. In: Schweppe, J. and Walters, M.A. (eds), *The Globalization of Hate: Internationalizing Hate Crime*. Oxford: Oxford University Press, pp. 79–95.

Berube, M. and Ducol, B. (2020) Jihadism in the Digital Era. In: Littlewood, J., Dawson, L. and Thompson, S.K. (eds), *Terrorism and Counter-Terrorism in Canada*. Toronto: University of Toronto Press, pp. 101–124.

Bhadi, R. (2003) No Exit: Racial Profiling and Canada's War Against Terrorism. *Osgoode Hall Law Journal,* 41(2/3), pp. 293–318.

Bhayani, G. and Thompson, S.K. (2016) SMART on Social Problems: Lessons Learned from a Canadian Risk-Based Collaborative Intervention Model. *Policing: A Journal of Policy and Practice,* 11(2), pp. 168–184.

Bjorgo, T. and Horgan, J. (2009) *Leaving Terrorism Behind: Individual and Collective Disengagement*. New York: Routledge.

Borum, R. (2011) Radicalization into Violent Extremism I: A Review of Social Science Theories. *Journal of Strategic Security,* 4(4), pp. 7–36.

Boxer, P., Guerra, N.G., Huesmann, L.R. and Morales, J. (2005) Proximal Peer-Level Effects of a Small-Group Selected Prevention Program on Aggression in Elementary School Children: An Investigation of the Peer Contagion Hypothesis. *Journal of Abnormal Child Psychology,* 33, pp. 325–338.

Brouillette-Alarie, S., Hassan, G., Varela, W., Ousman, S., Kilinc, D., Savard, É.L., Madriaza, P., Harris-Hogan, S., McCoy, J., Rousseau, C., King, M., Venkatesh, V., Borokhovski, E. and Pickup, D. (2022) Systematic Review on the Outcomes of Primary and Secondary Prevention Programs in the Field of Violent Radicalization. *Journal for Deradicalization,* 30, pp. 117–168.

Brown, D. (2022) 'Canada is Not Immune' Leading Black Voices Say in Response to Buffalo Mass Shooting. *CBC News,* 16 May, www.cbc.ca/news/canada/toronto/buffalo-shooting-canada-1.6455390

Canada Centre for Community Engagement and Prevention of Violence (2018) *National Strategy on Countering Radicalization to Violence.* Government of Canada, www.publicsafety.gc.ca/cnt/rsrcs/pblctns/ntnl-strtg-cntrng-rdclztn-vlnc/ntnl-strtg-cntrng-rdclztn-vlnc-en.pdf

Charters, D. (2008) *The (Un)Peaceable Kingdom: Terrorism and Canada Before 9/11.* Montreal: Institute for Research on Public Policy, https://irpp.org/research-studies/the-unpeaceable-kingdom/

Cochrane, C. (2015) *Left and Right: The Small World of Political Ideas.* Montreal and Kingston: McGill-Queen's University Press.

CPN-PREV (2021) CPN-PREV Partnerships, https://cpnprev.ca/partners/

CPN-PREV (2022) Prevention of Radicalisation and Extremist Violence in Canada, https://cpnprev.ca/

CSIS (2019) *CSIS Public Report 2019.* Canadian Security Intelligence Service, www.canada.ca/en/security-intelligence-service/corporate/publications/2019-public-report/threats-to-the-security-of-canada-and-canadian-interests.html

CSIS (2022) *CSIS Public Report 2020.* Canadian Security Intelligence Service, www.canada.ca/en/security-intelligence-service/corporate/publications/2020-public-report.html

Dawson, L. and Amarasingam, A. (2020) Canadian Foreign Fighters in Syria and Iraq, 2012–2016. In: Littlewood, J., Dawson, L. and Thompson, S.K. (eds), *Terrorism and Counter-Terrorism in Canada.* Toronto: University of Toronto Press, pp. 49–76.

Eisenman, D.P., Wold, C., Fielding, J., Long, A., Setodji, C., Hickey and S., Gelberg, L. (2006) Differences in Individual-level Terrorism Preparedness in Los Angeles County. *American Journal of Preventive Medicine,* 30, pp. 1–6.

Ellis, H. and Abdi, S. (2017) Building Community Resilience to Violent Extremism Through Genuine Partnerships. *American Psychologist,* 72(3), pp. 289–300.

Fischhoff, B., de Bruine, W.B., Perrin, W., Downs, J. (2004) Travel Risks in a Time of Terror: Judgments and Choices. *Risk Analysis,* 24, pp. 1301–1329.

Forcese, C. and Roach, K. (2015a) Criminalising Terrorist Babble: Canada's Dubious New Terrorist Speech Crime. *Alberta. Law Review,* 53(1), pp. 35–84.

Forcese, C. and Roach, K. (2015b) Bill C-51: The Good, the Bad… and the Truly Ugly. *The Walrus,* 13, ww.sfu.ca/~palys/Forcese&Kent-BillC-51-TheGoodBad&TrulyUgly.pdf

Goodwin, R., Willson, M. and Gaines, S. Jr. (2005) Terror Threat Perception and Its Consequences in Contemporary Britain. *British Journal of Psychology,* 96, pp. 389–406.

Graham, E. (2018) Formative evaluation toolkit. Prepared for the Administration for Children and Families. U.S. Department of Health and Human Services, www.acf.hhs. gov/sites/default/files/cb/formative_evaluation_toolkit.pdf

Hakim, R.T. and Hakim, N. (2016) The Concept of Jihad in Islam. *Journal of Humanities and Social Science,* 21(9), Ver. 7, pp. 35–42.

Hare, C. and Poole, K.T. (2014) The Polarisation of Contemporary American Politics. *Polity,* 46(3), pp. 411–429.

Huddy L., Feldman S., Capelos T. and Provost C. (2002) The Consequences of Terrorism: Disentangling the Effects of Personal and National Threat. *Political Psychology,* 23(3), pp. 485–509.

Jacoby, A. (2016) How the War Was 'One': Countering Violent Extremism and the Social Dimensions of Counter-Terrorism in Canada. *Journal for Deradicalization,* pp. 272–304.

Jiwani, Y. (2021) Gendered Islamophobia in the Case of the Returning ISIS Women: A Canadian Narrative. *Islamophobia Studies Journal,* 6(1), pp. 52–77.

Joosse, P. (2017) Leaderless Resistance and the Loneliness of Lone Wolves: Exploring the Rhetorical Dynamics of Lone Actor Violence. *Terrorism and Political Violence,* 29(1), pp. 52–78.

Kara, S. and Merali, A. (2020) Is 'Vicarious Retribution Model' Sufficient to Analyse Anti-Muslim Hate Crimes? *Journal of Muslim Minority Affairs*, 40(4), pp. 671–693.

Kubicek, B. and King, M. (2021) The Canada Centre and Countering Violent Extremism. In: Carvin, S., Juneau, T. and Forcese, C. (eds), *Top Secret Canada: Understanding the Canadian Intelligence and National Security Community*. Toronto: University of Toronto Press, pp. 181–198.

Lee, J.E.C. and Lemyre, L. (2009) A Social-Cognitive Perspective of Terrorism Risk Perception and Individual Response in Canada. *Risk Analysis*, 29(9), pp. 1265–1280.

Lenard, P.T. and Nagra, B. (2020) National Security: Exclusion and Isolation among Muslims in Canada. In: Littlewood, J., Dawson, L. and Thompson, S.K. (eds), *Terrorism and Counter-Terrorism in Canada*. Toronto: University of Toronto Press, pp. 265–282.

Littlewood, J., Dawson, L. and Thompson, S.K., eds (2020) *Terrorism and Counter-Terrorism in Canada*. Toronto: University of Toronto Press.

Littlewood, J., Thompson, S.K. and Dawson, L. (2020) Introduction. In: Littlewood, J., Dawson, L. and Thompson, S.K. (eds) *Terrorism and Counter-Terrorism in Canada*. Toronto: University of Toronto Press, pp. 3–21.

Lowndes, V. and Thorp, L. (2010) Preventing Violent Extremism: Why Local Context Matters. In: Eatwell, R. and Goodwin, M. (eds), *The New Extremism in 21st Century Britain*. London: Routledge, pp. 123–142.

MacLeod, Ian. (2011) *Terror Risk in Canada Lowest Among Major Western Economies: Study*. National Post, 4 August, https://nationalpost.com/news/canada/canadas-terror-risk-lowest-among-major-western-countries-study

McCauley, C., and Moskalenko, S. (2008) Mechanisms of Political Radicalization: Pathways Toward Terrorism. *Terrorism and Political Violence*, 20(3), pp. 415–433.

McLay, R. and Ramos, H. (2021) Do Polarisation Narratives Apply to Politics on the Periphery? The Case of Atlantic Canada. *Frontiers in Sociology*, 6, pp. 1–12.

Millett, K. and Ahmad, F. (2021) Echoes of Terror(ism): The Mutability and Contradictions of Countering Violent Extremism in Québec. *Canadian Social Studies*, 52(2), pp. 52–67.

Mills, C. E., Freilich, J.D. and Chermak, S.M. (2017) Extreme Hatred: Revisiting the Hate Crime and Terrorism Relationship to Determine Whether They Are 'Close Cousins' or 'Distant Relatives'. *Crime & Delinquency*, 63(10), pp. 1191–1223.

Nilson, C. (2014) Risk-Driven Collaborative Intervention: A Preliminary Assessment of Community Mobilization Prince Albert's Hub Model. Saskatoon, SK: Centre for Forensic Behavioural Sciences and Justice Studies, University of Saskatchewan, https://cfbsjs.usask.ca/documents/research/research_papers/RiskDrivenCollaborativeIntervention.pdf

Norris, F.H. (2005) Range, Magnitude, and Duration of the Effects of Disasters of Mental Health: Review Update. White River Junction, VT: Research Education in Disaster Mental Health Report, www.redmh.org/

Organisation for the Prevention of Violence (2022a) Who We Are, https://preventviolence.ca/about-the-opv/

Organisation for the Prevention of Violence (2022b) Organisational and Program Overview, www.seabrcw.ca/pdfs/opv.pdf

Organisation for the Prevention of Violence (2022c) Evolve Program, https://preventviolence.ca/evolve-program/

Parent, R. and Ellis, J.O. (2014) Right-wing Extremism in Canada. Working Paper No. 14-03, Canadian Network for Research on Terrorism, Security and Society, www.tsas.ca/wp-content/uploads/2018/03/TSASWP14-03_Parent-Ellis10.pdf

Pennycook, G., McPhetres, J., Bago, B. and Rand, D.G. (2022) Beliefs About Covid-19 in Canada, the United Kingdom and the United States: A Novel Test of Political Polarisation and Motivated Reasoning. *Personality and Social Psychology Bulletin*, 48(5), pp. 750–765.

Perry, B. and Scrivens, R. (2016) Uneasy Alliances: A Look at the Right-Wing Extremist Movement in Canada. *Studies in Conflict and Terrorism*, 39(9), pp. 819–841.

Perry, B. and Scrivens, R. (2018) A Climate for Hate? *Critical Criminology*, 26(2), pp. 169–187.

Perry, B. and Scrivens, R. (2019) *Right-Wing Extremism in Canada*. Cham: Palgrave.

Public Safety Canada (2022) About the Canada Centre, ww.publicsafety.gc.ca/cnt/bt/cc/bt-en.aspx

Purwanto, B., and Fenton, A.J. (2022) Inappropriate Use of Words "Jihadist" and "Islamist" in Western Media's Reports on Bombing Attacks. *Journal of Communications and Public Relations*, 1(2), pp. 13–20.

Quan, D. (2016) *Right-wing Extremist Groups 'Prevalent' Across Canada, Study Warns*. National Post, 10 February, https://nationalpost.com/news/canada/right-wing-extremist-groups-prevalent-across-canada-study-warns

ReDirect (2022) About Us, https://redirect.cpsevents.ca/about-us/

Roach, K. (2018) The Migration and Evolution of Programs to Counter Violent Extremism. *University of Toronto Law Journal*, 68(4), pp. 588–597.

Roach, K. and Forcese, C. (2015) *False Security: The Radicalization of Canadian Anti-Terrorism*. Toronto: Irwin Law.

Rosand, E. (2021) 20 Years After 9/11: Why Cities Matter More than Ever When It Comes to Preventing and Countering Violent Extremism. *ISD Dispatches*, 16 September. London: Institute for Strategic Dialogue, www.isdglobal.org/digital_dispatches/20-years-after-9-11-why-cities-matter-more-than-ever-when-it-comes-to-preventing-and-countering-violent-extremism/.

Rousseau, C., Hassan, G., Moreau, N. and Thombs, B. (2011) Perceived Discrimination and Its Association with Psychological Distress among Newly Arrived Immigrants Before and After September 11, 2011. *American Journal of Public Health*, 101(5), pp. 909–915.

Sayers, A.M. and Stewart, D.K. (2013) Breaking the Peace: The Wildrose Alliance in Alberta Politics. *Canadian Political Science Review*, 7(1), pp. 73–86.

See, S. (2018) The Intellectual Construction of Canada's 'Peaceable Kingdom' Ideal. *Journal of Canadian Studies*, 52(2), pp. 510–537.

Shanaah, S. and Heath-Kelly, C. (2022) What Drives Counter-Extremism? The Extent of P/CVE Policies in the West and Their Structural Correlates. *Terrorism and Political Violence*, DOI:10.1080/09546553.2022.2080063

SHERPA (2022) Recherche et Action sur les Polarisations Sociales, https://sherpa-recherche.com/sherpa/equipes-recherche/raps/ [in French]

Sommers, M. (2019) *Youth and the Field of Countering Violent Extremism*. Washington, DC: Promundo-US, https://promundoglobal.org/wp-content/uploads/2019/01/Youth_Violent_Extemism.pdf

Tetrault, J. (2021) What's Hate Got to Do With It? Right-Wing Movements and the Hate Stereotype. *Current Sociology*, 69(1), pp. 3–23.

Tetrault, J. (2022) Thinking Beyond Extremism: A Critique of Counter Terrorism Research on Right-Wing Nationalist and Far Right Social Movements. *British Journal of Criminology*, 62(2), pp. 431–449.

Thompson, S.K. and Leroux, E. (2020) *Final Report – Design and Performance: Developing Canadian Partnerships for Countering Violent Extremism*. Prepared for Public Safety Canada's Canada Centre for Community Engagement and Prevention of Violence.

Thompson, S.K. and Leroux, E. (2022) Lessons Learned from Dual Site Formative Evaluations of Countering Violent Extremism (CVE) Programming Co-led by Canadian Police. *Journal of Policing, Intelligence and Counter Terrorism*, DOI:10.1080/18335330.2022.2040741

Tishler, N. Ouellet, M. and Kilberg, J. (2020) A Survey of Terrorism in Canada: 1960–2015. In: Littlewood, J., Dawson, L. and Thompson, S.K. (eds), *Terrorism and Counter-Terrorism in Canada*. Toronto: University of Toronto Press, pp. 25–48.

United Nations (2022) *Update on the Impact of the Covid-19 pandemic on terrorism, counter-terrorism, and countering violent extremism*. Report. Security Council – Counter-Terrorism Committee, www.un.org/securitycouncil/ctc/content/update-impact-covid-19-pandemic-terrorism-counter-terrorism-and-countering-violent-extremism

Wang, J.H. and Moreau, G. (2022) Police-reported Hate Crime in Canada, 2020. *Juristat* 85-002-X, www150.statcan.gc.ca/n1/pub/85-002-x/2022001/article/00005-eng.htm

Welsh, B., Yohros, A. and Zane, S.N. (2020) Understanding Iatrogenic Effects for Evidence-Based Police: A Review of Crime and Violence Prevention Programs. *Aggression and Violence* 55, DOI: 10.1016/j.avb.2020.101511

Yarbrough, D.B., Shulha, L.M., Hopson, R.K. and Caruthers, F.A. (2011) *The Program Evaluation Standards: A Guide for Evaluators and Evaluation Users* (3rd ed.). Thousand Oaks, CA: Sage.

Yorktown Family Services (2022) Program Review 2021/2022: Estimated Time of Arrival (ETA).

19
UNITED STATES OF AMERICA

Brian Hughes

Introduction

In the context of policy and practice in the US, the exact meaning of 'resilience' can vary greatly. Typically, discussions of resilience fall along one of three tracks. First, there is resilience in the aftermath of violence, which takes the form of addressing the grief and trauma of affected individuals and the community around them. Second, there is resilience as self-defence. This takes the form of active shooter training, 'red flag' enforcement to remove firearms from violent individuals, and an ever-expanding web of dubiously effective surveillance technologies. In practice, these two conceptions of resilience predominate American discourse, intervention, and (perhaps most importantly) funding streams. However, a third more fundamental approach to resilience may be currently emerging in the US. This refers to resilience as 'deep' prevention – not merely responding to violence in its aftermath or attempting to mitigate it in the moment, but to develop communities where extremism and political violence are less likely to develop in the first place. This approach draws from practices of peacebuilding, anti-racist education, psychotherapy and addiction medicine, multi-faith reconciliation, and community organising.

Funding for the first two types of resilience work has steadily increased in recent decades, along with sharply rising rates of extremist organising and far-right political violence. This suggests that resilience as trauma care and resilience as self-defence are insufficient to stem the flow of political violence in the US. However, the more fundamental approach to resilience as prevention has been slow to develop due to two key obstacles of American political economy. First, there is the longstanding bloat of securitisation characterising federal and state budgets since the mid-twentieth century. Second, there is the persistent influence of historical White supremacy, expressed in underdeveloped minority political power and reactionary institutional structures.

The problem of extremism in the US, and the pressing question of how to build better community resilience to it, cannot be adequately addressed absent appreciation for this historical context and its contemporary structural outcomes. Broadly, this context refers to: history (particularly the history of overt and then structural White supremacy), culture (specifically the porous boundaries between extreme right and movement conservatism), politics (the continuity between factions within the Republican Party and the emergence of the so-called alt right and Trumpism), and technology (the role of techno-libertarianism in fostering an online ecosystem of extremist propaganda, organising, and recruitment). All of these dynamics – from the economic and cultural legacy of White supremacy to the failures of Reconstruction and successes of Civil Rights, the persistence of Confederate sympathy, and the rise of the White power and militia movements in the 1970s through the 1990s – have fed a vast reservoir of cultural resources and structural abetment to a radical right that is today organised and imagined through the decentralised networks of digital communication media.

Some historical conditions giving rise to American extremism

Far-right radicalism in the US is often treated as an acute outburst, either of illiberal political movements or extremist violence, that disrupts the ordinary smooth functioning of 'the world's oldest democracy'. This point of view is premised on the assumption that the radical right's 'values are alien to Western democratic values, but that a small potential exists for them in all Western societies' (Mudde 2010, p. 1170). As Mudde argues, that is not the case in Western Europe, and as this chapter argues, it is not the case in the US either. The radical right does not represent a 'normal pathology', but rather a 'pathological normalcy' (ibid.). It is 'well connected to mainstream ideas and much in tune with broadly shared mass attitudes and policy positions' (ibid., p. 1178). More fundamentally, the values and attitudes of the radical right are enmeshed in US history and all the social, political, economic, and cultural apparatuses whose origins reach back to its origins. Far from acute pathological outbursts, far-right extremism in the US is a natural outgrowth of deeply embedded conditions, which are often taken for granted. These conditions not only severely hamper resilience against extremist values, attitudes, organising, and violence but also they serve as a welcoming soil out of which extremism and even terrorism can grow.

The enslavement, exploitation, political disenfranchisement, and terrorisation of Africans in the US represents an essential point of origin for these conditions. 'Without the concessions' of the three-fifths compromise, exemption of slave-produced goods from export tariffs, and a 20-year extension of the slave trade itself, 'there would have been no union' (Sked 2014, p. 441). Following Reconstruction, the combination of racial terror and Jim Crow laws was used to suppress the Black vote, overrepresenting White interests in states where such circumstances prevailed, even while it tilted the legislative and regulatory agendas of their representatives further in the direction of White supremacy (Keyssar 2020). Throughout the US history, the extension of the racial franchise via 'becoming White' has acted as a political, cultural, and social gyroscope maintaining the balance of White supremacy (Allen 2012). The perpetuation of racialisation, Black marginalisation, and White supremacy is in many respects essential to the economic and political functioning of the US (Robinson 2000) – a necessity set into stark relief by the historical destruction of Black capital via 'race riots' (i.e., pogroms) such as the 1921 Tulsa Massacre and habitual abuse of eminent domain to seize or demolish profitable Black-owned property.

These historical events should be treated as extremist violence on their own terms – that is, based on an assumption that 'groups who don't share the same ethnic, religious, or political identity ... can only be resolved through separation, domination, or violence' (PERIL & SPLC 2021). This should in no way be mitigated by the fact that they were sanctioned by political authority and therefore not technically 'terrorism'. As Berger (2019) points out, extremism does not cease to be extremist simply because it assumes political power, or, indeed, is birthed from political power. We should also recognise that '[e]xtremist social movements can oscillate between violent and non-violent phases' (ibid., p. 4), which may reflect movements' relation to political power.

This history can be felt even in moments of political calm as an 'invisible' violence visited upon subordinated groups. Structural violence, as per Krieger et al., is 'the exploitive and oppressive social relationships that simultaneously define racial/ethnic groups and cause a system of inequalities that become embodied as racial/ ethnic health inequities' (1993, p. 938). This violence can be expressed, for example, in health disparities relating to environmental degradation that result in unequal access to housing and social services (Coolsaet 2020; Moreland-Capuia 2021; Zimring 2015). Or it can be seen in policing practices that incarcerate and execute Black men at rates disproportionate to rates of crime (Alexander 2012; Betancur and Herring 2013).

Symbolic violence, by contrast, resides in 'the imposition…of an ideology which legitimates and naturalises the status quo' (Chandler and Munday 2011). At the economic level, this is visible in the ideology of *producerism*, in which the virtuous, striving, and browbeaten producer struggles to fend off the parasite, a dependent subject that consumers' tax dollars and productive labour 'to subsidise a profligate and extravagant lifestyle' (HoSang and Lowndes 2019, p. 19). As HoSang and Lowndes point out, this interpellation of producer and parasite is implicitly racialised and gendered, even while it functions as a means for non-Whites to access some of the privileges of Whiteness.

However, when examining the consequences of structural and symbolic violence, we must also consider what is absent – that is, a missing *positivity* of legal, cultural, and material infrastructure that would *positively* structure the conditions of targeted groups. This condition was not ameliorated, in the case of Black Americans, following emancipation and reconstruction, due to organised campaigns of terror and capital seizure. Lacking, for example, capital due to the anti-Black pogroms of the late nineteenth and early twentieth centuries, Black Americans could not wield sufficient political or economic power to effect changes in policy or culture to their benefit. By the same token, the preservation of White supremacy created legal precedents and an incentive structure that further entrenched the chronic condition of White supremacy and acute expressions of racist terror. Of course, this fabric of chronic violence should be understood to extend beyond Black Americans, although theirs is perhaps the most visible example. Similar dynamics may be just as easily seen in the historical and structural legacy of male supremacy in the US (Ebin 2021; Griffith 2021; Oluo 2020), and in the interstices of countless less well-recognised oppressions (Fisher 2016).

Political reaction as an obstacle to resilience

American extremism itself must be understood within a larger fabric of reactionary politics and broadly supremacist extremism. Robin (2017) draws the distinction between the political left and right wings as one ultimately of public vs. private exercise of power. The left-wing political project works to expand public exercise of power whereas the right-wing works to preserve and establish new private domains. 'Historically, the conservative has favoured liberty for the highest orders and constraint for the lower orders' (ibid., p. 8). Mass democracy is, to the reactionary sensibility, 'a terrible disturbance in the private life of power' (ibid., p. 13). Taken on these terms, the reactionary dimensions of American governance become more apparent.

Suspicion, if not hostility, for the lower orders and their empowerment through mass democracy is evident in the most basic structures of the US federal system. The office of the presidency is determined not by popular vote but through the mediation of the electoral college. This is both a legacy of slavery and the demands made by slaveholding states on the nascent country (Keyssar 2020) and a broader bulwark against mass democracy, consciously implemented *as such* by the founders (Duquette et al. 2017; Hamilton et al. 2010; Wegman 2020). The Senate, too, incorporates a central organising principle intended to 'to check the impulses of the House and the popular will' (Hubert 2020, p. 126). The distribution of Senators (two per state) and longer, 'staggered' terms afforded to Senators are inherently minoritarian and conservative (Caro 2003; MacNeil and Baker 2013; Wirls and Wirls 2004). The Supreme Court is perhaps 'the ultimate supplier of antidemocracy' (Bowie 2021), offering 'a kind of interpretation not far removed from legislation' (Mace 1972, p. 1140) in the form of terminal rulings handed down by the unelected and lifetime-appointed products of elite legal institutions, the nine justices.

The tendency for American resilience programmes to redound toward security and surveillance is a persistent symptom of these anti-democratic and minoritarian tendencies. In the US, extremism prevention funding is primarily channelled through the Department of Homeland Security (DHS). None is provided through federal departments such as the Department of Health and Human Services or the Department of Education. These are structural conditions, and therefore not the specific fault of any one person or even administration. Rather, they are driven by deeply embedded processes and expectations which tend to favour a laissez-faire normalcy punctuated by executive action during moments of crisis.

Some cultural conditions giving rise to American extremism

These historical precedents and political infrastructures provide a rich, all-encompassing ground for extremism in the US to flourish – the foundation for 'pathological normalcy'. That is, they work generally to the detriment of preventative resilience and to the benefit of far-right extremism. One may read the consequences of this tilt toward reaction in key moments of recent political-cultural history leading up to the present day (Berlet and Lyons 2000). This section will do so from two points of departure: ideological and operational. The ideological and visionary point of departure is in the mid-century, with writers like Francis Parker Yockey and William Luther Pierce. The operational emerges from the post-Vietnam War White power movement with leaders like Louis Beam, Robert Jay Matthews, and David Lane. These men and the movements they represent set the precedent for much of the organisational and operational structures that continue to give shape and movement to the extreme right today.

The ideologues and visionaries of the mid-century American extreme right imagined a future of racial empire, global and even cosmic conquest. They did so in a milieu of far-right politics that frequently abutted the mainstream conservative movement. One case here is emblematic. Willis Carto was the founder of the 'Liberty Lobby' organisation (Michael 2008; Mintz 1985), 'one one of the most important postwar far-right groups in America' (Macklin 2012, p. 272). The Liberty Lobby was a group riddled with conspiratorial thinking, racism and anti-Semitism, and Holocaust denial (Michael 2008; Mintz 1985; Sokol 2009). Carto fundraised for David Duke's early, mainstream political campaigns, and the Liberty Lobby newsletter *Spotlight* counted among its loyal readership Oklahoma City bomber Timothy McVeigh (Sokol 2009).

Yet Carto and the Liberty Lobby were a cultural force to be reckoned with. At the peak of its publication in the late 1970s, Carto's newsletter *Spotlight* numbered 330,000 readers (ibid.). Liberty Lobby was represented in Congressional testimony before the Senate Finance Committee in 1962 (Macklin 2012). In addition to early work with the George Wallace presidential campaign, Carto had professional and political relationships with, among others, congressmen Ron Paul Sr. and James A Traficant Jr. (Weisenburger 2009). He published the writings of Joe Sobran, an American paleoconservative, *National Review* alumnus, and key influence on the alt right (Spencer and Gottfried 2015) in *Spotlight*'s successor publication *The American Free Press*.

Carto was also the greatest supporter of Francis Parker Yockey, an American author and central thinker in the postwar American extreme right. Yockey's book *Imperium: The Philosophy and History of Politics* is still in print and admired by White supremacists today; it is considered by some to stand alongside *The Turner Diaries* 'as signally important texts of the American Far Right' (Weisenburger 2009, p. 1107), both then and today (Gray 2018; Hughes et al. 2022; Lorber 2021). Carto visited Yockey in prison prior to Yockey's suicide and kept *Imperium* in print for decades to come (Weisenburger 2009).

Carto would maintain a relationship with American Nazi Party leader George Lincoln Rockwell until the latter's death in 1967 (Novak 2016). Then, following his involvement with arch-segregationist George Wallace's 1968 presidential campaign, Carto founded the National Youth Alliance (NYA), a far-right student group, which was joined by none other than William Luther Pierce (Durham 2002). Later, Pierce would seize power of the NYA from Carto, renaming it the National Alliance and go on to pen *The Turner Diaries* (famously also admired by McVeigh) in addition to serving as a central figure of post–Vietnam White power culture.

This mixture of extreme and mainstream spread both outward from movement ideologues like Carto to the mainstream conservative movement, but also went inward to the violent hard core of the American far-right. The confluence of mainstream and extreme, ideological, cultural, and operational, intersected along the axes of anti-communism, reaction to the Civil Rights movement, anti-counterculture, and fascist sympathy characterised the American right at the conclusion of the Vietnam War and dawn of the late-twentieth century White power movement. Broad cultural trends, such as 'dramatic, hard-won gains of feminism, civil rights, secularism, and gay liberation left the 1970s ripe for conservative backlash' (Belew 2018, p. 9). This backlash took its mainstream form in the Reagan counterrevolution and rise of Evangelical Christianity as a political bloc. Its fringe form emerged in the White power movement of groups like the Order, Aryan Nations, and affiliated militias.

While these expressions differ in some regards – one is mass-electoral, the other terroristic, one putatively democratic, the other anti-democratic – they were but two expressions of the same backlash. Both were 'rear-guard revolutions' of the type which Robin says define reaction: 'power besieged and power protected…even at the cost of the strength and integrity of the state' (2017, p. 15). The Reagan counterrevolution moved to 'starve the beast' of government through aggressive neoliberalisation (Bartlett 2007; Harvey 2005), thereby ensuring that the beneficiaries of those hard-won social gains would 'remain feudal subjects in the family, the factory, and the field' (Robin 2017, p. 15). The reverberations of this revolution may still be felt today in the US's lopsided approach to prevention. Neglected social services and bloated military budgets are the mere continuation of a profound shift in government priority inaugurated by the Reagan Revolution (Meeropol 2017).

The White power movement, for its part, would seek to return the beneficiaries of social progress to their proper place through 'a radical future that could be achieved only revolution…separation – the foundation of a utopian racial nation' (Belew 2018, p. 5). Despite their differing tactics and professed mutual antipathy, these two fronts fought in the same rear-guard action against the political, social, and economic enfranchisement of women, and racial and sexual minorities. The figure of the violent, utopian White power revolution emerges from the same ground of reaction as Reaganite cultural 'shmaltz' and its hard-nosed austerity economics.

Other connections exist between the political mainstream and figures in the White power movement. Despite his present-day marginality, David Duke once held a promising political career, first in the Louisiana state congress and for a brief moment on the national stage (Bridges 2018). Louis Beam, the White power terrorist who popularised the concept of 'leaderless resistance' (SPLC n.d.-b) affiliated his own KKK chapter with Duke's Knights of the Ku Klux Klan, which 'attempted to appeal to the mainstream in the New Right' (Belew 2018, p. 35). Robert Jay Matthews and David Lane, who led the White power terrorist organisation The Order, were first both members in the John Birch Society (from whose membership rolls Carto helped launch the Liberty Lobby), and Matthews first met Lane while recruiting for William Pierce's post-Carto National Alliance (SPLC n.d.-a). While these men were at least two steps removed from anything that could be described as the political mainstream, it is clear that they nevertheless emerged from the same complex of reactionary social conditions that gave rise to the broader late-twentieth-century right-wing.

This is the ordinary ferment of the American right-wing: a tangled web of influence, encounters, and interaction. Tugging it toward the mainstream, we see figures like Carto, while Pierce, Beam, and their ilk drag it towards its violent, terroristic core. In the US, the easy intermingling of such groups via culture war issues, anti-communism, and opposition to Black American empowerment continues to this day in the easy intermingling of White nationalism, anti-Semitism, conspiracy culture, and Republican Party politics. Groups such as Turning Point USA and movements such as the national conservatism tendency offer sites where the mutual legibility of extreme and mainstream are most apparent (ADL n.d.; Brooks 2021; Dunphy 2018; Kelley 2018). But these only serve to highlight pervasive conditions operating 'as-normal'.

The loose, unorganised, and emergent qualities of these relationships are the very fabric of the right-wing in the US – the very normalcy through which pathological extremism is threaded. It should never be taken as a claim – much less proof – of conspiracy between the extreme right, the far-right, and mainstream movement conservatism to launder fringe ideology into mainstream policy. Rather, these two webs of association between the extreme and terrorist right, on one hand, and the mainstream, on the other, ought to illustrate the banality of such associations.

Space precludes a full accounting here of the rich interpenetrations of postwar American right-wing tendencies. Tensions have long existed between the more cosmopolitan strains of American conservatism and its nativist tendencies. However, that tension is also reflective of the very linkages that connect the two and thereby legitimise the extreme by virtue of its association with the mainstream.

Political conditions giving rise to American extremism

Prior explorations of history and culture are, clearly, inextricably bound up with US politics and power. But it is worth examining one recent case of the mainstream and extreme's mutual co-creation for its clarity of dynamics, and for the central importance it played in the evolution of the contemporary far-right and extreme right. The evolution of the so-called alt-right as a hybrid of déclassé tendencies in American conservatism and the White power movement offers a clarifying case study in the ways that mainstream and extreme exist in a seamless continuity, emerging from the turnings of social change and political fortunes.

Throughout the 1980s, 1990s, and 2000s, the American conservative movement experienced an internal power struggle between camps that came to be known as the 'neoconservative' and 'paleoconservative' wings of the Republican Party (Berlet 2008; Gottfried and Spencer 2015). Paleoconservatives took generally economically protectionist, diplomatically isolationist, and demographically nativist positions. The neoconservatives, by contrast, espoused economic liberalisation on a global scale, enthusiastic military intervention abroad, and looser restrictions on immigration (aimed at driving down labour costs).

Politically, this struggle played out during the Nixon and Reagan administrations. And ultimately, the paleoconservative agenda was routed. However, paleoconservatives continued to drive aspects of conservative discourse from movement organs such as the *National Review*, *Commentary*, the Intercollegiate Institute, and others (Williams 2017). Ultraconservative writers like Patrick Buchanan, Peter Brimelow, John Derbyshire, Joe Sobran, Sam Francis, and many more clung to these positions, only to be forced out amid internal power struggles and public scandals over racist language and extremist positions.

As these writers, think-tankers, and one-time crafters of policy found themselves increasingly on the outs of the conservative movement, they gravitated toward a new ecosystem of far-right publications, which often demonstrated a strong paleoconservative bent. Publications like *Chronicles*, *Left and Right*, and *The Rockwell-Rothbard Report* provided 'an interconnected set of rhetorical pipelines and echo chambers [to] amplify and repeat the messages and…ideology of the group into the mainstream' (Berlet 2008, p. 580). That is, while the paleoconservative movement might not have enjoyed the same prestige of position it once did, it was far from contained outside of the broader conservative movement. Instead, mainstream conservatism sanitised itself (to the credit of some within the movement, with intent to exorcise paleoconservative racism and authoritarianism) while never fully silencing paleoconservatism's presence and influence. Nevertheless, by the end of the 1990s, paleoconservatism was in shambles, riven with internecine conflicts over matters of foreign interventionism and Austrian economics (Ashbee 2000, pp. 82–83).

This changed with the arrival of 'Web 2.0', the blogosphere, and inexpensive, user-friendly software for producing online publications. Almost immediately, paleoconservatism enjoyed a resurgence with the 2002 founding of *The American Conservative* (TAC) by Pat Buchanan, Taki Theodoracopulos, and Scott McConnell (Hawley 2017). Future alt-right leader Richard Spencer worked as an Assistant Editor there from 2007 to 2008, before moving on to *TakiMag*, another online publication operated by one of the *TAC*'s founders. *TAC* and *TakiMag* represent a nexus at which paleoconservatism helped to give birth to the alt-right. The original website, *AlternativeRight*.com, was launched with funding from none other than Peter Brimelow (let go as an editor from *National Review* after years of hosting White nationalist authors) and paleo-financier William H. Regnery II (ibid.). It hosted essays from paleoconservatives like Paul Gottfried and Sam Francis as well as mainstream libertarians like David Gordon and Thomas Woods.

More recently, the Trump presidency offers an object lesson in the inadequacy of 'normal pathology'–style analysis. Deep continuities show that Trumpism, like the Trump administration itself, is not aberrant to the US or the American conservative movement. In fact, it does not even represent a break from the Republican Party's neoconservative tendencies. To the contrary, Trumpism represented the *reunion* of neoconservative and paleoconservative tendencies (D'Haeseleer 2019; Guerlain 2018; Scotti 2016). Even while serving as an outlet for both paleo- and neoconservative agendas (not always harmoniously), American far-right extremists took the Trump administration as a beacon rallying them to acts of supremacist violence. One need only look to the events of August 2017 in Charlottesville, Virginia, and at the American Capitol on 6 January 2021 to see how different and in many cases incompatible fringe movements can be mobilised through a belief in the sanction of the executive (Miller-Idriss and Hughes 2021). Even the term 'paleoconservatism' has been reappropriated by members of the so-called Groyper movement in what amounts less to a novel political tendency than a rebranding of alt-right themes (Tanner and Burghart 2020).

Extremism of this sort clearly is not aberrant to the deeper fabrics of American politics any more than it is to American history. It is a natural outgrowth. Insofar as politics touches every corner of our communities, we cannot build true, lasting resilience until these factors are addressed. Without the concerted, arduous, and long-term efforts necessary to disentangle the cultural expressions of reaction, and the social relations giving rise to them, responses will never amount to more than triage.

Technological conditions giving rise to American extremism

The internet, Worldwide Web, and the applications that sit atop their infrastructure produce a socio-technical environment in which extremist politics thrive. As will be described below, this is not simply a matter of user choice and behaviour. It is not even so much an issue of platform governance (though tech companies and regulators have failed to adequately address even the most acute issues of extremism on digital platforms). The conditions that foster the growth of extremism online reside at the deepest level of design and engineering.

Notorious websites like 4chan and 8chan are the outcome of specific design and engineering choices made by their creators (Know Your Meme 2015). Their design and engineering features coordinate to foster a media environment that affords extreme conditions of speed and anonymity. The Chans' sense of breakneck speed comes about from design choices that afford posting over reading. High-traffic threads surface first, and low engagement threads quickly vanish. The Chans 'were never about communication, but about replication...There is no time for discourse in the sense of a considered exchange of ideas. The picture and slogan that gets pasted more, that floods the board, that soaks up more scroll time, wins' (Munn 2019). The breakneck flow of posts forestalls any serious exchange of ideas while offering special affordance to discourses such as racism, Islamophobia, anti-Semitism, and more. Their speed and volume are, ultimately, an affordance toward desensitisation. 'The first time a racial slur is encountered, it is shocking. The second time, the visceral disgust has been tempered. The third time, it is abhorrent but expected...The shock cannot be sustained; a new normal takes its place' (ibid.). Given 8chan's engineered preference for posting over reading, this process can take place in a matter of minutes.

This absorbs its user base at both the individual and collective levels into a *collective anonymity* and *anonymous collectivity*. Users 'do not hold individual identities while participating... instead, they join a collective identity' (Sparby 2017, p. 87). This collective anonymity produces 'a paradoxically monolithic, stable collective identity' (ibid.). The disinhibition of anonymity combines with the disinhibition of the mob and the abdicated social responsibility of 'bystander syndrome'. Anons are free to express their ugliest attitudes and beliefs, safe knowing that they become the possession of the collective. Likewise, they are freed from responsibility to intervene, disincentivised by the ugliness of backlash and the simultaneous vulnerability which expulsion from the anonymous collectivity offers.

Ostensibly, 4chan and 8chan exist to serve values of speech that not only tolerate speech acts that push the limit of the Brandenburg standard (that is, imminent lawless action), but that treat such speech as a positive good to be encouraged (McLaughlin 2019; Wells 2019). However, the Brandenburg standard of allowable speech tends to be significantly imbalanced against the interests of targeted groups (Matsuda et al. 2018; Schiffrin 2017). If neutral social conditions include a running threat of violence against certain classes of people, then this sort of free speech absolutism will inevitably place speech acts against those classes closer to an actual act of violence than a similar speech act against others (Calvert 1997; Hansford 2017). In any social space – online or off – built according to this free speech fundamentalism, not all voices 'speaking freely' will be equal. The Chans were thus engineered on an unequal social ground, amplified and accelerated by networked communication and mass data processing. The platforms' design thereby produced a monstrous expression of those original social values that inspired them and the power relationships which underpinned them.

As mainstream social media platforms remove extremist actors and content from their spaces, many shift operations to sites that are effectively clones of the more mainstream social media platforms where extremism is increasingly unwelcome (Squire 2019). The mere existence of alt-tech demonstrates the ways in which basic engineering and design characteristics produce the context in which extremist movements thrive. Namely, they offer one-stop, real-time public- and private-facing communication interfaces, with networking affordances that encourage people of similar outlooks and agendas to connect despite sharing no real-world acquaintance (Donovan et al. 2018). 'With few possibilities to meet in public without opposition, the Alt-Right has relied on creating an abundance of online media, forums, and opportunities for engagement that require internet infrastructure for the survival of their movement' (ibid., p. 54).

So-called alt-tech seeks to produce the same network effects as mainstream social media and is subject to the same lock-in effects. And while the balance of digital political economy tends toward their rapid deplatforming at the infrastructural (e.g. DNS) level, alt-tech has proven extremely adaptive and resilient. This resilience is due in part to the tech-libertarian principles that guide internet governance and the personal values of so many individuals in the tech industry (Golumbia 2016; Sandifer and Graham 2018). Some have even argued that this 'points to a new configuration of fascist ideology taking shape under the aegis of, and working in tandem with, neoliberal governance' via tech and the surveillance state (Pinto 2019, p. 319). At minimum, this flat, tech libertarianism produces a simplistic understanding of freedom at the expense of understanding the operations of power. And that flattening creates the regulatory context in which extremist virtual communities thrive.

Anti-extremism policy and practice in the US

The number of resilience-based programmes aimed at reducing the risk of extremism in American communities is notably insignificant as a proportion of the overall efforts aimed at counterterrorism, countering violent extremism, law enforcement, surveillance, lawfare, and other post hoc strategies for dealing with extremism.

Throughout its post-Vietnam peak, 'the Federal Bureau of Investigation (FBI), Bureau of Alcohol, Tobacco, and Firearms (ATF), U.S. Marshals Service, and Department of Justice monitored the White power movement' (Belew 2018, p. 12). Its attention again turned toward far-right extremism – particularly to unlawful militias – following the bombing of the Oklahoma City Alfred P. Murrah Federal Building in 1995. The FBI expanded its number of Joint Terrorism Task Forces (FBI 2020) and hired 500 new agents earmarked for domestic terrorism investigation (BBC News 2001). Congress and the President passed the Antiterrorism and Effective Death Penalty Act of 1996, which expanded victim services while stiffening penalties for terrorism-related crimes and designating foreign terrorist organisations while prohibiting material support for them (United States 1996). In general, this period seems positively characterised by an increased appreciation for the needs of victim-survivors (DOJ OVC 2000; Giannini 2008) – that is, resilience as post-trauma treatment.

Following the 9/11 terrorist attacks, focus on extremism in the US expanded massively, centring on Islamism at the expense of attention to far-right extremism. This period saw the creation of the DHS in 2003, a massive federal agency that synthesised 22 separate agencies (DHS 2012) with roughly a quarter-million employees and a projected annual budget in 2022 of $90.8 billion dollars (Painter 2021, p. 37). This 'led to economic growth in a variety of other "risk" arenas, i.e., new "security-based markets", such as bio-terrorism, cyber-terrorism, transportation and border security' (Alimahomed 2014, p. 84). The securitised approach to national security was continued under President Obama, even at the expense of social stability, as during the economic crisis when 'all discretionary spending would be halted for three years with the exception of any governmental spending on national security' (ibid.).

The Obama administration's 2011 pivot to a programme of 'Countering Violent Extremism' (CVE) came under fire for, among other things, unfairly targeting Muslim communities based on religious observance and for securitising the very community resilience programmes it aimed to grow. The American Civil Liberties Union (ACLU) warned that CVE programming could 'task community members to expansively monitor and report to law enforcement on the beliefs and expressive or associational activities of law-abiding Americans' (ACLU 2014). Doing so, the ACLU argued, 'reproduces the same harm as government surveillance and monitoring' (ibid.). Obama's CVE programme and its shortcomings are an excellent example of how this very dynamic operates. By placing ostensibly neutral expectations of free dialogue and security-related community services atop an Islamophobic culture and the larger security apparatus that metastasised in the wake of 9/11, CVE effectively treated American Muslims and their communities not as sites of potential resilience-building but as 'suspect communities' (Kundnani 2015), whose fragility in the face of Islamist extremism could practically be taken for granted.

Throughout that time, nonprofits and civil society organisations worked within the US to effect changes outside official state security apparatuses. The Southern Poverty Law Center, Anti-Defamation League, and other smaller organisations provided tracking, watchdog, and lawfare programmes to monitor and disrupt extremist activity where the government could not. This period also saw the rise of deradicalisation programmes like Life After Hate and Free Radicals, among others, who worked in individual capacities to assist extremists requesting help to leave their movements.

Following the mixed outcomes of CVE, the US government has reimagined its counter-extremism work, yet still focuses heavily on securitised and reactive approaches to the issue. Under the concept of a Center for Prevention Programs and Partnerships ('CP3'), the DHS has granted some $77 million to largely traditional security responses to the problem (DHS 2021a). Only approximately $20 million of that budget has been destined for programmes that are described as community-focused (DHS 2021b). Of these, the vast majority are dedicated to spotting radicalised individuals on the cusp of committing violent acts or innovating against new forms of terrorist violence – that is, resilience conceived as self-defence. Compared to the full $77 million CP3 allotment, even these self-defensive resources seem small. And compared to the combined budgets of the DHS, FBI, ATF, and other three-letter agencies, which number in hundreds of billions, it appears proportionally insignificant. Meaningful federal funding for truly preventative and resilience-based approaches remains, to date, largely untried. The US's approaches, historical and contemporary, remain held back by 'normal pathology' frameworks, which inform the vast majority of these efforts.

To be sure, a well-funded security apparatus is essential precisely because of the fertile environment for extremism that the US represents. And this apparatus ought to be directed at the gravest threat to public safety, which is currently the far-right. There is today some hope for a more focused preventative resilience approach, as the DHS' Targeted Violence and Terrorism Prevention grant programme appears to be devoting increasing resources to upstream strategies (Hennigan 2022). Today, the groups who are undertaking preventative resilience-based approaches using the small federal budget allotted to them make tremendous use of these scant resources. Their programmes are lean, efficient, and can even achieve outcomes far out of proportion to their meagre resources. But the hard work and excellence of these programmes can never compensate for so great a disparity between securitised and truly preventative measures. At present, the US does not possess structures of robust resilience against violent extremism. Developing these will be difficult, due to historical legacies of White supremacy and exacerbated anti-democratic political processes.

Concluding remarks

Chronic conditions of historical and political inequality hamper efforts to build preventative resilience to violent extremism in the US. The history of White supremacy, anti-democratic political structures, and an overly securitised approach to the problem of political violence stand in the way of such a preventative approach. At times, it may even seem as though *reactionary extremism itself* is more resilient than communities' ability to withstand it, while inclusive communities and the freedom they confer are quite fragile. Some positive changes in the US approach to resilience appear to be possible now at the federal level. However, without unravelling the tangled and extensive fabric of history, culture, politics, and technology that facilitate reaction, true preventative resilience will continue to face an uphill struggle.

References

ACLU (2014, December 18) *Coalition Letter to Obama Administration on Countering Violent Extremism (CVE) Program*. American Civil Liberties Union, www.aclu.org/other/coalition-letter-obama-administration-countering-violent-extremism-cve-program

ADL (n.d.) *Turning Point USA*. Anti-Defamation League, www.adl.org/resources/backgrounders/turning-point-usa

Alexander, M. (2012) *The New Jim Crow*. New York: The New Press.

Alimahomed, S. (2014) Homeland Security Inc.: Public order, private profit. *Race & Class*, 55(4), pp. 82–99, DOI:10.1177/0306396813519940

Allen, T. (2012) *The Invention of the White Race* (2nd edn). London: Verso Books.

Ashbee, E. (2000) Politics of paleoconservatism. *Society*, 37(3), 75–84, DOI:10.1007/BF02686179

Bartlett, B. (2007) 'Starve the beast': Origins and development of a budgetary metaphor. *The Independent Review*, 12(1), pp. 5–26.

BBC News. (2001) *The Enemy within*. BBC World: Americas, 7 June, http://news.bbc.co.uk/2/hi/americas/1374356.stm

Belew, K. (2018) *Bring the War Home: The White Power Movement and Paramilitary America*. Cambridge, MA: Harvard University Press.

Berger, J.M. (2019) Researching Violent Extremism: The State of Play. *RESOLVE Network*.

Berlet, C. (2008) The write stuff: U.S. serial print culture from conservatives out to Neo-Nazis. *Library Trends; Baltimore*, 56(3), pp. 570–600.

Berlet, C. and Lyons, M.N. (2000) *Right-wing Populism in America: Too Close for Comfort*. New York: Guilford Press.

Betancur, J.J. and Herring, C., eds (2013) *Reinventing Race, Reinventing Racism* [online]. Leiden and Boston: Brill.

Bowie, N. (2021) Antidemocracy. *Harvard Law Review*, 10 November [online], https://harvardlawreview.org/2021/11/antidemocracy/

Bridges, T. (2018) *The Rise and Fall of David Duke*. CreateSpace Independent Publishing Platform.

Brooks, D. (2021) The Terrifying Future of the American Right. *The Atlantic,* 18 November.

Calvert, C. (1997) Hate speech and its harms: A communication theory perspective. *Journal of Communication*, 47(1), pp. 4–19, DOI:10.1111/j.1460-2466.1997.tb02690.x

Caro, R.A. (2003) *Master of the Senate*. New York: Vintage Books.

Chandler, D. and Munday, R., eds (2011) Symbolic Violence. *A Dictionary of Media and Communication*. Oxford University Press [online], www.oxfordreference.com/view/10.1093/acref/9780199568758.001.0001/acref-9780199568758-e-2690

Coolsaet, B., ed. (2020) *Environmental Justice: Key Issues*. Abingdon, UK: Taylor and Francis, DOI: 10.4324/9780429029585

D'Haeseleer, B. (2019) *Perspective | How the Neocons Captured Donald Trump*. The Washington Post, 5 February, www.washingtonpost.com/outlook/2019/02/05/how-neocons-captured-donald-trump/

DHS (2012) *History*. Department of Homeland Security, 27 June, www.dhs.gov/history

DHS (2021a). *DHS Creates New Center for Prevention Programs and Partnerships and Additional Efforts to Comprehensively Combat Domestic Violent Extremism*. Department of Homeland Security, 11 May, www.dhs.gov/news/2021/05/11/dhs-creates-new-center-prevention-programs-and-partnerships-and-additional-efforts

DHS (2021b) *DHS Provides $20 Million to Local Communities to Prevent Targeted Violence and Terrorism*. Department of Homeland Security, 27 September, www.dhs.gov/news/2021/09/27/dhs-provides-20-million-local-communities-prevent-targeted-violence-and-terrorism

DOJ OVC (2000) *Responding to Terrorism Victims: Oklahoma City and Beyond*. Washington, DC: US Department of Justice.

Donovan, J., Lewis, B. and Friedberg, B. (2018) Parallel Ports. Sociotechnical Change from the Alt-Right to Alt-Tech. In: Fielitz, Maik and Thurston, Nick (Hg.), *Post-Digital Cultures of the Far Right*, Bielefeld: Transcript Verlag, pp. 49–66, DOI: 10.14361/9783839446706-004

Dunphy, J. (2018) A White Nationalist Praises Charlie Kirk & Offers Constructive Criticism. *Counter-Currents*, 13 June, https://counter-currents.com/2018/06/a-white-nationalist-praises-charlie-kirk-and-offers-constructive-criticism

Duquette, C.M., Mixon, F.G. and Cebula, R.J. (2017) Swing states, the winner-take-all electoral college, and fiscal federalism. *Atlantic Economic Journal*, 45(1), pp. 45–57, DOI:10.1007/s11293-016-9526-2

Durham, M. (2002) From imperium to internet: The National Alliance and the American extreme right. *Patterns of Prejudice*, 36(3), pp. 50–61, DOI: 10.1080/003132202128811484

Ebin, C. (2021) Threats to women/women as threats: Male supremacy and the anti-statist right. *Laws*, 10(2), 41, DOI:10.3390/laws10020041

FBI (2020) *The Oklahoma City Bombing: 25 Years Later* [story, 15 April]. Washington, DC: Federal Bureau of Investigation, www.fbi.gov/news/stories/25-years-after-oklahoma-city-bombing-041520

Fisher, S.D.E. (2016) Pauli Murray's Peter Panic: Perspectives from the margins of gender and race in Jim Crow America. *Transgender Studies Quarterly*, 3(1–2), pp. 95–103, DOI: 10.1215/23289252-3334259.

Giannini, M.M. (2008) Equal rights for equal rites? Victim allocution, defendant allocution, and the crime victims' rights act. *Yale Law & Policy Review*, 26(2), pp. 431–484.

Golumbia, D. (2016) *The Politics of Bitcoin: Software as Right-wing Extremism*. Minneapolis: University of Minnesota Press.

Gottfried, P., and Spencer, R.B. (2015) *The Great Purge: The Deformation of the American Conservative Movement*. Washington Summit Publishers.

Gray, P.W. (2018) 'The fire rises': Identity, the alt-right and intersectionality. *Journal of Political Ideologies*, 23(2), pp. 141–156, DOI:10.1080/13569317.2018.1451228

Griffith, R.M. (2021) *Making the World Over: Confronting Racism, Misogyny, and Xenophobia in U.S. History*. Charlottesville: University of Virginia Press.

Guerlain, P. (2018) US Foreign Policy of Chaos under Trump: The Wrecker and the Puppeteers. *Revue LISA/LISA e-Journal. Littératures, Histoire Des Idées, Images, Sociétés Du Monde Anglophone – Literature, History of Ideas, Images and Societies of the English-Speaking World*, vol. XVI-n°2, Article XVI-n°2, DOI:10.4000/lisa.10208

Hamilton, A., Madison, J., Jay, J. and Wright, B.F. (2010) *The Federalist*. Middletown, CT: Wesleyan University Press.

Hansford, J. (2017) The first amendment freedom of assembly as a racial project. *Yale Law Journal Forum*, 127, pp. 685–714.

Harvey, D. (2005) *A Brief History of Neoliberalism*. Oxford: Oxford University Press.

Hawley, G. (2017) *Making Sense of the Alt-Right*. New York: Columbia University Press.

Hennigan, B. (2022) *Buffalo Exposes Limits Of Biden's Domestic Terror Strategy*. Time, 20 May, https://time.com/6177847/biden-pledged-to-defeat-domestic-terror-buffalo-why-thats-not-enough/

HoSang, D.M. and Lowndes, J.E. (2019) *Producers, Parasites, Patriots: Race and the New Right-Wing Politics of Precarity*. Minneapolis: University of Minnesota Press.

Hubert, D. (2020) *Attenuated Democracy: A Critical Introduction to U.S. Government and Politics*. Salt Lake Community College, https://open.umn.edu/opentextbooks/textbooks/916

Hughes, B., Jones, D. and Amarasingam, A. (2022) Ecofascism: An examination of the far-right/ ecology nexus in the online space. *Terrorism and Political Violence*, 34(5) pp. 1–27, DOI:10.1080/09546553.2022.2069932

Kelley, B.J. (2018) *Turning Point USA's Blooming Romance with the Alt-Right*. Southern Poverty Law Center, 16 February, www.splcenter.org/hatewatch/2018/02/16/turning-point-usas-blooming-romance-alt-right

Keyssar, A. (2020) *Why Do We Still Have the Electoral College?* Cambridge, MA: Harvard University Press.

Know Your Meme (2015) *Q&A with Fredrick Brennan of 8chan*, https://knowyourmeme.com/blog/interviews/qa-with-fredrick-brennan-of-8chan

Krieger, N., Rowley, D.L., Herman, A.A., Avery, B. and Phillips, M.T. (1993) Racism, sexism, and social class: Implications for studies of health, disease, and well-being. *American Journal of Preventive Medicine*, 9(6, Supplement), pp. 82–122, DOI:10.1016/S0749-3797(18)30666-4

Kundnani, A. (2015) *A Decade Lost: Rethinking Radicalisation and Extremism*. Boone: Claystone Press.

Lorber, B. (2021) America First Is Inevitable. *Political Research Associates*, 15 January, https://politicalresearch.org/2021/01/15/america-first-inevitable

Mace, G. (1972) The antidemocratic character of judicial review. *California Law Review*, 60(4), pp. 1140–1149, DOI:10.2307/3479561

Macklin, G. (2012) Transatlantic connections and conspiracies: A.K. Chesterton and 'the new unhappy lords'. *Journal of Contemporary History*, 47(2), pp. 270–290, DOI: 10.1177/0022009411431723

MacNeil, N. and Baker, R. (2013) *The American Senate: An Insider's History*. Oxford: Oxford University Press.

Matsuda, M. J., Lawrence, C.R., Delgado, R. and Crenshaw, K.W. (2018) Introduction. In: Matsuda, M.J, Lawrence, C.R., Delgado, R. and Crenshaw, K.W. (eds), *Words that Wound: Critical Race Theory, Assaultive Speech, and the First Amendment*. Abingdon, UK: Routledge, pp. 1–15, DOI:10.4324/9780429502941-1

McLaughlin, T. (2019) The Weird, Dark History of 8Chan. *Wired*, 6 August, www.wired.com/story/the-weird-dark-history-8chan/

Meeropol, M.A. (2017) *Surrender: How the Clinton Administration Completed the Reagan Revolution*. Ann Arbor: University of Michigan Press, DOI:.10.3998/mpub.15199

Michael, G. (2008) *Willis Carto and the American Far Right*. Gainesville: University Press of Florida.

Miller-Idriss, C. and Hughes, B. (2021) *Blurry Ideologies and Strange Coalitions: The Evolving Landscape of Domestic Extremism*. Lawfare, 19 December, www.lawfareblog.com/blurry-ideologies-and-strange-coalitions-evolving-landscape-domestic-extremism

Mintz, F.P. (1985) *The Liberty Lobby and the American Right: Race, Conspiracy, and Culture*. Westport, CT: Greenwood Press.

Moreland-Capuia, A. (2021) *The Trauma of Racism: Exploring the Systems and People Fear Built*. Cham: Springer International Publishing AG.

Mudde, C. (2010) The populist radical right: A pathological normalcy. *West European Politics*, 33(6), pp. 1167–1186, DOI:10.1080/01402382.2010.508901

Munn, L. (2019) *Algorithmic Hate: Brenton Tarrant and the Dark Social Web*. Institute of Network Cultures, 19 March, https://networkcultures.org/blog/2019/03/19/luke-munn-algorithmic-hate-brenton-tarrant-and-the-dark-social-web/

Novak, M. (2016) *FBI Releases File on Willis Carto, Neo-Nazi Recently Buried at Arlington*. Gizmodo.com, 7 July, https://gizmodo.com/fbi-releases-file-on-willis-carto-neo-nazi-recently-bu-1783195062

Oluo, I. (2020) *Mediocre: The Dangerous Legacy of White Male America* (1st edn). Cypress, CA: Seal Press.

Painter, W.L. (2021) *DHS Budget Request Analysis: FY2022*. Washington, DC: Congressional Research Service.

PERIL and SPLC. (2021) *Preventing Youth Radicalization: Building Resilient, Inclusive Communities. The Parents & Caregivers Guide to Online Youth Radicalization* (Preventing Youth Radicalization: Building Resilient, Inclusive Communities). www.splcenter.org/peril-guide-online-youth-radicalization

Pinto, A.T. (2019) Capitalism with a transhuman face: The afterlife of fascism and the digital frontier. *Third Text*, 33(3), pp. 315–336, DOI:10.1080/09528822.2019.1625638

Robin, C. (2017) *The Reactionary Mind: Conservatism from Edmund Burke to Sarah Palin* (2nd edn). Oxford: Oxford University Press.

Robinson, C.J. (2000) *Black Marxism: The Making of the Black Radical Tradition*. Chapel Hill: University of North Carolina Press.

Sandifer, E. and Graham, J. (2018) *Neoreaction a Basilisk: Essays on and Around the Alt-Right*. Scotts Valley: CreateSpace Independent Publishing Platform.

Schiffrin, A. (2017) Disinformation and democracy: The internet transformed protest but did not improve democracy. *Journal of International Affairs*, 71(1), pp. 117–126.

Scotti, C. (2016) *Return of the Neocons: Trump's Surprising Cabinet Candidates*. The Fiscal Times.com, 17 November, www.thefiscaltimes.com/2016/11/17/Return-Neocons-Trump-s-Surprising-Cabinet-Candidates

Sked, A. (2014) Race in America: From civil war to civil rights. *Journal of Contemporary History*, 49(2), pp. 440–453, DOI:10.1177/0022009413516921

Sokol, J. (2009) Willis Carto and the American far right. *The Journal of American History*, 95(4), pp. 1248–1249.

Sparby, E.M. (2017) Digital social media and aggression: Memetic rhetoric in 4chan's collective identity. *Computers and Composition*, 45, pp. 85–97, DOI: 10.1016/j.compcom.2017.06.006

Spencer, R.B. and Gottfried, P.E. (2015) *The Great Purge: The Deformation of the American Conservative Movement*. Augusta, GA: Washington Summit Publishers.

SPLC. (n.d.-a) *David Lane*. Southern Poverty Law Center, www.splcenter.org/fighting-hate/extremist-files/individual/david-lane

SPLC. (n.d.-b) *Louis Beam*. Southern Poverty Law Center, www.splcenter.org/fighting-hate/extremist-files/individual/louis-beam

Squire, M. (2019) *Alt-Tech and the Radical Right, Part 1: Why the Shift?* Centre for Analysis of the Radical Right, 9 August, www.radicalrightanalysis.com/2019/08/09/alt-tech-and-the-radical-right-part-1-why-the-shift/

Tanner, C. and Burghart, D. (2020) *From Alt-Right To Groyper*. Institute for Research & Education on Human Rights, www.irehr.org/reports/alt-right-to-groyper/

United States (1996) *Antiterrorism and Effective Death Penalty Act of 1996*. Washington, DC: US Government Printing Office.

Wegman, J. (2020) *Let the People Pick the President: The Case for Abolishing the Electoral College / Jesse Wegman* (1st edn). New York: St. Martin's Press.

Weisenburger, S. (2009) Willis Carto and the American far right. *The Journal of Southern History*, 75(4), pp. 1106–1108.

Wells, C.E. (2019) Assumptions about 'terrorism' and the Brandenburg incitement test. *Brooklyn Law Review*, 85, p. 38.

Williams, L. (2017) 'The Alt-Right Side of History Will Prevail', Says the Finge Republican Bankrolling Richard Spencer. *Mother Jones*, 21 July, www.motherjones.com/politics/2017/07/alt-right-william-regnery-richard-spencer/

Wirls, D. and Wirls, S. (2004) *The Invention of the United States Senate*. Baltimore, MD: Johns Hopkins University Press.

Zimring, C.A. (2015) *Clean and White: A History of Environmental Racism in the United States*. New York: NYU Press.

INDEX

Note: In this index the page numbers for figures and tables are denoted by *italic* and **bold** text respectively. Endnotes are shown by "n" and the number of the note after the page number e.g., 206n1 refers to endnote number 1 on page 206.

4chan 293–294
8chan 293–294
9/11 attacks 11, 13, 38, 72, 119, 153, 169, 257, 272, 295; Australia 236, 237; Italy 213, 214; The Netherlands 139, 143, 145; New Zealand 259, 260, 262

abuses of power 130
academia, relative frequencies of concepts over time in 62, *63*, *64*, *66*
accumulating social resilience **206**
ACLU *see* American Civil Liberties Union (ACLU)
Actieprogramma Integrale Aanpak Jihadisme 145, 146, 147
Action Française 117, 118
Action Plans (Norwegian) 155, 156, 158–159, 160–161
Action Programme against Aggression and Violence (AgAG) 172–173
activism: anti-Muslim public 128; anti-racist 191, 192; civic 163; climate 71, **78**; environmental 258; extremist 193; far-right 12, 21, 118–119, 127, 128, 129, 185, 215; guerrilla 129; LGBTQ 184; Māori 258; Muslim political 126; ONR 201, 202; pro-social 87n2; right-wing 113; social 244; street 128; violent political 142
adaptation 37, 38, 190; in Grossman's conceptualisation of resilience to violent extremism 240, 247
Aden, Halima *82*, 82, 83

adversity 5, 38, 39, 41, 43, 72, 154, 197, 202, 241, 250, 266
AfD *see* Alternative for Germany (AfD) party
Afghanistan 13, 114, 212, 237, 255, 259, 260, 262, 267, 271
Africans, in the United States of America 287, 288
AgAG *see* Action Programme against Aggression and Violence (AgAG)
agonism 74, 80, 83, 86
AIVD *see* Algemene Inlichtingen en Veiligheidsdienst (AIVD)
Al-Fourqaan mosque 147
Algemene Inlichtingen en Veiligheidsdienst (AIVD) 143, 144, 145–146
Al-Qaeda (AQ) 75, **78**, 78, 127, 212, 228–229, 236, 237, 258
Al-Shabaab (AS) 14, 75, **78**, 78
Alternative for Germany (AfD) party 176, 177
alternative narratives *see* radical alternative narratives
alt-right 84, 133, 134, 291, 292, 293, 294
American Civil Liberties Union (ACLU) 295
American extremism 287–288, 289–294
angry citizens 170–171
Anni di piombo 210
antagonism 18, 74, 80, *81*, 82, 198
anti-authority violence 271, 275
anti-democracy 14, 18, 19, 20, 74, 75, 144, 145–146, 147, 206n1, 250, 289, 290, 296
anti-discrimination 174, 192, 203, 205
anti-egalitarian right 74, 116–117

Index

anti-extremism 116, 192; policy and practice, in United States of America 294–296
anti-fascism 142
anti-gender mobilisations 10, 118, 214
anti-immigration 42, 118, 133, 155, 171, 183, 201, 213, 214, 215, 221, 222–223, 224–225, 226
anti-Muslim attitudes 118, 122, 128, 156, 171, 183, 210, 214, 221, 222–223, 226
anti-pluralism 18, 19, 20
anti-racism 80, 163, 191, 192, 244; Roma 183, 186, 187, 191, 193
anti-Semitism 5, 117, 157, 289, 291, 293
anti-social extremism 20, 71, 73, 76, 79
antisocial resilience *43*
Antiterrorism Research Committee on Radicalisation and Jihadi Extremism 216
antiziganism 183, 186, 187, 191, 193
ANZCTC *see* Australia-New Zealand Counter-Terrorism Committee (ANZCTC)
AQ *see* Al-Qaeda (AQ)
Ardern, Jacinda 264–265
AS *see* Al Shabaab (AS)
ASIO *see* Australian Security Intelligence Organisation (ASIO)
Association of Those Persecuted by Communism 185
austerity 4, 26–27, 131, 134, 196, 210, 223, 232n10, 291
Australia 236–251, *247*
Australian Security Intelligence Organisation (ASIO) 41, 236, 239, 240, 251n15, 251n16
Australia-New Zealand Counter-Terrorism Committee (ANZCTC) 261, 262
authoritarianism 19, 226, 292
autocratic-fascist right, in Poland 198, **199**, 199–200, 205–206
Autonomy Foundation 12, 197, 204–205, 206

banlieues 115, 116, 119
BBE (Bijzondere Bijstandseenheid) 140, 141
BDJ *see* Bund Deutscher Jugend (BDJ)
Begum, Shamima 131–132
behavioural regimes 43, 45
beliefs 19, 22, 23, 34, 44, 245, 278, 293, 295; violence related 73, **78**, 238, 239, 246, 249, 257
belonging 39, 131, 162, 170, 187, 198, 248, 250, 273; European polarisation and resilience 59, 62, *63*, *64*, 64, 65, *66*, 68; to a group 53, 57, 60, 67, 74–75; multifaith 80–83, *81*, *82*; national 115, 121, 212, 213; sense of 74–75, 78, 79, 83, 87, 203, 249, 250; social 244; young people 73, 74, 80
bicultural status, of New Zealand 256, 266–267
Bijzondere Bijstandseenheid (BBE) 140, 141

Binnenlandse Veiligheidsdienst (BVD) 140, 142–143, 149n2, 149n4, 149n6, 149n7
Black Americans 287, 288
Black Lives Matter 71, **78**, 83, 103, 239
Blood and Honour Cultural Association 190, 191
BNC Informative Writing Sampler 52, *53*, *55*, 57, *58*, 59, *59*
BNP *see* British National Party (BNP)
bonding 35, 73, 246
bonding capital 39, 74
bonding social capital 35, 73, **78**, 85, 99, 100, 103, 104
border crisis 223, 224, 225, 227–228
border security 127, 132, 187, 188, 214, 295
both/and narratives of belonging 80, *82*, 82, 83, 86
Brandenburg standard, of allowable speech 293–294
BRaVE *see* Building Resilience, against Violent Extremism and Polarisation (BRaVE)
Breivik, Anders 5, 6, 145, 156
Brexit 9, 93, 128, 131, 134
bridging capital 39, 73, 74, 83, 86, 236, 245, 248, 257
bridging social capital 35, 73, **78**, 85–86, 99, 100, 103, 104
British National Party (BNP) 128
British values 22, 23, 24, 132, 134
broad approach, to counterterrorism 11, 139, 141, 142, 143–144, 145, 148, 149
Brummundal 155, 163
building pro-social resilience with young people, in Australia 245–246
building resilience: Australian conceptions of 236–237, 240–241, 242, 243, 246, 249, 250, 265, 275; online 99–100; to violence 40, 237, 249; to violent extremism 34, 37, 39, 40, 42, 44, 45, 74, 92, 93
Building Resilience to Violent Extremism (BRaVE) 8, 9, 34, 37, 39, 40, 42, 44, 45, 51, 52, 53, 55, 57, 58, 59, 61, 62, 69n1, 73, 257, 265; Australia 236–237, 240–241, 242–243, 245, 246, 247–248, 249, 250
Bund Deutscher Jugend (BDJ) 169
Burkini ban *81*, 81–82
BVD *see* Binnenlandse Veiligheidsdienst (BVD)

Canada 270–282
Canada Centre 275, 276, 277
Canadian Practitioner's Network for the Prevention of Radicalisation and Extremist Violence (CPN-PREV) 279, 280–281
Capitol Hill Riots 5, 10, 21, 92, 93, 98–99, 293; online resilience in response to 102–104
Carto, Willis 289–290, 291

CasaPound Italia 214, 215
Catholicism 117, 197, 198–199, 202, 203, 205, 213, 214–215, 218
CCE *see* Commission for Countering Extremism (CCE)
centralisation of extremism in British media 24–25
Centro nazionale sulla radicalizzazione (CRAD) 216
CFCM *see Conseil français du culte musulman* (CFCM)
Channel mentoring system 133
Chans 293, 294
Charlie Hebdo 114, 115, 119, 122
Christchurch Call to Action 7, 267
Christchurch mosque attack 7, 13, 14, 24, 78, 94, 126, 129, 156, 254, 259, 263, 266, 267; online resilience in response to the 100–101; prevention and resilience in response to 264–266; Royal Commission 254, 256, 261, 262, 264, 265, 266, 267
Christianity 187, 210, 213, 290
cities, violent extremism being seen as problem of 40–41
citizenship 36–37, 54, 57, 113–114, 120, 131–132, 143–144, 162, 212, 265
civic activism 163
Civic Coalition 196
civic nationalism 113–114
Civic Platform 196
civil disobedience 71
civil rights 14, 17–18, 19, 23, 25, 26, 28, 192, 228, 262, 287, 290
civil society actors 34, 45, 154, 156, 161, 162, 181, 189, 192, 230
Civitas 118
class 41, 79, 86, 87n2, 130, 183, 239, 294
climate activism 71, **78**
colonialism 14, 115, 116, 258
colour-blind values 122
Commission for Countering Extremism (CCE) 22
communal identity structures 38, 241
communal ideological or belief structures 38, 241
communication-based context 59–61, *59*
communitarianism 114, 115, 117
communities: engagement 10, 33, 74, 125, 144, 240, 242, 250, 275; resilience to violent extremism 14, 33–34, 35–36, 37, 38, 39, 73, 236, 286; trust 125, 132–133, 264
COMPACT programme 237, 243, 244–245, 246, *247*, 248–249
complex cultural identity 75, 80, 82, 83, 86, 246, 247
conducive environment, for radicalisation 9, 75, 76, 87

connectedness 43, 73, 162, 245, 246, 249, 257, 264–265
Conseil français du culte musulman (CFCM) 116
Conservative Party 126, 129, 171
conservative right 14, 96, 105n1, 117, 118, 184, 222, 231, 273; Italy 213, 214; Poland 199, 204, 206; United States of America 288, 289, 290, 292
conspiracy 5, 7, 38, 44, 60, 61, 113, 122, 129, 156, 177, 183, **189**, 215, 240, 291; online extremism 93, 95, 98, 99, 104; young people 74, 76, 79
CONTEST strategy 126
corroding social resilience 203, **206**
Council of Europe Convention on preventing and combating violence against women and domestic violence 184, 188, 199
counselling 65, 120, 173–175, 279, 280
counter-extremism 5, 7, 8, 10, 12, 18, 21, 25, 26–27, 28, 169; Hungary 181, 189, 190–191, 193; United Kingdom 125, 126, 127, 129, 133, 134
Countering Violent Extremism *see* CVE (Countering Violent Extremism)
counter-radicalisation 10, 120, 121, 142, 143, 144, 145, 216–217, 218, 248, 275
counterterrorism: broad approach to 11, 139, 141, 142, 143–144, 145, 148, 149; Dutch approach to 10–11, 139–142, 148; Trans-Tasman approach to 260–262
Covid-19 pandemic 3, 6, 7, 9, 10, 68, 73, 76, 94–96, 104, 129, 215; Australia 240, 250; Canada 271, 274; Greece 221, 223, 224; online resilience in response to 101–102
CPN-PREV *see* Canadian Practitioner's Network for the Prevention of Radicalisation and Extremist Violence (CPN-PR EV)
CRAD *see Centro nazionale sulla radicalizzazione* (CRAD)
criminality 12, 186, 191, 258, 278, 280
crises: border 223, 224, 225, 227–228; economic 12, 79, 196, 223, 228, 232n10, 295; financial 3, 4, 131, 144–145, 210, 223; Greek debt 221, 226
Cross Check 97–98
cultural context 57–59, *58*
cultural difference 114, 115
cultural diversity 37, 176, 242, 256, 273
cultural identity 39, 58, 73, 245, 257; complex 75, 80, 82, 83, 86, 246, 247; exclusivist 39; healthy 74
cultural sectarianism 114, 115, 117
cultural values 37, 39, 73, 245
culture, of New Zealand 256–257
CVE *see* Countering Violent Extremism (CVE); *see also* P/CVE (Preventing and Countering Violent Extremism)

Daesh *see* Islamic State in Iraq and Syria (IS/ISIS)
debt crisis, Greek 221, 226
deep prevention, resilience as 286
democracy: anti- *see* anti-democracy; mass 288–289; open 266
Democratic Charter movement 191
democratic order 142–143, 145–146
democratic values 154, 158, 160, 162, 174, 184, 287
Demonstration for All, The 118
demonstrations, in The Netherlands 147–148
DEMS *see* Diversity and Equality Management System (DEMS)
deportation 7, 212, 214, 216
deprivation 40, 76, 78, 116, 121, 176, 184; economic 76, 116, 121
de-radicalisation 6, 12–13, 120, 121, 174, 193, 278, 295; United Kingdom 126, 130, 133; young people 72, 76, 80
difference 22, 37, 55, 57, 59, 75, 133; cultural 114, 115
digital media 39, 79, 82, 86, 176, 279
dignity, human 9, 78, 86, 121
diminished prospects for the future, meme reflecting 75
Diminishing Opportunities for Violent Extremism (DOVE) 74
discrimination 40, 80, 173, 174, 176, 204, 205, 231, 250; anti- 174, 192, 203, 205; in Greece 221, 223, 224; minority 192; against Muslims 10, 78, 113, 116, 210, 211; racial 55, 162–163, 230; structural 5
disinformation 93, 95, 96, 98, 101, 102, 104, 122, 271
disintegration approach, to explaining resurgence of right-wing ideology 172
disrupted plots and terrorist attacks 236, 238
dissolution of boundaries, characterisation of racially motivated violence 171
diversity: cultural 37, 176, 242, 256, 273; in New Zealand 257
Diversity and Equality Management System (DEMS) 54
domestic refocus, phase of New Zealand's response to terrorism 259, 260
domestic terrorism 98, 211, 216, 263, 294
DOVE (Diminishing Opportunities for Violent Extremism) 74
DRIVE project 135n1
Duke, David 289, 291
Dutch approach, to counterterrorism 10–11, 139–142, 148
Dutch government 139, 140, 141, 146, 147, 148

ECHR *see* European Court of Human Rights (ECHR)

economic crisis 12, 79, 196, 223, 228, 232n10, 295
economic deprivation 76, 116, 121
EDL *see* English Defence League (EDL)
education *see* schools
égalité 113
8chan 293–294
either/or narratives of belonging 80, *81*
el Atrach, Abdelkarim 146, 147, 149n11
elites 14, 95, 130, 143, 186, 202, 289
empathy 37, 40, 75, 84, 87, 154
employment 9, 41, 42, 54, 71, 183, 227, 249, 250, 279; *see also* unemployment
empowerment 155, 164, 169, 175, **206**, 206, 230, 288, 291; young people 79, 80, 82, 83, 86
enacting social resilience 203, **206**
English Defence League (EDL) 128
environmental action 258
equality: gender 21, 80, *84*, 115, 118; racial 83–85, *84*, *85*; LGBTQ marches 198, 199, 203, **206**
Estimated Time of Arrival (ETA) Toronto programme 278, 279
ETA *see* Euskadi Ta Askatasuna (ETA)
ETA *see* Estimated Time of Arrival (ETA) Toronto programme
ethics 34, 73, 100, 162
ethnic minorities 55, 57, 60, 114, 115, 215
ethnicity 95, 133, 176, 183, 210, 228
ethno-nationalism 23, 182, 200
EU *see* European Union (EU)
European Commission 27, 51, 95
European Court of Human Rights (ECHR) 224, 226, 232n7, 232n8, 232n14
European Parliament 23, 128, 201
European Union (EU) 7–8, 12, 22, 27, 56, 145, 185; France 114, 117, 118, 121; Greece 222, 223, 225; Italy 215, 216; Poland 196, 200, 201
European Union Terrorism and Situation Trend report (TE-SAT) 2020 94–95
European values 22, 201
Euskadi Ta Askatasuna (ETA) 23
Evolve Program 280
exceptionalism, Italian 12, 210, 211, 218
exclusion: political 116; societal 27, 60, 82, 92, 99, 104–105, 131, 134, 135n1, 211, 250
exclusionary criteria of belonging 198
exclusionary discourse 4, 5, 19, 20, 21, 38, 40, 171, 181, 184, 192, 203
exclusionary *laicite* 114, 115, 119, 121
exclusivism 5, 18–19, 20–21, 38, 39, 44, 72, 74, 77, **78**, 79
EXIT project 11, 155, 160
extreme right 10, 11, 12, 41, 74, 92, 93, 95, 96, 104, 113, 117, 118–119, 142, 170–171, 171–173, 174, 175, 176, 177, 181, 184, 185, 186, 188, 214–215, 239, 286–287, 289, 290, 291

Index

extreme right politics, in Italy 214
extremism: American 287–288, 289–294; anti- 116, 192, 294–296; anti-social 20, 71, 73, 76, 79; counter- *see* counter-extremism; definition of 8, 18–19, 22, 27; Dutch 10–11, 139–142, 148; far-right *see* far-right extremism; Islamist 6, 126, 129, 133, 134, 258, 295; jihadist 10, 113, 114–116, 122, 122n1, 211–213, 216; non-violent 23, 148; online 92–105; Polish 197–200, **199**; political 225–228; reactionary 296; religion 228–229; right-wing 116–119, 198–200, **199**, 213–215; transnational *see* transnational extremism; violent *see* violent extremism; violent right-wing 11, 27–28, 169
extremist actors 45, 183, 184, 188, 193n1, 196, 204, 205, 294
extremist ideas 25–26, 155, 239
extremist responses, in Norway 155–158
extremist travellers *see* foreign fighters
extremist trends, in Norway 155–158
extremist values 238, 250, 287
extremist violence 5, 8, 27, 33, 35, 114, 156, 169, 230, 287–288; Canada 270, 271, 272–273, 274, 275, 277, 279, 280; Italy 210, 215; *see also* violent extremism

Facebook 92, 94, 96, 97–98, 99, 100–101, 102
faith 4, 11, 19, 22, 74, 114, 120, 169, 258; in Australia 248, 250; in Greece 229, 230, 231–232; multi- 80–83, *81*, *82*, 286; Muslim 20, 82, 116, 130, 134, 175, 212–213, 222; in United Kingdom 125, 134
far-right: activism 12, 21, 118–119, 127, 128, 129, 185, 215; extremism 6, 38, 40, 125, 127, 128, 184, 236, 238, 239, 249, 287, 289, 294, 295; in Hungary 181–189, **189**, 191, 192–193, 193n1; protest 147–148; violence 126, 127–128, 134
fascism 6, 12, 25, 117, 128, 214, 233n35; anti- 142; autocratic 198, **199**, 199–200, 205–206; in Hungary 183, 190; neo- 6, 12, 79, 98, 128, 185, 193n1, 214, 215; in Poland 197, 200, 201, 202; in United States of America 290, 294
FBI (Federal Bureau of Investigation) 22–23, 96, 294, 295
Federal Agency for Civic Education 177
Federal Bureau of Investigation (FBI) 22–23, 96, 294, 295
feminism **78**, 79, 83, *84*, 84, 86, 115, 290
Fidesz 12, 183, 185, 187–188, 193, 193n2
financial crises 3, 4, 131, 144, 210, 223
FN (*Front National*) 113, 117, 118, 119
force and violence 19–20
forced returns, at Greece's sea and land borders 224

foreign fighter families, return of 131–132
foreign fighters 6, 10, 34, 133, 271; Australia 236, 237; France 113, 114, 119; Italy 211, 216; The Netherlands 139, 144–146; New Zealand 258, 263; Norway 154, 156
Fortuyn, Pim 143
Forza Nuova 214
4chan 293–294
France 113–122; institutional values 115; 10, 120; Islam 10, 116, 120; New Right 10, 117, 214; republicanism 10, 113–114, 115, 116–117, 120, 121
fraternité 113
freedom of assembly 8, 18, 184, **189**
freedom of expression 8, 21, 61, 100, 102, 115, 119, 130, 190
freedom of speech 18, 26, 60–61, 122, 184, 249
Freedom Party 143, 145
French Revolution 113, 116–117
Front National (FN) 113, 117, 118, 119
Fundacja Autonomia 12, 197, 204–205, 206
fundamentalism 116, 193n1, 198–199, 206, 214, 230, 258, 294

gender equality 21, 80, *84*, 115, 118
gender ideology 12, 184, 188, 193n3, 199, 214
Generation Identity movement 128–129, 214
Germany 168–177
GIFCT *see* Global Internet Forum to Counter Terrorism, The (GIFCT)
Girls' Power Centres 204
global financial crisis 131, 144–145
Global Internet Forum to Counter Terrorism, The (GIFCT) 100–101
Global War on Terrorism (GWOT), phase of New Zealand's response to terrorism 259–260
globalisation 38, 114, 118, 125, 158, 239
Gogh, Theo van 143, 148
Golden Dawn 7, 13, 221, 223, 225–227, 229, 230–231
governance 4, 27, 35, 57, 83, 168, 200, 228, 288, 293, 294
governments, relative frequencies of concepts over time in *66*
great replacement theory 74, 78, 128
Greece 221–233; debt crisis 221, 226; national identity 222, 223, 228, 231; Orthodox Church 221, 222, 223, 226, 228–229, 231; values 229
Greniuch, Tomasz 201–202
group-focused enmity theory 198
guerrilla activism 129
GWOT *see* Global War on Terrorism (GWOT), phase of New Zealand's response to terrorism
GYEM *see* Working Group Against Hate Crimes (GYEM)
'gypsy crime/criminality' 186, 187, 191

Index

'hands off' approach, to counterterrorism 141–142, 148
harassment 98, 103, 174, **189**, 191, 224
Harper, Prime Minister Stephen 274
hate crime 8, 22, 27, 56, 95, 175, 201, 231; Canada 271, 272–273, 280; Hungary 188, 191, 192; New Zealand 256, 259
hate speech 13, 22, 56, 94, 132, **206**; Germany 175, 176; Greece 221, 228, 230, 231; Hungary 183, 186
Heitmeyer, Wilhelm 172, 198
hidden resilience capacity 43
historic abstracts and objectives with the BNC Informative Writing Sampler 55
historical context corpus 55–56
Hofstad Network 143, 149n8
HoGeSa (Hooligans Against Salafists) 170
Holocaust 187, 289
Home Office 125, 126–127, 132
homosexuality 176, 184, 188, 193n3
Hooligans Against Salafists (HoGeSa) 170
Horthy, Miklós 187
human dignity 9, 78, 86, 121
human rights 5, 10, 18, 25–28, 162, 198, 216; France 119, 121; Germany 172, 173, 174, 175, 176; Greece 224, 226, 227, 230, 232n16, 233n35; Hungary 188, 191; online extremism 96, 100, 104; United Kingdom 125, 127, 134
human security 143, 153
Hungarian Guard Traditionalist and Cultural Association 186, 188, 190, 191–192
Hungarian Hungarist Movement (MHM) 185, 190
Hungarian Justice and Life Party 184–185, 186–187, 188
Hungarian National Front 185, 190–191
Hungarian Socialist Party 185, 187
Hungarian Welfare Association 185
Hungary 181–193, **189**; national identity 182, 183; values 187

Identitarian movement 118, 128–129
identity *see* national identity
identity-driven violence 271, 275
ideological awakening, of young males 131
ideological radicalisation 210, 212, 213
ideologically motivated violent extremism (IMVE) 239, 271, 275, 281
ideologues 130, 158, 289, 290
illiberal phase, of Hungarian far-right 187–188
illiberalism 12, 68, 181, 189, 192, 197, 203, 204, 206n1, 287
immigration 12, 41, 56, 62, 131, 256, 273, 292; anti- *see* anti-immigration; France 113, 115, 117, 118, 121; Germany 171, 176; Greece 223, 224, 228–229; Italy 210, 211, 212, 213, 214, 215; The Netherlands 142, 143, 148
Imperium 290

IMVE *see* ideologically motivated violent extremism (IMVE)
incels/involuntary celibates 38, 75, **78**, 79–80, 83–84, *85*, 129, 133, 239, 271
incompatibility, antagonistic narratives of *81*
individual-level resilience 40, 250
Indonesia 139–140, 141, 149n1
inequality 4, 9, 10, 19, 27, 54, *75*, 296; Germany 173, 175; United Kingdom 125, 127, 129, 130, 131, 134, 135
influencers 79, 83–84, 87
injustice 78, 121, 139, 146, 147
Integral Action Programme Jihadism 145, 146, 147
integral approach, to counterterrorism in The Netherlands 144–146
interactive construction of extremists 146–147
interfaith dialogue and education 74, 120, 230
intergenerational inequality, meme reflecting *75*
international recalibration, of New Zealand's counterterrorism operations 260
international relations, New Zealand's small state approach to 255
international stabilisation, phase of New Zealand's response to terrorism 259–260
international terrorism 211, 216, 271
internet 9, 61, 79, 92–93, 94–95, 97, 100–101, 131; France 119, 120; Italy 212, 216, 217, 218; Norway 157, 158; United States of America 293, 294
intervention-based P/CVE programming, in Canada 276–281
Iraq 6, 34, 114, 119, 130, 131, 212, 225, 236, 237, 260, 261, 263
irregular violence 3, 17, 19, 27
IS/ISIS *see* Islamic State in Iraq and Syria (IS/ISIS)
Islam: French 10, 120; New 222, 232n2, 232n3; Old 222, 232n2, 232n3
Islamic State in Iraq and Syria (IS/ISIS) 10, 14, 36, 93, 95, 114, 212, 271; Australia 236, 237, 238, 246; United Kingdom 125, 127, 130, 131–132, 133; young people 75, **78**, 78, *81*
Islamism 156, 157, 229, 295; extremism 6, 126, 129, 133, 134, 258, 295; militancy 35, 145, 156, 157; terrorism 7, 158
Islamophobia 5, 10, 20–21, 27, 65, 148, 293; France 113, 122n1; Greece 221, 226, 231; Italy 213, 218; United Kingdom 126, 130, 133, 134, 135
Istanbul Convention 184, 188, 199
Italian exceptionalism 12, 210, 211, 218
Italy 210–218
ius soli 212, 213

Jewish people 10, 11, 38, 69n1, 79, 117, 118, 145, 170, 177, 182, 183, 184, 188, 215

jihadism 12, 13, 67, 130; France 114, 115, 116, 118, 119, 120; Italy 211, 212, 217; The Netherlands 144, 145, 146–147; Norway 161, 163
jihadist extremism: in France 10, 113, 114–116, 122, 122n1; in Italy 211–213, 216
jihadist radicalisation: in France 114–115, 116, 122; in Italy 210, 211, 212–213
jihadist violence 10, 113, 169
Jim Crow 287
Jobbik (*Jobbik Magyarországért Mozgalom*) 12, 183, 186, 187, 188, 190, 191, 193, 193n2
judiciary 115, 140, 141–142, 190, 201, **206**, 262
just cause 9, 71

Kepel, Gilles 114–115
Key Concept Analysis 52, 55–56, *55*
Koalicja Obywatelska 196
Kommunizmus Üldözötteinek Szövetsége (KÜSZ) 185

La Manif Pour Tous 118
laïcité 10, 82, 113, 114, 115, 120, 121, 122
LAOS *see* Popular Orthodox Rally (LAOS)
Law and Justice party 12, 196, 197–198, **199**, 199, 200, 201–202, 203, 204–205, 206
law and order 65, 66, *66*, 67, 68, 117, 214, 225
Le Pen, Jean-Marie 117
Le Pen, Marine 117, 118, 119
left-liberal rise and fall phase, of Hungarian far-right 185–187
legal infrastructure, relevant to right-wing extremist activity in Hungary **189**, 190
legislative practice 21–25, *24*
levelling up 54, 55
LGBTQ+ community 38, 94, 214, 231, 271; Hungary 183–184, 188, 192; Poland 198, 199, 200, 203, 204, 205, **206**, 206
liberal democracy 5, 18, 25, 28, 92, 153, 196, 197, 203, 204, 206, 257
liberté 113
Liberty Lobby 289–290, 291
linking capital 35, 36, 73, 74, 134, 257, 264; Australia 245–246, 247, 248–249, 250
linking social capital 35, 248; online extremism 100, 101, 102, 103–104; young people 73, **78**, 78–79, 85–86
Lizzo 83
London bombings 6, 130, 258
lone-actor/lone-wolf terrorism 12, 56, 156, 157, 211–212, 215, 216

Macedonia 223
Macron, President Emmanuel 100, 114, 115, 116, 119
Madrid attacks 6, 143, 148
Magyar Hungarista Mozgalom (MHM) 185, 190
Magyar Igazság és Élet Pártja (MIÉP) 184–185, 186–187, 188

Magyar Nemzeti Arcvonal (MNA) 185, 190–191
Magyar Népjóléti Szövetség (MNSZ) 185
maladaptive radicalisation 9, 72, 76, 78
maladaptive resilience 9, 33, 41, 42, 43, 76, 250
Māori people 256, 257, 258, 263
Marcus, George 45
marginalisation 36, 38, 74, 83, 131, 144, 168, 287; Hungary 187, 192; Italy 212–213, 215
mask wearing 97
mass democracy 288–289
Measures aimed at preventing radicalisation and jihadist extremism 216
mental health 26–27, 42, 84, 134, 277, 278, 279
messaging 9–10, 44, 75, 76, 84, 176, 203, 204, 240, 265
methodological note 7–8
MHM *see Magyar Hungarista Mozgalom* (MHM)
MIÉP *see Magyar Igazság és Élet Pártja* (MIÉP)
migration *see* anti-immigration; immigration
militant Islamism 35, 145, 156, 157
militias 14, 98, 188, 287, 290, 294
Minkenberg, Michael 193n1, 198, 199–200, 205–206, 206n1
minority discrimination 192
misinformation 5, 7, 61, 93, 95, 96–97, 99, 102, 104, 129, 177, 240, 271
misogyny 76, 79–80, 271, 275
MNA *see Magyar Nemzeti Arcvonal* (MNA)
MNSZ *see Magyar Népjóléti Szövetség* (MNSZ)
Moluccan activism 139–140, 141, 142, 148, 149, 149n1
mosques 24, 94; France 114, 118, 119; Greece 222, 226, 228, 229; Italy 212, 213; The Netherlands 142, 145, 147; New Zealand 254, 258, 259, 264, 265; Norway 156, 157; United Kingdom 128, 129
Movement for a Better Hungary 12, 183, 186, 187, 188, 190, 191, 193, 193n2
multiculturalism 13–14, 27, 37, 53, 54, 55, 128, 133, 143, 162–163, 182, 213, 274; Australia 236, 239, 240, 242, 243, 244, 245, 246, *247*, 247; New Zealand 256–257, 267
multifaith belonging, radical alternative narratives for 80–83, *81*, *82*, 286
multilateralism 13, 254, 255, 259, 260, 262, 266, 267
multisystemic resilience 9, 72, 73, 244; *see also* COMPACT programme
Muslim communities 10, 13, 36, 37, 55, 67, 87n1, 163, 217, 225, 272, 295; Australia 236, 241, 249; France 119, 120; The Netherlands 142, 144, 145, 148; United Kingdom 126, 128, 133, 134
Muslim faith 20, 82, 116, 130, 134, 175, 212–213, 222

Muslim minorities 36, 37, 74, 78, 126, 128, 130, 131, 222
Muslim political activism 126

National Action 129
National agreement for an Italian Islam 217
national belonging 115, 121, 212, 213
National Centre on Radicalisation 216
National Coordinator for Counter-Terrorism and Security 143–144, 145
National CVE Framework 242, 248
National Democratic Party (NPD) 169, 171, 172
National Front (FN) 113, 117, 118, 119
National Gathering 113, 117, 118, 119
national identity: Greek 222, 223, 228, 231; Hungarian 182, 183; other 82, 115, 197, 213, 214, 221, 256
national media 21–22, 27, 129, 224
national policy and programming, in Australia 241–243
National Radical Camp 12, 196, 197, **199**, 200–202, 203, 205, 206
National Rally 113, 117, 118, 119
national security 14, 23, 132, 140, 198, 236, 295; Canada 271, 272, 274; Italy 212, 216; New Zealand 258, 261, 265; Norway 156, 158
National Strategy on Countering Radicalisation to Violence 275–276
Nationale Coordinator Terrorisme en Veiligheid (NCTV) 143–144, 145
nationalism 19, 22, 38, 116–117, 291; civic 113–114; ethno- 23, 182, 200; Greek 222–223, 228; Hungarian 182, 185, 188; Polish 197, 198, 202
National-Socialist Underground (NSU) 170
Nazism 78–79, 118, 168, 171, 185, 290
NCTV *see Nationale Coordinator Terrorisme en Veiligheid* (NCTV)
neoconservatism 292–293
neo-fascism 6, 12, 79, 98, 128, 185, 193n1, 214, 215
neo-Nazis 7, 13, 95, 129, 143; Germany 170, 171, 172, 174; Greece 221, 223, 226, 227, 231; Hungary 185, 190, 193n1; Norway 155, 156, 157, 163; *see also* Golden Dawn
Netherlands, The 139–149
New Democracy 223, 225, 227, 232n9
New Islam 222, 232n2, 232n3
New Zealand 254–267
NGOs *see* non-governmental organisations (NGOs)
9/11 attacks 11, 13, 38, 72, 119, 153, 169, 257, 272, 295; Australia 236, 237; Italy 213, 214; The Netherlands 139, 143, 145; New Zealand 259, 260, 262
non-government responses, to right-wing extremism in Hungary 191–192

non-governmental organisations (NGOs) 52, 61, 121, 174, 191, 192, 204, 205, 217, 229, 230, 246
non-religious values 162–163
non-violent extremism 23, 148
normalisation 23, 26, 73, 119, 157, 173, 210, 214, 246, 255; United Kingdom 126, 130, 134
Norway 153–164; P/CVE policy discourse, and resilience 158–160
NPD *see* National Democratic Party (NPD)
NSU *see* National-Socialist Underground (NSU)

Obóz Narodowo-Radykalny (ONR) 12, 196, 197, **199**, 200–202, 203, 205, 206
O'Farrell, Lily 83–85, *85*
Oklahoma City bombing 289, 294
Old Islam 222, 232n2, 232n3
Omar, Ilhan 83, *84*
online extremism, and resilience 92–105
online resilience 99–100; in response to Capitol Hill riots 102–104; in response to Christchurch attack 100–101; in response to Covid-19 101–102
ONR *see Obóz Narodowo-Radykalny* (ONR)
open democracy 266
OPV *see* Organisation for the Prevention of Violence (OPV)
Orbán, Viktor 12, 181, 183, 185, 187–188, 189, 192, 193
Organisation for the Prevention of Violence (OPV) 279–280
Orthodox Church 221, 222, 223, 226, 228–229, 231
Öszödi beszéd (Öszöd speech) 185, 186
out-groups 18–19, 21, 22, 37, 74–75, 86, 187

paleoconservatism 292, 293
pandemic *see* Covid-19 pandemic
pathological normalcy 287, 289
Patriotic Alternative 129
P/CVE (Preventing and Countering Violent Extremism): Canada 276–277, 277–278, 279–282; France 119–121; Italy 216–218; Norway 158–160; *see also* CVE (Countering Violent Extremism)
P/CVE resilience models 40, 45
PEGIDA (Germany) 170
Pegida Nederland 147, 148
permissiveness 201, 202
Pew Research Center 103, 214, 228
Pierce, William Luther 289, 290, 291
PiS *see Prawo i Sprawiedliwość* (PiS)
platform exploitation, by extreme right 92–105
Platforma Obywatelska 196
pluralism 4, 13, 18, 19, 20, 37, 39, 169, 236, 249, 250

PMVE (Politically Motivated Violent Extremism) 275, 281
Poland 196–206, **199**, **206**
polarisation: in Canada 273–274; framing of 52–61, *53*, *55*, *58*, *59*; over time 61–67, *63*, *64*, *66*; social *see* social polarisation
police co-led situation tables 276, 277–278
policing 23–24, 25, 27, 34, 35, 67, 71, *81*, 119, 191, 201, 238, 271, 288; Greece 224, 225, 226, 230, 231; Italy 212, 213, 215, 217; The Netherlands 139, 140, 141–142, 146, 147, 148; New Zealand 259, 263, 264, 265, 266; Norway 153, 155, 156, 157, 158, 159, 160, 161, 162, 163; United Kingdom 126–127, 132
policy and programming, in Australia: national 241–243; state-based 243–245
policy development landscape, in the United Kingdom 131–132
political conditions, giving rise to American extremism 291–293
political exclusion 116
political extremism, in Greece 225–228
political instability 3, 153, 185–186, 217
political mobilisation, in Hungary 191–192
political parties 20, 41, 128, 142, 143, 170; Greece 222, 227, 229–230; Hungary 183, 184, 185, 186
political power 286, 287–288
political reaction, as obstacle to resilience 288–289
political violence 14, 17, 18, 21, 23, 25, 27, 28, 162, 188, 262, 286, 296; Dutch approach to 139–142, 143, 144, 148, 149
Politically Motivated Violent Extremism (PMVE) 275, 281
politics: extreme right 214; Hungarian post-socialist 181, 186–187, 188, 192–193; New Zealand 257; street 118, 215
Popular Orthodox Rally (LAOS) 222–223, 225, 226, 232n9, 232n10
populism 4, 10, 12, 14, 21, 61, 97, 125, 143, 153, 215, 273; France 113, 117, 118; Greece 221, 222
populist radical right 212, 213, 214
populist-authoritarian right, in Poland 198, 199, 206
post-socialist politics, in Hungary 181, 186–187, 188, 192–193
poverty 12, 27, 42, 131, 134, 211, 277
practitioners, relative frequencies of concepts over time in 63–65, *64*
Prawo i Sprawiedliwość (PiS) 12, 196, 197–198, **199**, 199, 200, 201–202, 203, 204–205, 206
Prevent programme 10, 24, 26, 78, 125, 126, 127–128, 129, 130, 131, 132–135, 238, 239
preventative resilience 14, 289, 296

Preventing and Countering Violent Extremism (P/CVE) *see* P/CVE (Preventing and Countering Violent Extremism)
prevention: in Grossman's conceptualisation of resilience to violent extremism 240, 246; primary 174, 276; secondary 174, 175, 276; tertiary 174, 276
prevention and resilience, phase of New Zealand's response to terrorism 259, 262, 264–266
preventive measures 11, 12–13, 121, 168, 177; Italy 212, 216, 217; The Netherlands 142, 143, 148, 149; Norway 155, 159, 160, 161, 162, 164
primary prevention 174, 276
prison 7, 13, 26, 67, 143–144, 170, 174, 266, 290; France 116, 120; Greece 221, 230–231; Italy 212, 216, 217; United Kingdom 125, 127
privilege 40, 74, 78, 97, 184, 213, 228, 250, 288
producerism 288
propaganda 44, 61, 78, *81*, 95, 99, 149n11, 174, 287; Australia 239, 240; Hungary 184, 188; Italy 212, 214; New Zealand 255, 265; Norway 157, 163
pro-social radicalism 71, 72, **78**, 79, 87n2
prosocial resilience: in Australia 245–246; in Norway 162–163
protective factors 8, 35, 36, 40, 41, *43*, 79, 163, 168, 248, 280
public sphere 76, 113, 181, 193, 197, 213, 218, 228
pushbacks, at Greece's sea and land borders 224, 228

QAnon 98, 99, 102, 113

racial discrimination 55, 162–163, 230
racial equality, radical alternative narratives for 83–85, *84*, *85*
racialisation 4, 10, 26, 27, 36, 74, 82, 115, 148, 215; United Kingdom 128, 131, 132; United States of America 287, 288
racism 5, 21, 26, 27, 40, 59, 115, 122, 155, 156, 173, 177; anti- 80, 163, 192, 244; anti-Roma 183, 186, 187, 191, 193; Greece 221, 223, 224, 226, 230, 232n29; The Netherlands 142, 146; Poland 198, 199–200; United States of America 289, 292, 293
racist or ethno-centrist – but non-fascist – right, in Poland 198
racist violence 170, 172, 224, 229, 230, 231
Racist Violence Recording Network (RVRN) 223, 224, 230
radical alternative narratives 86, 87, 130; for multifaith belonging 80–83, *81*, *82*; for racial equality 83–85, *84*, *85*
radical 'Islamist' movements **78**, 78; *see also* Al-Qaeda (AQ); Al-Shabaab (AS); Islamic State in Iraq and Syria (IS/ISIS)

Index

radical misogyny 76, 79–80
radical right 77, **78**, 78–79, 287
radicalisation: conducive environment for 9, 75, 76, 87; counter- 10, 120, 121, 142, 143, 144, 145, 216–217, 218, 248, 275; de- *see* de-radicalisation; ideological 210, 212, 213; jihadist 114–115, 116, 122, 210, 211, 212–213; maladaptive 9, 72, 76, 78; as resilience 76–78, 77, **78**; violent *see* violent radicalisation
radicalised violence 34, 42, 276, 282
radicalism 67, 76, 186–187, 196, 287; Polish variants of 197–200, **199**, 202–203, 205–206, 206n1
RAF *see* Red Army Faction (RAF)
RASP *see* Research and Action on Social Polarisation (RASP)
Rassemblement National 113, 117, 118, 119
reactionary extremism 296
recovery, in Grossman's conceptualisation of resilience to violent extremism 240, 246, 247
recruitment 42, 44, 74, 76, 78, 79, 119, 147, 212, 216, 287
Red Army Faction (RAF) 141
refugee crisis 4, 93, 118, 183, 187, 214, 221, 223, 228, 231
relative deprivation 76, 78
religion extremism, in Greece 228–229
religious faith *see* faith
religious governance 228
religious-fundamentalist right 193n1; in Poland 198–199, 206
religiously motivated violent extremism (RMVE) 239, 275, 281
repression 119, 134, 143, 144, 146, 149, 169
Republic of South Maluku (RMS) 139–140, 141
Republican in Name Only (RINO) 105n1
Republican Party 97, 98, 286–287, 291, 292
republican values 113, 120
republicanism, French 10, 113–114, 115, 116–117, 120, 121
Research and Action on Social Polarisation (RASP) 278
resentment 10, 12, 113, 132, 182, 213
resilience: accumulating social **206**; antisocial *43*; community 14, 33–34, 35–36, 37, 38, 39, 73, 236, 286; corroding social 203, **206**; framing of 52–53; individual-level 40, 250; maladaptive 9, 33, 41, 42, 43, 76, 250; multisystemic 9, 72, 73, 244; in Norwegian P/CVE policy discourse 158–160; in Norwegian practice 160–162; online building of 99–100; over time 61–67, *63*, *64*, *66*; political reaction as an obstacle to 288–289; preventative 14, 289, 296; prosocial 162–163, 245–246; radicalisation as 76–78, 77, **78**; social 202–204; societal 67, 73, 159;
socio-ecological 5, 41, 72; in US 286, 287, 288–289, 293, 294, 295, 296
resilience to violent extremism 33–45, *43*; in Australia 241, 243, 248, 249; in Canada 274–275; in Germany 168–169; in Greece 229–231; in Norway 154–155; in Poland 197, 202–203, 205, 206; and Prevent 133–135
resistance, in Grossman's conceptualisation of resilience to violent extremism 240, 245, 246, 247, 249
Resolution 2178 of UN Security Council 34
Rigby, Lee 24
right-wing extremism: France 116–119; Hungary **189**, 190–191; Italy 213–215; Norway 156, 157; Poland 198–200, **199**
right-wing terrorism 12, 169, 210, 211, 258–259
right-wing violence 168, 169–171, 172, 173, 175
risk assessment 144, 149, 281
risk factors 6, 74, 144, 148, 168
RMS *see* Republic of South Maluku (RMS)
RMVE *see* religiously motivated violent extremism (RMVE)
Roma people 57, 175, 182–183, 184, 186, 187, 191, 193
Roy, Olivier 114
Royal Commission of Inquiry into the Terrorist Attacks on Christchurch Mosques on 15 March 2019 254, 256, 261, 262, 264, 265, 266, 267
rule of law 20, 21, 22, 100, 143, 145, 146, 148, 204, 227
RVRN *see* Racist Violence Recording Network (RVRN)

safeguarding 25, 26, 134, 162, 238, 244, 246
Salafism 114, 121, 170; in The Netherlands 143–144, 148
scapegoating 74, 75, 79, 182, 201, 223
scholarship, on violent extremism 17, 18–21
schools 7, 13, 24, 26, 59, 67, 188, 205; Australia 246, 248; Canada 277, 278, 279; France 115, 120; Germany 173–175, 177; Greece 224, 227, 228; Italy 213, 216, 217; Norway 156, 162–163
secondary prevention 174, 175, 276
secularisation 114, 213, 218, 223
secularism 113, 115–116, 119, 122, 122n1, 218, 290
securitisation 5, 10, 11, 13, 23, 25, 26, 27, 35, 37, 153, 214, 223; Australia 241, 243; Norway 154, 160, 161, 162, 163, 164; United Kingdom 125, 130, 131, 132, 134; United States of America 286, 295, 296
security services 127, 140, 144, 156, 157, 160, 161, 162
self-defence, resilience as 286
sense of belonging 74–75, 78, 79, 83, 87, 203, 249, 250

Index

situation tables, police co-led 276, 277–278
skinheads 155, 157, 170, 184, 185
small state approach, to New Zealand's international relations 255
social activism 244
social belonging 244
social capital 10, 34, 35–36, 162, 248, 250; bonding 35, 39, 74, **78**, 78, 83, 85–86, 99, 100, 103, 104; bridging *see* bridging social capital; online extremism 92, 99–100, 101, 102, 103–105; young people 73, 75, 77–78, **78**, 85–86
social cohesion 37, 39, 40; in Australia 13, 37, 237–238, 240, 242–243, 244, 246, 247, 249, 250; in The Netherlands 142–143
social ecology 41, 44, 241, 245
social harms 34, 36, 37, 241, 244
social impacts, of violent extremism in Canada 272–273
social integration 35–36, 221
social media 3, 7, 9–10, 60, 128, 134, 146, 157, 176, 212, 215, 239, 265, 294; online extremism 93, 94, 95, 99, 104; young people 73, 76, 83, 83, 87
social mobility 131, 134
social networking 11, 35, 41, 42, 78, 79, 83, 87, 92, 99, 164
social polarisation 14, 125; in Greece 13, 221–225, 229, 230, 231; teams in Canada 276, 278–279
social resilience, in Poland 202–204
social values 99, 294
social work 171–173
social-ecological resilience 5, 41, 72
socialism 181, 182–183, 184, 185, 187, 197, 202, 239, 258
societal exclusion 27, 60, 82, 92, 99, 104–105, 131, 134, 135n1, 211, 250
societal resilience 67, 73, 159
socio-ecological phenomenon, resilience as 5, 72
socio-economic context 53–55, *53*
socio-economic deprivation 76, 121
socio-economic status 40, 155, 157, 183, 222
Soros, George 187–188
South Moluccans 140, 141
sovereign citizen movements 38, 239, 240
Soviet Union 182, 187, 191, 197
spending cuts 4, 26–27, 131, 134, 196, 210, 223, 232n10, 291
state counter-extremism, in Hungary 190–191
state-based policy and programming, in Australia 243–245
status 42, 73, 74, 78, 246, 250; socio-economic 40, 155, 157, 183, 222
stereotypes 74, 83, 134–135, 202
stigmatisation 45, 116, 117, 121, 143, 148, 203, 227, 248, 281

street politics 118, 128, 215
structural violence, definition of 288
supporting victims 173–175
surveillance 11, 26, 27, 35, 37, 76, 119, 130, 216, 266, 272; The Netherlands 144, 145, 149; Norway 155, 158, 160–161, 163–164; United States of America 286, 289, 294, 295
Suspect Communities (book) 36
suspect communities (concept) 295
symbolic violence 288
symbols 130, 145, 171, 172, 187, **189**, 190, 200, 201, 222
Syria 6, 34, 114, 119, 225; Australia 236, 237; The Netherlands 139, 145, 146, 147; New Zealand 261, 263; Norway 156, 157; United Kingdom 130, 131, 132
Szabó, Albert 185

targets, of violence 10, 11, 14, 36, 40–41, 113, 156
TD *see* Technischer Dienst (TD)
Te Tiriti O Waitangi 256
tech platforms 10, 92–93, 94, 95, 96, 97, 99, 100, 101–105, 105n4
Technischer Dienst (TD) 169
technological conditions, giving rise to American extremism 293–294
Terreurbrief (terror letter) 140–141
terrorism: counter- *see* counterterrorism; domestic 98, 211, 216, 263, 294; international 211, 216, 271; Islamist 7, 158; lone-actor/lone-wolf 12, 56, 156, 157, 211–212, 215, 216; right-wing 12, 169, 210, 211, 258–259
Terrorism Suppression Act 2002 (TSA) 262–263
terrorist attacks 4, 9, 11, 14, 72, 93, 148, 171, 295; Australia 236, 238, 240; France 114, 119, 121; Italy 211, 216, 217–218; New Zealand 254, 262, 263, 266, 267; Norway 156, 161; United Kingdom 125, 130, 133
terrorist groups 23, 43, 78, 237, 258, 260
terrorist innovation 43–44
terrorist-style violence 21–22, 23, 25, 27
tertiary prevention 174, 276
TE-SAT *see European Union Terrorism and Situation Trend report* (TE-SAT) 2020
thematic analysis, of European trends in polarisation and resilience 52, 53, 62, 68
Thrace 222, 226, 232n2, 232n3
threat assessment, by Australian Security Intelligence Organisation (ASIO) 239–240
threat landscape 38–41, 271, 272, 274
TikTok 95, 102, 103
totalitarianism **189**, 190, 193n3, 201
transactional risk economy 42, *43*
transnational extremism 4, 8, 14, 36–37, 38, 40, 43, 145, 184, 190, 237, 259
transparency 76, 100, 101, 104

310

Index

Trans-Tasman approach, to counterterrorism 260–262
trauma care, resilience as 286
Treaty of Waitangi 256
Trojan Horse hoax 24
Trump, Donald 7, 72, 95, 97, 98, 101, 102, 105n1, 272, 287, 292–293
TSA *see Terrorism Suppression Act 2002* (TSA)
Turkey 116, 170, 222, 223, 224, 226
Twitter 92, 95, 97, 98, 101–102, 104

UCOII *see Unione delle Comunita Islamiche in Italia* (UCCOII)
UCREL Semantic Analysis System (USAS) 52
UK Government 22, 23, 26, 125, 126, 127, 132, 133, 134
UKIP *see* United Kingdom Independence Party (UKIP)
UN Security Council's Resolution 2178 34
unemployment 12, 41, 115, 116, 172, 196, 211, 277; *see also* employment
Union of the Muslim Communities in Italy 217
Unione delle Comunita Islamiche in Italia (UCOII) 217
unique selling points, vulnerability of young people to 75, 76
United Kingdom 125–135
United Kingdom Independence Party (UKIP) 128
United States of America 286–296
universalism 8, 113–114, 117, 213
US Presidential election 10, 92, 93, 104
USAS *see* UCREL Semantic Analysis System (USAS)
Utøya massacre 5, 6, 145, 156

values: British 22, 23, 24, 132, 134; Catholic 117, 202; Christian 187, 213; colour-blind 122; community 74; conservative 105n1; core 21; cultural 37, 39, 73, 245; democratic 154, 158, 160, 162, 174, 184, 287; European 22, 201; extremist 238, 250, 287; French institutional 115; Greek 229; Hungarian 187; liberal 25; non-religious 162–163; pluralistic 4, 19, 37, 169; radical right 287; republican 113, 120; social 99, 294; of speech 293–294; Western 22, 23, 26, 287
Vér és Becsület Kulturális Egyesület 190, 191
victimisation 42, 146, 223, 271, 272, 277
victims 26, 56, 79, 84, 118, 155, 187, 224, 249, 280, 294–295; in Germany 169, 170, 175; in New Zealand 259, 262–265; supporting of 173–175
Világnemzeti Népuralmista Pártot (VNP) 185
violence: anti-authority 271, 275; behaviours 73, 246, 257, 265; beliefs 73, **78**, 238, 239, 246, 249, 257; building resilience to 40, 237, 249; exclusivist 5; extremist *see* extremist violence; far-right 126, 127–128, 134; identity-driven 271, 275; irregular 3, 17, 19, 27; jihadist 10, 113, 169; political *see* political violence; racist 170, 172, 224, 229, 230, 231; prevention of 35, 172–173, 204, 205, 276, 277, 282; radicalised 34, 42, 276, 282; right-wing 168, 169–171, 172, 173, 175; structural 288; symbolic 288; terrorist-style 21–22, 23, 25, 27; xenophobic 215, 271
violent action 4, 5, 11, 19, 44, 75, 76, 217, 262–263, 295; Australia 238, 239, 249; Germany 169, 170, 177; The Netherlands 142, 149
violent extremism: Australia 237–241; Britain 126–129; building resilience to *see* building resilience, to violent extremism; Canada 270, 271, 272, 275, 276, 280, 281; community resilience to 14, 33–34, 35–36, 37, 38, 39, 73, 236, 286; definition of 4; Greece 222–225; ideologically motivated (IMVE) 239, 271, 275, 281; Italian jihadist 211–213; New Zealand 258–259; Norway 154–155; religiously motivated (RMVE) 239, 275, 281; scholarship on 18–21; youth resilience to 9, 73–75, 77–78, 83, 245; *see also* building resilience, to violent extremism; extremist violence
violent radicalisation 9, 33, 37, 40, 116, 230; in Australia 238, 244, 248; in Canada 278, 281; of young people 71, 72, 73, 74, 75, 76, 77, 79–80
violent right-wing extremism 11, 27–28, 169
VNP *see Világnemzeti Népuralmista Pártot* (VNP)
voter fraud 96–97

Wagensveld, Edwin 147
Waitangi, Treaty of 256
War on Terror 23, 25, 28, 72, 119, 212, 225, 259; Norway 153, 161; United Kingdom 126, 130, 133, 134, 135
war volunteers *see* foreign fighters
Web 2.0 76
welfare state 158, 162, 224
Western values 22, 23, 26, 287
White power 14, 38, 287, 289, 290–291, 294
White supremacy 14, 286–287, 288, 296
Wilders, Geert 143, 145
Wmatrix software 60, 61
Working Group Against Hate Crimes (GYEM) 192
World Trade Centre attacks 72
World Value Survey (WVS) 182
World-National People's Power Party 185
WVS *see* World Value Survey (WVS)

XCheck 97–98
xenophobia 27, 67, 182, 183, 198, 221, 224, 230
xenophobic violence 215, 271

Years of Lead 210
Yockey, Francis Parker 289, 290
young democracy phase, of Hungarian far-right 184–185

young men 14, 79, 83–84, *84*, 130, 173
young people 71–87, *75*, 77, **78**, *81*, *82*, *84*, *85*, *86*
youth resilience, to violent extremism 9, 73–75, 77–78, 83, 245
Youth Resilience to Violent Extremism study 245
YouTube 92, 101, 102